W9-CBH-254

PRODUCTS LIABILITY

Aspen Casebook Series

PRODUCTS LIABILITY

Problems and Process
Eighth Edition

James A. Henderson, Jr.
Frank B. Ingersoll Professor of Law
Cornell Law School

Aaron D. Twerski
Irwin and Jill Cohen Professor of Law
Brooklyn Law School

Douglas A. Kysar
Joseph M. Field '55 Professor of Law
Yale Law School

Wolters Kluwer

Published by Wolters Kluwer in New York.

Wolters Kluwer Legal & Regulatory Solutions U.S. serves customers worldwide with CCH, Aspen Publishers, and Kluwer Law International products. (www.WKLegaledu.com)

To contact Customer Service, e-mail customer.service@wolterskluwer.com, call 1-800-234-1660, fax 1-800-901-9075, or mail correspondence to:

Wolters Kluwer
Attn: Order Department
PO Box 990
Frederick, MD 21705

Printed in the United States of America.

1 2 3 4 5 6 7 8 9 0

ISBN 978-1-4548-7086-9

Library of Congress Cataloging-in-Publication Data

Names: Henderson, James A., 1938- author. | Twerski, Aaron D., author. | Kysar, Douglas A., author.
Title: Products liability : problems and process / James A. Henderson, Jr., Aaron D. Twerski, Douglas A. Kysar.
Description: Eighth edition. | New York : Wolters Kluwer, 2016. | Includes index.
Identifiers: LCCN 2015044272 | ISBN 9781454870869
Subjects: LCSH: Products liability — United States.
Classification: LCC KF1296 .H43 2016 | DDC 346.7303/8–dc23
LC record available at http://lccn.loc.gov/2015044272

About Wolters Kluwer Legal & Regulatory Solutions U.S.

Wolters Kluwer Legal & Regulatory Solutions U.S. delivers expert content and solutions in the areas of law, corporate compliance, health compliance, reimbursement, and legal education. Its practical solutions help customers successfully navigate the demands of a changing environment to drive their daily activities, enhance decision quality and inspire confident outcomes.

Serving customers worldwide, its legal and regulatory solutions portfolio includes products under the Aspen Publishers, CCH Incorporated, Kluwer Law International, ftwilliam.com and MediRegs names. They are regarded as exceptional and trusted resources for general legal and practice-specific knowledge, compliance and risk management, dynamic workflow solutions, and expert commentary.

From Jim
To
Marcie

From Aaron
To
Kreindel

From Doug
To
Christine

Summary of Contents

Contents

PART II
Liability for Generic Product Risks

Preface to the Eighth Edition

The Eighth Edition of *Products Liability: Problems and Process* represents a substantial revision of prior iterations of the casebook. In addition to updating the book to reflect new cases, commentary, and problems, we have also significantly shortened and reorganized the material in order to make the book more user-friendly.

We have been aided in this process by Doug Kysar, who joins as a new co-author for this Edition. Doug brings additional perspective to the subject of products liability, which all three authors continue to regard as a fascinating, challenging, and important field of law. We hope that our enthusiasm comes through to the reader.

James A. Henderson, Jr.
Aaron D. Twerski
Douglas A. Kysar

October 2015

Acknowledgments

The authors wish to thank Beth Pollastro, at Brooklyn, and Jennifer Marshall, at Yale, who helped to prepare this edition of the casebook. Jylanda Diles, at Cornell, and Golda Lawrence, at Brooklyn, provided terrific assistance with prior editions. We are grateful to them all.

Research assistants provided invaluable help in assembling these materials. John Baumann (Cornell '86), Jay Bohn (Cornell '88), and Grace Lee (Brooklyn '87) helped us on the first edition. On the second edition, Ron Jenkins and David Ludwick (Cornell '93), Claire Kelly (Brooklyn '93), and Marni Schlissel (Brooklyn '92) provided invaluable assistance. On the third edition, Jordan Anger (Cornell '98), Hanna Liebman (Brooklyn '98), Allison Sealove (Brooklyn '97), and Victoria Ostrovsky (Brooklyn '97) were all of great help to us. On the fourth edition, Thomas Ciarlone (Cornell '01), Jesse Eggert (Cornell '01), Debbie Sternberg Tyler (Brooklyn '00), Kim Houghton (Brooklyn '01), and Michael Heydrich (Brooklyn '00) helped us meet very tight deadlines. On the fifth edition, Mason Barney (Brooklyn '05), Erez Davy (Brooklyn '05), Jennifer Lee (Brooklyn '05), Daniel London (Brooklyn '05), Carl Berry (Cornell '05), and Katharine Burns (Cornell '05) helped us to complete a very substantial revision of these materials. On the sixth edition, Helder Agostinho (Cornell '09), Daniel Hendrick (Cornell '09), and Michael Siegel (Cornell '09) helped with the revisions. On the seventh edition, Colin Leslie (Cornell '11), Steve Beytenbrod (Brooklyn '11), John-Paul Gonzalez (Brooklyn), Elina Shindelman (Brooklyn '11), Sarah A. Westby (Brooklyn '11), Noor I. Alam (Brooklyn '12), Yonah Jaffe (Brooklyn '12), and Shimon Sternhell (Brooklyn '12), provided valuable research assistance. For the eighth edition, we were aided ably by David Berke (Yale '17), Juliana Brint (Yale '17), Christine Kwon (Yale '17), Andy Mun (Yale '17), Nathan Nash (Yale '17), Paul Nolle (Brooklyn '17), Loren Oumarova (Yale '17), Shahriar Raafi (Brooklyn '17), Joey Samuels (Yale '17), Amanda Weingarten (Yale '16), David Weisner (Brooklyn '17), and Grace Zhang (Yale '16). We are grateful to them for their contributions.

Deans Peñalver at Cornell, Allard at Brooklyn, and Post at Yale also deserve thanks for their generous support.

We would like to thank the authors and publishers of the following works for permitting us to include excerpts from these works:

American Law Institute, Restatement of Torts (Second), §310, §311, §402A, and Comments *b, f, i, k,* and *n*; and §402B. Copyright © 1965, 1977 by The American Law Institute. Reprinted with permission.

American Law Institute, Restatement of Torts (Third): Apportionment of Liability §22, §23. Reporters Note to §7, §32. Copyright © 2000 by The American Law Institute. Reprinted with permission. U.C.C. §2-302 and Comment *1*; §2-313 and Comments *3* and *8*; §2-316 and Comment *1*; §2-719 and Comment *3*; §2-725. Copyright © 1995 by the American Law Institute and the National Conference of Commissioners on Uniform State Laws. Uniform Contribution Among Tortfeasors Act,

1995 and the National Conference of Commissioners on Uniform States Laws. Reprinted with permission.

American Law Institute, Restatement of Torts (Third): Products Liability, §1, §2, and Comments *c, d, e, f, g, i, j, k, m,* and *n*; §3 and Comment *b*; §4 and Comments *d,* and *e*; §5 and Comment *b*; §6 and Comments *b, d, e, f,* and *h*; §7 and Comments *a* and *b*; §8, §9, and Comments *a* and *b*; §10 and Comments *a* and *j*; §15, §16, §17, §18, §19, §20, §21, and Comment *e*. Copyright © 1998 by The American Law Institute. Reprinted with permission.

Henderson & Twerski, Manufacturer's Liability for Defective Product Designs: The Triumph of Risk Utility, 74 Brooklyn L. Rev. 1061, 1077-1099 (2009). Copyright © 2009 by The Brooklyn Law Review. Reprinted by permission of the authors, The Brooklyn Law Review.

Henderson & Twerski, Drug Designs *Are* Different. Copyright © 2001 by The Yale Law Journal Company, Inc. Reprinted by permission of the authors, The Yale Law Journal Company, and Fred B. Rothman & Company from The Yale Law Journal, vol. 111, No. 1, pages 151-153, 155-159, 162-164, 168-169, 171-172, 180-181.

Henderson & Twerski, Closing the American Products Liability Frontier: The Rejection of Liability Without Defect, 66 N.Y.U. L. Rev. 1263, 1298-1300, 1305-1306, 1316-1318. Copyright © 1991 by the New York University Law Review. Reprinted by permission of the New York University Law Review.

Henderson & Twerski, Doctrinal Collapse in Products Liability: The Empty Shell of Failure to Warn, 65 N.Y.U. L. Rev. 265, 292-294. Copyright © 1990 by the New York University Law Review. Reprinted by permission of the New York University Law Review.

Posner, A Theory of Negligence, 1 J. Legal Stud. 29, 32. Copyright © 1972 by the University of Chicago. Reprinted with permission of the author and the publisher.

Ramseyer, Liability For Defective Products: Comparative Hypotheses And Evidence From Japan, 61 Am. J. Comp. L. 617 (2013).

Reimann, Liability for Defective Products at the Beginning of the Twenty-First Century: Emergence of a Worldwide Standard?, 51 Am. J. Comp. L. 751 (Fall 2003)

Uniform Law Commission, Uniform Contribution Among Tortfeasors Act. Copyright © 1939 and 1955 by The National Conference of Commissioners on Uniform State Laws. All Rights Reserved.

Wertheimer, The Smoke Gets in Their Eyes: Product Category Liability and Alternative Feasible Designs in the Third Restatement, 61 Tenn. L. Rev. 1429. Copyright © 1994 by The Tennessee Law Review Association, Inc. Reprinted by permission of the Tennessee Law Review Association, Inc.

Wolfram, Modern Legal Ethics 594-596, 653-657. Copyright © 1986 by West Publishing Co. Reprinted with permission of the author and the West Group.

PRODUCTS LIABILITY

PART I

Liability for Manufacturing Defects

Part I serves two purposes. First, it sets forth the law governing the liability of manufacturers for harm caused by manufacturing defects. And second, it introduces basic subjects, such as allocation of responsibility among potential defendants (Chapter One), causation (Chapter Two), and affirmative defenses (Chapter Three), that cut across the entirety of American products liability. Although most of the materials in Part I involve manufacturing defects, not all of them do. Because some of the important doctrinal issues to be addressed in this part — for example, issues of causation — can best be illustrated by cases and problems involving generically defective products, some of the materials in this part involve such alternative examples of defectiveness. Consistent with our basic plan of attack, however, whenever the defectiveness issue is central to the analysis we will limit ourselves in this part to manufacturing defects. In those instances involving generically defective products we will assume away the problems of defining "defectiveness" and focus instead on other issues of doctrine and policy concerning how courts do, and should, deal generally with questions of liability for defective products. We will wait to wrestle with the conceptual problems of generic defectiveness — defective design and failure-to-warn — until Part II.

CHAPTER ONE

Product Distributor's Strict Liability for Defect-Caused Harm

To recover for harm (personal injury and property damage) caused by a defective product, American tort law demands that the plaintiff establish: (1) that the plaintiff's harm results from a product defect; and (2) that the defect existed when the product left the hands of the defendant. Before the onset of the products liability revolution in the early 1960s, it was also necessary to establish that the defendant-distributor of the defective product had been negligent in either manufacturing or distributing the defective product. As we shall see shortly, courts have dispensed with the need to prove negligence in at least one significant category of products liability cases. When the plaintiff can establish a manufacturing defect — that the product unit does not conform to the manufacturer's own intended design — the plaintiff is no longer required to prove that the distributor was at fault. It is sufficient to prove that the product was defective and that the defect caused the plaintiff's harm.

In this chapter we will briefly (very briefly) review the basic principles of negligence from first-year Torts and then turn our attention to a problem that continues to haunt both litigants and courts in seeking to fairly adjudicate product liability claims. When products cause harm, victims often suspect that a product defect was the culprit. Let us assume that the plaintiff is correct. The product that caused the injury was indeed defective at the time of the accident. Plaintiff is only halfway home. The plaintiff must also establish that the product was defective when it left the hands of the defendant. Surely a defendant who distributed a perfectly good product that was rendered defective by someone else afterwards does not bear legal responsibility for the plaintiff's harm.

One's first impression may be that proving that the defect originated at the time of distribution is not likely to be a problem. To the contrary, we assure you that the problem is most serious. Once the distributor lets a product out of its hands, the product is at the mercy of a host of people. Consumers can be counted on to abuse and misuse products. Merchants and repairers have access to the innards of a product. Age and heavy use can take a serious toll on product integrity. As you will see, proving that a defect originated at the time of sale may at times be even more difficult than proving that a product defect caused the accident.

This chapter also considers the boundaries of strict liability, how liability gets allocated among members of the distributive chain, and how products liability interfaces with workers compensation.

A. THE ROLE OF NEGLIGENCE IN THE FORMATIVE PERIOD

1. Negligence from First-Year Torts

These materials assume that you have taken the basic first-year torts course and that you are generally familiar with the principles governing liability for negligent conduct. You will recall that Judge Learned Hand articulated a classic formulation of the negligence standard in United States v. Carroll Towing Co., 159 F.2d 169 (2d Cir. 1947). Judge Hand took the position that whether an actor's injury-causing conduct was negligent depended on three variables: (1) the probability that injury would result from the actor's conduct; (2) the gravity of the harm that could be expected to result should injury occur; and (3) the burden of adequate precautions to avoid or minimize injury. In one of the most famous (or infamous, depending on your philosophical outlook) tort quotes, Hand suggested that his test could be reduced to algebraic terms: "If the probability be called P; the injury L [loss]; and the burden B [i.e., the burden of precaution to avoid the risk of loss]; liability depends upon whether B is less than L multiplied by P: i.e., whether $B < PL$." Id. at 173.

After *Carroll Towing*, a quarter of a century passed before Professor (now Judge) Richard Posner pointed out that the Learned Hand negligence tort formula was in lockstep with an economic test of negligence. In what has come to be recognized as a landmark article expressing the law-and-economics perspective on the subject, Posner argued that the Learned Hand formula stood for the following proposition:

> Discounting (multiplying) the cost of an accident if it occurs by the probability of occurrence yields a measure of the economic benefit to be anticipated from incurring the costs necessary to prevent the accident. The cost of prevention is what Hand meant by the burden of taking precautions against the accident. It may be the cost of installing safety equipment or otherwise making the activity safer, or the benefit forgone by curtailing or eliminating the activity. If the cost of safety measures or of curtailment — whichever cost is lower — exceeds the benefit in accident avoidance to be gained by incurring that cost, society would be better off, in economic terms, to forgo accident prevention. A rule making the enterprise liable for the accidents that occur in such cases cannot be justified on the ground that it will induce the enterprise to increase the safety of its operations. When the cost of accidents is less than the cost of prevention, a rational profit-maximizing enterprise will pay tort judgments to the accident victims rather than incur the larger cost of avoiding liability. Furthermore, overall economic value or welfare would be diminished rather than increased by incurring a higher accident-prevention cost in order to avoid a lower accident cost. If, on the other hand, the benefits in accident avoidance exceed the costs of prevention, society is better off if those costs are incurred and the accident averted, and so in this case the enterprise is made liable, in the expectation that self-interest will lead it to adopt the precautions in order to avoid a greater cost in tort judgments. [Posner, A Theory of Negligence, 1 J. Legal Stud. 29, 32 (1972).]

Hand's notion that a reasonable manufacturer would not invest unlimited resources in preventing defects, even if it were to bear all defect-related costs, may seem a bit heartless to some of you. If a manufacturer could eliminate even more defects, together with the accident costs those defects cause, shouldn't the manufacturer spend additional money on quality control even if the savings in accident costs prevented by further spending are less than the costs of preventing them? We defer this and related questions until we reach the section below on strict liability. For now, let us consider negligence for what it is, even if some of you harbor doubts about its ethical adequacy as a liability standard.

Some writers who agree generally that negligence is an appropriate liability standard insist that Learned Hand's approach in *Carroll Towing* rests on unrealistic assumptions about the rationality of human decisionmaking. See generally Gregory C. Keating, Reasonableness and Rationality in Negligence Theory, 48 Stan. L. Rev. 311 (1996). For a comprehensive survey of the literature, reaching the conclusion that some Learned Hand critics have overstated the case against rational choice, see Jeffrey J. Rachlinski, The Uncertain Psychological Case for Paternalism, 97 Nw. U. L. Rev. 1165, 1168 (2003) ("[T]he primary lesson that legal scholars have taken from the cognitive psychology of judgment and choice, the notion that people make systematically erroneous choices, is mistaken."). See also Benjamin C. Zipursky, Law and Morality: Tort Law: Sleight of Hand, 48 Wm. & Mary L. Rev. 1999 (2007) (breach in negligence is to be judged by ordinary care standard; no evidence that negligence decisions are based on the Learned Hand formula). In any event, Judge Hand himself expressed doubt over the wisdom of trying to reduce the negligence concept to precise mathematical formulas. See Moisan v. Loftus, 178 F.2d 148 (2d Cir. 1949). But the basic idea that Hand tried to capture with his "B < PL" formulation has come to be recognized as an appropriate way of expressing the basis for liability for negligently caused harm. See Restatement (Third) of Torts: Liab. For Physical and Emotional Harm §3 (2010). Although some judges prefer to express the negligence test in the more humanistic terms of "what a reasonable person would have done," even that formulation is consistent with the notion that reasonable persons weigh the costs of activities against their benefits in deciding upon courses of action.

From whatever perspective one measures the interests at stake in making the necessary cost-benefit trade-offs, this much is clear: If a manufacturer fails to invest in quality control at least to the point where the next incremental investment in safety would not save more than it would cost to make it — if the manufacturer fails to take all cost-effective safety measures — the manufacturer is negligent and is liable for all of the harm that its defective products cause. Concomitantly, if the manufacturer takes all cost-effective quality control measures, the injured plaintiff will not be able to point to a further safety measure that the manufacturer could have taken where "B < PL," and the manufacturer is not negligent (and thus is not liable to the injured plaintiff). This will result even if a considerable number of victims, like the plaintiff, are being harmed because of product defects. The negligence system leaves it to the victims, themselves, to insure against the defect-related accident costs that are not worth preventing. These so-called "residual accident costs" remain where they have fallen — on the accident victims and their casualty loss insurers. Thus, the only accident-related costs that reasonable manufacturers bear under a negligence regime are the costs of the quality control measures that they must take to avoid being negligent. (Defect-related accidents also hurt their reputations in the market; but the market imposes those costs, not the tort system.)

Strictly speaking, these costs of quality control are not "insurance" costs but rather "prevention" costs. As Posner's excerpt, above, explains, one incurs prevention costs in trying to stop accidents from happening. In contrast, casualty loss insurance serves to spread the costs of accidents that are cheaper to incur than to prevent. Those who may suffer loss transfer the risks to commercial insurers, who aggregate, or "pool," similar risks of loss, charging an appropriate premium, thereby spreading the high costs of individual losses among all the insureds in the relevant risk pool. Spreading such "primary accident costs" lowers the social dislocations, or "secondary costs," of the residual accidents that are not worth preventing. Under negligence, manufacturers engage in accident prevention and accident victims insure against the residual accident losses that are too costly for the manufacturer to prevent by the exercise of care. Of course, victims also play a role in accident prevention under the rules governing contributory negligence; we will address that aspect at the end of Part I.

Why would a rational tort system adopt negligence as the basis of manufacturers' liability for manufacturing defects? Traditional notions of fairness play an important role. Certainly it is fair to impose liability on manufacturers who unreasonably expose users and consumers to risks of harm. Likewise, it is only fair, the supporters of traditional negligence will argue, that a manufacturer who does all that a reasonable person would do to prevent defects should not be held liable for accidents that it is in the best interests of society, including product users and consumers, to allow to happen. People who purchase and use products have a right to expect that manufacturers will behave reasonably. But purchasers know that some defects are unavoidable and should take that possibility into account in deciding whether to purchase and use such products. Moreover, each individual purchaser understands better than anyone else his or her own tolerance toward risk and is in the best position to know how much dislocation costs a defect-related accident will cause and thus how much casualty loss insurance coverage to obtain. Thus, each consumer pays her own premiums for her own insurance covering the residual costs not worth trying to prevent—a rock star who wants 50 million dollars coverage should pay her own premiums and not expect law students who buy the same products she does to help pay her insurance costs. Thus, it can be argued that a system of negligence-based liability is not only fair to everyone involved but is also efficient, in that it achieves the proper levels of both accident prevention and casualty loss insurance.

We will return to reconsider the merits of this assessment when we reach the subject of strict tort liability.

2. *The Fall of the Privity Rule*

An interesting chapter in the development of negligence-based liability for defective products, now chiefly of historical interest, involved the question of whether the negligent manufacturer of a defective product could be held liable to an injured person with whom the manufacturer had not directly contracted. The question should seem odd to you. *Of course* a negligent manufacturer's responsibility extends beyond its immediate buyers. Indeed, under traditional principles of proximate cause a negligent manufacturer should be liable for all the harms that a reasonable person would have foreseen at the time of original sale of the defective product. But what seems clear to us today was not always so clear. Beginning in England in the first half of the nineteenth century, courts adopted a general rule that the negligent supplier of a defective product was liable only to those with whom he had directly dealt in the supply contract; anyone not in "privity of contract" with the supplier could not recover for the supplier's negligence no matter how directly and foreseeably his injuries were causally linked to that negligence.

This rule limiting a product supplier's tort liability is generally referred to as the "privity rule." By common consent, its origins are traced to the opinion of Lord

Abinger, C.B., in Winterbottom v. Wright, 10 M. & W. 109 (Exch. 1842), in which the plaintiff sought to recover in negligence for injuries suffered when a horse-drawn mail coach collapsed while plaintiff was driving it. The defendant had supplied the coach in question, along with others, to the Postmaster General pursuant to a contract that called for the defendant to keep the coach in good repair. The plaintiff alleged that the defendant negligently failed to fulfill his contractual promise to keep the coach in repair, causing it to collapse and injure the plaintiff.

In granting judgment for defendant, the English court concluded that, given the absence of any contractual relationship between the defendant and the plaintiff, no recovery could be had in negligence. Refusing to permit the contract between the defendant and the Postmaster General to be turned into a tort, Lord Abinger observed:

> There is no privity of contract between [the plaintiff and the defendant]; and if the plaintiff can sue, every passenger, or even any person passing along the road, who was injured by the upsetting of the coach, might bring a similar action. Unless we confine the operation of such contracts as this to the parties who entered into them, the most absurd and outrageous consequences, as to which I can see no limit, would ensue. [10 M. & W. at 114.]

Although the privity rule in *Winterbottom* came generally to be recognized by American courts, by the end of the nineteenth century a number of exceptions were developed judicially. In an early New York case, Thomas v. Winchester, 6 N.Y. 307 (1852), falsely labeled poison was sold to a druggist, who in turn sold it to a customer. The customer, who was seriously injured due to the mislabeling, recovered damages from the defendant who had affixed the erroneous label even though the injured plaintiff had no direct privity relationship with the defendant. The defendant's negligence, the court said, "put human life in imminent danger." Once the privity barrier had been overcome for products that created "imminent danger," injured plaintiffs besieged courts with claims against remote manufacturers, contending that, indeed, their injuries were brought about by products whose danger levels were very high and thus met the threshold test for bypassing the privity rule.

The seeming arbitrariness of the privity rule, together with the conceptual confusion surrounding exceptions to the rule, finally came to an end with the decision of the New York Court of Appeals in MacPherson v. Buick Motor Co., 111 N.E. 1050 (N.Y. 1916). The case involved an allegedly defective wooden wheel on a 1911 Buick Runabout automobile that collapsed and caused an accident that injured the plaintiff. The plaintiff's negligence-based complaint against Buick was dismissed for lack of privity, whereupon the intermediate appellate court remanded for trial, holding that the privity rule did not bar plaintiff's claim. On remand, the jury found for the plaintiff on the grounds that Buick had been negligent in failing to inspect the wheel for defects and a manufacturing defect had caused the accident. The trial court entered judgment for the plaintiff. The intermediate court affirmed, and Buick appealed to the Court of Appeals, New York's highest court. Judge Benjamin N. Cardozo, one of America's greatest appellate judges and the author of a number of famous opinions on the subject of tort law, wrote for the majority in affirming the judgment below.

The holding in MacPherson v. Buick eventually gained widespread acceptance and is now universally recognized. See generally W. Prosser & P. Keeton, Law of Torts 683 (5th ed. 1984); Restatement (Second) of Torts, §395, Comment *a* (1965). See generally

James A. Henderson, Jr., MacPherson v. Buick Motor Co.: Simplifying the Facts While Reshaping the Law, in Tort Stories 41 (Robert L. Rabin & Stephen D. Sugarman eds. 2003). Today, lack of privity is not a bar to negligence-based recovery for personal injuries against suppliers of defective products. The privity doctrine does, however, retain considerable vitality in products liability cases when recovery is sought for economic harm, reflecting the fact that plaintiffs in those cases must base their claims on contract, rather than tort.

3.   *The Rise of Res Ipsa Loquitur*

During the period following the fall of the privity rule, American courts increasingly relied on the doctrine of res ipsa loquitur in negligence-based manufacturing defect cases. Res ipsa loquitur ("the thing speaks for itself") allows an inference of negligence to be drawn from the occurrence of an accident involving an instrumentality (in a products liability case, the product itself) within the defendant's control under circumstances where such an accident would not ordinarily occur in the absence of negligence.

Thus, from the fact that a defective product failed in use and caused an accident, courts allowed triers of fact to infer that the manufacturer of the product negligently caused the defect to occur. One difficulty with res ipsa loquitur from the plaintiff's perspective was proving that the defect was present when the product left the hands of the manufacturer — that is, that the product was in the defendant's control when it became defective. Direct proof was sometimes available, but not always. In these latter instances, if the product failed immediately after first distribution, when practically new, and if the product was being used normally, the inference could be drawn that the defect originated with the manufacturer. But if the product was not new or had been subjected to rough handling after purchase, or if the plaintiff could not account for what had happened between distribution of the product and its subsequent failure in use, then the plaintiff faced more substantial difficulties in proving that a defect at the original time of sale — an "original defect" — caused his injuries.

One aspect of the res ipsa doctrine that has caused confusion over the years is the frequently repeated statement that the accident must be an event that does not ordinarily happen if the defendant is exercising due care. Some plaintiffs have sought to prove this by demonstrating that when an actor in the same position as was the defendant exercises care, the event rarely happens — for example, only once in a thousand times — whereas when actors behave negligently the event occurs only once in a hundred times. In theory, this ought not to be sufficient to reach the jury, because although the event occurs more frequently when the actor is negligent, there is no indication regarding the relative frequency with which the actor behaves negligently. If negligence only rarely is present, then in any given instance an absence of negligence may be the more likely explanation. Thus, in the words of the Oregon Supreme Court's opinion in Brannon v. Wood, 444 P.2d 558, 562 (Or. 1968) (a medical malpractice case), "[t]he test is not whether a particular injury rarely occurs, but rather, when it occurs, is it ordinarily the result of negligence." See generally David Kaye, Probability Theory Meets Res Ipsa Loquitur, 77 Mich. L. Rev. 1456 (1979).

Escola v. Coca-Cola Bottling Co.
150 P.2d 436 (Cal. 1944)

GIBSON, C.J.

Plaintiff, a waitress in a restaurant, was injured when a bottle of Coca-Cola broke in her hand. She alleged that defendant company, which had bottled and delivered the alleged defective bottle to her employer, was negligent in selling "bottles containing said beverage which on account of excessive pressure of gas or by reason of some defect in the bottle was dangerous . . . and likely to explode." This appeal is from a judgment upon a jury verdict in favor of plaintiff. . . .

. . . [B]eing unable to show any specific acts of negligence [plaintiff] relied completely on the doctrine of res ipsa loquitur.

Defendant contends that the doctrine of res ipsa loquitur does not apply in this case, and that the evidence is insufficient to support the judgment. . . .

Res ipsa loquitur does not apply unless (1) defendant had exclusive control of the thing causing the injury and (2) the accident is of such a nature that it ordinarily would not occur in the absence of negligence by the defendant.

Many authorities state that the happening of the accident does not speak for itself where it took place some time after defendant had relinquished control of the instrumentality causing the injury. Under the more logical view, however, the doctrine may be applied upon the theory that defendant had control at the time of the alleged negligent act, although not at the time of the accident, *provided* plaintiff first proves that the condition of the instrumentality had not been changed after it left the defendant's possession. As said in Dunn v. Hoffman Beverage Co., 126 N.J.L. 556 [20 A.2d 352, 354], "defendant is not charged with the duty of showing affirmatively that something happened to the bottle after it left its control or management; . . . to get to the jury the plaintiff must show that there was due care during that period." Plaintiff must also prove that she handled the bottle carefully. The reason for this prerequisite is set forth in Prosser on Torts [1941], at page 300, where the author states:

> Allied to the condition of exclusive control in the defendant is that of absence of any action on the part of the plaintiff contributing to the accident. Its purpose, of course, is to eliminate the possibility that it was the plaintiff who was responsible. If the boiler of a locomotive explodes while the plaintiff engineer is operating it, the inference of his own negligence is at least as great as that of the defendant, and res ipsa loquitur will not apply until he has accounted for his own conduct.

It is not necessary, of course, that plaintiff eliminate every remote possibility of injury to the bottle after defendant lost control, and the requirement is satisfied if there is evidence permitting a reasonable inference that it was not accessible to extraneous harmful forces and that it was carefully handled by plaintiff or any third person who may have moved or touched it. If such evidence is presented, the question becomes one for the trier of fact and, accordingly, the issue should be submitted to the jury under proper instructions.

In the present case no instructions were requested or given on this phase of the case, although general instructions upon res ipsa loquitur were given. Defendant, however, has made no claim of error with reference thereto on this appeal.

Upon an examination of the record, the evidence appears sufficient to support a reasonable inference that the bottle here involved was not damaged by any extraneous force after delivery to the restaurant by defendant. It follows, therefore, that the bottle was in some manner defective at the time defendant relinquished control because sound and properly prepared bottles of carbonated liquids do not ordinarily explode when carefully handled.

The next question, then, is whether plaintiff may rely upon the doctrine of res ipsa loquitur to supply an inference that defendant's negligence was responsible for the defective condition of the bottle at the time it was delivered to the restaurant. Under the general rules pertaining to the doctrine, as set forth above, it must appear that bottles of carbonated liquid are not ordinarily defective without negligence by the bottling company. . . .

An explosion such as took place here might have been caused by an excessive internal pressure in a sound bottle, by a defect in the glass of a bottle containing a safe pressure, or by a combination of these two possible causes. The question is whether under the evidence there was a probability that defendant was negligent in any of these respects. If so, the doctrine of res ipsa loquitur applies.

The bottle was admittedly charged with gas under pressure, and the charging of the bottle was within the exclusive control of defendant. As it is a matter of common knowledge that an overcharge would not ordinarily result without negligence, it follows under the doctrine of res ipsa loquitur that if the bottle was in fact excessively charged an inference of defendant's negligence would arise. If the explosion resulted from a defective bottle containing a safe pressure, the defendant would be liable if it negligently failed to discover such flaw. If the defect were visible, an inference of negligence would arise from the failure of defendant to discover it. Where defects are discoverable, it may be assumed that they will not ordinarily escape detection if a reasonable inspection is made, and if such a defect is overlooked an inference arises that a proper inspection was not made. A difficult problem is presented where the defect is unknown and consequently might have been one not discoverable by a reasonable, practicable inspection. In [an earlier] case we refused to take judicial notice of the technical practices and information available to the bottling industry for finding defects which cannot be seen. In the present case, however, we are supplied with evidence of the standard methods used for testing bottles.

A chemical engineer for the Owens-Illinois Glass Company and its Pacific Coast subsidiary, maker of Coca-Cola bottles, explained how glass is manufactured and the methods used in testing and inspecting bottles. He testified that his company is the largest manufacturer of glass containers in the United States, and that it uses the standard methods for testing bottles recommended by the glass containers association. A pressure test is made by taking a sample from each mold every three hours — approximately one out of every 600 bottles — and subjecting the sample to an internal pressure of 450 pounds per square inch, which is sustained for one minute. (The normal pressure in Coca-Cola bottles is less than 50 pounds per square inch.) The sample bottles are also subjected to the standard thermal shock test. The witness stated that these tests are "pretty near" infallible.

It thus appears that there is available to the industry, a commonly-used method of testing bottles for defects not apparent to the eye, which is almost infallible. Since Coca-Cola bottles are subjected to these tests by the manufacturer, it is not likely that they contain defects when delivered to the bottler which are not discoverable by visual inspection. Both new and used bottles are filled and distributed by defendant. The used bottles are not again subjected to the tests referred to above, and it may be inferred that defects not discoverable by visual inspection do not develop in bottles after they are manufactured. Obviously, if such defects do occur in used bottles there is a duty upon the bottler to make appropriate tests before they are refilled, and if such tests are not commercially practicable the bottles should not be re-used. This would seem to be particularly true where a charged liquid is placed in the bottle. It follows that a defect which would make the bottle unsound could be discovered by reasonable and practicable tests.

Although it is not clear in this case whether the explosion was caused by an excessive charge or a defect in the glass, there is a sufficient showing that neither cause would ordinarily have been present if due care had been used. Further, defendant had exclusive control over both the charging and inspection of the bottles. Accordingly, all the requirements necessary to entitle plaintiff to rely on the doctrine of res ipsa loquitur to supply an inference of negligence are present.

It is true that defendant presented evidence tending to show that it exercised considerable precaution by carefully regulating and checking the pressure in the bottles and by making visual inspections for defects in the glass at several stages during the bottling process. It is well settled, however, that when a defendant produces evidence to rebut the inference of negligence which arises upon application of the doctrine of res ipsa loquitur, it is ordinarily a question of fact for the jury to determine whether the inference has been dispelled.

The judgment is affirmed.

SHENK, J., CURTIS, J., CARTER, J., and SCHAUER, J., concurred.

TRAYNOR, J.

I concur in the judgment, but I believe the manufacturer's negligence should no longer be singled out as the basis of a plaintiff's right to recover in cases like the present one. In my opinion it should now be recognized that a manufacturer incurs an absolute liability when an article that he has placed on the market, knowing that it is to be used without inspection, proves to have a defect that causes injury to human beings. MacPherson v. Buick Motor Co., 217 N.Y. 382 [111 N.E. 1050], established the principle, recognized by this court, that irrespective of privity of contract, the manufacturer is responsible for an injury caused by such an article to any person who comes in lawful contact with it.

. . . Even if there is no negligence, however, public policy demands that responsibility be fixed wherever it will most effectively reduce the hazards to life and health inherent in defective products that reach the market. It is evident that the manufacturer can anticipate some hazards and guard against the recurrence of others, as the public cannot. Those who suffer injury from defective products are unprepared to meet its consequences. The cost of an injury and the loss of time or health may be an overwhelming misfortune to the person injured, and a needless one, for the risk of injury can be insured by the manufacturer and distributed among the public as a cost of doing business. It is to the public interest to discourage the marketing of products having defects that are a menace to the public. If such products nevertheless find their way into the market it is to the public interest to place the responsibility for whatever injury they may cause upon the manufacturer, who, even if he is not negligent in the manufacture of the product, is responsible for its reaching the market. However intermittently such injuries may occur and however haphazardly they may strike, the risk of their

authors' dialogue 1

JIM: You know, the thing that bugs me about *Escola* is how the plaintiff got away with her claim that the bottle was defective when it was delivered to the restaurant. I buy Traynor's point about applying strict liability instead of negligence. But how can he and the rest of the court practically assume away the defect issue?

AARON: I'm not sure they did that, Jim. The plaintiff introduced proof that the bottle had been handled normally, including when she retrieved it, herself, from the cooler. Why shouldn't that suffice?

JIM: It's proving a negative, Aaron. In effect, the court in *Escola* not only allows a presumption of manufacturer's negligence, but also a presumption of original defect. And *Escola* isn't the only case we've considered thus far that's done that.

AARON: What do you mean?

JIM: I wrote a "tort story" about *MacPherson*,[1] and I read the trial transcript in that case.

AARON: And?

JIM: Cardozo says in his opinion in *MacPherson* that the plaintiff was driving his nearly new Buick down the road when all of a sudden the wheel collapsed due to defective wooden spokes. He assumes a manufacturing defect and goes on to demolish the privity defense.

AARON: That makes sense to me. I assume plaintiff's experts examined the spokes and found them to be defective, and the jury bought their story. What's the problem?

JIM: The problem is that the car was more than a year old when the accident happened; had been driven safely many miles on rough country roads, hauling heavy gravestones (MacPherson was a stone carver); and had hit a telephone pole at fairly high speed when the wheel collapsed. The likelihood of the wheel actually being rotten when MacPherson originally bought the car was very low.

AARON: What's your point in telling me this? It doesn't change the law in either *MacPherson* or *Escola*, does it?

JIM: No, it doesn't. Cardozo and Traynor seem to have been so bent on changing the law that they winked at the facts. But the defect issue will come back to haunt them, mark my words.

AARON: Get down off the soapbox, Jim, before it collapses under you. We'll get to the defect issue soon enough. (See Section C, infra.)

---

1. See James A. Henderson, Jr., *MacPherson v. Buick Motor Co.:* Simplifying the Facts While Reshaping the Law, Tort Stories 41 (Robert L. Rabin & Stephen D. Sugarman eds. 2003).

occurrence is a constant risk and a general one. Against such a risk there should be general and constant protection and the manufacturer is best situated to afford such protection.

The injury from a defective product does not become a matter of indifference because the defect arises from causes other than the negligence of the manufacturer, such as negligence of a submanufacturer, of a component part whose defects could not be revealed by inspection or unknown causes that even by the device of res ipsa loquitur cannot be classified as negligence of the manufacturer. The inference of negligence may be dispelled by an affirmative showing of proper care. . . . An injured person, however, is not ordinarily in a position to refute such evidence or identify the cause of the defect, for he can hardly be familiar with the manufacturing process as the manufacturer himself is. In leaving it to the jury to decide whether the inference has been dispelled, regardless of the evidence against it, the negligence rule approaches the rule of strict liability. It is needlessly circuitous to make negligence the basis of recovery and impose what is in reality liability without negligence. If public policy demands that a manufacturer of goods be responsible for their quality regardless of negligence there is no reason not to fix that responsibility openly. . . .

As handicrafts have been replaced by mass production with its great markets and transportation facilities, the close relationship between the producer and consumer of a product has been altered. Manufacturing processes, frequently valuable secrets, are ordinarily either inaccessible to or beyond the ken of the general public. The consumer no longer has means or skill enough to investigate for himself the soundness of a product, even when it is not contained in a sealed package, and his erstwhile vigilance has been lulled by the steady efforts of manufacturers to build up confidence by advertising and marketing devices such as trademarks. Consumers no longer approach products warily but accept them on faith, relying on the reputation of the manufacturer or the trademark. Manufacturers have sought to justify that faith by increasingly high standards of inspection and a readiness to make good on defective products by way of replacements and refunds. The manufacturer's obligation to the consumer must keep pace with the changing relationship between them. . . .

B. THE MODERN RULE OF STRICT LIABILITY IN TORT

Strict products liability is liability in tort for harm caused by defective products without any necessity for the plaintiff to show negligence on the part of the defendant. Although it was many decades in the making, it finally came into American products liability law in the early 1960s. We shall consider, in Section D, the categories of commercial product suppliers to whom strict tort liability applies. In the discussions that follow we will assume that it applies to product manufacturers, wholesalers, and retailers. We shall also consider in Chapter Eight the elements of harm that may, and may not, be recovered under strict liability. For the purposes of this chapter, we will assume that the elements of harm for which plaintiffs may recover include personal injuries and property damage.

1.   Implied Warranty as a Bridge to Strict Liability in the 1950s and Early 1960s

Strict products liability evolved out of two different bases of liability: negligence and implied warranty. Prior to recognition of strict products liability by American courts in the 1960s, each of these theories of liability had a "good news, bad news" quality for products plaintiffs. Thus, while the privity requirement had been eliminated in negligence cases by the 1940s, due mainly to Cardozo's opinion in MacPherson v. Buick Motor Co., discussed in Section A, supra, it remained necessary for plaintiffs to prove negligence. Res ipsa loquitur was frequently available, as in Escola v. Coca-Cola Bottling Co., reprinted in the preceding section. But even there the jury could, in any given instance, refuse to draw an inference of negligence from the mere fact of a product defect. Historically, an alternative method of recovery that required the plaintiff to establish only defect (not fault) was available. Plaintiff could bring an action for breach of the implied warranty of merchantability. Under the Uniform Sales Act and later under the U.C.C. §2-314(2)(c), accompanying every sale of goods (unless disclaimed) is a warranty that the product is "reasonably fit for the ordinary purposes for which such goods are used." Defective products satisfy the statutory definition of unmerchantability and provide a predicate for a cause of action. Very simply, the implied warranty of merchantability can be characterized as "strict liability in contract."

But along with the "good news" that accompanied Code warranties, the "bad news" was quite substantial. First, because the cause of action was contractual, privity between the parties was required. *MacPherson*, supra, dealt the death blow to privity in causes of action based on negligence. The privity doctrine remained very much alive, however, in cases involving implied warranties. Admittedly, plaintiffs could sue immediate sellers with whom they were in privity, such as retailers, for breach of implied warranty. However, this right was often a mirage. Retail sellers were often judgment-proof. In some cases they disclaimed liability as allowed by the U.C.C. §2-316. Furthermore, the U.C.C. statute of limitations provides for a maximum of four years from tender of delivery (sale), U.C.C. §2-725. By contrast, a tort statute of limitations generally runs from the time of injury, thus in many cases providing a longer time to bring suit.

The landmark decision that stripped the implied warranty action of its contractual impediments involved an action for breach of the implied warranty of merchantability. In Henningsen v. Bloomfield Motors, Inc., 161 A.2d 69 (N.J. 1960), plaintiff brought suit for injuries sustained when a new Plymouth that her husband had purchased two weeks earlier went out of control. Mrs. Henningsen was driving when she heard a loud noise "from the bottom, by the hood." It "felt as if something cracked." The steering wheel spun in her hands; the car veered sharply to the right and crashed into a highway sign and a brick wall. The trial judge dismissed negligence counts against Chrysler, the manufacturer of the car. The judge submitted the issue of breach of implied warranty of merchantability to the jury, which found against both the retailer and the manufacturer.

The auto manufacturer, Chrysler, appealed the verdict against it on the grounds that it was not in privity with the injured plaintiff. In striking down the privity defense the court said:

> Under modern conditions the ordinary layman, on responding to the importuning of colorful advertising, has neither the opportunity nor the capacity to inspect or to determine the fitness of an automobile for use; he must rely on the manufacturer who has

control of its construction, and to some degree on the dealer who, to the limited extent called for by the manufacturer's instructions, inspects and services it before delivery. In such a marketing milieu his remedies and those of persons who properly claim through him should not depend "upon the intricacies of the law of sales. The obligation of the manufacturer should not be based alone on privity of contract. It should rest, as was once said, upon 'the demands of social justice.'" . . .

Accordingly, we hold that under modern marketing conditions, when a manufacturer puts a new automobile in the stream of trade and promotes its purchase by the public, an implied warranty that it is reasonably suitable for use as such accompanies it into the hands of the ultimate purchaser. Absence of agency between the manufacturer and the dealer who makes the ultimate sale is immaterial. [161 A.2d at 83-84.]

We are pleased to report that either by judicial decision or through legislative enactment[2] lack of privity is no longer a viable defense in personal injury litigation. As we shall see in a later chapter, in cases involving pure economic loss the privity defense retains considerable vitality.

After clearing the way for plaintiff's recovery by eliminating privity as a requirement for suit, the *Henningsen* court went on to invalidate the disclaimer of tort liability that was part of the standard automobile contract of sale. We defer discussion of the efficacy of disclaimers to later in this book.

The *Henningsen* decision, as important as it was, sought to impose strict liability against manufacturers within the terminology framework of the Uniform Commercial Code. Only a short time elapsed before American courts recognized that the language used by the U.C.C. to talk about liability provided a clumsy tool to utilize for prosecuting personal injury cases. Only two years after *Henningsen*, the time had come to announce that strict liability was a purely tort doctrine. See Greenman v. Yuba Power Products, Inc., 377 P.2d 897 (Cal. 1962). As fate would have it, the task of authoring the landmark opinion accomplishing this change fell to Justice Traynor, whose concurrence in *Escola* earlier had urged the replacement of res ipsa loquitur with strict liability in tort:

Although in these cases strict liability has usually been based on the theory of an express or implied warranty running from the manufacturer to the plaintiff, the abandonment of the requirement of a contract between them, the recognition that the liability is not assumed by agreement but imposed by law, and the refusal to permit the manufacturer to define the scope of its own responsibility for defective products make clear that the liability is not one governed by the law of contract warranties but by the law of strict liability in tort. Accordingly, rules defining and governing warranties that were developed to meet the needs of commercial transactions cannot properly be invoked to govern the manufacturer's liability to those injured by its defective products unless those rules also serve the purposes for which such liability is imposed.

We need not recanvass the reasons for imposing strict liability on the manufacturer. They have been fully articulated in the cases cited above. The purpose of such liability is to insure that the costs of injuries resulting from defective products are borne by the manufacturers that put such products on the market rather than by the injured persons who are powerless to protect themselves.

---

2. U.C.C. §2-318 (Alternative C) provides that both express and implied warranties extend "to any person who may reasonably be expected to use, consume, or be affected by the goods and who is injured in person by breach of the warranty."

2.   *Adoption of §402A of the Restatement (Second) of Torts in 1965*

Rarely has a single provision of any Restatement of the law had a greater impact on courts than did the adoption in 1965 of the strict liability rule in §402A. And rarely has a single individual been so closely associated with the development of a legal doctrine as was Professor William Prosser with the development of strict products liability. In what are perhaps the two best-known law review articles on the subject, Prosser developed the reasoning leading up to, and immediately following, judicial recognition of strict privity-free liability. See William S. Prosser, The Assault upon the Citadel (Strict Liability to the Consumer), 69 Yale L.J. 1099 (1960); Prosser, The Fall of the Citadel (Strict Liability to the Consumer), 50 Minn. L. Rev. 791 (1966). Prosser was in a unique position to predict the future path of American products liability law. As Reporter for the Restatement (Second) of Torts he played a leadership role in getting the American Law Institute to include a general strict products liability provision in its restatement of tort law. Based primarily on the *Greenman* decision, supra, and designated §402A, the new rule of strict tort liability was destined to dominate, and in some instances to confuse and confound, the law of products liability to the present day.

Restatement (Second) of Torts
(1965)

§402A. Special Liability of Seller of Product for Physical Harm to User or Consumer
   (1) One who sells any product in a defective condition unreasonably dangerous to the user or consumer or to his property is subject to liability for physical harm thereby caused to the ultimate user or consumer, or to his property, if
      (a) the seller is engaged in the business of selling such a product, and
      (b) it is expected to and does reach the user or consumer without substantial change in the condition in which it is sold.
   (2) The rule stated in Subsection (1) applies although
      (a) the seller has exercised all possible care in the preparation and sale of his product, and
      (b) the user or consumer has not bought the product from or entered into any contractual relation with the seller.

In Pulley v. Pacific Coca-Cola Bottling Co., 415 P.2d 636 (Wash. 1966), the plaintiff found a slimy cigarette in a new bottle of coke and became upset upon drinking it prior to that discovery. In her strict liability claim that followed, defendant Coca-Cola attempted to introduce evidence of their extreme care in trying to avoid such contamination, implying the cigarette must have entered the bottle post-sale. The trial court disallowed the evidence and the trial court entered judgment for plaintiff on a jury verdict. The Supreme Court of Washington affirmed, concluding that defendant's proof of due care was irrelevant and prejudicial in a strict liability.

3. Codification of the Strict Liability Rule in the Restatement (Third) of Torts in 1998

In 1992 the American Law Institute began the task of revising §402A by commissioning a project to write the Restatement (Third) of Torts: Products Liability. Two of the authors of this casebook were Reporters for the project, which was finally approved and promulgated in 1998. It provides a systematic formulation of American products liability in the familiar "black letter/comment" format. Courts have been reacting to the new Restatement since the late 1990s, for the most part favorably. It covers quite a bit more ground than §402A, and no court will adopt all of its provisions at once. Moreover, some of its provisions are controversial, and courts will differ in their reactions. We will include portions of it, where relevant, throughout these materials. Here are the first two sections which serve as the linchpins for the entire Products Liability Restatement project.

Restatement (Third) of Torts: Products Liability
(1998)

§1. LIABILITY OF COMMERCIAL SELLER OR DISTRIBUTOR FOR HARM CAUSED BY DEFECTIVE PRODUCTS

One engaged in the business of selling or otherwise distributing products who sells or distributes a defective product is subject to liability for harm to persons or property caused by the defect.

§2. CATEGORIES OF PRODUCT DEFECT

A product is defective when, at the time of sale or distribution, it contains a manufacturing defect, is defective in design, or is defective because of inadequate instructions or warnings. A product:

(a) contains a manufacturing defect when the product departs from its intended design even though all possible care was exercised in the preparation and marketing of the product;

(b) is defective in design when the foreseeable risks of harm posed by the product could have been reduced or avoided by the adoption of a reasonable alternative design by the seller or other distributor, or a predecessor in the commercial chain of distribution, and the omission of the alternative design renders the product not reasonably safe;

(c) is defective because of inadequate instructions or warnings when the foreseeable risks of harm posed by the product could have been reduced or avoided by the provision of reasonable instructions or warnings by the seller or other distributor, or a predecessor in the commercial chain of distribution, and the omission of the instructions or warnings renders the product not reasonably safe.

COMMENT:

c. Manufacturing defects. As stated in Subsection (a), a manufacturing defect is a departure from a product unit's design specifications. More distinctly than any other type of defect, manufacturing defects disappoint consumer expectations. Common examples of manufacturing defects are products that are physically flawed, damaged, or incorrectly assembled. In actions against the manufacturer, under prevailing rules concerning allocation of burdens of proof, plaintiff ordinarily bears the burden of establishing that such a defect existed in the product when it left the hands of the manufacturer. Occasionally a defect may arise after manufacture, for example, during shipment or while in storage. Since the product, as sold to the consumer, has a defect that is a departure from the product unit's design specifications, a commercial seller or distributor down the chain of distribution is liable as if the product were defectively manufactured. As long as the plaintiff establishes that the product was defective when it left the hands of a given seller in the distributive chain, liability will attach to that seller. Such defects are referred to in this Restatement as "manufacturing defects" even when they occur after manufacture.

PROBLEM ONE

Your firm represents Hilda Brooks, age 58, in a products liability action against Zonar Manufacturing Co. Zonar manufactures surgical implants. Ms. Brooks underwent surgery on her leg about a year ago, during which her doctor implanted a surgical pin known as a Schneider intramedullary rod into her fractured bone to provide support and stabilization during the healing process. Ms. Brooks remained in a wheelchair for approximately six months after surgery and was then permitted to place partial weight on the affected leg, first while using a single crutch and later a cane. Several months after she began walking on the leg a routine X-ray revealed a break in the rod, which, according to one of the doctors, had probably occurred several days earlier.

Because of the breaking of the intramedullary rod, Ms. Brooks's doctors recommended surgery to correct the situation. As it turned out the breaking of the rod led the doctors to perform two separate operations. The first operation was not wholly successful and a second surgical intervention was necessary.

The case is in the midst of trial. Plaintiff presented the testimony of two metallurgists and a mechanical engineer. The metallurgists' analyses revealed the presence of various imperfections in the rod, including a small crack about a quarter-inch from the break, pitting on the surface of the rod, and inclusions (foreign objects in the steel). Their testimony indicated that any of these imperfections could have existed at the time the rod left the manufacturer and that their presence could initiate a crack in the metal and create areas of stress concentration, weakening the metal so that fatigue failure would occur at a stage considerably below the ordinary anticipated endurance level. It was the opinion of both metallurgists that, if the rod was properly designed for implantation in the human body and not bent prior to use, the failure resulted from a defect that existed at the time of manufacture. The mechanical engineer took measurements of the rod and of plaintiff, ascertained weight distribution, and determined the stress placed upon the rod in walking and in rising from a sitting position. Given the tensile strength of the rod and its endurance limit, the rod, in his opinion, could not have fractured unless a defect existed.

Defendant's expert, qualified both in the fields of metallurgy and mechanical engineering, testified that fracture of the rod occurred as a result of fatigue failure. Her extensive research in the field of implants had shown that because maximum stress occurs at the point of non-union of the bone, fatigue failure of the implant commonly occurs at that same point. It was this witness's opinion that the computations of plaintiff's expert were inaccurate because, in determining the endurance limit of the implanted rod, consideration had not been afforded the additional stresses brought by muscle pull, which, in her experience, can surpass the stresses of bodily weight. She further testified that no defect existed in the rod; its failure, rather, resulted from the stress of a cyclic load over an extended period of time in the area of non-union of the bone.

Defendant's counsel, Robert Best, is seeking to bolster his expert's opinion by introducing the testimony of Allen Franklin, the director of quality control at Zonar. The trial judge excused the jury and heard Best's offer of proof. Best told the court that Franklin will testify that, unlike most quality control procedures that merely test random samples of the product to assure quality, Zonar submits every surgical implant to rigorous inspection which, Franklin insists, would have caught any defect.

Defendant's attempt to introduce this testimony came late this afternoon. Judge Moses decided to recess for the day and has requested both sides to brief the issue and to present her with memos in the morning.

The State of New California has adopted strict liability in tort. It has not specifically ruled on the issue of the admissibility of quality control techniques in a strict liability case. Mr. Young, the partner who is trying the case, has asked you to prepare a memo arguing against the admissibility of Franklin's testimony. Young also wants you to anticipate Best's arguments and prepare rebuttals to them.

4. Policy Objectives Supporting Strict Liability in Tort

The place to begin the analysis is with Justice Roger Traynor's concurrence in *Escola*, supra, the exploding Coke bottle case from California decided in 1944. You will recall that Traynor urged his colleagues to stop relying on res ipsa loquitur in favor of adopting strict liability in tort. It is worth setting forth his reasoning verbatim (150 P.2d at 462):

> . . . Even if there is no negligence, however, public policy demands that responsibility be fixed wherever it will most effectively reduce the hazards to life and health inherent in defective products that reach the market. It is evident that the manufacturer can anticipate some hazards and guard against the recurrence of others, as the public cannot. Those who suffer injury from defective products are unprepared to meet its consequences. The cost of an injury and the loss of time or health may be an overwhelming misfortune to the person injured, and a needless one, for the risk of injury can be insured by the manufacturer and distributed among the public as a cost of doing business. It is to the public interest to discourage the marketing of products having defects that are a menace to the public. If such products nevertheless find their way into the market it is to the public interest to place the responsibility for whatever injury they may cause upon the manufacturer, who, even if he is not negligent in the manufacture of the product, is responsible for its reaching the market. However intermittently such injuries may occur and however haphazardly they may strike, the risk of their occurrence is a constant risk and a general one. Against such a risk there should be general and constant protection and the manufacturer is best situated to afford such protection.

Several aspects of Justice Traynor's analysis may seem, at least at first glance, somewhat puzzling. First, he says responsibility should be fixed wherever it will reduce the hazards inherent in defective products. But doesn't a negligence rule, properly administered, achieve that risk-reduction objective? That is, doesn't the traditional negligence rule require manufacturers to prevent all the defects that are worth preventing? How will strict liability improve on that situation? Another potential puzzlement arises in connection with Traynor's observation that, with respect to defects that do reach the market and cause harm despite the manufacturer's reasonable efforts at quality control, "the manufacturer is best situated to afford general and constant protection." What sort of protection does strict liability in tort afford the product purchaser who, on Traynor's assumption, has already been injured by the product defect?

PROBLEM TWO

Assume that a manufacturer distributes products that occasionally contain defects that cause injury. Quality control measures in the form of inspection for defects are available by which to reduce the incidence of defects, each successive measure costing more than the last. Without any inspection (quality control), 10 defect-caused accidents will occur per 100,000 product units, at an expected cost of $1,000/accident. Assume that the manufacturer's costs of investments in quality control and the corresponding reductions in accidents are reflected in the chart set forth in Table 1. Assume further that the only costs associated with manufacturing defects are those included in the chart and that negligent manufacturers are liable for "residual accident costs." How far would a rational manufacturer invest in quality control under a negligence rule perfectly and costlessly applied? How far, under strict liability? See if you can answer these questions using the data given in the chart in Table 1. Then fill in columns (6), (7), and (8), either to help reach the answers or to confirm their validity. Surprised? Might there even be an argument that a manufacturer will provide greater quality control under a negligence regime than under strict liability?

It is useful to consider the fairness implications of the move from negligence to strict liability. Under negligence, it will be recalled, accident victims bear the burden of insuring against the residual accident losses that are not worth avoiding. Under strict liability, manufacturers insure against those residual losses and pass on the insurance costs to purchasers as part of the prices paid for the products. Observe that the premiums charged for the insurance are priced on a pro-rata, per product basis. A rock star who buys a bottle of soda pays the same loss insurance premium as does a law student. And yet the loss insurance is worth much, much more to the rock star than to the typical law student. (Do you see why?) Under negligence, where each would-be victim buys his own insurance, the rock star pays much more in premiums, reflecting the fact that the rock star's insurance is worth much more. But under strict liability, both the rock star and the law student pay the same premium. In effect, under strict liability the law student subsidizes the rock star. Is this fair?

Table 1

reduction in flaw-caused accidents (per 100K prod's)	(1) marginal accident cost reduction (per unit quality control)	(2) total accident cost reduction (cumulative)	(3) total residual accident costs (per 100K prod's)	(4) marginal costs of quality control (per unit quality control)	(5) total costs quality control (cumulative)	(6) total social costs of quality control and accidents	(7) total producer's cost (quality control and liability) under negligence	(8) total producer's costs (quality control and liability) under strict liability
10 → 9	1,000	1,000	9,000	100	100			
9 → 8	1,000	2,000	8,000	300	400			
8 → 7	1,000	3,000	7,000	700	1,100			
7 → 6	1,000	4,000	6,000	1,200	2,300			
6 → 5	1,000	5,000	5,000	1,900	4,200			
5 → 4	1,000	6,000	4,000	2,800	7,000			
4 → 3	1,000	7,000	3,000	5,400	12,400			
3 → 2	1,000	8,000	2,000	11,000	23,400			

C.   DEFECT AS THE LINCHPIN OF
STRICT PRODUCTS LIABILITY

Strict liability for manufacturing defects is settled law in every jurisdiction in this country. This might lead you to think that products liability plaintiffs harmed by manufacturing defects "have got it made in the shade." Well, think again. While courts no longer require plaintiffs to show that a manufacturer was negligent in allowing a defect to escape into the stream of commerce, they continue to require plaintiffs to prove that a defect caused the accident and that the defect existed when the defendant sold or otherwise commercially distributed the product. Proving an "original defect" (a defect that existed at the time of original distribution) is as difficult now as it was back in Judge Traynor's day. To understand the role of defect as the linchpin of strict products liability, two questions must be answered: (1) What, exactly, makes a product defective? and (2) How does the plaintiff prove original defect? This section seeks to answer these questions.

1.   What Makes a Product Defective? (The Conceptual Dimension)

Without defining the term "defect," §402A of the Restatement (Second) of Torts (1965) refers to "any product in a defective condition unreasonably dangerous to the user or consumer." What purpose does the "unreasonably dangerous" modifier serve? Consider the following case.

Cronin v. J. B. E. Olson Corp.
501 P.2d 1153 (Cal. 1972)

SULLIVAN, J.

In this products liability case, the principal question which we face is whether the injured plaintiff seeking recovery upon the theory of strict liability in tort must establish, among other facts, not only that the product contained a defect which proximately caused his injuries but also that such defective condition made the product unreasonably dangerous to the user or consumer. We have concluded that he need not do so. Accordingly, we find no error in the trial court's refusal to so instruct the jury. Rejecting as without merit various challenges to the sufficiency of the evidence, we affirm the judgment.

On October 3, 1966, plaintiff, a route salesman for Gravem-Inglis Bakery Co. (Gravem) of Stockton, was driving a bread delivery truck along a rural road in San Joaquin County. While plaintiff was attempting to pass a pick-up truck ahead of him, its driver made a sudden left turn, causing the pick-up to collide with the plaintiff's truck and forcing the latter off the road and into a ditch. As a result, plaintiff was propelled through the windshield and landed on the ground. The impact broke an aluminum safety hasp which was located just behind the driver's seat and designed to hold the bread trays in place. The loaded trays, driven forward by the abrupt stop and impact of the truck, struck plaintiff in the back and hurled him through the windshield. He sustained serious personal injuries.

The truck, a one-ton Chevrolet stepvan with built-in bread racks, was one of several trucks sold to Gravem in 1957 by defendant Chase Chevrolet Company (Chase), not a party to this appeal. Upon receipt of Gravem's order, Chase purchased the trucks from defendant J. B. E. Olson Corporation (Olson), which acted as sales agent for the assembled vehicle, the chassis, body, and racks of which were manufactured by three subcontractors. The body of the van contained three aisles along which there were welded runners extending from the front to the rear of the truck. Each rack held ten bread trays from top to bottom and five trays deep; the trays slid forward into the cab or back through the rear door to facilitate deliveries.

Plaintiff brought the present action against Chase, Olson and General Motors Corporation[3] alleging that the truck was unsafe for its intended use because of defects in its manufacture, in that the metal hasp was exceedingly porous, contained holes, pits and voids, and lacked sufficient tensile strength to withstand the impact. Defendants' answers denied the material allegations of the complaint and asserted the affirmative defense of contributory negligence. Subsequently, upon leave of court, the additional defense of assumption of the risk was asserted.

At the trial, plaintiff's expert testified, in substance, that the metal hasp broke, releasing the bread trays, because it was extremely porous and had a significantly lower tolerance to force than a non-flawed aluminum hasp would have had. The jury returned a verdict in favor of plaintiff and against Olson in the sum of $45,000 but in favor of defendant Chase and against plaintiff. Judgment was entered accordingly. This appeal by Olson followed.

Defendant attacks the sufficiency of the evidence to support the verdict and the trial court's instruction on strict liability. The challenge to the evidence is multi-pronged, claiming in effect that plaintiff produced no evidence on several essential issues. We first turn to this challenge, considering defendant's arguments in the order presented.

[The court concludes that the plaintiff introduced sufficient evidence to support the conclusion that the hasp was defective when originally supplied by the defendant. A collision of the sort involved here is reasonably foreseeable, and the hasp was intended to prevent what happened here. Plaintiff's expert testified that if the hasp had not been weak and porous, it would have prevented the plaintiff's injuries. The court next turns to the question of whether the trial judge erred in instructing the jury that it might find the hasp defective, and the defendant liable, without finding the hasp to have been unreasonably dangerous.]

The history of strict liability in California indicates that the requirement that the defect made the product "unreasonably dangerous" crept into our jurisprudence without fanfare after its inclusion in section 402A of the Restatement (Second) of Torts in 1965. The question raised in the instant matter as to whether the requirement is an essential part of the plaintiff's case is one of first impression.

We begin with section 402A itself. According to the official comment to the section, a "defective condition" is one "not contemplated by the ultimate consumer, which will be unreasonably dangerous to him." (Rest. 2d Torts, §402A, com. *g.*) Comment *i*, defining "unreasonably dangerous," states, "The article sold must be dangerous to an extent beyond that which would be contemplated by the ordinary consumer who purchases it, with the ordinary knowledge common to the community as to its

---

3. Defendant General Motors Corporation, manufacturer of the chassis, was voluntarily dismissed by plaintiff prior to trial.

characteristics." Examples given in comment *i* make it clear that such innocuous products as sugar and butter, unless contaminated, would not give rise to a strict liability claim merely because the former may be harmful to a diabetic or the latter may aggravate the blood cholesterol level of a person with heart disease. Presumably such dangers are squarely within the contemplation of the ordinary consumer. Prosser, the reporter for the Restatement, suggests that the "unreasonably dangerous" qualification was added to foreclose the possibility that the manufacturer of a product with inherent possibilities for harm (for example, butter, drugs, whiskey and automobiles) would become "automatically responsible for all the harm that such things do in the world." (Prosser, Strict Liability to the Consumer in California (1966) 18 Hastings L.J. 9, 23.)

The result of the limitation, however, has not been merely to prevent the seller from becoming an insurer of his products with respect to all harm generated by their use. Rather, it has burdened the injured plaintiff with proof of an element which rings of negligence. As a result, if, in the view of the trier of fact, the "ordinary consumer" would have expected the defective condition of a product, the seller is not strictly liable regardless of the expectations of the injured plaintiff. If, for example, the "ordinary consumer" would have contemplated that Shopsmiths posed a risk of loosening their grip and letting the wood strike the operator, another Greenman might be denied recovery. In fact, it has been observed that the Restatement formulation of strict liability in practice rarely leads to a different conclusion than would have been reached under laws of negligence.

Of particular concern is the susceptibility of Restatement section 402A to a literal reading which would require the finder of fact to conclude that the product is, first, defective and, second, unreasonably dangerous. A bifurcated standard is of necessity more difficult to prove than a unitary one. But merely proclaiming that the phrase "defective condition unreasonably dangerous" requires only a single finding would not purge that phrase of its negligence complexion. We think that a requirement that a plaintiff also prove that the defect made the product "unreasonably dangerous" places upon him a significantly increased burden and represents a step backward in the area pioneered by this court.

We recognize that the words "unreasonably dangerous" may also serve the beneficial purpose of preventing the seller from being treated as the insurer of its products. However, we think that such protective end is attained by the necessity of proving that there was a defect in the manufacture or design of the product and that such defect was a proximate cause of the injuries. Although the seller should not be responsible for all injuries involving the use of its products, it should be liable for all injuries proximately caused by any of its products which are adjudged "defective."

We can see no difficulty in applying [this] formulation to the full range of products liability situations, including those involving "design defects." A defect may emerge from the mind of the designer as well as from the hand of the workman.

Although it is easier to see the "defect" in a single imperfectly fashioned product than in an entire line badly conceived, a distinction between manufacture and design defects is not tenable.

The most obvious problem we perceive in creating any such distinction is that thereafter it would be advantageous to characterize a defect in one rather than the other category. It is difficult to prove that a product ultimately caused injury because a widget was poorly welded—a defect in manufacture—rather than because it was made of inexpensive metal difficult to weld, chosen by a designer concerned with economy — a defect in design. The proof problem would, of course, be magnified when the article in question was either old or unique, with no easily available basis for comparison. We wish to avoid providing such a battleground for clever counsel. Furthermore, we find no reason why a different standard, and one harder to meet, should apply to defects which plague entire product lines. We recognize that it is more damaging to a manufacturer to have an entire line condemned, so to speak, for a defect in design, than a single product for a defect in manufacture. But the potential economic loss to a manufacturer should not be reflected in a different standard of proof for an injured consumer.

In summary, we have concluded that to require an injured plaintiff to prove not only that the product contained a defect but also that such defect made the product unreasonably dangerous to the user or consumer would place a considerably greater burden upon him than that articulated in *Greenman*. We believe the *Greenman* formulation is consonant with the rationale and development of products liability law in California because it provides a clear and simple test for determining whether the injured plaintiff is entitled to recovery. We are not persuaded to the contrary by the formulation of section 402A which inserts the factor of an "unreasonably dangerous" condition into the equation of products liability.

We conclude that the trial court did not err by refusing to instruct the jury that plaintiff must establish that the defective condition of the product made it unreasonably dangerous to the user or consumer.

The judgment is affirmed.

WRIGHT, C.J., McCOMB, J., PETERS, J., TOBRINER, J., MOSK, J., and BURKE, J., concurred.

Some of the *Cronin* court's confidence that "unreasonably dangerous" is not necessary may lie in the relative ease with which manufacturing defects may be conceptualized. As reflected in all of the materials considered up to this point, manufacturing defects are imperfections in a few product units out of many, which cause the few units to fail dangerously during use. As we shall discover in later chapters dealing with liability for defective product design, courts encounter conceptual difficulties trying to construct objective legal standards of reasonableness with which to determine the adequacy of product designs.

The simple "imperfectly fashioned" and "departure from the intended design" definitions of "manufacturing defect" in *Cronin* and §2(a) of the Restatement (Third), respectively, raise interesting questions. For example, an anonymous critic of the Products Liability Restatement noted that liability would ensue under §2(a) if a defective connection of a wire in a car radio caused static and diverted the attention of the driver to fiddle with the dial, thus taking the driver's eye off the road and resulting in an accident. Was the critic right? Why were the Reporters so bullheaded in their insistence, with regard to manufacturing defects, that there be no requirement that the defect render the product "not reasonably safe?" And what about the buyer who finds a minor imperfection in the paint of his new automobile? Does he have a tort claim for having received a less-than-perfect, and therefore legally defective, product? Would a "not reasonably safe" requirement help sort out such claims?

2. How Does the Plaintiff Prove Original Defect? (The Practical Dimension)

One obvious way for a plaintiff to prove an original product defect is through the testimony of an expert who has examined the product and is able to opine that a defect at time of sale caused the accident. *Cronin*, supra, involved such testimony in connection with the failure of a metal hasp in a bread truck. Experts in that case examined the hasp and found the metal to be dangerously porous. This sort of direct evidence of original defect appears in many of the reported decisions in this and subsequent chapters. Even more important to plaintiffs is circumstantial proof of defect. Typically, the product malfunctions under circumstances that support an inference of original defect. The Products Liability Restatement addresses this phenomenon in the following way:

Restatement (Third) of Torts: Products Liability
(1998)

§3. CIRCUMSTANTIAL EVIDENCE SUPPORTING INFERENCE OF PRODUCT DEFECT

It may be inferred that the harm sustained by the plaintiff was caused by a product defect existing at the time of sale or distribution, without proof of a specific defect, when the incident that harmed the plaintiff:

(a) was of a kind that ordinarily occurs as a result of product defect; and

(b) was not, in the particular case, solely the result of causes other than product defect existing at the time of sale or distribution.

COMMENT:

b. Requirement that the [harmful incident] be of a kind that ordinarily occurs as a result of product defect. The most frequent application of this Section is to cases involving manufacturing defects. When a product unit contains such a defect, and the defect affects product performance so as to cause a harmful incident, in most instances it will cause the product to malfunction in such a way that the inference of product defect is clear. From this perspective, manufacturing defects cause products to fail to perform their manifestly intended functions. Frequently, the plaintiff is able to establish specifically the nature and identity of the defect and may proceed directly under §2(a). But when the product unit involved in the harm-causing incident is lost or destroyed in the accident, direct evidence of specific defect may not be available. Under that circumstance, this Section may offer the plaintiff the only fair opportunity to recover.

When examination of the product unit is impossible because the unit is lost or destroyed after the harm-causing incident, a somewhat different issue may be presented. Responsibility for spoliation of evidence may be relevant to the fairness of allowing the inference set forth in this Section. In any event, the issues of evidence spoliation and any sanctions that might be imposed for such conduct are beyond the scope of this Restatement, Third, Torts: Products Liability. . . .

ILLUSTRATIONS:

1. John purchased a new electric blender. John used the blender approximately 10 times exclusively for making milkshakes. While he was making a milkshake, the blender suddenly shattered. A piece of glass struck John's eye, causing harm. The incident resulting in harm is of a kind that ordinarily occurs as a result of product defect.

2. Same facts as Illustration 1, except that John accidentally dropped the blender, causing the glass to shatter. The product did not fail to function in a manner supporting an inference of defect. Whether liability can be established depends on whether the plaintiff can prove a cause of action under §§1 and 2 [based on direct proof of defect].

c. No requirement that plaintiff prove what aspect of the product was defective. The inference of defect may be drawn under this Section without proof of the specific defect. Furthermore, quite apart from the question of what type of defect was involved, the plaintiff need not explain specifically what constituent part of the product failed. For example, if an inference of defect can be appropriately drawn in connection with the catastrophic failure of an airplane, the plaintiff need not establish whether the failure is attributable to fuel-tank explosion or engine malfunction.

d. Requirement that the incident that harmed the plaintiff was not, in the particular case, solely the result of causes other than product defect existing at the time of sale. To allow the trier of fact to conclude that a product defect caused the plaintiff's harm under this Section, the plaintiff must establish by a preponderance of the evidence that the incident was not solely the result of causal factors other than defect at time of sale. The defect need not be the only cause of the incident; if the plaintiff can prove that the most likely explanation of the harm involves the causal contribution of a product defect, the fact that there may be other concurrent causes of the harm does not preclude liability under this Section. But when the harmful incident can be attributed solely to causes other than original defect, including the conduct of others, an inference of defect under this Section cannot be drawn.

Evidence may permit the inference that a defect in the product at the time of the harm-causing incident caused the product to malfunction, but not the inference that the defect existed at the time of sale or distribution. Such factors as the age of the product, possible alteration by repairers or others, and misuse by the plaintiff or third parties may have introduced the defect that causes harm.

ILLUSTRATION:

6. While driving a new automobile at high speed one night, Driver drove off the highway and crashed into a tree. Driver suffered harm. Driver cannot remember the circumstances surrounding the accident. Driver has brought an action against ABC Company, the manufacturer of the automobile. Driver presents no evidence of a specific defect. However, Driver's qualified expert presents credible testimony that a defect in the automobile must have caused the accident. ABC's qualified expert presents credible testimony that it is equally likely that, independent of any defect, Driver lost control while speeding on the highway. If the trier of fact believes the testimony of Driver's expert, then an inference of defect may be established under this Section. If, however, ABC's expert is

believed, an inference of product defect may not be drawn under this Section because Driver has failed to establish by a preponderance of the evidence that the harm did not result solely from Driver's independent loss of control at high speed.

Speller v. Sears, Roebuck & Co.
790 N.E.2d 252 (N.Y. 2003)

GRAFFEO, J.

In this products liability case, [the trial court denied defendants' motion for summary judgment and defendants brought an interlocutory appeal to the Appellate Division, which reversed and] granted summary judgment dismissing plaintiffs' complaint. Because we conclude that plaintiffs raised a triable issue of fact concerning whether a defective refrigerator caused the fire that resulted in plaintiffs' injuries, we reverse and reinstate the complaint against these defendants.

Plaintiffs' decedent Sandra Speller died in a house fire that also injured her seven-year-old son. It is undisputed that the fire originated in the kitchen. Plaintiffs commenced this action against Sears, Roebuck and Co., Whirlpool Corporation and the property owner alleging negligence, strict products liability and breach of warranty. Relevant to this appeal, plaintiffs asserted that the fire was caused by defective wiring in the refrigerator, a product manufactured by Whirlpool and sold by Sears. After discovery, defendants Sears and Whirlpool moved for summary judgment seeking dismissal of the complaint. Relying principally on a report issued by the New York City Fire Marshal, defendants rejected the refrigerator as the source of the fire, instead contending that a stovetop grease fire was the cause of the conflagration. Thus, they argued that their product was outside the chain of causation that resulted in plaintiffs' damages.

In opposition to defendants' motion for summary judgment, plaintiffs submitted excerpts from the depositions of two experts and an affidavit from a third, as well as other materials. Plaintiffs' experts refuted the conclusions reached in the Fire Marshal's report, opining that the fire started in the upper right quadrant of the refrigerator, an area with a concentration of electrical wiring. All three rejected the stove as the source of the fire. Plaintiffs also submitted portions of the deposition of a Whirlpool engineer retained as an expert by defendants. Although the engineer disputed that the fire originated in the refrigerator, he acknowledged that a fire would not occur in a refrigerator unless the product was defective.

Supreme Court denied defendants' request for summary judgment, holding that plaintiffs' submissions raised a triable issue of fact as to whether the fire was caused by a defect in the refrigerator. The Appellate Division reversed and granted the motion, dismissing the complaint as against Sears and Whirlpool. The Court reasoned that defendants' evidence suggesting an alternative cause of the fire shifted the burden to plaintiffs to come forward with specific evidence of a defect. Characterizing the submissions of plaintiffs' experts as "equivocal," the Court concluded that plaintiffs failed to satisfy their burden of proof to withstand summary judgment. (294 A.D.2d 349, 350 [2002].) This Court granted plaintiffs leave to appeal. . . .

In this case, plaintiffs' theory was that the wiring in the upper right quadrant of the refrigerator was faulty, causing an electrical fire which then spread to other areas of the kitchen and residence. Because that part of the refrigerator had been consumed in the fire, plaintiffs noted that it was impossible to examine or test the wiring to determine the precise nature of the defect. Thus, plaintiffs sought to prove their claim circumstantially by establishing that the refrigerator caused the house fire and therefore did not perform as intended.

New York has long recognized the viability of this circumstantial approach in products liability cases. . . . In order to proceed in the absence of evidence identifying a specific flaw, a plaintiff must prove that the product did not perform as intended and exclude all other causes for the product's failure that are not attributable to defendants. . . . In this regard, New York law is consistent with the Restatement, which reads: [The court sets out §3, supra.]

Here, in their motion for summary judgment, defendants focused on the second prong of the circumstantial inquiry, offering evidence that the injuries were not caused by their product but by an entirely different instrumentality — a grease fire that began on top of the stove. This was the conclusion of the Fire Marshal who stated during deposition testimony that his opinion was based on his interpretation of the burn patterns in the kitchen, his observation that one of the burner knobs on the stove was in the "on" position, and his conversation with a resident of the home who apparently advised him that the oven was on when the resident placed some food on the stovetop a few hours before the fire.

In order to withstand summary judgment, plaintiffs were required to come forward with competent evidence excluding the stove as the origin of the fire. To meet that burden, plaintiffs offered three expert opinions: the depositions of an electrical engineer and a fire investigator, and the affidavit of a former Deputy Chief of the New York City Fire Department. Each concluded that the fire originated in the refrigerator and not on the stove.

In his extensive deposition testimony, the electrical engineer opined that the fire started in the top-right-rear corner of the refrigerator, an area that housed the air balancing unit, thermostat, moisture control and light control. He stated that the wiring in this part of the appliance had been destroyed in the fire, making it impossible to identify the precise mechanical failure and, thus, he could only speculate as to the specific nature of the defect. He testified that the "most logical probability" was that a bad connection or bad splice to one of the components in that portion of the unit caused the wire to become "red hot" and to ignite the adjacent plastic. He tested the combustibility of the plastic and confirmed that the "plastic lights up very easily, with a single match" and continues to burn like candle wax. The engineer observed that the doors of the refrigerator were "slightly bellied out," indicating they were blown out from the expanding hot gases inside the refrigerator. The wall behind the refrigerator was significantly damaged and the upper right quadrant was burned to such a degree that it was not likely to have been caused by an external fire. Interpreting the burn patterns differently from the Fire Marshal, the electrical engineer found that the cabinets above the stove, although damaged, were not destroyed to the extent he expected to find if there had been a stovetop grease fire.

Plaintiffs' fire investigator similarly opined that the fire originated in the refrigerator's upper right corner, in part basing his conclusion on his observations of the scene three days after the fire and his examination of the appliances. He also interviewed a witness to the fire. He testified that he eliminated the stove as the source of the fire after his examination of that appliance and the cabinets above it. Contrary to the testimony of the Fire Marshal, he observed that all of the burner knobs on the stove were in the same position, either all "off" or all "on." He further examined the burn patterns, noting that if the blaze had been caused by a grease fire on the stove, the cabinets directly above would have been consumed in the fire. Instead, they were merely damaged. He acknowledged that he did not know exactly how the fire started inside the refrigerator but indicated he suspected there had been a poor connection in the wiring that caused the wire to smolder until it ignited the highly combustible foam insulation inside the unit.

The former Deputy Chief of the New York City Fire Department asserted in his affidavit that the "fire damage to the area around the refrigerator when compared to that of the stove clearly shows the longer and heavier burn at the refrigerator," indicating the fire originated there. He also stated that he had ruled out all other possible origins of the fire. Upon review of these expert depositions and affidavit, we conclude that plaintiffs raised a triable question of fact by offering competent evidence which, if credited by the jury, was sufficient to rebut defendants' alternative cause evidence. In other words, based on plaintiffs' proof, a reasonable jury could conclude that plaintiffs excluded all other causes of the fire.

We therefore disagree with the Appellate Division's characterization of plaintiffs' submissions as equivocal. Plaintiffs' experts consistently asserted that the fire originated in the upper right quadrant of the refrigerator and each contended the stove was not the source of the blaze. Both parties supported their positions with detailed, non-conclusory expert depositions and other submissions which explained the bases for the opinions.

Defendants contend that after they came forward with evidence suggesting an alternative cause of the fire, plaintiffs were foreclosed from establishing a product defect circumstantially but were then required to produce evidence of a specific defect to survive summary judgment. We reject this approach for two reasons. First, such an analysis would allow a defendant who offered minimally sufficient alternative cause evidence in a products liability case to foreclose a plaintiff from proceeding circumstantially without a jury having determined whether defendant's evidence should be credited. Second, it misinterprets the court's role in adjudicating a motion for summary judgment, which is issue identification, not issue resolution. Where causation is disputed, summary judgment is not appropriate unless "only one conclusion may be drawn from the established facts" (Kriz v. Schum, 75 N.Y.2d 25, 34 [1989]). That is not the case here where plaintiffs directly rebutted defendants' submissions with competent proof specifically ruling out the stove as the source of the blaze. Because a reasonable jury could credit this proof and find that plaintiffs excluded all other causes of the fire not attributable to defendants, this case presents material issues of fact requiring a trial.

Accordingly, the order of the Appellate Division should be reversed, with costs, and the motion of defendants Sears, Roebuck and Co. and Whirlpool Corporation for summary judgment denied.

. . .

Chief Judge KAYE and Judges SMITH, CIPARICK, WESLEY, ROSENBLATT and READ concur.

Order reversed, etc.

The issue of circumstantial proof in *Speller* continues to arise in products litigation. In Bradley v. Earl B. Feiden, Inc., 8 N.Y.3d 265 (2007), the plaintiff offered expert testimony to prove that a kitchen fire originated in his three-week-old refrigerator and that, specifically, a defective defrost timer in the refrigerator caused the fire. The defendant's experts excluded the defrost timer as the cause and suggested that an electric can opener started the blaze. The plaintiff's experts ruled out the can opener theory. In response to special interrogatories, the jury found that the fire started in the refrigerator and not the can opener, but also found that, although the defrost timer did not cause the refrigerator fire, some other defect in the refrigerator did cause it. After judgment on the jury verdict for the plaintiff, the defendant appealed, arguing, in part, insufficiency of plaintiff's proof. The New York Court of Appeals affirmed the judgment for plaintiff. Even though the jury rejected the specific defrost timer claim, a reasonable jury could still have found that the fire started in the refrigerator and that an unspecified defect in the refrigerator must have caused the fire.

In Z.C. v. Wal-Mart Stores, Inc., 574 F. App'x 52 (2d Cir. 2014), the young plaintiff dropped a BB gun which discharged and caused harm to his right eye. After the accident, plaintiff's father destroyed the gun, and another BB gun that plaintiff also was playing with, preventing experts from determining which gun had discharged or what defect caused the discharge. The trial court granted summary judgment for the defendant seller and the court of appeals affirmed. Evidence that the guns were not new and had been used roughly prior to the accident undermined plaintiff's attempt to argue that the defect originated at the time of original sale by defendant.

A plaintiff may introduce evidence of similar product failures in other product units as probative of the alleged manufacturing defect in the product in question. In deciding whether to admit evidence of other accidents, trial courts consider the degree of similarity between the accidents and the potential for undue prejudice and jury confusion. See Nissan Motor Co. v. Armstrong, 145 S.W.3d 131 (Tex. 2004). In *Armstrong*, the plaintiff alleged that a throttle defect caused an accident. The trial court admitted into evidence Nissan's database of 757 customer complaints involving unintended acceleration of its ZX sports cars and entered judgment on a plaintiff's verdict. The intermediate court affirmed, deeming the evidence probative of the throttle defect alleged by plaintiff. The Supreme Court of Texas reversed, ruling that the unsworn, unsubstantiated records of similar but not identical incidents were of limited probative value and unduly prejudicial. Accord Achtar v. Toyota Motor Corp., 2008 WL 1919573 (Ky. Ct. App. 2008). Courts are more likely to admit evidence of other incidents that involve equivalent circumstances. See Nelson v. Stanley Works, No. C902436, 2004 WL 2094374, at *5 (Minn. Ct. App. 2004) (testimony regarding a second tool of the same model, used in the same manner, manufactured at the same plant, and broken in a similar manner to an allegedly defective power tool was relevant and admissible to show a manufacturing flaw); Sparks v. Mena, 294 S.W.3d 156 (Tenn. Ct. App. 2008) (evidence of failure of safety shield on surgical knife was supported by 18 similar failures when safety shield failed to close and thus caused injury to surgical patients; that the manufacturer found no defect when the surgical knives were returned for inspection does not bar their use as evidence).

The limits of circumstantial proof can be observed in cases in which unexpected accidents occur but the circumstances do not point to any manufacturing defect. In these situations, rival hypotheses may be just as probable as the plaintiff's theory of defect and the court will likely bar the plaintiff from reaching a jury. See, e.g., Ruminer v. General Motors, 483 F.3d 561 (8th Cir. 2007). In *Ruminer*, the plaintiff was injured when he crashed his Chevrolet Suburban into a tree. The plaintiff did not point to a specific defect but argued that, because the car's occupant protection system failed to prevent injuries, the jury could infer that the system was unreasonably dangerous. The trial court granted summary judgment for the defendant. The Eighth Circuit, applying Arkansas law, affirmed, holding that the plaintiff had not disproved rival hypotheses and reasoning that "common experience does not dictate that if an individual is injured in a car accident, the injury is most likely a result of a defect in the automobile's occupant protection system." 483 F.3d at 565.

The age of the product and its successful use by plaintiff over time is a relevant consideration in deciding whether an inference of defect can be drawn. In Barnish v. KWI Building Co., 980 A.2d 535 (Pa. 2009), the Pennsylvania Supreme Court held that a product can perform successfully for many years and yet still be defective. However, plaintiff must explain how the product could be defective and yet still function properly for a period of time. Because plaintiff failed to explain how a spark detection system that functioned properly for ten years was defective when it left the control of the manufacturer, the defendant was entitled to summary judgment.

Spoliation is not limited to the destruction of the product that is the subject of litigation. In BIC Pen Corp. v. Carter, 2008 WL 5090757 (Tex. App. 2008), plaintiff, a six-year-old, suffered burns over 55 percent of her body when her five-year-old brother ignited a BIC cigarette lighter. Plaintiff contended that the lighter did not meet BIC's fork force and sparkwheel rotation force specifications and the lighter was therefore easier to operate by a child than it would have been had it complied with the specifications. Plaintiff had sought discovery of testing reports performed by BIC on lighters manufactured the same week as the lighter in question. BIC destroyed the documents after the discovery request was made. The trial court gave a spoliation instruction informing the jury that they could presume that the destroyed documents were unfavorable to BIC. On appeal the Court upheld the instruction against the argument of BIC that the actual lighter that caused the fire was available for inspection, reasoning that the destroyed documents may have identified more precise specifications for the manufacture of the lighter.

A few states provide for an independent tort action if a defendant destroys evidence in bad faith, with the intention of defeating the plaintiff's claim. See Rizzuto v. Davidson Ladders, Inc., 905 A.2d 1165 (Conn. 2006). In *Rizzuto*, the plaintiff was injured while using a ladder in a Home Depot store and gave notice to the defendants to preserve the ladder for evidence. The defendant's expert inspected the ladder and concluded that it was not defective. The defendant then destroyed the ladder before the plaintiff had an opportunity to inspect it. The trial court denied the plaintiff's intentional spoliation claim on the ground that spoliation was not a cognizable tort. The Supreme Court of Connecticut reversed, finding that an independent tort for damages is justified because the "defendants' bad faith intentional destruction of the ladder deprived [plaintiff] of the evidence he needed to establish a prima facie case of product liability." 905 A.2d at 1173. The high court held that the plaintiff could recover the full amount of compensatory damages that he would have received if the underlying action had been pursued successfully. A number of states that once provided for a tort remedy for spoliation have reversed course, however, concluding that nontort remedies are more desirable. See, e.g., Cedars-Sinai Med. Center v. Superior Court, 954 P.2d 511 (Cal. 1998) (concluding that a tort remedy imposes undesirable social costs and undermines policies that favor the remedying of litigation-related misconduct within the underlying lawsuit).

For further discussion of spoliation in civil litigation, see Sheldon M. Finkelstein, Evelyn R. Storch & James Simpson, Spoliation, or Please Don't Leave the Cake Out in the Rain, 32 Litig. 28 (2006).

PROBLEM THREE

Hanna Liebman was driving to the supermarket in her three-year-old, four-door Stardom Sedan manufactured by BMC Inc. Liebman was driving on her side of the road when she was suddenly hit head-on by a car driven by Sheldon Varik. Varik had apparently dozed off for a few seconds. His car veered over the center line and collided with Liebman. She was seriously injured in the accident when her face hit the windshield of her BMC Stardom. Varik carries the minimum $20,000 liability insurance policy mandated by the State of New California; Liebman's injuries are in excess of one million dollars. All events transpired in New California and its law will govern the case.

Liebman insists that she was wearing her three-point shoulder harness seat belt at the time of the accident. (Her car is an earlier model, distributed before airbags were mandatory.) She has a clear and unmistakable recollection of buckling up before embarking on her trip. Furthermore, she insists that she always wears her seat belt. Her contention is that the seat belt malfunctioned and did not restrain her at the time of impact. All experts in the case agree that if Liebman had been wearing her seat belt and if her seat belt had been working properly, Liebman's head would not have hit the windshield and almost all of her injuries would have been avoided. However, plaintiff's experts who examined the seat belt mechanism after the crash can find no defect in the retraction mechanism. The mechanism worked perfectly in all of the tests they conducted in an effort to discover a defect.

You are the trial judge in the case of Liebman v. BMC Inc. BMC has moved for directed verdict on the grounds that the seat belt was not defective. Liebman's lawyers argue that, if Liebman was telling the truth and she did, in fact, wear her seat belt, then the seat belt mechanism must have failed in some unexplained fashion. The issue of Liebman's credibility, they contend, is for the jury to decide. Will you grant the defendant's motion for directed verdict? If you conclude the issue of defect is for the jury, are there additional problems with plaintiff's proving that the defect existed at time of sale?

D. THE BOUNDARIES OF STRICT PRODUCTS LIABILITY

The boundaries of interest in this section determine which claims are, and which are not, part of the products liability system. Traditionally, whether a plaintiff's claim falls within or without the boundaries determines whether the defendant is strictly liable or liable only for negligence. Plaintiffs whose claims fall outside the boundaries are not necessarily without remedy in tort; but they must prove that the defendant was at fault. Of course, proving negligence may not be possible on the facts, so in many cases the boundary determination will determine liability. Moreover, in recent decades a majority of states have enacted statutes that modify the common law in many respects. Because these statutes typically refer to "products liability claims," the boundary questions in this section determine whether or not such statutes apply.

The operative language in §1 of the Products Liability Restatement, setting the boundaries of the subject, is: "One engaged in the business of selling or otherwise distributing products who sells or distributes a defective product is subject to liability. . . ." The materials that follow are designed to answer the following questions: (1) What are (and what are not) products?; (2) What commercial activities constitute "selling or otherwise distributing?"; and (3) When is a product seller or distributor "in the business of selling or distributing?"

1. What Are (and What Are Not) Products?

The place to begin is with the definition of "product" in the Products Liability Restatement:

Restatement (Third) of Torts: Products Liability
(1998)

---

§19. DEFINITION OF PRODUCT

For purposes of this Restatement:

(a) A product is tangible personal property distributed commercially for use or consumption. Other items, such as real property and electricity, are products when the context of their distribution and use is sufficiently analogous to the distribution and use of tangible personal property that it is appropriate to apply the rules stated in this Restatement.

(b) Services, even when provided commercially, are not products.

(c) Human blood and human tissue, even when provided commercially, are not subject to the rules of this Restatement.

The baseline principle that products are tangible personal property is straightforward enough, though some tangible personalty cases present interesting factual variations. For example, in Sease v. Taylor's Pets, Inc., 700 P.2d 1054 (Or. Ct. App.), *rev. denied*, 704 P.2d 514 (Or. 1985), the Oregon appellate court had no trouble holding a pet shop strictly liable for having sold a rabid skunk. More basically, it will be observed that the "product" concept in all but one of the operative sections of the Products Liability Restatement is limited to *new* products — the liability of commercial sellers of used products is dealt with separately in §8.

Before proceeding to consider extensions of the "product" concept beyond tangible personalty, it will be helpful to consider those commercial activities that clearly do *not* involve the sale or distribution of products: the purveyors of pure "services," referred to in subsection 19(b), supra. Examples of these commercial activities include services furnished by health care providers, architects, attorneys, engineers, and others. In Milford v. Commercial Carriers, Inc., 210 F. Supp. 2d 987 (N.D. Ill. 2002), the court refused to impose strict liability on a company that provided blueprints and designs for the construction of an automobile carrier that injured its operator. Other examples of judicial refusals to extend strict liability to service providers include Truglio v. Hayes Construction Co., 785 A.2d 1153 (Conn. App. Ct. 2001) (builder of sidewalk using liquid concrete, as opposed to preformed slabs, held to have performed service); and Jackson v. L.A.W. Contracting Corp., 481 So. 2d 1290 (Fla. Ct. App. 1986) (road resurfacing company). In many instances, service providers are associated closely enough with the distribution of defective products that strict liability claims against them are at least arguable. But once the court concludes that these defendants are essentially providing services, the plaintiffs must prove negligence.

A frequently litigated example of this type of case involves repairers, who may arguably be viewed as placing a repaired product into commerce, whether or not they actually supply any parts. Repairers who furnish no replacement parts in the course of their work have been treated as providers of services, liable only if found negligent. See Ayala v. V. & O. Press Co., 126 A.D.2d 229 (N.Y. App. Div. 1987). See also Meadows v. Anchor Longwall & Rebuild, Inc., 2006 U.S. Dist. LEXIS 51514 (W.D. Pa. 2006) (firm that removed, cleaned, inspected, repaired, and rebuilt a mining shield was a provider of services and thus not strictly liable for harm caused by a defective component in the shield). The *Ayala* decision also limited the negligence-based liability of a repairer, holding that a repairer was not required to warn the user of a design defect in the machine he was repairing when he restored the machine to the condition of its original design. See also Seo v. All-Makes Overhead Doors, 119 Cal. Rptr. 2d 160 (Cal. Ct. App. 2002) (finding no duty on the part of repairer of remote-controlled gate to correct or warn of defects). Courts, however, have held repairers who supply allegedly defective parts strictly liable for harm caused by defects in those replacement parts. See, e.g., Bell v. Precision Airmotive Corp., 42 P.3d 1071 (Alaska 2002). Similarly, strict liability has been applied to product rebuilders. See Michalko v. Cooke Color & Chem. Corp., 451 A.2d 179 (N.J. 1982) (rebuilder of machine strictly liable for defects, including design defects, despite fact that rebuilder merely followed buyer's specifications). See also Carollo v. Al Warren Oil Co., 355 Ill. App. 3d 172 (2004) (defendant spent over 200 hours assembling and rebuilding tanker truck). But see Barry v. Stevens Equip. Co., 335 S.E.2d 129 (Ga. Ct. App. 1985) (summary judgment for defendant product rebuilder in strict liability action affirmed).

Returning to the examples of "products" not involving tangible personalty referred to in subsection 19(a), supra, a generally accepted extension of strict products liability doctrine is the inclusion of commercial sellers of new housing in the category of commercial sellers of products. Historically, the major impediment to the inclusion of such sellers was the notion that the term "product" implied personalty, and did not readily apply to real property. See, e.g., Lowrie v. City of Evanston, 365 N.E.2d 923 (Ill. App. Ct. 1977). Additionally, courts assumed that purchasers of real property were as able as sellers to inspect for defects, and most of the cases did not involve personal injuries. The widespread development of mass-production techniques in the housing industry in the decades following World War II provided the factual basis for the eventual elimination of these conceptual impediments. Real estate developers began manufacturing tract houses, and courts came to realize that the individual purchasers of mass-produced homes are typically in no better position to inspect for defects than are the purchasers of mass-produced automobiles. Moreover, in many cases the structural components alleged to have been defective at time of sale were manufactured items that clearly would have qualified as "products" had they not been attached to realty when sold by the defendant.

Extension of the boundaries of strict liability to include commercial sellers of mass-produced housing began with the Supreme Court of New Jersey. See Schipper v. Levitt & Sons, Inc., 207 A.2d 314 (N.J. 1965); Patitucci v. Drelich, 379 A.2d 297 (N.J. Super. Ct. App. Div. 1977). See generally Sean M. O'Brien, Note, Caveat Venditor: A Case for Granting Subsequent Purchasers a Cause of Action Against Builder-Vendors for Latent Defects in the Home, 20 J. Corp. L. 525 (Spring 1995). With few exceptions, courts in other states have followed New Jersey's lead, even in cases involving the commercial sale of new, custom-built homes. See, e.g., Bastian v. Wausau Homes Inc., 620 F. Supp. 947 (N.D. Ill. 1985); Elderkin v. Gaster, 288 A.2d 771 (Pa. 1972); Rutledge v. Dodenhoff, 175 S.E.2d 792 (S.C. 1970). But see Wakefield v. Bohlin, 2006 WL 290483 (Cal. Ct. App. 2006).

An area in which quite a lot of judicial activity has occurred is the generation and delivery of electrical power. A small number of courts have refused to consider electricity a product. See, e.g., Curtiss v. Northeast Utilities, 1994 WL 702690, at *3 (Conn. Super. Ct. 1994) (plaintiff's cattle were injured by coming into contact with defendant's electricity lines; court found that "it strains credibility to hold a utility company strictly liable unless negligence is involved" and added that electricity cannot be "defective" because it is natural and not manufactured as such).

The majority position considers electricity a product once it has passed through a consumer's meter, as that indicates that it has been harnessed and made safe for consumer use and been placed into the stream of commerce. See Travelers Indemnity Co. of Am. v. Connecticut Light & Power Co., 2008 WL 2447351 (Conn. Super. Ct. 2008); Bryant v. Tri-County Elec. Membership Corp., 844 F. Supp. 347 (W.D. Ky. 1994); Otte v. Dayton Power & Light Co., 523 N.E.2d 835 (Ohio 1988). For more on this subject, see Roger W. Holmes, Strict Products Liability for Electric Utility Companies: A Surge in the Wrong Direction, 29 Suffolk U.L. Rev. 161 (1995).

One area of products liability that poses some particularly interesting conceptual questions involves the sale of information. As the following decision illustrates, the physical manifestations of a book fall neatly within the definition of a product because they are "tangible." Thus, poisonous glues used in the binding will bring strict liability. But what about poisonous ideas within?

Winter v. G. P. Putnam's Sons
938 F.2d 1033 (9th Cir. 1991)

SNEED, Circuit Judge.

Plaintiffs are mushroom enthusiasts who became severely ill from picking and eating mushrooms after relying on information in The Encyclopedia of Mushrooms, a book published by the defendant. Plaintiffs sued the publisher and sought damages under various theories. The district court granted summary judgment for the defendant. We affirm.

Facts and Proceedings Below

The Encyclopedia of Mushrooms is a reference guide containing information on the habitat, collection, and cooking of mushrooms. It was written by two British authors and originally published by a British publishing company. Defendant Putnam, an

American book publisher, purchased copies of the book from the British publisher and distributed the finished product in the United States. Putnam neither wrote nor edited the book.

Plaintiffs purchased the book to help them collect and eat wild mushrooms. In 1988, plaintiffs went mushroom hunting and relied on the descriptions in the book in determining which mushrooms were safe to eat. After cooking and eating their harvest, plaintiffs became critically ill. Both have required liver transplants.

Plaintiffs allege that the book contained erroneous and misleading information concerning the identification of the most deadly species of mushrooms. In their suit against the book publisher, plaintiffs allege liability based on products liability, breach of warranty, negligence, negligent misrepresentation, and false representations. Defendant moved for summary judgment asserting that plaintiffs' claims failed as a matter of law because 1) the information contained in a book is not a product for the purposes of strict liability under products liability law; and 2) defendant is not liable under any remaining theories because a publisher does not have a duty to investigate the accuracy of the text it publishes. The district court granted summary judgment for the defendant. Plaintiffs appeal. We affirm.

Discussion

A book containing Shakespeare's sonnets consists of two parts, the material and print therein, and the ideas and expression thereof. The first may be a product, but the second is not. The latter, were Shakespeare alive, would be governed by copyright laws; the laws of libel, to the extent consistent with the First Amendment; and the laws of misrepresentation, negligent misrepresentation, negligence, and mistake. These doctrines applicable to the second part are aimed at the delicate issues that arise with respect to intangibles such as ideas and expression. Products liability law is geared to the tangible world.

A. Products Liability

The language of products liability law reflects its focus on tangible items. In describing the scope of products liability law, the Restatement (Second) of Torts lists examples of items that are covered. All of these are tangible items, such as tires, automobiles, and insecticides. The American Law Institute clearly was concerned with including all physical items but gave no indication that the doctrine should be expanded beyond that area.

The purposes served by products liability law also are focused on the tangible world and do not take into consideration the unique characteristics of ideas and expression. Under products liability law, strict liability is imposed on the theory that "[t]he costs of damaging events due to defectively dangerous products can best be borne by the enterprisers who make and sell these products." Prosser & Keeton on The Law of Torts, §98, at 692-93 (W. Keeton ed. 5th ed. 1984). Strict liability principles have been adopted to further the "cause of accident prevention . . . [by] the elimination of the necessity of proving negligence." Id. at 693. Additionally, because of the difficulty of establishing fault or negligence in products liability cases, strict liability is the appropriate legal theory to hold manufacturers liable for defective products. Id. Thus, the seller is subject to liability "even though he has exercised all possible care in the preparation and sale of the product." Restatement §402A comment *a*. It is not a question of fault but simply a determination of how society wishes to assess certain costs that arise from the creation and distribution of products in a complex technological society in which the consumer thereof is unable to protect himself against certain product defects.

Although there is always some appeal to the involuntary spreading of costs of injuries in any area, the costs in any comprehensive cost/benefit analysis would be quite different were strict liability concepts applied to words and ideas. We place a high priority on the unfettered exchange of ideas. We accept the risk that words and ideas have wings we cannot clip and which carry them we know not where. The threat of liability without fault (financial responsibility for our words and ideas in the absence of fault or a special undertaking or responsibility) could seriously inhibit those who wish to share thoughts and theories. As a New York court commented, with the specter of strict liability, "[w]ould any author wish to be exposed . . . for writing on a topic which might result in physical injury? e.g., How to cut trees; How to keep bees?" Walter v. Bauer, 109 Misc. 2d 189, 191, 439 N.Y.S.2d 821, 823 (Sup. Ct. 1981) (student injured doing science project described in textbook; court held that the book was not a product for purposes of products liability law), aff'd in part & rev'd in part on other grounds, 88 A.D.2d 787, 451 N.Y.S.2d 533 (1982). One might add: "Would anyone undertake to guide by ideas expressed in words either a discrete group, a nation, or humanity in general?"

Strict liability principles even when applied to products are not without their costs. Innovation may be inhibited. We tolerate these losses. They are much less disturbing than the prospect that we might be deprived of the latest ideas and theories.

Plaintiffs suggest, however, that our fears would be groundless were strict liability rules applied only to books that give instruction on how to accomplish a physical activity and that are intended to be used as part of an activity that is inherently dangerous. We find such a limitation illusory. Ideas are often intimately linked with proposed action, and it would be difficult to draw such a bright line. While "How To" books are a special genre, we decline to attempt to draw a line that puts "How To Live a Good Life" books beyond the reach of strict liability while leaving "How To Exercise Properly" books within its reach.

Plaintiffs' argument is stronger when they assert that The Encyclopedia of Mushrooms should be analogized to aeronautical charts. Several jurisdictions have held that charts which graphically depict geographic features or instrument approach information for airplanes are "products" for the purpose of products liability law. See Brocklesby v. United States, 767 F.2d 1288, 1294-95 (9th Cir. 1985) (applying Restatement for the purpose of California law), cert. denied, 474 U.S. 1101 (1986); Saloomey v. Jeppesen & Co., 707 F.2d 671, 676-77 (2d Cir. 1983) (applying Restatement for the purpose of Colorado law); Aetna Casualty & Surety Co. v. Jeppesen & Co., 642 F.2d 339, 342-43 (9th Cir. 1981) (applying Nevada law); Fluor Corp. v. Jeppesen & Co., 170 Cal. App. 3d 468, 475, 216 Cal. Rptr. 68, 71 (1985) (applying California law). Plaintiffs suggest that The Encyclopedia of Mushrooms can be compared to aeronautical charts because both items contain representations of natural features and both are intended to be used while engaging in a hazardous activity. We are not persuaded.

Aeronautical charts are highly technical tools. They are graphic depictions of technical, mechanical data. The best analogy to an aeronautical chart is a compass. Both may be used to guide an individual who is engaged in an activity requiring certain knowledge of natural features. Computer software that fails to yield the result for which it was designed may be another. In contrast, The Encyclopedia of Mushrooms is like a book on how to use a compass or an aeronautical chart. The chart itself is like a physical "product" while the "How to Use" book is pure thought and expression. Given these considerations, we decline to expand products liability law to embrace the ideas and expression in a book. We know of no court that has chosen the path to which the plaintiffs point. . . .[4]

[The court's discussion of misrepresentation and negligence is omitted. In connection with plaintiff's claim that Putnam negligently failed to discover the alleged errors in the book, the court has held that a publisher has no duty to investigate the accuracy of an author's statement in published works.]

In Garcia v. Kusan, Inc., 655 N.E.2d 1290 (Mass. App. Ct. 1996), the court held that the instructions and rule book for indoor hockey are not a product for purposes of applying strict liability. Plaintiff was struck in the eye by a hockey stick during a game that took place at his elementary school. He could not identify the stick as one sold by the defendant manufacturer. Instead, he claimed that the instructions and rules accompanying hockey sticks sold to the school constituted a defective product. The court held that the rule book sans the hockey sticks was not a defective product. See also Gorran v. Atkins Nutritionals, Inc., 464 F. Supp. 2d 315 (S.D.N.Y. 2006) (diet information in Atkins diet books did not constitute a product); Isham v. Padi Worldwide Corp., 2007 WL 2460776 (D. Hawaii) (scuba diving program is not a product and claim that the diving program contained defects that departed from the actual, intended design of the program are not subject to strict products liability); Way v. Boy Scouts of Am., 856 S.W.2d 230 (Tex. App. 1993) (advertising supplement in *Boys' Life* magazine describing shooting and firearms is not a product; decedent, a young boy killed after he was encouraged to experiment with guns as a result of advertisement, could not bring an action for strict products liability). Similarly, in Abraham v. Entrepreneur Media, Inc., 2009 WL 4016515 (E.D.N.Y.), a plaintiff failed to convince a court that investment advice given by a newspaper that had allegedly been grossly negligent in gathering information about a stock (company was on the "Hot 100" list of fastest growing corporations) was subject to a tort duty of care. Citing *Winter*, the court held that the plaintiff's cause of action was without merit. Although there are as yet no reported cases, there are numerous instances where a GPS navigation device has directed users in a manner that resulted in personal injury. Is a GPS like an aeronautical chart; a

---

4. See Jones v. J. B. Lippincott Co., 694 F. Supp. 1216, 1217-18 (D. Md. 1988) (nursing student injured treating self with constipation remedy listed in nursing textbook; court held that Restatement 402A does not extend to dissemination of an idea or knowledge); Herceg v. Hustler Magazine, Inc., 565 F. Supp. 802, 803-04 (S.D. Tex. 1983) (person died after imitating "autoerotic asphyxiation" described in magazine article; court held that contents of magazines are not within meaning of Restatement 402A); Walter v. Bauer, 109 Misc. 2d 189, 190-91, 439 N.Y.S.2d 821, 822-23 (Sup. Ct. 1981) (student injured doing science project described in textbook; court held that the book was not a defective product for purposes of products liability law because the intended use of a book is reading and the plaintiff was not injured by reading), *aff'd in part & rev'd in part on other grounds*, 88 A.D.2d 787, 451 N.Y.S.2d 533 (1982); Smith v. Linn, 386 Pa. Super. 392, 398, 563 A.2d 123, 126 (1989) (reader of Last Chance Diet book died from diet complications, court held that book is not a product under Restatement §402A), *aff'd*, 587 A.2d 309 (1991), cf. Cardozo v. True, 342 So. 2d 1053, 1056-57 (Fla. Dist. Ct. App.) (transmission of words is not the same as selling items with physical properties so that where a bookseller merely passes on a book without inspection, the thoughts and ideas within the book do not constitute a "good" for the purposes of a breach of implied warranty claim under the U.C.C.), *cert. denied*, 353 So. 2d 674 (Fla. 1977).

service; or more like a "How to Do" book? John E. Woodward, Oops, My GPS Made Me Do it!: GPS Manufacturer Liability Under a Strict Products Liability Paradigm When GPS Fails to Give Accurate Directions to GPS End Users, 34 U. Dayton L. Rev. 429 (2009), explores the possible theories that might govern such a case.

In one area the question of whether or not information falls under the definition of a product for strict liability purposes appears to have been answered in the negative. The information contained within interactive video game software does not constitute a product for strict liability purposes. In Wilson v. Midway Games, Inc., 198 F. Supp. 2d 167 (D. Conn. 2002), a mother sued the producers of Mortal Kombat, a console video game in which human opponents brutally slaughter one another, when her son was fatally stabbed by his adolescent friend shortly after playing Mortal Kombat. The stabbing occurred in a manner eerily resembling an episode contained within the game. Citing *Winter*, supra, the *Wilson* court conceptually divided commercial information into two categories: instruction manuals, cookbooks, navigational charts, etc. on the one hand; and exhortation, inspiration, and suggestion, on the other. The court opined that it is at least arguable that information falling within the first category should be considered a product, whereas information falling within the second category should not. Dismissing the mother's complaint for failure to state a claim upon which relief could be granted, the court reasoned that, because information contained within video game software is closer to the second category, it should not be considered a product for strict liability purposes. Other courts have reached similar results. See James v. Meow Media, Inc., 300 F.3d 683 (6th Cir. 2002) (parents of school shooting victim failed to state a strict liability claim against game software makers, movie producers, and parties maintaining pornographic websites because those parties did not deal in "products"); Sanders v. Acclaim Entertainment, 188 F. Supp. 2d 1264 (D. Colo. 2002) (Columbine victims' families failed to state a strict liability claim against game software makers who allegedly inspired school shooting because intangible thoughts and ideas are not products).

PROBLEM FOUR

Claire Kelly has asked you to represent her in an action against Exotic Eating Magazine. Claire became critically ill after eating a batch of muffins that she made following a recipe in Exotic Eating Magazine. Exotic Eating always requests new recipes from its readers. One reader, Marni Schlissel from Michigan, decided to submit her recipe for muffins, which had always been a big hit at family gatherings. The recipe for Marni's Marvelous Muffins called for an unusual amount of extract of wintergreen, one-half cup, to give them that special something. Extract of wintergreen is a tasty ingredient readily available in markets in the Midwest.

The magazine's testers in New York always check the availability of the recipe ingredients. When the testers couldn't find extract of wintergreen, they published the recipe with what they considered to be a reasonable substitute, oil of wintergreen. Unfortunately, oil of wintergreen is really methyl salicylate and is used primarily to rub sore muscles. Taken internally in anything more than minute quantities it becomes very toxic.

Claire made a big batch of Marni's Marvelous Muffins following the magazine's recipe step by step. As she was very hungry when she made them, she proceeded to eat three of the muffins, which she actually enjoyed before she passed out and was rushed to the hospital with toxic poisoning.

You've just read the *Winter* decision and it controls in your jurisdiction. Does Ms. Kelly have a cause of action?

POSTSCRIPT ON BLOOD AND OTHER HUMAN TISSUE

Before leaving the question of "What are products?," it remains to consider the issue addressed in subsection 19(c) of the Products Liability Restatement, supra. When a hospital or a blood bank sells a unit of blood contaminated with hepatitis or the HIV virus, and the recipient-purchaser contracts hepatitis or AIDS, should the seller be strictly liable in tort? Except for the fact that these viruses cannot be detected and eliminated, the appropriate answer would seem to be "yes" — the defendant sold a product with a defect that caused harm to the plaintiff. Hepatitis and HIV viruses are arguably "foreign" rather than "natural" ingredients in the human bloodstream and thus constitute defects. What, then, of the fact that there is no foolproof method to detect them? On one view, that should not matter; as a practical matter, manufacturers of fabricated products such as automobiles cannot find and eliminate all "theoretically detectable" manufacturing defects, either. See, e.g., Rostocki v. Southwest Fla. Blood Bank, Inc., 276 So. 2d 475, 477 (Fla. 1973).

Reacting to the possibility that courts might impose (or have imposed) strict liability in these "bad blood" cases, states have, nearly without exception, enacted shield statutes aimed at preventing such outcomes. Borne of a legislative perception that strict liability would threaten sources of these vital products, shield statutes protect sellers of blood from strict products liability and have even been interpreted to implicitly shield distributors of other parts of the human body. See, e.g., Condos v. Muskoloskeletal Transplant Found., 208 F. Supp. 2d 1226 (C.D. Utah 2002) (legislature intended to shield distributors of bone tissue by enacting Utah's Blood Shield Statute). The decisions are collected in Products Liability Reporter (CCH) ¶ 1630 (updated periodically). Some jurisdictions distinguish between commercial and nonprofit sellers of blood products and human tissue. See, e.g., Ariz. Rev. Stat. Ann. §32-1481(B); La. Rev. Stat. Ann. §9:2797. Most have held that the policy protecting nonprofit sellers extends to commercial sellers as well. See, e.g., Doe v. Travenol Laboratories, 698 F. Supp. 780 (D. Minn. 1988).

The Products Liability Restatement preserves these immunities by fiat — without saying that blood is not a product, §19(c) simply places blood and other human tissue outside the scope of the Restatement. Why do you suppose the Institute handled the issue in that way? What about human sperm? In Donovan v. Idant Laboratories, 625 F. Supp. 2d 256 (E.D. Pa. 2009) (applying New York law), a mother who was inseminated from the sperm purchased from a commercial sperm bank sued on behalf of herself and the child born from the sperm when it turned out that the child had a genetic disease (Fragile X syndrome). The court held that sperm was a product under New York law but that New York courts would bar a claim for wrongful life.

Quite apart from the question of strict liability, suppliers of bad blood are everywhere liable for harm caused by their negligence. In this connection, careful donor selection and special handling can reduce, but not eliminate, the relevant risks. Thus, sellers who fail to take these steps may be held liable for negligently causing injury to recipients who contract hepatitis. The hot question dividing the courts concerns the standard to which blood banks will be held in administering the negligence rule. The blood bank industry has argued that they should be held to the professional standard of care that governs medical care providers. Under this approach, adherence to customary practice constitutes an absolute defense to liability. Several courts, however, have refused to recognize adherence to custom as a blanket defense for blood banks. In United Blood Services v. Quintana, 827 P.2d 509 (Colo. 1992), a plaintiff who contracted the HIV virus from contaminated blood brought suit against United Blood Services for its negligence in screening and testing the blood. After extensive discussion, the court concluded that a blood bank should be held to a professional standard of care. The court took note of the important role of custom in deciding whether a blood bank was negligent. It said:

> To be sure, there is a presumption that adherence to the applicable standard of care adopted by a profession constitutes due care for those practicing that profession. The presumption, however, is a rebuttable one, and the burden is on the one challenging the standard of care to rebut the presumption by competent evidence. . . . 827 P.2d at 521.

For discussion of the AIDS blood contamination cases, see Ross D. Eckert, The AIDS-Blood Transfusion Cases: A Legal and Economic Analysis of Liability, 29 San Diego L. Rev. 203 (1992); Kathryn W. Pieplow, AIDS, Blood Banks and the Courts: The Legal Response to Transfusion-Acquired Disease, 38 S.D.L. Rev. 609 (1993). In an article by Clark C. Havighurst, Trafficking in Human Blood: Titmuss (1970) and Products Liability, 72 Law & Contemp. Probs. 1 (2009), the author argues that had strict liability governed the sale of blood it would have significantly reduced the number of blood-borne AIDS cases.

2. Which Activities Constitute "Selling or Otherwise Distributing" in a Commercial Context?

Once again, consider the Products Liability Restatement's definitions of these terms:

Restatement (Third) of Torts: Products Liability
(1998)

---

§20. DEFINITION OF ONE WHO SELLS OR OTHERWISE DISTRIBUTES

For purposes of this Restatement:

    (a) One sells a product when, in a commercial context, one transfers ownership thereto either for use or consumption or for resale leading to ultimate use or consumption. Commercial product sellers include, but are not limited to, manufacturers, wholesalers, and retailers.

    (b) One otherwise distributes a product when, in a commercial transaction other than a sale, one provides the product to another either for use or consumption or as a preliminary step leading to ultimate use or consumption. Commercial nonsale product distributors include, but are not limited to, lessors, bailors, and those who provide products to others as a means of promoting either the use or consumption of such products or some other commercial activity.

(c) One also sells or otherwise distributes a product when, in a commercial transaction, one provides a combination of products and services and either the transaction taken as a whole, or the product component thereof, satisfies the criteria in Subsection (a) or (b).

Subsection 20(a) describes the paradigm, the commercial product seller, to which most of the cases in these materials conform. The term "sells" implies a consideration; but in the commercial setting even gifts for which no price is charged are really transfers of title for a tacit consideration in the form of customer good will. Thus, when a business supplies free samples by way of advertising, courts apply strict liability in such cases. See, e.g., McKisson v. Sales Affiliates, Inc., 416 S.W.2d 787 (Tex. 1967). See also Levondsky v. Marina Assoc., 731 F. Supp. 1210 (D. N.J. 1990) (defective glass in which free drink was served by casino). Observe that the operative concept here is "sells"; all sellers in the commercial chain, from manufacturers down to retailers, are strictly liable for defects existing at the time of sale.

Subsection 20(b) is also quite straightforward, though more interesting. As indicated in the black letter, commercial product lessors have been included in the category of suppliers held strictly liable for product defects. See, e.g., Cintrone v. Hertz Truck Leasing & Rental Serv., 212 A.2d 769 (N.J. 1965); Francioni v. Gibsonia Truck Corp., 372 A.2d 736 (Pa. 1977). In *Cintrone*, the Supreme Court of New Jersey held the commercial lessor of a truck fleet strictly liable for injuries to a driver-employee of the lessee. Relying on implied warranty concepts, the court concluded that "the relationship between the parties fairly calls for an implied warranty of fitness for use, at least equal to that assumed by a new car manufacturer." 212 A.2d at 777. In Kemp v. Miller, 453 N.W.2d 872 (Wis. 1990), the court gave a ringing endorsement to *Cintrone*. The Wisconsin court held that the commercial lessor "impliedly represents that those products will be fit for use throughout the term of the lease." The court specifically held that the lessor's liability extended "not only to design and manufacturing defects but also to defects which arise after the product leaves the manufacturer's control." 453 N.W.2d at 879. See generally Richard C. Ausness, Strict Liability for Chattel Leasing, 48 U. Pitt. L. Rev. 273 (1987).

Subsection 20(b) also explicitly includes commercial bailors. Thus, courts have applied strict liability to suppliers of demonstration models loaned out to promote product sales. See Delaney v. Towmotor Corp., 339 F.2d 4 (2d Cir. 1964); Beatie v. Martin Chevrolet-Buick, Inc., 786 A.2d 549 (Del. 2001) (court cites Restatement (Third) of Torts: Products Liability in holding car dealership strictly liable for harm caused by defect in promotional vehicle used by employee as a perquisite, though not in a technical bailment relationship, because vehicle was supplied for the purpose of promoting the sale or lease of other vehicles); Thorpe v. Bullock, Inc., 348 S.E.2d 55 (Ga. Ct. App. 1986) (where defendant supplier allowed a restaurant to use a deep fryer free of charge as an inducement for the restaurant to buy the fryer, supplier was just as liable as if it had sold the fryer, in that it had placed it in the stream of commerce). Defective products that cause harm prior to actual purchase receive the same treatment. See Barker v. Allied Supermarket, 596 P.2d 870 (Okla. 1979) (product harmed plaintiff before purchase in self-service store). The Eleventh Circuit, interpreting Florida law, was less charitable. In McQuiston v. K-Mart Corp., 796 F.2d 1346 (11th Cir. 1986), plaintiff suffered permanent injuries to her wrist when she lifted the lid of a cookie jar sitting on a display shelf and the lid came apart. Plaintiff had not decided to buy the cookie jar; she was just looking for a price tag on the inside of the lid. The court held that there was no action against the retailer for breach of the implied warranty of merchantability because the purchaser had not yet formed an intent to purchase. The court differentiated this case from an injury caused when plaintiff had taken the item off the shelf in a self-service store with the definite intent to purchase the item.

Commercial actors whose conduct facilitates the sale and distribution of products by others, without themselves providing products for use and consumption, are generally excluded from strict products liability. Thus, trademark licensors who provide promotional material but do not supply products are held strictly liable only when they actively control or participate substantially in the design, manufacture, or distribution of the licensee's product. See Products Liability Restatement §14, Comment *d* (1998). The case law supports this proposition. For example, in Torres v. Goodyear Tire & Rubber Co., 786 P.2d 939 (Ariz. 1990), the Arizona Supreme Court held Goodyear, a trademark licensor who was actively involved in its licensee's operation, strictly liable for plaintiffs' injuries resulting from a defective Goodyear tire produced and distributed by its licensee. The court relied on Goodyear's extensive degree of control over its licensees' manufacture and production of tires. Accord Auto Ins. Co. of Hartford Connecticut v. Murray Inc., 571 F. Supp. 2d 408 (W.D.N.Y. 2008) (whether trademark licensor is liable in strict products liability depends on the degree of active control of the licensee's product). By contrast, strict liability may not be imposed where the licensor's involvement with the licensee is tenuous. See, e.g., Tyler v. Pepsico, 400 S.E.2d 673 (Ga. 1990), where Pepsico, a soft drink franchisor, was not held strictly liable for injuries sustained by a plaintiff struck in the eye by the aluminum cap of an exploding bottle. The Georgia court reasoned that although Pepsico supplied syrup to the bottler, Pepsico and the bottler operated as distinct and separate entities, and the bottler exclusively received the proceeds from bottle sales. See generally David J. Franklyn, The Apparent Manufacturer Doctrine, Trademark Licensors and the Third Restatement of Torts, 49 Case W. Res. L. Rev. 671 (1999); S. Sandrock, Tort Liability of a Non-Manufacturing Franchisor for Acts of Its Franchisee, 48 U. Cin. L. Rev. 699 (1979).

An interesting wrinkle involving sales facilitators is presented when plaintiffs seek to include product certifiers such as Good Housekeeping and Underwriters Laboratories, who give their seals of approval to the products, as defendants in strict liability actions. The very purpose of such a seal is to induce consumer confidence in the safety and the quality of the product. Might not this be a component part of the product? Nonetheless, the few cases extant have permitted only causes of action based in negligence and have refused to impose strict liability against such certifiers. See Hempstead v. General Fire Extinguishing Corp., 269 F. Supp. 109 (D. Del. 1967); Hanberry v. Hearst Corp., 81 Cal. Rptr. 519 (Cal. Ct. App. 1969); accord United States Lighting Serv. v. Llerrad Corp., 800 F. Supp. 1513 (N.D. Ohio 1992) (after defective energy-saving lights caused damage, plaintiff installer sought to recover from defendant independent testing laboratory, which had rated the product as adequate. Summary judgment was denied so that issues of negligence of the testing laboratory in rating the product could be litigated).

Auctioneers are another category of sales facilitators excluded from strict products liability. See, e.g., New Texas Auto Auction Services, L.P. v. Gomez De Hernandez, 249 S.W.3d 400 (Tex. 2008) (citing to Restatement, of Torts, Third; Products Liability §20, Comment *g*.) In Musser v. Vilsmeier Auction Co., 562 A.2d 279 (Pa. 1989), the court refused to apply strict liability against an auctioneering firm that auctioned some 90 used tractors and analogized the role of the auctioneer to that of a financier: They both help facilitate the sale of the product but neither has any role in the selection of goods for sale.

Consistent with the foregoing, courts refuse to hold commercial actors who finance sales transactions, even when the financing party plays a role that formally makes it part of the distributive chain. In Abco Metals Corp. v. J.W. Imports Co., Inc., 560 F. Supp. 125, 131 (N.D. Ill. 1982), *aff'd sub nom.* Abco Metals Corp. v. Equico Lessors, Inc., 721 F.2d 583 (7th Cir. 1983), the court described the role of financial lessors:

> [It] does not actually provide the equipment to the lessee, but rather provides the money which allows the user of already selected equipment to purchase it. To a substantial extent, a financial lessor may be analogized to a bank that loans money to its clients. Rather than simply loaning the money for the purchase to the ultimate user of the equipment, the transaction is set up as a "lease," with the lessor "purchasing" the equipment for the specific purpose of "renting" it to the user. . . . Normally the lessor has no familiarity with the particular equipment involved and rarely does the lessor intend to take possession of the equipment when the lease term is completed.

The court went on to explain why it was inappropriate to hold financial lessors liable as a member of the distributive chain:

> The inescapable conclusion is that Equico had no input into the production or marketing of this machine. It was not, therefore, in the original chain of distribution and was not a party capable of preventing a defective product from entering the stream of commerce.

Id. at 585. See Potts v. UAP-GA AG CHEM, Inc., 567 S.E.2d 316 (Ga. 2002); D'Huyvetter v. A. O. Smith Harvestore Prod., 475 N.W.2d 587 (Wis. Ct. App. 1991).

Magrine v. Krasnica
**227 A.2d 539 (N.J. Super. 1967), *aff'd sub nom.*, Magrine v. Spector,
241 A.2d 637, *aff'd*, 250 A.2d 129 (N.J. 1969)**

LYNCH, J.S.C. (temporarily assigned) [sitting without a jury].

The novelty of this case lies in the attempt by plaintiff, a patient of defendant dentist, to extend the rule of "strict liability" against defendant for personal injuries caused by the breaking of a hypodermic needle in plaintiff's jaw while being used by defendant in an injection procedure. The break was due to a latent defect in the needle.

Novelty, of itself, does not foreclose consideration of plaintiff's contentions in this field of developing tort law. Neither does it justify a headlong leap to impose strict liability unless, based on proper policy considerations and reason, such liability should be found. Plaintiff concedes that there is no precedent — anywhere — holding a dentist, or any other "user" of an article, strictly liable for injuries caused by a latent defect therein. Since the case is one of first impression, the court feels impelled to set forth its reasoning at some length.

The case is submitted for decision on a stipulation setting forth the following facts: On November 22, 1963 plaintiff was a patient of defendant. He was administering a local anesthetic with a hypodermic needle inserted in the left temporomandibular space, a point at the extreme end of the lower gum beyond the last tooth. The needle extended 15/8" beyond the syringe. It had been assembled by the doctor just before the injection and had been used approximately eight times for about three weeks prior to the accident. It is the custom of the doctor to use about four needles a month and to discard them at the end of the month. As the injection was being made the needle "separated" at the hub, the place where the needle entered the syringe, leaving the entire 15/8″ length of the needle in plaintiff's jaw. Defendant does not know what caused the needle to break, but he believes there must have been some sort of defect in it. He does not know from whom he purchased the needle. However, he testified on oral deposition that the needle was manufactured by a certain Precision Bur Company of New York, but in answers to interrogatories he had suggested other possible manufacturers.

Paragraph 22 of the stipulation of facts reads as follows:

> Plaintiffs make no assertion or claim that defendant failed to do what a reasonably prudent person would have done under the circumstances or that defendant did what a reasonably prudent person would not have done. Plaintiffs rely upon strict liability, breach of warranty and breach of contract to recover. They do not assert the negligence of defendant except insofar as negligence may be included in the above theories of liability.

We have seen the rapid development of the "strict liability" concept in the products liability field . . . [including transactions outside] [Cintrone v. Hertz Truck Leasing & Rental Service, 45 N.J. 434, 212 A.2d 769 (1965)] (lessor of a "U-Drive-It" truck held strictly liable for injuries caused by a defect in the vehicle).

Inspired by the holding in *Cintrone*, and the authorities cited therein, to the effect that "strict liability" is not confined to "sales" transactions, plaintiff conceives that the gates are wide open, at least to the extent that the doctrine should be applied "to service contracts, and particularly to those involving the use of manufactured implements in the performance of the service."

Plaintiff's argument moves from the major premise that "strict liability" is not confined to "sales," through the minor premise that the basic policy considerations of the doctrine apply to the use of a needle by a dentist, and concludes that he should be held liable though free from negligence. Since the major premise is established (*Cintrone*), it therefore remains for us to analyze the policy considerations projected by our decisions and other authorities and determine to what extent, if any, they postulate a judgment for plaintiff.

Quoting from 2 Harper and James, Law of Torts, §28.19, p. 1576 (1956), plaintiff asserts that the relevant policy considerations are as follows:

> Warranties may be imposed or annexed to a transaction by law, because one party to the transaction is in a better position than another (1) "to know the antecedents that affect . . . the quality of the thing . . . dealt with; (2) to control those antecedents; (3) and to distribute losses which occur because the thing has a dangerous quality; (4) when that danger is not ordinarily to be expected; (5) so that other parties will be likely to assume its absence and therefore refrain from taking self-protective care."

At first glance it would appear that, indeed, defendant dentist is in a "better position" "to know the antecedents that affect . . . the quality" of the needle he used and "to control those antecedents" than his patient—this for the reason that he selected his own supplier and presumably the particular needle. *Literally*, therefore, the first policy consideration would appear to be satisfied. But does the statement of

Harper and James coincide with the sense of the concept as applied by our Supreme Court?

[A discussion of prior case law is omitted.]

Thus, in all of our recent cases strict liability was imposed (except with respect to a retail dealer) upon those who were in "a better position" in the sense that they *created* the danger (in making the article or possessed a better capacity or expertise to control, inspect and discover the defect . . . than the party injured. In these respects the dentist here was in no better position than plaintiff. He neither created the defect nor possessed any better capacity or expertise to discover or correct it than she.

It is further very clear that strict liability was imposed in our New Jersey cases for the *essentially basic reason* that those so held liable put the product "in the stream of trade and promote its purchase by the public." . . . Defendant dentist did not put the needle in the stream of commerce or promote its purchase.

It may be logically argued that the foregoing analysis does not effectively distinguish defendant from the retail dealer who, for example, sells food in a sealed container, or otherwise has no opportunity to discover a defect in the article he sells, and who nevertheless is liable for breach of warranty. In this respect such retail dealer is in no better position to discover the defect than the dentist here. Nevertheless, the situations are distinct. In the first place, the Uniform Sales Act and the Uniform Commercial Code, *legislative* enactments, apply to sales and there can be no judicial construction which could deny a warranty against a retail seller. At common law the implied warranty was originally confined to food. Even so, several courts have refused to impose warranty liability on the "innocent" retailer who has no means of discovering the defect in the goods. Such reasoning is not without a concept of fairness. Prosser suggests that other courts may follow this position but that he would hold such a dealer liable. Of more meaningful significance is a recognition that the *essence of* the transaction between the retail seller and the consumer relates to the *article sold.* The seller is *in the business* of supplying the product to the consumer. It is that, and that alone, for which he is paid. A dentist or a physician offers, and is paid for, his professional services and skill. That is the *essence* of the relationship between him and his patient.

Plaintiff also invokes the policy consideration of "spreading of the risks" — the concept which suggests that defendant could cover his liability by insurance, or he could be held harmless by impleading his supplier or manufacturer. The "risk distributing theory" is a relevant consideration. But again, we must appreciate the context in which it has been applied in our cases. In . . . *Cintrone* it was considered in holding liable the manufacturer or lessor, who put the goods in the stream of commerce. Such a party may fairly be assumed to have substantial assets and volume of business, and a large area of contacts over which the risk can be widely spread. It is the "large-scale" enterprise which should bear the loss. The impact of liability upon such a defendant is minuscule in comparison with that of an individual dentist or physician. His means of "spreading the risk" could be by insurance or impleading his supplier or manufacturer. "Malpractice" insurance, however, does not cover implied warranty unless the policy "expressly covers contract claims." In this very case defendant dentist is represented not only by counsel for his insurance carrier but also by his personal counsel because the carrier denies coverage. In any event, there are definite limits as to how far the argument of "risk-spreading" by insurance can go. . . .

So, here, if the dentist or physician were to obtain insurance covering strict liability for equipment failure, the risk would be spread upon his patients by way of increased fees. Can anyone gainsay the fact that medical and dental costs, and insurance therefore, are already bearing hard there? Witness the constant cry over increasing medical-surgical insurance premiums in New Jersey. As a matter of principle, the spreading of losses to their patients subverts, rather than supports, the policy consideration that the loss should be imposed on those best able to withstand it, i.e., the manufacturer or other entity which puts the article into the stream of commerce. . . .

Something can be said, by way of logical argument, in plaintiff's favor, for the policy consideration that if the dentist be held liable he, as the retail seller of food in a sealed container, can implead the manufacturer and thus be used as a conduit to place the loss where it belongs. This, too, should be regarded as only a "makeweight" argument. While we fully appreciate the appeal of the suggestion that the retail dealer — or the dentist here — is the most convenient conduit to "fight out" liability with the ultimate manufacturer, we are not satisfied that in this case such circuity of action is appropriate. . . . Here, as the stipulation says, defendant "does not know from whom the needle was purchased; he testified on oral depositions that the needle was manufactured by a certain Precision Bur Co. of New York, New York, but in answers to interrogatories Dr. Krasnica had suggested other possible manufacturers." Thus, plaintiff is not without remedy to reach the supplier by proper use of discovery procedures. If it be shown that identification of the supplier does not eventuate in this particular case, and *both* plaintiff and defendant are denied recourse to him, then our answer is that this is a "hard case" from which bad law should not flow. It is not the usual situation, for ordinarily the manufacturer can be reached. In our view it would be bad law to sustain plaintiff's contentions because the relevant policy considerations do not justify imposition of strict liability upon a dentist in the first, or last, instance. Further, the vast body of malpractice law, presumably an expression of the public policy involved in this area of health care, imposes upon a dentist or physician liability only for negligent performance of his services-negligent deviation from the standards of his profession. In the performance of his professional skill he has control of what he does. As to the instrument he uses, he has no control with respect to a latent defect therein. Why, then, should he be held strictly liable for the instruments he uses, as to which he has no control over latent defects, and liable only for negligence in the performance of his professional services, which he does control? "Suggestive analogy" is useful, but reason and consistency of principle should not be totally disregarded. . . .

We must consider, also, the consequences if we were to adopt the rule of strict liability here. The same liability, in principle, should then apply to any user of a tool, other equipment or any article which, through no fault of the user, breaks due to a latent defect and injures another. It would apply to any physician, artisan or mechanic and to any user of a defective article — even to a driver of a defective automobile. In our view, no policy consideration positing strict liability justifies application of the doctrine in such cases. No more should it here. . . .

Judgment for defendant.

As *Magrine* suggests, providers of medical services are generally not treated as commercial sellers of the medical products they use and otherwise provide in the course of treatment. Thus, hospitals are not considered sellers of medical supplies utilized during surgery. See, e.g., Cafazzo v. Central Medical Health Servs., Inc., 668 A.2d 521 (Pa. 1995) (defective mandibular prosthesis implanted in plaintiff); In re Breast Implant Prod. Liab. Litig., 503 S.E.2d 445 (S.C. 1998) (breast implants);

Easterly v. HSP of Tex., Inc., 772 S.W.2d 211 (Tex. App. 1989) (catheter included in an epidural kit during the administration of anesthesia broke and was left in the patient's spine). But see Bell v. Poplar Bluff Physicians Group, Inc., 879 S.W.2d 618, 620 (Mo. Ct. App. 1994), *overruled by* Budding v. SSM Healthcare Sys., 19 S.W.3d 678 (Mo. 2000) (court refused to apply strict liability against hospital that supplied temporomandibular interpositional joint implant; statute requires that negligence be established against health-care providers). Pharmacists also escape strict liability for the generic hazards presented by prescription products. See Madison v. American Home Prod. Corp., 595 S.E.2d 493 (S.C. 2004). See also Restatement (Third) of Torts: Products Liability §6(e) (1998).

Magrine is an example of the type of case described in Restatements Third, subsection 20(c), supra, often referred to as a "sales-service hybrid" or "nonsale supplier transaction." In general, other than in the medical context, courts have been willing to impose strict liability on providers of services as long as a product-sale component can be identified. In Newmark v. Gimbel's Inc., 258 A.2d 697 (N.J. 1969), a well-known decision involving an allegedly defective hair treatment product used on a beauty parlor customer, the Supreme Court of New Jersey reversed the trial court's refusal to give a strict liability instruction to the jury. The court likened the defendant's position to that of a retailer and distinguished *Magrine*, supra, on several grounds, among them that the beauty parlor operator was a nonprofessional offering a mechanical and routine service; that he advertised for customers; and that he charged customers directly for the products consumed in the course of treatment.

In responding to these sale-service hybrids, some courts have adopted a "predominant purpose" test. See, e.g., Linden v. Cascade Stone Co., 699 N.W.2d 189 (Wis. 2005) (contractor's predominant purpose was to provide a product). A good example of the sort of sales-service hybrid in which courts are likely to find that the service component dominates, and thus are likely to refuse to impose strict liability, is Ferrari v. Grand Canyon Dories, 38 Cal. Rptr. 2d 65 (Cal. Ct. App. 1995), *rev. denied*, 1995 Cal. LEXIS 2964 (Cal. 1995), in which the plaintiff was a passenger on a white water rafting trip arranged by the defendant commercial tour provider. Plaintiff was injured when she hit her head on the raft's metal frame, and alleged that the raft was defective in that the frame was not buffered by padding and no helmets were provided. In rejecting plaintiff's claim that the tour supplier was subject to strict liability as lessor of the raft, the court analogized the situation to an airline passenger suing the airline rather than the plane manufacturer for a defect in the plane. The court explained the various roles: "The manufacturer's role is that of a provider of a product, the airplane. On the other hand, the airline operating the plane would be primarily involved in providing a service, i.e., transportation. The airline is itself the end user of the product and imposition of strict liability would be inappropriate." Id. at 71. Citing to *Ferrari* the court in Ontiveros v. 24 Hour Fitness Corp., 86 Cal. Rptr. 3d 767 (Cal. Ct. App. 2008), held that a fitness club member could not sue in products liability for injuries suffered while using a defective stair step exercise machine. For a further look at the sale-service issue, see Ellen Taylor, Applicability of Strict Liability Warranty Theories to Service Transactions, 47 S.C. L. Rev. 231 (1996).

Nonsale suppliers may conveniently be divided into two subcategories: those who charge their customers specifically and directly for the use of the product provided, and those who treat the costs of furnishing the product as part of their overhead, to be reflected in the prices they charge for their other products and services. Several courts have imposed strict products liability on nonsale suppliers in the first subcategory. For example, the Superior Court of Delaware imposed strict liability on the operator of a skating rink for injuries to a patron caused by an alleged defect in a pair of rented roller skates. Wilson v. Dover Skating Center, Ltd., 566 A.2d 1020 (Del. Super. Ct. 1989). The court concluded that the rink was the owner-lessor of the skates and that, as such, it was in the best position to inspect the skates for defects and take defective pairs out of circulation. The court also determined that the rental of the skates was an integral part of the rink's business and was used as an inducement to garner additional customers.

Compared with the preceding group, nonsale suppliers in the second subcategory, who do not specifically charge customers for using the products, are involved in many more reported cases across a broader range of fact patterns. The comparative abundance and variety of these decisions stems in part from the fact that many commercial enterprises furnish products for the temporary use and convenience of their customers or employees. Examples of nonliability include supermarkets that provide shopping carts [see, e.g., Keen v. Dominick's Finer Foods, Inc., 364 N.E.2d 502 (Ill. App. Ct. 1977)] and hotels that supply bathmats in their bathrooms [see, e.g., Wagner v. Coronet Hotel, 458 P.2d 390 (Ariz. Ct. App. 1969)]. See also Fee Trans. Servs., Inc. v. Fulgham, 154 S.W.3d 84 (Tex. 2004) (furnishing of trailer to independent contractor so he could work for transportation company did not impose strict liability on transportation company when trailer malfunctioned). A similar result obtained where an aerobatics flight student was killed in a crash. Cook v. Gran-Aire, Inc., 513 N.W.2d 652 (Wis. Ct. App. 1994), *rev. denied*, 520 N.W.2d 89 (Wis. 1994). The court found that no sale or lease had taken place despite a separate charge for the use of the plane, because the plane had never left the possession or control of the flight school insofar as the instructor at all times had access to separate flight controls. See also Feik v. Sieg Co., 823 F. Supp. 588 (C.D. Ill. 1993) (auto parts store that lent a compressor vise to a customer so that he could self-install new struts not strictly liable; the loan was not part of the consideration for the purchase, nor was the use of a compressor a necessary incident to the sale).

3. When Is a Product Seller or Other Distributor "In the Business of Selling or Distributing"?

The general rule that strict liability applies only to commercial product distributors can be traced back to the origins of products liability law in commercial sales warranties. The limitation was built into §402A of the Restatement (Second) of Torts, considered the wellspring of American products liability law. In its terms, that section applies to product distributors "engaged in the business of selling" such products. (§402A(1)(a)). Comment *f* states that strict liability:

> applies to any manufacturer of such a product, to any wholesale or retail dealer or distributor, and to the operator of a restaurant. It is not necessary that the seller be engaged solely in the business of selling such products. Thus the rule applies to the owner of a motion picture theatre who sells popcorn or ice cream, either for consumption on the premises or in packages to be taken home.
>
> The rule does not, however, apply to the occasional seller of food or other such products who is not engaged in that activity as a part of his business. Thus it does not

apply to the housewife who, on one occasion, sells to her neighbor a jar of jam or a pound of sugar.

As noted at the beginning of this section, the Products Liability Restatement applies to "one engaged in the business of selling or otherwise distributing products." Two categories of product suppliers are excluded from coverage: (1) those who supply unsafe and defective products, but in noncommercial contexts; and (2) those who supply unsafe and defective products in a commercial context, but are not in the business of selling the type of product supplied. In cases involving the first type of supplier, courts unanimously refuse to impose strict liability, even when the supplier sells the product. See, e.g., Elley v. Stephens, 760 P.2d 768 (Nev. 1988) (husband and wife sellers not strictly liable for harm caused to buyers by manufacturing defect in their "prefab" home). Inevitably, some cases come close to the line between commercial and noncommercial activity, but most are fairly easy to categorize. Thus, when someone gives, lends, or sells to a neighbor a defective product that subsequently causes an injury, the transferor is liable in tort only if the injured party can prove negligence.

In contrast to the product suppliers in the first category just considered, the suppliers in the second category who routinely escape strict liability are those who, although clearly commercial, are not in the business of supplying the type of product that injured the plaintiff. Thus, courts refuse to apply strict liability to isolated sales of products by commercial enterprises not in the business of selling the same type of product as those causing injury. (These cases are frequently said to involve "casual sales.") See, e.g., Ridenhour v. Colson Caster Corp., 687 S.W.2d 938 (Mo. Ct. App. 1985) (contractor not strictly liable for lending defective scaffolding as a matter of convenience to plaintiff's employer, subcontractor). However, one should not assume that a one-time sale of a particular product will necessarily be found to be casual. In Sprung v. MTR Ravenburg, Inc., 788 N.E.2d 620 (N.Y. 2003), the New York Court of Appeals found that a strict liability claim against a specialty sheet metal manufacturer for a defective retractable floor should not be precluded by the fact that the manufacturer

---

authors' dialogue 2

JIM: You remember Judge Vincent McKusick, an adviser to the Products Liability Restatement project?

AARON: How could I not remember Vince? He had recently retired as Chief Justice of the Supreme Judicial Court of Maine. He was one of the most helpful, thoughtful advisors we had.

JIM: Do you remember what he told us at the very beginning of the Restatement project, in early 1993, about trying to define the boundaries — what are products, and who can be said to have sold or distributed them?

AARON: Yeah. He said it would be harder than trying to nail a jellyfish to the wall. I'd say he exaggerated a bit. The boundaries are clear enough to make the system workable. But they're flexible enough to make it interesting.

had never before produced such a floor. The court justified this holding because the sale was not incidental to the manufacturer's normal business, but rather a regular sort of sale for the manufacturer. Id. at 623-624.

In Jaramillo v. Weyerhaeuser Company, 906 N.E. 2d 387 (N.Y. 2009), the United States Court of Appeals for the Second Circuit certified a question to the New York Court of Appeals regarding whether a company that sold one of its used machines (itself purchased used) to a different company can be held strictly liable for a workplace accident involving that machine, which occurred 16 years later. The New York high court answered the question in the negative. Although sales of its used, unneeded productive machinery were a significant part of defendant's earnings and occurred on a regular basis, they were nonetheless "casual, occasional" sales as opposed to "ordinary, regular" sales. The New York Court concluded:

> This case is controlled by two policy considerations . . . The "onerous" burden of strict liability is only imposed on "certain sellers" because of "continuing relationships with manufacturers" and a "special responsibility to the public, which has come to expect [these sellers] to stand behind their goods". The second of these policy goals is clearly absent here: buyers of Weyerhaeuser's used (third-hand, in fact) equipment at irregularly-scheduled "as is, where is" surplus sales cannot reasonably "expect [Weyerhaeuser] to stand behind [someone else's] goods." As to the first policy goal, while Weyerhaeuser may have had a closer relationship with the manufacturers [of the machines] than a customer would have with a supplier of run-of-the-[mill] equipment not unique to its particular industry, this relationship was still general in nature and even more attenuated with respect to the machines that Weyerhaeuser sold as surplus. Indeed, the machines involved in Jaramillo's accident was actually bought used by Weyerhaeuser from a third party rather than new from the manufacturer. Simply put, there is no reason to believe that imposing strict liability on Weyerhaeuser's sales of its scrap, used machines would create any measurable "pressure for the improved safety of products" on . . . manufacturers. Indeed, the most likely effect would be exactly what the District Court predicted: Weyerhaeuser would stop selling its used machinery, thus depriving small businesses of the ability to purchase otherwise unaffordable equipment.

In light of our precedents and the policy considerations underlying strict products liability, we answer the certified question in the negative.

E.   ALLOCATING RESPONSIBILITY INSIDE AND OUTSIDE THE COMMERCIAL CHAIN OF DISTRIBUTION

1.   Allocating Responsibility Between Product Distributors and Other Defendants and Among Members of the Distributive Chain

a.   Joint and Several Liability

At early common law, two situations in which defendants acted tortiously toward the plaintiff gave rise to what is now referred to as joint and several liability: (1) if the defendants acted in concert to cause the harm, and (2) if the defendants acted independently but caused indivisible harm. Liability in the case of concerted action is a form of vicarious liability, in which all the defendants will be responsible for the harm actually caused by only one of them. An example of this is where *A* and *B* engage in an automobile race on a public street and *A* runs over the plaintiff. *B* will be liable to the plaintiff just as much as *A*, although *B* did not actually hit the plaintiff. Joint and several liability will also be imposed if the defendants act independently, each actually causing harm to the plaintiff but under circumstances in which it is impossible to apportion harm between defendants. Thus, if the plaintiff were a passenger in *A*'s automobile, which collided with *B*'s automobile due to the fault of both drivers, *A* and *B* will be jointly and severally liable for the harm to the plaintiff.

The common law distinguished these two types of cases in determining whether defendants could be joined procedurally in a single action. If the defendants acted in concert, they were joint tortfeasors and could be joined in one action or sued separately, or severally, hence the phrase *joint and several liability*. But if defendants acted independently to cause indivisible harm, courts at common law would not allow joinder. In those cases, defendants were severally liable only. Technically, only defendants acting in concert were called joint tortfeasors. However, modern rules of procedure permit joinder in indivisible harm cases (see Fleming James et al., Civil Procedure 557, 5th ed., 2001), and today courts refer to defendants causing such harm as joint tortfeasors. The term *joint and several liability* has now become a shorthand phrase to reflect a substantive rather than a procedural rule. It means that each joint tortfeasor is responsible for the totality of the plaintiff's judgment. A plaintiff cannot recover more, in total, than the amount of his judgment plus any interest owing at the time of satisfaction. Furthermore, there is no requirement that jointly and severally liable defendants be joined procedurally as defendants.

As the following materials indicate, modern tort law provides opportunities for the defendant initially singled out by the plaintiff to shift some (or all) of the liability to other defendants who should share (or bear entirely) the financial burden. Given these more recent developments, of what significance, today, is the theoretical "jointness" of the defendant's liability to the plaintiff? The most important implication is a practical one: If the other defendants are judgment proof, the jointly liable defendant against whom the plaintiff successfully proceeds ends up holding the entire financial bag. Thus, in an egregious case that catalyzed reform efforts, a defendant adjudged 1 percent at fault footed 86 percent of the damages bill. See Walt Disney World Co. v. Wood, 515 So. 2d 198 (Fla. 1987).

With the adoption of comparative fault by most American jurisdictions, the question arises whether joint tortfeasor's liability should be limited to each tortfeasor's allocated fault apportionments, thus eliminating traditional joint tortfeasor liability. In other words, a defendant would be "severally liable," i.e., liable for only the percentage of harm allocated to him or her by the fact finder. The legislatures have been busy enacting statutes to deal with apportionment issues, and a majority of states have adopted some form of limitation on joint and several liability. A significant minority of jurisdictions retain the common law joint and several system. See Reporters' Notes to §§17, A18, Restatement (Third) of Torts: Apportionment of Liability (2000).

A significant minority of states have abolished joint and several liability outright, some with relatively narrow exceptions. See Reporters' Notes to §§17, B18, Restatement (Third) of Torts: Apportionment of Liability (2000). Some of these statutes impact products liability litigation in dramatic and arguably unintended ways. For example, in State Farm Ins. Cos. v. Premier Manufactured Sys., Inc., 142 P.3d 1232 (Ariz. 2007), a statute mandated several liability only, even among members of the distributive chain. The plaintiff argued that juries would likely allocate small percentages of responsibility to retailers and wholesalers, and much larger percentages to manufacturers. If the manufacturer were insolvent or otherwise unavailable to pay its share, the plaintiff would be left holding the bag for the lion's share of the total verdict. Even though the court admitted that such a result undermines the purpose of holding all product sellers strictly liable, the court held the statute to be unequivocal and constitutional and limited the nonmanufacturers to several liability only. Most of the reform has been effected through legislation; very few states have abolished joint and several liability judicially, though a few did so initially and then followed up with statutory codification. Tennessee rejected the common law joint and several doctrine by case law when it adopted comparative fault. See McIntyre v. Balentine, 833 S.W.2d 52 (Tenn. 1992). Later, in Owens v. Truckstops of America, Inc., 915 S.W.2d 420 (Tenn. 1996), the Supreme Court of Tennessee distinguished the entire distributive chain from other tortfeasors in the context of products liability cases. Thus, in Tennessee, all tortfeasors are severally liable only, but retailers, manufacturers, and other members of the distributive chain are jointly and severally liable for the percentage of fault allocated to the entire distributive chain.

While retention of the common law rule and outright abolition constitute polar extremes, many states have adopted middle-ground positions by statute, limiting, in some fashion, the plaintiff's recovery to the percentage of fault assigned to each defendant. The statutes are often Byzantine in their complexity. Many contain myriad qualifications — e.g., abolishing joint and several liability only when defendants meet a threshold percentage of fault, or only when the plaintiff is not at fault, or for some causes of action and not others, or for only noneconomic loss (pain and suffering). Many states employ combinations of these conditions. For summaries of these statutes, see Reporters' Notes to §§17, D19, E18, Restatement (Third) of Torts: Apportionment of Liability (2000).

A common feature of joint and several reform measures is application of a percentage threshold that triggers a reversion to joint liability. If the defendant is determined to be more than, say, 50 percent at fault, then liability is joint and several rather than several only. For example, in Montana and New Hampshire, if a defendant is more than 50 percent at fault, he is jointly and severally liable; otherwise several liability applies. Wisconsin's threshold is 51 percent (Wis. Stat. Ann. §895.045) and New Jersey's is 60 percent; 1995 N.J. Stat. Ann. §2A:15-5.3. A few states tie several-only recovery to a plaintiff's fault (i.e., only a faultless plaintiff will be entitled to a joint and several award).

Many of the statutes include exceptions for certain types of torts. An interesting example is New Mexico's law, N.M. Stat. Ann. §41-3A-1, which retains joint and several liability for intentional tort claims, claims of vicarious liability, strict products liability claims, and claims that the courts find implicate a "sound basis in public policy" that demands application of the joint and several rule.

Some states have abolished joint and several for noneconomic damages (e.g., pain and suffering) only. See Reporters' Notes to §§17, C21, Restatement (Third) of Torts: Apportionment of Liability (2000). Several states have opted for a kinder, gentler modification of the common law joint tortfeasor doctrine, patterned after the Uniform Comparative Fault Act. According to this model, in the event one of several tortfeasors is insolvent, that tortfeasor's share is reallocated among the remaining parties, including the plaintiff, if the plaintiff was negligent.

A related issue is whether to allocate fault to nonparties. Some states allow the factfinder to take into account the fault of nonparties, including settling tortfeasors and immune parties. Supporters of this position point out that without considering the fault of nonparties or immune parties, the goal of limiting a defendant's liability to his percentage of fault is undercut. Defendants will pay more than their several shares of awards since the fault of nonparties will be borne by the available defendants. Detractors retort that plaintiffs may not be fairly compensated for their losses when recovery is reduced based on the fault of a nonparty. Furthermore, plaintiffs complain that it is difficult to litigate the fault of nonparties who are not identified.

The possible ramifications arising from the abolition of joint and several liability have yet to be fully tapped. Consider ADT Security Services Inc. v. Swenson, 687 F. Supp. 2d 884 (D. Minn. 2009). In this case the decedent's ex-boyfriend (Van Keuren) attacked her in her home. The decedent and her then-current boyfriend (Hawkinson) purchased an ADT security system to protect them from another attack from her ex-boyfriend. The system was to sound an alarm when the telephone wires were cut or if sliding glass doors were broken. When the system did not work, Van Keuren broke into the decedent's home and killed both the decedent and Hawkinson while the decedent's children were watching. In an action brought on behalf of the children, the question arose whether ADT was jointly and severally liable for all of the harm to the children or whether the damages should be apportioned according to fault, i.e., should ADT be liable only for its percentage of fault and Van Keuren for his percentage of fault.

Here is the interesting question. Minnesota has abolished joint and several liability with the following exceptions relevant to this case. If a tortfeasor is liable for more than 50 percent of the fault or the tortfeasor committed an intentional tort, the common law rule of joint and several liability is still in force. Clearly, as between the murderer (Van Keuren) and ADT the percentage of fault attributed to ADT is less than 50 percent. The intentional tortfeasor is certainly liable for all the damages, but it is not clear at all whether the negligent tortfeasor is liable for the percentage of fault allotted to the intentional tortfeasor (Van Keuren). The Court found refuge in a provision of the Restatement (Third) of Torts: Apportionment of Liability, §14 (2000):

> A person who is liable to another based on a failure to protect the other from the specific risk of an intentional tort is jointly and severally liable for the share of comparative responsibility assigned to the intentional tortfeasor in addition to the share of comparative responsibility assigned to the person.

Whatever might be the result with other intentional torts, in the case at bar the function of the ADT system was to protect against an intentional intruder. If there were to be several liability only, a jury would certainly allot the overwhelming percentage of fault to the murderer and thus leave the plaintiff (children) with little compensation.

The pace and vigor that have characterized joint and several liability reform have led to understandable complexity. Many jurisdictions have developed a patchwork of case law-based clarifications and amendments on top of statutory complexities. To trace these developments, useful discussions of the joint tortfeasor tort reform movement can be found in Kathleen M. O'Connor & Gregory P. Sreenan, Apportionment of Damages: Evolution of a Fault-Based System of Liability for Negligence, 61 J. Air L. & Com. 365 (1996) (includes a complete rundown of each jurisdiction's overarching scheme). See also Arthur Best, Impediments to Reasonable Tort Reform: Lessons from the Adoption of Comparative Negligence, 40 Ind. L. Rev. 1 (2007), and F. Patrick

Hubbard, The Nature and Impact of the "Tort Reform" Movement, 35 Hofstra L. Rev. 437, 488 (2006).

b. Letting Retailers and Wholesalers Out of the Litigation

One interesting development has been the movement (or at least the beginnings of a movement) to let retailers and wholesalers off the strict liability hook (or at least partway off). Later in this chapter we consider the rules governing contribution and indemnity among the various members in the distributive chain. The tendency is for the liability to be passed up the chain from retailers and wholesalers to the manufacturer by means of implied rights of indemnity. Although this tendency reduces the ultimate exposures to liability of retailers and wholesalers, those categories of sellers are routinely joined as defendants and, even if eventually they (or their insurers) escape liability to the plaintiff, they incur substantial costs defending against liability and otherwise protecting their interests.

Earlier, in the days when implied warranty and res ipsa loquitur were the vehicles by which product sellers' liabilities were expanded, some jurisdictions recognized exceptions for retailers and wholesalers to whom products came wrapped in packaging that prevented inspection for defects. Despite the fact that these "sealed package," or "sealed container," exceptions for retailers and wholesalers were not recognized by the Restatement (Second) of Torts, §402A, a number of states have retained them, often by statute. See Del. Code Ann. tit. 18, §7001 (1999) (product sold in "sealed container" and in "unaltered form" provides a defense to action for manufacturing or design defect unless (1) the seller expressly warranted the product; (2) the manufacturer is insolvent, immune from suit, or not subject to suit in the state; or (3) the manufacturer is not ascertainable through reasonable effort); Md. Code Ann. Cts. & Jud. Proc. §5-405(b) (2006) (using language similar to the Delaware statute, but further barring the sealed container defense if the court determines by clear and convincing evidence that the judgment would be unenforceable against the manufacturer).

The "sealed container" doctrine has even been extended to shield defendants from strict liability in cases where products are sold outside of their containers. In Jones v. GMRI, Inc., 551 S.E.2d 867 (N.C. Ct. App. 2001), the North Carolina Court of Appeals applied that state's "sealed container" statute, N.C.G.S.A. §99B-2(a), which provides that:

> No product liability action, except an action for breach of express warranty, shall be commenced or maintained against any seller when the product was acquired and sold by the seller in a sealed container or when the product was acquired and sold by the seller under circumstances in which the seller was afforded no reasonable opportunity to inspect the product in such a manner that would have, or should have, in the exercise of reasonable care, revealed the existence of the condition complained of, unless the seller damaged or mishandled the product while in his possession. . . .

551 S.E.2d at 870. At trial, the jury found that contaminated meatballs served by the defendant restaurant arrived in a "sealed container" and were cooked, giving the defendant "no reasonable opportunity to inspect." The court entered judgment for the defendant. The appellate court affirmed because defendant was entitled to judgment by the "plain meaning" of the statute given the jury's findings.

Some observers feel that imposing strict liability on retailers and wholesalers is unfair, at least when the manufacturer is available to be a defendant. Consider the Model Uniform Product Liability Act, 44 Fed. Reg. 62,714 (1979).

§105. Basic Standards of Responsibility for Product Sellers Other than Manufacturers

(A) A product seller, other than a manufacturer, is subject to liability to a claimant who proves by a preponderance of the evidence that claimant's harm was proximately caused by such product seller's failure to use reasonable care with respect to the product.

Before submitting the case to the trier of fact, the court shall determine that the claimant has introduced sufficient evidence to allow a reasonable person to find by a preponderance of the evidence that such product seller has failed to exercise reasonable care and that this failure was a proximate cause of the claimant's harm.

In determining whether a product seller, other than a manufacturer, is subject to liability under Subsection (A), the trier of fact shall consider the effect of such product seller's own conduct with respect to the design, construction, inspection, or condition of the product, and any failure of such product seller to transmit adequate warnings or instructions about the dangers and proper use of the product.

Unless Subsection (B) or (C) is applicable, product sellers shall not be subject to liability in circumstances in which they did not have a reasonable opportunity to inspect the product in a manner which would or should, in the exercise of reasonable care, reveal the existence of the defective condition.

(B) A product seller, other than a manufacturer, who makes an express warranty about a material fact or facts concerning a product is subject to the liability set forth in Subsection 104(D) [dealing with liability for express warranty].

(C) A product seller, other than a manufacturer, is also subject to the liability of manufacturer under Section 104 if:

(1) The manufacturer is not subject to service of process under the laws of the claimant's domicile; or

(2) The manufacturer has been judicially declared insolvent in that the manufacturer is unable to pay its debts as they become due in the ordinary course of business; or

(3) The court determines that it is highly probable that the claimant would be unable to enforce a judgment against the product manufacturer.

(D) Except as provided in Subsections (A), (B), and (C), a product seller, other than a manufacturer, shall not otherwise be subject to liability under this Act.

The Model Uniform Product Liability Act (MUPLA), one of the most significant proposals at the state level for reform of American products liability law, was developed by a special task force of the United States Department of Commerce. Promulgated in 1979, MUPLA is aimed at bringing uniformity to what has increasingly become a confusing patchwork of varying state law. One of the interesting aspects of §105, supra, is that such a reform may stand a better chance of enactment into law than reform aimed at helping manufacturers, because wholesalers and retailers represent a large and politically powerful group, better able than are manufacturers to present the "little guy" image at legislative hearings. In any event, a large number

authors' dialogue 3

JIM: The MUPLA provision letting wholesalers and retailers off the hook unless they themselves were negligent or expressly warranted the product seems to make good sense. I can see why so many state legislatures have enacted such legislation.

AARON: In general I agree with you. Letting them out makes a lot of sense. But neither MUPLA nor the state statutes are sensitive to problems that plaintiffs will face once the middlemen are taken out of the picture. Here, as elsewhere, legislators cannot foresee all the fallout from the rules that they enact into law.

JIM: I don't see the problem. The legislation allows for recovery when the manufacturer is not subject to the jurisdiction of the court of the claimant's domicile and also allows recovery when the manufacturer is insolvent or when it is highly probable that it will become insolvent.

AARON: But that's not enough protection for plaintiffs. Consider the following scenario. Plaintiff files suit against XYZ Corp. in January 2000 for the sale of a defective product that caused her injury. The wholesaler and retailer move to dismiss because they were not negligent nor did they expressly warrant the product. In January 2000 there is no hint that XYZ is in financial trouble, so the trial court grants the middlemen's motions. The case muddles along in state court for five years before it comes to trial. In January, 2005, XYZ Corp. files for Chapter 11. Thus when the case is ready for trial, XYZ is no longer a solvent defendant. The wholesaler and retailer, however, were dismissed from the suit in 2000. If plaintiff tries to sue them in 2004-5, the tort statute of limitations will have run. Plaintiff is out of luck.

of states have passed legislation along the line of MUPLA §105. The Utah Court of Appeals applied the Utah Liability Reform Act (ULRA), based on MUPLA, in Sanns v. Butterfield Ford, 94 P.3d 301 (Utah Ct. App. 2004). In that case, the plaintiff sued the retailer and manufacturer of a van after the van tipped over and caused the plaintiff's injury. The Utah Court of Appeals affirmed the trial court's entry of summary judgment in favor of the retailer defendant. Basing its decision on the ULRA, the court noted that the retailer was a "passive seller" and reasoned that, as such, the retailer should not be exposed to the time and expense of defending the action when the manufacturer was a party to the lawsuit. The retailer was not subject to strict liability because it had no knowledge of any design or manufacturing defect, and it did not participate in the design, manufacture, engineering, testing, or assembly of the van.

Even if the manufacturer is solvent and available to the plaintiff and the retailer deals in products that it receives and sells in sealed containers, the retailer may nevertheless be liable under the "apparent manufacturer" doctrine. Under this doctrine, a retailer may be liable as a manufacturer if it sells or distributes as its own a product manufactured by another, usually through label or advertising. Chevron v. Aken Maritime, Inc., 604 F.3d 888 (5th Cir. 2010) (applying Louisiana law) (recognizing the doctrine as protecting the interests of consumers who rely on the vendor's reputation).

JIM: By gosh you're right, Aaron. But there is an easy fix. The MUPLA-based statute should be changed so that the statute of limitations against the middlemen is tolled and that, if the manufacturer becomes insolvent at any time before trial, the wholesaler and retailer can be brought back into the litigation.

AARON: If the middlemen cannot close their books on the case at the time suit against the manufacturer is brought, what good does the MUPLA-based legislation do them? They have to insure against products liability losses. And what is worse, they will be forced to reenter a case four years from the original time of suit. They would have to reopen discovery so that they could properly defend themselves. It's no fun to have to enter a case many years after the injury event.

JIM: I think that middlemen could purchase insurance rather cheaply if their only exposure were that they would be held liable if the manufacturer subsequently became insolvent. As for discovery, it is unlikely that the manufacturer who sought to defend the case when it was still solvent would not have developed sufficient information to mount a defense. Why would they not share such information with their middlemen? I'm not making light of the problem you raise. With major companies going into insolvency, the problem is real. But with the change in legislation that I suggest, it seems to me that plaintiffs will have adequate protection and middlemen will not be hurt too badly. No legislative resolution on this issue will be letter perfect. But middlemen legitimately want out of products liability suits in which they are truly nonplayers; the law ought to accommodate them.

DOUG: Excuse me for butting in Jim and Aaron, but I couldn't help overhearing your conversation. I think I could learn a lot from listening in. I hope you don't mind if I pull up a well designed and manufactured chair.

But see Goesel v. Boley International Ltd., 664 F. Supp. 2d 923 (N.D. Ill. 2009) (the Illinois statute exculpating nonmanufacturers from strict liability trumps the "apparent manufacturer" doctrine and limits strict liability to the exceptions specifically set forth in the statute.) The apparent manufacturer doctrine is set forth in Restatement (Third) of Torts: Products Liability §14 (1998).

PROBLEM FIVE

Florence Green wants you to represent her in a products liability action. Ms. Green's story is simple and straightforward. The week before her parents' anniversary she went to Jack's Liquor Mart to buy several bottles of Shangri-La Champagne. She took the bottles home and refrigerated them in preparation for the anniversary party she was giving. When the party was in full swing she went to the refrigerator and removed a bottle of champagne. When she tried to open the bottle it suddenly exploded and caused disfiguring cuts to her face. Jack's Liquor Mart is a high-volume discount liquor supermarket. It purchased 100 cases of Shangri-La Champagne from Triangle Liquor Distributors, which had purchased the champagne from the Shangri-La Winery. The bottles used by the Winery were manufactured by Glass Perfect, Inc. to the specifications of Shangri-La.

Your initial investigation reveals that Jack's Liquor Mart is a frequent litigant in exploding champagne bottle cases. The problem stems from the self-service aspect of the store. Customers have free access to the bottles and bottle abuse by customers who think it rather funny to shake up a bottle of champagne or otherwise mishandle the bottle (for example, by scratching it with a pocket knife) is not uncommon. The owner of Jack's Liquor Mart (Jack Keehl) has done his best to cut down this practice by putting several guards on duty, but he frankly admits that he cannot stop a prankster who is intent on doing damage. The expert who has examined this broken glass is certain that the bottle was defective when it exploded but he cannot determine where in the distributive chain such defect came into being.

In evaluating the case you discover that New California has enacted legislation identical to the provision of the Model Uniform Product Liability Act §105, set forth supra. You must now decide whether the case has sufficient merit for you to pursue it.

c. Contribution Among Members of the Distributive Chain

At early common law, if the plaintiff recovered against one of several joint tortfeasors, the liable tortfeasor was without legal recourse against the others to compel them to share the burden of liability. The harshness of this early rule has been ameliorated to some extent, and today most states provide for contribution among joint tortfeasors, either by statute or by judicial decision. A number of states have adopted the Uniform Contribution Among Tortfeasors Act, in either its 1939 or its 1955 version. See Reporters' Notes to §23 of Restatement (Third) of Torts: Apportionment of Liability (2000). The basic principles are contained in the following excerpts from the 1955 Uniform Act:

§1.   [RIGHT TO CONTRIBUTION]

(a) Except as otherwise provided in this Act, where two or more persons become jointly or severally liable in tort for the same injury to person or property or for the same wrongful death, there is a right of contribution among them even though judgment has not been recovered against all or any of them.

(b) The right of contribution exists only in favor of a tortfeasor who has paid more than his pro rata share of the common liability, and his tort recovery is limited to the amount paid by him in excess of his pro rata share. No tortfeasor is compelled to make contribution beyond his own pro rata share of the entire liability.

(c) There is no right of contribution in favor of any tortfeasor who has intentionally [willfully or wantonly] caused or contributed to the injury or wrongful death.

(d) A tortfeasor who enters into a settlement with a claimant is not entitled to recover contribution from another tortfeasor whose liability for the injury or wrongful death is not extinguished by the settlement nor in respect to any amount paid in a settlement which is in excess of what was reasonable. . . .

§2. [Pro Rata Shares]

In determining the pro rata shares of tortfeasors in the entire liability . . . their relative degrees of fault shall not be considered. . . .

The Uniform Act calls for the trier of fact initially to allocate fault among joint tortfeasors on a pro rata basis. Under that approach, if there are three such defendants, each is assigned one-third of the liability burden. In contrast to this pro rata approach, the majority of states have now adopted approaches that might be referred to as "equitable allocation," in which the share of liability initially allocated to each defendant is determined on the basis of that defendant's comparative share of the negligence, or fault. This is accomplished either by statute or by judicial decision. See, e.g., Blazovic v. Andrich, 590 A.2d 222 (N.J. 1991); Schneider National, Inc. v. Holland Hitch Co., 843 P.2d 561 (Wyo. 1992). Thus, if defendant *A* is found by the judge or jury to have been 40 percent negligent; defendant *B,* 50 percent; and defendant *C,* 10 percent, and all of the defendants are solvent and nonimmune, they would owe $40,000, $50,000, and $10,000, respectively, of a $100,000 judgment. Note that the problem of contribution among tortfeasors is eliminated if a tortfeasor's liability is limited to the tortfeasor's percentage of the fault. Since a tortfeasor will not pay more than the equitable share assigned to that tortfeasor, that person will not be entitled to contribution.

In Zeller v. Cantu, 478 N.E.2d 930 (Mass. 1985), the Massachusetts Supreme Judicial Court concluded that its version of the Uniform Contribution Act, calling for pro rata contribution, had not been impliedly repealed by the enactment of the Comparative Fault Act. The court imposed pro rata liability on a doctor and a surgical blade manufacturer.

The Restatement (Third) of Torts: Apportionment of Liability §23 (2000) adopts the following approach:

§23. Contribution

(a) When two or more persons are or may be liable for the same harm and one of them discharges the liability of another by settlement or discharge of judgment, the person discharging the liability is entitled to recover contribution from the other, unless the other previously had a valid settlement and release from the plaintiff.

(b) A person entitled to recover contribution may recover no more than the amount paid to the plaintiff in excess of the person's comparative share of responsibility.

(c) A person who has a right of indemnity against another person under §22 does not have a right of contribution against that person and is not subject to liability for contribution to that person.

An important difference between products liability cases and other kinds of tort cases is that, in products cases, the defendants are usually members of the same commercial chain of distribution and thus have opportunities to address the contribution question ahead of time, by contract. These contract provisions tend to allocate responsibility on an "all-or-nothing" basis, and thus might be considered "contracts of indemnity." In any event, courts give them effect as between the contracting parties in the distributive chain.

d. Indemnity Rights Up the Distributive Chain

A plaintiff injured by a defective product typically sues all the members of the distributive chain who can be served. Wholesalers and retailers may be held strictly liable for selling defective products even though they were not at fault and had no way of discovering that the product was defective. It is not surprising that these nonmanufacturing sellers seek indemnity from parties above them in the distributive chain. If the sellers are, in fact, totally free from fault, then each seller is entitled to indemnity from any predecessor in the distributive chain. See, e.g., Promaulayko v. Johns Manville Sales Corp., 562 A.2d 202 (N.J. 1989); Lowe v. Dollar Tree Stores, Inc., 835 N.Y.S.2d 161 (N.Y. App. Div. 2007) (retailer's right of indemnification includes attorneys' fees, costs, and disbursements for defending against tort action). In Godoy v. Abamaster of Miami, Inc., 302 A.D.2d 57 (N.Y. App. Div. 2003), the plaintiff brought an action for defective design against a retailer, a wholesale distributor, and an importer-distributor after she lost four fingers while operating a commercial meat grinder. Although the jury apportioned 50 percent of the fault to the distributor and only 10 percent to the distributor-importer, the court found that the evidence did not support the finding that either defendant was more negligent than the other. Finding *Promaulayko's* reasoning persuasive, the court held that in the absence of the manufacturer, the party closest to the manufacturer, the importer-distributor, should indemnify the distributor lower in the commercial chain of distribution.

However, when the wholesaler or retailer has been negligent in its distribution of the product, there is little reason to allow full indemnity up the chain. Thus, in Frazer v. A.F. Munsterman, Inc., 527 N.E.2d 1248 (Ill. 1988), the Illinois Supreme Court denied indemnity in favor of the retail distributor of a trailer manufactured with defective brakes by the third-party defendant. Indemnity was inappropriate, the Illinois high court reasoned, because the distributor had been found negligent in providing its customer with an inadequate trailer hitch. The jury should apportion liability between the manufacturer and the retail distributor under the Illinois contribution act. Refusing to allow full "upstream" indemnity does not undermine the policies underlying strict products liability, the court concluded. (One Justice dissented vigorously.) And in Thatcher v. Commonwealth Edison Co., 527 N.E.2d 1261 (Ill. 1988), the Illinois Supreme Court applied the rule in *Frazer* to bar indemnity on behalf of a downstream purchaser-user who settled the injured tort-plaintiff's claim against it. Although the settlement prevented a jury finding on the issue of negligence, the high court held the settlement to be a sufficient admission of fault to bar the upstream claim of full indemnity. (One justice dissented, arguing that mere settlement is not the equivalent of an admission or finding of fault and that the issue of the settling defendant's culpability, if any, should be tried.) 527 N.E.2d at 1264.

In General Motors Corp. v. Hudiburg Chevrolet, Inc., 199 S.W.3d 249 (Tex. 2006), a dealer hired an independent contractor to assemble a truck chassis and body. The

Supreme Court of Texas held that the dealer could not recover indemnity against the manufacturer of the defective chassis if the defect in the assembled truck arose in part from the way it was assembled at the retail level. The court concluded that even if the dealer was liable to the injured plaintiff only on the basis of strict liability, the dealer's nonnegligent involvement in the final assembly precluded its rights to indemnity against the chassis manufacturer, notwithstanding the fact that the chassis was itself defective. Presumably, fault-based apportionment between the parties would be available even if full indemnity was not.

Other courts, however, insist that even a retailer whose negligent failure to inspect contributed to the plaintiff's injury should be entitled to full indemnity against the manufacturer. In Schneider National, Inc. v. Holland Hitch Co., 843 P.2d 561 (Wyo. 1992), the operator of a trucking company was allowed full indemnity against the manufacturer of a defective trailer hitch that broke and caused the trailer to disengage and kill passengers in an oncoming car despite the claim by the hitch manufacturer that the trucker had acted negligently in failing to inspect the tractor and trailer. The trucking company impleaded the manufacturer of the hitch for full indemnity. The court held that it was appropriate to hold the hitch manufacturer for the entirety of the loss under strict liability since it was the "cheapest cost avoider." Similarly, in East Penn Mfg. Co. v. Pineda, 578 A.2d 1113 (D.C. App. 1990), a retailer who was an experienced seller of batteries and was negligent in failing to place an adequate warning on a battery, warning of dangers attendant to jump-starting, sought full indemnity from the battery manufacturer. The court found an implied duty to indemnify because the seller reasonably relied on the manufacturer's knowledge and skill in making a defect-free product and the seller's negligence consisted, at most, of a failure to discover the defect.

If contribution rules allow joint tortfeasors to recover against each other based on the percentage of fault rather than on a pro rata basis, there seems to be no good reason to allow a defendant whose fault contributed to the injury to recover total indemnity. The majority of cases clearly point in that direction. See Debra T. Landis, Annotation, Products Liability: Seller's Right to Indemnity from Manufacturer, 79 A.L.R.4th 278 (1990). The Restatement (Third) of Torts: Apportionment of Liability §22 (2000) provides:

§22. INDEMNITY

(a) When two or more persons are or may be liable for the same harm and one of them discharges the liability of another in whole or in part by settlement or discharge of judgment, the person discharging the liability is entitled to recover indemnity in the amount paid to the plaintiff, plus reasonable legal expenses, if:

(1) the indemnitor has agreed by contract to indemnify the indemnitee, or

(2) the indemnitee was vicariously liability

(b) A person who is otherwise entitled to recover indemnity pursuant to contract may do so even if the party against whom indemnity is sought would not be liable to the plaintiff.

In Brunjes v. Lasar Mfg. Co., 835 N.Y.S.2d 385 (N.Y. App. Div. 2007), the appellate court relied in part on §22(a)(ii) in ruling that the retail seller of a commercial meat mixer would presumably have indemnity rights against the "upstream" distributor, but that the trial court's conditional granting of summary judgment for the retailer was premature. Given that the tort-plaintiff alleged negligent installation and servicing by the retailer, the question of the retailer's right of indemnification would have to wait until the underlying tort claims were resolved. Presumably, if both the upstream distributor and the retailer were found at fault, apportionment between them would occur.

e. Settlement and Release Between the Plaintiff and Members of the Distributive Chain

It is most often to the advantage of both plaintiff and defendant to settle out of court. Indeed, without pervasive settlement practice the litigation system, which is already overburdened, would bog down completely. When joint tortfeasors are involved, the plaintiff may be able to reach agreement with only one of the tortfeasors. At common law, if the plaintiff settled with one joint tortfeasor, all were automatically released. This rule discouraged settlements since plaintiffs would be unwilling to settle with one party for a reasonable dollar amount if it might require abandoning claims against the remaining tortfeasors. The automatic release rule has now been rejected by all states, and plaintiff is able to release one tortfeasor and retain actions against the others. See Restatement (Third) of Torts: Apportionment of Liability §40(b) (2000).

Another problem has arisen, however. Does the defendant who settles with the plaintiff and receives a release from liability remain open to a contribution action by the defendant who decides to eschew settlement and litigate? May the litigating defendant who loses the lawsuit turn to the settling defendant and demand contribution for the damages paid out as a result of the judgment? There are no easy solutions to these problems. If contribution against the settling defendant is permitted, defendants will be discouraged from entering into settlements; under such a rule, settlement may not buy the settling party peace, but may only delay the lawsuit for a later day. On the other hand, if contribution against the settling defendant is not allowed and the judgment is reduced only by the dollar amount of the settlement, a "sweetheart settlement" between friendly parties may leave the nonsettling tortfeasor holding the bag. A succession of Uniform Contribution Among Tortfeasor Acts have dealt with this problem in different ways. The 1939 Act left the settling tortfeasor liable for contribution and the 1955 Act adjusted the rule slightly by releasing the settling tortfeasor from contribution if, but only if, the settlement had been made in good faith. Section 23 of the Restatement (Third) of Torts: Apportionment of Liability (2000), reproduced supra, bars contribution against the settling party who obtains a release from the plaintiff.

The Uniform Comparative Fault Act, promulgated in 1979, takes a markedly different approach to resolving this problem. The act provides for allocation of fault for each party in the action. Section 6 of the Act provides:

> A release, covenant not to sue, or similar agreement entered into by a claimant and a person liable discharges that person from all liability for contribution, but it does not discharge any other persons liable upon the same claim unless it so provides. However, the claim of the releasing person against other persons is reduced by the amount of the released person's equitable share of the obligation, determined in accordance with the provisions of [another] Section.

A simple hypothetical demonstrates how this works. Consider the following example propounded in a leading treatise:

> Assume plaintiff (P) has suffered $100,000 in damages because of the combined negligence of two defendants (D1 and D2). Plaintiff settles with D1 for $10,000 and proceeds to trial against D2. In a jurisdiction following the Uniform Act, the jury finds P 10 percent at fault, D1 60 percent at fault, and D2 30 percent at fault. Had P not settled with D1, P would have received a judgment against both defendants for 90 percent of P's damages (D1's 60 percent plus D2's 30 percent) or $90,000. Under the Uniform Act's principle of joint-and-several liability, P could have recovered $90,000 from either joined defendant. But because P has settled with D1, P's judgment under the Uniform Act is reduced by D1's share of the fault; thus P receives a judgment not for 90 percent of the damages but only for 90 percent less 60 percent (D1's share), or 30 percent. This amounts to a $30,000 judgment against D2; when added to the $10,000 received in settlement from D1, P has received a total of $40,000 — as opposed to the $90,000 P would have received had P not settled. Settling with D1 has cost plaintiff $50,000. [Comparative Negligence: Law and Practice §19.10[6] (1995).]

In short, plaintiff settled out not only the dollar amount of the claim with the settling tortfeasor but also the percentage of fault that will ultimately be attributed to him. Under this approach, which is adopted in §16 of the Restatement (Third) of Torts: Apportionment of Liability (2000), plaintiff can no longer profitably enter into a sweetheart settlement with the settling tortfeasor. If the defendant's fault percentage is higher than plaintiff has estimated, the difference comes out of the plaintiff's pocket.

Although the solutions under the Uniform Comparative Fault Act and the new Restatement governing allocation of liability have merit, they can discourage some legitimate settlements from taking place because a plaintiff may be unwilling to barter away a hitherto undetermined percentage of the lawsuit. Consider, for example, a plaintiff injured as a result of the combined fault of automobile driver error and defective brakes. Assume that the driver has low liability insurance limits and no assets otherwise available to pay a judgment. The insurer might be willing to tender the face value of the policy in settlement and close the case, but the plaintiff may not be willing to accept the settlement and issue the release. By releasing the settling tortfeasor from liability the plaintiff forgoes the right subsequently to collect that defendant's percentage of fault from the solvent, otherwise jointly and severally liable tortfeasor. This may hurt the plaintiff substantially if the jury assigns a high percentage of fault to the settling defendant. Is there any sensible way out of this morass?

F. ASSIGNING RESPONSIBILITY COLLECTIVELY TO THE DISTRIBUTIVE CHAIN

This section examines techniques whereby an injured victim may overcome difficulties in establishing where in the commercial distributive chain (manufacturer, wholesaler, retailer, etc.) the product came to be defective. For the purpose of this discussion, we will assume that the product was defective when the purchaser bought it from the retailer, but that it is not clear when the defect arose. A diagram will help to clarify the analysis. Figure 1 sets forth a diagram of a vertical distributive chain from top to bottom, coupled with a horizontal chain across the bottom from left to right. Note that the diagram presents two variations regarding the horizontal chain. The first is that the user/victim is the direct purchaser of the product from the vertical chain ((5) in the diagram). The second is that the victim is not the purchaser but rather is a third party, either a user or a nonuser in the horizontal chain ((6) in the diagram). Both variations can present the plaintiff with serious problems in identifying the defect in the hands of a financially solvent and legally responsible party.

Figure 1

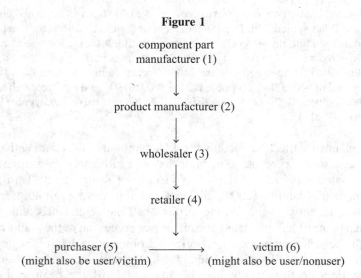

In order to recover in negligence against one or more defendants in the chain, the plaintiff must prove that it (or they) acted negligently in causing the defect to occur or remain undetected. Even if the plaintiff can prove that some defendants' efforts at quality control were negligently inadequate, each defendant will point to the others as the source of the defect. The manufacturers (1) and (2), wholesaler (3), and retailer (4) will insist that "A member of the chain above me caused the defect, and I could not reasonably be expected to have discovered it." The component part manufacturer, manufacturer, and wholesaler will argue that "A member of the chain below me caused the defect." All four defendants will also argue, of course, that the defect occurred after the last commercial sale of the product; while it was being used, but we have assumed away that possibility in our hypothetical in order to simplify the analysis of "gap in the chain" problems that persist even when the plaintiff can prove that he bought a dangerously defective product.

Under strict liability, some, but not all, of the finger pointing is eliminated. Strict liability holds the defendant liable for commercially selling a defective product. Whether the defect is discoverable or not by the seller is irrelevant. Thus, the parties down the distributive chain (i.e., manufacturer, wholesaler, retailer) cannot point up the chain and contend that the defect was created before the product came into their hands. That might be the basis of a defense under negligence but it is not under strict liability. However, the finger pointing down the chain continues to be a viable line of defense under strict liability. Remember, it is almost always legitimate for a defendant to contend that the product was nondefective when the defendant distributed it and that the defect was introduced after the product left the defendant's hands. Thus, if any member of the distributive chain is insolvent, underinsured, or immune from suit, the plaintiff may be forced to seek recovery up the chain. The classic answer by defendants up the chain will be that the product was tampered with or otherwise became defective down the chain.

The materials that follow consider several approaches by which plaintiffs may be able to overcome these difficulties of proof by holding the entire commercial chain jointly and severally liable for harm caused by a defect existing at the time the product was finally delivered to the plaintiff or to the plaintiff's predecessor in the horizontal chain of use and consumption.

Most courts will not allow a plaintiff who can prove that a product was defective when he bought it to join the entire commercial chain, including the manufacturer, without also proving that the product was defective from the very beginning. However, a minority of states have been more generous to injured plaintiffs and have allowed them to join the members of the chain as defendants without identifying the original source of the defect existing at the time of retail sale. Thus, in Prutch v. Ford Motor Co., 618 P.2d 657 (Colo. 1980), the Colorado Supreme Court held that plaintiff need not establish where in the distributive chain the defect arose. The court said:

> To impose an impossible or unreasonably onerous burden of proof is to deny many consumers a meaningful remedy. Thus, the plaintiff's burden should be no more than to establish that the defect arose in the course of manufacture-distribution and before the plaintiff purchased the item. . . . A plaintiff . . . therefore, should be able to satisfy the burden of proof by evidence that at the time of purchase or acquisition the product was flawed, . . . and damages resulted. . . .
>
> Manufacturers, distributors and sellers in the chain usually have greater access to information identifying a defect's source than does the buyer. Moreover, they are in a position to protect themselves against losses from conduct of another in the chain, as by "hold harmless" and indemnity agreements or other contractual arrangements. . . .
>
> Requiring each defendant in the chain of distribution to show that the product was not defective when it left its control imposes no unreasonable burden on defendants. Such a procedure simply redistributes the burden to those who have superior knowledge of the truth and better access to evidence. [Id. at 660.]

An Arizona appellate court added its endorsement. See Mineer v. Atlas Tire Co., 806 P.2d 904 (Ariz. Ct. App. 1990).

Very occasionally, special factual circumstances have moved a court to impose tort liability collectively on all members of the distributive chain of demonstrably defective product even though different members were liable on different legal theories—e.g., negligence and strict liability—and some possible defendants had not been joined in plaintiff's action. Thus, in Anderson v. Somberg, 338 A.2d 1 (N.J.), *cert. denied*, 423 U.S. 929 (1975), plaintiff suffered spinal injuries when a rongeur, a forceps-like surgical instrument, broke in his spine during back surgery. Plaintiff brought jointly and severally action against: (1) the surgeon who performed the operation, for negligent malpractice; (2) the hospital in which the operation took place, for negligently providing the doctor with defective instrument; (3) the medical supply distributor who furnished the defective instrument to the hospital, for breach of warranty; and (4) the manufacturer of the rongeur, on the basis of strict liability.

The jury returned a verdict in favor of all the defendants. The intermediate appellate reversed for a new trial, one judge concurring. The majority held that the jury on remand should be instructed to find for plaintiff against at least one defendant and otherwise, against all four. A concurrence would not have required a plaintiff's verdict, but would have instructed the jury that the plaintiff had made out a very strong case that at least one defendant was liable. The New Jersey high court affirmed the order for new trial, adopting the approach of the majority below. One judge on the Supreme Court dissented, voting to reverse the appellate court and affirm the trial court's judgment for defendant. The dissenter observed:

> Consider further . . . that a jury does undertake, despite a failure of adequate proof, to carry out the mandate of this instruction. How is a verdict to be reached? The absence of sufficient evidence upon which a verdict might justly rest, coupled with the compulsion to reach a verdict against *someone*, removes from the case any semblance of rationality. It then becomes a mere game of chance. There being no rational guide, each jury may proceed as the whimsy of the moment dictates. Thus we have trial by lot, or by chance — no more a rational process than were trial by ordeal or trial by combat. And yet it is the very essence of the judicial process that a determination reached by a court shall be the result of a rational study and analysis of applicable fact and law. . . .

Notwithstanding these decisions, the general rule remains that the plaintiff must establish that the product was defective in the hands of each defendant sought to be held strictly liable. If a gap cannot be covered by evidence sufficiently probative to point the finger at a particular defendant, then the plaintiff loses against that defendant. See, e.g., Moreno v. Sayre, 208 Cal. Rptr. 444 (Cal. Ct. App. 1984); SCM Corp. v. Letterer, 448 N.E.2d 686 (Ind. Ct. App. 1983); Marderosian v. The Stroh Brewery Co., 333 N.W.2d 341 (Mich. Ct. App. 1983).

G.   ASSIGNING RESPONSIBILITY FOR PRODUCT-RELATED WORKPLACE ACCIDENTS

Mix together the following ingredients: (1) a steady stream of serious and often permanently disabling injuries to employees flowing from hundreds of thousands of workplace accidents in this country each year; (2) the growing expectation among our citizenry that whenever serious injury occurs in a commercially managed environment, the managers of that environment should probably be liable in tort to the injured person; and (3) a century-old tradition under American worker compensation statutes that the compensation remedy, which is typically only a monetary fraction of the potential tort remedy, is exclusive — the employee may not bring a negligence action against his employer for work-related accidental injuries. Stir these ingredients over a moderate flame and what have you got? A volatile and potentially explosive mixture. Add one further ingredient: Many of these workplace accidents occur in the context of employees using dangerous and allegedly defective machinery manufactured by corporations that are not immune from tort liability to the injured employees. Now what have you got? One of the fastest growing and most perplexing areas of modern American products liability law.

1. *Direct Attack by the Employee Against the Employer*

In connection with many of the products liability claims brought by employees against the manufacturers of products that have caused them to suffer workplace injuries, the employer has played a sufficiently substantial role in causing the accident to justify joining the employer as a co-defendant with the manufacturer. That such joinder almost never occurs reflects the reality that employers enjoy an immunity under worker compensation statutes from employer tort liability for all workplace injuries, including injuries caused by defective products. Thus, workers' compensation is the exclusive remedy available to employees against their employers. Injured employees may recover against the manufacturers of defective machines that caused workplace injuries. But an employee's exclusive remedy against her employer is no-fault compensation benefits. This bar to employer tort liability is subject to limited exceptions, which are identified in the subsections that follow. But in most instances, injured employees cannot recover in tort directly from their employers. The prevailing view is that the statutory bar is an appropriate quid pro quo for the employers having provided a no-fault compensation remedy for workplace injuries.

The employer's worker compensation immunity from tort should be, and is, difficult to break. It was intended to provide broad-based protection, and courts have by and large interpreted the immunity so as to protect the employer from almost all tort-based suits. But dissatisfaction has arisen in some quarters with the all-encompassing sweep of immunity. The most significant exception to worker compensation immunity was to allow recovery for intentional torts committed by the employer against employees. In many instances statutes specifically exempted intentional torts from worker compensation immunity, and when they did not do so, state courts inferred such an exception. The question then arose as to the meaning of intent in the worker compensation context. Did it mean desire to do harm, or was it sufficient that the employer knew with substantial certainty that harm would occur. The Ohio experience is noteworthy. For a quarter of a century the Ohio Supreme Court struck down as unconstitutional legislative attempts to limit the right of employees to recover for intentional torts. See, e.g., Blankenship v. Cincinnati Micron Chemicals Inc., 433 N.E.2d 572 (Ohio 1982) (exposing employees to toxic chemicals constituted intentional tort). Indeed, in Johnson v. B.P. Chemicals, 707 N.E.2d 1107 (Ohio 1999), the court scolded the legislature for attempting to write legislation to make it difficult for employees to sue in tort for intentional torts. In a statute passed in 2005, Ohio Rev. Code Ann. 2745.01, the legislature defined the term "substantially certain" to mean that "an employer acts with deliberate intent to cause an employee to suffer an injury, a disease, a condition, or death." In Kaminski v. Metal & Wire Products Co., 927 N.E.2d 1066 (Ohio 2010), the Ohio Supreme Court upheld the legislation and noted that the legislation conformed Ohio law to that of the majority of jurisdictions in the United States.

Several states still seek to circumvent the worker compensation bar by allowing employees to sue their employers directly. A number of courts including Louisiana follow the substantial-certainty test once used in Ohio, which sometimes is interpreted to allow certain actions that are not "true" intentional torts to circumvent exclusivity. See, e.g., Robinson v. North Am. Salt Co., 865 So. 2d 98 (La. Ct. App. 2003) (injury from working on moving conveyor belt while in man- lift device); Trahan v. Trans-Louisiana Gas Co., 618 So. 2d 30 (La. Ct. App. 1993) (exposure to chemicals); Wainwright v. Moreno's, Inc., 602 So. 2d 734 (La. Ct. App. 1992) (foreman ordered plaintiff to remain in a ditch despite warnings of an imminent cave-in). Yet most states steadfastly adhere to the actual-intent standard, either by judicial decision or legislative enactment. See Wise v. CNH Am., LLC, 142 P.3d 774, 776 (Mont. 2006) (intentional injury defined as intentional and deliberate act with specific and actual intent of causing injury to employee).

Several state legislatures have enacted statutes expressly providing for an intentional tort exception. For example, New Jersey's Workers Compensation Act reads in part: "If an injury or death is compensable under this article, a person shall not be liable to anyone at common law or otherwise on account of such injury or death for any act or omission occurring while such person was in the same employ as the person injured or killed, except for intentional wrong." N.J. Stat. Ann. §34:15-8. In the following case, the Supreme Court of New Jersey considered what constitutes an "intentional wrong" within the meaning of the Act.

Laidlow v. Hariton Machinery Co.
790 A.2d 884 (N.J. 2002)

LONG, J.

The Workers' Compensation system has been described as an historic "trade-off" whereby employees relinquish their right to pursue common-law remedies in exchange for prompt and automatic entitlement to benefits for work-related injuries. Millison v. E. I. du Pont de Nemours & Co., 101 N.J. 161, 174, 501 A.2d 505 (1985). That characterization is only broadly accurate. In fact, not every worker injured on the job receives compensation benefits and not all conduct by an employer is immune from common-law suit. The Legislature has declared that certain types of conduct by the employer and the employee will render the Workers' Compensation bargain a nullity. Thus, for example, a worker whose death or injury is "intentionally" self-inflicted or results from a "willful" failure to make use of a safety device, furnished and required by the employer, will be ineligible for benefits. Likewise, an employer who causes the death or injury of an employee by committing an "intentional wrong" will not be insulated from common-law suit. N.J.S.A. 34:15-8; Millison, supra, 101 N.J. at 169.

The described limitations involve intentional wrongful conduct committed either by the worker or the employer. Underlying those limitations is the idea that such conduct neither constitutes "a natural risk of" nor "arises out of" the employment, the very notions at the heart of the Workers' Compensation bargain in the first instance.

The focus of this appeal is conduct by an employer that is alleged to constitute an intentional wrong under N.J.S.A. 34:15-8. We are called on to revisit our holding in Millison; resolve conflicting interpretations of it; and apply that decision to a case in which an injured employee claims that his employer has removed a safety device from a dangerous machine, knowing that the removal was substantially certain to result in injury to its workers and, in addition, deliberately and systematically deceived safety inspectors into believing that the machine was properly guarded. We hold that, in those circumstances, the employee's allegations, if proven, meet both the conduct and context prongs of Millison, thus entitling the employee to pursue his common-law remedies.

I

Rudolph Laidlow (Laidlow) suffered a serious and debilitating injury when his hand became caught in a rolling mill he was operating at his place of employment, AMI-DDC, Inc. (AMI). Laidlow sustained a crush and degloving injury resulting in partial amputations of the index, middle, ring and small fingers of his dominant left hand. Laidlow sued AMI on an intentional tort theory. He also named his supervisor, Richard Portman (Portman), in the suit for discovery purposes. AMI answered, denying the allegations of the complaint, and moved for summary judgment on the basis of the Workers' Compensation bar. . . .

AMI is in the business of manufacturing electrical products. Laidlow has been employed by AMI since August 7, 1978. On December 11, 1992, Laidlow was performing his job as a "set up man," which required him to work with a rolling mill that changed the dimension of heated metal bars when they were inserted into the mill. Laidlow manually inserted the bars into a "channel" that guided them into the mill, and often had to apply pressure to the bars with his hand in order to feed them into the rollers. On the day of the accident, Laidlow's glove became caught by the unguarded nip point as he was pushing a bar of silver into the channel. His gloved hand was pulled toward the mill's rollers. An eyewitness, Laidlow's co-worker Steven Smozanek, described the incident as follows: "The rollers are approximately 18 inches in diameter, and as he was feeding the bar into the roller, it pulled his hand against the roller, not into the roller, and as it pulled the hand against the roller, it just ripped the glove and the skin right off his hand."

On a prior occasion, Laidlow's glove had also become hooked on a bar, but he was able to slip his hand out of the glove before it was pulled into the machine. Smozanek described a similar incident when he was working on the mill and his gloved hand had snagged on a bar, but he too was able to pull his hand out of the glove just in time to escape injury. Those close calls were reported to AMI.

After the rolling mill was purchased by AMI in 1978, the company arranged to have a safety guard installed. However, the safety guard was "never" engaged; from 1979 to the date of Laidlow's accident in 1992, the guard always was "tied up." According to Laidlow, the guard was placed in its proper position only when Occupational Safety and Health Administration (OSHA) inspectors came to the plant. On those occasions, Portman, Laidlow's supervisor, would instruct employees to release the wire that was holding up the safety guard. As soon as the OSHA inspectors left, the safety guard would again be disabled.

Laidlow operated the mill without the safety guard in place for approximately twelve to thirteen years. During that period, except for the "near misses" referred to earlier, there were apparently no accidents with the mill until Laidlow was seriously injured during the incident at issue here.

Laidlow spoke to Portman regarding the safety guard three times during the period immediately preceding his accident. Approximately two weeks prior to the accident, Laidlow asked Portman to restore the guard. Several weeks before that, he spoke to Portman because a new operator was going to work on the mill and Laidlow thought the guard should be restored to its operative position. Additionally, one week before the incident, Laidlow again expressed concern that a new, inexperienced operator would be working on the mill, and told Portman that it was dangerous not to use the guard. According to Laidlow, the guard was never restored. Portman responded to his requests by stating that "it was okay" and "not a problem," and by "walk[ing] away."

Laidlow never refused to operate the mill without the safety guard in place nor spoke with any other superior in the company about the safety guard.

AMI concedes that the guard was removed for "speed and convenience." In addition, Gerald Barnes, a professional engineer retained by Laidlow, certified that AMI "knew there was a virtual certainty of injury to Mr. Laidlow or a fellow work[er] arising from the operation of the mill without a guard."

On those facts, the trial court concluded that Laidlow failed to demonstrate an "intentional wrong" under N.J.S.A. 34:15-8 and that Workers' Compensation was his exclusive remedy. Accordingly, the trial court granted AMI's motion for summary judgment, along with a similar motion filed by Portman.

The Appellate Division affirmed the dismissals, concluding that there was no evidence of an intentional wrong by AMI to warrant an exception from the Workers' Compensation bar. The panel relied on the lack of any accident over a twelve-year period and determined that OSHA violations alone, in the absence of proof of deliberate intent to injure, would not satisfy the intentional wrong standard. The court dismissed the suit against Portman because Laidlow failed to demonstrate any need to pursue discovery.

Judge Lintner dissented, contending that the record, fairly read, presented a jury issue regarding intentional wrong; that the lack of injuries over the twelve-year period was not dispositive of the issue of substantial certainty of injury; that, coupled with the guard's removal, AMI's deceptive practices with regard to OSHA provided conclusive evidence of "context" under *Millison;* and that Laidlow should have been allowed to obtain discovery from Portman because Portman was in a unique position to provide evidence of what the employer knew.

The appeal is before us as of right under Rule 2:2-1(a)(2) based on the dissenting opinion below. We granted Amicus status to the Trial Lawyers of America (ATLA-NJ) and New Jersey Manufacturer's Insurance Company (NJM).

II

In essence, Laidlow's argument is that the combination of the employer's disabling of the safety guard and deception of OSHA presents a triable issue on whether such conduct meets the definition of an "intentional wrong." AMI counters that under *Millison*, an intentional wrong requires a "deliberate intention to injure" and that Laidlow concedes that no one at AMI harbored such an intention. AMI also maintains that *Millison* specifically declared that the removal of a safety device fails to meet the intentional wrong standard. To the extent that recent Appellate Division decisions suggest the contrary, AMI argues that those cases should be disapproved. Furthermore, AMI argues that even if removal of a safety guard could qualify in some circumstances as an intentional wrong, the absence of any prior injury on its machine and Laidlow's successful experience in operating the machine without an accident for over twelve years obviates that possibility in this case. . . .

III

Our decision in *Millison* is obviously at the root of this case and a review of our holding there is essential. In *Millison*, we were faced with the question of "what categories of employer conduct will be sufficiently flagrant so as to constitute an 'intentional wrong,' thereby entitling a plaintiff to avoid the 'exclusivity' bar of N.J.S.A. 34:15-8?'' *Millison,* supra, 101 N.J. at 176, 501 A.2d 505. . . .

That is the so-called exclusive remedy provision of the Workers' Compensation Act, often referred to as the Workers' Compensation bar. *Millison* confronted that provision in the context of an occupational disease caused by exposure to asbestos during employment.

The appeal in *Millison* challenged a trial court's grant of summary judgment to an employer based on N.J.S.A. 34:15-8 in connection with plaintiffs' claim that the employer knowingly exposed them to an occupational disease. That court simultaneously denied summary judgment to the company doctors with respect to whom plaintiffs alleged the fraudulent concealment of their asbestos-related diseases. The Appellate Division affirmed the grant of summary judgment to the employer and reversed the denial of summary judgment to the physicians because there was no evidence that they "deliberately intended" to injure the workers.

We granted plaintiffs' petition for certification. Before us, plaintiffs argued that "their charges that defendants knowingly and deliberately exposed employees to a hazardous work environment and fraudulently concealed existing occupational diseases are sufficient to fall within the Act's limited 'intentional wrong' exception and to take their injuries outside the intended scope of the Compensation Act.'' *Millison,* supra, 101 N.J. at 170.

In addressing that contention, we recounted the history of the intentional wrong exception that had led the Appellate Division to its conclusion that only an employer's deliberate intent to injure was sufficient to vault the exclusivity bar. We also identified the precedents underlying the Appellate Division's ruling. [Description of earlier rulings requiring "deliberate intention" omitted.]

We recognized that those cases traced their rationale to Professor Larson's narrow and limited approach to intentional wrong and quoted extensively from his treatise. Specifically, we cited the following section:

> Even if the alleged conduct goes beyond aggravated negligence, and includes such elements as knowingly permitting a hazardous work condition to exist, knowingly ordering claimant to perform an extremely dangerous job, willfully failing to furnish a safe place to work, or even willfully and unlawfully violating a safety statute, this still falls shorts of the kind of actual intention to injure that robs the injury of accidental character.
>
> . . .
>
> If these decisions seem rather strict, one must remind oneself that what is being tested here is not the degree of gravity or depravity of the employer's conduct, but rather the narrow issue of intentional versus accidental quality of the precise event producing injury. The intentional removal of a safety device or toleration of a dangerous condition may or may not set the stage for an accidental injury later. But in any normal use of the words, it cannot be said, if such an injury does happen, that this was deliberate infliction of harm comparable to an intentional left jab to the chin. 2A A. Larson, The Law of Workmen's Compensation §68.13 at 13-22 to 13-27 (1983) (footnotes omitted).

What is critical, and what often has been misunderstood, is that we cited Professor Larson and the cases relying on his approach for informational, not precedential, purposes. *Millison,* in fact, specifically rejected Professor Larson's thesis that in order to obtain redress outside the Workers' Compensation Act an employee must prove that the employer subjectively desired to harm him. In place of Larson's theory, we adopted Dean Prosser's broader approach to the concept of intentional wrong.

Under Prosser's approach, an intentional wrong is not limited to actions taken with a subjective desire to harm, but also includes instances where an employer knows that the consequences of those acts are substantially certain to result in such harm. See W. Prosser and W. Keeton, The Law of Torts, §80 at 569 (5th ed. 1984).

In abandoning Larson's purely subjective approach in favor of substantial certainty, we stated: "In adopting a 'substantial certainty' standard, we acknowledge that every undertaking, particularly certain business judgments, involve some risk, but that willful employer misconduct was not meant to go undeterred." Id. at 178. . . .

In addition to adopting Prosser's "substantial certainty" test relative to conduct, in *Millison* we added a crucial second prong to the test:

> Courts must examine not only the conduct of the employer, but also the context in which that conduct takes place: may the resulting injury or disease, and the circumstances in which it is inflicted on the worker, fairly be viewed as a fact of life of industrial employment, or is it rather plainly beyond anything the legislature could have contemplated as entitling the employee to recover only under the Compensation Act? Id. at 179, 501 A.2d 505.

By the addition of the context prong, *Millison* required courts to assess not only whether the employer acted with knowledge that injury was substantially certain to occur, but also whether the injury and the circumstances surrounding it were part and parcel of everyday industrial life or plainly outside the legislative grant of immunity. In other words, under *Millison,* if only the conduct prong is satisfied, the employer's action will not constitute an intentional wrong within the meaning of N.J.S.A. 34:15-8. That standard will be met only if both prongs of *Millison* are proved. . . .

"Recapping, . . . under *Millison,* in order for an employer's act to lose the cloak of immunity of N.J.S.A. 34:15-8, two conditions must be satisfied: (1) the employer must know that his actions are substantially certain to result in injury or death to the employee, and (2) the resulting injury and the circumstances of its infliction on the worker must be (a) more than a fact of life of industrial employment and (b) plainly beyond anything the Legislature intended the Workers' Compensation Act to immunize. . . .

V

We turn now to the case at bar. . . . [W]e are satisfied that under our well-established standards for . . . summary judgment should have been denied to AMI and the case sent to a jury on the issue of substantial certainty.

The evidence with inferences in favor of Laidlow is powerful. The rolling mill is a dangerous machine because it requires an employee to manually feed material into a nip point. . . . Apparently recognizing that principle, after its purchase AMI provided a safety guard for the rolling mill. Yet, for 13 years, from 1979 to 1992 when Laidlow was injured, the guard was inactivated by AMI nearly 100percent of the time the machine was in use. During that period, Laidlow and a fellow employee had experienced close calls with the nip point of the unguarded mill. Those were potentially serious accidents in which the employees' gloves were ripped off by the machine and their fingers saved only by the cloth in the gloves. Those close calls were reported to AMI to no avail. They were persuasive evidence that AMI knew not only that injury was substantially certain to occur, but also that when it did occur it would be very serious, as Laidlow's injury turned out to be. Within the month prior to his accident, Laidlow asked his supervisor three times to restore the guard because the unguarded machine was dangerous and because new and inexperienced employees would be operating it. Nothing was ever done. . . .

AMI argues that the absence of prior accidents obviates a possible finding of "substantial certainty" by a jury. We disagree. To be sure, reports of prior accidents like prior "close-calls" are evidence of an employer's knowledge that death or injury are substantially certain to result, but they are not the only such evidence. Likewise, the absence of a prior accident does not mean that the employer did not appreciate that its conduct was substantially certain to cause death or injury. In short, we disagree with AMI and the Appellate Division that the absence of a prior accident on the rolling mill ended any inquiry regarding intentional wrong. That is simply a fact, like the close-calls, that may be considered in the substantial certainty analysis. . . .

A finding that the substantial certainty prong was satisfied does not end our inquiry. Laidlow's allegations, if proved, also must satisfy the context prong of *Millison* to preclude AMI from summary judgment. We have concluded that if Laidlow's allegations are proved, however, the context prong of *Millison* would be met. Indeed, if an employee is injured when an employer deliberately removes a safety device from a dangerous machine to enhance profit or production, with substantial certainty that it will result in death or injury to a worker, and also deliberately and systematically deceives OSHA into believing that the machine is guarded, we are convinced that the Legislature would never consider such actions or injury to constitute simple facts of industrial life. On the contrary, such conduct violates the social contract so thoroughly that we are confident that the Legislature would never expect it to fall within the Worker's Compensation bar. . . .

VII

The judgment of the Appellate Division is reversed. The matter is remanded for trial after plaintiff is afforded a reasonable opportunity to complete discovery concerning Portman.

In subsequent cases involving summary judgment for the employer, the New Jersey high court remanded for reconsideration in light of *Laidlow*. In Crippen v. Central Jersey Concrete Pipe Co., 823 A.2d 789 (N.J. 2003), an employee suffocated after falling into a loading hopper. The intermediate court of appeals reaffirmed its grant of summary judgment for the employer, concluding that "*Laidlow* [did] not alter [its] prior analysis." Id. at 794. The supreme court disagreed and reversed, finding summary judgment inappropriate where the employer violated an OSHA directive to remedy dangerous conditions and intentionally misrepresented to OSHA that the conditions had been abated. The supreme court also reversed summary judgment in Mull v. Zeta Consumer Products, 823 A.2d 782 (N.J. 2003), although the plaintiff did not allege OSHA deception. The court concluded, under the context prong, that the removal of safety devices, combined with the employer's alleged knowledge of the machine's dangerous condition from prior accidents and employee complaints and prior OSHA violation notices did not constitute simple facts of industrial life. See also Fermaintt v. McWane, Inc., 694 F. Supp. 2d 399 (N.J. 2010) (finding that neither the "conduct" prong nor the "context" prong was satisfied when an employer disabled an anti-rollback device causing a cast iron pipe to fall upon and kill the plaintiff; there were no previous history of near-miss accidents nor a pattern of OSHA violations).

The cases reveal a wide range of views as to what constitutes the kind of intent that will allow a plaintiff to break the exclusive remedy provision of worker's compensation. Close attention to the case law and the facts of the particular case is crucial. For an extensive review of the case law see Robles v. Hovensa, L.L.C., 2008 WL 2439881 (V.I. 2008).

Products liability cases present plaintiffs with another stratagem for bypassing the exclusive remedy provision of worker compensation. In Douglas v. E & J Gallo Winery, 137 Cal. Rptr. 797 (Cal. Ct. App. 1977) (superseded by statute), employees were injured by a defective scaffold furnished by their employer from a supply it had manufactured for sale to others. The court held that an employer could function in a "dual capacity." In its employer capacity it was required to pay worker compensation benefits and was immune from tort liability. Receipt of such benefits would not, however, prevent the employee from suing the manufacturer in its parallel capacity as a product manufacturer. This dual capacity doctrine was expanded in Bell v. Industrial Vangas, Inc., 637 P.2d 266 (Cal. 1981), to impose tort liability on behalf of a route salesman who was injured while he was delivering flammable gas to the premises of a customer. The employer was not the manufacturer of the allegedly defective product but was involved in its marketing and distribution. Such a seller would be liable for strict liability in tort had the plaintiff been a nonemployee. Bell is discussed in Glen R. Olson, Note, Bell v. Industrial Vangas: The Employer-Manufacturer and the Dilemma of Dual Capacity, 34 Hastings L.J. 461 (1982).

The dual capacity doctrine has been controversial. Professor Larson impugns the dual capacity exception, concluding that no state retains a dual capacity doctrine along the lines of the Douglas case. 2A Arthur Larson, Workmen's Compensation §72.81 (1993). The California legislature responded to Bell by mandating that worker compensation be the exclusive remedy even if the employer functioned in a dual capacity. Cal. Lab. Code §3602. The statute reflects concern that an unlimited dual capacity doctrine would swallow the entirety of the tort liability bar. The dissenters in Bell observed that the potential for abuse was substantial: "If an employer is to be held civilly liable to injured workers in the employer's capacity as a 'manufacturer,' what compelling reason can exist for denying similar liability for injuries attributable to the employer's other relationships, including his status as 'Landowner,' 'motor vehicle operator' or 'cafeteria proprietor?'" 637 P.2d at 278. See also Byrd v. Munsey Prods. of Tenn., 1985 Tenn. App. LEXIS 3029 (Tenn. Ct. App. 1985). The courts in Nelson v. Superior Court, 50 Cal. Rptr. 3d 684, 690 (Cal. Ct. App. 2007), and Fleetwood Enters., Inc. v. Workers' Compensation Appeals, 37 Cal. Rptr. 3d 587, 592 (Cal. Ct. App. 2006), both noted in footnotes that the dual capacity doctrine has been substantially restricted in California by statute.

The Supreme Court of Ohio reacted differently from the Bell Court, supra, in a case involving the dual capacity doctrine. In Schump v. Firestone Tire & Rubber Co., 541 N.E.2d 1040 (Ohio 1989), the plaintiff, who worked for a tire manufacturer, received injuries while driving a truck equipped with his employer's tires. The Ohio high court refused to apply the dual capacity doctrine, holding that the truck was equipped with the employer's tires in accordance with company policy and that any injury resulting from a defective tire was sustained as an employee and not as a consumer. The court held that the dual capacity doctrine would apply only when there was a showing that an employer occupied two independent and unrelated relationships with an employee and that it had assumed a role other than that of an employer. In Jessop v. Angelo Benedetti, Inc., 2003 WL 23114 (Ohio App. 8 Dist. 2003), the plaintiff was severely injured after his boot became caught in the blade of a piece of paving equipment. The court upheld summary judgment, finding no liability under the dual capacity doctrine where the employer designed and developed the machine solely for the business use of its employees and not for sale or lease. Illinois, which also recognizes the dual capacity doctrine, rejected an injured employee's contention that the employer acted as a "quasi-manufacturer" by modifying a trim press in Murcia v. Textron, Inc., 795 N.E.2d 773 (Ill. App. Dist. 2003). The court found that the dual capacity doctrine did not apply where the modification was incidental to the employer's business of manufacturing machine parts and was undertaken in its capacity as employer.

2. Allocating Responsibility Between the Worker Compensation System and the Products Liability System

Kotecki v. Cyclops Welding Corp.
585 N.E.2d 1023 (Ill. 1991)

MORAN, J.

Mark A. Kotecki (Kotecki) brought an action in LaSalle County for personal injury, allegedly caused by defendant Cyclops Welding Corporation's (Cyclops) negligence in the design and construction of an agitator, used on the premises of Carus Chemical Company (Carus), Kotecki's employer. Cyclops then filed a third-party complaint against Carus, seeking contribution. Carus moved to strike the ad damnum clause of the third-party claim for contribution. The trial court denied the motion. . . . [Interlocutory-appeal followed.]

The sole issue on appeal is whether an employer, sued as a third-party defendant in a product liability case, is liable for contribution in an amount greater than its statutory liability under the Workers' Compensation Act.

As this is an interlocutory appeal, all of the facts are gleaned from the pleadings. Kotecki, in his complaint, alleges that he sustained personal injury when he caught his hand in the motor of an agitator; that the injury occurred while he was acting in the scope of his employment with Carus; and that Cyclops negligently designed, constructed, and installed the agitator on the Carus property without sufficient guarding devices for the motor and drive system.

Cyclops then filed a third-party complaint against Carus, alleging various acts of negligence. Cyclops thus sought contribution from Carus under the Contribution Act (Ill. Rev. Stat. 1987, ch. 70, par. 301 et seq.), in an amount proportionate with the degree of fault attributable to Carus' culpability, if it is found liable to Kotecki at trial. . . .

Any discussion of the effect of workers' compensation on the Contribution Act must begin with Skinner v. Reed-Prentice Division Package Machinery Co. (1977), 70 Ill. 2d 1. In *Skinner,* the court held that a defendant manufacturer sued in strict tort liability had a right of contribution against the employer (whose conduct may have contributed to the injury) of an injured worker. The plaintiff, Rita Skinner, was injured while she was using an injection molding machine and she sued the machine's manufacturer under strict product liability. The manufacturer filed a third-party action against her employer for contribution, alleging negligence. This court found that the trial court's dismissal of the third-party action was error. (*Skinner,* 70 Ill. 2d at 16.) It additionally found that there is a right of contribution among joint tortfeasors, and that the doctrine would apply prospectively only. *Skinner,* 70 Ill. 2d at 16.

Following this court's decision in *Skinner,* the legislature passed the Contribution Among Joint Tortfeasors Act (Ill. Rev. Stat. 1989, ch. 70, pars. 301 through 305) (Contribution Act). For the purposes of this case, the statute states in pertinent part:

> [W]here 2 or more persons are subject to liability in tort arising out of the same injury to person or property, or the same wrongful death, there is a right of contribution among them, even though judgment has not been entered against any or all of them. Ill. Rev. Stat. 1989, ch. 70, par. 302(a). . . .

Carus essentially argues that although it is clear that an employer can be held liable for contribution to a manufacturer, this court has never stated if that amount is limited by the employer's workers' compensation liability. Cyclops . . . argues that . . . a manufacturer has a right to contribution from the employer, and the amount that the employer can be required to pay is limited only by the extent of the damages that are attributable to the employer's negligence. . . .

Cyclops . . . argues that this court should not examine any potential limitations on the amount that an employer could be required to contribute because the legislature is currently considering various pending bills in this area of the law. (Cyclops cited potential legislative amendments to the Workers' Compensation Act or the Contribution Act which would bar a third party from filing a third-party complaint against an employer. However, all of the bills that Cyclops cites either were tabled or left pending at the end of the legislative term.) Nevertheless, as this court has noted:

> We believe that the proper relationship between the legislature and the court is one of cooperation and assistance in examining and changing the common law to conform with the ever-changing demands of the community. There are, however, times when there exists a mutual state of inaction in which the court awaits action by the legislature and the legislature awaits guidance from the court. Such a stalemate is a manifest injustice to the public. When such a stalemate exists and the legislature has, for whatever reason, failed to act to remedy a gap in the common law that results in injustice, it is the imperative duty of the court to repair that injustice and reform the law to be responsive to the demands of society. (Alvis v. Ribar (1981), 85 Ill. 2d 1, 23-24 (despite the presence of six bills in the legislature, the court abolished the doctrine of contributory negligence).) . . .

The underlying controversy between workers' compensation and contribution was succinctly stated by the Minnesota Supreme Court:

> If contribution or indemnity is allowed, the employer may be forced to pay his employee — through the conduit of the third-party tortfeasor — an amount in excess of his statutory workers' compensation liability. This arguably thwarts the central concept behind workers' compensation, i.e., that the employer and employee receive the benefits of a guaranteed, fixed-schedule, nonfault recovery system, which then constitutes the exclusive liability of the employer to his employee. [Citation.] If contribution or indemnity is not allowed, a third-party stranger to the workers' compensation system is made to

bear the burden of a full common-law judgment despite possibly greater fault on the part of the employer. This obvious inequity is further exacerbated by the right of the employer to recover directly or indirectly from the third party the amount he has paid in compensation regardless of the employer's own negligence. [Citations.] Thus, the third party is forced to subsidize a workers' compensation system in a proportion greater than his own fault and at a financial level far in excess of the workers' compensation schedule. (Lambertson v. Cincinnati Corp. (1977), 312 Minn. 114, 119-20, 257 N.W.2d 679, 684.) . . .

The majority (45) of other jurisdictions do not allow a contribution action against an employer, from a defendant sued in tort, by an injured employee. (See Sherman, Contribution from Employers: Availability, Good Faith Settlements and What the Future May Hold, 75 Ill. B.J. 568, 572 n.52 (June 1987) (collecting cases).) At the other end of the spectrum, only New York allows a defendant to recover unlimited contribution from negligent employers. (See Dole v. Dow Chemical Co. (1972, 30 N.Y.2d 143, 381 N.Y.S.2d 382, 282 N.E.2d 288.) . . .

The Minnesota Supreme Court adopted a rule finding that, as in Illinois, an employer could be required to contribute, but that the amount of an employer's contribution would be limited by its workers' compensation liability. (*Lambertson,* 312 Minn. at 130, 257 N.W.2d at 689.) . . . The Minnesota rule arguably strikes a balance between the competing interests of the employer, as a participant in the workers' compensation system, and the equitable interests of the third-party defendant in not being forced to pay more than its established fault. Notably, this approach has been adopted by legislation in Idaho. See Runcorn v. Shearer Lumber Products, Inc. (1984), 107 Idaho 389, 395, 690 P.2d 324, 330. . . .

We find that the Minnesota rule provides the fairest and most equitable balance between the competing interests of the employer and the third-party defendant. . . . Limiting the amount of contribution of an employer to its liability under workers' compensation:

> allows the third party to obtain limited contribution, but substantially preserves the employer's interest in not paying more than workers' compensation liability. While this approach may not allow full contribution recovery to the third party in all cases, it is the solution we consider most consistent with fairness and the various statutory schemes before us. *Lambertson,* 312 Minn. at 130, 257 N.W.2d at 689.

The language of the Workers' Compensation Act clearly shows an intent that the employer only be required to pay an employee the statutory benefits. These limited benefits are paid in exchange for a no-fault system of recovery. The Contribution Act . . . requires that the employers contribute to tort judgments if they are partially responsible for an employee's injuries. . . .

Reversed and remanded, with directions.

The injured employee's ability to recover worker compensation benefits against the employer and then to prosecute a products liability claim against the manufacturer has raised questions regarding the proper method for allocating the liabilities between the two systems. According to an early study, employer negligence is implicated in more than half of all employment-related products liability claims. See Insurance Services

Office, Product Liability Closed Claim Survey: A Technical Analysis of Survey Results Report 10, 64-66 (1977). Even when employer negligence is established, states differ sharply as to how the losses are to be allocated. Among the major positions one finds:

(1) No Contribution. The majority rule places the entirety of the loss on the manufacturer of the defective product, with no right of contribution against the employer. See, e.g., Harsh Int'l v. Monfort Indus., 662 N.W.2d 574 (Neb. 2003) (explaining that a majority of jurisdictions will not allow a third-party action against the employer). In fact, in most states the employer who pays (or whose insurer pays) benefits to the injured employee has a subrogation lien against the ultimate tort recovery. Manufacturers are justifiably angered by the majority position, because the no-fault worker compensation system ends up bearing no responsibility whatsoever for harm caused, at least in part, by the employers' faulty conduct. By denying manufacturers contribution rights against employers and allowing subrogation, courts do more than protect the worker compensation system from tort recovery — they protect worker compensation from its own underlying obligation to the employee. Given the high level of dissatisfaction with the no contribution rule, its majority status is likely to change. Both courts and legislatures will be forced to acknowledge the legitimate complaints of manufacturers.

(2) Total Contribution. For many years New York permitted a manufacturer of a defective product to bring a third-party claim for contribution based on the proportionate fault of the parties. See Dole v. Dow Chem. Co., 282 N.E.2d 288 (N.Y. 1972). New York stood alone in this regard; no other state allowed total contribution. The New York approach drew heavy criticism because it exposed an employer to tort damages in excess of its liability under worker compensation law. In 1996 the New York legislature cut back significantly on *Dole*. N.Y. Workers' Comp. Law §11 (McKinney 2001) now provides that the right to contribution by a third party against an employer for injuries suffered by an employee acting within the scope of his or her employment will be allowed only if the employee suffered a "grave injury." The statute defines "grave injury" to mean only one or more of the following:

> . . . death, permanent and total loss of use or amputation of an arm, leg, hand or foot, loss of multiple fingers, loss of multiple toes, paraplegia or quadriplegia, total and permanent blindness, total and permanent deafness, loss of nose, loss of ear, permanent and severe facial disfigurement, loss of an index finger or an acquired injury to the brain caused by an external physical force resulting in permanent total disability. [Ch. 635, Laws of 1996.]

After some initial indications that the gravity of the employee's injuries might be a question of fact for the jury, it now appears that the New York courts will not permit contribution unless the employee's injuries are expressly listed in the statute. See, e.g., Meis v. ELO Org., LLC, 767 N.E.2d 146 (N.Y. 2002) (finding that the loss of a thumb is not listed in §11 as a "grave injury" and plaintiff failed to demonstrate that he suffered a "permanent and total loss of use" of the hand); Castro v. United Container Mach. Group, Inc., 761 N.E.2d 1014 (N.Y. 2001) (holding that the loss of multiple fingertips did not meet the "loss of multiple fingers" requirement and thus was not a "grave injury" under §11); Castillo v. 711 Group, Inc., 882 N.E.2d 885 (N.Y. 2008) (amputation removing both joints of index finger qualified as loss of index finger, whereas amputation of only one joint did not); Ibarra v. Equipment Control, Inc., 268 A.D.2d 13 (N.Y. App. Div. 2000) (finding that employee's loss of vision in one eye, even if total, does not constitute "total and permanent blindness"); Fleming v. Graham, 886 N.E.2d 769, 773-74 (N.Y. 2008) ("A disfigurement is severe if a reasonable person viewing the plaintiff's face in its altered state would regard the condition as abhorrently distressing, highly objectionable, shocking or extremely unsightly. Though plaintiff's face showed numerous scars they did not rise to the level of "severe" disfigurement).

(3) Limited Contribution. Kotecki, supra, is a leading case. As noted in Kotecki, Minnesota adopted a rule allowing third parties to seek contribution from negligent employers in Lambertson v. Cincinnati Corp., 257 N.W.2d 679 (Minn. 1977). The court applied comparative fault principles and held that the amount to be contributed must reflect the negligent employers' percentage of fault, but cannot exceed the total worker compensation liability for the injury. Illinois courts continue to apply Kotecki even where the employee did not pursue his workers' compensation rights, Pavelich v. All Am. Homes, Inc., 606 N.E.2d 859 (Ill. App. 2d Dist. 1992), or where willful and wanton employer misconduct is alleged, Lannom v. Kosco, 616 N.E.2d 731 (Ill. App. Ct. 1993). The Kotecki limit can, however, be waived contractually. Virginia Surety Co. v. Northern Ins. Co. of N.Y., 866 N.E.2d 149 (Ill. 2007) (acknowledging that Kotecki cap can be waived). The limited contribution approach was adopted in the Draft Uniform Product Liability Act but was rejected in the final draft of the Act because establishing the percentage of employer fault imposed significant transaction costs.[5]

(4) Severing the Systems. An interesting approach to resolving the conflict between the worker compensation system (which provides the employee limited benefits) and the tort system (which provides the employee total recovery) is to apportion fault between the parties and then to hold the manufacturer liable for its share of damages in tort and the employer (or its insurer) for the worker compensation benefits. For example, in a case where the worker compensation recovery is $10,000 and the total tort damages are $200,000, if the manufacturer is held 75 percent at fault and the employer is held 25 percent at fault, the employee recovers $150,000 from the manufacturer and $10,000 from the employer. This approach was adopted by the district court in Shellman v. United States Lines, Inc., only to be promptly reversed, 528 F.2d 675 (9th Cir. 1975), cert. denied, 425 U.S. 936 (1976). A similar holding involving the Longshoremen and Harbor Workers' Compensation Act was reversed by the United States Supreme Court. Edmonds v. Compagnie Generale Transatlantique, 577 F.2d 1153 (4th Cir. 1978) (en banc), rev'd, 443 U.S. 256, reh'g denied, 444 U.S. 880 (1979). The reasoning behind severing the systems is that the employee has made his bargain with the worker compensation system and should be limited to that system's measure of damages against the employer. Thus, this approach severs the joint tortfeasor doctrine and allocates damages according to the provisions of the two differing systems. Although courts and scholars have expressed interest in the solution, it is not the governing law in any jurisdiction that retains the joint tortfeasor doctrine. Many states have abrogated joint

---

5. Model Uniform Product Liability Act §114, Analysis 44 Fed. Reg. at 62,740 (1979).

authors' dialogue 4

JIM: At the end of the day, I can't help thinking that our courts and legislatures have made a mess of the interface between worker compensation and products liability. I think they may be going too far in allowing employees to sue employers in tort, and not far enough in allowing manufacturers to interplead employers for contribution.

AARON: Your preference for contribution seems a bit arbitrary. If you want the employer to bear some (all) of the tort liability, why not let it happen directly, via an intentional tort action?

JIM: First of all, courts are distorting the concept of intentionality in allowing employees to sue their employers directly. These doctrinal distortions may spill over into other areas and, suddenly, almost every negligence action becomes an intentional tort. Heck, even selling perfectly good knives can be an intentional tort, given that it is certain that some people will cut themselves. The better way to handle the employer's role in creating unreasonable product-related risks in the workplace is via the allocation of responsibility by juries under comparative fault, as part of the products liability action against the manufacturer. Juries can assess the appropriate responsibilities as between manufacturers who commercially design and market the machinery and employers who manage the workplaces in which the accidents occur.

DOUG: Jim, if your idea is sound, why haven't more states adopted it?

JIM: I don't know, really. Maybe it's politics. Most states deny tort recovery against the employers and deny contribution on behalf of manufacturers, leaving products liability to bear all the tort-measured losses. Most states even pay back the worker comp carriers out of the plaintiff's products recovery, holding the employer's side completely harmless for what, in many instances, is clearly the employer's fault.

AARON: But then, why the beginnings of a trend in favor of expanding knowledge-based intentional tort recoveries against employers?

JIM: Maybe it's more acceptable, politically. Who can argue against allowing tort recovery for *intentional* wrongdoing?

DOUG: Interesting, though, that it is courts pushing these intentional tort recoveries for reasons of *political* acceptability. This seems to be one area where the courts are not shy about playing a strong role in determining the allocation of responsibility, even when it appears overtly political to do so. I'll be curious to see as we go along when this judicial bravado waxes and wanes.

and several liability and limit a defendant's liability to the defendant's proportional share of fault. See Section C, infra.

(5) Dollar-for-Dollar Reduction of Plaintiff's Tort Recovery. The solution that has engendered the most support in debates over a federal products liability act would

allow the defendant manufacturer to deduct the plaintiff's worker compensation benefits from the amount of any tort judgment. Under this proposal, it would make no difference whether the employer was negligent. Worker compensation benefits would be assessed exclusively against the compensation system. No subrogation lien would be allowed and no contribution action against the employer could be brought. The drafters of the Model Uniform Product Liability Act (MUPLA) have backed this approach as does the leading authority on worker compensation. Section 114(a) of MUPLA provides:

> In the case of any product liability claim brought by or on behalf of an injured person entitled to compensation under a state Worker Compensation statute, damages shall be reduced by the amount paid as Worker Compensation benefits for the same injury plus the present value of all future Worker Compensation benefits payable for the same injury under the Worker Compensation statute.

It might be argued that the MUPLA provision would accomplish "mirror image" injustice. Just as current law shifts employer-caused costs onto manufacturers, the proposal would allow the manufacturer to shift partial liability to the no-fault worker compensation system for an injury that was entirely the fault of the manufacturer. Such a reaction, however, is probably not justified. The worker compensation system, which was established to provide limited recovery for a work-related injury, would, in fact, be paying for a work-related injury. To deny the employer who was truly not at fault his third-party action against the manufacturer may appear to be somewhat unfair. But does it violate basic principles of fairness to recognize that when a no-fault system operates side-by-side with a fault system, it is best to permit each system to work separately? It might be possible to "fine tune" the proposal and allow dollar-for-dollar reduction only when the employer is at fault, and even to allow the subrogation lien when he is not. But that would require that fault be tried and apportioned between the employer and manufacturer. Such an approach would increase transaction costs, presenting apportionment questions for jury resolution in the workplace setting where apportionment of fault may be especially difficult.

CHAPTER TWO

Causation

It should come as no surprise that the plaintiff in a products liability case must establish a causal connection between the defendant's defective product and the plaintiff's harm. In products cases sounding in tort, courts approach the causation issue very much as they do in nonproducts cases studied in the first-year torts course; and in cases sounding in warranty, all of the relevant Uniform Commercial Code sections impose causation requirements. Beyond this, generalizations are difficult. For one thing, the relevant terminology tends to be confusing. Some courts distinguish cause-in-fact from proximate cause, others employ only one (or the other) of these terms, while still others rely on phrases such as "direct cause" or "substantial cause." Notions of "intervening cause" and "superceding cause" also generate considerable mischief. The best advice to the student regarding terminology is to be aware that jurisdictions differ in the ways they talk about causation, and to use the terminology appropriate to the jurisdiction in which he or she is briefing or arguing a given case. We have organized the following causation materials around the persistent substantive issues presented in the cases, rather than around the vicissitudes of terminology.

Several distinct (or at least distinguishable) questions arise in connection with the causation issue. Suppose that the plaintiff suffers harm after using or consuming a product that she can show was defective at time of sale and seeks to hold the defendant manufacturer liable for the harm. Four questions must be answered in the affirmative for the plaintiff to establish causation:

(1) Did the product harm the plaintiff?
(2) Did the defendant supply the product?
(3) Did the defect in the defendant's product contribute to harming the plaintiff?
(4) Did the defective product proximately cause the plaintiff's harm?

These questions provide the structure for this chapter. All of them can arise in cases involving manufacturing defects; but typically some of them — for example, the first question involving whether the product, in fact, caused the plaintiff's harm — are easily answered in the affirmative. Thus, when a plaintiff buys a new bicycle that suddenly breaks because of a defect while being used normally and causes personal injury, typically no one disputes that the bicycle in question harmed the plaintiff. Instead, the first causation question will usually be contested only in cases involving generic product hazards. For example, did the misleadingly marketed cigarettes that plaintiff smoked for 20 years cause plaintiff's lung cancer? Notwithstanding the fact that some of the causation issues considered in this chapter involve generic product risks rather than manufacturing defects, all four causation issues are considered here for convenience. The existence of a defect may be assumed in all of these cases for purposes of considering causation, and therefore "defect" does not present problems that will confuse the analysis.

A.   DID THE PRODUCT ACTUALLY CAUSE THE PLAINTIFF'S HARM?

1.   But-For Causation in General

But for causation comes into play in two different contexts. The first, of concern in this section, tests whether the product in question was a necessary condition to the plaintiff suffering harm. The second, of concern in Section C, infra, tests whether the defective aspect of the product, rather than simply the product itself, was a necessary condition. The first but-for issue is universally dealt with as part of cause-in-fact. As for the second, while many courts also treat it as part of cause-in-fact, some deal with it as part of proximate cause. Section 26 of Restatement (Third) of Torts: Liability for Physical and Emotional Harm (2010) falls into the first camp. Thus, it asserts that tortious conduct "is a factual cause of harm when the harm would not have occurred absent the [tortious] conduct." In the cause-in-fact context considered in this section, the question is whether the plaintiff would have suffered the same harm if the product had never been produced in the first instance. That is, but-for the product itself (rather than the product defect), would the plaintiff have been harmed anyway? If the answer is "Yes, the plaintiff would have been harmed even if the product had never existed," then the product in question is not a cause-in-fact of the plaintiff's harm.

But-for actual causation breaks down logically into two components. The first, sometimes referred to as "general," or "generic," causation, concerns whether the product sold by the defendant is inherently capable of causing the sort of harm suffered by the plaintiff. If it is not, the defendant wins the actual causation issue as a matter of law. The second cause-in-fact issue is specific causation—whether the product in question actually harmed this particular plaintiff. Most products liability cases involve only specific causation; the general causation issue is not raised by the facts. When, for example, an allegedly defective automobile runs over the plaintiff and the issue is whether a defect in the vehicle caused the accident, general causation is not an issue—no one questions that automobiles are inherently capable of physically harming people. But what if the plaintiff claims that fumes from the automobile's exhaust caused him to contract lung cancer? In that instance, the manufacturer may argue not only that the automobile was not defective, but also that exhaust fumes from a single vehicle are not inherently capable, as a general matter, of causing lung cancer. Indeed, even if the defendant in the "fumes hurt the plaintiff" case admits that the vehicle's exhaust system was defective, it may still have the general causation argument that, in any event, vehicles generally cannot—and, therefore, this particular vehicle did not—cause people to contract lung cancer. Even if it were clear as a general matter that toxic exhaust fumes from motor vehicles can cause people to contract cancer, the manufacturer may still argue that the particular automobile involved in the case did not cause the plaintiff's illness. This second actual causation issue in our exhaust fumes hypothetical—whether the particular automobile in question harmed the plaintiff—is the issue of specific causation, the issue presented in most products liability cases involving actual causation.

2. Special Problems of Proof: Reliance on Experts

The issues of generic and specific causation raise very interesting questions regarding the proper use of expert testimony. Questions of causation often tend to arise at the fringes of scientific knowledge and often involve expert testimony that is questionable from the standpoint of scientific methodology. Defendants frequently challenge the admissibility and adequacy of plaintiff's expert proof. To understand how these issues get resolved it will be necessary to trace a bit of history. In 1923, in Frye v. United States, 293 F. 1013 (D.C. Cir. 1923), the District of Columbia Court of Appeals was asked whether evidence derived from a lie-detector test was admissible against a defendant in a murder trial. The court devised a standard for admissibility of scientific evidence that would become the rule for most, if not all, American courts for the next 70 years:

> Just when a scientific principle or discovery crosses the line between the experimental and demonstrable stages is difficult to define. Somewhere in this twilight zone the evidential force of the principle must be recognized, and while courts will go a long way in admitting expert testimony deduced from a well-recognized scientific principle or discovery, the thing from which the deduction is made must be sufficiently established to have gained general acceptance in the particular field in which it belongs. 293 F. at 1014.

Thus, when faced with an objection to a party's scientific evidence, the court applying the *Frye* test must determine whether the method by which that evidence was obtained was generally accepted by experts "in the particular field in which it belongs." If the judge determines that the methodology is not generally accepted by the relevant field, the judge will disallow the evidence. If the plaintiff's cause of action depends on the disallowed evidence, this often marks the end of the case.

No other area of products liability in recent years reflects more vividly the problems just described than cases involving the widely used prescription drug, Bendectin. Approved in 1956 by the FDA as a safe treatment for morning sickness during pregnancy, Bendectin was used by over 30,000,000 women between 1957 and 1983. Richardson-Merrell, Inc., the manufacturer, withdrew the drug from the market in 1983 due to widespread fears that it caused severe birth defects in the children of women who ingested the drug while pregnant. Whether these fears were grounded in fact is still disputed, but the fears were real enough. A large number of tort claims had been filed based on scientific studies, including epidemiological studies, allegedly revealing the drug to be a teratogen, or birth defect-causing agent. By the mid-1980s, Bendectin litigation appeared to be a growth area for plaintiffs' lawyers. See, e.g., Oxendine v. Merrell Dow Pharmaceuticals, 506 A.2d 1100 (D.C. 1986) (Bendectin manufacturer held liable based on epidemiological proof of causation).

Notwithstanding the optimism that reigned in the early to mid-1980s among plaintiffs' lawyers regarding the future of Bendectin litigation, the tide began turning against them as the established scientific community concluded in a number of major research projects that the link between the drug and the birth defects had not been established at an adequate level of statistical significance—that is, observed correlations between ingestion and injury could, for all the data showed, have been the product of random chance, i.e., the birth defects may not have exceeded the general background risk of birth defects in the population as a whole. Courts began issuing summary judgments for the defendant, Merrell, with increasing frequency. Not all federal courts agreed with this trend, however, and a fair amount of confusion reigned. All of these developments culminated in an epochal Supreme Court decision.

In Daubert v. Merrell Dow Pharmaceuticals, Inc., 509 U.S. 579 (1993), the Supreme Court vacated the judgment of the court of appeals in favor of the defendant in a Bendectin case. The court of appeals had ruled for defendant after excluding plaintiff's expert's testimony based on *Frye.* The Supreme Court reversed and remanded, holding that "general acceptance" is not a necessary precondition to the admissibility of scientific evidence under the Federal Rules of Evidence:

> Faced with a proffer of expert scientific testimony . . . the trial judge . . . must make a preliminary assessment of whether the testimony's underlying reasoning or methodology is scientifically valid and properly can be applied to the facts at issue. Many considerations will bear on the [first] inquiry [regarding scientific validity], including whether the theory or technique in question can be (and has been) tested, whether it has been subjected to peer review and publication, its known or potential error rate and the existence and maintenance of standards controlling its operation, and whether it has attracted widespread acceptance within a relevant scientific community. The [validity] inquiry is a flexible one, and its focus must be solely on principles and methodology, not on the conclusions that they generate. Throughout, the judge should also be mindful of other applicable Rules. . . . Cross examination, presentation of contrary evidence, and careful instruction on the burden of proof, rather than wholesale exclusion under an uncompromising "general acceptance" standard, is the appropriate means by which evidence based on valid principles may be challenged.

Rather than necessarily making it easier or more difficult for plaintiffs to get their scientific testimony admitted into evidence, the Supreme Court in *Daubert* appears to have aimed at giving federal courts more control over the admissibility issue, instead of deferring under *Frye* to the scientific community.

The *Daubert* ruling, based on the Court's interpretation of Federal Rule of Evidence 702, has had its greatest impact on federal courts. See Tamraz v. Lincoln Elec. Co., 620 F.3d 665 (6th Cir. 2010) (district court abused its discretion in admitting doctor's testimony that defendant's welder's products caused plaintiff's Magnesium-Parkinson's disease because doctor's conclusions were based on speculation and did not constitute scientific evidence). Macy et. al. v. Whirlpool Corp., 2015 WL 3505511 (5th Cir. 2015) (upholding district court's exclusion of expert testimony based on *Daubert*). But not all federal courts apply the same level of scrutiny in reviewing expert testimony. See Tucker v. Smithkline Beecham Corp., 2010 WL 1266487, *21 (S.D. Ind. 2010) (holding that "absence of a 'gold standard' published, peer-reviewed, placebo-controlled study demonstrating a statistically significant increased incidence in suicide or suicidal events with Paxil, does not render [experts] opinion inadmissible [under *Daubert*]"); Bitler v. A.O. Smith Corp., 400 F.3d 1227, 1236 (10th Cir. 2004) (affirming admission of expert testimony without requiring expert to test his theory). For an article concluding that defendants justifiably believe that the *Daubert* standard is more restrictive to expert testimony than was the case under *Frye* see Andrew Juris, Scott DeVito, The Stricter Standard: An Empirical Assessment of *Daubert's* Effect on Civil Defendants, 72 Cath. U.L. Rev. 675 (2013) (examining removal practice; defendants remove cases to federal courts to get the benefit of *Daubert*); see also Edward J. Imwinkelried, The Epistemological Trend in the Evolution of the Law Expert Testimony: A Scrutiny at Once Broader, Narrower and Deeper, 47 Ga. L. Rev. 863 (2013) (*Daubert* signaled a change from deference to experts to an examination of the validity of testimony).

Daubert is not limited to the federal courts. Thirty state courts have adopted *Daubert* standards for the admissibility of expert testimony. Fourteen states continue allegiance to the *Frye* — general acceptance standard. Seven states have yet to commit. But, even states that insist that *Frye* governs rely on *Daubert* methodology in applying the *Frye* rule. See, e.g., Cornell v. 360 W. 51st Street Realty, LLC, 9 N.E. 3 884 (N.Y. 2014); Hallmark v. Edlridge, 189 P.3d 646, 650 (Nev. 2008); Palmer v. Mobil Oil Corp., 87 N.E.2d 1114 (N.Y. 2006). For a comprehensive survey of the status of all state courts as of 2015 see American Bar Association; Website, Section of Litigation, 50 State Survey of *Daubert/Frye* Applicability, available at http://apps.americanbar .org/litigation/committees/trialevidence/daubert-frye-survey.html (June 2015).

The Supreme Court has revisited the *Daubert* principle in several decisions. See, e.g., General Elec. Co. v. Joiner, 522 U.S. 136 (1997) (holding that a court of appeals should utilize the "abuse of discretion" standard in reviewing a trial court's decision to exclude expert testimony under *Daubert*); Kumho Tire Co. v. Carmichael, 526 U.S. 137 (1999) (holding that a trial court correctly applied the *Daubert* standard when excluding the testimony of a witness who purported to be an expert in tire defects). These decisions are discussed further in Rider v. Sandoz.

Rider v. Sandoz Pharmaceutical Corp.
295 F.3d 1194 (11th Cir. 2002)

Before ANDERSON, HULL and RONEY, Circuit Judges.
RONEY, Circuit Judge.
This case involves an issue that has repeatedly come before federal courts: whether expert testimony purporting to link the drug Parlodel with hemorrhagic stroke is admissible to prove causation. Bridget Siharath and Bonnie Rider (plaintiffs) brought this action, alleging that their postpartum hemorrhagic strokes were caused by ingestion of Parlodel. Defendant Sandoz Pharmaceuticals Company (Sandoz), maker of Parlodel, moved to suppress the testimony of the plaintiffs' expert witnesses and for summary judgment. The district court [for the Northern District of Georgia] held that the plaintiffs' expert testimony was not sufficiently reliable to meet the standards established by Daubert v. Merrell Dow Pharm., 509 U.S. 579, 113 S. Ct. 2786, 125 L. Ed. 2d 469 (1993), and granted summary judgment in favor of Sandoz. Plaintiffs appeal. We affirm. . . .

I. Background

Bridget Siharath and Bonnie Rider both took the drug Parlodel to suppress lactation after childbirth. The active ingredient in Parlodel is bromocriptine, an ergot alkaloid compound. Both women subsequently suffered hemorrhagic strokes.

Siharath and Rider filed suit against Sandoz, alleging that Parlodel caused their hemorrhagic strokes. After discovery, Sandoz moved, in limine, to exclude the opinions and testimony of the plaintiffs' experts on causation, and for summary judgment. Because the motions, documentary evidence, experts, and issues were the same in both cases, the district court addressed the motions together. The district court held a *Daubert* hearing to determine whether the evidence was admissible.

The district court, in a three-day hearing, examined the evidence presented in great detail and found that the plaintiffs' claims were based on speculation and conjecture rather than the scientific method. The court drew a careful distinction between clinical process, in which conclusions must be extrapolated from incomplete data, and the scientific method, in which conclusions must be drawn from an accepted process, and concluded that the plaintiffs' experts were relying on the former. Accordingly, the district court excluded the evidence and granted summary judgment in favor of Sandoz. . . . This appeal followed.

II. *The Legal Standard*

Toxic tort cases, such as this one, are won or lost on the strength of the scientific evidence presented to prove causation. For many years the standard for admissibility of such evidence was the "general acceptance" test set forth in Frye v. United States, 293 F. 1013 (D.C. Cir. 1923). When the Federal Rules of Evidence were enacted in 1975, a question arose as to whether the "general acceptance" test had been supplanted by the reliability test articulated in Rule 702. The question was resolved in three cases decided by the Supreme Court. Daubert v. Merrell Dow Pharm., 509 U.S. 579, 113 S. Ct. 2786, 125 L. Ed. 2d 469 (1993); Gen. Elec. Co. v. Joiner, 522 U.S. 136, 118 S. Ct. 512, 139 L. Ed. 2d 508 (1997); Kumho Tire Co., Ltd. v. Carmichael, 526 U.S. 137, 119 S. Ct. 1167, 143 L. Ed. 2d 238 (1999). These cases are commonly referred to as the *Daubert* trilogy.

Since *Daubert*, courts are charged with determining whether scientific evidence is sufficiently reliable to be presented to a jury. The *Daubert* court made it clear that the requirement of reliability found in Rule 702 was the centerpiece of any determination of admissibility. The Supreme Court identified four factors used to determine the reliability of scientific evidence: 1) whether the theory can and has been tested; 2) whether it has been subjected to peer review; 3) the known or expected rate of error; and 4) whether the theory or methodology employed is generally accepted in the relevant scientific community.

In *Joiner*, the Supreme Court established the standard for reviewing trial court rulings of admissibility, and held that such rulings would be made under an abuse of discretion standard. The *Joiner* court also established the important test of analytical "fit" between the methodology used and the conclusions drawn. The court reasoned that just because a methodology is acceptable for some purposes, it may not be acceptable for others, and a court may not admit evidence when there is "simply too great an analytical gap between the data and the opinion proffered."

In *Kumho Tire*, the Supreme Court made it clear that testimony based solely on the experience of an expert would not be admissible. The expert's conclusions must be based on sound scientific principles and the discipline itself must be a reliable one. The key consideration is whether the expert "employs in the courtroom the same level of intellectual rigor that characterizes the practice of an expert in the relevant field." The court emphasized that judges have considerable leeway in both how to test the reliability of evidence and determining whether such evidence is reliable. . . .

III. The Plaintiffs' Theory of Causation

Plaintiffs sought to introduce the testimony of five experts. All five possessed impressive credentials and were found to be well qualified by the district court, three over the defendants' objection. . . . Two of the experts, Doctors Kulig and Dukes, testified at the *Daubert* hearing. The experts presented a detailed argument for the cause of the plaintiffs' hemorrhagic strokes that may be summarized as follows:

1) The active ingredient in Parlodel is bromocriptine, a member of the class of drugs known as ergot alkaloids.
2) Other ergot alkaloids can cause vasoconstriction, which suggests that bromocriptine causes vasoconstriction.
3) Animal studies also suggest that bromocriptine causes vasoconstriction.
4) Vasoconstriction can cause high blood pressure and ischemic stroke (stroke caused by decreased blood flow to the brain).
5) If vasoconstriction and high blood pressure can cause ischemic stroke, it can also cause hemorrhagic stroke (stroke caused by a rupturing of a blood vessel).
6) Thus, Parlodel caused the plaintiffs' hemorrhagic strokes.

IV. The Evidence Presented

The scientific evidence presented by plaintiffs in support of their theory of causation may be grouped into six categories: 1) epidemiological studies that, on the whole, may point weakly toward causation; 2) case reports in which injuries were reported subsequent to the ingestion of Parlodel; 3) dechallenge/rechallenge tests that implied a relationship between Parlodel and stroke; 4) evidence that ergot alkaloids (a class of drug that includes bromocriptine) may cause ischemic stroke; 5) animal studies indicating that under some circumstances, bromocriptine may cause vasoconstriction in dogs and other animals; and, 6) the FDA statement withdrawing approval of Parlodel's indication for the prevention of lactation.

A.   Epidemiology

Epidemiology, a field that concerns itself with finding the causal nexus between external factors and disease, is generally considered to be the best evidence of causation in toxic tort actions. Plaintiffs presented four epidemiological studies. Three of the four appear to have found no relationship or a negative relationship between Parlodel and stroke. Another may suggest a positive relationship. Nonetheless, both parties agree that none of the studies present statistically significant results and that the epidemiological evidence in this case is inconclusive. . . .

It is well-settled that while epidemiological studies may be powerful evidence of causation, the lack thereof is not fatal to a plaintiff's case. . . . This Court has long held that epidemiology is not required to prove causation in a toxic tort case. Accordingly, this case presents the difficult question of whether the evidence submitted to prove causation, in the absence of epidemiology, was sufficient to meet the requirements of *Daubert*.

B.   Case Reports

Much of the plaintiffs' expert testimony relied on case reports in which patients suffered injuries subsequent to the ingestion of Parlodel. Although a court may rely on anecdotal evidence such as case reports, courts must consider that case reports are merely accounts of medical events. They reject only reported data, not scientific methodology. Some case reports are a very basic form report of symptoms with little or no patient history, description of course of treatment, or reasoning to exclude other possible causes. The contents of these case reports were inadequate, even under the plaintiffs' expert's standards, to demonstrate a relationship between a drug and a potential side effect.

Some case reports do contain details of the treatment and differential diagnosis. Even these more detailed case reports, however, are not reliable enough, by themselves, to demonstrate the causal link the plaintiffs assert that they do because they report symptoms observed in a single patient in an uncontrolled context. They may rule out other potential causes of the effect, but they do not rule out the possibility that the effect manifested in the reported patient's case is simply idiosyncratic or the result of unknown confounding factors. As such, while they may support other proof of causation, case reports alone ordinarily cannot prove causation. The record demonstrates that the district court carefully considered the case reports and properly concluded that the case reports did not by themselves provide reliable proof of causation.

C.   Dechallenge/Rechallenge Data

Plaintiffs' experts provided dechallenge/rechallenge data that they argue suggests a link between Parlodel and stroke. A test is a "dechallenge" test when a drug that is suspected of causing a certain reaction is withheld to see if the reaction dissipates. The drug may then be reintroduced in a "rechallenge" to see if the reaction reoccurs. These reports, which may be analogized to controlled studies with one subject, can be particularly useful in determining whether a causal relationship exists. Nonetheless, because none of the studies involved a patient with the particular injury suffered by the plaintiffs, they do not provide data useful in determining whether Parlodel caused the plaintiffs' injuries. . . .

[T]hese dechallenge/rechallenge reports suggest at most a possibility that Parlodel may cause localized vasoconstriction, and may suggest that it causes hypotension. They cannot be considered reliable evidence of a relationship between Parlodel and stroke because neither of them involve stroke. Moreover, dechallenge/rechallenge tests are still case reports and do not purport to offer definitive conclusions as to causation. . . .

D.   Chemical Analogies

Bromocriptine is one of many drugs in a class known as ergot alkaloids. Plaintiffs sought to introduce evidence that because other ergot alkaloids cause vasoconstriction, then it is proper to conclude bromocriptine must do so as well. There is an insufficient basis in the record for this Court to hold that the district court abused its discretion by not drawing such a conclusion. Ergot alkaloids encompass a broad class of drugs with great chemical diversity, and "[e]ven minor deviations in chemical structure can radically change a particular substance's properties and propensities." The district court, after a detailed review of the properties of ergot alkaloids, concluded that plaintiffs failed to come forward with even a theory as to why the mechanism that causes some ergot alkaloids to act as vasoconstrictors would more probably than not be the same mechanism by which bromocriptine acts to cause vasoconstriction. The district court did not abuse its discretion in doing so.

E. Animal Studies

Plaintiffs offered evidence of animal studies in which bromocriptine demonstrated vasoconstrictive properties in dogs and certain other animals. Plaintiffs did not offer any animal studies that suggest that bromocriptine causes stroke, or even high blood pressure. The district court discussed each of these studies and was within its discretion in concluding that plaintiffs offered insufficient evidence on which that court could base a conclusion that the effect of bromocriptine would be the same on humans as it is on animals.

F. FDA Findings

Plaintiffs presented evidence that the FDA issued a statement withdrawing approval of Parlodel's indication for the prevention of lactation. The district court concluded that the language in the FDA statement itself undermined its reliability as proof of causation. In the statement, the FDA did not purport to have drawn a conclusion about causation. Instead, the statement merely states that possible risks outweigh the limited benefits of the drug. This risk-utility analysis involves a much lower standard than that which is demanded by a court of law. A regulatory agency such as the FDA may choose to err on the side of caution. Courts, however, are required by the *Daubert* trilogy to engage in objective review of evidence to determine whether it has sufficient scientific basis to be considered reliable. The district court did not abuse its discretion in concluding that the FDA actions do not, in this case, provide scientific proof of causation.

V. *Applying the Evidence to the Plaintiffs' Theory of Causation*

The deficiencies in the evidence reveal three gaps in the causal argument advanced by the plaintiffs. First, plaintiffs suggest that because bromocriptine is an ergot alkaloid, it causes vasoconstriction. Although some other ergot alkaloids do cause vasoconstriction, plaintiffs offered insufficient evidence for the district court to find that bromocriptine does so as well. This is not a case where the Court finds the evidence offered to be unreliable. In this case the record contains no evidence at all of this hypothesis. Instead, it contains principally speculation and conjecture. . . .

Second, the plaintiffs urge the Court to extrapolate the results of animal studies to humans. As with the plaintiffs' evidence of chemical properties, the district court did not err in finding no basis for doing so. Plaintiffs' experts admitted that with respect to animal studies generally, what happens in an animal would not necessarily happen in a human being. Accordingly, it is necessary for plaintiffs to offer some rationale for the suggestion that the vascular structures of humans and animals are sufficiently similar in this context to conclude that bromocriptine's effects on animals may be extrapolated to humans. Plaintiffs have not done so. . . .

Third, plaintiffs argue that because there is some evidence that bromocriptine causes ischemic stroke, it also causes hemorrhagic stroke. This is the most untenable

---

authors' dialogue 5

AARON: I don't like the way the lower courts are applying *Daubert*. Clearly the Supreme Court believed it was making things somewhat easier on plaintiffs by admitting expert testimony that satisfies its criteria even if the expert's methodology has not been generally accepted in the scientific community. But by making "general acceptance" one of the criteria, the new approach seems to have retained all the difficulties of the traditional *Frye* rule for plaintiffs and added further hurdles for them to overcome. Now, even if an expert's methodology is accepted by part of the relevant scientific community, and thus the testimony might have been admissible under *Frye*, it can be excluded if the trial court concludes that the expert's methodology fails to meet the other *Daubert* criteria. At the very least, *Daubert* is adding greatly to the costs of bringing iffy causation claims into court. I guess I'm fearful that *Daubert* may be making it too difficult for plaintiffs to prove their claims.

JIM: I followed you up until the last part. Why *shouldn't* we make it more difficult for plaintiffs to bring "iffy claims" into court? Without *Daubert*, plaintiffs can always get some voodoo doctor to come in and opine that the plaintiff's stomach cancer was caused by the defendant's pop-up toaster, or the microwave oven. Besides, I'm not sure that, in fact, courts are being all that hard on plaintiffs.

DOUG: Now *you've* gone too far, Jim. For all you know, a poorly designed microwave could very well cause cancer. Why not allow the plaintiff to try and prove it through a qualified expert, even if the expert's theories are not yet accepted by the scientific establishment? I'm sure the first scientists linking cigarettes to cancer were dismissed as quacks. Why should the legal system wait for the glacial process of scientific consensus-building?

JIM: As I read the case, all *Daubert* asks is that the expert explain herself and show that she is relying on sound scientific method. Surely that is not too much to ask.

AARON: Maybe what we're saying is that there's no middle ground. Courts have to choose between being too hard and too easy on expert theorizing that is out of the mainstream. You, a throwback to the Cro-Magnon period, prefer being too hard. And I, the quintessential Renaissance man, prefer being too easy, if that is the only alternative.

JIM: I'm feeling queasy.

---

link in the causal chain. Strokes are broadly classified into two categories: ischemic and hemorrhagic. Ischemic strokes occur as a result of lack of blood flow to the brain. Hemorrhagic strokes occur as a result of bleeding within the brain. Thus, although the two conditions share a name, they involve a wholly different biological mechanism. The evidence that suggests that Parlodel may cause ischemic stroke does not apply to situations involving hemorrhagic stroke. This is a "leap of faith" supported by little more than the fact that both conditions are commonly called strokes. Plaintiffs argue that as a result of the vasoconstriction caused by Parlodel, blood pressure may increase to the point that blood vessels in the brain rupture. Plaintiffs have offered no reliable evidence that Parlodel increases blood pressure to such dangerous levels. Even if they had, they failed to offer proof of how such an increase in blood pressure can precipitate a hemorrhagic stroke.

Since the shortcomings in the evidence render the theory unreliable, the district court did not abuse its discretion in excluding the plaintiffs' evidence of causation.

VI. Conclusion

In the absence of epidemiology, plaintiffs may still prove medical causation by other evidence. In the instant case, however, plaintiffs simply have not provided reliable evidence to support their conclusions. To admit the plaintiffs' evidence, the Court would have to make several scientifically unsupported "leaps of faith" in the causal chain. The *Daubert* rule requires more. Given time, information, and resources, courts may only admit the state of science as it is. Courts are cautioned not to admit speculation, conjecture, or inference that cannot be supported by sound scientific principles. "The courtroom is not the place for scientific guesswork, even of the inspired sort. Law lags science; it does not lead it." Rosen v. Ciba-Geigy Corp., 78 F.3d 316, 319 (7th Cir. 1996). . . .

We hold that the district court did not abuse its discretion in concluding that the Plaintiffs' scientific proof of causation is legally unreliable and inadmissible under the standards set by the *Daubert* trilogy.

AFFIRMED.

A large majority of federal courts have rejected expert testimony in Parlodel cases on grounds similar to *Rider*. See, e.g., Glasttetter v. Novartis Pharm. Corp., 252 F.3d 986 (8th Cir. 2001) (postpartum stroke case); Soldo v. Sandoz Pharm. Corp., 244 F. Supp. 2d 434 (W.D. Pa. 2003) (postpartum stroke case). However, in Hyman & Armstrong v. Gunderson, 279 S.W.3d 93 (Ky. 2008), reh'g denied (2009), in a case where a woman who took Parlodel postpartum and suffered seizures and death, the Kentucky Supreme Court sharply criticized *Rider* saying that it "equate[s] reliability with scientific certainty . . . which is far from what the Supreme Court intended in *Daubert*." The court noted that the lack of epidemiological studies to support causation was not determinative since "one cannot ethically experiment on human beings, exposing them to the near certainty of some number of deaths, simply to satisfy some evidentiary standard." The Kentucky court relied on the factors denigrated by the *Rider* court to support the admissibility of the expert testimony. Thus, animal studies, case reports, chemical analogies, and differential diagnosis were sufficient to support a finding of causation. This same theme was sounded by the court in Schott v. I-Flow Corp., 2010 WL 1008478 (S.D. Ohio 2010). The court relied on expert opinion based on a host of criteria, not including epidemiological studies, to support the proposition that use of an infusion pump to administer anesthetic into the shoulder joint causes serious and permanent damages to the shoulder joint. The court held that the inability to obtain epidemiological studies on groups of humans was not determinative because to conduct such studies would be unethical for exposing subjects to the risk of serious and permanent injury.

An issue not directly addressed in the *Rider* opinion but lurking in the background is whether *Daubert* permits the utilization of pieces of evidence each not sufficiently reliable to support a finding of causation but when taken together may make out general causation. The question whether scientists should be able to make out causation by this "weight of the evidence" approach came to a head in the following controversial case.

Milward v. Acuity Specialty Products Group, Inc.
639 F.3d 11 (1st Cir. 2011)

LYNCH, Chief Judge.

Brian and Linda Milward brought negligence claims against defendant chemical companies alleging that the rare type of leukemia that Brian Milward suffers, Acute Promyelocytic Leukemia (APL), was caused by his routine workplace exposure to benzene-containing products that had been manufactured or supplied by defendants. Milward worked as a refrigeration technician and asserted that he was exposed to benzene from 1973 until the time he filed this complaint and jury demand in October 2007. He had been diagnosed with APL in October 2004.

At defendants' request, the district court bifurcated the suit into two phases. The first phase concerned whether the expert opinion offered by plaintiffs on "general causation" was admissible under Federal Rule of Evidence 702. "'General causation' exists when a substance is capable of causing a disease." *Restatement (Third) of Torts: Liability for Physical and Emotional Harm* §28 cmt. c(3) (2010) ("*Restatement*"). If plaintiffs' expert evidence had been ruled admissible, the second phase would have considered all other issues, including negligence, exposure, and the "specific causation" of Milward's leukemia. "'Specific causation' exists when exposure to an agent caused a particular plaintiff's disease." *Id.* §28 cmt. c(4).

This case never reached the second phase. The district court ruled that the testimony of plaintiffs' expert on general causation, Dr. Martyn Smith, was inadmissible under Federal Rule of Evidence 702. The court so ruled after reviewing written statements and materials and conducting a four-day evidentiary hearing in which it heard testimony from plaintiffs' experts Dr. Smith, a toxicologist, and Dr. Carl Cranor, an expert on scientific methodology; and from defendants' experts Dr. David Garabrant, an epidemiologist, Dr. David Pyatt, a toxicologist, and Dr. John Bennett, a pathologist. The district court, in a detailed opinion, ruled that "Dr. Smith's proffered testimony that exposure to benzene can cause APL lacks sufficient demonstrated scientific reliability to warrant its admission under Rule 702." The court entered final judgment for defendants and plaintiffs timely appealed.

The appellate standard of review for Rule 702 rulings is abuse of discretion. *Gen. Elec. Co. v. Joiner,* 118 S. Ct. 512, (1997).

We reverse the district court's exclusion of Dr. Smith's general causation testimony. Dr. Smith's testimony is admissible. We stress that it is up to the jury to decide whether to accept his opinion that exposure to benzene can cause APL — a proposition that plaintiffs must prove by a preponderance of the evidence.

I.

The Supreme Court in *Daubert v. Merrell Dow Pharmaceuticals, Inc.,* 113 S. Ct. 2786 (1993), vested in trial judges a gatekeeper function, requiring that they assess proffered expert scientific testimony for reliability before admitting it. The Court held that Rule 702 displaced the "general acceptance" test of *Frye v. United States,* 293 F. 1013 (D.C. Cir.1923), under which "the admissibility of an expert opinion or technique turned on its 'general acceptance' *vel non* within the scientific community." Under Rule 702:

> If scientific, technical, or other specialized knowledge will assist the trier of fact to understand the evidence or to determine a fact in issue, a witness qualified as an expert by knowledge, skill, experience, training, or education, may testify thereto in the form of an opinion or otherwise, if (1) the testimony is based upon sufficient facts or data, (2) the testimony is the product of reliable principles and methods, and (3) the witness has applied the principles and methods reliably to the facts of the case. Fed. R. Evid. 702. . . .

Although *Daubert* stated that trial courts should focus "on principles and methodology, not on the conclusions that they generate," *Daubert,* 113 S. Ct. 2786, the Court subsequently clarified that this focus "need not completely pretermit judicial consideration of an expert's conclusions," In *Joiner,* the Court explained that "conclusions and methodology are not entirely distinct from one another" and "nothing in either *Daubert* or the Federal Rules of Evidence requires a district court to admit opinion evidence that is connected to existing data only by the *ipse dixit* of the expert." *Joiner,* 118 S. Ct. 512. Expert testimony may be excluded if there is "too great an analytical gap between the data and the opinion proffered." *Id.* "[T]rial judges may evaluate the data offered to support an expert's bottom-line opinions to determine if that data provides adequate support to mark the expert's testimony as reliable."

This does not mean that trial courts are empowered "to determine which of several competing scientific theories has the best provenance." *Id.* at 85. "*Daubert* does not require that a party who proffers expert testimony carry the burden of proving to the judge that the expert's assessment of the situation is correct." *Id.* . . .

So long as an expert's scientific testimony rests upon "'good grounds,' based on what is known," *Daubert,* . . . 113 S. Ct. 2786, it should be tested by the adversarial process, rather than excluded for fear that jurors will not be able to handle the scientific complexities, . . . 113 S. Ct. 2786. "Vigorous cross-examination, presentation of contrary evidence, and careful instruction on the burden of proof are the traditional and appropriate means of attacking shaky but admissible evidence." *Id.;* . . .

II. . . .

The question before us is whether the district court abused its discretion in concluding that the other requirements of Rule 702, concerning the reliability of Dr. Smith's opinion, were not met. We will first discuss some basic facts about leukemia, the weight of the evidence methodology, and Dr. Smith's use of that methodology, and we will then turn to an evaluation of the district court's ruling.

Leukemia is a cancer of the blood cells. There are different types of leukemia, which are generally classified in two ways. The first classification is between leukemia's acute and chronic forms: acute leukemia is characterized by a rapid increase in the number of immature blood cells, while chronic leukemia is characterized by the excessive buildup of relatively mature but abnormal white blood cells. The second classification is between the types of stem cells affected: leukemia can be either "myeloid" or "lymphoid." Combining these two classifications provides a total of four main categories of leukemia: acute myeloid leukemia (AML); chronic myeloid leukemia (CML); acute lymphoid leukemia (ALL); and chronic lymphoid leukemia (CLL). Within each of these categories, there are typically several subcategories.

Brian Milward's leukemia, APL, is subtype M3 and is an extremely rare disease. APL accounts for only five to ten percent of all cases of AML, which is itself rare, with an annual incidence of 3.5 cases per 100,000 people. APL is characterized by a deficiency of mature blood cells in the myeloid cell line and an excess of immature cells called promyelocytes.

APL is in part caused by the chromosomal translocation of a gene known as the retinoic acid receptor-alpha gene (RARα) on chromosome 17. Although APL and the other subtypes of AML have been the subject of extensive research, there is not yet a scientific consensus as to the causes of the genetic translocation that induces APL.

Dr. Smith's opinion is that what is known about both AML and APL supports the inference that exposure to benzene can cause APL. He reached this opinion using a "weight of the evidence" methodology in which he considered five lines of evidence drawn from the peer-reviewed scientific literature on leukemia and benzene. We first discuss the reliability of this methodology in general, and then turn to Dr. Smith's application of it.

A. The Reliability of the Weight of the Evidence Methodology

Dr. Smith's opinion was based on a "weight of the evidence" methodology in which he followed the guidelines articulated by world-renowned epidemiologist Sir Arthur Bradford Hill in his seminal methodological article on inferences of causality. *See* Arthur Bradford Hill, *The Environment and Disease: Association or Causation?*, 58 Proc. Royal Soc'y Med. 295 (1965).

Hill's article explains that one should not conclude that an observed association between a disease and a feature of the environment (e.g., a chemical) is causal without first considering a variety of "viewpoints" on the issue. These viewpoints include: the strength or frequency of the association; the consistency of the association in varied circumstances; specificity of the association; the temporal relationship between the disease and the posited cause; the dose response curve between them; the biological plausibility of the causal explanation given existing scientific knowledge; the coherence of the explanation with generally known facts about the disease; the experimental data that relates to it; and the existence of analogous causal relationships. *See id.* at 295–99.

This "weight of the evidence" approach to making causal determinations involves a mode of logical reasoning often described as "inference to the best explanation," in which the conclusion is not guaranteed by the premises. *See Bitler v. A.O. Smith Corp.*, 391 F.3d 1114, 1124 n. 5 (10th Cir. 2004). As explained by plaintiffs' expert on methodology Dr. Cranor, Distinguished Professor of Philosophy at the University of California, Riverside, inference to the best explanation can be thought of as involving six general steps, some of which may be implicit. The scientist must (1) identify an association between an exposure and a disease, (2) consider a range of plausible explanations for the association, (3) rank the rival explanations according to their plausibility, (4) seek additional evidence to separate the more plausible from the less plausible explanations, (5) consider all of the relevant available evidence, and (6) integrate the evidence using professional judgment to come to a conclusion about the best explanation.

In this mode of reasoning, the use of scientific judgment is necessary. "No algorithm exists for applying the Hill guidelines to determine whether an association truly reflects a causal relationship or is spurious." *Restatement* §28 cmt. c(3). Because "[n]o scientific methodology exists for this process . . . reasonable scientists may come to different judgments about whether such an inference is appropriate." *Id.* §28 reporters' note cmt. c(4). . . .

Defendants argue that "regardless of its level of acceptance in the scientific community, a pure 'weight of the evidence' approach like that utilized by Dr. Smith . . . is hardly the type of reliable scientific evidence contemplated by *Daubert*." No serious argument can be made that the weight of the evidence approach is inherently unreliable. Rather, admissibility must turn on the particular facts of the case. Here, the question is whether Dr. Smith, in reaching his opinion, applied the methodology with "the same level of intellectual rigor" that he uses in his scientific practice. *Kumho Tire,* 526 U.S. at 152, 119 S. Ct. 1167.

B. Dr. Smith's Application of the Methodology

In concluding that the weight of the evidence supported the conclusion that benzene can cause APL, Dr. Smith relied on his knowledge and experience in the field of toxicology and molecular epidemiology and considered five bodies of evidence drawn from the peer-reviewed scientific literature on benzene and leukemia.

First, Dr. Smith considered the near-consensus among governmental agencies, experts, and active researchers in the field that benzene can cause AML as a class. The existence of this causal connection has been established since the late 1970s. Dr. Smith noted that epidemiological studies have found a statistically significant increased incidence of AML in benzene-exposed workers and have identified a dose-response relationship.

Second, Dr. Smith considered evidence concerning the etiology, or origins, of leukemia indicating that all types of AML derive from a genetically damaged pluripotent stem cell. Dr. Smith referred to a recent peer-reviewed article that provided a review of the current literature and reported numerous studies demonstrating that both AML and CML are stem cell diseases. He cited peer-reviewed studies finding that in the APL and Core Binding Factor (CBF) subtypes of AML, as well as in CML, the stem cell mutation is often in part caused by a chromosomal translocation. He also cited evidence that APL and CBF share common genetic susceptibility factors, common risk factors, and the same incidence pattern occurring at a constant incidence with age after age 20. Dr. Smith concluded that the best explanation for this evidence is that all AMLs, including APL, have a common etiology.

Third, Dr. Smith considered toxicology studies establishing that metabolites of benzene cause significant chromosomal damage at the stem cell level in the bone marrow — the type of damage that is known to cause APL and other types of AML. He also cited peer-reviewed work published by his lab showing that leukemia cases associated with benzene exposure are more likely to contain clonal chromosome aberrations than leukemias arising in the general population.

Fourth, Dr. Smith considered two sets of studies concerning the inhibition of a cellular enzyme known as topoisomerase II (or "topo II") that is essential for the maintenance of proper chromosome structure and segregation. One set of studies— including both test tube and animal studies—has established that two benzene metabolites are catalytic inhibitors of topo II. A second set of studies has established that a variety of chemotherapeutic agents that are catalytic inhibitors of topo II cause APL. Dr. Smith explained that taken together, these studies provided evidence of a known biological mechanism by which exposure to benzene could cause APL.

Fifth, Dr. Smith considered the small set of epidemiological studies that provide data on the relationship between benzene exposure and subtypes of AML. He concluded that the evidence showed an increased risk factor for APL, which although not statistically significant was consistent with causality, and provided no grounds for concluding otherwise.

Dr. Smith explained that taking into account all of the evidence described above— the fact that benzene causes AML as a class, that all subtypes of AML likely have a common etiology, that benzene is known to cause the general types of cellular damage that are known to cause APL, that benzene is known to inhibit an enzyme whose inhibition is known to cause APL, and that APL has been reported in benzene-exposed workers in a number of epidemiological studies—he reached the opinion that the weight of the evidence supports the conclusion that benzene exposure is capable of causing APL. Dr. Smith's opinion rests on a scientifically sound and methodologically reliable foundation, as is required by *Daubert*.

III.

In finding Dr. Smith's opinion inadmissible under Rule 702, the district court relied on (a) its evaluation of the mechanistic and epidemiological evidence on which Dr. Smith based his opinion, and (b) its understanding of the scientific concept of "biological plausibility" as used by Dr. Smith when he explained his conclusions. As we explain below, on both of these points, the district court erred. In the end, the court's exclusion of the testimony was based on its evaluation of the weight of the evidence, which is an issue that is the province of the jury, and on its misperception of the methodology and analysis that provided the basis for Dr. Smith's opinion.

A. The Evidentiary Basis of Dr. Smith's Opinion

1. Mechanistic Evidence

The district court's exclusion of Dr. Smith's testimony was based to a significant extent on its rejection of what it took to be his three key subsidiary conclusions regarding the weight of the mechanistic evidence. We briefly summarize the court's analysis on these points before turning to our discussion of the ways in which the court erred in its analysis.

First, the court held that there was insufficient evidence to support Dr. Smith's opinion that all subtypes of AML likely have a common etiology. The court reasoned that the "clear differences" among AML subtypes—in particular, APL's unique response to certain types of therapy, and the subtypes' different chromosomal abnormalities—made "a broad extrapolation from AML generally to APL specifically" inappropriate. *Milward,* 664 F. Supp. 2d at 144. The court also noted that a series of recent studies had "led investigators to think that the 'leukemic stem cell' may exist in more mature, differentiated cell lines," such that "the 'leukemic stem cell' may not be a stem cell in the usual sense, but rather a differentiated cell that has somehow acquired the ability to reproduce itself, as a stem cell can." *Id.* at 145. If the various AML subtypes did not arise from the same progenitor or stem cell, the court reasoned, they might well not share a common etiology. Finally, the court emphasized that there was "no scientific consensus" on this issue, and that the question of when the key chromosomal translocation occurs was considered by researchers to be "*a question that remains unanswered in the APL field.*" *Id.* (quoting S. Wojiski et al., *PML–RARα Initiates Leukemia by Conferring Properties of Self–Renewal to Committed Promyelocytic Progenitors,* 23 Leukemia 1462, 1469 (2009) (emphasis added)) (internal quotation marks omitted).

Second, the court held that what was known about the types of chromosomal translocations caused by benzene did not offer sufficient support for Dr. Smith's opinion that it is biologically plausible that benzene causes the characteristic t(15;17)(q22;q12) translocation seen with APL. The court explained that this opinion would be warranted if benzene's impact on chromosomes were randomly experienced, but it noted that a paper co-authored by Dr. Smith concluded that "benzene can initiate or promote leukemia induction by a *nonrandom* selective effect" on specific chromosomes. *Id.* at 147 (emphasis added). This defeated "the generalization that because . . . benzene causes damage to some chromosomes, it is 'biologically plausible' that it causes damage to other chromosomes." *Id.*

Third, the court held that there was insufficient evidence to support the inference that benzene metabolites inhibit topo II in such a way as to cause the chromosomal translocation seen in cases of APL. The court's conclusion was in part based on evidence that "[t]here are different classes of topo II inhibitors and the different classes have been associated with different AML subtypes." *Id.* Highlighting one article's finding that leukemias induced by benzene do not appear to exhibit the defining characteristics associated with four other classes of topo II inhibitors, *id.* at 148, the court held that to "the extent that Dr. Smith's opinion rests on the proposition that all topo II inhibitors act similarly to cause a similar effect, then, it does not appear to be based on reliable scientific knowledge," *id.* at 147.

In reaching these three conclusions about some of the evidence on which Dr. Smith based his opinion, the court both placed undue weight on the lack of general acceptance of Dr. Smith's conclusions and crossed the boundary between gatekeeper and trier of fact.

Although general acceptance is still a relevant consideration under *Daubert,* the court's demands went too far. On the question of the origins of APL, for example, the court explained that in the absence of consensus about the target cell for the leukemic mutation, Dr. Smith's opinion that all forms of AML likely share a common origin was "at best a plausible hypothesis." *Milward,* 664 F. Supp. 2d at 146. The court explained that the fact that "other plausible hypotheses . . . might be true as well, including the hypothesis that the genetic mutation that leads to APL occurs in relatively mature cells," meant that Dr. Smith's opinion was not "based on sufficient facts and data to be accepted as a reliable scientific conclusion." *Id.; see also id. at 148* (focusing on lack of consensus as to the topo II question). But the fact that another explanation might be right is not a sufficient basis for excluding Dr. Smith's testimony. "Lack of certainty is not, for a qualified expert, the same thing as guesswork." *Primiano v. Cook,* 598 F.3d 558, 565 (9th Cir. 2010).

In addition, the alleged flaws identified by the court go to the weight of Dr. Smith's opinion, not its admissibility. There is an important difference between what is *unreliable* support and what a trier of fact may conclude is *insufficient* support for an expert's conclusion. . . .

In Dr. Smith's weight of the evidence approach, no body of evidence was itself treated as justifying an inference of causation. Rather, each body of evidence was treated as grounds for the subsidiary conclusion that it would, if combined with other evidence, support a causal inference. The district court erred in reasoning that because no one line of evidence supported a reliable inference of causation, an inference of causation based on the totality of the evidence was unreliable. *Cf. NutraSweet Co. v. X–L Eng'g Co.,* 227 F.3d 776, 789 (7th Cir. 2000) (holding that an expert's reliance on individual pieces of evidence, insufficient in themselves to prove a point, "did not render his opinion speculative"). The hallmark of the weight of the evidence approach is reasoning to the best explanation for all of the available evidence. . . .

IV.

The record clearly demonstrates that Dr. Smith's opinion was based on an analysis in which he employed the "same level of intellectual rigor" that he employs in his academic work. *Kumho Tire,* 119 S. Ct. 1167. In excluding Dr. Smith's testimony, the district court did not properly apply *Daubert* and exceeded the scope of its discretion. We reverse the district court's judgment for the defendants and its exclusion of Dr. Smith's testimony, and we remand for proceedings consistent with this opinion. So ordered.

At first blush, it seems quite reasonable to allow scientists to make out causation based on the totality of the evidence. Harsh criticism of the *Milward* opinion came from Professor David Bernstein, The Misbegotten Judicial Resistance to the Daubert Revolution, 89 Notre Dame L. Rev. 27, 62-67 (2013). He argues "to allow an expert to testify simply because he purports to be extrapolating from the evidence in light of the weight he chooses to give to each item of evidence would be to leave the evidentiary gates wide open. Every quack and huckster claiming that he is relying on an evidentiary mosaic to invent causation without reference to reliable scientific evidence could claim he is utilizing a 'weight of the evidence methodology.'" See also Aaron D. Twerski and Lior Sapir, Sufficiency of the Evidence Does Not Meet Daubert Standards: A Critique of the Green-Sanders Proposal, 23 Widener L.J. 641, 660 (2014) ("How one puts together a set of 'might be' pieces of evidence requires an explanation as to whether reliable scientific methods were utilized to reach his conclusion. The fact that Dr. Smith's opinion was the best that he could draw on the underdeveloped state of the evidence is precisely the level of opinion that the *Daubert* trilogy was designed to preclude."). For a spirited defense of *Milward* and the "weight of evidence" standard see Michael D. Green, Pessimism About Milward, 3 Wake. Forest J.L. & Pol'y 41 (2013).

After reading *Rider* and *Milward* do you have any confidence that any trier of fact (either judge or jury) could fairly resolve the general causation question?

Even if a plaintiff can demonstrate an increased risk due to exposure to a toxic agent plaintiff still faces the daunting task of proving specific causation, i.e., that the plaintiff's injury was caused by the toxic agent. On remand from the Supreme Court, in

Daubert the Ninth Circuit Court of Appeals found that plaintiff could not establish specific causation because plaintiff was unable to show that Bendectin more than doubled the risk of birth defects. The court said:

> California tort law requires plaintiffs to show not merely that Bendectin increased the [general] likelihood of injury, but that [specifically] it more likely than not caused their injuries. . . . In terms of statistical proof, this means that plaintiffs must establish not just that their mothers' ingestion of Bendectin increased somewhat the likelihood of birth defects, but that it more than doubled it — only then can it be said that Bendectin is more likely than not the source of their injury. Because the background rate of limb reduction defects is one per thousand births, plaintiffs must show that among children of mothers who took Bendectin the incidence of such defects was more than two per thousand. [43 F.3d 1311, 1320.]

But must the issue of specific causation depend entirely on the probabilistic proof of general causation? Might not plaintiffs prove specific causation by other means? The Restatement of Liability for Physical and Emotional Harm §28 (2010) comment *c* has weighed in on the issue of expert scientific testimony. The lengthy discussion in the comment and the accompanying Reporters' Note are well worth reading. The Comment takes the position that as long as proper evidence of increased risk is available, a court may utilize other evidence to prove that the plaintiff before the court suffered from exposure to the risk. The Reporters' Note contains an exhaustive list of cases supporting the opposing views. Many insist that a doubling of the risk is a *sina qua non* to support a finding of causation. Other cases take the position that, even when evidence on general causation does not double the risk, other factors may support a finding of specific causation. Thus, for example, evidence of differential diagnosis, such as offered by the plaintiff in *Rider*, may help a court to determine that the plaintiff in question, more probably than not, was harmed by the toxic agent.

It is interesting that on remand from *Milward* to determine specific causation the trial court granted the defendant's motion for summary judgment. The court found the plaintiff's expert opinion on causation to be unreliable. The expert based her opinion on differential diagnosis, i.e., she ruled out other causes and thus inferred that benzene was the cause of the plaintiff's leukemia. The court found the opinion to lack credibility since between 70-80 percent of AML cases are idiopathic–meaning that they have no known cause. With such a high percentage of AML cases brought about because of non-benzene causes there are no grounds for a differential diagnosis. The fact that general causation evidence may have established that benzene can be a cause of AML does not suffice to conclude that it more probably than not was the cause of the plaintiff's illness. Milward v. Acuity Specialty Products Group, Inc., 969 F. Supp. 2d 101 (D. Mass. 2013) (appeal pending).

PROBLEM SIX

Ilisa Mazarek, a 28-year-old woman, has come to see you about bringing an action against TFL Laboratories, the manufacturer of Perfect-Coil, an intrauterine device (IUD). Ilisa has been married for seven years and has been unable to conceive. She has consulted numerous obstetricians and has had a full battery of tests. Her husband, Michael, has been tested for sterility and his sperm has been found healthy.

In April of this year, Ilisa made an appointment with Dr. Suzanne Blanzer, who reviewed all the test results that had been gathered previously. Blanzer then asked Ilisa whether she had ever used an IUD. Ilisa said that while in college she had used a plastic IUD called Perfect-Coil. Dr. Blanzer then told her that it could well be that the IUD was the source of her trouble. She said that recent research performed at the Harvard Medical School and at the University of Washington in Seattle revealed that women who had used IUDs (especially plastic IUDs) had twice the risk of later infertility than non-IUD users. The studies were published in the most recent issue of a prestigious medical journal. According to the Harvard study, 89 of the 283 infertile women (31.4 percent) had used an IUD as compared with 646 of 3,833 in the fertile control group (16.7 percent). The Seattle results were even more pronounced. The difference between infertile and fertile women was 35.2 percent to 13.8 percent.

Apparently, use of an IUD contributes to a higher than normal risk of pelvic inflammatory disease. These infections can damage the fallopian tubes, causing infertility. The head of the Harvard study clearly believes a causal relationship was established between IUDs and infertility because of the unlikelihood of chance or bias in the results and the consistency of the results with findings in other studies.

Dr. Blanzer told Ilisa that there was no way to determine with certainty whether her fallopian tubes had been damaged as a result of infections brought about by use of the IUD. "Although many fallopian tube infections cause pain, it certainly is possible that you had one or more infections without realizing, or that you had some minor abdominal pain and paid little attention to it." Dr. Blanzer told Ilisa that she would treat her to help enhance her chances of conceiving. "Nonetheless," she said, "you must face the facts. The great likelihood is that you will not conceive." Dr. Blanzer then raised a question that Ilisa had never been asked before by any other obstetrician. She asked whether Ilisa had a number of different sexual partners before or during her marriage. The reason she asked was that the Boston researchers had found an increased risk of infertility for all IUD users who had several sexual partners as compared to monogamous users. In fact, regardless of the type of contraception used, the researchers found that women who had multiple sexual partners faced an increased risk of developing pelvic infection.

Ilisa told Dr. Blanzer that during marriage she had been totally faithful but that she had not been a paragon of virtue in her younger years. When asked to be more precise, she said, "I was far from promiscuous. In any event, it's my business and nobody else knows. That's the way it is. That's the way it's going to be."

You must decide whether to take the case. You are to assume that New California has adopted the *Daubert* approach to expert testimony. You have heard that a consortium of plaintiff's lawyers has filed thousands of lawsuits against TFL Laboratories. Nonetheless, considerable skepticism exists as to whether the claimants can prevail. Would other kinds of factual investigation be helpful before you decide to proceed?

B.   DID THE DEFENDANT SUPPLY THE PRODUCT?

In many instances, the plaintiff will have little difficulty establishing that the defendant was in fact a supplier of the product that allegedly injured plaintiff. Controversy instead will focus on whether the product was defective. In some instances, however, plaintiff faces critical gaps in the evidence establishing what actually happened. The most difficult gap-in-the-proof causation cases are those in which the plaintiff is harmed

authors' dialogue 6

AARON: Jim and Doug. After reading *Rider* and *Milward* do you really believe that a jury will be able to weigh competing expert opinions as to whether a drug or chemical substance can or did cause a given illness?

DOUG: Come on Aaron. Experts disagree about causation all the time. The jury listens to the testimony and the cross-examination and decides which expert is more credible.

JIM: On this one, for a change, I agree with Aaron. The experts all seem to agree in these two cases that they are making an educated guess. Putting all the fancy language aside that is the crux of the matter. There is a difference between firm opinions and educated guesses.

AARON: Right on. Courts should allow experts to testify to the former and reject the latter.

DOUG: Ok, wise guys. What should we do? Judges have to make that call. Judges are human. Sometime they will say a case is on one side of the line and sometime on the other side. If you don't like that would you send the parties off to decide the issue by a duel to death with lances?

AARON: I'll tell you, but you won't like it. Maybe we should go back to the *Frye* rule. Scientific evidence must meet general acceptance in the relevant scientific community. Courts are not capable of testing cutting-edge science in the context of a several-week trial. Talk to trial judges. Almost to a person they will tell you they hate *Daubert* hearings. Even if judges don't hold formal hearings, and rely instead on paper submissions in motions for summary judgment, they spend weeks on end trying to figure out whether an expert's opinion is based on good scientific methodology. Let the scientists do their work first and get some consensus before hitting the courtroom with speculative theories.

JIM: Aaron, you may be right, but we will never put the genie back in the bottle. The American judiciary, both state and federal, has been *Daubertized*.

AARON: Just one more word. It is now clear that there is not much predictability as to how a court will come out in a *Daubert* challenge. The United States Supreme Court is responsible for this terrible mess. The ink wasn't dry on *Daubert* and it was clear to most observers that they had created a monster.

by a defective product that is both unidentified by trademark or insignia and cannot be directly linked to the defendant. In the classic example of such a defendant-identification case, the plaintiff is harmed by a defective unit of a type of product manufactured and distributed by many companies, under circumstances where the plaintiff cannot prove which company actually produced and distributed the defective, harm-causing product unit. These difficult causation cases usually involve generically dangerous products rather than manufacturing defects. Perhaps the best-known example involved personal injuries allegedly resulting from plaintiffs' prenatal exposure to the prescription drug, diethylstilbestrol (DES). The plaintiffs in these cases were women whose mothers took DES many years earlier, while pregnant, to prevent miscarriage. Reliable expert testimony showed that the drug affected the plaintiffs while in their mothers' wombs, resulting in reproductive tract cancers in the plaintiffs many years later. Hundreds of thousands of women were involved. Many of the plaintiffs could not prove which drug company distributed the DES their mothers took. (As many as 300 companies may have produced the generic drug during the relevant period.) Some courts responded in ways that allowed the injured plaintiffs to overcome otherwise fatal gaps in their proofs of actual causation by joining as defendants all, or most, of the company's manufacturing and distributing DES in the relevant geographical areas during the time periods relevant to their cases. The leading case is Sindell v. Abbott Labs., 607 P.2d 924 (Cal.), cert. denied, 449 U.S. 912 (1980).

The California high court in *Sindell* considered and rejected the "alternative liability" theory from earlier California case law that would have held all the defendants jointly and severally liable unless they could prove that they did not market the DES that harmed the plaintiff. Not only did the companies lack any comparative advantage in determining which company's drug had caused the cancer, but the numbers of victims were much greater than in the earlier cases, and not all of the possible defendants could be joined in one legal action. And allocating liability pro rata among companies overlooked the reality that some companies produced many times the quantities of DES compared with other, smaller companies. To overcome these difficulties, the *Sindell* court adopted what has come to be known as the "market-share theory." According to the market-share approach, when a plaintiff joins the manufacturers who produced, in the aggregate, a substantial share of the relevant DES market, the burden shifts to each defendant to prove it did not produce the drug that the plaintiff's mother ingested. Those companies that do not carry this burden are held liable to the plaintiff for the percentage of damages approximating their individual share of the relevant DES market. The court reasoned that it was fair to shift the burden of proof on causation to the defendants in light of the fact that each defendant's market share, and therefore its share of the damages, would approximate the probability that it caused the plaintiff's injuries. See also Collins v. Eli Lilly Co., 342 N.W. 2d 37, 50-52 (Wis. 1984) (market share based on a "risk distribution" theory).

The courts that have adopted the market share approach have been forced to grapple with three difficult issues: (1) how to define the market; (2) whether a defendant who can prove that its product did not injure the plaintiff should escape liability under the market share theory; and (3) if only a given percentage of defendants who participated in the market at the time of injury can be accounted for, who should bear the loss for the missing market shares?

Several courts have held that market shares should be calculated based on the sales of all manufacturers of the product in the national market, whether or not particular defendants could have supplied the particular units that harmed the plaintiff. The New York Court of Appeals was the first to adopt this approach. In Hymowitz v. Eli Lilly Co., 539 N.E.2d 1069, 1077-1078 (N.Y. 1989) the court said:

> We are aware that the adoption of a national market will likely result in a disproportion between the liability of individual manufacturers and the actual injuries each manufacturer caused in this State. Thus our market share theory cannot be founded upon the belief that, over the run of cases, liability will approximate causation in this State (see, Sindell v. Abbott Laboratories). Nor does the use of a national market provide a reasonable link between liability and the risk created by a defendant to a particular plaintiff . . . Instead,

we choose to apportion liability so as to correspond to the overall culpability of each defendant, measured by the amount of risk of injury each defendant created to the public-at-large. Use of a national market is a fair method, we believe, of apportioning defendants' liabilities according to their total culpability in marketing DES for use during pregnancy. Under the circumstances, this is an equitable way to provide plaintiffs with the relief they deserve, while also rationally distributing the responsibility for plaintiffs' injuries among defendants. . . .

Florida has opted for a much narrower definition of the market. In Conley v. Boyle Drug Co., 570 So. 2d 275, 283 (Fla. 1990) the court argued:

[T]he relevant market for determining liability should be as narrowly defined as the evidence in a given case allows. Thus, where it can be determined that the DES ingested by the mother was purchased from a particular pharmacy, that pharmacy should be considered the relevant market. Likewise, where the county or state of ingestion is as specific an area as can be established, that geographic area will serve as the relevant market.

Closely related to the market size question is whether a defendant can escape paying its market share if it can establish that it was not responsible for the harm to the particular plaintiff. Until *Hymowitz*, the courts had answered the question in the affirmative. Though *Hymowitz* is a minority view in denying the defendant the right to prove itself out of a market share, it is arguably defensible in principle. Market share posits the view that causation should be viewed writ large over a broad market. Of what importance is it that a defendant establishes that its pill was not sold to a particular patient? Switching back and forth between traditional causation and proportional causation in this class of cases seems odd. Furthermore, the transaction costs of litigating and establishing different market shares depending on the posture of any individual case are likely to be enormous.

As for the question of joint and several liability in the market-share setting, several courts have been troubled by the fact that, under *Sindell*, a defendant who had proved its market share would be liable to pay for the harm caused by unnamed or insolvent defendants. Most courts, including California, have now concluded that joint and several liability ought not to be applied against market share defendants.

The controversy concerning the wisdom of applying market share has been even more shrill when plaintiffs have sought to apply the approach to manufacturing defects. In Sheffield v. Eli Lilly & Co., 192 Cal. Rptr. 870 (Cal. Ct. App. 1983), the plaintiff developed encephalitis as a result of being inoculated with defective polio vaccine. Plaintiff made exhaustive attempts to discover which drug manufacturer had made the particular batch of defective vaccine supplied to Wayne County, Indiana, where she took her shot. Since the plaintiff was unable to identify the manufacturer, she sought to apply the market-share theory against all the manufacturers of polio vaccine. In rejecting this extension of *Sindell*, the court explained:

The "deep pocket" theory may be socially desirable as a vehicle to insure that all victims of a defective product will be compensated from an industry-wide fund; but if applied indiscriminately to penalize the careful and careless producer alike it fails to act as a deterrent to the latter or provide an incentive to product safety industry-wide, and it may result in keeping beneficial but potentially dangerous products off the market. . . . It is clear, . . . that one manufacturer cannot force its competitors to discover or guard against defects in its products. The imposition of such a liability over that portion of the pharmaceutical industry producing the beneficial safe product would inhibit drug research and development, unreasonably raise the cost of health care, and punish drug manufacturers who have done no wrong. 192 Cal. Rptr. at 876.

At least one court has not been so hesitant. The Supreme Court of Hawaii, in Smith v. Cutter Biological, Inc., 823 P.2d 717 (Haw. 1991), adopted market-share liability in an action in which a hemophiliac allegedly contracted the AIDS virus from a tainted blood product.

For all the notoriety surrounding market share, a majority of courts have rejected the theory outright. See, e.g., Smith v. Eli Lilly & Co., 560 N.E.2d 324 (Ill. 1990); Zaft v. Eli Lilly & Co., 676 S.W.2d 241 (Mo. 1984); Mulcaby v. Eli Lilly & Co., 366 N.W.2d 67, 76 (Iowa 1986). See also Ga. Code Ann §51-1-11 (2015) (rejecting market share liability). Even those jurisdictions that recognize market share liability have refused to expand it beyond the DES cases. See, e.g., Brenner v. American Cyanamid Co., 263 A.D.2d 165 (N.Y. App. Div. 1999) (lead paint); Spencer v. Baxter Int'l, Inc., 163 F. Supp. 2d 74 (D. Mass. 2001) (contaminated blood products); Mills v. Allegiance Healthcare Corp., 178 F. Supp. 2d 1 (D. Mass. 2001) (latex gloves); Hamilton v. Beretta, 750 N.E.2d 1055 (N.Y. 2001) (handguns); Jackson v. Glidden Co., 2007 WL 184662 (Ohio 2007) (lead paint); Ferris v. Gatke, 132 Cal. Rptr. 2d 819 (Cal. Ct. App. 2003) (asbestos); State Farm Fire & Cas. Co. v. Middleby Corp., 2011 WL683883 (Del. Sup. Ct. 2011) (gas control valves). For a rare exception see Thomas v. Mallett, 701 N.W.2d 523 (Wis. 2005) (allowing market share in lead paint case). For a critique of *Thomas,* see George Priest, Market Share Liability in Personal Injury and Public Nuisance Litigation: An Economic Analysis, 18 Sup. Ct. Econ. Rev. 109 (2010).

PROBLEM SEVEN

Your firm represents Louise Larkin, age 37, who seeks to recover for injuries sustained while undergoing surgery six months ago. Having suffered from ovarian cysts for several years, Ms. Larkin was advised by her physician, about a year ago, to undergo abdominal surgery to correct the condition. Both the surgeon and the anesthesiologist recommended spinal, rather than general, anesthesia. Fully informed of the benefits and risks associated with the surgery, Ms. Larkin consented to the operation. During the administering of the spinal anesthesia, the hypodermic needle broke off in Ms. Larkin's spine, causing serious complications that may lead to permanent partial paralysis. Investigation has revealed that the needle in question was new, and that it broke due to a latent manufacturing defect.

Efforts to trace the identity of the manufacturer of the needle have thus far proven futile. The hospital in which the surgery was performed supplied the needle in question, along with the other equipment to be used in the operation. The hospital purchases such needles in bulk, from several different medical supply distributors in your city. When items such as hypodermic needles come into the hospital supply department, they are treated as fungible goods, within appropriate categories of type, size, and the like. No effort is made to keep track of from whom, or when, any particular hypodermic needle was purchased. Given the need for standardization of items of this sort, no effort appears to have been made by manufacturers to allow products such as hypodermic needles to be distinguished from similar items produced by others. Thus, there appears to be no way by which the needle may be shown to have been produced by a particular manufacturer or sold to the hospital by a particular distributor. For the last several years the hospital has purchased this sort of hypodermic needle from three different distributors, who purchased their needle supplies from at least ten, and possibly as many as twenty, needle manufacturers. Two, at least, of the twenty manufacturers are foreign-based; one of the domestic manufacturers who may have produced the needle declared bankruptcy last month.

Assuming that Magrine v. Krasnica and Anderson v. Somberg (Chapter One, supra) are decisions of the highest court in your state, what are the chances of reaching the jury against one or more of the possible defendants in Ms. Larkin's case? In undertaking your analysis, make whatever reasonable assumptions of fact you believe are necessary.

C. DID THE DEFECT IN THE DEFENDANT'S PRODUCT CONTRIBUTE TO HARMING THE PLAINTIFF?

In the cases in this section, the plaintiff can prove that the defendant produced the harm-causing product and that the product contained a dangerous defect, but has difficulty establishing that the presence of the defect in the product contributed to the product's having caused the harm. The inquiry is not into what actually happened, which is typically clear enough, but into what would have happened if the manufacturing defect had not been present. As explained earlier, this inquiry is frequently referred to as a but-for inquiry. The question to be answered is this: But for the presence of the defect, would the plaintiff have suffered the same (or similar) harm anyway? Again, this is a different question than is asked in the defendant-identification cases considered in the preceding section. Unlike the earlier-considered cases, gaps in proof are not typically present. In most cases, it is clear that the defendant's product (or conduct) has caused plaintiff's harm; what is at issue is what role, if any, the defective condition of the product played in causing the harm. As mentioned earlier, the new Restatement of general tort principles merges this question with the first question in Section A, supra, under the umbrella heading "factual cause." See Restatement of Liability for Physical and Emotional Harm §26 (2010).

1. The Traditional Burden In Proving Causation

Midwestern V.W. Corp. v. Ringley
503 S.W.2d 745 (Ky. 1973)

STEPHENSON, Justice.

A Hardin Circuit Court jury awarded Wanda Ringley damages for personal injuries and property damage as a result of an accident when her automobile skidded and struck a telephone pole. The verdict was against Kelly Vance Motors, Inc., the Volkswagen dealer from whom Wanda purchased the car, Volkswagenwerk Aktiengesell, the manufacturer of the car, Volkswagen of America, Inc., the importer, a wholly owned subsidiary of the factory, and Midwestern Volkswagen Corporation, the distributor who purchased the car from the importer and sold the automobile to Kelly Vance Motors. The manufacturer, importer, and distributor appeal from the judgment in favor of Wanda Ringley and also appeal from a joint and several judgment in favor of Kelly Vance Motors against them for indemnity. Kelly Vance Motors does not appeal.

Wanda purchased a new Volkswagen automobile from Kelly Vance Motors. The warranty against defects in manufacturing covered a period of twenty-four months. Shortly after Wanda purchased the automobile, while applying the brakes to come to an abrupt stop, ... the automobile pulled to the right. Wanda returned the automobile to Kelly Vance Motors and reported the incident, and when she picked up the automobile, she was advised that it had been repaired. She testified she had no further difficulty until shortly thereafter when a similar incident occurred, and again the automobile was returned to Kelly Vance Motors and again she was advised that the car was repaired. Wanda testified that she had no further difficulty until a little more than a month after the car was purchased when a similar instance of the automobile's pulling to the right after the brakes were applied resulted in Wanda's again returning the automobile to Kelly Vance Motors for the assigned reason that the "brakes grab and pull to one side."

Eight days after picking up the automobile, Wanda undertook to pass an automobile on a wet road and, according to Wanda, she observed a pool of water in the road ahead of her. She testified that she applied the brakes, that the right-front wheel grabbed sending her automobile into a spin and out of control. The automobile struck a telephone pole resulting in severe personal injuries.

According to witnesses who testified for Wanda, it was discovered that the right-front brake drum was "out of round" to a degree exceeding factory specifications. They testified that this was a defect in the manufacturing process which would cause the automobile to pull to the right when the brakes were applied.

Wanda's version of the accident was contradicted, as was the testimony of the extent that the "out of round" condition of the brake drum exceeded factory specification, or that the brake drum was "out of round" at all. All of this presents no problem as a jury issue was presented. Numerous errors are asserted; however, we conclude that appellants' assertion that Wanda failed to prove causation is dispositive of the case.

All of Wanda's witnesses testified that an "out of round" brake drum on the right front would cause the automobile to pull to the right when the brakes were applied. On cross-examination, they testified that dirt and dust in the left brake lining would cause the automobile to pull to the right. There was testimony that the brake drums were blown out when the automobile was taken to Kelly Vance Motors. They further testified on cross-examination that water in the left brake lining would cause the automobile to pull to the right; that improper adjustment of the right-front brake drum would cause the automobile to pull to the right. There was testimony by one of the witnesses that an examination of the right-front brake after the accident revealed that it was adjusted too tightly. Wanda's witnesses further testified on cross-examination that improper tire pressure and improper alignment could cause pulling.

The voluminous transcript is composed chiefly of testimony attempting to establish a defect in manufacturing. None of Wanda's expert witnesses testified that the "out of round" brake drum "probably" caused the automobile to pull to one side at the time of the accident. The testimony was that an "out of round" brake drum was dangerous and would cause the automobile to pull when the brakes were applied, also that other conditions asked about would cause the automobile to pull when the brakes were applied.

The jury found for Wanda under an instruction based on the doctrine of manufacturer's strict liability. This doctrine of strict liability does not relieve Wanda from the plaintiff's burden of introducing evidence of causation. Although the jury may draw reasonable inferences from the evidence of a defect in manufacturing, it is incumbent on the plaintiff to introduce evidence that will support a reasonable inference that the defect was the 'probable' cause of the accident as distinguished from a 'possible' cause among other possibilities; otherwise, the jury verdict is based on speculation or surmise. . . .

The only evidence which would even tend to establish a probability is encompassed in one question and answer during the cross-examination of one of Wanda's witnesses:

Q. Likewise, is there any way of telling now whether, at the time of this accident Miss Ringley had, what the reason was for the car pulling to the right, or whichever direction it was, any way of telling what actually happened on that occasion?

A. The only thing I can tell what caused it is the brake drum being out of round and the lining has been chattering, and it will show chattering points just a little on the lining.

We conclude that this answer is so equivocal that it cannot be said that the witness was testifying as to a probability.

Finally, Wanda cites Gaidry Motors v. Bannon, Ky., 268 S.W.2d 627, as authority for submission of her case to the jury. There the purchaser of a used car drove only fourteen blocks from the used-car lot; and when applying the brakes at an intersection, the car brakes grabbed, causing the car to skid and injure a pedestrian. Mechanics testified that there was grease on one of the brake drums and that this condition would cause the brakes to grab. This court held that the evidence was sufficient to submit the case to the jury on the question of proximate cause. We feel that the brief interval of time between the purchase of the used car and the accident and the absence of any other explanation for the mechanical failure are the distinguishing factors between *Gaidry* and the instant case.

We conclude that Wanda failed to establish a jury issue as to causation and that the trial court erred in not directing a verdict for the appellants.

The judgment is reversed with directions to enter a judgment dismissing the claim against the appellants.

In Greene v. B.F. Goodrich Avionics Sys., Inc., 409 F.3d 784 (6th Cir. 2005), the Sixth Circuit, applying Kentucky law and citing *Ringley*, held that the lower court erred by not granting judgment NOV to the defendant helicopter gyroscope manufacturer, reasoning that plaintiff failed to show that an allegedly defective vertical gyroscope was the probable cause, not merely a possible cause, of her husband's helicopter accident. See also Burgett v. Troy-Bilt, LLC, 579 Fed. App'x 372, 379 (6th Cir. 2014). Courts in other jurisdictions have granted defendants' motions for summary judgment because plaintiffs' failed to prove the defect was more probably than not the cause of the alleged injury. See, e.g., Estate of Thompson v. Kawasaki Heavy Industries, Ltd., 922 F. Supp. 2d 780, 792 (N.D. Iowa 2013) (applying Iowa law).

---

authors' dialogue 7

JIM: I know you disagree, but I think *Midwestern VW* was wrongly decided.

AARON: You are right.

JIM: *Midwestern VW* is wrong?

AARON: No. You are right that I disagree with you. The plaintiff should be required to play by the rules. It shouldn't suffice for the plaintiff to have a one-car accident, hurt herself badly, and then find some small departure-from-the-specs in a brake drum on which to blame the manufacturer. The plaintiff's expert has got to be more precise and informative.

JIM: But all that means is that the plaintiff's lawyer was a little sloppy. Next time the expert will simply say the magic words and the plaintiff will reach the jury. Why punish Wanda Ringley?

AARON: Let's not forget *Daubert* and its progeny. (See pp. 88-103, supra.) Those cases, together with the holding in *Midwestern VW*, will help sort out the worthy claims from the unworthy. But we shouldn't fudge doctrine to compensate for sloppy lawyering. You know the old adage "bad facts make bad law"? Well, bad lawyers also make bad law when judges go soft on them.

DOUG: Aaron's right, Jim. If you feel sorry for Wanda, let her sue her attorney.

JIM: Ouch!

PROBLEM EIGHT

Milton Ratabush invited his mother, Belle, to come and live with him for a few months after the death of his father. Belle is an alert, but somewhat frail, 75-year-old woman. The first week she was at Milton's home she mentioned to Dotty (Milton's wife) that it was hard for her to use the shower because the bathtub surface was slippery. Milton immediately purchased a package of "No-Slip" strips manufactured by Drydock, Inc. The package contained four 36-inch strips. Directions on the package indicated that two strips should be sufficient to provide the desired traction for the tub.

Two weeks after Milton installed two "No-Slip" strips in his bathtub, Belle fell and broke her hip while showering in the tub. When Milton examined the strips on the floor of the tub, he discovered that they had become loose around the edges at a number of places. An expert's examination of the two unused strips revealed gaps in the distribution of the glue-like substance that is supposed to provide adhesion to the tub.

This is not the first time that Belle has suffered injury due to a fall. Last year she suffered a momentary blackout while walking upstairs. She fell and broke her arm. Belle has no recollection of the accident in Milton's home. When Dotty found her in the bathtub, she had blacked out. Her doctor maintains that the blackout could have occurred after the fall as a result of the intense pain caused by the breaking of the hip. Belle does not remember what precipitated her fall.

Milton has consulted you about bringing suit against Drydock on his mother's behalf. Will you take the case?

2. Enhanced Injury

In some instances, a product defect is not the cause of the accident that brought about the plaintiff's injury. Instead, the defect may cause add-on injuries. This phenomenon appears most frequently in crashworthiness cases involving automobiles. Typically, subsequent to an auto crash either the driver or a passenger alleges that the auto was not adequately designed to withstand a crash. A reasonably alternative design, it is claimed, would have protected the plaintiff from suffering such severe injuries. However, even had a better design been incorporated in the auto the plaintiff may have suffered injuries as a result of the crash. The auto company should only be liable for the injuries that could have been avoided by the safer design. Where plaintiff can prove the extent of the add-on injuries recovery is limited to the dollar amount assigned to the add-on. In some instances, however, plaintiff may not be able to prove with any degree of certainty the amount of the add-on injuries. How to deal with this difficult causation issue has been the subject of extensive case law that will be discussed in Chapter Four.

3. Loss-of-a-Chance

In loss-of-a-chance cases, the defendant's conduct — here, the defendant's product — does not actually cause the plaintiff's harm, but rather the defendant's negligence — the defect in the product — prevents the plaintiff from being rescued from preexisting risks from outside sources. A seminal decision on loss-of-a-chance causation is Herskovits v. Group Health Coop. of Puget Sound, 664 P.2d 474 (Wash. 1983). Although not a products liability decision, it deserves consideration here because it deals forthrightly with the issue of whether there should be liability when all we can ever know is that the defendant's wrongful conduct contributed marginally to increase the risk that ultimately materialized in injury. Herskovits involved a wrongful death action against a hospital and its employees; plaintiff proved that the defendant's negligence reduced the decedent's chances of surviving cancer. At no point in time relevant to the liability issue did the decedent have better than a 50 percent chance of survival. No expert witness was able to testify that the defendant's negligent delay in diagnosis "probably" or "more likely than not" caused the decedent's death, in the sense that if the defendant had not been negligent, the decedent more likely than not would have survived. The trial court granted defendant's motions for summary judgment. The Washington high court reversed, concluding:

> The ultimate question raised here is whether the relationship between the increased risk of harm and Herskovits' death is sufficient to hold Group Health responsible. Is a 36 percent (from 39 percent to 25 percent) reduction in the decedent's chance for survival sufficient evidence of causation to allow the jury to consider the possibility that the physician's failure to timely diagnose the illness was the proximate cause of his death? We answer in the affirmative. To decide otherwise would be a blanket release from liability for doctors

and hospitals any time there was less than a 50 percent chance of survival, regardless of how flagrant the negligence. . . .

Causing reduction of the opportunity to recover (loss of chance) by one's negligence, however, does not necessitate a total recovery against the negligent party for all damages caused by the victim's death. Damages should be awarded to the injured party or his family based only on damages caused directly by premature death, such as lost earnings and additional medical expenses, etc. [664 P.2d at 476-479.]

In Matsuyama v. Birnbaum, 890 N.E.2d 819 (Mass. 2008), the Massachusetts Supreme Court after an exhaustive review of authority noted that a strong majority of states to have considered adopting "loss of chance" liability have done so. In joining this trend, the *Matsuyama* court described how they would calculate damages:

To illustrate, suppose in a wrongful death case that a jury found, based on expert testimony and the facts of the case, that full wrongful death damages would be $600,000 (step 1), that the patient had a 45% chance of survival prior to the medical malpractice (step 2), and that the physician's tortious acts reduced the chances of survival to 15% (step 3). The patient's chances of survival were reduced 30% (i.e., 45% minus 15%) due to the physician's malpractice (step 4), and the patient's loss of chance damages would be $600,000 multiplied by 30%, for a total of $180,000 (step 5). . . . Id. at 840 (1987).

However, some courts have rejected the "loss of chance" doctrine and insist that plaintiffs establish causation based on the balance of probabilities. See, e.g., Kemper v. Gordon, 272 S.W.3d 146 (Ky. 2008), reh'g denied (2009). One state has legislatively prohibited courts from imposing loss of chance liability. See S.D. Codified Laws 20-9-1.1 (2010). Another has limited its use unless the opportunity to achieve a better result was at least 50 percent, Mich. Comp Laws. Ann §600.2912(a). For an extensive review of judicial and legislative authority see Alice Férot, The Theory of Loss of Chance: Between Reticence and Acceptance, 8 FIU. L. Rev. 591 (2013); and Brian Casaceli, Losing a Chance to Survive: An Examination of the Loss of Chance Doctrine Within the Context of a Wrongful Death Action, 9 J. Health & Biomedical L. 521 (2014). The Restatement of Liability for Physical and Emotional Harm (2010) recognizes the loss-of-chance cause of action in §26, comment *n*. After observing that a number of courts have reconceptualized the concept of plaintiff's harm so as to allow recovery in cases where the plaintiff is deprived of a less-than-fifty-percent chance of recovery, the comment opines regarding the possible future of the "lost opportunity" tort:

To date, the courts that have accepted lost opportunity as cognizable harm have almost universally limited its recognition to medical-malpractice cases. Three features of that context are significant: 1) a contractual relationship exists between patient and physician (or physician's employer), in which the raison d'être of the contract is that the physician will take every reasonable measure to obtain an optimal outcome for the patient; 2) reasonably good empirical evidence is often available about the general statistical probability of the lost opportunity; and 3) frequently the consequences of the physician's negligence will deprive the patient of a less-than-50-percent chance for recovery. Whether there are appropriate areas beyond the medical-malpractice area to which lost opportunity might appropriately be extended is a matter that the Institute leaves to future development.

For a useful summary of judicial developments in nonproduct settings, including scholarly commentaries, see Reporters' Note to comment *n*. When an epidemiological study shows an increased risk of disease due to exposure to an unreasonably dangerous toxin, why should courts not apply proportional causation reflecting the percentage of increased risk to plaintiff? See Boaz Shnoor, Loss of Chance: A Behavioral Analysis of the Difference Between Medical Negligence and Toxic Torts, 33 Am. J. Trial Advoc. 71 (2009).

PROBLEM NINE

Jon Brett was placed in the intensive care unit (ICU) of the local hospital after suffering a severe heart attack. His condition was critical, but he did not require constant bedside attention because his condition was continually monitored by a Kardia Heart Monitor. The hospital relies on such monitoring machines for early warning of changes in the condition of ICU patients. Because of a manufacturing defect, the monitor malfunctioned and hospital personnel were not alerted immediately to the onset of Brett's second heart attack. By the time the hospital personnel became aware of the situation, Brett's condition was beyond remedy, and he died. Brett's wife and children have come to you seeking to hold Kardia liable for his death.

Your preliminary research indicates that, in general, early warnings increase survival rates of second heart attacks by about 20 percent. Factors such as advanced age, severity of the first heart attack, weight, and high blood pressure can reduce the chance of survival. Data are not available as to how much each of the factors reduce a given individual's chance of survival, and there are also no reliable statistics as to the synergistic effects of these factors. Although Brett was a trim age 45, his first heart attack was severe, and he suffered from high blood pressure.

Assuming that your high court will recognize *Herskovits*, supra, as controlling authority and making reasonable assumptions of fact where necessary, what is your preliminary assessment of your chances of reaching the jury with a claim against Kardia?

D. DID THE DEFECTIVE PRODUCT PROXIMATELY CAUSE THE PLAINTIFF'S HARM?

Union Pump Co. v. Allbritton
898 S.W.2d 773 (Tex. 1995)

OWEN, Justice.

The issue in this case is whether the condition, act, or omission of which a personal injury plaintiff complains was, as a matter of law, too remote to constitute legal causation. Plaintiff brought suit alleging negligence, gross negligence, and strict liability, and the trial court granted summary judgment for the defendant. The court of appeals reversed and remanded, holding that the plaintiff raised issues of fact concerning proximate and producing cause. Because we conclude that there was no legal causation as a matter of law, we reverse the judgment of the court of appeals and render judgment that plaintiff take nothing.

On the night of September 4, 1989, a fire occurred at Texaco Chemical Company's facility in Port Arthur, Texas. A pump manufactured by Union Pump Company caught fire and ignited the surrounding area. This particular pump had caught on fire twice before. Sue Allbritton, a trainee employee of Texaco Chemical, had just finished her shift and was about to leave the plant when the fire erupted. She and her supervisor Felipe Subia, Jr., were directed to and did assist in abating the fire.

Approximately two hours later, the fire was extinguished. However, there appeared to be a problem with a nitrogen purge valve, and Subia was instructed to block in the valve. Viewing the facts in a light most favorable to Allbritton, there was some evidence that an emergency situation existed at that point in time. Allbritton asked if she could accompany Subia and was allowed to do so. To get to the nitrogen purge valve, Allbritton followed Subia over an aboveground pipe rack, which was approximately two and one-half feet high, rather than going around it. It is undisputed that this was not the safer route, but it was the shorter one. Upon reaching the valve, Subia and Allbritton were notified that it was not necessary to block it off. Instead of returning by the route around the pipe rack, Subia chose to walk across it, and Allbritton followed. Allbritton was injured when she hopped or slipped off the pipe rack. There is evidence that the pipe rack was wet because of the fire and that Allbritton and Subia were still wearing fireman's hip boots and other firefighting gear when the injury occurred. Subia admitted that he chose to walk over the pipe rack rather than taking a safer alternative route because he had a "bad habit" of doing so.

Allbritton sued Union Pump, alleging negligence, gross negligence, and strict liability theories of recovery, and accordingly, that the defective pump was a proximate or producing cause of her injuries. But for the pump fire, she asserts, she would never have walked over the pipe rack, which was wet with water or firefighting foam.

Following discovery, Union Pump moved for summary judgment. To be entitled to summary judgment, the movant has the burden of establishing that there is no genuine issue of material fact and that it is entitled to judgment as a matter of law. A defendant who moves for summary judgment must conclusively disprove one of the elements of each of the plaintiff's causes of action. Lear Siegler, Inc. v. Perez, 819 S.W.2d 470, 471 (Tex. 1991). All doubts must be resolved against Union Pump and all evidence must be viewed in the light most favorable to Allbritton. Id. The question before this Court is whether Union Pump established as a matter of law that neither its conduct nor its product was a legal cause of Allbritton's injuries. Stated another way, was Union Pump correct in contending that there was no causative link between the defective pump and Allbritton's injuries as a matter of law?

Negligence requires a showing of proximate cause, while producing cause is the test in strict liability. Proximate and producing cause differ in that foreseeability is an element of proximate cause, but not of producing cause. Id. Proximate cause consists of both cause in fact and foreseeability. Cause in fact means that the defendant's act or omission was a substantial factor in bringing about the injury which would not otherwise have occurred. A producing cause is "an efficient, exciting, or contributing cause, which in a natural sequence, produced injuries or damages complained of, if any." Common to both proximate and producing cause is causation in fact, including the requirement that the defendant's conduct or product be a substantial factor in bringing about the plaintiff's injuries. . . . Lear Siegler, 819 S.W.2d at 472 n.1 (quoting Restatement (Second) of Torts 431 cmt. e (1965)).

At some point in the causal chain, the defendant's conduct or product may be too remotely connected with the plaintiff's injury to constitute legal causation. As this Court noted in City of Gladewater v. Pike, 727 S.W.2d 514, 518 (Tex. 1987), defining the limits of legal causation "eventually mandates weighing of policy considerations." See also Springall v. Fredericksburg Hospital and Clinic, 225 S.W.2d 232, 235 (Tex. Civ. App. — San Antonio 1949, no writ), in which the court of appeals observed:

> [T]he law does not hold one legally responsible for the remote results of his wrongful acts and therefore a line must be drawn between immediate and remote causes. The doctrine of "proximate cause" is employed to determine and fix this line and "is the result of an effort by the courts to avoid, as far as possible the metaphysical and philosophical niceties in the age-old discussion of causation, and to lay down a rule of general application which will, as nearly as may be done by a general rule, apply a practical test, the test of common experience, to human conduct when determining legal rights and legal liability."

Id. at 235 (quoting City of Dallas v. Maxwell, 248 S.W. 667, 670 (Tex. Commn. App. 1923, holding approved)).

Drawing the line between where legal causation may exist and where, as a matter of law, it cannot, has generated a considerable body of law. Our Court has considered where the limits of legal causation should lie in the factually analogous case of Lear Siegler, Inc. v. Perez, supra. The threshold issue was whether causation was negated as a matter of law in an action where negligence and product liability theories were asserted. Perez, an employee of the Texas Highway Department, was driving a truck pulling a flashing arrow sign behind a highway sweeping operation to warn traffic of the highway maintenance. Id. at 471. The sign malfunctioned when wires connecting it to the generator became loose, as they had the previous day. Id. Perez got out of the truck to push the wire connections back together, and an oncoming vehicle, whose driver was asleep, struck the sign, which in turn struck Perez. Id. Perez's survivors brought suit against the manufacturer of the sign. In holding that any defect in the sign was not the legal cause of Perez's injuries, we found a comment to the Restatement (Second) of Torts, section 431, instructive on the issue of legal causation:

> In order to be a legal cause of another's harm, it is not enough that the harm would not have occurred had the actor not been negligent. . . . The negligence must also be a substantial factor in bringing about the plaintiff's harm. The word "substantial" is used to denote the fact that the defendant's conduct has such an effect in producing the harm as to lead reasonable men to regard it as a cause, using that word in the popular sense, in which there always lurks the idea of responsibility, rather than in the so-called "philosophic sense," which includes every one of the great number of events without which any happening would not have occurred.

Lear Siegler, 819 S.W.2d at 472 (quoting Restatement (Second) of Torts §431 cmt. *a* (1965)).

As this Court explained in *Lear Siegler*, the connection between the defendant and the plaintiff's injuries simply may be too attenuated to constitute legal cause. 819 S.W.2d at 472. Legal cause is not established if the defendant's conduct or product does no more than furnish the condition that makes the plaintiff's injury possible. Id. This principle applies with equal force to proximate cause and producing cause. Id. at 472 n.1.

This Court similarly considered the parameters of legal causation in Bell v. Campbell, 434 S.W.2d 117, 122 (Tex.1968). In *Bell*, two cars collided, and a trailer attached to one of them disengaged and overturned into the opposite lane. A number of people gathered, and three of them were attempting to move the trailer when they were struck by another vehicle. Id. at 119. This Court held that the parties to the first accident were not a proximate cause of the plaintiffs' injuries, reasoning:

> All acts and omissions charged against respondents had run their course and were complete. Their negligence did not actively contribute in any way to the injuries involved in this suit. It simply created a condition which attracted [the plaintiffs] to the scene, where they were injured by a third party.

Id. at 122.

In *Bell*, this Court examined at some length decisions dealing with intervening causes and decisions dealing with concurring causes. The principles underlying the various legal theories of causation overlap in many respects, but they are not coextensive. While in *Bell*, this Court held "the injuries involved in this suit were not proximately caused by any negligence of [defendants] but by an independent and intervening agency," id., we also held "[a]ll forces involved in or generated by the first collision had come to rest, and no one was in any real or apparent danger therefrom[,]" Id. at 120, and accordingly, that the "[defendants'] negligence was not a concurring cause of [the plaintiffs'] injuries." Id. at 122. This reasoning applies with equal force to Allbritton's claims.

Even if the pump fire were in some sense a "philosophic" or "but for" cause of Allbritton's injuries, the forces generated by the fire had come to rest when she fell off the pipe rack. The fire had been extinguished, and Allbritton was walking away from the scene. Viewing the evidence in the light most favorable to Allbritton, the pump fire did no more than create the condition that made Allbritton's injuries possible. We conclude that the circumstances surrounding her injuries are too remotely connected with Union Pump's conduct or pump to constitute a legal cause of her injuries. See *Lear Siegler*, 819 S.W.2d at 472.

Accordingly, we reverse the judgment of the court of appeals and render judgment that plaintiff take nothing.

In a dissenting opinion, Justice Spector held that the defendant is not entitled to summary judgment:

> The record reflects that at the time Sue Allbritton's injury occurred, the forces generated by the fire in question had not come to rest. Rather, the emergency situation was continuing. The whole area of the fire was covered in water and foam; in at least some places, the water was almost knee-deep. Allbritton was still wearing hip boots and other gear, as required to fight the fire. . . . 898 S.W.2d at 785-786.

In Marshall v. Nugent, 222 F.2d 604 (1st Cir. 1955), the court of appeals addressed the same line-drawing problem as the court in *Lear Siegler* posed hypothetically. In that case, defendant's driver drove his truck in a dangerous manner around a curve on an icy mountain road. In doing so, he forced a car in which the plaintiff was a passenger

---

authors' dialogue 8

DOUG: The dissent in *Union Pump* is right, isn't it?

AARON: I don't think so. It seems to me that the majority got it right on the money. What the plaintiff did by taking the shortcut was her own private frolic. As long as she had a safer way out of the fire area, and chose not to take it, the pump manufacturer should be off the hook.

JIM: But then you aren't talking proximate cause, Aaron. You're talking assumption of the risk, or plaintiff's contributory fault, aren't you?

AARON: What difference does it make what you call it? The manufacturer should not be liable for the risks she brought on herself.

JIM: The difference it makes is that if it's her own negligence that is doing the work for you, most states have adopted comparative fault. If you are right that she acted negligently, the jury should apportion responsibility between the parties, not bar her recovery altogether.

AARON: I see what you're saying, but I think I'm talking proximate cause, here. It is not reasonably foreseeable that a defect in a pump would lead to someone taking a dangerous shortcut after the defect-caused fire is out. When proximate cause is absent, defendant wins the whole enchilada — the plaintiff takes nothing.

DOUG: What if the plaintiff had not taken the shortcut, and had slipped on the wet floor and hurt herself coming out the safer way?

AARON: Then I agree that the proximate cause issue should have been for the jury.

JIM: So the difference for you really is the element of plaintiff's fault, isn't it?

AARON: I don't think so. It's foreseeability. What if she had decided to perform handsprings to celebrate the fire being put out, and had suffered injury doing that? Defendant should win that case on proximate cause grounds as a matter of law, shouldn't it?

JIM: I guess so. But taking a more dangerous shortcut is the result of momentary inadvertence that the manufacturer should pay for once its defective pump causes a fire that causes commotion and requires firefighting. Willfully reckless conduct by the plaintiff may break the proximate cause link as a matter of law. But as long as she has her firefighting gear on and is walking out of the area through foamy water, proximate cause should not be an outright bar to recovery as a matter of law. Plaintiff should have reached the jury.

DOUG: My goodness, Jim, you're actually on the plaintiff's side!

JIM: You won't tell anyone, will you?

---

off the road and into a snowbank. No one was hurt. The truck driver stopped to assist in extricating the car from the snowbank, and suggested that the plaintiff go up the hill to warn oncoming traffic. The plaintiff started up the hill, and within two minutes was struck and seriously injured by a car driven by co-defendant Nugent.

At trial, the jury found for the plaintiff. In upholding the trial court's decision to allow the question of the truck driver's liability to go to the jury, the Court of Appeals held that it is the jury who must decide the policy issues involved with causation analysis, that is "whether under all the circumstances the defendant ought to be recognized as privileged to do the act in question or to pursue his course of conduct with immunity from liability for harm to others which might result." 222 F.2d at 611. In such "borderline cases" the court leaves the issue of proximate cause to the jury "with appropriate instructions." As for the extent to which a jury might hold a negligent driver liable for injuries stemming from his actions, the court said:

> In a traffic mix-up due to negligence, before the disturbed waters have become placid and normal again, the unfolding of events between the culpable act and the plaintiff's eventual injury may be bizarre indeed; yet the defendant may be liable for the result. . . . In such a situation, it would be impossible for a person in the defendant's position to predict in advance just how his negligent act would work out to another's injury. Yet this in itself is no bar to recovery. 222 F.2d at 610.

The approach in the *Marshall* decision appears more willing to give the issue of proximate causation to the jury than does the approach in *Union Pump*. Wherein, exactly, lies the difference?

In Stahlecker v. Ford Motor Co., 667 N.W.2d 244 (Neb. 2003), the trial court dismissed a complaint in which the plaintiff alleged that a defect in a tire manufactured and sold by the defendants caused the tire to fail during use, rendering the automobile inoperable in a remote area. The plaintiff's decedent was left "alone and stranded" as a result of the tire failure, leading to her being assaulted and killed by a passerby. The Supreme Court of Nebraska affirmed the judgment for defendants, concluding (667 N.W.2d at 258):

> Although the operative amended petition alleges sufficient facts to establish that Ford and Firestone negligently placed defective products on the market which caused Amy to become stranded at night in a remote location, it alleges no facts upon which either Ford or Firestone would have a legal duty to anticipate and guard against the criminal acts which were committed at that location by another party. Therefore, the criminal acts constitute an efficient intervening cause which necessarily defeats proof of the essential element of proximate cause.

Section 29 of the new Restatement of Liability for Physical and Emotional Harm (2010) jettisons the phrase "proximate cause" in favor of "limitations on liability." It simply asserts that "An actor is not liable for harm different from the harms whose risks made the actor's conduct tortious." Is this formulation adequate in working out sensible solutions to the causation issue presented in *Union Pump, Lear Siegler*, and *Marshall*, supra? Comment *j* to §29 makes the following observation:

> Negligence limits the requirement of reasonable care to those risks that are foreseeable. Thus, when scope of liability arises in a negligence case, the risks that make an actor negligent are limited to foreseeable ones, and the factfinder must determine whether the harm that occurred is among those reasonably foreseeable potential harms that made the actor's conduct negligent. . . .
>
> For the strict-liability bases for liability, the standard in this Section is more cogently applied than a foreseeability standard. . . . [A good example is the] strict liability [that] is

imposed for manufacturing defects. Focusing on the risks created by a manufacturing defect, rather than attempting to manipulate the concept of foreseeability, better illuminates the requisite analysis. . . .

See generally David G. Owen, Products Liability Law, ch. 12 (2008).

PROBLEM TEN

A partner in the law firm in which you are an associate has asked for your help in a case involving a claim against your client, an automobile manufacturer, for increased injuries arising from an auto accident six months ago. The plaintiff, Edna Abrams, age 19, was a passenger in the back seat of a four-door sedan manufactured by your client. The car ran off the road to avoid another vehicle and struck a utility pole. Edna was not wearing a seat belt and catapulted forward from the back seat through the front windshield, suffering severe injuries. The back seat contained two-point, lap-type seat belts in working condition. Edna swears she decided not to buckle her seat belt because her father had always told her that a lap belt was worse than no belt at all. Had Edna been wearing her lap-type seat belt, she would have been injured much less severely. Edna claims that the back seat of the sedan should have been equipped with three-point shoulder harness seat belts, and that the car was defectively designed without them. She swears that if the car had contained a three-point belt in the back seat, she would have buckled it. Her expert will testify that if she had been wearing a three-point shoulder harness seat belt, she would have escaped injury altogether.

Your partner explains that the auto design in question satisfied applicable safety regulations when it was sold. He is concerned that the issue of defect will reach the jury and that the question of but-for causation will turn on Edna's testimony that she would have buckled up a three-point belt had it been available. The partner asks, "The question of whether or not to believe her will be for the jury, will it not? And yet it seems to me that she should be barred on the basis of lack of a proximate cause connection between the alleged defect and her injuries — after all, she didn't buckle up the available belt when doing so would have greatly reduced her injuries. Can you find me a hook to support a judgment for defendant as a matter of law?"

PROBLEM ELEVEN

Unitop, Inc. manufactures a full line of commercial meat slicing machines. Its top-of-the-line unit, Model 505, is a sophisticated piece of machinery. One of the safety features on Model 505 is an automatic shut-off which closes down the slicer when the guard holding the meat to the slicer advances within 1/2 inch of the slicing blade. In Unitop's experience, even with the metal guard which holds the meat to the slicing blade, users who are momentarily distracted can get their hands near the blade and suffer injury. The automatic cut-off forces the user to engage a button (Single-Slice Button) for each slice to be made after the 1/2-inch level has been reached. Since users have to engage the button for each slice, they tend to focus attention on what they are doing and thus are more apt to avoid injury.

Mo's Deli purchased a Model 505 two years ago. Morris (Mo) Blitner liked the machine but detested the 1/2-inch automatic cut-off feature because it interrupted the smooth flow of work. Six months ago, Mo discovered that the Single-Slice Button was not working. Apparently due to inadequate soldering, the wires loosened and then shorted out. Mo's one-year warranty on the Model 505 had run out. The cost of repairing the wiring of the Single-Slice Button would have been $150. It was much simpler for Mo to disengage the automatic cut-off mechanism and be done with it.

One week after removing the automatic cut-off, Mo, while slicing pastrami, was engaged in serious discussion with a customer (a stockbroker) who had a particularly good tip on some commodities futures. Mo was not paying sufficient attention to what he was doing and his fingers hit the blades. (The remaining piece of unsliced pastrami had reached a thickness where the automatic cut-off would have been operative if it were still connected.) Mo subsequently brought a tort action against Unitop, which has moved for summary judgment based on the uncontested facts set forth herein. As the law clerk for Judge Malcolm Sweet, before whom the case is pending, you have been assigned to draft an opinion with regard to this matter.

CHAPTER THREE
Affirmative Defenses

A. CONDUCT-BASED DEFENSES: BACKGROUND PRINCIPLES

1. Introduction

The question of what share of responsibility should be borne by a plaintiff who contributes to his own injury has troubled the courts in nonproducts tort litigation. The problem is even more acute in products liability cases. Unlike the usual tort case where the parties are complete strangers to each other prior to the injury-causing accident, in the products case the defendant provides the user with a defective product that becomes the instrumentality of harm. The conceptual difficulties stem from the fact that the possibility of user misconduct must be taken into account in the original design and marketing decisions — if a pattern of user misconduct is foreseeable, the manufacturer may have a duty to exercise due care to protect against it. Given the manufacturer's heightened responsibility, it will likely be difficult to assess the user's proper share of the overall liability when a claim is litigated. Consider, for example, a drill press with a defective safety guard at the point of operation. When the failure of the safety guard to function properly is a cause of injury to the user, is it fair to bar the plaintiff or reduce his recovery as a result of his negligent conduct that also contributed to the accident? If the very reason for installing an effective safety guard is to prevent injuries to users who negligently or inadvertently place their hands at the danger point, does it make sense to cut back on the initial assessment that the injury is best avoided by the manufacturer?

Furthermore, to some extent, a consumer's interaction with a product is a function of highly sophisticated marketing processes. It ill behooves a manufacturer who has encouraged various forms of risky user behavior to argue that the consumer failed to follow societal norms for careful product use. On the other hand, to free the user from all responsibility when interacting with a defective product seems equally unwise. A defective product will often signal to the user that something is wrong. Should a user be free to disregard such danger signals? And what of user conduct that would be deemed negligent irrespective of the product's defectiveness? Should product prices reflect accident costs that, in truth, are only marginally related to product defects?

2. *Contributory Negligence*

During the period in which the operative theory for recovery for defective products was based in negligence, contributory negligence and assumption of the risk operated as total bars to plaintiff's recovery in most jurisdictions.

With the introduction of strict products liability, courts felt free to reexamine the appropriateness of contributory fault as a complete defense. Again, the Restatement (Second) of Torts §402A was influential in setting the tone. Comment *n* provides:

> *n. Contributory negligence.* Since the liability with which this Section deals is not based upon negligence of the seller, but is strict liability, the rule applied to strict liability cases applies. Contributory negligence of the plaintiff is not a defense when such negligence consists merely in a failure to discover the defect in the product, or to guard against the possibility of its existence. On the other hand the form of contributory negligence which consists in voluntarily and unreasonably proceeding to encounter a known danger, and commonly passes under the name of assumption of risk, is a defense under this Section as in other cases of strict liability. If the user or consumer discovers the defect and is aware of the danger, and nevertheless proceeds unreasonably to make use of the product and is injured by it, he is barred from recovery.

The Restatement (Second) of Torts §402A was written in 1964, when the overwhelming majority rule was that contributory negligence served as a total defense to negligence. Since then comparative fault has swept the country. Contributory fault remains as a total bar to recovery (even in nonproducts liability cases) in five jurisdictions: Alabama, Maryland, North Carolina, Virginia, and the District of Columbia. Given the fact that the majority of jurisdictions have adopted some form of comparative fault, the real question is not whether contributory negligence should serve as a total bar to a products liability claim, but whether comparative negligence should operate as a partial defense in that context. This problem will be dealt with in the following section.

3. *Comparative Fault*

Before taking sides on the question of applying comparative fault to various kinds of user conduct in products liability cases, it will be useful to identify the different strains that make up the cacophony known generically as "comparative fault" or "comparative negligence."

Comparative negligence has been adopted in American jurisdictions in various forms. The Reporters' Note to §7 of the Restatement (Third) of Torts: Apportionment of Liability (2000) describes the various forms of comparative responsibility as follows:

> Under a modified system, the plaintiff is barred from recovery if the factfinder assigns the plaintiff a percentage of responsibility equal to or above 50 percent or 51 percent. If the factfinder assigns the plaintiff a percentage of responsibility below that percentage, the plaintiff's recovery is reduced by the percentage the factfinder assigns to the plaintiff. Under a pure system, the plaintiff's recovery is always reduced by the percentage of responsibility the factfinder assigns to the plaintiff, regardless of its magnitude. The plaintiff is never barred from recovery merely because of the percentage of responsibility

the factfinder assigns to the plaintiff. This [Restatement] adopts pure comparative responsibility. A court should use modified comparative responsibility only when a statute requires it to do so. . . .

Currently, thirteen jurisdictions utilize pure comparative fault. Twelve jurisdictions have adopted a modified comparative responsibility system that bars plaintiff from recovering if his percentage of negligence is found to be 50 percent or more. Twenty-one jurisdictions utilize a modified comparative responsibility system with a 51 percent bar.

Although most jurisdictions have elected to adopt either a pure or modified form of comparative responsibility, two other forms of comparative responsibility systems deserve mention. South Dakota allows a plaintiff to recover only if his negligence is slight in comparison to the gross negligence of a defendant. Michigan has adopted a unique form of comparative responsibility. Under Michigan Law, if a plaintiff's percentage of fault is greater than the aggregate fault of the defendant(s), the court reduces economic damages by the percentage of comparative fault and the plaintiff will not be allowed to recover noneconomic damages. When the plaintiff's percentage of fault is less than the aggregate fault of the defendant(s), the court will reduce the plaintiff's recovery for both economic and noneconomic loss. Thus, Michigan seems to have created a hybrid system of comparative responsibility utilizing aspects of both pure and modified comparative responsibility. See Mich. Comp. Laws Ann. §600.2959.

B. APPLICATION OF COMPARATIVE FAULT IN PRODUCTS LIABILITY

It does not follow from the adoption of comparative fault as a general matter that it should be applied in products liability cases. One must first decide whether it is appropriate (or even possible) to compare a product defect with the plaintiff's fault. The Products Liability Restatement takes a strong position on this matter favoring the application of comparative fault in products liability cases.

Restatement (Third) of Torts: Products Liability
(1998)

§17. Apportionment of Responsibility Between or Among Plaintiff, Sellers, and Distributors of Defective Products, and Others

(a) A plaintiff's recovery of damages for harm caused by a product defect may be reduced if the conduct of the plaintiff combines with the product defect to cause the harm and the plaintiff's conduct fails to conform to generally applicable rules establishing appropriate standards of care.

(b) The manner and extent of the reduction under Subsection (a) and the apportionment of plaintiff's recovery among multiple defendants are governed by generally applicable rules apportioning responsibility.

1.   Can Fault and Defect Be Compared?

a.   Manufacturing Defects: Comparing Apples and Oranges

Early on in the products liability era, the United States Court of Appeals for the Third Circuit struggled with the question of whether one could compare fault with defect. Other courts have followed in its footsteps. In Murray v. Fairbanks Morse, 610 F.2d 149 (3d Cir. 1979), plaintiff was injured while installing an electrical control housed in a one-and-a-half-ton unit onto a platform. The manufacturer of the unit had attached two iron cross members to the open bottom of the unit. A cherry picker lifted the unit over the platform and sought to align it with pre-drilled holes so that it could be fastened with bolts. The holes were not perfectly aligned so plaintiff chose to use a crow bar to rock the heavy unit into alignment. The accident occurred when plaintiff put his weight on one of the cross members. It gave way and plaintiff fell ten feet onto a concrete floor incurring severe injury to his spine. Plaintiff claimed that the control panel was defective because it had only been tack-welded to the unit. Defendant contended that plaintiff's method of installation was highly dangerous. The jury awarded the plaintiff $2 million but found the plaintiff to be 5 percent at fault. The trial court reduced plaintiff's damages accordingly.

Since defendant was held strictly liable for the defective weld, the court was faced with the question of how it could compare product defect (no fault) with plaintiff conduct (fault). The court reasoned as follows:

> The substitution of the term fault for defect, however, would not appear to aid the trier of fact in apportioning damages between the defect and the *conduct* of the plaintiff. The key conceptual distinction between strict products liability theory and negligence is that the plaintiff need not prove faulty conduct on the part of the defendant in order to recover. The jury is not asked to determine if the defendant deviated from a standard of care in producing his product. There is no proven faulty conduct of the defendant to compare with the faulty conduct of the plaintiff in order to apportion the responsibility for an accident. . . . A comparison of the two is therefore inappropriate. . . .
>
> In apportioning damages we are really asking how much of the injury was caused by the defect in the product versus how much was caused by the plaintiff's own actions. We agree with the Ninth Circuit when it noted that comparative causation "is a conceptually more precise term than 'comparative fault' since fault alone without causation does not subject one to liability." Pan-Alaska Fisheries, Inc. v. Marine Construction & Design Co., 565 F.2d 1129, 1139 (9th Cir. 1977). The appropriate label for the quality of the act is insignificant. . . . Thus, the underlying task in each case is to analyze and compare the causal conduct of each party regardless of its label. Although fault, in the sense of the defendant's product or the plaintiff's failure to meet a standard of care, must exist before a comparison takes place, the comparison itself must focus on the role each played in bringing about the particular injury. . . .

Did the *Murray* court resolve the problem of how to compare plaintiff conduct with product defect? How does one compare causation? If a semi-trailer with defective brakes collides with a negligently driven Volkswagen bug, does the semi-trailer bear more casual responsibility for the accident? Isn't comparative causation simply nonsense? See Aaron D. Twerski, The Many Faces of Misuse: An Inquiry into the Emerging Doctrine of Comparative Causation, 29 Mercer L. Rev. 403 (1978).

b. Generic Defects: Comparing Fault Under Risk-Utility Balancing

The difficulties a court may have in comparing fault when faced with a manufacturing defect claim would seem to melt away when the claim is based on defective design or failure to warn. In manufacturing defect cases the defendant need not be at fault. The defendant may have used the best quality control extant and still be liable. In design and failure-to-warn cases, where defect is determined by risk-utility balancing, one can easily compare the negligence of the defendant-manufacturer in making a bad risk-utility decision with the negligent conduct of the plaintiff. Courts occasionally note the difference between manufacturing and design defect cases when applying comparative fault principles. See Webb v. Navistar International Transportation Corp., infra. However, most courts just go their merry way applying comparative fault to all forms of product defect.

c. Should Fault and Defect Be Compared?

Webb v. Navistar International Transportation Corp.
692 A.2d 343 (Vt. 1996)

DOOLEY, J. . . .

I

[In this case, the plaintiff's father had been driving the family tractor on a highway late one evening. The plaintiff, riding as a passenger, was standing behind the tractor body on a "draw bar" — essentially a large hitch. The owner's manual and a cautionary decal on the tractor both stated that passengers should not ride in that position. An (allegedly) drunk driver crashed into the tractor's rear where the plaintiff was standing. Plaintiff suffered severe leg injuries. Plaintiff sued the tractor manufacturer on various products liability theories related to the accident. In this appeal, the Supreme Court of Vermont reviewed a favorable jury verdict for the plaintiff on design defect and failure-to-warn claims related to the tractor's lighting system (and how those defects allegedly contributed to the accident). The trial court failed to instruct the jury that it could apportion fault between the parties. In its decision, the Vermont Supreme Court had to decide whether to permit comparative allocation of fault in products liability actions.]

I do not believe, . . . that the judgment in this case can be affirmed. I agree with defendant that comparative liability principles are applicable in strict products liability actions and should have been charged to the jury in this case. Because the split in the Court reserves the details of implementing comparative principles for another day, I state only the reasons we adopt a comparative causation rule. . . .

The primary reason that courts adopt comparative liability principles in strict products liability actions is "because it is fair to do so." . . . Adopting comparative liability principles "will accomplish a fairer and more equitable result" because the plaintiff's award is reduced by an amount equal to the degree to which the plaintiff is responsible for the accident. . . . Most courts reject the framework that places the burden of loss on one party where two parties contributed to causing the injury. . . . Comparative liability principles also further fairness by preventing a negligent plaintiff from recovering as much as a plaintiff who has taken all reasonable precautions. . . .

Moreover, there is no reason to impose the cost of a plaintiff's negligence upon the manufacturer to spread among other consumers of the product . . . see also Restatement (Third) of Torts: Products Liability §7 cmt. *a* (Tentative Draft No. 1, 1994) (unfair to impose costs of substandard plaintiff conduct on manufacturers, who will be impelled to pass on costs to all consumers, including those who use and consume product safely). The instant case is illustrative. Here, plaintiff stood on the draw bar of the tractor while it traveled down a public road. Although he understood the importance of the warning against such action, he chose to disregard the warning. As a result, he blocked the view of the reflective triangle and the single amber flashing light that may have been operable. Moreover, he failed to maintain the reflectors and the other flashing light. If the jury may reduce plaintiff's recovery to the extent that his injuries were caused by his negligence, defendant is not held liable for the cost of injuries attributed to plaintiff's negligence and does not pass this cost on to those farmers who heed the warnings posted on their tractors. Strict products liability was intended to spread the cost of injuries resulting from defective products; it was never intended to spread the cost of injuries resulting from user negligence. . . .

Apportioning liability more effectively spreads recoveries from manufacturers for selling defective products than the "all or nothing" framework. Under the "all or nothing" framework, some plaintiffs receive windfalls because they collect damages for injuries caused by their own negligence in addition to damages for injuries caused by the product defect. On the other hand, some plaintiffs receive nothing because the court or jury has determined that their negligence constitutes misuse, assumption of risk or an intervening cause, concepts often difficult to distinguish. . . . Applying principles of comparative liability will reduce the total damages awarded to some plaintiffs but will also extend recoveries to some plaintiffs formerly barred from any recovery; thus, recoveries will be more equitably distributed among plaintiffs.

A minority of courts have rejected comparative liability principles in the context of strict products liability actions and continue to impose the "all or nothing" framework set forth in the Restatement (Second) of Torts §402A. See, e.g., Bowling v. Heil Co., . . . 511 N.E.2d 373, 380 [Ohio 1987] (finding no rationale to persuade it that comparative fault principles should apply to products liability actions); *Kimco Dev. Corp.*, 637 A.2d at 606 [Pa. 1993] (declining to extend negligence concepts to strict products liability area). . . .

We draw two reasons from those decisions for retaining the "all or nothing" rule. First, several courts have suggested that it is too confusing to inject negligence concepts into strict liability actions, see, e.g., *Kimco Dev. Corp.*, 637 A.2d at 606 (conceptual confusion would ensue should negligence and strict liability concepts be commingled), and that juries will be unable to compare a defective product with a plaintiff's negligent conduct to apportion liability. . . .

Most courts have rejected this concern as semantic and theoretical. "We are convinced that in merging the two principles what may be lost in symmetry is more than gained in fundamental fairness," *Daly*, . . . 575 P.2d at 1172 [Cal. 1978], and "fairness and equity are more important than conceptual and semantic consistency." *Kaneko*, 654 P.2d at 352 [Haw. 1982]. Further, apportioning liability will be less difficult for juries than the current framework, which requires juries to distinguish between defenses that courts and scholars are often unable to differentiate. As the Supreme Court of Texas noted, assumed risk and unforeseeable misuse are nothing more than extreme variants of contributory negligence. See *Duncan*, 665 S.W.2d at 423 [Tex. 1984]. And the line between contributory negligence — resulting in total recovery — and assumed risk or misuse — resulting in no recovery — is difficult to draw. . . . There is no need to draw shadowy lines between misuse, assumption of risk and contributory negligence, however, . . . all defenses may constitute a basis for apportioning liability. . . .

Second, the "all or nothing" courts maintain that comparative principles would undermine the purposes of imposing strict liability on manufacturers because this approach reduces the incentive to produce safe products and fails to allocate the risk for loss from injury to manufacturers who are in a better position to absorb it. See *Kimco Dev. Corp.*, 637 A.2d at 606-07. On the contrary, applying principles of comparative liability in strict products liability actions is completely consistent with the purposes of imposing strict liability on manufacturers. Indeed, it will have no effect on the principal purpose of adopting this doctrine; the plaintiff is still relieved from proving negligence of the manufacturer or privity of contract with it. . . .

Nor is it clear that adopting comparative principles will significantly reduce the incentive to produce safe products. . . . Recoveries may be reduced in some cases, but more plaintiffs will recover if assumption of the risk and product misuse are no longer total bars to recovery. Overall, the cost of a defect may be the same under either approach. . . .

On balance the reasons to adopt comparative principles greatly outweigh the reasons to reject this approach. The comparative approach is fairer to all parties, and properly implemented, will not reduce the incentive to produce safe products.

IV

. . . I reach this conclusion as part of the development of the common law of products liability in this state and not because of the Vermont comparative negligence statute, 12 V.S.A. §1036. The statute applies only to "an action . . . to recover damages for *negligence*." (Emphasis added.) We must presume that the Legislature intended the plain meaning of the statutory language. . . . The wording covers actions based on negligence, but not on strict liability. The majority of courts confronting this question have reached the same conclusion. . . .

Even though the comparative negligence statute does not apply, we could construct a comparable causation rule that would mirror its terms. In this case, the main significance of such a rule is that plaintiffs could not recover if the causal effect of the negligence of Bruce Webb was greater than the causal effect of the liability of defendant. Using this test, Justice Morse would hold that, as a matter of law, a majority of plaintiffs' damages were caused by the negligence of Bruce Webb so that plaintiffs cannot recover at all.

I do not subscribe to the "half-or-nothing" framework of [the comparative negligence statute] for products liability cases. The rule is inconsistent with the policy of ensuring that manufacturers bear the cost of casting defective products into the market. The manufacturer must remain responsible for damages resulting from the defect, regardless of the extent to which other factors contributed to the injuries. . . .

The dissent characterizes the adoption of comparative causation as a major step toward abolishing the doctrine of strict products liability. I find this conclusion to be greatly exaggerated. I doubt that a balanced and properly designed rule on comparative causation will significantly reduce the incentive for manufacturers to produce safe products; indeed, it may increase the incentive. . . .

If comparative principles ever apply in a strict liability case, they should apply here. The jury could find that a number of Bruce Webb's actions or omissions reflected lack of due care for his safety. Some of these actions or omissions do not involve the condition of the tractor and are not related to plaintiffs' liability theory. For example, irrespective of what lighting was available or in use, the jury could find that Bruce Webb was negligent in riding on the draw bar and covering up a reflector and an amber light while the tractor was being operated on a highway. On remand, I would allow at least that determination.

Reversed and remanded.

MORSE, Justice, concurring.

I agree with Justice Dooley that principles of comparative fault should apply to some products liability claims. We disagree, however, on the basis for comparative fault. Justice Dooley believes we should reverse and remand this case for a third trial because the trial judge failed to instruct the jury on comparative causation. I would reverse because on the facts no reasonable juror could find Bruce Webb less than fifty-one percent responsible for the accident, and thus, under 12 V.S.A. §1036 (comparative negligence), judgment would have been entered for defendant.

No matter how the claim is labeled, the 402A claim here is essentially a negligence claim that defendant did not design the tractor carefully enough or warn plaintiff reasonably of the dangers. In any products liability design/warning case, ever since the doctrine was first formulated, the plaintiff has been required to prove that the product was negligently designed or negligently warned. Accordingly, it follows that 12 V.S.A. §1036, our comparative negligence statute, should control. Section 1036 provides in part:

> Contributory negligence shall not bar recovery *in an action* by any plaintiff, or his legal representative, *to recover damages for negligence* resulting in death, personal injury or property damage, if the negligence was not greater than the causal total negligence of the defendant or defendants, but the damage shall be diminished by general verdict in proportion to the amount of negligence attributed to the plaintiff. (Emphasis added.)

The plain language of the statute indicates that it applies in an action to recover damages for negligence. Because plaintiffs' defective design/warning claim is a negligence claim, §1036 must therefore apply. Other courts have similarly applied their comparative negligence statutes to such claims. . . .

If there were such a thing as true "strict liability" whereby a manufacturer is liable for injury no matter how carefully the product is designed and warned for safety, I would agree the comparative negligence statute should not apply. (I have not as yet come across such a cause of action in the product design/warning field.) When a product is defective in the sense it did not turn out as it was intended in the manufacturing process, the manufacturer should be strictly liable for proximate resulting harm. But that is not this case.

Under §1036, recovery is barred if a plaintiff's total negligence is greater than the negligence of the defendant. Applying §1036 in this case, I would reverse the jury verdict and enter judgment for defendant because the evidence showed as a matter of law that [plaintiff's] negligence was greater than the negligence of defendant due to defective design or inadequate warnings. Neither the lighting system of the tractor nor the allegedly inadequate warning against use of the field light on a public road was a significant cause of the accident. Rather, [plaintiff] failed to maintain the flashing lights, and consequently, could not mind the warning decal on the tractor to "use flashing warning lights at all times on public roads." Had the flashing lights worked and been turned on as instructed by the warning, the field light would not have operated. Any deficiency in the lighting system of the tractor was exceedingly minor when compared with plaintiff's failure to keep the flashing lights in working order. Moreover, plaintiff aggravated the situation further by riding on the draw bar and blocking view of the reflective slow-moving-vehicle triangle and the single flashing amber light that may have been working. A reasonable juror would have to conclude that the major fault and cause for the accident was attributable to plaintiff.

Accordingly, I would reverse. . . .

JOHNSON, Justice, dissenting. . . .

I

Justice Dooley and Justice Morse would hold, under varying circumstances, that when a plaintiff alleges injury caused by a defective product, the defendant that produced or distributed the product can reduce or eliminate its liability for damages by showing that the plaintiff's negligent conduct was a contributing cause of the injury. I believe that such a holding would take a major step toward abolition of the doctrine of strict products liability by undermining the principal purpose of the doctrine — to promote the manufacture and distribution of safe products. I see no justification in law, policy, or the facts of this case to extend the doctrine of comparative fault to strict products liability actions.[1]

Notwithstanding assertions to the contrary in Justice Dooley's opinion, my position is followed by a significant number of jurisdictions. 1 A. Best, Comparative Negligence: Law and Practice §9.20[6], at 41-42 (1996) (significant number of jurisdictions continue to reject or limit application of comparative negligence in strict products liability actions); Annotation, Applicability of Comparative Negligence Doctrine to Actions Based on Strict Liability in Tort, 9 A.L.R.4th 633, 638-41 (1981) (reviewing cases in which courts have refused to compare fault); see, e.g., Kinard v. Coats Co., . . . 553 P.2d 835, 837 (Colo. Ct. App. 1976) (better-reasoned position is that comparative negligence has no application to products liability actions); Lippard v. Houdaille Indus., Inc., 715 S.W.2d 491, 493 (Mo. 1986) (en banc) (refusing to apply comparative fault principles to products liability actions); Bowling v. Heil Co., . . . 511 N.E.2d 373, 380 (Ohio 1987) (better-reasoned decisions are those that have declined to inject plaintiff's negligence into law of products liability); Kimco Dev. Corp. v. Michael D's Carpet Outlets, . . . 637 A.2d 603, 605-06 (Pa. 1993) (agreeing with cited jurisdictions refusing to extend negligence concepts to products liability actions).

Further, although a majority of jurisdictions compare fault in products liability actions, that majority is hopelessly divided on when and what to compare and how to implement the comparison. . . . Some courts compare any and every type of contributory negligence, other courts compare only contributory negligence that rises to the level of assumption of risk or unforeseeable misuse, and still others compare all

---

1. For the reasons stated by Justice Dooley, I oppose Justice Morse's position, which would unabashedly return strict products liability actions to the realm of negligence law, at least with respect to warning/design cases.

types of contributory negligence except when the negligence can be labeled as a failure to discover or guard against the risk posed by the defective product. . . .

III

The principal argument for comparing plaintiffs' negligence in products liability actions is couched in terms of fairness. It is fairer to compare, so the argument goes, because the comparison avoids imposing upon manufacturers and careful consumers the costs caused by negligent consumers. But the real issue is whether a higher value should be placed on the deterrence of product defects than is placed on laying the correct amount of blame on the particular actors involved in an accident that was statistically predictable. . . .

Some courts have reasoned that comparing negligence does not greatly affect the incentive to produce safe products because a manufacturer's liability is reduced only to the extent that the trier of fact finds that the user's conduct contributed to the injury, and manufacturers are not able to predict in any given case whether contributory negligence will reduce the plaintiff's judgment. . . . This reasoning does not hold up under scrutiny.

Although manufacturers may not be able to anticipate careless behavior in any given case, they know with virtual certainty that a product will cause a calculable number of accidents, and they will often be able to predict the extent of plaintiffs' negligence by evaluating accidents on a statistical basis. H. Latin, The Preliminary Draft of a Proposed Restatement (Third) of Torts: Products Liability — Letter, 15 J. Prod. & Tox. Liab. 169, 179 (1993); D. Sobelsohn, Comparing Fault, 60 Ind. L.J. 413, 438 (1985). From their calculations, manufacturers can approximate the total liability exposure that those accidents will create, and will then incur increased production costs for safety features only when it makes economic sense to do so. In this way, "the effect of reductions in liability costs as a result of comparative apportionment can make a major difference on the manufacturer's marginal investments in safety." Latin, supra, at 179.

To the extent that product liability would be reduced by comparing plaintiffs' negligence, the incentive to produce safe products would also be reduced. . . . M. Davis, Individual and Institutional Responsibility: A Vision for Comparative Fault in Products Liability, 39 Vill. L. Rev. 281, 344 (1994) (if manufacturers need only compensate those injured during careful use, losses resulting from defective product will never be fully considered in evaluating needed investment in safety). For example, if a particular feature of a product results in accidents costing $1 million, and redesign of the product to eliminate the dangerous feature would cost $900,000, the manufacturer would not have any incentive to redesign the product if the manufacturer could predict that a certain percentage of consumers would negligently contribute to their injuries while using the product, thereby making it cheaper for the manufacturer to pay tort claims rather than redesign the defective product. . . .

We can be certain that, based on statistical accident data and marketing analyses, manufacturers make conscious, calculated choices regarding the safety of their products, choices that are affected by legal principles. If the law provides an economic incentive for a manufacturer to add safety features to a particular product, thousands of people may be spared injury. If, on the other hand, reduced tort damages from comparing plaintiffs' negligence convinces a manufacturer that it would not make economic sense to add safety features to its product, many consumers, including careful ones, may later be injured by the defective product. Assuming that they are able to fend off a defendant's claims of comparative negligence, those careful consumers may obtain full monetary damages, but at the expense of their health or even their lives. This is *not* a fair result. . . .

But there is another important reason why I am persuaded that it is unfair to use comparative principles in strict liability cases. The victim's negligence may be the result of a moment's inattention to some detail, carelessness in a time of crisis, or miscalculation as to the danger involved in using a product a certain way. These types of ordinary negligence, to which all of us fall prey at times, cannot be regarded as equivalent to the manufacturer's responsibility to design safe products and warn the public of dangers that accompany use of their products. . . .

This is where the superficial appeal to fairness falls apart. As a general proposition, we can all agree that each person should bear responsibility for his or her own conduct. It is for this reason that comparative negligence has been accepted as fair in other contexts. But the doctrine of comparative negligence arose in cases where the fault of the parties was of a similar order — carelessness versus carelessness. In strict products liability cases, however, we have fault of very different kinds. The garden-variety carelessness that may contribute to an injury in the use of a product is simply not of the same magnitude as the design, manufacture and release into commerce of a dangerously defective product or a product whose dangers are hidden by inadequate warnings. It is *not* fair, therefore, to treat the two as equivalent. . . .

Plaintiffs who voluntarily assume a known risk should, in my judgment, be barred from recovery. Limiting the assumption-of-risk defense tends to penalize legitimate commercial interests unfairly rather than promote fairness to consumers. Justice Dooley's opinion proclaims that comparing conduct amounting to a voluntary assumption of a known risk benefits consumers, but it undermines the doctrine of strict liability, which provides a powerful incentive for manufacturers and vendors to create and purvey only those products that are safe for everyone. In short, the majority imagines a problem negatively affecting consumers and then creates a cure far worse than the "problem" it seeks to rectify.

Second, while it may not always be easy to distinguish assumption of risk from ordinary contributory negligence, the subjective component of assumption of risk makes the defense qualitatively distinct from other forms of contributory negligence . . . (plaintiff must voluntarily encounter risk despite being subjectively aware of existence of risk and appreciating extent of danger; many courts distinguish assumption of risk from contributory negligence on point that only assumption of risk involves application of subjective standard to plaintiff's conduct); see also Zahrte v. Sturm, Ruger & Co., . . . 661 P.2d 17, 18 (Mont. 1983) (subjective element of assumption of risk makes it distinct from contributory negligence). . . .

In sum, (1) manufacturers have the opportunity to make calculated, informed choices concerning product safety; (2) economic factors and legal principles drive their decisions; (3) those decisions can affect the health and safety of thousands or even millions of people; and (4) enterprises can more easily absorb and equitably pass on to the public the costs of defective products as part of doing business. On the other hand, (1) consumers lack the expertise and information about products possessed by manufacturers; (2) liability law provides no incentive for them to be more careful; (3) their contributory negligence is foreseeable, such that its costs can be equitably spread among all product users; and (4) most importantly, their negligence is simply not equivalent in kind to the act of designing and manufacturing a defective product. For these reasons, there is nothing unfair about imposing full liability on a manufacturer who places in the stream of commerce a defective product that is a proximate cause of the plaintiff's injuries, even if the plaintiff's negligence contributed to those injuries. Products should be designed to protect not only ideal consumers, but also careless, illiterate, ignorant, and inattentive ones as well. . . .

I would affirm the judgment below. I am authorized to say that Justice Gibson joins in my opinion.

Having read *Webb*, how do you come out on the question of reducing plaintiff's recovery based on comparative fault? The dissent's protestation notwithstanding, the overwhelming majority of courts apply comparative fault to products liability claims. Two Restatement projects have endorsed this view. See Restatement of Torts (Third): Products Liability §17 (1998) set forth supra; Restatement of Torts (Third): Apportionment of Liability §1, comment *b* (2000).

The *Webb* dissent correctly points out that some courts refuse to apply comparative fault when the plaintiff's negligence only consists of not discovering the defect. See Murray, supra. See also Star Furniture Co. v. Pulaski Furniture Co., 297 S.E.2d 854, 862 (W.Va. 1982) ("[T]o penalize a consumer for failing to discover defects or to guard against them places a burden on consumers which strict liability was intended to remove."). Alternatively, some courts will only apply comparative fault when the plaintiff's conduct is deemed to constitute assumption of risk. See, e.g., Suter v. San Angelo Foundry & Mach. Co., 406 A.2d 140 (N.J. 1979). However, Suter adds the caveat that this assumption of risk approach does not apply to an employee who is injured in an employment setting, since an employee has no meaningful choice as to whether to work on a machine. Accord McGee v. Stihl Inc., 2011 WL 6130417 (D.N.J. 2011). But these carve-outs are a distinct minority view. Well over 20 states mandate the application of comparative fault to products liability actions and allow for no exceptions to the rule. See, e.g., N.Y. C.P.L.R. §1411 (McKinney 2015); Huffman v. Caterpillar Tractor Co., 908 F.2d 1470 (10th Cir. 1990) (holding that the Colorado comparative fault statute covers all forms of culpable conduct). Both the Products Liability Restatement and the Apportionment Restatement set forth, supra, take the position that courts should not make fine distinctions among various types of plaintiff conduct as a matter of law. Instead, juries should weigh all forms of plaintiff conduct in deciding how much fault to apportion to the parties.

The issues of plaintiff's misuse and product alteration have given rise to inordinate confusion. We will straighten out this mess as best we can. Product misuse and alteration may manifest themselves at three different stages of a products liability case. First, if an injury is caused by the kind of product misuse that cannot reasonably be designed against, then the product is simply not defective. A buzzsaw cannot be rendered reasonably safe for purposes of cutting a child's hair (or anyone's hair, for that matter). See, e.g., Jurado v. Western Gear Works, 619 A.2d 1312 (N.J. 1993).

In the second category, the product is defective, but the fact-finder must evaluate whether the use for which the product was employed was so unreasonable or unforeseeable that the plaintiff has not met his burden of showing proximate cause. In these cases, the issue should be whether the plaintiff has established a prima facie case. See, e.g., Smith v. Louis Berkman Co., 894 F. Supp. 1084, 1091 (W.D. Ky. 1995); White v. Caterpillar, Inc., 867 P.2d 100, 107-08 (Colo. Ct. App. 1993) (upholding misuse instruction where the misuse, rather than the defect, caused the injury; however, the court noted that misuse is not an absolute bar if the manufacturer could have reasonably anticipated the consumer's misuse); Reott v. Asia Trend, Inc., 55 A.3d 1088, 1090 (Pa. 2012) (finding manufactures can raise affirmative defense that highly reckless conduct in use of product was "the sole or superseding cause of the injuries sustained"); but see Kenser v. Premium Nail Concepts, Inc., 338 P.3d 37 (Mont. 2014) (ruling defendant could not invoke misuse as defense given foreseeability of the harm-causing use).

In the third category of misuse, the plaintiff's misuse or modification of the product contributes — along with the defect in the defendant's product — to causing the harm. Usually, these cases are submitted for comparative fault allocation, which results in a reduction of damages. In Jimenez v. Sears, Roebuck & Co., 904 P.2d 861 (Ariz. 1995), the plaintiff bought an electric disc grinder, read the manual, checked to see if the machine was working properly, and proceeded to use the tool. After 45 minutes, the disc shattered, injuring the plaintiff Jimenez. Jimenez was familiar with the type of tool and disregarded a suggestion in the manual to wear a leather apron. The defendant alleged that the plaintiff also must have turned the safety guard away from him during the tool's operation. The court held that, under Arizona's comparative fault statute, misuse was an apportionable contributing cause rather than a bar to recovery when it was a concurrent cause of the plaintiff's harm. See also Weigle v. SPX Corp., 729 F.3d 724, 739 (7th Cir. 2013) ("Misuse is not a complete defense but is considered an aspect of comparative fault."); States v. R.D. Werner Co., 799 P.2d 427 (Colo. Ct. App. 1990); Standard Havens Prods., Inc. v. Benitez, 648 So. 2d 1192, 1197 (Fla. 1994) ("[P]roduct misuse reduces a plaintiff's recovery in proportion to his or her own comparative fault."); Barnard v. Saturn Corp., 790 N.E.2d 1023 (Ind. Ct. App. 2003) (holding that plaintiff's misuse of car jack should be taken into account under principles of comparative fault, but should not serve as a complete bar to recovery).

A considerable body of literature has grown up around the subject of comparative fault and its applicability to products litigation. See, e.g., Mary J. Davis, Individual and Institutional Responsibility: A Vision for Comparative Fault in Products Liability, 39 Vill. L. Rev. 281 (1994); Dix Noel, Defective Products: Abnormal Use, Contributory Negligence, and Assumption of Risk, 25 Vand. L. Rev. 93, 117-18 (1972) (arguing contributory negligence should diminish plaintiff's damages); Richard C. Henke, Comparative Fault in Products Liability: Comparing California and New Jersey, 19 T.M. Cooley L. Rev. 301 (2002).

SOCIAL CONTROL OF PRODUCT-RELATED ACCIDENTS: THE SEAT BELT DEFENSE AND GOVERNMENTAL CONTROL OF DRIVERS' BEHAVIOR

As of 2015, all states except New Hampshire have passed some form of Mandatory Seat Belt Use Laws (MULS). The seat belt defense has often been a serious topic of debate. Auto manufacturers contend that, even if they have contributed to causing the plaintiff's injury through a vehicle defect, the plaintiff co-authored the injury by failing to buckle up. Many jurisdictions have addressed this issue through statute. The seat belt statutes break down into four categories:

(1) *Failure to wear a seat belt cannot reduce recovery.* Illinois specifically provides that "failure to wear a seat belt shall not be considered evidence of

negligence, shall not limit the liability of an insurer, and shall not diminish any recovery for damages arising out of . . . operation of a motor vehicle.'' 625 Ill. Comp. Stat. 5/12-603.1(c) (2015). Similar statutes have been enacted in many other states (e.g., Connecticut, Georgia, Idaho, Kansas, Louisiana, Maryland, Massachusetts, Montana, Nevada, New Mexico, North Carolina, North Dakota, Oklahoma, Pennsylvania, Washington, and Wyoming).

(2) *Failure to wear a seat belt may be used to reduce recovery.* The New York statute provides that failure to wear a seat belt may be introduced into evidence in order to reduce (but not bar) recovery N.Y. Veh. & Traf. Law §1229-c(8) (McKinney 2015). In Colorado, only awards for pain and suffering can be reduced through the seat belt defense, but not awards for economic loss or medical payments. Colo. Rev. Stat. §42-4-237(7) (2015).

(3) *Reduction is permitted, subject to a cap.* Statutes in Iowa, Michigan, Missouri, and Oregon allow for reduction of damages based on the failure to wear a seat belt, but that reduction is capped by statute. Iowa Code §321.445.4(b)(2) (instituting a 5 percent damage reduction cap); Mich. Comp. Laws §257.710e(7) (5 percent cap); Mo. Rev. Stat. §307.178(4)(2) (1 percent); Or. Rev. Stat. §31.760(1) (5 percent); W.Va. Code §17C-15-49(d) (5 percent). Given the low percentage limits in these jurisdictions, it may be hardly worth the cost of hiring a defense expert to testify that the failure to wear a seat belt aggravated the injury.

(4) *Reduction is only permitted in products liability cases.* Perhaps somewhat bizarrely, several states only allow seat belt evidence in crashworthiness cases. See, e.g., Ark. Code Ann. §27-37-703(a); Ind. Stat. Ann. §9-19-10-7(c); Tenn. Code Ann. §55-9-604(a).

However, the Restatement (Third) of Torts: Apportionment of Liability §3 (2000) takes a radically different position from the prevailing view. The Restatement says that the factfinder should consider the plaintiff's conduct in failing to wear a seat belt when assigning percentages of responsibility.

d. The Crashworthiness Imbroglio: Should Fault Be Compared with Enhanced Injury

Wolf v. Toyota Motor Corporation
2013 WL 6596833 (Del. Sup. Ct. 2013)

COOCH, R.J.

I. INTRODUCTION

These motions stem from a tragic accident which resulted in the deaths of three members of the Ward family: father John, wife Joy, and daughter Sarah. On the morning of August 23, 2009, the Ward family was involved in a head-on collision on SR 30 in Sussex County when Darien Custis (''Custis''), driving a 1994 Mercedes–Benz owned by John F. Warfield (''Warfield''), was distracted by reaching for a bottle of iced tea on the car's floor. The sole survivor in the Ward's Toyota was 8 year old daughter Hailey. Custis was essentially unhurt in the accident and later pled guilty to vehicular homicides involving John, Joy, and Sarah. Natalie Wolf, as the Administratrix of the Ward family estates and Guardian and Next Friend of Hailey, filed a "crashworthiness" products liability claim against the Toyota Defendants. . . . Plaintiffs claim that defects in the Toyota Camry driven by the Wards "enhanced" their injuries. Plaintiffs elected not to include Custis or Warfield as defendants in their complaint. The claim against Warfield is that of negligent entrustment. . . . The Toyota Defendants filed a motion requesting leave to join Custis and Warfield as third-party defendants under Superior Court Civil Rule 14(a). For the reasons set forth below, the Court's Order of . . . denying the Toyota Defendants' Motion for Leave to File a Third-Party Complaint is vacated. . . .

This Court is not the first to consider, in a "crashworthiness" claim, "whether to isolate the action against the motor vehicle manufacturer for this individual defect and the injury alleged to be caused by the defect, or to allow a jury to hear all of the evidence regarding how the accident happened in the first place." Two distinct and opposite conclusions have been reached across the United States:

> The majority view holds that a manufacturer's fault in causing enhanced injuries may be reduced by the fault of those (*i.e.,* the plaintiff or third parties) who caused the initial collision. The minority position, by contrast, maintains that because a manufacturer is solely responsible for its product's defects, it should also be solely liable for the enhanced injuries caused by those defects.

A. The "Majority View"

The apparent majority of courts addressing whether to consider the circumstances of the initial collision hold that concurrent causation and comparative fault apply in "crashworthiness" claims:

> "[A] plaintiff may still recover against a manufacturer for the enhanced injury caused by the product defect, but evidence is permitted as to the cause of the initial impact and injuries in addition to the defect and enhanced injuries, and the jury is tasked with apportioning fault to each responsible party for the damages proximately caused by that party."
>
> "The majority view recognizes that jurors are asked everyday to consider the complex issues of contributory/comparative negligence and proximate cause and there is no reason to change what we ask them to do simply because the case involves a question of enhanced injury."
>
> Over twenty states and the RESTATEMENT (THIRD) OF TORTS: PRODUCTS LIABILITY allow fault of the plaintiff or a defendant other than the manufacturer to be considered in a "crashworthiness" claim. Multiple cases and law review articles include Delaware in that list, citing the 1997 Delaware Superior Court case of *Meekins v. Ford Motor Company*.

B. The "Minority View"

The apparent minority view [as set forth in D'Amario v. Ford Motor Co.] holds it is "impermissible" in "crashworthiness" claims "to allow the fact finder to compare the fault or negligence of the plaintiff and other potentially liable parties and nonparties in causing the accident with the fault or negligence of the manufacturer in designing or manufacturing a motor vehicle.'' This view holds that the accident is essentially divided into two impacts and two separate causes of action: the accident itself and a second subsequent collision resulting from the vehicle's design. The minority view holds that any ''comparative negligence of the plaintiff and other third party tortfeasors in causing the accident is deemed irrelevant and inadmissible'' and juries are restricted from hearing it. ''In essence, the trial snapshot of evidence . . . begin[s] at the instant the crash or accident ha[s] occurred.''

C. Delaware Law: Meekins v. Ford Motor Company . . .

The apparent single case in Delaware law that addresses the issue of whether a jury should consider all the circumstances of a collision where enhanced injury damages are sought is *Meekins*. *Meekins* was a ''crashworthiness'' claim in which the plaintiff sustained injury when an airbag, deployed as a result of a collision, crushed his fingers against the steering wheel. Plaintiff contended the injury was a result of a defectively designed airbag. Defendant Ford contended the injury was a result of ''the violent turning of the steering wheel engendered by the collision,'' charging the plaintiff with contributory negligence. The late Superior Court Judge N. Maxson Terry, Jr. held in *Meekins* that a plaintiff's negligence should be considered when apportioning fault in a ''crashworthiness'' claim:

> Our tort law has historically recognized the fact that there may be more than one prox-imate cause of an injury. Jurors have had no difficulty in apportioning fault equitably between multiple parties where negligent conduct is the proximate cause of injuries. The existence of other proximate causes of an injury does not relieve a plaintiff driver under Delaware's comparative negligence statute from responsibility for his own conduct which proximately caused him injury. Further, I can discern no policy reason why, in an enhanced injury case, the rule should be any different. Public policy seeks to deter not only manufacturers from producing a defective product but to encourage those who use the product to do so in a responsible manner.

The *Meekins* court also held that:

> ''[it] is obvious that the negligence of a plaintiff who causes the initial collision is one of the proximate causes of all of the injuries he sustained, whether limited to those the original collision would have produced or including those enhanced by a defective prod-uct in the second collision.''

The *Meekins* court also discussed, although in *dicta,* that the negligence of all possible negligent parties should be considered, and presented a hypothetical much like the case at bar:

> But what if a plaintiff collides with another vehicle and the driver of that vehicle is negligent? Assume also that the enhanced injuries caused to the plaintiff by a design defect in his car are clearly identifiable. Under ordinary rules of proximate cause the other driver would have potential liability for all of the plaintiff's injuries, but logically, following the enhanced injury theory of the plaintiff, only the manufacturer should have the liability because the other driver's conduct in causing the initial collision would not have caused the injury absent the design defect. Thus, carrying the theory to its logical conclusion, plaintiff should have no recovery against the other driver for his

negligence in causing the collision. This result would run counter to well settled principles of tort law.

D. The Majority Rule Approach Is the Better Reasoned Approach: Manufacturer Defendants in a "Crashworthiness" Claim May File a Third-Party Complaint Against Original Tortfeasor to Allow for Proper Allocation of Fault and to Present a More Complete Account of the Accident to the Jury.

Before deciding to adopt the majority rule and now allowing the original tortfeasors to be joined as third-party defendants in the case, this Court considered the policy arguments for and against both approaches to this issue. Some majority view proponents contend that the jury should be able to consider all of the facts when determining a claim. There is a concern from majority view proponents that the minority view serves as "a shield preventing the admissibility of clearly relevant and material accident fact evidence, particularly driver intoxication evidence, thereby creating litigation predicated on less than complete facts concerning the causes of the claimed injuries and damages." In other products liability proceedings, juries are expected to listen to and to make determinations about long and complicated testimony about which they may have no prior experience, yet in "crashworthiness" products liability claims minority view courts have concluded that juries are unable to handle this task due to a risk of "confusion." Some majority rule proponents contend any issues of jury confusion or prejudice could be mitigated by the "tools" already available to the judge. They also argue the minority view undermines the great responsibility for truth-seeking placed on jurors in our court system. . . .

Apportionment is another issue some majority rule supporters argue is better addressed by the majority approach. They maintain that comparative fault systems are often meant for the fact finder to "hear evidence regarding all potential proximate causes of injury and apportion responsibility accordingly." If under the minority view the accident is treated as two separate sets of collisions and injuries, there are additional majority concerns of how to properly allocate fault when an injury, such as death, is determined "indivisible." Many proponents of the majority view argue that states have comparative fault statutes that are broad enough that the jury, even considering evidence of the initial crash, could find that the "entire injury was caused by the defect, or that a specific injury would not have been caused but for the defect." . . .

Numerous proponents of the minority view are likewise concerned about apportionment, but they argue that asking jurors to apportion fault between an original tortfeasor and the manufacturer causes "cognitive dissonance" that prejudices plaintiffs. They caution that the majority view's deterrent for negligent drivers may go too far, to the point of burying the liability of a manufacturer under the morally reprehensible behavior of another party. This is especially a concern when accidents include intoxicated drivers. Some articles claim that jurors are just not able to look beyond an intoxicated driver to properly assess manufacturer liability. "Given that the law already punishes the socially reprehensible misconduct of drunk drivers, good public policy should not allow the manufacturer to escape its share of liability for exacerbated injuries suffered by the plaintiff." . . .

The Court is persuaded in this case that the majority rule is the better reasoned approach to the issue at bar. As stated above, practical issues of apportionment are better resolved by allowing the Toyota Defendants to file a third-party claim against the original tortfeasors. . . . This Court respects the difficult responsibility placed on jurors in these cases and thinks that, if jurors can determine the facts and apportion fault in other types of claims, they should be able to do the same in a "crashworthiness" case. This view is consistent with *Meekins,* the only Delaware case addressing this issue. This Court thus aligns itself with the majority of states on this issue, noting also that Delaware law provides that there can be more than one proximate cause of Plaintiffs' injuries.

VI. CONCLUSION

The trial courts orders denying Motion for Leave to File a Third–Party Complaint is vacated.

A strong majority of jurisdictions agree that comparative fault applies even in crashworthiness cases. See, e.g., Dannenfelser v. Daimler Chrysler Corp., 370 F. Supp. 2d 1091 (D. Haw. 2005); Quinton v. Toyota Motor Corp., 2013 WL2470083 at *2 (D.S.C. 2013); Gartman v. Ford Motor Co., 430 S.W.2d 215, 220 (Ark. Ct. App. 2013); Jahn v. Hyundai Motor Co., 773 N.W.2d 550 (Iowa 2009) (overruling previous decisions to the contrary and adopting Products Liability Restatement §16, including comment *f*); Davis v. Daimler Chrysler Co., 2009 WL 323428 (Conn. Sup.) (plaintiff's comparative negligence in causing the initial collision is a proper issue in a crashworthiness case; court adopts Products Liability Restatement §16 comment *f*).

In Egbert v. Nissan Motor Ltd., 228 P.3d 737 (Utah 2010), the Court was faced with the question as to whether there should be fault apportionment between the negligence of a driver who caused the accident and the auto manufacturer whose car was not adequately crashworthy. The injuries to the plaintiff were single and indivisible. The Court held that because Utah had abolished joint and several liability a jury must be instructed to apportion fault between the defendant-driver and the auto manufacturer. The Court said that Products Liability Restatement did not directly address this issue in §16. The authors believe that §16, Illustration 8 does speak to the issue and is in full agreement with the Utah court's decision. For a thoughtful discussion of this issue see Ellen M. Bublick, The Tort-Proof Plaintiff: The Drunk in the Automobile, Crashworthiness Claims, and *the Restatement (Third) of Torts*, 74 Brook. L. Rev. 707 (2009).

e.   Should Plaintiff's Fault Be Compared with Defendant's Breach of Express or Implied Warranty?

In the pre-comparative fault era when contributory negligence was a complete bar, courts were reluctant to recognize contributory negligence as a defense to an express warranty action. In Bahlman v. Hudson Motor Co., 288 N.W. 309 (Mich. 1939), plaintiff purchased a car relying on the representation that the roof was rugged and was made from a single sheet of steel. Plaintiff was injured when, due to his negligence, the car turned over. A jagged edge of the roof lacerated his head. As the accident demonstrated, those representations that the roof was rugged and made from a single steel sheet were false. The court held that the auto manufacturer's representations were not only relevant to non-negligent accidents and thus refused to recognize contributory negligence as a defense. Now that comparative negligence has removed the threat of plaintiff fault operating as a total bar, courts appear willing to entertain comparative fault as a defense to personal injury actions based on express warranty. In this vein, the Restatement (Third) of Torts: Apportionment of Liability §1(b) endorses across-the-board applicability of comparative fault to all tort actions regardless of the theory on which the cause of action is predicated. Other cases are in accord. See, e.g., Trishan Air, Inc. v. Dassault Falcon Jet Corp., 532 Fed App'x 784 (9th Cir. 2013) (applying California's comparative fault statute to express warranty actions); Lougbridge v. Goodyear Tire & Rubber Co., 207 F. Supp. 2d 1187 (D. Colo. 2002) (applying Colorado's comparative fault statute to an express warranty claim).

As to whether comparative fault should apply to products liability cases brought under the U.C.C. §2-314 (breach of implied warranty of merchantability), courts agree that the same comparative fault principles that apply to strict liability in tort apply to the implied warranty as well. See JCW Electronics v. Garza, 257 S.W.3d 701, 707 (Tex. 2008).

f. No Duty/Primary Assumption of Risk: Reintroducing Plaintiff's Conduct as a Total Bar

One form of contributory fault — assumption of risk — may still operate as a total bar to a plaintiff's products liability claim. You will remember from first-year Torts that many courts draw a distinction between what they call "primary assumption of the risk," which operates as a no-duty rule negating liability entirely, and "secondary assumption of the risk," which is a form of contributory fault and usually only reduces the plaintiff's damages. At some level the no-duty analysis is clearly appropriate. For example, if a person asks a neighbor to borrow the family car and the neighbor responds, "You're welcome to use it but you should know that the brakes are dangerous," liability should not be imposed on the neighbor when the brakes fail and the borrower is injured. The owner of the car has fulfilled his responsibility to the borrower by disclosing the risk. Whether the borrower acted voluntarily or under the compulsion of personal need is of no moment. The car owner has no duty to rescue the borrower from the implications of his own choice to use the car and take his chances. In such a case the car owner should bear no liability, and comparative negligence should play no role. Similarly, a baseball park will generally not be held liable for injuries suffered by a fan sitting outside of the screened-in portion of the field. The risks of fast-moving foul balls are well known and the costs (both monetary and nonmonetary) attendant to screening the entire ball field are high. A court would be justified in holding as a matter of law that the owner of the ball field did not breach a duty to spectators. Akins v. Glens Falls City School District, 424 N.E.2d 531 (N.Y. 1981).

When contributory negligence and assumption of the risk were total bars it mattered little whether the terminology used to describe the "no-recovery" result was no duty, no breach, assumption of the risk, or even "the XYZ syndrome." Now that courts and legislatures have assimilated contributory negligence and assumption of the risk into comparative negligence, the nomenclature matters a great deal. Characterizing the case as one in which there is "no duty" will absolve the defendant from liability, whereas labeling it as an affirmative defense may well mean that the plaintiff will recover a reduced verdict. See Turcotte v. Fell, 502 N.E.2d 964, 967 (N.Y. 1986); Benejam v. Detroit Tigers, Inc., 246 Mich. App. 645 (Mich. Ct. App. 2001).

Whether a given fact pattern is weighty enough to trigger a no-duty analysis is not self-evident. Most courts are reluctant to find primary assumption of the risk. As the Court noted in Keller v. CNH America, LLC., 2009 WL 1766695 (D. Minn. 2009), "the defendant pleading primary assumption of the risk must demonstrate that by proceeding with the activity, the plaintiff intended to relieve the defendant of any duty to protect against a risk that was inherent, obvious and unavoidable." But some courts seem more ready to bar the plaintiff entirely on highly questionable facts.

Green v. Allendale Planting Co. & the KBH Corp.
954 So. 2d 1032 (Miss. 2007)

EASLEY, J.

This case is an action for damages for personal injuries brought by Larry Green (Green) in the Circuit Court of Bolivar County against KBH Corporation (KBH) for injuries he sustained while attempting to determine the cause of an unusual noise he heard while operating a mule boy, owned by his employer, Allendale, and manufactured by KBH. . . .

Allendale purchased the mule boy in question from KBH approximately three to four weeks prior to Green's accident.[2] Allendale did not make any modifications to the mule boy and had not experienced any problems with it. Although it was Green's first cotton season operating the mule boy, he was an experienced farm hand. Green had operated various farm implements that could be attached to tractors such as cultivators, plows, bush hogs, disks, and grain carts. Moreover, Green had been employed at Allendale for approximately twelve years before the accident.

On September 28, 2001, the day of the accident, Green was operating the mule boy when he heard a loud, unusual noise coming from the back of the mule. Green left the mule boy running and stepped down from the tractor. In order to determine the exact cause of the noise, Green knelt down in close proximity to the four metering chains. Green lost his balance. In an attempt to reestablish his balance, Green's hand came into contact with the moving chains, and he lost three fingers. [Plaintiff brought suit against KBH alleging failure to warn about the dangers attendant to use of the mule boy and defective design based on the absence of a safety guard that would have prevented his injuries.]

---

2. According to KBH, a mule boy is a tractor-pulled and powered farm implement manufactured by KBH designed to receive cotton from a cotton picker in the field and then transport it to module builders. After a cotton picker's bin is full, the cotton is dumped from the cotton picker's bin into the mule boy's basket. The mule boy's hydraulic system lifts the basket above the module builder and tilts it into a dumping position so that the cotton can be transferred into the module builder for compacting. When the mule boy is elevated to the dumping position, there are four sets of metering chains connected with "chain slat" crossbars which are designed to allow an exact amount of cotton to be unloaded into the module builder. The metering chains rotate around what is the mule boy's lower side when raised and activated, and the cotton is deposited in a controlled manner by the tractor driver into the module builder below.

[T]he trial court concluded that there was no genuine issue of material fact regarding whether he voluntarily and deliberately exposed himself to a dangerous condition. The court further held that Green's own testimony established that his actions were deliberate and voluntary. Green voluntarily knelt down next to the moving chains, with the knowledge that they were dangerous. His actions were sufficient to indicate acceptance of the dangerous condition. . . .

The trial court granted summary judgment in favor of KBH, finding that KBH established a complete defense to Green's failure to warn and defective design claims brought pursuant to the M.P.L.A. . . .

Miss. Code Ann. §11-1-63(d) (Rev. 2002) precludes liability for defective design when the plaintiff assumes the risk of his injuries. Subsection (d) provides:

> In any action alleging that a product is defective pursuant to paragraph (a) of this section, the manufacturer or seller shall not be liable if the claimant (i) had knowledge of a condition of the product that was inconsistent with his safety; (ii) *appreciated the danger in the condition*; and (iii) *deliberately and voluntarily chose to expose himself to the danger* in such a manner to register assent on the continuance of the dangerous condition.

(Emphasis added.)

Assumption of the risk applies where a person *freely and voluntarily* chose to encounter a dangerous condition. Elias v. New Laurel Radio Station, 245 Miss. 170, 179, 146 So. 2d 558, 561 (1962). "Assumption of risk arises from a mental state of willingness, or a mental state approaching consent." Id. The Court defined the doctrine of assumed risk as follows:

> On the applicability of the doctrine of assumed risk, incurred risk, etc., 65 C.J.S., Negligence, Sec. 174, p. 849 states: "Accordingly, it has been held to be the rule, generally referred to as the doctrine of assumption of risk, and sometimes referred to as the doctrine of 'incurred risk,' or 'taking the risk or hazard,' or 'running the risk,' that one who voluntarily exposed himself or his property to a known and appreciated danger due to the negligence of another may not recover for injuries sustained thereby, even though he was in the exercise of ordinary care or even of the utmost care. Corollaries of this rule are that to acquiesce in, or consent to, a course of negligent conduct is to assume the risks incident thereto, *that one having a choice of reasonably convenient ways assumes the risk of a dangerous one, and that one who voluntarily attempts a rash, imprudent, and dangerous undertaking is to be presumed to have assumed the risk incidental thereto.*
>
> "The doctrine, accordingly, can apply only where a person may reasonably elect whether or not he shall expose himself to a particular danger; and it has no application where a continued exposure to risk is due to a lack of reasonable opportunity to escape after the danger is appreciated, or is the result of influence, circumstances, or surroundings which are a real inducement to continue. Thus, if plaintiff surrendered his better judgment on an assurance of safety or a promise of protection he did not assume the risk unless the danger was so obvious and so extreme that there could be no reasonable reliance on the assurance."
>
> No person can assume a risk that he does not know exists.

Id. at 178-79 (emphasis added).

Often the question of whether the plaintiff appreciated and understood the risk is a question of fact for the jury, however, "in certain circumstances the facts may show as a matter of law that the plaintiff understood and appreciated the danger." Herod v. Grant, 262 So. 2d 781, 783 (Miss. 1972). "However, in the absence of evidence that the injured person knew of the danger, or that the danger was so obvious that he must be taken to have known of it, it cannot be held that he assumed the risk of injury therefrom.'' Id. The Court held:

> The elements that must be found in order to constitute a defense of assumption of risk are generally stated in some such terms as the following: (1) [k]nowledge on the part of the injured party of a condition inconsistent with his safety; (2) appreciation by the injured party of the danger in the condition; and (3) a deliberate and voluntary choice on the part of the injured party to expose his person to that danger in such a manner as to register assent on the continuance of the dangerous condition.

Id. at 782.

. . .

Here, Green admitted in his deposition testimony that he had knowledge and appreciated the dangerous condition of the mule boy. Green testified that the chains could be seen moving when the mule boy was running. In fact, he stated that ''anybody could see the chains moving.'' The mule boy operated by a piece of metal running between four sets of chains. The tractor had to be turned on for the chains to move. Green testified that there was nothing wrong with the mule boy. In fact, he stated that the mule boy was new. Green testified that when using any piece of farm equipment, he used his common sense. Green testified that he was aware that farm equipment, especially a piece of equipment with a moving part, can be dangerous. Green testified that he was aware that the chains were moving and the tractor was running when he went to look at the mule boy.

Green takes issue with the trial court's finding that he voluntarily and deliberately approached the dangerous condition. Nothing was presented to the trial court that indicated that Green was instructed or encouraged to get near the mule boy's moving chains. When Green got off the tractor, he did not turn the mule boy off before approaching it. Green does not allege that the on/off switch was defective or failed to operate. He simply failed to turn off the machine before getting near it. Green clearly testified that the tractor was still on and the chains were still moving when he approached the mule boy. Green testified that he was not trying to repair the mule boy.

Green conceded that he was aware that the machine was dangerous. Green testified in his deposition that he knew if he got too close, he would be pulled into the moving chains. Yet, he ignored the danger and approached the running mule boy. Green testified that he lost his balance when he tried to squat down; he then slipped. When he tried to keep from falling, he put out his hand to catch himself. His hand was grabbed by the machine, and he was injured.

Here, the record reveals from Green's deposition that he understood and appreciated the danger. Further, the moving chains were open and obvious to Green. Green proceeded to approach the mule boy without first turning off the machine, even though he appreciated that it was a dangerous situation. The trial court was correct in granting summary judgment in favor of KBH.

We find that the trial court did not err in granting summary judgment in favor of . . . the KBH Corporation. Therefore, the judgment of the Circuit Court of Bolivar County, Mississippi, is affirmed in toto.

. . .

DISSENT: GRAVES, J.

. . .

The majority erroneously concludes that KBH established an affirmative defense to Green's defective design claims. "Assumption of the risk is [most often] a jury question in all but the clearest of cases." Daves v. Reed, 222 So. 2d 411, 415 (Miss. 1969) (omitting citations). Nevertheless, the majority contends that the danger of coming in close contact with the moving chains was so obvious that the trial court could conclude as a matter of law that Green assumed the risk of his injuries, by deliberately and voluntarily exposing himself to a known danger. Green accidently fell and injured his hand. He did not voluntarily expose himself to a known danger. A jury question exists as to whether Green's injuries were the result of KBH's failure to install a safety guard to cover the metering chains.

The majority correctly asserts that Green was aware of the danger of coming in close contact with the moving chains attached to the mule boy. However, the majority erroneously concludes that Green's failure to turn off the mule boy before approaching it was an indication that he voluntarily and deliberately chose to expose himself to a dangerous condition.

Although Green placed himself in close proximity to the moving chains attached to the mule boy, he did not deliberately and voluntarily choose to place his hand inside the machine. Green's hand got caught in the machine when he accidently fell. Therefore, a jury question exists as to whether Green's injuries were the result of the acts or omissions of KBH and its failure to install a safety guard to cover the metering chains. The affidavits of Green's expert, Robert T. Tolbert, and the OSHA regulations raise a fact question as to whether Green's injuries may have potentially been prevented by attaching a safety guard over the moving chains. See also Lenoir v. Porter, 672 F.2d 1240, 1245 (5th Cir. 1980) (holding a jury question existed as to whether the employee's hand would have gotten caught in the machine if the limit bar had been present). Accordingly, I would reverse and remand the grant of summary judgment in favor of KBH back to the trial court for a decision on the merits.

Mississippi continues to read its assumption of risk statute broadly. In McSwain v. Sunrise Medical, Inc., 689 F. Supp. 2d 835 (S.D. Miss. 2010), plaintiff purchased a custom-made wheelchair that was delivered without anti-tip tubes. Plaintiff was barred from recovery when the wheelchair tipped causing injury. He was aware that the wheelchair needed the anti-tip tubes and unsuccessfully attempted to install them from his old wheelchair; his knowledge of risk constituted assumption of risk. See also Smith v. Cent. Mine Equip. Co., 559 Fed App'x 679 (10th Cir. 2014) (applying Okla. Law) (employee's continued use of defectively designed drill rig warranted summary judgment; employee was fully aware of danger).

Several jurisdictions do not permit comparative fault as a defense to strict liability but do recognize assumption of the risk as an absolute bar. Thus, unlike the majority of states that have assimilated assumption of the risk into comparative fault, these courts must make the hard call whether the plaintiff's conduct fulfills the requisites of assumption of the risk. Two cases from Ohio and Pennsylvania on almost identical fact patterns exemplify the problem. Zigler v. Avco Corp., 846 N.E.2d 547 (Ohio Ct. App. 2005); Hadar v. Avco Corp., 886 A.2d 225 (Pa. Super. Ct. 2005). In both cases,

Authors' dialogue 9

JIM: Aaron, I know that you have long favored an independent role for assumption of the risk, separate and apart from the no-duty analysis. My own view is that there is no reason to keep assumption of the risk around. In cases where primary assumption of the risk would bar the plaintiff's claim, a no-duty analysis can do the job. I see no need to have two doctrines where one will do.

AARON: You know, Jim, I have come around to your way of thinking. In fact, I have begun to consider the possibility that, at least in products cases, even your no-duty analysis should not entirely bar recovery. We should simply compare the conduct of the plaintiff with the defendant's defect and apportion fault under comparative negligence or comparative responsibility.

JIM: Goodness, Aaron. You have made a one-hundred-and-eighty-degree change in your thinking. What prompts you to take the position that primary assumption of the risk or no-duty should play no role in products liability cases?

DOUG: Before you answer, Aaron, I will throw in my two cents. The no-duty analysis — including primary assumption of risk — has a role in products liability. To understand why, we need look no further than the *Blankenship* case discussed two pages below. While I sympathize with the 'bungee bouncer's unfortunate plight, it is hard to argue that he should recover a single cent from the crane manufacturer. Such meritless claims should be killed in the cradle through primary assumption of risk, ideally in summary judgment motions. However, the role for no-duty/primary assumption of risk should be circumscribed in the products liability context for the same reasons that products liability arose doctrinally in the first place. In terms of product-related decision-making and information, consumers are severely disadvantaged relative to manufacturers. It is thus necessarily more difficult for consumers to make informed risk assumptions with products as opposed to other tort contexts. Accordingly, cases like *Green* are entirely inappropriate for no-duty/primary assumption of risk.

AARON: Interesting — I still disagree, though. Think of your classic cases of primary assumption of risk: the passenger who voluntarily gets into the car with a drunk driver or a friend who borrows a car after being told that the car's steering mechanism is broken. In both cases, those doctrines would deny plaintiff any recovery. The relationship between the plaintiff and the defendant — the defendants in these examples being the drunk driver and the car-lending friend rather than the car manufacturers — is such that it is sensible to say that the plaintiff has expressly relieved the defendant of the normal obligations that the defendant would otherwise owe. In the products context, however, the defendant manufactures a defective product. Does it make sense to say that the plaintiff, by her conduct, relieves the defendant of obligations to her with regard to the defect? If the plaintiff were to say to the drunk driver "I want to ride with you but I insist that you drink two cups of coffee," defendant may respond by saying, "Get lost. You take me as I am. If not, you can walk to your destination." In the products case, however, there is no discourse, no options offered. That is what leads me to reject your position, Doug. The user may have choices other than being forced to use the product in its dangerous state, but I do not see the user relieving the defendant of its responsibility for making a defective product.

JIM: Oh, no, Aaron. There are cases of primary assumption of the risk that operate similarly with respect to products. For example, if I leave a box of dangerous firecrackers out in the park and mark them with a sign saying, "Danger — Explosive Fireworks," I may be liable to a child who plays with the fireworks and gets hurt. But if you, an adult, come along and say, "I want to play with the fireworks, I'll take my chances," then you should be barred by primary assumption of the risk.

DOUG: I don't necessarily agree with that specific example, Jim, but I do agree with the broader concept. There are some misuses that involve so much self-imposed, unforeseeable, and unpreventable risk-taking that primary assumption of risk (or a no-duty analysis — in my view, these two terms are getting at the same thing, with the former as a subspecies of the latter) is appropriate. I buy into some of your reasoning, Aaron, but I don't go as far with it.

AARON: My approach would be the most straightforward. Getting rid of the no-duty rule, including primary assumption of risk, will simplify things without changing many outcomes. Even without the no-duty analysis, the plaintiff will likely be totally barred and, if not, her recovery will be dramatically reduced. In cases that would otherwise fall within the rubric of no-duty/primary assumption of the risk, plaintiffs are likely to be denied recovery because the defect is not the proximate cause of the harm. Moreover, plaintiffs still have to surmount the hurdle, in two-thirds of the states, of modified comparative fault. A plaintiff whose assumption of risk is so clear that a court would free the defendant of liability on no-duty grounds is not likely to be treated with mercy by a jury. They would almost certainly find her fault to be more than 50 percent, thereby barring recovery completely. The only problem left is that some jurisdictions have pure comparative fault. In some cases, a plaintiff might recover 10 or 20 percent of the total verdict. Big deal. That's a small price to pay for simplicity. All products liability cases should go to juries on comparative fault.

JIM: I can't believe what you just said. You have not only abandoned assumption of risk, but you now take the position that clear no-duty cases should go to juries. I just think you're wrong. It is the function of courts to make the call in clear no-duty cases.

inexperienced workers were operating mechanized corn pickers. In the process they encountered clogging of the machines. In order to unclog the machines, operators are instructed to turn off the power and remove the debris (usually corn husks) by hand. Instead of turning the power off, the operators pulled on some corn husks, hoping that this would unclog the machines. The chains of the machines pulled the corn husks and the plaintiffs' arms into the machine causing serious damage to both plaintiffs. Plaintiffs alleged design and failure to warn against the defendant-manufacturers of the corn pickers. In both cases, trial judges granted the defendants' motion of summary judgment and in both cases the appellate courts reversed. Given the relative inexperience of the operators and the fact that they were not touching the corn picker itself but were in contact only with the corn husks, there were legitimate questions of fact as to whether they had adequate knowledge of the risk that their arms would be sucked into the corn pickers.

Mississippi applies comparative fault to strict products liability cases. The wisdom of the legislature in enacting assumption of risk as an absolute bar is questionable. *Green* seems to call for comparative fault rather than primary assumption of risk. It is difficult to believe that plaintiff sought to relieve the defendant-manufacturer of the mule boy of its obligation to properly guard the exposed chains of the machine. For a case holding that primary assumption of the risk is inappropriate when plaintiff establishes a design defect that would have protected plaintiff from being disposed to the danger, see Ford v. Polaris Indus., 43 Cal. Rptr. 3d 215 (Cal. Ct. App. 2006).

A more appropriate case for primary assumption of risk is Blankenship v. CRT Tree, 2002 WL 31195215 (Ohio App. Ct. 2002). Plaintiff, an employee of CRT (a tree cutting business) gave in to the entreaties of a fellow employee who operated a hydraulic crane to engage in bungee bouncing. Unlike bungee jumping where one jumps off a high structure while wearing a harness that is attached to a bungee cord, in "bungee bouncing" the person is attached with a bungee cord to a crane. When the operator takes up and lets out the cable of the crane, it creates a bouncing motion for the participant. Plaintiff fell from a height of 105 feet while bungee bouncing and suffered serious injury. He sued a host of defendants including the crane manufacturer alleging that the crane was defective due to a lack of safety precautions, warnings, and instructions.

The trial court granted defendant's motion for summary judgment. On appeal the court held that the plaintiff was barred from recovery by primary assumption of the risk. The court said that the dangers attendant to bungee bouncing from such an elevated height are well known. The activity is so fraught with high danger that defendant owed no duty to a plaintiff who voluntarily engaged in such activity.

It is worth noting that Alabama, one of the few states that has not yet adopted comparative fault, will bar a plaintiff completely from recovery in a products liability case either on grounds of assumption of risk or contributory negligence. See J.H.O.C. v. Volvo Trucks North America, 303 Fed. App'x 828 (11th Cir. 2008) (failure to repair truck six months after recall notice constitutes assumption of risk); Burleson v. RSR Group Florida, Inc., 981 So. 2d 1109 (Ala. 2007) (plaintiff killed when gun without safety device discharged; plaintiff's storing of the gun fully loaded with cartridges amounted to contributory negligence as a matter of law).

PROBLEM TWELVE

Maryanne Hammond woke her husband, Jim, at 3:00 A.M. one Tuesday morning three weeks ago. Maryanne was seven months pregnant and her water had just ruptured. While examining herself Maryanne noticed that the umbilical cord was visible. From what she had learned at her childbirth classes she knew she had a "prolapsed cord," and that unless she got to the hospital immediately, the baby would be in serious jeopardy. Jim dressed quickly and went outside to start the car. As fate would have it, his car would not start. Jim quickly ran to his next-door neighbor and rang the bell repeatedly. Trish Devaney staggered to the door and found Jim frantic. Jim told Trish that he had to have her car to take his wife to the hospital.

Trish Devaney owned a new Chevy Chevette that had about 10,500 miles on it. She immediately agreed to let Jim have the car. When Trish handed Jim the keys she told him to drive carefully. "Jim," she said, "the steering has not felt right. I don't know what's wrong. I got a recall letter from GM about defects in the steering column. I haven't had the time to take the car in to check it out." Jim responded, "Steering is the least of my problems now."

Jim was wrong. On the way to the hospital, while making a sharp left turn, the steering mechanism failed and Jim lost control of the car. Jim was seriously injured. Maryanne lost the baby and suffered severe internal injuries. (The baby was born alive, but survived for only a short period.) Jim had not wanted to worry Maryanne on their way to the hospital, and had not said anything to her about the car having steering problems.

Assuming that Green v. Allendale Printing Co., supra, was recently cited with approval by the Supreme Court of New California, do Jim and Maryanne have causes of action against General Motors, either on their own behalf or as representatives of their deceased child?

g. Is Comparative Fault a Defense that Only Defendants Can Raise, or Can Plaintiffs Use It as an Affirmative Gambit?

Generally, it is the obligation of the defendant to plead and prove that the plaintiff's conduct was negligent and that his or her negligence contributed to the harm. But in an interesting case, Philip Morris USA v. Arnitz, 933 So. 2d 693 (Fla. Dist. Ct. App. 2006), plaintiff turned the tables and insisted on pleading his own comparative fault. He had good reason for doing so. Plaintiff began smoking in the 1960s when he was 15 years old. Beginning in 1970, he made numerous unsuccessful attempts to quit smoking. In 2000, he was diagnosed with lung cancer and emphysema. Plaintiff alleged that Philip Morris (PM) cigarettes were defectively designed because PM had used over 110 additives to increase the addictive quality of its cigarettes and that it had "flue-cured" its tobacco (i.e., exposed the tobacco to toxic exhaust fumes from propane heaters) that increased the carcinogenic nature of the tobacco. In his complaint, the plaintiff admitted that he too was at fault for smoking and that he did not try hard enough to quit. In effect, the plaintiff's claim was that he knew that smoking was dangerous but he did not know of the increased risk presented by cigarettes due to the aforementioned defects in the product.

Now it gets interesting. PM had originally pled comparative fault as an affirmative defense but then decided to withdraw that defense from the case. It did, however, seek to present plaintiff's knowledge of the risks of smoking to show that "cigarettes were not 'dangerous to the extent beyond that which would be contemplated by the ordinary consumer.'" If PM could, in fact, establish that proposition, then plaintiff would have failed to make out a prima facie case of liability under Florida law. Plaintiff, recognizing that he stood a chance to lose on this issue if it were presented to the jury as an "all or nothing" proposition, admitted some comparative fault hoping that he would get at least a partial recovery. The ploy worked. The jury found plaintiff 60 percent at fault and PM 40 percent at fault. PM contended that comparative fault was an affirmative defense and, if it decided not to plead the defense, that was the end of it. PM claimed that plaintiff should not be allowed to assert an affirmative defense. The court, in agreeing with plaintiff, said:

> Here, Philip Morris asserts that it must be allowed the choice in which defenses it raises. However, . . . Arnitz, as plaintiff, must be allowed to choose the theory under which his case is tried . . . Arnitz admitted that he was partly responsible for his injuries because he continued to smoke after he became aware of the health risks associated with smoking; but he also contended that the Philip Morris brand cigarettes had a design defect that made them even more dangerous and that he and other consumers were unaware of this increased health risk. We conclude that the trial court did not err in allowing Arnitz to present his theory of the case to the jury and, based on the pleadings, in instructing the jury on comparative negligence.

Id. at 698.

C.   NON-CONDUCT-BASED DEFENSES

1.   Time-Based Defenses

a.   Open-Ended Time Bars

The traditional tort statute of limitations begins to run when the cause of action accrues—at the time of injury to the plaintiff. Time bars for tort claims differ from state to state. Some are as short as one year, others as long as six years from the time of injury. The vast majority of jurisdictions bar actions after two or three years have passed. These statutes of limitations provide little in the way of repose to manufacturers. The injury may not occur until 40 years after the sale to the initial purchaser. The one- to six-year period after injury assumes that evidence regarding the injury to the plaintiff will not be stale; but to the extent that proof of defect is intertwined with questions as to how the product was used over the years, a time bar that is activated by injury to the plaintiff provides little protection against much stale and unreliable evidence that will be brought to bear on proof of defect.

Depending on the jurisdiction, however, the statute of limitations starts to run in a products liability action when some or all of the following factors are established: (1) plaintiff knows or reasonably should know of the injury; (2) plaintiff knows or reasonably should know of the causal connection between the injury and the harmful product; and (3) plaintiff knows or reasonably should know of a particular defendant's identity.

b.   Fixed-Period Time Bars

A fixed-period time bar selects an event that the defendant can control or reasonably predict as the trigger that commences the running of the time period. Typically the triggering event is sale by the manufacturer or the time when the product was first purchased for use. After a fixed time period (ranging from 4 to 12 years), a plaintiff is totally barred from bringing his action. These statutes accomplish repose at the expense of considerable unfairness to injured claimants. It should be noted that U.C.C. §2-725 belongs to this category of repose statutes. It provides:

(1) An action for breach of any contract for sale must be commenced within four years after the cause of action has accrued. By the original agreement the parties may reduce the period of limitation to not less than one year but may not extend it.

(2) A cause of action accrues when the breach occurs, regardless of the aggrieved party's lack of knowledge of the breach. A breach of warranty occurs when tender of delivery is made, except that where a warranty explicitly extends to future performance of the goods and discovery of the breach must await the time of such performance, the cause of action accrues when the breach is or should have been discovered.

The applicability of the U.C.C. statute of limitations to personal injury actions has been a matter of substantial debate in the courts. Many courts will allow the plaintiff to choose between the tort or U.C.C. statute of limitations, whichever is longer. See, e.g., Redfield v. Mead Johnson & Co., 512 P.2d 776 (Or. 1973). In any event, the U.C.C. four-year-from-time-of-sale cutoff generally bars only plaintiff's U.C.C. action for breach of warranty and does not bar the tort suit. See, e.g., Victorson v. Bock Laundry Mach. Co., 335 N.E.2d 275 (N.Y. 1975).

To close the open loop of the injury-triggering device, many states have enacted products liability repose statutes. The Oregon statute, Or. Rev. Stat. §30.905(2) (2015), is illustrative:

(2) A product liability civil action for personal injury or property damage must be commenced before the later of:
  (a) Ten years after the date of which the product was first purchased for use or consumption; or
  (b) The expiration of any statute of repose for an equivalent civil action in the state in which the product was manufactured, or, if the product was manufactured in a foreign country, the expiration of any statute of repose for an equivalent civil action in the state into which the product was imported.

Several state statutes require that an action be brought within ten years from the date of purchase or within one year after the expiration of the anticipated life of the product (expiration date placed on the product), whichever is shorter. See Montgomery v. Wyeth, 540 F. Supp. 2d 933 (E.D. Tenn. 2008) (Court laments the unfairness of the statute and urges Tennessee legislature to change the statute).

Plaintiffs can occasionally circumvent statutes of repose by insisting on literal readings of such statutes. In Barber Greene Co. v. Urbantes, 517 So. 2d 768 (Fla. Ct. App. 1988), a 12-year statute of repose governing products liability actions was held not to apply when the products in question were leased rather than sold. Given that courts usually equate leasing and selling elsewhere in products liability law, the distinction in this case at first blush makes no sense. However, the statute reads as follows:

Actions for products liability . . . must be begun within the period prescribed in the chapter, . . . but in any event within 12 years after the date of delivery of the completed product to its original purchaser. . . .

Based on the statutory language, the court held that the statute did not apply to a lease situation. For a critique of statutes of repose see J. Alex Bruggenschmidt, Asbestos For the Rest of Us: The Continued Viability of Statutes of Repose in Product Liability, 76 Def. Couns. J. 54 (2009) (arguing that statutes of repose are unfair to those who develop diseases after long latency periods). An interesting problem arises when plaintiffs try to bypass the statutory time period by bringing an action for breach of a post-sale duty to warn. This issue is explored in depth in Frank E. Kulbaski III, Statutes of Repose and the Post-Sale Duty to Warn: Time for a New Interpretation, 32 Conn. L. Rev. 1027 (2000).

PROBLEM THIRTEEN

Margaret O'Reilly purchased a new Buick Skylark from Darien Motors in September, five years ago. The following July, she was driving the Skylark on the Meadowlane Parkway that runs between Midwood and Santa Anna in New California. She was traveling 75 m.p.h. in a 50 m.p.h. zone when she lost control of her steering. Her car collided with a cement embankment and turned over. O'Reilly was seriously injured as a result of the accident. She considered whether to see a lawyer about bringing an action against General Motors, but she thought that she had lost control of the car due to her speeding. She decided that there was no chance of success and dismissed the lawsuit from her mind.

In September of last year, O'Reilly received a registered recall letter from General Motors. The letter stated that General Motors had been experiencing difficulties with steering mechanisms in Buick Skylarks of the model year she had purchased. Apparently the problem stemmed from a bad batch of steel that had been used on Buick Skylark steering shafts that were manufactured during a certain week. All cars that had serial numbers ending with the letters "AOH" had steering shafts made of steel from the suspect batch. O'Reilly had purchased an AOH car. The letter instructed O'Reilly to bring the car to any local Buick dealer for replacement of the steering mechanism.

When O'Reilly received the recall letter she immediately called you to inquire about proceeding with a lawsuit against General Motors. You told O'Reilly that there might well be statute of limitations problems in this case. However, you explained that without the allegedly defective steering column it would be impossible to establish defect. O'Reilly responded that, strange as it might seem, the car was available for examination. Apparently the New California Safety Council sets up public exhibits in all the major cities to demonstrate the evils of speeding. O'Reilly said that they called her about two months after the accident to ask her for the crushed vehicle to use as an exhibit. She agreed. "The car is in the Midwood Town Square for you to see."

After exploring the matter with those responsible for maintaining the exhibit, you arranged for the vehicle to be dismantled for an examination by an engineer. The report has just arrived at your office. The expert's unequivocal opinion is that the break in the steering column resulted from a fatigue crack rather than from impact. In short, the expert is confident that the steering mechanism failed prior to impact and was a substantial cause of O'Reilly's loss of control of her car.

Now you have a statute of limitations problem. Can you overcome the argument that O'Reilly's case is barred by New California's two-year statute of limitations, which governs all tort actions?

NOTE: CONSTITUTIONALITY OF STATUTES OF REPOSE

Plaintiffs unhappy with summary dismissal of their actions under repose statutes that bar them even before the injury occurs, have challenged their constitutionality under various provisions of state constitutional law. See, e.g., Berry v. Beech Aircraft Corp., 717 P.2d 670 (Utah 1985) (constitutional challenge based on "open courts" provision of the state constitution). Other courts have challenged repose statutes on the grounds that they are arbitrary and unfair. In Lankford v. Sullivan, Long & Hagerty, 416 So. 2d 996 (Ala. 1982), the Alabama Supreme Court held unconstitutional a repose statute that required that a products liability action "must be brought within ten years after the manufactured product is first put to use." It found that it was unlikely that the repose statute would resolve the problems allegedly caused by the "long tail" permitted by an injury-accrual statute. The court then commented:

> The statute, by tying the period to date of use, as opposed to the accrual date of the cause of action, would permit a purchaser of a defective product to sue for injuries received nine years and eleven months after the first use, whereas it would bar the action of a purchaser who was injured by the same defective product ten years and one month after he first used the product.
>
> Another arbitrary aspect of the statute, which might more properly be classified as a due process problem, is that it does not provide for an extension of the limitation period for someone injured shortly before the expiration period. Suppose a person was injured on the last day of the ten-year period; presumably he would have to file suit that very day or else be barred by the statute. Thus the limitation period effected by the statute ranges from one day to one year, depending upon when the injury occurs. This is clearly arbitrary. The statute has no savings clause to provide for those injuries occurring near the expiration of the ten-year period. [Id. at 1003.]

The New Hampshire court in Heath v. Sears, Roebuck & Co., 464 A.2d 288 (N.H. 1983), waxed even more eloquent in its decision striking down that state's repose statute:

> Except in topsy-turvy land, you can't die before you are conceived, or be divorced before you marry, or harvest a crop never planted, or burn down a house never built, or miss a train running on a non-existent railroad. For substantially similar reasons, it has always heretofore been accepted, as a sort of logical "axiom," that a statute of limitations does not begin to run against a cause of action before that cause of action exists, i.e., before a judicial remedy is available to a plaintiff.
>
> [Id. at 295-296, quoting from Dincher v. Marlin Firearms Co., 198 F.2d 821, 823 (2d Cir. 1952).]

But other courts are not as sympathetic to the constitutional challenges. See, e.g., Pullum v. Cincinnati, Inc., 476 So. 2d 657, 659 (Fla. 1985) (upholding a Florida statute under an equal protection attack; "holding that . . . [t]he legislature, in enacting this statute of repose, reasonably decided that perpetual liability places an undue burden on manufacturers, and it decided that twelve years from the date of sale is a reasonable time for exposure to liability for manufacturing of a product''); AlliedSignal Inc. v. Ott, 785 N.E.2d 1068 (Ind. 2003) (plaintiff exposed to asbestos after repose period had run from time of delivery is barred and statute is constitutional); McIntosh v. Melroe Co., 729 N.E.2d 972, 973 (Ind. 2000) (holding that Indiana's statute of repose that runs from the time of a product's initial delivery ''is a permissible legislative decision to limit the liability of manufacturers of goods over ten years old and does not violate [constitutional guarantees]'').

PART II

Liability for Generic Product Risks

The phrase "generic product risks" embraces two important categories of products liability cases: those in which the plaintiff claims that the design of the defendant's product exposed her to unreasonable risks of injury ("defective design") and those in which the plaintiff claims that the defendant supplied a product without adequate instructions or warnings ("defective marketing"). In both categories, every product unit designed and marketed in the same way shares the same risk potential. Unlike manufacturing defects, if you condemn one unit as generically defective, you condemn them all. That, of course, is why litigation over the adequacy of product design and marketing provides the impetus for reforming the products liability system; a manufacturer can wake up one morning and find itself confronted with the real possibility that all the products it has sold for the last 20 years (all 450 billion of them) are legally defective.

Why take up defective design before defective marketing? Given that it is easier for a manufacturer to provide adequate warnings and accurate portrayals of its products than it is to redesign its products, arguably warnings should come first. However, good engineering demands that a manufacturer's first responsibility is to reduce risk as much as reasonably possible by building hardware into products that eliminate the risks of injury. Warnings serve as a backup once one has, so to speak, maxed out with regard to design. Consider, for example, a punch press that is unguarded at the point of operation. An inattentive or forgetful plaintiff may stick his hand into the danger point and suffer serious injury. Even the boldest warning, "Danger — Keep Hands Away," will not eliminate the possibility that a forgetful employee may inadvertently get his hand caught. A safety guard may be preferable to a warning because it physically prevents the accident from happening by blocking entrance to the danger point. As we shall see, the thesis that a manufacturer should undertake reasonable design as the first step in seeking to accomplish safer products is a governing principle in the Products Liability Restatement §2, Comment *l*. We thus direct our attention first to design because it really does come first. Not until we have exhausted available avenues for reasonable design do we look to whether further steps might have been taken to safeguard against residual risks through the mechanism of warning.

Chapter Four deals with liability for defective design. Chapter Five examines the legal standards by which defendants are held liable for failure to instruct or to warn. Although the distinction between design and marketing is clear enough in most cases, you should appreciate that it gives way under pressure. For example, plaintiffs frequently combine claims of defective design with claims of failure to warn: "You should have designed the top so that it would not fall off, or at least should have warned me that it might fall off." Or: "You should have made the top less likely to

155

fall off, and should have warned me in any event.'' Whether juries in such cases keep straight the distinction between design and warning is open to question. Chapter Six considers the liability of sellers for express statements about product performance. Actions for breach of express warranty or misrepresentation are almost always generic to an entire product line.

CHAPTER FOUR
Liability for Defective Design

We begin this chapter with fair warning. The material that follows is tough stuff. Courts have given voice to several different standards for determining when a product is defectively designed. Many courts take the position that the plaintiff must proffer credible evidence that a reasonable alternative design was available at the time of sale that would have prevented the harm suffered by the plaintiff. The Products Liability Restatement takes this position. Some courts appear to allow a plaintiff to establish a claim if the product that caused the harm disappointed consumer expectations. Under this view, the nature of the alternative design that should have been adopted remains vague and indeterminate. The rhetoric surrounding this issue is often extreme in favor of one test or another. You will have to struggle with the cases to determine whether the rhetoric reflects important policy differences that have a significant impact on the outcomes of cases or whether the rhetoric provides little more than good sound bites. In reality, there may be more fundamental agreement as to what it takes to make out a cause of action for design defect than meets the eye.

In seeking to fashion a legal standard for defective design, it will be useful to look at the problems that attend establishing a design for any complex system. Consider the decisions faced by a traffic engineer in designing a system for regulating city traffic: where to place red lights, whether to stagger the lights so that drivers do not have to stop at every block, what speed limits to set on various thoroughfares, what parking restrictions to put in place, etc. A moment's reflection reveals that the engineer will have to concern herself with competing values. The more stoplights that are in place, the easier it will be to have safe pedestrian crossings. If she decides to stagger the lights and increase the speed limit to facilitate faster driving, safe pedestrian crossings may be compromised. The presence of parked cars complicates the picture. Though parking may be necessary to allow for access to shopping, parked cars may eliminate a lane of traffic essential to maintaining a steady flow of traffic.

If one were to ask what is a reasonable way to design a traffic system in a given neighborhood, the answer is not readily apparent. One might design such a system many different ways, depending on which values one wishes to give primacy. Is fast flow of traffic of primary importance? Pedestrian access to shopping? Pedestrian safety? The late Professor Lon Fuller labeled this kind of problem "polycentric." Such problems may be ill-suited for litigation, at least when they are presented to courts to decide under an open-ended standard of reasonableness. If after the occurrence of an accident a claim was made that the traffic system was not reasonably designed, a court would have a devil of a time dealing with the issue. When each point for decision is related to all the others as are the strands of a spiderweb, if one strand is pulled, a complex pattern of readjustment will occur throughout the web. As one issue is resolved another pops up. As the second is resolved a third must be confronted. And as the third issue is being resolved it may be necessary to go back and reexamine the first two issues.

In an article written at the very outset of the design defect era, Professor Henderson argued that product designs are inherently polycentric. He contended that:

> Because absolute safety is not attainable and — in any event — is not the sole desirable objective of the product's design, the engineer must place relative values upon a multitude of factors. The decisions he must make regarding these factors are as interrelated and interdependent as the strands of an intricate web. [Changing one's assessment of any single factor changes one's assessment of all, or most, of the other factors.] Intelligent answers to the question of "How much product safety is enough?" — the question that will concern us throughout — can only be provided by a process that considers such factors as market price, functional utility, and aesthetics, as well as safety, and achieves the proper balance among them. Ultimately, the question reduces to "What portion of society's limited resources are to be allocated to safety, thereby leaving less to be devoted to other social objectives?"

James A. Henderson, Jr., Judicial Review of Manufacturers' Conscious Design Choice: The Limits of Adjudication, 73 Colum. L. Rev. 1531, 1540 (1973).

Henderson's critique of design defect litigation brought forth the following response from a coauthor of this casebook. In an article entitled The Use and Abuse of Warnings in Products Liability: Design Defect Litigation Comes of Age, 61 Cornell L. Rev. 495, 526 (1976), Professor Aaron D. Twerski, with colleagues Weinstein, Donaher, and Piehler, argued:

> In the cases discussed by Professor Fuller, courts are thrown a complex problem and asked to resolve it on no basis other than general notions of fairness and equity. Such litigation is unfocused and diffuse. There is no central focal point that becomes the axis about which all considerations must turn. In product design litigation the opposite is true. Admittedly, absolute safety is unattainable and is not the only consideration germane to a design defect case. But the focal point of the case is clearly defined. It revolves around the question of whether the product has met a minimal level of product safety acceptability, i.e., the product is not unreasonably dangerous. To the extent that factors such as cost, aesthetics and functional utility are examined, they are examined not in isolation but in relation to safety.

Suffice it to say that both authors have moderated their views. Twerski acknowledges that polycentricity can be a serious problem in design litigation. Henderson now believes that a well-formulated test for design defect that concentrates on marginal comparisons of alternative designs — essentially the test for defect reflected in the Restatement of Products Liability — serves to reduce the justiciability concerns that he expressed in his early piece. In any event, design litigation is not a cakewalk. In analyzing the various tests propounded by the courts for defect, it is important to keep in mind the underlying difficulty in judging any complex design system and to ask how any suggested test for determining defect addresses the problem of evaluating the trade-offs that are inherent in design.

One further word of caution is in order. We have noted that the legal test for defectiveness should establish the standard against which to measure the product that caused the injury. Whatever the legal standard finally adopted, courts are creating ex nihilo. The hypothetical alternative product may be something new, or at the very least something different. Bringing this kind of creative process to the courtroom is both exciting and frightening. It tests the limits of traditional adjudication in ways that have not often been confronted in litigation practice. The student is thus cautioned not to let the search for a legal test for design defect distract attention from the battle over how a hypothetical standard is proved in court. At the coliseum, the spectator should keep his eye first and foremost on the combatants, not the referee. With these admonitions in mind, we invite you to enter the arena. The gladiators are ready and the lions, very hungry.

A. PRELIMINARY PUZZLEMENTS

1. Do We Need Governmental Review of Product Designs? Why Not Leave Responsibility for Design Safety Entirely to the Market?

Recall from Chapter One that traditional justifications for imposing strict liability for manufacturing defects rest on judicial assumptions regarding the inability of product users and consumers to understand relevant risks or to act effectively to reduce them. But even if the market cannot effectively regulate the production of manufacturing defects, are not users and consumers capable of adequately understanding and managing the generic risks presented by product designs? Most generic risks either are obvious or, if not, are generally known or warned about by commercial product distributors. That being the case, the market should function well to achieve appropriate levels of product safety. And if the risks are hidden and the warnings inadequate, plaintiff need not pursue a case for design defect. A failure-to-warn claim provides a much easier road to recovery. Thus, it can be argued that courts need not review product designs at all.

That there is merit to this argument is suggested by the fact that, until fairly recently, American courts did *not* review product designs when the generic risks were obvious, which was the case more often than not. Referred to as the "patent danger rule," this single-factor barrier to liability reigned in many jurisdictions. The leading case adopting the patent danger rule is Campo v. Scofield, 95 N.E.2d 802 (N.Y. 1950). The plaintiff in *Campo* had his hands crushed in the rollers of a piece of farm machinery. The plaintiff argued that the machinery was defectively designed in that the risk of user injury was unreasonably great. The New York high court held for the defendant as a matter of law on the basis that the risk was obvious to the user and therefore should be the user's, and not the defendant's, responsibility. The *Campo* decision was followed in many American jurisdictions, and at one time represented the majority view. Many courts adopting the rule used it to explain why someone who cuts himself with a sharp knife cannot recover from the knife manufacturer — the sharpness of the knife is obvious, therefore it is up to the user to be careful not to suffer injury.

California was one of the first jurisdictions to overturn the patent danger rule. In Pike v. Frank G. Hough Co., 467 P.2d 229 (Cal. 1970), the court held that, although a blind spot due to the absence of rearview mirrors was obvious to the operator of a high earthmoving machine, such obviousness should not constitute an absolute bar to the defendant's liability in negligence toward a bystander run over by the mirrorless machine. That the patent danger rule's days were numbered was made clear in *Micallef v. Miehle Co.*, 348 N.E.2d 571 (N.Y. 1976), in which the New York Court of Appeals overruled *Campo*. Since that time, a strong majority of states have rejected the patent danger rule. See, e.g., Ogletree v. Navistar Int'l Transp. Co., 500 S.E.2d 570 (Ga. 1998); Sperry-New Holland v. Prestage, 617 So. 2d 248 (Miss. 1993); Holm v. Sponco Mfg. Inc., 324 N.W.2d 207 (Minn. 1982); Auburn Mach. Works Co. v. Jones, 366 So. 2d 1167 (Fla. 1979); Byrns v. Riddel, Inc., 550 P.2d 1065 (Ariz. 1976). But see McCollum v. Grove Mfg. Co., 293 S.E.2d 632, *aff'd*, 300 S.E.2d 374 (N.C. 1983).

What is the theoretical basis for overturning the patent danger rule and embarking on what, in many jurisdictions, has become a vigorous and robust process of judicial review of product designs even when the risks are obvious? As is so often the case, the answer from an instrumental, efficiency-based standpoint is that courts recognize that users and consumers are often unable to cope adequately with even obvious product-related risks. For example, a modern court confronted with the *Campo* fact pattern is likely to view the worker's plight more sympathetically than did the New York court in 1950. Although many generic product risks are obvious, not all of them are. Nor may all such risks be effectively warned against. Sooner or later, people working with farm machinery are going to be inattentive even if they "know" that the machines are generically quite dangerous. For example, a machine designed so that a single moment's inadvertence may cost the user a finger or a hand is too unforgiving to pass muster. It is better to design the machine so as to forgive a certain amount of momentary forgetfulness and inadvertence. And when the injured victim is not a user but a bystander, as in the *Pike* decision, supra, the argument for building greater safety into the design is even stronger.

The Products Liability Restatement §2, Comment *d* rejects the patent danger rule as an absolute defense to a claim for design defect. The obviousness of the danger is only one factor to be taken into account in deciding whether the product should have been more safely designed. Reflected in this rejection is the Restatement's commitment to a standard for defective design based on whether, even if the relevant risks are obvious, the defendant's design could have been made safer at reasonable cost. A minority of American courts have rejected such a risk-utility approach in favor of a standard based on whether the defendant's design disappoints consumer expectations. Not surprisingly, as we shall see later in this chapter, courts adopting this "consumer expectations" test for design defects have tended to conclude that obvious risks do not render a product design defective.

Even when performing a vigorous risk-utility review of product designs, courts still face the question of whether their analyses of the tradeoffs involved in product design are more reliable than the analyses of manufacturers and consumers interacting through market transactions. The example of optional safety devices, which are widespread in both consumer and industrial product markets, demonstrates this dilemma. Optional safety devices can be seen as private solutions to risk-management problems, giving purchasers the power to make refined decisions about how much to invest in product safety. Courts have struggled with the question of whether to, in essence, delegate responsibility to private decision makers by refusing to hold product manufacturers liable when they fail to include optional safety devices as part of standard product equipment. Two of the authors of this book have argued that courts should apply a no-duty rule when sellers offer optional safety features but consumers choose not to use them. See James A. Henderson, Jr. & Aaron D. Twerski, Optional Safety Devices: Delegating Product Design Responsibility to the Market, 45 Ariz. St. L.J.

1399 (2013). In their article, Professors Henderson and Twerski suggest that a product should not be considered defectively designed "based on the omission of a safety device when the product seller offers the device as an option at the time of sale and a reasonable seller would expect those who purchase for use and consumption to make reasonable decisions regarding whether or not to include the safety device in the design." Id. at 1424. For a case adopting this approach, see Parks v. Ariens Co., 2015 WL 3960901 (N.D. Iowa 2015). For further discussion of the potential for "private" market-derived solutions to product risk-benefit decision making, see Richard C. Ausness, "Danger Is My Business": The Right to Manufacture Unsafe Products, 67 Ark. L. Rev. 827 (2014); James A. Henderson, Jr., The Constitutive Dimensions of Tort: Promoting Private Solutions to Risk-Management Problems, 40 Fla. St. U. L. Rev. 221 (2013); Richard C. Ausness, Risky Business: Liability of Product Sellers Who Offer Safety Devices as Optional Equipment, 39 Hofstra L. Rev. 807 (2011).

2. If We Need Governmental Review of Product Designs, Why Not Rely Exclusively on Nonjudicial Regulatory Agencies? Why Rely on Tort?

Even if one concludes that governmental review of product design safety is required, it does not necessarily follow that courts should be doing the lion's share of the reviewing and related standard-setting. Nonjudicial regulatory agencies exist at both the federal and state levels that are already bearing some of the design-review responsibility. We will consider throughout these materials the roles played by these agencies in connection with the tort liability system. For example, violation of applicable safety regulations set by agencies renders a product design defective as a matter of law. The question here is why our liability system should not defer even more substantially to the governmental design standards established nonjudicially — why not allow conformance by manufacturers to agency safety regulations to preclude tort liability altogether? Two steps might be taken that would expand judicial deference to regulatory standards more dramatically. First, as discussed in Section I of this chapter, American courts could utilize federal preemption principles to abrogate the traditional rule that product safety statutes and regulations establish minimum — rather than exclusive — standards, thereby deferring entirely to nonjudicial governmental regulators when an applicable safety standard exists. And second, both state and federal legislatures could create new agencies and empower them to establish exclusive design safety standards for most, if not all, products distributed, used, and consumed in this country. The question thus presents itself: why do we rely so heavily on courts, rather than other governmental regulators, to review product design safety and to establish appropriate standards?

An important part of the answer to this question must lie in tradition. Since the development of the negligence concept in the mid-nineteenth century, the rule has been that legislatures and administrative agencies are deemed to set minimum standards. If an actor violates these standards, he is presumptively negligent and his product designs are presumptively defective. But if he conforms to such standards, courts applying law are free to set higher, more exacting standards. A 55 mile-per-hour speed limit means that going 60 m.p.h. is negligent; but circumstance may require a reasonable driver to go slower. Although proof that the defendant was driving ten m.p.h. under the posted limit is relevant and comes into evidence, the trier of fact may nevertheless find the defendant to have been driving unreasonably fast under the particular circumstances.

But pointing to tradition begs the question of why tradition took that form and why it should continue to hold sway. Many of the product design standards set by federal regulatory agencies do not appear on their face — as does a speed limit — to be merely minimum standards. Are there institutional differences between courts and administrative agencies that explain why, aside from limited instances of federal preemption, courts are encouraged to second-guess agencies when it comes to setting product design standards? Differences in technical expertise do not explain why courts dominate; on the whole, administrative agencies appear more technically expert than courts. Perhaps a more important characteristic is the perceived political independence of courts. Administrative agencies are often accused of being vulnerable to being "captured" by the industries they regulate. This phenomenon could be expected to increase in frequency and severity once it was clear that, by conforming to the design standards established by such agencies, manufacturers could immunize themselves from exposure to tort liability. By contrast, American courts are thought to be far less vulnerable to political "capture" by affected parties. Moreover, even independent agencies would be slow in getting around to all the products that would require regulation. And the task of continually updating administrative safety regulations, which presumably could be applied only prospectively after promulgation, would be onerous. By contrast, judicial threats of future tort liability minimize these difficulties by encouraging manufacturers to apply reasonableness standards ahead of time, to their own conduct. This process of self-application, together with the absence of constraints on the retroactive enforcement of new liability rules, render the tort system more flexible than administrative regulation, and more automatically adaptable to changing technical and social conditions.

It would seem to follow that our traditional reliance on courts as the primary governmental agencies for reviewing product design safety and setting design standards makes sense and is here to stay. Courts are generally perceived to be politically independent, fair, and impartial. And reliance on general rules of reasonableness that product manufacturers apply to their own conduct, subject to judicial review after-the-fact in determining tort liability, appears to be sufficiently flexible to avoid bogging down our systems of product distribution in bureaucratic mountains of red tape. Tort law may be far from the perfect solution, but it appears better than the alternatives.

3.   If We Must Rely on the Tort System, Why Limit Liability to Defect-Caused Harm? Why Not Adopt Broad-Based Enterprise Liability?

In Part I, supra, dealing with manufacturing defects, it seemed intuitively correct to rely on the concept of defect as the trigger for the defendant seller's liability. At the very least, manufacturers should be liable when the product unit that harms plaintiff fails to conform to the design intended by the manufacturer — when the purchaser, quite literally, does not get what he paid for and the defect proximately causes serious harm. But when the plaintiff *does* get what he paid for — when the product unit in question conforms to the intended design — the proper judicial response is less intuitively obvious. One response would be to deny liability altogether, at least when the risks inherent in the design are obvious and there has been no deceptive marketing. We considered that possibility in the previous section and indicated that American courts have rejected it overwhelmingly. Even when a product unit conforms exactly to its intended design, courts will impose liability if the risks presented by the design exceed the legal standard to which the design must conform — if the design, itself, is "defective." In this section, we want you to consider whether it should be necessary to ask whether a design is defective before imposing liability on the manufacturer. The question to be addressed is the one in the heading to this section: "Why limit liability to defect-caused harms?"

The alternative here being considered is broad-based enterprise liability — liability based merely on the fact that the defendant's product has caused the plaintiff's harm. Such liability would truly be strict liability. All that a plaintiff would be required to show is that the defendant's product caused, presumably in a but-for sense, her harm. Instrumentally, such a system would internalize all the accident costs associated with product use and consumption, leaving manufacturers, operating out of self-interest, to work out the best designs and marketing schemes to achieve optimal levels of accident costs. And from a fairness standpoint, enterprise liability without any requirement of defect would simply ask manufacturers to "pay for what they break." After all, manufacturers volunteer to distribute inherently risky products in order to make a profit; it is only fair, one could argue, that they compensate victims when the products cause harm. Plaintiff's comparative fault could be taken into account in measuring recoveries, but the plaintiff would not be required to prove defect in order to establish a prima facie case.

The question you should consider is whether such a broad-based system of strict liability without any requirement of defect would be viable. Could courts consistently determine which product(s) caused which harms? Would manufacturers be able to obtain insurance covering their exposures to liability under a system of enterprise liability?

B. WHEN THE FACT OF THE ACCIDENT SPEAKS FOR ITSELF — INFERRING DEFECT FROM PRODUCT MALFUNCTION

Before turning to complex design defect cases where courts must go outside the manufacturer's design choice to discover standards against which to measure the design chosen by the manufacturer, it is necessary to identify the easy design defect case. Indeed, the easy design defect case is so basic that often it is not even identified as one of design defect. You will recall that Chapter One set forth §3 of the Products Liability Restatement, which provides that one can draw a res ipsa-like inference of defect without proof of the specific nature of the defect "when the incident that harmed the plaintiff: (a) was of a kind that ordinarily occurs as a result of product defect, and (b) was not, in the particular case, solely the result of causes other than product defect existing at the time of sale or distribution."

Most often these res ipsa-type inferences are drawn when a product contains a manufacturing defect that causes it to fail in circumstances under which an inference of defect is compelling. However, it is possible that when a product fails to perform its manifestly intended function the culprit was a design error. Like the manufacturing defect case where the built-in standard against which the product is measured is the product's "intended design," when the product fails in its core uses, the built-in standard against which it is measured is the product's "intended function." Comment *b* to §3 and accompanying illustrations clarify this point:

COMMENT:

. . .

b. Requirement that the harm be of a kind that ordinarily occurs as a result of product defect. . . . Although the rules in this Section [allowing for an inference of defect to be drawn based on product malfunction] most often apply to manufacturing defects, occasionally a product design causes the product to malfunction in a manner identical to that which would ordinarily be caused by a manufacturing defect. Thus, an aircraft may inadvertently be designed in such a way that, in new condition and while flying within its intended performance parameters, the wings suddenly and unexpectedly fall off, causing harm. In theory, of course, the plaintiff in such a case would be able to show how other units in the same production line were designed, leading to a showing of a reasonable alternative design under §2(b). As a practical matter, however, when the incident involving the aircraft is one that ordinarily occurs as a result of product defect, and evidence in the particular case establishes that the harm was not solely the result of causes other than product defect existing at time of sale, it should not be necessary for the plaintiff to incur the cost of proving whether the failure resulted from a manufacturing defect or from a defect in the design of the product. Section 3 allows the trier of fact to draw the inference that the product was defective whether due to a manufacturing defect or a design defect. Under those circumstances, the plaintiff need not specify the type of defect responsible for the product malfunction. . . .

ILLUSTRATIONS:

3. Mary purchased a new automobile. She drove the car 1,000 miles without incident. One day she stopped the car at a red light and leaned back to rest until the light changed. Suddenly the seat collapsed backward, causing Mary to hit the accelerator and the car to shoot out into oncoming traffic and collide with another car. Mary suffered harm in the ensuing collision. As a result of the collision, Mary's car was set afire, destroying the seat assembly. The incident resulting in the harm is of a kind that ordinarily occurs as a result of product defect. Mary need not establish whether the seat assembly contained a manufacturing defect or a design defect.
4. Same facts as in Illustration 3, except that the seat-back assembly failed when Mary, while stopped at the red light, was rear-ended by another automobile at 40 m.p.h. Mary cannot make out liability under this Section. The product did not fail to function in a manner supporting an inference of defect since the collapse of the seat is not the kind of incident that ordinarily occurs as a result of product defect. Liability must be established under the rules set forth in §§1 and 2.

Where to draw the line between cases that allow for an inference of defect without specifying the nature of the defect and cases that require proof of an external standard against which to measure the defendant's design is a matter of common sense. This problem has been with us for a long time. In the negligence context, courts have always had to struggle regarding how far one could push the res ipsa doctrine and when to require direct proof of defendant's fault. Nonetheless, no one can conclude that res ipsa has eaten up the entirety of negligence law. Similarly, the cases in which one can draw an appropriate inference of product defect from product failure are usually factually compelling and intuitively apparent. When that is the case, a plaintiff should not be put through the pains of proving a reasonable alternative design or establishing defect by some other external standard. The circumstantial inference of defect should carry the day.

An interesting example of a court being called upon to draw the line between inferring defect from product malfunction and determining defect based on risk-utility analysis is *Hartford Fire Ins. Co. v. Dent-X Int'l, Inc.*, 2007 WL 911841 (D. Conn. 2007). A destructive fire occurred within a dental x-ray film processor that the defendant manufacturer argued had been left on all weekend, in contravention of clear instructions and warnings that the machine must be cleaned and turned off at each workday's end. The plaintiff's expert insisted that the machine had been turned off properly and nevertheless caught fire. The federal district court, quoting and applying §3 of the Restatement (Third) of Torts: Products Liability (1998), held that (1) the jury could conclude that the machine had been properly turned off and thereafter malfunctioned; and (2) even if the jury found that the machine had been left on over the weekend, the jury could nevertheless find that the machine malfunctioned by catching on fire. Expert testimony regarding how the machine might have been redesigned to prevent such a fire was not required, the district court reasoned, because "the jury could conclude that leaving the machine on over the weekend was foreseeable." 2007 WL 911841, at *5. Did the federal district court properly apply §3's malfunction theory?

Of course, when a res ipsa-like inference of design defect based on the internal standard of intended purpose is not available, plaintiffs have the option of putting themselves through the pain and expenses of establishing defective design by means of an external, objective standard of reasonableness. The materials in the following sections pursue the implications of plaintiffs pursuing the latter option.

C.   RISK-UTILITY: THE REASONABLE ALTERNATIVE DESIGN STANDARD FOR DETERMINING DESIGN DEFECT

It should not be surprising that in searching for a test for design defect, courts would look to the risk-utility test developed by Learned Hand in *United States v. Carroll Towing Co.*, 159 F.2d 169 (2d Cir. 1947) (see Chapter One). If that test is capable of determining whether a bargee was reasonable in leaving his vessel rather than incurring the costs occasioned by his remaining on board, it should also be able to determine whether a product is reasonably designed without certain safety features. Indeed, the *Carroll Towing* decision may be said to have involved the question of "How should a reasonable barge operation be designed?" This is arguably true of all first-year negligence cases, is it not?

In *Thibault v. Sears, Roebuck & Co.*, 395 A.2d 843 (N.H. 1978), the court indicated that when a warning could not eliminate the risk of harm, it would judge the adequacy of the design using risk-utility standards. In that case, the plaintiff had his foot caught under the housing of a power lawnmower while mowing up and down on a steep slope. Despite the instruction booklet warning not to mow up and down, the plaintiff thought he could do so, given the length of the slope. While mowing, he lost his balance and fell. He instinctively gripped the handle of the mower, and when he came to rest at the end of the slope, his foot was under the housing, badly mangled. The plaintiff contended that the injury could have been avoided had the mower been equipped with a rear trailing guard. In reviewing the elements of plaintiff's prima facie case, the court said:

> In a strict liability case alleging defective design, the plaintiff must first prove the existence of a "defective condition unreasonably dangerous to the user." In determining unreasonable danger, courts should consider factors such as social utility and desirability. The utility of the product must be evaluated from the point of view of the public as a whole, because a finding of liability for defective design could result in the removal of an entire product line from the market. Some products are so important that a manufacturer may avoid liability as a matter of law if he has given proper warnings. In weighing utility and desirability against danger, courts should also consider whether the risk of danger could have been reduced without significant impact on product effectiveness and manufacturing cost. For example, liability may attach if the manufacturer did not take available and reasonable steps to lessen or eliminate the danger of even a significantly useful and desirable product. [Id. at 846.]

As case law developed, it became clear that, in cases that did not involve product malfunction, the availability of a reasonable alternative design was not merely a consideration to be taken into account in determining defect — it was a requisite for the imposition of liability for defective design.

1. Defining the Standard for Determining Design Defect

Smith v. Louisville Ladder Co.
237 F.3d 515 (5th Cir. 2001)

W. EUGENE DAVIS, Circuit Judge.

This is an appeal from a judgment entered on a jury verdict for the plaintiff, Rodger Nelson Smith ("Smith"), in a products liability action against Louisville Ladder Corp. ("Louisville"). . . . We conclude that the record evidence does not support any of Smith's theories of recovery. We therefore reverse and render judgment for Louisville.

I

Rodger Smith worked as a technician for Longview Cable Company ("Longview"), which provided cable television service in the Longview, Texas area. At the time of his accident in April 1995, Smith had been employed by Longview for approximately one and one-half years. Longview purchased the extension ladder and hook assembly in use at the time of Smith's accident from Louisville.

On the day of Smith's injury, he was assigned a routine repair job that required him to rest the ladder against a cable strand located some twenty feet off the ground. Smith placed the cable line inside the U-shaped hooks that extended from the top of the ladder and rested the ladder against the cable. The base of the ladder was on the ground approximately five feet from a utility pole to which the overhead cable was attached. Because of its weight, the cable sloped down slightly as it moved from the pole.

Smith climbed the ladder without securing the ladder to the pole or any other stationary object. Smith's plan was to secure himself to the ladder with his safety belt when he reached the top of the ladder and then use a hand line to attach the ladder to the utility pole. After Smith climbed to the top of the ladder, he reached for his safety belt and his weight shifted, causing the ladder to slide to his left down the natural slope of the cable. The ladder slid sideways for some distance with Smith hanging onto the ladder. When the ladder reached a position at or near the low point of the line between the two utility poles to which it was attached, one of the hooks came off the line, and the ladder twisted and came to an abrupt halt. Unable to maintain his grip on the ladder, Smith fell to the ground and was seriously injured.

Lateral slides of ladders along cables were well recognized risks in the telecommunications industry, and Smith, himself, had experienced several of these slides during his employment with Longview. However, in the earlier slides Smith had attached his safety belt to the ladder before the slide began and because he did not fall from the ladder he suffered no injury. . . .

Following trial, the jury found in favor of Smith . . . and after taking Smith's 15% contributory negligence into account, awarded Smith $1,487,500. The district court entered judgment on the verdict and denied Smith's post-judgment motions. This appeal followed.

II

A. Design Defect

Smith focused most of his time and attention at trial on his theory that the Louisville extension ladder with hook assembly was defective because of the hook's ability to come off the cable during a slide. Smith's expert, Dr. Packman, testified that when the hook disengaged from the cable near the end of Smith's slide, the ladder to which Smith was clinging twisted more violently than it would have had the hook remained attached to the cable and he concluded that this additional twist contributed to Smith's fall. Packman introduced the concept of a simple latching device that, when engaged, would close the opening in the hook, encircle the cable and prevent the hook from disengaging from the strand. Under Dr. Packman's concept, the latch remains disengaged until the hook is placed over the cable and the ladder is resting on the cable. The operator, from his position on the ground, would then remotely activate a spring loaded latch by pulling a line running from the latch to the bottom of the ladder. Once the latch was engaged, the hook would no longer be open and in the event of a slide, the hook could not disengage from the cable.

Louisville Ladder argues that Smith did not establish that the hook with Dr. Packman's latch was a "safer alternative design" within the meaning of the Texas statute. To establish a design defect, Section 82.005 of the Texas Civil Practice and Remedies Code requires a claimant "to prove by a preponderance of the evidence that: (1) there was a safer alternative design; and (2) the defect was a producing cause of the personal injury property damage or death for which the claimant seeks recovery." Subsection (b) states:

> (b) In this section, "safer alternative design" means a product design other than the one actually used that in reasonable probability. . . .
>
>   (1) would have prevented or significantly reduced the risk of the claimant's personal injury, property damage, or death without substantially impairing the product's utility; and
>
>   (2) was economically and technologically feasible at the time the product left the control of the manufacturer or seller by the application of existing or reasonably achievable scientific knowledge.

We found only one Texas case discussing the proof necessary to establish a safer alternative design under this statute. In General Motors Corp. v. Sanchez, 997 S.W.2d 584 (Tex. 1999), the plaintiff's expert testified that his alternative design of the General Motors transmission would prevent internal forces in the transmission from moving the gear selector toward "reverse" rather than "park" when the driver inadvertently leaves the lever in a position between "reverse" and "park." According to plaintiff's expert, his proposed design change would eliminate this spontaneous movement 99% of the time. The court held that this testimony was sufficient to allow the jury to conclude that plaintiff had established a safer alternative design. Id. at 592.

In our case, Smith completely relies on Dr. Packman's evidence and testimony to establish a safer alternate design. Packman testified that his spring loaded latch, by preventing the hook from disengaging from the cable, would make the jolt at the end of the slide less violent, and, therefore, the worker would have a better chance of hanging onto the ladder. He conducted videotaped experiments for the purpose of establishing this fact. In the first experiment, he placed a 200-pound weight on a ladder with hooks like those found on the Louisville Ladder and then precipitated a slide to demonstrate the jerk that would occur when one of the hooks disengaged from the strand. For the second experiment, Dr. Packman videotaped a slide involving hooks that encircled the cable. This experiment demonstrated a less violent jerk at the end of the slide.

The only conclusion Dr. Packman was able to reach was that his alternative design would result in a less violent jerk on the ladder at the end of slide. Unlike the expert who testified in *General Motors*, Dr. Packman was unable to quantify this reduction in force and was unable to say that Smith or another worker could stay on the ladder in a slide where the hook was prevented from disengaging from the cable. The most Dr. Packman could say was that his design alteration would diminish the possibility of the worker's falling off because there was some reduction in the jerk.

Furthermore, Dr. Packman's concept of the latching device to close the open end of the hook around the cable was a preliminary concept. At the time of trial he admitted that he had considered several possible ways a man on the ground (or some distance up the ladder) could operate the latch mechanism but had not settled on any particular method. He agreed that his design was preliminary and that he was not ready to recommend it to a manufacturer. In addition, Packman conceded that a person climbing the ladder would find his proposed mechanism somewhat awkward and that using the mechanism could cause the ladder to get out of balance and slide. He was also questioned about a concern that the line to operate the latch mechanism running the length of the ladder has the potential of being a hazard to the person climbing the ladder. Packman agreed that he never evaluated the risks associated with his proposed alternate design due in part to the fact that it was never completed. Packman also conceded that he did not purport to conduct a risk-benefit analysis of his proposed redesign. . . .

After careful review of the record, we conclude that no reasonable jury could have found from the evidence that the latching device Dr. Packman proposed adding to the hook assembly was a safer alternative design as defined by the Texas statute. Dr. Packman conceded that his proposed alternate design would not assist in preventing the hook from sliding on the cable. He also agreed that the only benefit a worker would derive from the alternate design was a reduced jerk at the end of the slide. He was therefore unable to say that his alternate design would have prevented Mr. Smith's fall. Therefore, we conclude that the evidence fails to establish that the alternative design would have "significantly" reduced the risk of Mr. Smith's injury.

Furthermore, Dr. Packman conceded that he made no risk-benefit analysis including what additional hazards would be created in implementing his proposed alternative design. Thus, Dr. Packman's testimony does not establish that his proposed design would not have substantially impaired the ladder's utility. The jury's finding of design defect, therefore, cannot stand. . . .

[The court's discussion of other grounds for liability is omitted.]

IV

For the above stated reasons, we conclude that Smith failed to present sufficient evidence at trial to support any of his theories of recovery. The district court's judgment is, therefore, reversed and judgment is rendered in favor of Louisville.

REVERSED and RENDERED.

DENNIS, Circuit Judge dissenting: . . .

The Texas Supreme Court and appeals courts have drawn on common law, statutes, and the Restatements in expounding the state's products liability laws. . . .

In Turner v. General Motors Corp., the Texas Supreme Court discussed the strict liability standard of "defectiveness" as applied in design defect cases. The court held that, in a design defect case, evidence is admissible upon the factors of risk and utility, such as the product's utility to users and to the public as a whole balanced against the likelihood and severity of injury from its use; the availability of an alternative product that would fill the same need without being unsafe or unreasonably costly; the ability to eliminate the product's unsafe character without significantly impairing its utility or increasing its cost; the consumer's awareness of the product's inherent dangers; the avoidability of those dangers because of their obvious nature or because of warnings supplied by the manufacturer; and the ordinary consumer's expectations. However, the court also held that the jury must be instructed only in general terms to consider the utility of the product and the risks involved in its use, and that the jury should not be instructed to balance specifically enumerated factors. . . . "The Texas Supreme Court has never explicitly made proof of each balancing factor a distinct element of a strict liability claim. . . . And certainly, that the jury is instructed in ultimate terms without detailing the criteria is at odds with the notion that proof of each is required." (citations, footnotes and internal quotations omitted). . . .

In 1993, Texas codified the safer alternative design factor, making it an essential element of a design defect claim. TPLA §82.005. Section 82.005 does not attempt to state all the elements of a design defect claim, however. For example, it does not define design defect or negate the common law requirement that such a defect render the product unreasonably dangerous. The statute was not intended to, and does not, supplant the Texas common law risk-utility analysis Texas has for years employed in determining whether a defectively designed product is unreasonably dangerous. That analysis still permits strict liability parties to direct their evidence to the various balancing criteria listed in *Turner*, while the jury can be instructed only in general terms and cannot be required to perform a balancing of enumerated factors. Id. at 256 n.6. The only change rendered by section 82.005 is that it converts two elements — a safer alternative design and producing cause — to necessary, though not sufficient, elements in proving a defective design claim. . . .

Subsequent to the enactment of section 82.005, the Texas Supreme Court, in expounding Texas's strict tort liability design defect law, has often relied upon other sources consistent with section 82.005, especially the Restatement (Third) of Torts: Products Liability. . . .

For all of the foregoing reasons, I believe that the Texas Supreme Court would follow Restatement Third: Products Liability §2 and its comments with respect to design defects, especially when those provisions are consistent with and complementary to Texas statutory and common law. In addition to those already adopted or followed by the Texas Supreme Court, other provisions of the section 2 comments have particular relevance in the present case.

[The opinion excerpts Comment *f* to §2(b), set out infra.]

Factors

The majority clearly errs in proceeding to decide this case as if, under Texas law, the plaintiff in a design defect case is absolutely required to present an expert to mathematically quantify risk and utility evidence and to balance risk and utility factors. In a Texas design defect case, evidence is admissible as to many factors, including risk and utility, such as utility of the product to the user, usefulness to the public, and the gravity and likelihood of injury from its use, availability of a suitable substitute product taking into consideration cost of production and any impairment to usefulness, public knowledge or obviousness of dangers of the product, suitable warnings, and expectations of the ordinary consumer. A plaintiff is not necessarily required to introduce proof on all of these factors; their relevance and the relevance of other factors, will vary from case to case. See Temple EasTex, Inc. v. Old Orchard Creek Partners, Ltd., 848 S.W.2d 724, 731 (Tex. App.-Dallas 1992); Restatement (Third) of Torts: Products Liability §2, comment *f* (1998). Moreover, under Texas law, it is *the jury's function* to weigh risks and utilities by deciding whether the product was defectively designed, taking into consideration the utility of the product and the risk involved in its use. . . . The jury can be instructed only in general terms, however, and cannot be required to balance specifically enumerated factors. . . . The notion of mathematical "quantification" appears to be the majority's own invention; no Texas case or law demands expert mathematical quantification of risk or utility factors as a sufficiency of evidence or proof requirement in a products liability case. . . .

The majority departs from Texas law again in holding that the alternative design presented by Dr. Packman was not valid because he had not introduced a model of a spring loaded cable hook. The Texas products liability law does not, however, require the plaintiff to produce a prototype in order to make out a prima facie case. " 'Qualified expert testimony on the issue suffices, even though the expert has produced no prototype, if it reasonably supports the conclusion that a reasonable alternative design could have been practically adopted at the time of sale.' " *Sanchez*, 997 S.W.2d 584, 592 (Tex. 1999) (quoting Restatement (Third) of Torts: Products Liability §2, cmt. *f* (1998)). . . .

Based on the foregoing data, Dr. Packman testified that in his opinion the alternative design that he proposed, consisting of a cable hook held closed during engagement by a spring latch, would have prevented or significantly reduced the risk of Mr. Smith's injury; that the alternative design was feasible because the technology of the spring latch was simple, well-known and had been in existence for a very long time; that spring latches were readily available — indeed, agreeing to the statement that they were "available in hardware stores pretty much everywhere" — when the ladder was manufactured; that its attachment to the cable hook would not have impaired the utility of the product significantly; and that a spring-loaded latch was already incorporated into the ladder's design by Louisville Ladder in the ladder's rung-lock mechanism, making the spring latch concept an "absolutely obvious" one of which the defendant was fully aware. Mr. Van Bree, the defendant's representative, testified that Louisville Ladder did, indeed, incorporate the spring-latch design into its rung-lock mechanism, though it had not tested the idea of incorporating the concept into the cable hook. . . .

[T]he evidence upon which the majority relies — that due to the imponderable variables none of the experts, including Dr. Packman, were able to mathematically quantify either the likelihood and gravity of the risk or the amount of risk reduction through the use of the alternative design; that Dr. Packman did not manufacture a prototype of his suggested alternative design; that Dr. Packman testified only that the alternative design would prevent cable hook disengagement and thereby reduce torsional forces and in turn reduce the risk and severity of accidents; and that Dr. Packman frankly conceded that he could not testify as to whether the alternative design would have prevented Mr. Smith's accident altogether — "although relevant, is certainly not dispositive." *Reeves*, 530 U.S. 133, . . . In concluding that this testimony so overwhelmed the evidence favoring Mr. Smith that no rational trier of fact could have found that Mr. Smith proved that the defendant's open cable hook was defectively designed for the purposes for which it was sold, the majority impermissibly substitutes its judgment concerning the weight of the evidence for the jury's. . . . I must dissent.

Restatement (Third) of Torts: Products Liability
(1998)

---

§1. LIABILITY OF COMMERCIAL SELLER OR DISTRIBUTOR FOR HARM CAUSED BY DEFECTIVE PRODUCTS

One engaged in the business of selling or otherwise distributing products who sells or distributes a defective product is subject to liability for harm to persons or property caused by the defect.

§2. CATEGORIES OF PRODUCT DEFECT

A product . . .

(b) is defective in design when the foreseeable risks of harm posed by the product could have been reduced or avoided by the adoption of a <u>reasonable alternative design</u> by the seller or other distributor, or a predecessor in the commercial chain of distribution, and the omission of the alternative design renders the product not reasonably safe.

COMMENT:

f. Design defects: factors relevant in determining whether the omission of a reasonable alternative design renders a product not reasonably safe. Subsection (b) states that a product is defective in design if the omission of a reasonable alternative design renders the product not reasonably safe. A broad range of factors may be considered in determining whether an alternative design is reasonable and whether its omission renders a product not reasonably safe. The factors include, among others, the magnitude and probability of the foreseeable risks of harm, the instructions and warnings accompanying the product, and the nature and strength of consumer expectations regarding the product, including expectations arising from product portrayal and marketing. See Comment *g*. The relative advantages and disadvantages of the product as designed and as it alternatively could have been designed may also be considered. Thus, the likely effects of the alternative design on production costs; the effects of the alternative design on product longevity, maintenance, repair, and esthetics; and the range of consumer choice among products are factors that may be taken into account. A plaintiff is not necessarily required to introduce proof on all of these factors; their relevance, and the relevance of other factors, will vary from case to case. Moreover, the factors interact with one another. For example, evidence of the magnitude and probability of foreseeable harm may be offset by evidence that the proposed alternative design would reduce the efficiency and the utility of the product. On the other hand, evidence that a proposed alternative design would increase production costs may be offset by evidence that product portrayal and marketing created substantial expectations of performance or safety, thus increasing the probability of foreseeable harm. Depending on the mix of these factors, a number of variations in the design of a given product may meet the test in Subsection (b). On the other hand, it is not a factor under Subsection (b) that the imposition of liability would have a negative effect on corporate earnings or would reduce employment in a given industry.

When evaluating the reasonableness of a design alternative, the overall safety of the product must be considered. It is not sufficient that the alternative design would have reduced or prevented the harm suffered by the plaintiff if it would also have introduced into the product other dangers of equal or greater magnitude.

While a plaintiff must prove that a reasonable alternative design would have reduced the foreseeable risks of harm, Subsection (b) does not require the plaintiff to produce expert testimony in every case. Cases arise in which the feasibility of a reasonable alternative design is obvious and understandable to laypersons and therefore expert testimony is unnecessary to support a finding that the product should have been designed differently and more safely. For example, when a manufacturer sells a soft stuffed toy with hard plastic buttons that are easily removable and likely to choke and suffocate a small child who foreseeably attempts to swallow them, the plaintiff should be able to reach the trier of fact with a claim that buttons on such a toy should be an integral part of the toy's fabric itself (or otherwise be unremovable by an infant) without hiring an expert to demonstrate the feasibility of an alternative safer design. Furthermore, other products already available on the market may serve the same or very similar function at lower risk and at comparable cost. Such products may serve as reasonable alternatives to the product in question.

In many cases, the plaintiff must rely on expert testimony. Subsection (b) does not, however, require the plaintiff to produce a prototype in order to make out a prima facie case. Thus, qualified expert testimony on the issue suffices, even though the expert has produced no prototype, if it reasonably supports the conclusion that a reasonable alternative design could have been practically adopted at the time of sale. . . .

A test that considers such a broad range of factors in deciding whether the omission of an alternative design renders a product not reasonably safe requires a fair allocation of proof between the parties. To establish a prima facie case of defect, the plaintiff must prove the availability of a technologically feasible and practical alternative design that would have reduced or prevented the plaintiff's harm. Given inherent limitations on access to relevant data, the plaintiff is not required to establish with particularity the costs and benefits associated with adoption of the suggested alternative design.

In sum, the requirement of Subsection (b) that a product is defective in design if the foreseeable risks of harm could have been reduced by a reasonable alternative design is based on the common-sense notion that liability for harm caused by product designs should attach only when harm is reasonably preventable. For justice to be achieved, Subsection (b) should not be construed to create artificial and unreasonable barriers to recovery.

The necessity of proving a reasonable alternative design as a predicate for establishing design defect is, like any factual element in a case, addressed initially to the courts. Sufficient evidence must be presented so that reasonable persons could conclude that a reasonable alternative could have been practically adopted. Assuming that a court concludes that sufficient evidence on this issue has been presented, the issue is then for the trier of fact. This Restatement takes no position regarding the specifics of how a jury should be instructed. So long as jury instructions are generally consistent with the rule of law set forth in Subsection (b), their specific form and content are matters of local law.

Does the Texas statute in *Smith* mirror §2(b) of the Products Liability Restatement? Many state legislatures and courts require that, in order to succeed in a case alleging defective design, a plaintiff must establish the availability of a reasonable alternative design. Louisiana, Mississippi, New Jersey, and North Carolina have enacted reasonable alternative design statutes similar to that of Texas. Still other states have adopted the reasonable alternative design requirement as part of their common law of products liability, often with reference to §2(b) of the Products Liability Restatement.

In Wright v. Brooke Group, Ltd., 652 N.W.2d 159 (Iowa 2002), in response to a certified question from the United States District Court requesting direction as to the appropriate standard for determining whether cigarettes are unreasonably dangerous, the Iowa Supreme Court adopted §2 of the Products Liability Restatement. The court held that the consumer expectations test was not appropriate for deciding whether a product was defectively designed. Instead, the court opted for a risk-utility test and held that such a test required plaintiff to prove a reasonable alternative design. The court said, "[W]e think that [the Restatement] sets forth an intellectually sound set of legal principles for product defect cases." Id. at 167. In another certified question case, Jones v. NordicTrack, Inc., 550 S.E.2d 101 (Ga. 2001), plaintiff tripped over a blunt chrome leg that protruded from a NordicTrack Ski Exerciser. Defendant argued that the machine was not "in use" at the time of the injury. The court held that there was no such requirement as a predicate to bringing a case for design defect in Georgia; the question instead was whether the product met risk-utility guidelines. Citing the Products Liability Restatement §2, the court asserted that under risk-utility standards "the 'heart' of a design defect case is the reasonableness of selecting from among alternative product designs and adopting the safest feasible one." Id. at 103. See also Morales v. E.D. Etnyre & Co., 382 F. Supp. 2d 1278 (D.N.M. 2005) (*Erie* guess that New Mexico would adopt §2(b) of the Restatement of Products Liability).

In Burke v. U-Haul Int'l, 501 F. Supp. 2d 930, 933 (W.D. Ky. 2007), the plaintiffs were injured when their vehicle overturned while towing a dolly designed by and rented from the defendant. The district court, applying Kentucky law, stated that "[i]n the typical design defect claim Kentucky law requires proof of a feasible alternative design." Id. at 933. The court denied the defendant's renewed motion for judgment as a matter of law because the plaintiffs "met the requirement of showing a feasible alternative." Id.

A number of other courts require plaintiff to prove a reasonable alternative design in order to make out a prima facie case. See, e.g., Miller v. Ingersoll-Rand Co., 148 Fed App'x 420 (6th Cir. 2005) (applying Michigan law, summary judgment for defendant manufacturer affirmed on ground that plaintiff had not proven that alternative designs would have been feasible or would have prevented plaintiff's injuries); Quintana-Ruiz v. Hyundai Motor Corp., 303 F. 3d 62 (1st Cir. 2002) (applying Puerto Rico law) (insufficient evidence to support a jury verdict for plaintiff that air bag should have had a higher deployment threshold; evidence of technological feasibility of alternative design does not suffice where there was evidence that the higher deployment threshold would have increased the risk of injury in lower intensity crashes); Branham v. Ford Motor Co., 701 S.E.2d 5 (S.C. 2010) (the exclusive test in a products liability design case is the risk-utility test with its requirement of showing a feasible alternative design; court adopts §2(b) of Products Liability Restatement); Vines v. Beloit Corp., 631 So. 2d 1003, 1006 (Ala. 1994) (summary judgment granted to defendant after plaintiff failed to show reasonable alternative design for machine which processes pulp wood into paper). Similar expressions are found in cases from Arkansas, Delaware, District of Columbia, Indiana, Maine, Massachusetts, Minnesota, Montana, New York, Utah, Virginia, and West Virginia. Not all jurisdictions, however, have joined the trend of requiring a reasonable alternative design. See, e.g., Vautour v. Body Masters Sports Industries, Inc., 147 N.H. 150, 156 (2001) (noting that "while proof of an alternative design is relevant in a design defect case, it should be neither a controlling factor nor an essential element"); Bustos v. Hyundai Motor Co., 243 P.3d 440, 452 (N.M. Ct. App. 2010) ("Under New Mexico law, the existence of a reasonable alternative design is a relevant consideration by a jury but . . . a specific finding on this issue is not required.").

With the adoption of the reasonable alternative design requirement, courts have had to face the problem that divided the Fifth Circuit in *Smith*. What quantum of proof is necessary to make out a reasonable alternative? It is relatively rare in tort cases for courts to direct a verdict for a defendant on disputed issues of fact as the majority did in *Smith*. In products liability design defect cases, however, it is not unusual at all for courts to step in and declare that plaintiff has not provided sufficient credible evidence to make out a reasonable alternative design. The reason that courts police design defect cases more aggressively is that the stakes are much higher than they are in the afore-mentioned run-of-the-mill negligence case. The societal impact of an erroneous risk-utility decision in the traditional negligence context is limited. Tort cases are fact-sensitive and each case has its own peculiar fact pattern upon which the jury must decide whether the defendant met the societal standard of reasonable care. In design defect cases, once a product has been declared defectively designed the entire product line of that genre of product is open to attack in repetitive litigation. A plaintiff's verdict that withstands appellate scrutiny sends a message to the manufacturer (and ofttimes to an entire industry) that its design standards are not up to snuff. Courts are reluctant to countenance design claims based on a weak factual predicate.

Consider the recent case of Mays v. General Binding Corp., 565 Fed. App'x 94 (3d Cir. 2014) (applying New Jersey law), in which plaintiff elementary school teacher suffered an electrostatic shock while using a laminating machine. Plaintiff relied on an expert who made a report saying that alternative designs "were and are readily available"; specifically, the report identified "designed-in features including well-grounded induction bars, ionization neutralizers, and web cleaners,'' as alternatives to the technology already used by manufacturer defendant. The expert did not, however, specify whether the suggested features were "economically or practically feasible." Furthermore, manufacturer's expert showed that none of nine competing laminators on the market incorporated the alternative designs proposed by plaintiff's expert. Based on this evidence, the appellate court agreed with the trial court, mentioning that "[a]n alternative design lacking in specificity or a factual basis cannot support a cause of action for damages because tort law is not designed to accommodate claims that would absolutely minimize accidents." Id. at 96. The appellate court found the expert's report insufficient to raise a triable issue of fact and upheld the trial court's summary judgment for the defendant.

Bourne v. Marty Gilman, Inc.
452 F.3d 632 (7th Cir. 2006)

KANNE, Circuit Judge.

When Ball State student Andrew Bourne rushed onto a football field with a crowd that tore down a goalpost, the post fell on his back and rendered him paraplegic. He and his parents sued Gilman Gear, manufacturer of the post, in diversity under Indiana law arguing that the post was defective and unreasonably dangerous because (1) it was foreseeable that fans will tear down goalposts, (2) the average fan would not understand the extent of the risk, and (3) there are alternative designs that would reduce that risk. The district court granted summary judgment for Gilman Gear because the risk was obvious. We affirm.

I. History

We have taken the facts of this sad but straightforward case from the parties' summary judgment papers, beginning with Bourne's testimony that, in October 2001 when he was 21-years old, he attended his first-ever tailgating party outside the game. Near the end of the fourth quarter, he joined a crowd to storm the field in celebration of an imminent Ball State victory. Bourne himself did not rip down the post. He jumped and tried to grab it, missed, and walked away. With his back to the post, he heard a snap, and the post fell on his back, causing his injuries. Although he knew that the post would collapse, he expected it to do so gradually.

As both parties agree, Ball State itself encouraged the crowd to pull down goalposts with a flashing sign on the scoreboard that read, "The goalpost looks lonely." Indeed, the school had earlier resolved that controlling the crowd might prove even more dangerous than letting it tear down the goalposts. (Ball State is not a party now because it settled for a paltry $300,000, a limit imposed by state tort reform in the 1970s.)

Neil Gilman, the president of Gilman Gear, testified that his company has known all along that fans sometimes tear down posts; he also described his company's posts. The posts, he explained, are about 40-feet tall and weigh 470 pounds. They are aluminum rather than steel because steel is heavier, harder to install, and tends to rust. And they are the so-called "slingshot" style with one vertical support holding up the structure. This slingshot style was introduced in 1969 so as to minimize the danger posed to players in the end zone by the old H-shaped goalposts with two vertical supports.

Notably, Gilman Gear did not design the posts itself; instead, it bought the design in 1985. To facilitate "rolling" of the metal in its newly assumed manufacturing process, Gilman Gear switched to a different, less-brittle type of aluminum alloy than was used by the prior maker. When asked if his company had "considered engineering controls" to address hazards created by pulling down posts, Gilman said no.

To avert summary judgment, the Bournes submitted the affidavit of their expert, Vaughn Adams, a Ph.D. in Safety Engineering, who testified that reasonable manufacturers should foresee that goalposts will be torn down by fans. Adams compiled non-exhaustive numbers of football games in which students tore down posts: 16 in 2000, 10 in 2001, 17 in 2002, 12 in 2003, and 3 by October 2004. Adams also noted Gilman's testimony that he knew about some or all of those tear-downs (though not all were Gilman Gear posts). Additionally, Adams cited two newspaper articles reporting incidents of injury other than Bourne's, though he did not attempt to compile statistics.

In short, Adams's and the Bournes' theory is that, when fans try to pull them down, Gilman Gear's aluminum posts will at first bend but then suddenly "snap," abruptly falling on unwary fans whose lay knowledge of metallurgy lulls them into believing that goalposts fall gradually enough to permit a safe retreat. Adams, however, did not testify to any science on which he based his opinion. For example, he offered only speculation to support his premise that social and cultural pressure misleads the average fan into believing that goalposts collapse slowly enough that ripping them down is safe. Moreover, although he hinted that Gilman Gear's change in aluminum alloy in 1985 rendered the posts more dangerous, he cited no evidence comparing the posts before and after the change. Instead, his conclusions apparently rested on availability of alternative designs. The first of these alternative designs is the "double-offset gooseneck," which reinforces the single vertical support with another support right next to it. Second is a "hinged" goalpost, first introduced by the University of Iowa in the 1990s, which permits the athletic facility to lower the posts immediately after a game. (Gilman Gear itself began making and selling these posts after Bourne's injury; at least one other company makes them, too.) Third, there is the "fan-resistant" or "indestructible" goalpost made by Merchants Environmental Industries, Inc. This third kind is made out of steel, less likely to break than aluminum. But just as Adams did not conduct tests on any posts manufactured by Gilman Gear, he did not test any other company's posts or cite to any scientific data. Instead, he presented just a few marketing materials distributed by makers of these alternative designs. While posts like the one that injured Bourne cost $4,700 per pair, the hinged posts cost $6,500 and the "indestructible" posts between $23,000 and $32,000. The cost of the double-gooseneck rigs is not in the record. Adams assumed that a cost-benefit analysis shows the pricier alternatives to be preferable in light of their greater safety and lower rate of replacement. He also opined that Gilman Gear was negligent for failing to test its posts to determine when they would break.

In granting summary judgment for Gilman Gear, the district court held that Indiana law barred recovery for the Bournes because it was obvious to a reasonable person that a collapsing goalpost poses a risk of serious injury. The court reasoned that Andrew Bourne's subjective failure to appreciate the magnitude of the risk that a collapsing post might strike his back and take away the use of his legs did not alter the fact that the risk of injury was obvious as a matter of law and, consequently, that the post was not unreasonably dangerous. In so holding the district court acknowledged that in Indiana the so-called "open and obvious" rule is no longer an absolute bar to a claim under the

Products Liability Act against a manufacturer, but the court reasoned that the principle remains relevant and, in this case, was decisive.

II. Analysis

On appeal the Bournes maintain that the "open and obvious" rule cannot bar a claim for defective design under the Indiana Products Liability Act. Relying on Mesman v. Crane Pro Servs., 409 F.3d 846, 849-52 (7th Cir. 2005), they insist that they can win despite the obviousness of the risk if they can nonetheless prove through the application of the classic formulation of negligence that Gilman Gear should have adopted a reasonable alternative design.

The relevant law is codified in the Indiana Products Liability Act. Ind. Code §§34-20-1-1 to 34-20-9-1. Although the Act originally applied only to strict liability (for manufacturing defects and failure to warn), it was amended in 1995 to apply to claims of defective design, which traditionally sound in negligence. *Mesman*, 409 F.3d at 851. Compare Ind. Code §33-1-1.5-1 (1995) with id. (1990). The law was re-codified in 1998, but without relevant change. Compare Ind. Code §§34-20-1-1 to 34-20-9-1 (effective July 1, 1998) with Ind. Code §§33-1-1.5-1 to 33-1-1.5-10 (1997).

A plaintiff bringing an action under the Act must establish that (1) he or she was harmed by a product; (2) the product was sold "in a defective condition unreasonably dangerous to any user or consumer"; (3) the plaintiff was a foreseeable user or consumer; (4) the defendant was in the business of selling the product; and (5) the product reached the consumer or user in the condition it was sold. See Ind. Code §34-20-2-1; see also Moss v. Crosman Corp., 136 F.3d 1169, 1171 (7th Cir. 1998).

At the outset, we note that Indiana is a comparative-fault state and contributory negligence is not a complete bar unless the plaintiff bears more than 50 percent of the blame for his own injury. Ind. Code. §§34-20-8-1; 34-51-2-7, -8; see also Smith v. Baxter, 796 N.E.2d 242, 244-45 (Ind. 2003). What is more, misuse is not a bar unless the misuse was "not reasonably expected by the seller." Ind. Code §34-20-6-4; see also Morgen v. Ford Motor Co., 797 N.E.2d 1146, 1149-50 (Ind. 2003). Likewise, the statute protects "any bystander injured by the product who would reasonably be expected to be in the vicinity of the product during its reasonably expected use." Ind. Code §34-6-2-29; see also Stegemoller v. ACandS, Inc., 767 N.E.2d 974, 975 (Ind. 2002). Mindful of these rules and Neil Gilman's testimony that his company actually foresaw the fans' vandalism, Gilman Gear does not argue that the claim should be barred on the basis of misuse or Bourne's fault. Consequently, we need not pass on whether this is a case in which no reasonable jury could find that the plaintiff was less responsible for his own injury than others were, see, e.g., Barnard v. Saturn Corp., a Div. of Gen. Motors Corp., 790 N.E.2d 1023, 1031 (Ind. Ct. App. 2003).

The only question presented by the parties is whether the goalpost was "in a defective condition unreasonably dangerous to any user or consumer." Actually, this is two questions because Indiana law requires the plaintiff to show that a product is both "in a defective condition" and that it is "unreasonably dangerous." McMahon v. Bunn-O-Matic Corp., 150 F.3d 651, 657 (7th Cir. 1998) (citing Koske v. Townsend Eng'g Co., 551 N.E.2d 437, 440-41 (Ind. 1990)).

The district court started and finished its inquiry with the [second] prong, whether the post was "unreasonably dangerous." "Unreasonably dangerous" means "any situation in which the use of a product exposes the user or consumer to a risk of physical harm to an extent beyond that contemplated by the ordinary consumer who purchases the product with the ordinary knowledge about the product's characteristics common to the community of consumers." Id. §34-6-2-146. Applying that rule in this case, the district court decided that any reasonable person on the field should have known the general danger posed by a falling goalpost. Consequently, the court concluded, recovery was barred under precedent holding that a user's knowledge of a general risk precludes recovery even if he did not know the extent or specific degree of that risk. Whether or not Andrew knew the post could suddenly "snap" and paralyze him, he should have known that it could fall and seriously injure him, and the district court considered that the end of the matter.

The Bournes' principal objection to this ruling is that the district court explained that their recovery was barred because the danger was "obvious" as a matter of law. They rely on our recent opinion in *Mesman* explaining that, after the Indiana legislature in 1995 expanded its code of products liability to cover all theories of liability including defective design, Indiana law no longer permits a manufacturer to avoid liability in a design defect case simply because a defect is "open and obvious." See *Mesman*, 409 F.3d at 850-51. After all, a product may be designed with a feature that, although obvious, is nonetheless unreasonably prone to cause accidents. For example, a machine may have an exposed moving blade or other part such that the user, though he knows of it, may nonetheless slip and fall and cut off his hand. Since that injury is easily foreseeable and cheaply preventable by attaching a guard, the manufacturer ought not get off the hook. Indeed, that interpretation makes sense; the accident magnet is just as obvious to the designer as the user, and the rule should not work just one way. . . .

Despite the use of some imprecise language here (the court should have said that the goalpost was not unreasonably dangerous as a matter of law, rather than declaring that the danger posed by the goalpost was obvious as a matter of law), the gist of the district court's ruling is sound. Indeed, the district court, like the *Mesman* court and the Indiana Supreme Court, expressly recognized that the "open and obvious" rule has been abrogated. The district court was correct, furthermore, that obviousness remains a relevant inquiry because, as noted above, the question of what is unreasonably dangerous depends upon the reasonable expectations of consumers and expected uses. In some cases, the obviousness of the risk will obviate the need for any further protective measures, or obviousness may prove that an injured user knew about a risk but nonetheless chose to incur it. Although obviousness typically factors in the equation for the jury (it is evidence but "not conclusive evidence," *Mesman*, 409 F.3d at 851), there are some cases where the case is so one-sided that there is no possibility of the plaintiff's recovery. And the bottom line is that Indiana law does not permit someone to engage in an inherently dangerous activity and then blame the manufacturer.

Undeterred, the Bournes nevertheless maintain that, because the goalpost can be made safe (unlike a BB gun), a window remains open for them to show defective design because the goalpost exposed Andrew to a greater risk than he should have expected. In other words, the product exposed him "to a risk of physical harm to an extent beyond that contemplated by the ordinary consumer who purchases the product with the ordinary knowledge about the product's characteristics common to the community of consumers." Ind. Code §34-6-2-146. Even indulging that argument, the Bournes must lose because they cannot show a defect with the evidence that they have adduced.

A defective product is one sold in a condition "(1) not contemplated by reasonable persons among those considered expected users or consumers of the product; and (2) that will be unreasonably dangerous to the expected user or consumer when used in reasonably expectable ways of handling or consumption." Ind. Code §34-20-4-1. That definition is decidedly unhelpful. But fortunately the statute more clearly explains that a plaintiff alleging a design defect cannot prevail without showing that the manufacturer was negligent. See id. §34-20-2-2. That requires applying the classic formulation of negligence: B < PL. *Mesman*, 409 F.3d at 849 (citing United States v. Carroll Towing Co., 159 F.2d 169, 173 (2d Cir. 1947)). A caveat (hinted at above) is that there is no duty for a manufacturer to redesign a product that cannot be made safe, like a BB gun. See Ind. Code §34-20-4-4 ("A product is not defective under this article if the product is incapable of being made safe for its reasonably expectable use, when manufactured, sold, handled, and packaged properly.").

The Bournes are not the first to make this type of argument. In *McMahon*, a woman injured by hot coffee that spilled into her lap sued the manufacturer of the coffeepot on the theory that its design was defective insofar as it made the coffee hotter than necessary, and hotter than she, as a reasonable consumer, expected. A better design, she argued, would produce a slightly cooler cup of coffee. To this end, she submitted the testimony of an expert who opined that the coffeepot could easily, and cost effectively, be made to produce a cooler, yet tasty, cup of coffee. But just because the safer pot could be made did not mean that the manufacturer's pot was defective. Instead, it was her burden to show that the cost-benefit formula demanded adopting the alternative design. Yet her expert did not explain the basis for his conclusion regarding the risks, benefits, and costs of reducing the temperature of the coffee. Nor was the case one in which there was no possible benefit from hotter coffee such that *res ipsa loquitur* might apply. For that reason, and because an expert's conclusory assertions are of no evidentiary value, summary judgment was affirmed.

The Bournes' case shares the same fatal flaw. Their expert's affidavit is their only evidence that the design is defective. But just like the expert in *McMahon*, Adams's testimony is comprised of mere conclusions. For the premise that fans are unaware of the risks, he offers only speculation that social pressure and publicity falsely assure them that pulling down posts is safe. (Perhaps seeing the weakness, the Bournes contend simply that people would not rip down posts if they knew the risks.) As mentioned above, Adams's suggestion that Gilman Gear's change in aluminum alloy in 1985 made the product less safe is nothing but innuendo. Moreover, Adams does not provide a basis on which a finder of fact could evaluate the frequency of injuries caused by goalposts, or calculate the extent to which risk would actually be reduced by the alternative designs, or justify the cost of those alternatives relative to the benefits of aluminum posts. Although Gilman Gear points out such flaws, explaining that Adams's affidavit actually proves the infrequency of injury relative to the number of games, the Bournes retort simply that Adams's testimony was not meant to provide those statistics. As if unaware of their burden, they say neither statistics nor testing is required because the competitors actually sell safer (according to Adams) posts (although they are 38 percent to 700 percent more expensive). But that will not do: mere existence of a safer product is not sufficient to establish liability. Otherwise, the bare fact of a Volvo would render every KIA defective.

Finally, Adams does not even consider the possibility of unintended increases in risk to intended users, like the students or staff who would have to hurriedly lower the hinged post to police the crowd at the end of a game. But the costs of those incidental effects must be weighed in the balance. See *Pries*, 31 F.3d at 545 (criticizing an expert's testimony for failing to consider whether a proposed alternative design to protect the victim of a particular auto accident might not increase risks to other users).

After all, Indiana neither requires manufacturers to be insurers nor to guard against all risks by altering the qualities sought by intended users.

III.   Conclusion

Because the district court's conclusion that Indiana law does not require manufacturers to protect consumers and users from themselves is fundamentally correct, and because any jury's application of the B < PL formula based on this record would be mere speculation, we AFFIRM the judgment of the district court.

Are the *Bourne* court's analysis and conclusions consistent with §2(b) and Comment *f* of the Restatement, set out following Smith v. Louisville Ladder Co., supra? By emphasizing the obviousness of the dangers of pulling down goalposts, does the federal court interpret Indiana law to be reinstating the patent danger rule discussed in Section A, supra? Is the insufficiency of the plaintiff's expert testimony in *Bourne* basically the same as in *Smith*?

In a majority of cases, the question of whether the plaintiff has proven a reasonable alternative design is for the jury. See, e.g., Lapsley v. Xtek, Inc., 689 F.3d 802 (7th Cir. 2012) (affirming jury verdict for plaintiff based on claim that manufacturer should have included an alternative thrust plate within heavy industrial product at steel rolling mill which led to an accident that permanently disabled plaintiff worker); Brochtrup v. Mercury Marine, 426 Fed. App'x 335 (5th Cir. 2011) (upholding jury verdict of damages to plaintiff who argued that propeller of boat engine could have been designed in a manner that would have prevented bodily contact with propeller); Tingey v. Radionics, 193 Fed. App'x 747 (10th Cir. 2006) (replacing injury-causing mechanical toggle switch on medical treatment machine with computer circuitry would not be feasible because it would require redesigning entire machine; but a jury applying Utah law could find that simply removing the toggle switch would be feasible and would not unduly interfere with machine's beneficial performance); Buongiovanni v. General Motors Corp., 1998 WL 1107329 (Pa. Com. Pl. 1998) (upholding $28 million jury verdict for plaintiff predicated on claim that seat of her Chevette was not sufficiently rigid and caused the seat to collapse backward when the car was struck from behind injuring the plaintiff; expert testimony supported the contention that reasonable alternative design could have been adopted and whether the more rigid seat would create additional risks in other scenarios was for the jury to decide).

Scholarly commentary written prior to the Restatement project agrees overwhelmingly with the risk-utility/reasonable alternative design approach. See, e.g., M. Stuart Madden, Products Liability vol. 1 at 299 (2d ed. 1988) ("[T]he majority rule posits that plaintiff cannot establish a prima facie case of defective design without evidence of a technologically feasible, and practicable, alternative to defendant's product that was available at the time of manufacture."). In the post-Restatement era, including law review articles written during the project in an effort to influence its direction, the commentators have been forceful on both sides of the RAD debate. See, e.g., Dominick Vetri, Order Out of Chaos: Products Liability Design-Defect Law, 43 U. Rich. L. Rev. 1373 (2009); David G. Owen, Design Defects, 73 Mo. L. Rev. 291 (2008); James A. Henderson, Jr. & Aaron D. Twerski, Achieving Consensus on Defective Product

Design, 83 Cornell L. Rev. 867 (1998); Richard L. Cupp, Jr., Defining the Boundaries of "Alternative Design" Under the Restatement (Third) of Torts: The Nature and Role of Substitute Products in Design Defect Analysis, 63 Tenn. L. Rev. 329 (1996); Marshall S. Shapo, In Search of the Law of Products Liability, The ALI Restatement Project, 48 Vand. L. Rev. 631 (1995).

In an effort to survey the landscape since the publication of the Restatement, two of the authors undertook a state-by-state analysis of relevant law, including Puerto Rico and the District of Columbia. See Aaron D. Twerski & James A. Henderson, Jr., Manufacturer's Liability for Defective Product Designs: The Triumph of Risk-Utility, 74 Brook. L. Rev. 1061 (2009); see also Mike McWilliams & Margaret Smith, An Overview of the Legal Standard Regarding Product Liability Design Defect Claims and A Fifty State Survey on the Applicable Law in Each Jurisdiction, 82 Def. Couns. J. 80 (2015). Updating the findings of these contributions to the summer of 2015, we find that 23 jurisdictions have wholly adopted section 2(b)'s RAD requirement, 18 by case law and 5 by statute. Twelve jurisdictions combine risk-utility balancing and consumer expectations into a two-prong test; however, these jurisdictions have limited the use of consumer expectations to res ipsa-like cases that would appropriately fall under Restatement §3. Five states do not require a RAD, and one has rejected both the risk-utility test and consumer expectations tests, but cases in these six states have not reached the jury without the plaintiff providing a RAD. Five jurisdictions follow the consumer expectations test solely, and six have not yet determined their approach.

PROBLEM FOURTEEN

Fun Playgrounds, Inc., one of your firm's clients, manufactures and markets playground systems to schools and municipalities in the State of New California. Rather than selling individual pieces of equipment such as slides, monkey bars, etc., they design and install the entire playground. This includes providing the layout for the playground equipment; the grass, walkways, benches, and protective padding; and fencing, signs, water fountains, and lighting. After a layout plan is agreed upon, Fun Playgrounds installs all the equipment.

New Country Day School, an upscale private elementary school, contracted with Fun Playgrounds to install an elaborate playground on its grounds. After completion, during the first week that the playground was put to use, Bobby Spark, a precocious 5-year-old, suffered severe brain damage while using the playground. Bobby had climbed up seven rungs of an eight-rung ladder attached to a slide. Scott Kenner, a classmate, was at the top of the ladder. Apparently, Bobby was impatient with Scott for taking too much time before getting on the slide, and gave Scott a push. Scott responded in kind. Bobby fell backwards off the ladder and landed on his head.

Bobby's parents have consulted with a plaintiff's law firm about the possibility of bringing a products liability action against Fun Playgrounds. The firm has notified the client of the pending claim in writing. The case has been assigned to you for evaluation, and you have conducted a preliminary investigation. Your experts tell you that Bobby's brain damage was almost certainly occasioned by the intensity of the contact of the playground surface with his head. The protective padding over the portions of the playground surface surrounding larger pieces of equipment is three inches of pulverized rubber material. The experts say that if the padding had been six

authors' dialogue 10

DOUG: Aaron and Jim, as Reporters for the Products Liability Restatement, you sure have taken your share of lumps from courts and commentators who don't like the reasonable alternative design test. Why is it that reasonable people disagree with such a common sense test for defect?

JIM: Well for one, the acronym (RAD) hasn't helped any. It sounds like some kind of disease.

AARON: Come on, Jim, he's asked a serious question.

JIM: Okay, okay. It seems so foreboding, so "RADical." Just look at the majority decision in *Smith v. Lousiville Ladder*. If the test were some loosey-goosey risk-utility balancing, the majority might have let the jury verdict stand. But once they focused on Reasonable Alternative Design, the court felt that plaintiff had not proved enough to pass directed verdict muster.

AARON: Aha, I get it. Some people don't like what we did because we sort of rub their noses in the fact that plaintiffs must do more than merely assert defectiveness, point to the plaintiff's injury, and let the jury decide. They've got to introduce evidence to support their claims. Being an Orthodox Jew, let me tell you one of my favorite jokes. One member of the clan decides that he wants once in his life to taste ham. (You know that ham is strictly forbidden under Jewish law.) Anyway, this guy goes to the deli and points to the ham in the display counter and says, "Give me a half-pound of that." To which the salesperson responds, "Do you mean the ham, sir?" To which the guy with the guilty conscience says, "Who asked you to name it?" You get the point. I'm having enough trouble with eating ham. Don't rub my nose in it. Maybe that's why what we did is unpopular in some circles. We have made them face the music and admit what they're doing.

JIM: I think that there is something to what you say. But it may be more than facing the music. Our critics think the music is too shrill and loud. I think that they would like a "kindler, gentler" version of RAD, one that has a better chance of getting the judges away from directing verdicts and letting almost all cases go to juries.

inches thick Bobby would probably have escaped with only minor injuries. Your research as to the thickness of padding for young children's playgrounds reveals that standard padding in the playground industry is three inches thick. Playground safety regulations require only three inches; Fun's playgrounds conform to all applicable regulations. The classic text on playground design suggests that if you exceed three inches for padding, children find that the playground is too safe and unchallenging. If the children find the playground boring they will tend to avoid the playground and go and play in the street, where they tend to engage in more dangerous activities. The text goes on to say that there are real limitations regarding the levels of safety that can, or should, be designed into playground equipment. The text strongly suggests that

AARON: Look, Jim, we tried to soften things up by saying that a plaintiff does not have to produce a prototype and that, in our view, risk-utility balancing is not an exact science. But I'll be damned if I want to present mush to courts.

DOUG: Isn't the problem, though, that a few courts *were* applying mush as their design defect test and it worked awfully well to get plaintiffs past summary judgment and into settlement talks? So as Reporters, you faced the choice of, on the one hand, giving the ALI's imprimatur to a squishy, formless minority test or, on the other hand, appearing to be "against" the interests of plaintiffs and their representatives.

AARON: There really wasn't a choice, Doug, because even in the courts that claim to endorse mush, they almost never in actual practice let cases go to a jury unless the plaintiff presents a RAD. We just came along and politely told those courts, look, no matter what you're telling your rabbi, you're eating ham.

JIM: Let me play devil's advocate and offer an argument against RAD that might have some merit. Some courts have read *Daubert* (the U.S. Supreme Court decision requiring scientific rigor) very strictly and have precluded experts from testifying as to a RAD on the grounds that the RAD has not been subjected to adequate testing. By demanding prototype testing, courts can put a screeching halt to some pretty good RAD cases.

AARON: The cure for that is to read *Daubert* with some common sense. Whether a scientific thesis has been tested and subjected to peer review is only one factor in *Daubert.* There is nothing wrong with RAD. There may be a whole lot wrong with judges who read *Daubert* as if it were the Ten Commandments.

JIM: You're probably right. But, our test sure plays into the hands of the hard hats. I still believe that what we have done is right. RAD is an intellectually honest way of dealing with the design standard. And you know, maybe the majority opinion in *Smith* was right. The expert expressed confidence in his RAD but then he said his design was preliminary and he was not prepared to recommend it to a manufacturer for implementation. Maybe the expert in *Smith* gets an "A" for honesty, but a RAD should certainly be more than a good idea. At the very least, the expert should testify that RAD could be immediately implemented. "I need to think about it some more" is not a very good RAD.

DOUG: Oy vey.

---

much of the residual risk of playground injury must be dealt with by providing adult supervision over children of tender age.

You have shared this information with a senior partner who asks you to write a memorandum as to whether a claim for reasonable alternative design against Fun Playgrounds, Inc., based on the adequacy of the padding would withstand a motion for summary judgment. He also asks whether the plaintiff might have some other ground for a design defect claim against Fun Playgrounds. The claims have not yet been filed, but he wants to know what may be coming. In preparing your analysis, you are to assume that *Smith v. Louisville Ladder Corp.*, reprinted above, is a decision of the Supreme Court of New California.

PROBLEM FIFTEEN

Carmencita Castro has consulted your law firm regarding a potential case against Chrysler. Your initial investigation and research reveals the following: Ms. Castro suffered grievous injuries in a nighttime, head-on collision with a Chrysler automobile being driven by Norman Whitehead on a highway outside of Pittsburgh, New California. The state police tested Mr. Whitehead shortly after the collision, and his blood alcohol level was recorded at 0.19, well in excess of legal intoxication. An expert for the plaintiff testified that at that level most people would have been unconscious. Mr. Whitehead's intoxication caused him to drive his automobile across the median line of the highway into Ms. Castro's lane, hitting Ms. Castro's automobile head-on.

The potential case against Chrysler would be based on a claim that the auto manufacturer should have foreseen that drunken drivers would attempt to operate its automobiles, and should have accordingly provided one or another of three devices in its basic design that would have prevented Mr. Whitehead from starting his automobile on the night in question. The first of these devices is a chemical breath analysis test built into the dashboard of the vehicle, which the driver would have to pass (by blowing into a plastic tube) before the vehicle could be started. The second is a test of alertness in which the steering wheel would be used to keep a needle on the dashboard within certain marks before the car would start. The third anti-drunk-driver device is a system in which five digits are flashed for a brief time on a screen, after which the driver must key in the first three digits, depress the brake pedal, and then key in the last two digits before the car can be started. When a driver "flunks" one of these tests, he is given one more chance, after which he must wait an hour (regardless of whether he would be able to pass the test within a shorter time period) before being given another chance. All three devices are aimed at keeping intoxicated persons, whose alertness and coordination are presumably impaired, from being able to start their automobiles.

Anti-drunk-driver devices are clearly within existing technology. The literature on this subject in technological journals claims that any one of the devices would prevent 80 to 90 percent of legally intoxicated drivers from starting their cars. It is reasonable to assume that had an anti-drunk-driver device been installed in Whitehead's car, it would almost certainly have prevented him from starting his car on the night in question.

When the adoption of anti-drunk-driver devices was first suggested by People Against Drunk Driving (PADD), auto manufacturers dismissed the idea. They claimed that the reliability of the devices is questionable, and that their high cost of initial installation (in excess of $1,000 per vehicle) would be only a modest down payment on the costs of maintenance and the aggravations caused by malfunctions. Moreover, subsets of the innocent driver population whose coordination and reflexes may be somewhat below normal (elderly drivers, nervous drivers, and the like) would be "trapped" by the devices, and denied their freedom of movement. Chrysler also argues that the breath analysis device would pick up "false signals" from various forms of perfumes and mouthwashes, and would be especially unreliable. And problems of bypassing the devices, including drunk drivers having the tests taken by less intoxicated passengers, or drivers starting their cars and then proceeding to get drunk, would reduce the utility of such devices.

The senior partner in your firm has misgivings about investing time in a contingent fee case that may go nowhere. He expects that Chrysler will move to dismiss, or if that fails, move for summary judgment. He asks you to prepare a memorandum addressing whether plaintiff could withstand either of these preliminary motions.

In preparing your memorandum you are to assume that Smith v. Louisville Ladder Co., reprinted above, is a decision of the Supreme Court of New California.

2. The Time Dimension: Post-Distribution Increases in Knowledge of Risks

As of what point in time should the reasonableness of the defendant's design choices be judged? As of the original time of distribution? The time of the accident? The time of trial? At first blush, it may seem odd that any such questions should arise. No one, it might be presumed, should be held liable for risk information or for technological developments that arose after the distribution of the product. For any insurance system to work, the risks insured against must be ascertainable and quantifiable ahead of time. It follows that to impose liability on manufacturers for risks that were not knowable at the time the products were distributed would render products claims uninsurable. See generally Patricia Munch Danzon, Tort Reform and the Role of Government in Private Insurance Markets, 13 J. Legal Stud. 517 (1984); Alan Schwartz, Products Liability, Corporate Structure and Bankruptcy: Toxic Substances and the Remote Risk Relationship, 14 J. Legal Stud. 689 (1985).

However, before common sense can triumph, many obstacles have to be overcome. Once courts began to focus on risk-utility balancing in design cases, the question arose whether strict liability is perceptibly different from negligence. One obvious difference between negligence and strict liability might be the time when knowledge of risks became available to the manufacturer or seller. Negligence, with its focus on the conduct of the manufacturer, would impose liability only when the defendant knew, or a reasonable manufacturer should have known, of the risks that harmed the plaintiff. In contrast, it might be thought that strict liability would impose liability even though a reasonable manufacturer would not have had access to knowledge of risks that only later became available. Thus, courts that are committed to applying a strict liability standard might deem a product "unreasonably dangerous" even though the manufacturer had acted reasonably in designing and marketing the product.

The possibility of attributing to the manufacturer knowledge of risks that could not have been acquired using reasonable care has created apprehension in the business community. Courts and legislatures have responded to this concern by allowing defendants to make "Who could have known?" arguments in response to strict liability claims based on knowledge of risks acquired only after sale or distribution. Most American courts have rejected claims based on risks whose existence became known only after sale. See Products Liability Restatement, §2, Comment *m*; Pavelko v. Breg, Inc., 2011 WL 782664 (D. Colo. Feb. 28, 2011) (granting summary judgment for defendant because the risk of pain pumps to shoulder cartilage was medically identified in 2006 for the first time, while plaintiff's shoulder surgery was performed in 2003). Although the formulations differ from jurisdiction to jurisdiction, in the end and for all practical purposes they reinstate the negligence standard as the operative rule in most cases.

Having said this much, it must be acknowledged that a minority of jurisdictions have at one time or another expressed the view that in design defect cases, the seller is charged at time of trial with knowledge of risks that were scientifically unknowable at time of sale. See, e.g., In re Hawai'i Fed. Asbestos Cases, 699 F. Supp. 233, 235 (D.

Haw. 1988), *aff'd*, 960 F.2d 806 (9th Cir. 1992) (stating that foreseeability on part of manufacturer does not matter, as that requirement confuses negligence with strict liability, and Hawai'i follows strict liability); Voss v. Black & Decker Mfg. Co., 450 N.E.2d 204, 208 (N.Y. 1983) (observing that the standard for design defect is whether, *"if the design defect were known at the time of manufacture*, a reasonable person would conclude that the utility of the product did not outweigh the risk inherent in marketing [the product]") (emphasis added); Phillips v. Kimwood Mach. Co., 525 P.2d 1033, 1036-1037 (Or. 1974) ("A dangerously defective article would be one which a reasonable person would not put into the stream of commerce *if he had knowledge of its harmful character*.") (emphasis added).

In Green v. Smith & Nephew AHP, Inc., 629 N.W.2d 727 (Wis. 2001), plaintiff brought suit against the manufacturer of latex gloves, contending that the gloves contained an excessive level of allergy-causing latex proteins. As a precaution against contracting AIDS, plaintiff health care worker had begun using the latex gloves in 1986 when handling patients. Over the next several years she developed a serious rash over various parts of her body as well as an asthmatic condition. Although latex gloves sold by other manufacturers contained greatly reduced protein levels, there was no scientific knowledge of any allergic reaction to latex proteins at the time of manufacture and sale. The claim was thus that the gloves sold by the defendant with high latex protein were defective and unreasonably dangerous irrespective of the manufacturer's knowledge (or lack thereof) at the time of production. The defendant argued that it should not be held liable for designing gloves with a high latex protein content since it neither knew nor could have known of the risk of harm presented by condition of the product. The jury was instructed that whether defendant knew or could have known of the risk was irrelevant for a claim based in strict liability. The jury found for the plaintiff. Affirming, the Wisconsin Supreme Court held that foreseeability of harm is not necessary in a case based on strict liability. Most other jurisdictions disagree. On a nearly identical claim, a California appellate court in Morson v. Superior Court, 109 Cal. Rptr. 2d 343 (Cal. Ct. App. 2002), took the view that under risk-utility balancing it would be necessary to consider what was technologically knowable in order to decide whether latex gloves were defectively designed.

Despite this difference of view, the debate concerning unknowable risks in the context of design defect cases may be of more philosophical interest than actual practical impact. In failure-to-warn litigation, the issue of risk foreseeability has concrete significance. As we shall see in Chapter Five dealing with failure to warn, all but a small minority of courts impose liability in failure-to-warn cases only when the risk of harm is reasonably foreseeable. However, the overwhelming majority of design defect cases concern mechanical problems whose risks are rarely unforeseeable; the principles of mechanics, at least as they apply to consumer products, have not changed much since the time of Sir Isaac Newton. Admittedly, in cases of products that have toxic qualities such as drugs and chemicals, the problem of slumbering risks that suddenly appear after many years of exposure to the product is real. And in coming years the problem may grow as the fruits of nanotechnology make their way more widely into consumer product markets. Nanotechnology offers a potentially revolutionary scientific advance precisely because nanoscale particles do not behave in the predictable Newtonian fashion of their macroscale counterparts. At present, scientists are confident that both the benefits and risks of nanotechnology could be significant but also that uncertainty pervades the area. See Douglas A. Kysar, Ecologic: Nanotechnology, Environmental Assurance Bonding, and Symmetric Humility, 28 UCLA Envtl. L. &

Pol'y J. 201 (2010). Such uncertainty has not stopped manufacturers from introducing nanomaterials into an every-growing array of products, including electronics, clothing, paint, cosmetics, and medical supplies. Hence, courts may one day be forced to reckon more frequently and more deeply with the question of foreseeability in design defect litigation.

3.   The Time Dimension: Post-Distribution Improvements in Risk-Avoidance Techniques

a.   State of the Art

The preceding section deals with the fact that knowledge about product-related risks increases through time. In this section, we confront the related phenomenon that knowledge regarding ways of reducing and avoiding such risks also increases through time. Thus, persons using or consuming a product known to be risky might do so in the reasonable belief that the risks are unavoidable, only to discover at some future time that a means of avoiding those risks (while still enjoying the benefits of use or consumption) is possible. If such knowledge would not have been available to the defendant earlier, is the manufacturer to be held to time-of-trial knowledge despite the exercise of reasonable care?

If the answer is "yes," then the manufacturer will be held strictly liable for harm caused by its nonnegligent conduct. If the answer is "no" — if the plaintiff must prove that a reasonable manufacturer would have discovered the risk-avoidance technique back at the time of sale — then the test for liability for failing to adopt the safeguard will be negligence. A third possibility would be to make the discoverability of the risk-avoidance technique a relevant consideration, but to place upon the defendant the burden of proof on that issue. Presumably, plaintiffs would reach the jury with the issue in most, if not all, cases under such a "shift the burden" approach.

In any event, the issue thus framed has come to be labeled as the "state-of-the-art" issue in American products liability. Some courts apply the phrase to knowledge-of-risk cases, but a majority limit its use to the risk-avoidance issue. As is so frequently the case, the phrase means different things to different people. In some jurisdictions, a defendant's product design conforms to the state of the art at the time of distribution if it includes all safety features available at that time that have proven themselves in the marketplace to be cost effective. This comes close to allowing the defendant to use conformance to industry custom as an affirmative defense, does it not? In other jurisdictions, a defendant's design conforms to the state of the art only if it includes all safety features that would have been available by the imaginative use of cutting-edge technology.

Boatland of Houston, Inc. v. Bailey
609 S.W.2d 743 (Tex. 1980)

McGEE, J.

This is a product defect case involving an alleged defect in the design of a 16-foot bass boat. The plaintiffs were the widow and adult children of Samuel Bailey, who was killed in a boating accident in May of 1973. They sued under the wrongful death statute, alleging that Samuel Bailey's death occurred because the boat he was operating was defectively designed. The boat had struck a partially submerged tree stump, and Bailey was thrown into the water. With its motor still running, the boat turned sharply and circled back toward the stump. Bailey was killed by the propeller, but it is unclear whether he was struck when first thrown out or after the boat circled back toward him.

Bailey's wife and children sought damages under a strict liability theory from the boat's seller, Boatland of Houston, Inc. At trial, they urged several reasons why the boat was defectively designed, including inadequate seating and control area arrangement, unsafe stick steering and throttle design, and the failure of the motor to automatically turn off when Bailey was thrown from the boat.

The trial court rendered a take-nothing judgment based on the jury's failure to find that the boat was defective and findings favorable to Boatland on several defensive issues. The court of civil appeals, with one justice dissenting, reversed and remanded the cause for a new trial because of errors in the admission of evidence and the submission of the defensive issues. We reverse the judgment of the court of civil appeals and affirm that of the trial court.

Evidence of Design Defect

The alleged design defects are causally related to Bailey's being thrown from the boat and struck by the propeller and not to the boat's hitting the stump. Nevertheless, the same rules of strict liability govern cases in which the defect caused the initial accident and cases in which the defect caused the injuries. Turner v. General Motors Corp., 584 S.W.2d 844, 848 (Tex. 1979).

In Turner v. General Motors Corp., this court discussed the strict liability standard of "defectiveness" as applied in design defect cases. Whether a product was defectively designed requires a balancing by the jury of its utility against the likelihood of and gravity of injury from its use. The jury may consider many factors before deciding whether a product's usefulness or desirability are outweighed by its risks. Their finding on defectiveness may be influenced by evidence of a safer design that would have prevented the injury. Turner v. General Motors Corp., supra at 849. Because defectiveness of the product in question is determined in relation to safer alternatives, the fact that its risks could be diminished easily or cheaply may greatly influence the outcome of the case.

Whether a product was defectively designed must be judged against the technological context existing at the time of its manufacture. Thus, when the plaintiff alleges that a product was defectively designed because it lacked a specific feature, attention may become focused on the feasibility of that feature — the capacity to provide the feature without greatly increasing the product's cost or impairing usefulness. This feasibility is a relative, not an absolute, concept; the more scientifically and economically feasible the alternative was, the more likely that a jury may find that the product was defectively designed. A plaintiff may advance the argument that a safer alternative was feasible with evidence that it was in actual use or was available at the time of manufacture. Feasibility may also be shown with evidence of the scientific and economic capacity to develop the safer alternative. Thus, evidence of the actual use of, or capacity to use, safer alternatives is relevant insofar as it depicts the available scientific knowledge and the practicalities of applying that knowledge to a product's design. This method of presenting evidence of defective design is not new to the Texas law of product liability.

As part of their case-in-chief, the Baileys produced evidence of the scientific and economic feasibility of a design that would have caused the boat's motor to automatically shut off when Bailey fell out. According to the Baileys, the boat's design should have incorporated an automatic cut-off system or the boat should have been equipped with a safety device known as a "kill switch."

The deposition of J. C. Nessmith, president of Boatland, was read, in which he stated that there were presently several types of "kill switches" available, and that they were now installed by Boatland when it assembled and sold bass boats.

The deposition of Bill Smith, who was a passenger in the boat with Bailey at the time of the accident, was also read. Smith had not heard of automatic kill switches before the accident, but afterwards he got one for his own boat.

The deposition testimony of George Horton, the inventor of a kill switch designed for open-top carriers, was also introduced. Horton began developing his "Quick Kill" in November of 1972 and applied for a patent in January of 1973. According to Horton, his invention required no breakthroughs in the state of the art of manufacturing or production. He stated that his invention was simple: a lanyard connects the operator's body to a device that fits over the ignition key. If the operator moves, the lanyard is pulled, the device rotates, and the ignition switch turns off. When he began to market his "Quick Kill," the response by boat dealers was very positive, which Horton perceived to be due to the filling of a recognized need. He considered the kill switch to be a necessary safety device for a bass boat with stick steering. If the kill switch were hooked up and the operator thrown out, the killing of the motor would prevent the boat from circling back where it came from. Horton also testified that for 30 years racing boats had been using various types of kill switches. Thus, the concept of kill switches was not new.

Robert Swint, a NASA employee who worked with human factors engineering, testified that he had tested a bass boat similar to Bailey's. He concluded that the boat was deficient for several reasons and that these deficiencies played a part in Bailey's death. According to Swint, when the boat struck a submerged object and its operator became incapacitated, the seating and control arrangement caused the boat to go into a hard turn. If the operator were thrown out, the boat was capable of coming back and hitting him. Swint also stated that a kill switch would have cut off the engine and the motor would not have been operative when it hit Bailey.

Jim Buller, who was fishing in the area when Bailey was killed, testified that his own boat did not have a kill switch at that time, but he ordered one within "a matter of days."

Boatland elicited evidence to rebut the Baileys' evidence of the feasibility of equipping boats with kill switches or similar devices in March of 1973, when the boat was assembled and sold. The Baileys had been granted a running objection to all evidence of this nature. In response to the Baileys' evidence that kill switches were presently used by Boatland, Nessmith testified that he did not know of kill switches until the spring of 1973, and first began to sell them a year later.

In response to the Baileys' evidence that the "Quick Kill" was readily available at the time of trial, Horton stated on cross-examination that until he obtained the patent for his "Quick Kill" in 1974 he kept the idea to himself. Before he began to manufacture them, he investigated the market for competitive devices and found none. The only applications of the automatic engine shut-off concept in use at the time were homemade, such as on racing boats. He first became aware of competitive devices in August of 1974.

Boatland introduced other evidence to show that kill switches were not available when Bailey's boat was sold. The deposition of Jimmy Wood, a game warden, was read in which he stated that he first became aware of kill switches in 1975. He testified that he had a "Quick Kill" on his boat since 1976, and he thought it was the only kill switch made. Willis Hudson, who manufactured the boat operated by Bailey, testified that he first became aware of kill switches in 1974 or 1975 and to his knowledge no such thing was available before then. Ralph Cornelius, the vice-president of a marine appliance dealership, testified that kill switches were not available in 1973. The first kill switch he saw to be sold was in 1974, although homemade "crash throttles" or foot buttons had long been in use.

Apart from evidence of the feasibility of an automatic motor cut-off design, evidence was introduced pertaining to whether such a design would have prevented Bailey's injuries. After considering the feasibility and effectiveness of an alternative design and other factors such as the utility and risk, the jury found that the boat was not defective. The trial court rendered judgment for Boatland. The Baileys complained on appeal that the trial court erred in admitting Boatland's evidence that kill switches were unavailable when Bailey's boat was assembled and sold. The court of civil appeals agreed, holding that the evidence was material only to the care exercised by Boatland and thus irrelevant in a strict liability case.

In its appeal to this court, Boatland contends that the court of civil appeals misconstrued the nature and purpose of its evidence. According to Boatland, when the Baileys introduced evidence that kill switches were a feasible safety alternative, Boatland was entitled to introduce evidence that kill switches were not yet available when Bailey's boat was sold and thus were not a feasible design alternative at that time.

The primary dispute concerning the feasibility of an alternative design for Bailey's boat was the "state of the art" when the boat was sold. The admissibility and effect of "state of the art" evidence has been a subject of controversy in both negligence and strict product liability cases. In negligence cases, the reasonableness of the defendant's conduct in placing the product on the market is in issue. Evidence of industry customs at the time of manufacture may be offered by either party for the purpose of comparing the defendant's conduct with industry customs. An offer of evidence of the defendant's compliance with custom to rebut evidence of its negligence has been described as the "state of the art defense." In this connection, it is argued that the state of the art is equivalent to industry custom and is relevant only to the issue of the defendant's negligence and irrelevant to a strict liability theory of recovery.

In our view, "custom" is distinguishable from "state of the art." The state of the art with respect to a particular product refers to the technological environment at the time of its manufacture. This technological environment includes the scientific knowledge, economic feasibility, and the practicalities of implementation when the product was manufactured. Evidence of this nature is important in determining whether a safer design was feasible. The limitations imposed by the state of the art at the time of manufacture may affect the feasibility of a safer design. Evidence of the state of the art in design defect cases has been discussed and held admissible in other jurisdictions. In this case, the evidence advanced by both parties was relevant to the feasibility of designing bass boats to shut off automatically if the operator fell out, or more specifically, the feasibility of equipping bass boats with safety switches.

The Baileys offered state of the art evidence to establish the feasibility of a more safely designed boat: They established that when Bailey's boat was sold in 1973, the general concept of a boat designed so that its motor would automatically cut off had been applied for years on racing boats. One kill switch, the ''Quick Kill,'' was invented at that time and required no mechanical breakthrough. The Baileys were also allowed to show that other kill switches were presently in use and that the defendant itself presently installed them.

Logically, the plaintiff's strongest evidence of feasibility of an alternative design is its actual use by the defendant or others at the time of manufacture. Even if a safer alternative was not being used, evidence that it was available, known about, or capable of being developed is relevant in determining its feasibility. In contrast, the defendant's strongest rebuttal evidence is that a particular design alternative was impossible due to the state of the art. Yet the defendant's ability to rebut the plaintiff's evidence is not limited to showing that a particular alternative was impossible; it is entitled to rebut the plaintiff's evidence of feasibility with evidence of limitations on feasibility. A suggested alternative may be invented or discovered but not be feasible for use because of the time necessary for its application and implementation. Also, a suggested alternative may be available, but impractical for reasons such as greatly increased cost or impairment of the product's usefulness. When the plaintiff has introduced evidence that a safer alternative was feasible because it was used, the defendant may then introduce contradictory evidence that it was not used.

Thus in response to the Baileys' evidence of kill switch use in 1978, the time of trial, Boatland was properly allowed to show that they were not used when the boat was sold in 1973. To rebut proof that safety switches were possible and feasible when Bailey's boat was sold because the underlying concept was known and the ''Quick Kill,'' a simple, inexpensive device had been invented, Boatland was properly allowed to show that neither the ''Quick Kill'' nor any other kill switch was available at that time.

It could reasonably be inferred from this evidence that although the underlying concept of automatic motor cut-off devices was not new, kill switches were not as feasible an alternative as the Baileys' evidence implied. Boatland did not offer evidence of technological impossibility or absolute nonfeasibility; its evidence was offered to show limited availability when the boat was sold. Once the jury was informed of the state of the art, it was able to consider the extent to which it was feasible to incorporate an automatic cut-off device or similar design characteristic into Bailey's boat. The feasibility and effectiveness of a safer design and other factors such as utility and risk, were properly considered by the jury before it ultimately concluded that the boat sold to Bailey was not defectively designed.

In cases involving strict liability for defective design, liability is determined by the product's defective condition; there is no need to prove that the defendant's conduct was negligent. Considerations such as the utility and risk of the product in question and the feasibility of safer alternatives are presented according to the facts as they are proved to be, not according to the defendant's perceptions. Thus, even though the defendant has exercised due care his product may be found defective. When the Baileys introduced evidence of the use of kill switches, Boatland was entitled to introduce rebuttal evidence of nonuse at the time of manufacture due to limitations imposed by the state of the art. Evidence offered under these circumstances is offered to rebut plaintiff's evidence that a safer alternative was feasible and is relevant to defectiveness. It was not offered to show that a custom existed or to infer the defendant's compliance there-with. We would be presented with a different question if the state of the art in 1973 with respect to kill switches had not been disputed and Boatland had attempted to avoid liability by offering proof that Bailey's boat complied with industry custom. . . .

Conclusion

For the reasons stated above the judgment of the court of civil appeals is reversed. The judgment rendered by the trial court, that the Baileys take nothing against Boatland, is affirmed.

POPE, J., concurring, in which BARROW, J., joins [opinion omitted].

On Rehearing

CAMPBELL, J., dissenting.

I dissent.

"State of the art" does not mean "the state of industry practice." "State of the art" means "state of industry knowledge." At the time of the manufacture of the boat in question, the device and concept of a circuit breaker, as is at issue in this case, was simple, mechanical, cheap, practical, possible, economically feasible and a concept seventy years old, which required no engineering or technical breakthrough. The concept was known by the industry. This fact removes it from "state of the art."

Boatland is a retail seller. It is not the manufacturer. From the adoption of strict liability in this case, and consideration of public policy, each entity involved in the chain of commercial distribution of a defective product has been subject to strict liability for injuries thereby caused, even though it is in no way responsible for the creation of a defective product or could not cure the defect. The remedy for a faultless retail seller is an action for indemnity against the manufacturer.

In products liability, the measure is the dangerously defective quality of the specific product in litigation. The focus is on the product, not the reasoning behind the manufacturer's option of design or the care exercised in making such decisions. Commercial availability or defectiveness as to Boatland is not the test. Defectiveness as to the product is the test. If commercial unavailability is not a defense or limitation on feasibility to the manufacturer, it cannot be a defense to the seller.

The manufacturer of the boat, Mr. Hudson, testified as follows as concerns the concept of a "kill switch." It is practically without dispute that this is one of the simplest mechanical devices and concepts known to man. Its function is, can be, and was performed by many and varied simple constructions. It is more a concept than an invention. The concept has been around most of this century. It is admittedly an easily incorporated concept. Was an invention required in order to incorporate a circuit breaker on a bass boat? Absolutely not! Did the manufacturer have to wait until George Horton invented his specific "Quick Kill" switch before it could incorporate a kill switch of some sort on its bass boats? Absolutely not! Mr. Hudson uses an even simpler electrical circuit breaker on his boats.

Mr. Hudson testified he could have made a kill switch himself, of his own, and of many possible designs, but simply did not do it. Why didn't he do it? He didn't think about it. He never had any safety engineer examine his boats. He hadn't heard of such, he puts them on now, but still thinks people won't use them.

Was the manufacturer faced with a limitation or state of the art due to commercial unavailability? No. If the manufacturer of this boat were the defendant in this case, would the majority hold under this evidence that the commercial unavailability of someone else's simple product is a limitation on the manufacturer's capability (feasibility) to incorporate a device performing the same safety function on its boat? Not if any semblance of strict product liability is to be preserved. . . .

What is this Court faced with in this case? Nothing more than a defendant seller attempting to avoid liability by offering proof that Bailey's boat complied with industry practice (which it did at that time) but not because of any limitations on manufacturing feasibility at that time. This is an industry practice case. The evidence does not involve "technological feasibility." The law of the majority opinion is that a simple device, not supplied by the manufacturer, is a defense in a strict liability suit, against a retailer, even though the industry practice was created by the manufacturing industry.

There is no dispute that commercially marketed "kill switches" for bass boats were unavailable to Boatland at the time it sold the boat. Horton's "Quick Kill" was unavailable. The important point is that there is no dispute that at the time of the manufacture of Mr. Bailey's boat, a circuit breaker, whether electrical or mechanical could have easily and cheaply been incorporated into the boat.

Evidence of commercial unavailability to this retail seller should not be admissible. If it is, the majority opinion has created a new and separate test for defectiveness for a retail seller in a strict liability case. . . .

I would hold that the trial court erred in permitting such evidence by Boatland to go to the jury, and would affirm the judgment of the Court of Civil Appeals. . . .

Restatement (Third) of Torts: Products Liability
(1998)

§2. CATEGORIES OF PRODUCT DEFECT

COMMENT:

d. Design defects: general considerations. . . . How the defendant's design compares with other, competing designs in actual use is relevant to the issue of whether the defendant's design is defective. Defendants often seek to defend their product designs on the ground that the designs conform to the "state of the art." The term "state of the art" has been variously defined to mean that the product design conforms to industry custom, that it reflects the safest and most advanced technology developed and in commercial use, or that it reflects technology at the cutting edge of scientific knowledge. The confusion brought about by these various definitions is unfortunate. This Section states that a design is defective if the product could have been made safer by the adoption of a reasonable alternative design. If such a design could have been practically adopted at time of sale and if the omission of such a design rendered the product not reasonably safe, the plaintiff establishes defect under Subsection (b). When a defendant demonstrates that its product design was the safest in use at the time of sale, it may be difficult for the plaintiff to prove that an alternative design could have been practically adopted. The defendant is thus allowed to introduce evidence with regard to industry practice that bears on whether an alternative design was practicable. Industry practice may also be relevant to whether the omission of an alternative design rendered the product not reasonably safe. While such evidence is admissible, it is not necessarily dispositive. If the plaintiff introduces expert testimony to establish that a reasonable alternative design could practically have been adopted, a trier of fact may conclude that the product was defective notwithstanding that such a design was not adopted by any manufacturer, or even considered for commercial use, at the time of sale.

The strong majority position is that state-of-the-art evidence, whatever is meant by the phrase, is admissible in product design cases. See generally Gary C. Robb, A Practical Approach to Use of State of the Art Evidence in Strict Products Liability Cases, 77 Nw. U. L. Rev. 1 (1982). See also Smith v. Cent. Mine Equip. Co., 876 F. Supp. 2d 1261, 1270 (W.D. Okla. 2012) (applying Oklahoma law), aff'd, 559 F. App'x 679 (10th Cir. 2014) (noting that "compliance with industry custom and practice or 'state of the art' does not relieve a manufacturer from liability if the manufacturer otherwise failed to exercise due care" but it is "relevant to the negligence determination"); Sturm Ruger & Co., Inc. v. Day, 594 P.2d 38, 45 (Alaska 1979) ("While not, strictly speaking, a defense in products liability action, state of the art may be considered in determining whether a product is defective"), cert. denied, 454 U.S. 894 (1981), overruled on other grounds, Dura Corp. v. Harned, 703 P.2d 396 (1985); Potter v. Chicago Pneumatic Tool Co., 694 A.2d 1319, 1346 (Conn. 1997) (reprinted infra) ("the overwhelming majority of courts have held that, in design defect cases, state-of-the-art evidence is relevant to determining the adequacy of the product's design"); Kelley v. Hedwin Corp., 707 S.E.2d 895, 898 (Ga. Ct. App. 2011) ("Georgia courts employ the risk-utility test according to the following nonexhaustive list of factors . . . [including] the state of the art at the time the product is manufactured."). Compare Ky. Rev. Stat. Ann. §411.310(2) (authorizing presumption of no defect upon proof of manufacturer's adherence to state of the art in design, manufacturing methods, and testing) and Ariz. Rev. Stat. Ann. §12-683(1) (authorizing affirmative defense upon proof that product plans, manufacturing methods, inspection, testing, and labeling conformed with state of the art). For other states recognizing a state-of-the-art defense, see Indiana Code §34-20-5-1; Iowa Code Ann. §668.12; N.J. Stat. Ann. §2A:58C-3(a)(1); Ohio Rev. Code Ann. §2307.75(F). Occasionally, a court may find itself entangled trying to sort out the parties' respective burdens of proof regarding state-of-the-art evidence. See, e.g., Cavanaugh v. Skil Corp., 751 A.2d 518 (N.J. 2000) (attempting to reconcile plaintiff's burden to prove reasonable alternative design with New Jersey statute allowing for state-of-the-art defense).

A minority of courts continue to take the position that strict liability leaves no place for a "state of the art" argument. See, e.g., Habecker v. Clark Equip. Co., 36 F.3d 278, 285 (3d Cir. 1994) (applying Pennsylvania law) (agreeing with plaintiff that state-of-the-art evidence is "unequivocally impermissible in a Pennsylvania products liability trial"); Murphy v. Chestnut, 464 N.E.2d 818 (Ill. App. Ct. 1984) (state-of-the-art not a valid defense to strict liability claim); Johnson v. Hannibal Mower Corp., 679 S.W.2d 884 (Mo. Ct. App. 1984) (evidence of compliance of lawnmower with standards of American National Standards Institute is inadmissible because compliance with state of the art is irrelevant to strict liability claim; that manufacturer had built the safest product possible under existing technology had no bearing on the claim).

b. Admissibility of Evidence of Subsequent Remedial Measures

The question frequently arises whether a plaintiff should be permitted to introduce evidence of design changes adopted by the defendant subsequent either to distribution or accidental injury. Defendants often try to exclude such evidence on two grounds. First, defendants argue that the highly prejudicial nature of the evidence outweighs its probative value. Although the fact that such a change was made is admittedly relevant to the negligence issue, it is altogether too easy for jurors to jump blindly from the fact of post-sale design change to the conclusion of pre-sale fault. Alternatively, defendants contend that such evidence should be categorically excluded under the traditional rule in negligence cases barring evidence of subsequent remedial measures (Federal Rules of Evidence 407 and its state analogues). This rule is based primarily on the public policy concern that, were it not for the assurance that such evidence would be excluded from litigation, parties might refrain from making safety-related adjustments for fear that the evidence will be used against them.

The competing policy considerations on this issue received a thorough workout in an opinion authored by Judge Richard Posner. In Flaminio v. Honda Motor Co., Ltd., 733 F.2d 463 (7th Cir. 1984), the plaintiff was injured in a single-vehicle accident allegedly caused by vibration in the front end of the motorcycle he was driving. Affirming the district court's exclusion of evidence of subsequent remedial measures in a strict liability case, Judge Posner explained:

> Rule 407 of the Federal Rules of Evidence makes evidence of subsequent remedial measures "not admissible to prove negligence or culpable conduct in connection with the event," but adds: "This rule does not require the exclusion of evidence of subsequent measures when offered for another purpose, such as proving ownership, control, or feasibility of precautionary measures, if controverted, or impeachment.". . . .
>
> [W]e agree with the majority view that the rule does apply to strict liability cases. We are not persuaded by the purely semantic argument to the contrary that since "culpable conduct" is not the issue in such a case — the defendant is liable, at least prima facie, even if he is not blameworthy in the sense of being willful or negligent, provided that he caused the plaintiff's injury — the rule is inapplicable by its own terms. Wisconsin law rejects this argument in holding that a defendant's blameworthiness must, under the state's comparative-negligence statute, be compared with the plaintiff's blameworthiness in strict liability cases, even though the defendant was not blameworthy in a negligence sense. A major purpose of Rule 407 is to promote safety by removing the disincentive to make repairs (or take other safety measures) after an accident that would exist if the accident victim could use those measures as evidence of the defendant's liability. One might think it not only immoral but reckless for an injurer, having been alerted by the accident to the existence of danger, not to take steps to correct the danger. But accidents are low-probability events. The probability of another accident may be much smaller than the probability that the victim of the accident that has already occurred will sue the injurer and, if permitted, will make devastating use at trial of any measures that the injurer may have taken since the accident to reduce the danger.
>
> The analysis is not fundamentally affected by whether the basis of liability is the defendant's negligence or his product's defectiveness or inherent dangerousness. In either case, if evidence of subsequent remedial measures is admissible to prove liability, the incentive to take such measures will be reduced. Id. at 468-469.

Rule 407 has been amended to exclude evidence of subsequent remedial measures in products liability cases regardless of whether plaintiff proceeds under negligence or strict liability. The current version of Rule 407 reads as follows:

> When measures are taken that would have made an earlier injury or harm less likely to occur, evidence of the subsequent measures is not admissible to prove:

- negligence;
- culpable conduct;
- a defect in a product or its design; or
- a need for a warning or instruction.

But the court may admit this evidence for another purpose, such as impeachment or — if disputed — proving ownership, control, or the feasibility of precautionary measures.

State courts have split on the question posed in *Flaminio*. Some hold that the subsequent repair rule does not apply to exclude evidence in strict liability actions. See, e.g., Forma Scientific, Inc. v. BioSera, 960 P.2d 108 (Colo. 1998); Ford Motor Co. v. Fulkerson, 812 S.W.2d 119 (Ky. 1991); Robinson v. G.G.C., Inc., 808 P.2d 522 (Nev. 1991); Sanderson v. Steve Snyder Enterprises, Inc., 491 A.2d 389 (Conn. 1985); Friedrichs v. Huebner, 329 N.W.2d 890 (Wis. 1983); Ault v. Int'l Harvester Co., 528 P.2d 1148 (Cal. 1974) (en banc); Linert v. Foutz, 20 N.E.3d 1047 (Ohio Ct. App. 2014); Magnante v. Pettibone-Wood Manufacturing Co., 228 Cal. Rptr. 420 (Cal. Ct. App. 1986). Similar expressions can be found in some state evidentiary schemes. See Alaska R. Evid. 407; Haw. Rev. Stat. Ann. §626-1, Rule 407; Iowa R. Evid. 5.407.

Other courts, recognizing the distinction between negligence and strict liability to be artificial in design defect cases, apply the rule to bar evidence in strict liability actions as well. See, e.g., Duchess v. Langston Corp., 769 A.2d 1131 (Pa. 2001); Hyjek v. Anthony Indus., 944 P.2d 1036 (Wash. 1997); Cyr v. J.I. Case Co., 652 A.2d 685 (N.H. 1994); Cover v. Cohen, 461 N.E.2d 864 (N.Y. 1984); Hallmark v. Allied Prods. Cos., 646 P.2d 319 (Ariz. 1982). Again, some state evidentiary codes contain similar amendments. See, e.g., Ala. R. Evid. 407; Ariz. R. Evid. 407; Me. R. Evid. 407; Miss. R. Evid. 407; Mont. R. Evid. 407; Rule 11-407 NMRA; Pa. R. Evid. 407; Tex. R. Evid. 407. See also Arthur A. Best & W. Matthew Pierce, The Incongruous Relationship Between Federal Rule of Evidence 407 and the Restatement (Third) of Torts Products Liability Elements of Proof, 91 Denv. U.L. Rev. Online 61 (2014); Craig A. Livingston & John C. Hentschel, Finding Fault with *Ault* — Why the Exclusion of Subsequent Design Change Evidence in Product Liability Cases Makes Sense, Even in California, 78 Def. Couns. J. 285, 291 (2011).

In Griffin v. Suzuki Motor Corp., 124 P.3d 57 (Kan. 2005), the trial court admitted plaintiff's evidence that a successor vehicle to the model that rolled over and injured the plaintiff had been designed to reduce the risks of roll-over. The trial court also admitted evidence regarding vehicle testing standards that had been developed subsequent to the sale of plaintiff's vehicle. The plaintiff argued that the later model did not represent a design change subject to the Kansas statutory version of Rule 407, but rather a whole new concept, with a new name and a new marketing approach. The intermediate court of appeals reversed the judgment for plaintiff, remanding for a new trial. The Supreme Court of Kansas affirmed the ruling of the court of appeals, observing that if the subsequent model was so fundamentally different as to escape the reach of the post-sale-remedial measure exclusionary rule, it could not legitimately serve as a reasonable alternative design.

An interesting issue is whether a change in design made subsequent to sale but before plaintiff's injury is a "subsequent remedial measure." Much of the confusion stems from the ambiguous reference to an "event" as the triggering point for the rule's application. From a public policy standpoint, one could argue that the sale, not the accident, is the important event. Certainly prejudice to the defendant derives from post-sale modifications; and regarding mass-produced and distributed products, post-sale modifications are likely to be post-accident also, regarding at least some victims, if not the actual plaintiff. Notwithstanding these considerations, the Iowa Supreme Court in Tucker v. Caterpillar, Inc., 564 N.W.2d 410 (Iowa 1997), held that evidence of a warning decal and manual issued after manufacture but before plaintiff's accident was not barred under Iowa's subsequent remedial measure rule. Holding that the term "event" referred to the accident or injury underlying the litigation, the Court reasoned that "public policy concerns about deterring safety improvements do not support exclusion of evidence of such measures taken *before* an accident." Id. at 413. But see General Motors Corp. v. Moseley, 447 S.E.2d 302 (Ga. Ct. App. 1994), *overruled on other grounds*, 496 S.E.2d 459 (1998) (considering long-term nature of planning and implementation of design change, fact that change preceded injury did not bar rule's application). Note that the amended Federal Rule of Evidence 407 has resolved the issue for the federal courts by clarifying that the rule applies only after an alleged "injury or harm."

Evidence of post-accident modifications made by a third-party generally is not barred by the exclusionary rule. In Magnante v. Pettibone-Wood Mfg. Co., 228 Cal. Rptr. 420 (Cal. Ct. App. 1986), an intermediate California appellate court admitted evidence that a worker's employer had modified the design of a truss boom after an accident. The court held that even those courts that apply the "subsequent repair rule" to all products liability actions would permit evidence of changes made by someone who did not distribute the product. Admitting evidence of those modifications could not discourage manufacturers from making design changes to their products. See also Diehl v. Blaw-Knox, 360 F.3d 426 (3d Cir. 2004) (applying Pennsylvania law); Ford Motor Co. v. Nuckolls, 894 S.W.2d 897 (Ark. 1995); Hartman v. Opelika Mach. Welding Co., 414 So. 2d 1105 (Fla. Dist. Ct. App. 1982), *petition denied*, 426 So. 2d 27 (Fla. 1983); Denolf v. Frank L. Jursik Co., 238 N.W.2d 1 (Mich. 1975); Emerson v. Garvin Group, LLC, 399 S.W.3d 42 (Mo. Ct. App. E.D. 2013).

Under the explicit terms of Rule 407, a plaintiff may introduce evidence of post-injury changes to show design feasibility. See, e.g., Poulter v. Cottrell, Inc., 50 F. Supp. 3d 953 (N.D. Ill. 2014) (after incident of auto hauler falling from rig, auto rig manufacturer initiated retro-fit program to add grab bars, guard rails, and cat walks to all rigs sold; the court found the evidence admissible to determine the feasibility of alternative design). On the other hand, the defendant can keep the undesired evidence out of the case by admitting the feasibility of the plaintiff's alternative design. See, e.g., Jacobson v. BMW of North America, 2010 WL 1499809 (3d Cir. 2010); Ahlberg v. Chrysler Corp., 481 F.3d 630, 633 (8th Cir. 2007) (applying Iowa law). Moreover, some courts limit the concept of feasibility to technological feasibility alone. Thus, a defendant, while admitting feasibility in the technical sense, may be able to dispute the practicability of an alternative design in terms of added costs and offsetting risks without opening the door for plaintiff to introduce evidence of subsequent design changes. See, e.g., In re Joint E. Dist. & S. Dist. Asbestos Litig., 995 F.2d 343, 345 (2d Cir. 1993) (stating that "'feasibility' is not an open sesame whose mere invocation parts Rule 407 and ushers in evidence of subsequent repairs and remedies"). For a decision grappling with the appropriate scope of the feasibility exception, see Duchess v. Langston Corp., 769 A.2d 1131 (Pa. 2001).

In addition to general evidentiary rules, a number of states also circumscribe the use of subsequent remedial measures in products liability litigation through specific tort reform measures. A statute in Michigan provides an example:

> With regard to the production of a product that is the subject of a product liability action, evidence of a philosophy, theory, knowledge, technique, or procedure that is learned, placed in use, or discontinued after the event resulting in the death of the person or injury to the person or property, which if learned, placed in use, or discontinued before the event would have made the event less likely to occur, is admissible only for the purpose of proving the feasibility of precautions, if controverted, or for impeachment. [Mich. Comp. Laws Ann. §600.2946(3).]

See also Ariz. Rev. Stat. Ann. §12-686; Colo. Rev. Stat. §13-21-404; Idaho Code §6-1406(1).

4. How Do Negligence and Strict Liability Theories Differ? Should Design Claims Be Submitted to Juries on Both Theories?

One can easily understand the substantive difference between negligence and strict liability theories in connection with manufacturing defects. Manufacturing defects are defined mechanically as departures from the intended design. Strict liability means that the manufacturer is liable for harm caused by such defects without the need for risk-benefit analysis to determine fault. But the test for defective design in most jurisdictions rests squarely on risk-utility analysis judged only as of time of sale. Thus, it would appear that defective design is substantially the same as negligent design; if a court insists that it is imposing strict liability on manufacturers for their defective designs, it is strict liability in name only. An early products liability case in Kentucky acknowledged as much, opining that "the distinction between the so-called strict liability principle and negligence is of no practical significance so far as the standard of conduct required of the defendant is concerned. In either event the standard required is reasonable care." Jones v. Hutchinson Mfg., Inc., 502 S.W.2d 66, 69-70 (Ky. 1973). More recent courts also have concluded that strict liability and negligence theories are equivalent in design defect cases. See, e.g., Runge v. Stanley Fastening Systems, L.P., 2011 WL 6755161 (S.D. Ind. 2011); Forslund v. Stryker Corp., 2010 WL 3905854 (D. Minn. 2010); Rupolo v. Oshkosh Truck Corp., 749 F. Supp. 2d 31 (E.D. N.Y. 2010).

Earlier it was suggested that the risk-utility test for defective design derives from Learned Hand's famous "$B < PL$" formulation of negligence. Comment d to §2 of the Products Liability Restatement explains:

> Assessment of a product design in most instances requires a comparison between an alternative design and the product design that caused the injury, undertaken from the viewpoint of a reasonable person. That approach is also used in administering the traditional reasonableness standard in negligence. See Restatement, Second, Torts §283, Comment c. The policy reasons that support use of a reasonable-person perspective in connection with the general negligence standard also support its use in the products liability context.

Given that most American courts adopt a risk-utility approach to questions of defective product design, why do a majority of courts insist on talking about "manufacturers' strict liability" for harm caused by design defects? One answer might be that the courts employ time-of-trial hindsight in holding manufacturers strictly liable for post-sale increases in knowledge of risks and risk-avoidance techniques. But the materials in this section indicate that most American jurisdictions, consistent with their adopting a negligence approach to design, do *not* attribute time-of-trial knowledge to manufacturers. As an alternative explanation, the authors of this casebook are convinced that the persistence of "strict liability for design defects" judicial language can be traced to §402A of the Restatement (Second) of Torts, which fails to distinguish manufacturing defects from design defects and imposes a single "strict liability" rule covering all types of product defects. The authors believe that many courts are trapped, if you will, in the rhetoric of §402A's commitment to a strict liability rule that makes no sense substantively in the context of product design. Thus, for most courts, the continuing talk of strict liability is (mostly) harmless semantics.

But a few courts insist that, although strict liability in the product design and marketing context is close to being identical with negligence, the two theories are different at their core. One well-known example, Anderson v. Owens-Corning Fiberglas Corp., 810 P.2d 549 (Cal. 1991), deals with failure to warn and is noted in Chapter Five, infra. Interestingly, the California high court in *Anderson* expressly rejects reliance on time-of-trial knowledge of product risks that were unknowable at time of distribution, while insisting that strict liability for failure to warn is nevertheless different from negligence. Another such case is Blue v. Environmental Eng'g Inc., 828 N.E.2d 1128 (Ill. 2005), involving an allegedly defective trash compactor design. The Supreme Court of Illinois, while acknowledging that negligence and strict liability are quite similar, insists that they are different: The risk-utility test involving reasonable alternative designs applies to strict liability design claims but not to negligence claims. One may question the coherence of this distinction. The court tries to explain the difference by observing that under strict liability the focus is on the product, whereas under negligence the focus is on the manufacturer's conduct, a distinction commonly drawn in products liability jurisprudence. See, e.g., Mack v. General Elec. Co., 896 F. Supp. 2d 333, 344 (E.D. Pa. 2012); Lind v. Beaman Dodge, Inc., 356 S.W.3d 889 (Tenn. 2011); Branham v. Ford Motor Co., 701 S.E.2d 5, 9 (S.C. 2010).

But would not the conduct of failing to adopt a reasonable alternative design invariably constitute negligence and, simultaneously, render the defendant's design unreasonably dangerous (and thus defective)? Cf. Jablonski v. Ford Motor Co., 923 N.E.2d 347 (Ill. App. Ct. 2010) (questioning the reasoning and precedential value of *Blue*), *overruled on other grounds*, 955 N.E.2d 1138 (Ill. 2011). For discussion, see Aaron D. Twerski, Chasing the Illusory Pot of Gold at the End of the Rainbow: Negligence and Strict Liability in Design Defect Litigation, 90 Marq. L. Rev. 7 (2006).

Lecy v. Bayliner Marine Corp.
973 P.2d 1110 (Wash. Ct. App. 1999)

Cox, J. . . .

In late September 1992, after chartering a motor yacht designed and manufactured by Bayliner, Karen and Henry Lecy and Marco and Pamela Bacich set off on a pleasure cruise from Anacortes to the San Juan Islands. Soon after entering navigable waters between two islands, the boat encountered some turbulence. The wind increased and the swells rose to between two and three feet in height. The couples gathered in the upper cabin. While there, Henry Lecy apparently fell against the port-side cabin door. Lecy and the door both went overboard. He drowned in spite of the rescue efforts of his companions.

Karen Lecy commenced a wrongful death action against Bayliner and others. She later amended her complaint to add a claim for negligent infliction of emotional distress. The Baciches commenced a separate action for negligent infliction of emotional distress against the same defendants. The actions were consolidated for trial.

Over Bayliner's objection, the trial court gave a special verdict form that included interrogatories and alternative answers for strict liability and negligence. Using that form, the jury found that the vessel's door system was not unreasonably dangerous either as to its design or its construction. But the jury then found that Bayliner was negligent in the design of that door system. Based on that finding, the jury further found that Bayliner's negligent design of the door system was the proximate cause of Henry Lecy's death and the emotional distress claims of the Bachiches and Karen Lecy. The jury assessed substantial damages for each of these claims. . . .

Bayliner contends that the trial court erred by denying its CR 50(b) motion for judgment notwithstanding the jury verdict. . . .

Bayliner . . . contends that it was entitled to judgment as a matter of law under federal maritime law because the jury's finding in Bayliner's favor on the strict liability claim precluded it, as a matter of law, from considering the negligent design claim. We agree. . . .

The threshold question that we must resolve in our analysis is what substantive law governs. The parties correctly conclude that the law of admiralty applies. Admiralty jurisdiction applies when (1) the claims arise from an event that occurred on navigable waters and (2) the activity has the potential to affect maritime commerce. Both prongs of this test are met here. The accident occurred on navigable waters. And the operation of a pleasure vessel on navigable waters bears a sufficient relation to maritime commerce to invoke admiralty jurisdiction. "With admiralty jurisdiction comes the application of substantive admiralty law."

The more difficult and crucial question is what substantive rule of admiralty governs. We first resolve that question and then proceed to apply that rule to this case.

Derived from both state and federal sources, "general maritime law is an amalgam of traditional common-law rules, modifications of those rules, and newly created rules." When there are no clear precedents in the law of admiralty, courts may "look to the law prevailing on the land." Courts should also be guided by the aim of maintaining uniformity in admiralty law. State law should be applied only where there is no governing federal statute or judicially created admiralty rule and where there is no likelihood of jeopardizing the uniformity of admiralty practice. In applying state law, courts should apply the general common law rather than the law of any particular state so as to further the goal of uniformity.

Substantive maritime law recognizes both strict liability and negligence in the area of product liability. But the parties here have not presented us with any maritime case that has addressed the precise question at issue here — whether a jury finding of no strict liability for design may be harmonized with a jury finding of negligent design. Our search reveals none. Thus, we turn to land-based federal and state cases and the Restatement (Third) of Torts for guidance.

At the time the parties argued the jury instructions, Bayliner objected to the wording of the special verdict form. In essence, Bayliner took the position that if the jury answered "no" to the interrogatory based on the strict liability for design defect, it should not be permitted to proceed to consider whether Bayliner had been negligent in the design of the door system. The trial court rejected the argument and gave the jury the special verdict form that allowed it to consider both theories, strict liability in design and negligent design.

At issue here is whether the special verdict form was proper in view of the jury's later answers to the interrogatories in that form. The relevant interrogatories and answers are set forth below:

> QUESTION NO. 1: Was the door system for the port side of the pilot house of the vessel Checkmate unreasonably dangerous as designed by Bayliner?
> . . . ANSWER: NO.
> . . .
> QUESTION NO. 6: Was the defendant negligent in the design of the door system in question?
> . . . ANSWER: YES.

If the jury's answers to the special interrogatories that comprise a special verdict conflict, we attempt to harmonize the answers. But we cannot do so here.

Federal and state case law in other jurisdictions is generally in agreement that a jury's rejection of strict liability for design defect precludes a finding of negligent design. In *Lambert*, for instance, a California appellate court recently concluded that the jury's answers to interrogatories on a special verdict form were irreconcilable. The jury answered "no" to the question of whether the Blazer had a design defect, but answered "yes" to the question of whether General Motors was negligent in the design of the 1985 Blazer. The court concluded that the jury's finding of no design defect in the Blazer was fatally inconsistent with its conclusion that General Motors had negligently designed it. The court rejected Lambert's attempt to rescue the verdict by arguing that the jury may have found General Motors negligent for failing to test the vehicle or for failing to warn customers about its weak roof. In the absence of any defect, reasoned the court, these alleged omissions could not have made any difference. Testing cannot reveal a defect that does not exist, and a manufacturer cannot be negligent for failing to warn about a nonexistent defect.

In *Tipton*, the Sixth Circuit reached a similar result. There, by its answers to the interrogatories on a special verdict form, the jury found that the tire in question was not defective or unreasonably dangerous, but that Michelin had negligently designed or manufactured the tire. The court concluded that these answers were irreconcilable because both the strict liability and the negligence theory depended on a finding that the tire was defective. Thus, once the jury found that there was no defect in the tire, it was precluded from finding that Michelin had negligently designed or manufactured that tire. . . .

The Restatement (Third) of Torts lists cases that confirm this general trend. And the Fifth Circuit land-based cases, upon which Bayliner heavily relies, are expressly noted. The Restatement commentators also refer to the "mischief caused by dual instructions on both negligence and strict liability." The standard for product defect liability set forth in the Restatement is based on whether the product is "not reasonably safe" and whether the risk was foreseeable. Thus, reason the commentators, juries will necessarily consider the conduct of the manufacturer and do not need a separate negligence instruction to invite such consideration. . . . [Comment *n* to §2(b) of the Restatement admonishes courts not to give juries the same design claim under two or more different doctrinal headings. See p. 218, infra.]

Lecy and the Baciches rely on . . . Davis v. Globe Mach. Mfg. Corp. [684 P.2d 692 (Wash. 1984)]. There, Davis brought a products liability claim on the basis of both strict liability and negligence. The negligence claim was based on the manufacturer's alleged failure to warn. The trial court dismissed the negligence claim at the close of Davis' case. Davis appealed that dismissal. Globe argued that the issue was moot because the jury found the product reasonably safe under the strict liability test. On the strict liability claim, the jury responded "no" to the following interrogatory: "Did the defendant supply a product which was 'not reasonably safe' at the time it left defendant's control or fail to give an adequate warning necessary to make the use of the product reasonably safe?" The Supreme Court rejected Globe's argument, stating:

> Negligence and strict liability are not mutually exclusive [theories of recovery] because they differ in focus: *negligence focuses upon the conduct of the manufacturer while strict liability focuses upon the product. . . .*

But the court nonetheless concluded that the trial court properly dismissed the negligence claim because there was not sufficient evidence to support it.

Relying on the italicized statement above, Lecy and the Baciches argue that the jury verdict here can be reconciled under *Davis* because negligence focuses on the conduct of the manufacturer, while strict liability focuses on the product. But the record before us refutes this argument, and *Davis* is therefore distinguishable.

Here, the court gave the jury the standard instruction for strict liability for design defect. The focus of the instruction is on what makes a product not reasonably safe (or unreasonably dangerous) as designed. A product may be unreasonably dangerous . . . if:

> at the time of manufacture, the likelihood that the product would cause the plaintiff's harm or similar harms, and the seriousness of those harms, outweighed the manufacturer's burden to design a product that would have prevented those harms and any adverse effect a practical, feasible alternative would have on the product's usefulness. . . .

Because the instruction on unreasonably dangerous design required the jury to engage in risk-utility balancing, it simply cannot be argued that this inquiry did not involve consideration of the manufacturer's conduct in designing the door system. Thus, the reliance on *Davis* for the proposition that strict liability and negligence do not overlap because the former is focused solely on the product while the latter is focused on the manufacturer's conduct is misplaced. Contrary to the contentions of Lecy and the Baciches, the jury here *did* consider the reasonableness of the manufacturer's conduct when it arrived at its conclusion that the door system was not unreasonably dangerous as designed.

Moreover, *Davis* cannot guide our decision here. While it states the uncontested proposition that strict liability and negligence are not mutually exclusive theories, it was not presented with the question — and thus did not decide — whether a finding of reasonably safe design precludes a finding of negligent design. . . .

In sum, we conclude that the reasoning of the case law from other jurisdictions and the commentary in the Restatement (Third) of Torts reflects the general common law approach to the question presented here. Applying this rule, we conclude that the jury's finding that the door system was not unreasonably dangerous as designed precludes it from finding that the door system was negligently designed.

We emphasize that our holding is limited to the situation where the jury finds a product not unreasonably dangerous *as designed*, but then purports to find that same product was negligently *designed*. We recognize that where, for instance, the jury is presented with a strict liability *design* defect claim and a negligent *manufacture* claim, a jury's rejection of strict liability may not preclude its finding of negligence. Because the two bases of liability are separate and do not necessarily overlap, the jury may properly reject strict liability, yet find negligence. . . .

We reverse the judgment and remand for a new trial.

Note that §2(b) sets forth a functional test for design defect. Risk-utility balancing is to be used to determine whether a reasonable alternative design was available at time of distribution. The Restatement makes no mention of whether the doctrinal theory to support liability is strict liability, negligence or the implied warranty of merchantability. Presumably, any legal doctrine can be utilized as long as the plaintiff meets the functional requirements of §2(b). For the reasons developed in Subsection 1, supra, a strong majority of courts agree with *Lecy* that a negligence/no defect verdict is inconsistent. In Garrett v. Hamilton Controls, Inc., 850 F.2d 253, 257 (5th Cir. 1998) (applying Texas law), the court hit the nail on the head:

> A manufacturer logically cannot be held liable for failing to exercise ordinary care when producing a product that is not defective because: (1) if a product is not unreasonably dangerous because of the way it was manufactured, it was not negligent to manufacture it that way and (2) even if the manufacturer was somehow negligent in the design or production of the product, that negligence cannot have caused the plaintiff's injury because the negligence did not render the product "unreasonably dangerous."

See also Kosmynka v. Polaris Indus., Inc., 462 F.3d 74 (2nd Cir. 2006) (jury found that defendant negligently designed all-terrain vehicle but found for defendant on strict liability and implied warranty claims; judgment for plaintiff reversed and remanded, based on inconsistent verdicts under New York law); Golonka v. General Motors Corp., 65 P.3d 956, 965 (Ariz. Ct. App. 2003) ("When a plaintiff's claim for strict liability design and negligent design are factually identical, and the jury employs a risk/benefit analysis to determine that the manufacturer is not at fault for strict liability design, the jury cannot consistently find the product manufacturer at fault for negligent design."). A minority of courts have taken the position that a negligence/no defect verdict is not necessarily inconsistent. See, e.g., Trull v. Volkswagon of Am., Inc. 320 F.3d 1 (1st Cir. 2002) (applying New Hampshire law); Moeller v. Garlock Sealing Technologies, LLC, 2009 WL 1208179, (W.D. Ky. 2009), *rev'd on other grounds*, 660 F.3d 950 (6th Cir. 2011) (applying Kentucky law); In re Vioxx Products Liability Litigation, 523 F. Supp. 2d 471, 474 (E.D. La. 2007) (applying South Carolina law); Livingston v. Isuzu Motors, Ltd., 910 F. Supp. 1473 (D. Mont. 1995) (applying Montana law); Sharp ex. rel Gordon v. Case Corp., 595 N.W.2d 380, 388 (Wis. 1999).

Courts also set verdicts aside on the ground of inconsistency in failure-to-warn cases. See, e.g., Oxford v. Foster Wheeler LCC, 177 Cal. App. 4th 700 (Cal. App. 2009) (jury verdict against plaintiffs on strict liability claim and for plaintiffs on negligence claim were set aside as inconsistent).

The Restatement of Products Liability deals with these issues in Comment *n* to §2, "*Relationship of definitions of defect to traditional doctrinal categories.*" Comment *n* is indifferent as to whether the reasonable alternative design requirement should be clothed in negligence or strict liability language. It insists only that multiple theories not be used for the same functional test. Thus, a plaintiff could choose to argue either that the manufacturer acted negligently in failing to adopt a reasonable alternative design or that the defendant was strictly liable for failing to adopt a reasonable alternative design. But the same design claim should not be given under two different legal theories:

> A . . . difficult question arises as to whether a case should be submitted to a jury on multiple theories of recovery. Design and failure-to-warn claims may be combined in the same case because they rest on different factual allegations and distinct legal concepts. However, two or more factually identical defective-design claims or two or more factually identical failure-to-warn claims should not be submitted to the trier of fact in the same case under different doctrinal labels. Regardless of the doctrinal label attached to a particular claim, design and warning claims rest on a risk-utility assessment. To allow two or more factually identical risk-utility claims to go to a jury under different labels, whether "strict liability," "negligence" or "implied warranty of merchantability," would generate confusion and may well result in inconsistent verdicts.

Although the issue of which theory should be utilized was of little moment to the Restaters, an important study by two professors concludes that a plaintiff's choice of theory may have a significant impact on a jury. Professors Richard L. Cupp, Jr., and Danielle Polage undertook an empirical study of the impact of negligence versus strict liability instructions on mock jurors. Their results are reported in The Rhetoric of Strict Products Liability Versus Negligence: An Empirical Analysis, 77 N.Y.U. L. Rev. 874 (2002). The authors conclude that use of negligence terminology rather than strict liability was more likely to result in jurors' willingness to award any damages; when awards of damages were made they were greater when negligence was the theory presented to them. Thus, a negligence instruction may improve the plaintiff's chances both in terms of imposing liability and receiving a higher damages award.

5. Can a Warning Substitute for a Reasonable Alternative Design?

At the outset of this chapter we discussed the rise and fall of the patent danger rule. We indicated that at the turn of the century courts had soundly rejected the notion that a manufacturer had no duty to adopt a reasonably safer design merely because a product's dangers were open and obvious. The Products Liability Restatement §2, Comment *g*, is in full accord. Though the patent danger rule is dead, defendants often advocate an argument that is a first cousin to it. When a product is accompanied with stark and ominous warnings, defendants contend that the warnings should suffice and that there is no need to adopt a reasonable alternative design. Courts have not taken kindly to this argument.

Uniroyal Goodrich Tire Co. v. Martinez
977 S.W.2d 328 (Tex. 1998)

PHILLIPS, Chief Justice, delivered the opinion of the Court, in which GONZALEZ, SPECTOR, ABBOTT and HANKINSON, Justices, join.

We must decide whether a manufacturer who knew of a safer alternative product design is liable in strict products liability for injuries caused by the use of its product that the user could have avoided by following the product's warnings. The court of appeals held that the mere fact that a product bears an adequate warning does not conclusively establish that the product is not defective. . . . Because we agree, we affirm the judgment of the court of appeals.

I

Roberto Martinez, together with his wife and children, sued Uniroyal Goodrich Tire Company ("Goodrich"), The Budd Company, and Ford Motor Company for personal injuries Martinez suffered when he was struck [on October 31, 1990] by an exploding 16″ Goodrich tire that he was mounting on a 16.5″ rim. Attached to the tire was a prominent warning label containing yellow and red highlights and a pictograph of a worker being thrown into the air by an exploding tire. The label stated conspicuously:

DANGER

NEVER MOUNT A 16″ SIZE DIAMETER TIRE ON A 16.5″ RIM. Mounting a 16″ tire on a 16.5″ rim can cause severe injury or death. While it is possible to pass a 16″ diameter tire over the lip or flange of a 16.5″ size diameter rim, it cannot position itself against the rim flange. If an attempt is made to seat the bead by inflating the tire, the tire bead will break with explosive force.
. . .
    NEVER inflate a tire which is lying on the floor or other flat surface. Always use a tire mounting machine with a hold-down device or safety cage or bolt to vehicle axle.
    NEVER inflate to seat beads without using an extension hose with gauge and clip-on chuck.
    NEVER stand, lean or reach over the assembly during inflation.
. . .
    Failure to comply with these safety precautions can cause the bead to break and the assembly to burst with sufficient force to cause serious injury or death.

Unfortunately, Martinez ignored every one of these warnings. While leaning over the assembly, he attempted to mount a 16″ tire on a 16.5″ rim without a tire mounting machine, a safety cage, or an extension hose. Martinez explained, however, that because he had removed a 16″ tire from the 16.5″ rim, he believed that he was mounting the new 16″ tire on a 16″ rim. Moreover, the evidence revealed that Martinez's employer failed to make an operable tire-mounting machine available to him at the time he was injured, and there was no evidence that the other safety devices mentioned in the warning were available.

In their suit, the Martinezes did not claim that the warnings were inadequate, but instead alleged that Goodrich, the manufacturer of the tire, Budd, the manufacturer of the rim, and Ford, the designer of the rim, were each negligent and strictly liable for designing and manufacturing a defective tire and rim. Budd and Ford settled with the Martinezes before trial, and the case proceeded solely against Goodrich.

At trial, the Martinezes claimed that the tire manufactured by Goodrich was defective because it failed to incorporate a safer alternative bead design that would have kept the tire from exploding. This defect, they asserted, was the producing cause of Martinez's injuries. Further, they alleged that Goodrich's failure to adopt this alternative bead design was negligence that proximately caused Martinez's injury.

The bead is the portion of the tire that holds the tire to the rim when inflated. A bead consists of rubber-encased steel wiring that encircles the tire a number of times. When the tire is placed inside the wheel rim and inflated, the bead is forced onto the bead-seating ledge of the rim and pressed against the lip of the rim, or the wheel flange. When the last portion of the bead is forced onto this ledge, the tire has "seated," and the air is properly sealed inside the tire. The bead holds the tire to the rim because the steel wire, unlike rubber, does not expand when the tire is inflating. The tire in this case was a 16″ bias-ply light truck tire with a 0.037″ gauge multi-strand weftless bead, or tape bead, manufactured in 1990. A tape bead consists of several strands of parallel unwoven steel wires circling the tire with each layer resting on top of the last, similar to tape wound on a roll. After a number of layers have been wound, the end of the bead is joined, or spliced, to the beginning of the same bead to form a continuous loop.

The Martinezes' expert, Alan Milner, a metallurgical engineer, testified that a tape bead is prone to break when the spliced portion of the bead is the last portion of the bead to seat. This is commonly called a hang-up. Milner testified that an alternative bead design, a 0.050″ gauge single strand programmed bead, would have prevented Martinez's injuries because its strength and uniformity make it more resistant to breaking during a hang-up. Milner explained that the 0.050″ single strand programmed bead is stronger because it is 0.013″ thicker and that it is uniform because it is wound, or programmed, by a computer, eliminating the spliced portion of the bead that can cause the tire to explode during a hang-up. . . .

Milner explained that the computer technology required to manufacture the programmed bead was developed in 1972 and widely available by 1975. Milner testified that Goodyear began using a 0.051″ gauge single strand programmed bead in its radial light truck tires in 1977, and that Yokohama began using a single strand programmed bead in its radial light truck tires in 1981. Milner also testified that General Tire began using a single strand programmed bead in its bias-ply light truck tires in 1982. Finally, Milner testified that Goodrich itself began using the single strand programmed bead in its 16″ radial light truck tires in 1991. Based upon this evidence and his expert opinion, Milner testified that the tire manufactured by Goodrich with a tape bead was defective and unreasonably dangerous. Because Goodrich had also been sued in thirty-four other lawsuits alleging accidents caused by mismatching Goodrich tires, Milner asserted that Goodrich was grossly negligent in failing to adopt the 0.050″ single strand programmed bead in its bias-ply 16″ light truck tires.

Milner also testified that the rim designed by Ford and manufactured by Budd was defective because its size was not clearly marked on it and because it could have been redesigned to prevent a 16″ tire from passing over its flange.

The jury found that Goodrich's conduct was the sole proximate cause of Martinez's injuries and that Goodrich was grossly negligent. Furthermore, the jury found that the tire manufactured by Goodrich was defective, while the wheel rim designed by Ford and manufactured by Budd was not defective. The jury allocated 100% of the producing cause of Martinez's injuries to the acts and omissions of Goodrich.

The court of appeals affirmed the award of actual damages. . . . However, the court of appeals reversed and rendered the award of punitive damages, holding that there was no evidence to support the jury's finding of gross negligence.

Only Goodrich applied to this Court for writ of error. As in the court of appeals, Goodrich's principal argument here is that no evidence supports the jury finding that the tire was defective because "the tire bore a warning which was unambiguous and conspicuously visible (and not claimed to be inadequate); the tire was safe for use if the warning was followed; and the cause of the accident was mounting and inflating a tire in direct contravention of those warnings." . . .

II

A

This Court has adopted the products liability standard set forth in section 402A of the Restatement (Second) of Torts. . . .

To prove a design defect, a claimant must establish, among other things, that the defendant could have provided a safer alternative design. . . .

The newly released Restatement (Third) of Torts: Products Liability carries forward this focus on reasonable alternative design. See Restatement (Third) of Torts: Products Liability. §2(b). . . .

To determine whether a reasonable alternative design exists, and if so whether its omission renders the product unreasonably dangerous (or in the words of the new Restatement, not reasonably safe), the finder of fact may weigh various factors bearing on the risk and utility of the product. [The court excerpts Comment *f* from the Products Liability Restatement, supra.]

Goodrich urges this Court to depart from this standard by following certain language from Comment *j* of the Restatement (Second) of Torts. Comment *j* provides in part:

> Where warning is given, the seller may reasonably assume that it will be read and heeded; and a product bearing such a warning, which is safe for use if it is followed, is not in defective condition, nor is it unreasonably dangerous.

Restatement (Second) of Torts §402A cmt. *j* (1965). The new Restatement, however, expressly rejects the Comment *j* approach:

> Reasonable designs and instructions or warnings both play important roles in the production and distribution of reasonably safe products. In general, when a safer design can reasonably be implemented and risks can reasonably be designed out of a product, adoption of the safer design is required over a warning that leaves a significant residuum of such risks. For example, instructions and warnings may be ineffective because users of the product may not be adequately reached, may be likely to be inattentive, or may be insufficiently motivated to follow the instructions or heed the warnings. However, when an alternative design to avoid risks cannot reasonably be implemented, adequate instructions and warnings will normally be sufficient to render the product reasonably safe. . . . *Warnings are not, however, a substitute for the provision of a reasonably safe design.*

Restatement (Third) of Torts: Products Liability §2 cmt. *l* (emphasis added). The Reporters' Notes in the new Restatement refer to Comment *j* as "unfortunate language" that "has elicited heavy criticism from a host of commentators." Restatement (Third) of Torts: Products Liability §2, Reporters' Note, cmt. *l* (citing Howard Latin, Good Warnings, Bad Products, and Cognitive Limitations, 41 U.C.L.A. L. Rev. 1193 (1994) (utilizing the work of cognitive theorists to demonstrate that warnings should only be used as a supplement to a design that already embodies reasonable safety and not as a substitute for it); Aaron D. Twerski, *et al.*, The Use and Abuse of Warnings in Products Liability: Design Defect Comes of Age, 61 Cornell L. Rev. 495, 506 (1976)). Similarly, this Court has indicated that the fact that a danger is open and obvious (and thus need not be warned against) does not preclude a finding of product defect when a safer, reasonable alternative design exists. . . . ("A number of courts are of the view that obvious risks are not design defects which must be remedied. (citations omitted). However, our Court has held that liability for a design defect may attach even if the defect is apparent.") . . .

B

[W]e agree with the new Restatement that warnings and safer alternative designs are factors, among others, for the jury to consider in determining whether the product as designed is reasonably safe. *See* Restatement (Third) of Torts: Products Liability §2 cmt. *f.* While the dissenting justices say that they also agree with the Restatement's approach, they would, at least in this case, remove the balancing process from the jury. Instead, they would hold that Goodrich's warning rendered the tape bead design reasonably safe as a matter of law.

The dissenting justices first argue that Goodrich's warning was clear and that it could have been followed, and consequently Martinez was injured only by "[i]gnoring . . . his own good sense." *Post* at 343. Even if this were true, it is precisely because "it is not at all unusual for a person to fail to follow basic warnings and instructions," General Motors Corp. v. Saenz, 873 S.W.2d 353, 358 (Tex. 1993), that we have rejected the superseded Comment *j*. The dissent also notes that there have been few reported mismatch accidents involving tires with this particular warning label. While this is certainly relevant, and perhaps would persuade many juries, we cannot say that it conclusively establishes that the tire is reasonably safe when weighed against the other evidence. The jury heard firsthand how an accident can occur despite the warning label, and how a redesigned tire would have prevented that accident. The jury also heard evidence that Goodrich's competitors had incorporated the single strand programmed bead by the early 1980s, and that Goodrich itself adopted this design in 1991, a year after manufacturing the tire that injured Martinez. Under these circumstances, there is at least some evidence supporting the jury's finding of product defect. . . .

Because we conclude that there is some evidence to support the judgment of the court below on the theory of products liability, we need not consider Goodrich's claim that there is no evidence as to negligence. For the foregoing reasons, we affirm the judgment of the court of appeals.

HECHT, J., files a dissenting opinion, in which ENOCH and BAKER, JJ. join, and in which OWEN, J., joins in all but Part II. . . .

Since it is human nature to disregard instructions, a rule that any product is reasonably safe as long as it bears an adequate warning of the risks of its use is not feasible. Such behavior, however, does not warrant the opposite rule that warnings are irrelevant in determining whether a product is reasonably safe. I agree with the Court that comment *l* to Section 2 of the Restatement (Third) of Torts: Products Liability now has it about right: [The dissent quotes comment *l*, set forth in the majority opinion.]

I do not agree, however, that the Court correctly reads or follows comment *l*. Comment *l* limits but does not foreclose the role of warnings in making products reasonably safe, even when there is a safer alternative design. The Court stresses the last sentence of comment *l* and brushes past the first sentence. Taken as a whole, the comment says, correctly, I think, that a safer alternative design that eliminates a risk is required over a warning that leaves a significant residuum of risk because product users may not get the warning, may be inattentive, or may not be motivated to heed the warning. . . .

Section 2(b) of the Restatement (Third) of Torts: Products Liability states the applicable rule: [The court sets out §2(b).]

There are two components to this rule: the possibility of a safer, reasonable alternative design, *and* a product that is not reasonably safe without that design. Both are required. Even if a reasonable alternative design would make a product safer, the product is not defective unless the omission of the design makes the product not reasonably safe. The comparison is not between the two designs, but between the product alternatively designed and the product including any warning. Comment *f* to Section 2 explains: [The court excerpts from Comment *f*, supra.]

Given the ease with which injury can be avoided, there is no evidence that redesigning the bead wire will eliminate a "significant residuum of risk" in the tire as designed with the warning label. In fact, Martinez's own evidence is to the contrary. The record establishes that there has been only one other claimed injury caused by attempting to mount a 16″ tire with a warning label on a 16.5″ wheel. The record does not reflect whether that claim was ever proved. Thousands of 16″ tires have been manufactured with warning labels; millions of 16.5″ wheels have been manufactured without warning labels. Martinez's evidence (which should not have been admitted) shows thirty-four claims against Goodrich for injuries caused by mismatching unlabeled 16″ tires on 16.5″ wheels. There has been one other claim involving a labeled tire. The tire industry should not be compelled to redesign bead wires to make tires harder to explode — or pay damages for failing to do so — simply because one or perhaps two mechanics over the years failed to follow directions or their own good sense. . . .

The record in this case shows that Goodrich's tire including the warning label was not defectively designed as a matter of law. Even if that were not so, Goodrich is entitled to have its liability determined in a fair trial in which at least some responsibility for the accident is assigned to Martinez. . . . Because the Court denies Goodrich any relief, I respectfully dissent.

Having read the majority and dissent, on whose side do you come down? Note that both the majority and dissent embrace §2, Comment *l*. They differ only as to its application to the facts. What do you make of the dissent's argument that §2(b) requires proof of a reasonable alternative design *and* proof that the omission of the reasonable alternative design renders the product *not reasonably safe?* The dissent utilized the "not reasonably safe" requirement as the conceptual tool that allowed it, in light of the clear warnings provided with the product, to deny liability even though a safer alternative design was clearly available. Can you think of other reasons why the Restaters might have adopted a test for defect that required that both of these elements be established? If the safer alternative design suggested by plaintiff is reasonable, does it not necessarily follow that its omission renders the product not reasonably safe?

For other cases adopting the view of the *Uniroyal* majority, see Rogers v. Ingersoll-Rand Co., 144 F.3d 841 (D.C. Cir. 1998) (warnings on a milling machine about the dangers that arise when machine is backing up does not shield the manufacturer from liability where defect in system prevented alarm from operating); Delaney v. Deere & Co., 999 P.2d 930, 942 (Kan. 2000) (observing that "just because there is a warning on a piece of equipment does not prevent the equipment from being dangerous"); Lewis v. American Cyanamid Co., 715 A.2d 967 (N.J. 1998) ("when considering plaintiff's reasonably foreseeable misuses, [the jury] must decide whether the [product's] design was defective despite the presence of warnings cautioning against such misuses"). See also White v. ABCO Eng'g Corp., 221 F.3d 293, 305-06 (2d Cir. 2000) (applying New Jersey law), (determining that despite clearly adequate warnings, manufacturer of conveyor could be held liable for failure to provide side guarding); Kampen v. American Isuzu Motors, 157 F.3d 306 (5th Cir. 1998) (applying Louisiana law) (approving Comment *l* but ruling that specific warning against misuse rendered the product use one that was not reasonably anticipated by the manufacturer); Leaf v. Goodyear Tire & Rubber Co., 590 N.W.2d 525 (Iowa 1999) (casting doubt as to propriety in design defect case of utilizing Comment *j* presumption that warning will be heeded when provided; Restatement §2 Comment *l* may be more appropriate governing standard); Eads v. R. D. Werner Co., 847 P.2d 1370 (Nev. 1993) (concluding that warning a ladder can tip is not dispositive on the issue of defect when stronger side rails would have made the ladder more stable).

D.   RISK-UTILITY: PRODUCT CATEGORY LIABILITY

The Products Liability Restatement confronts the question of whether liability should be imposed on an entire category of inherently dangerous products even though no alternative designs are available by which to reduce the risks.

Restatement (Third) of Torts: Products Liability
(1998)

---

§2.   CATEGORIES OF PRODUCT DEFECT

. . .

COMMENT:

. . .

d. Design defects: general considerations. . . . The requirement in Subsection (b) that the plaintiff show a reasonable alternative design applies in most instances even though the plaintiff alleges that the category of product sold by the defendant is so dangerous that it should not have been marketed at all. See Comment *e*. Common and widely distributed products such as alcoholic beverages, firearms, and above-ground swimming pools may be found to be defective only upon proof of the requisite conditions in Subsection (a), (b), or (c). If such products are defectively manufactured or sold without reasonable warnings as to their danger when such warnings are appropriate, or if reasonable alternative designs could have been adopted, then liability under §§1 and 2 may attach. Absent proof of defect under those Sections, however, courts have not imposed liability for categories of products that are generally available and widely used and consumed, even if they pose substantial risks of harm. Instead, courts generally have concluded that legislatures and administrative agencies can, more appropriately than courts, consider the desirability of commercial distribution of some categories of widely used and consumed, but nevertheless dangerous products.

A prominent exception to the trend against imposing product category liability was the case of O'Brien v. Muskin Corp., 463 A.2d 298 (N.J. 1983). Despite warnings against diving, plaintiff dove into a shallow above-ground pool manufactured by defendant. Plaintiff's hands separated upon hitting the slippery vinyl bottom of the pool and he struck his head causing injuries. The trial court refused to charge the jury on plaintiff's design defect claim and the state high court reversed, holding that a product manufacturer could be found liable for users' injuries even in the absence of a reasonable alternative design:

> The assessment of the utility of a design involves the consideration of available alternatives. If no alternatives are available, recourse to a unique design is more defensible. The existence of a safer and equally efficacious design, however, diminishes the justification for using a challenged design.
>
> The evaluation of the utility of a product also involves the relative need for that product; some products are essentials, while others are luxuries. A product that fills a critical need and can be designed in only one way should be viewed differently from a luxury item. Still other products, including some for which no alternative exists, are so dangerous and of such little use that under the risk-utility analysis, a manufacturer would bear the cost of liability of harm to others. That cost might dissuade a manufacturer from placing the product on the market, even if the product has been made as safely as possible. Indeed, plaintiff contends that above-ground pools with vinyl liners are such products and that manufacturers who market those pools should bear the cost of injuries they cause to foreseeable users.
>
> A critical issue at trial was whether the design of the pool, calling for a vinyl bottom in a pool four feet deep, was defective. The trial court should have permitted the jury to consider whether, because of the dimensions of the pool and slipperiness of the bottom, the risks of injury so outweighed the utility of the product as to constitute a defect. In removing that issue from consideration by the jury, the trial court erred. To establish sufficient proof to compel submission of the issue to the jury for appropriate fact-finding under risk-utility analysis, it was not necessary for plaintiff to prove the existence of alternative, safer designs. Viewing the evidence in the light most favorable to plaintiff, even if there are no alternative methods of making bottoms for above-ground pools, the jury might have found that the risk posed by the pool outweighed its utility.
>
> In a design-defect case, the plaintiff bears the burden of both going forward with the evidence and of persuasion that the product contained a defect. To establish a prima facie case, the plaintiff should adduce sufficient evidence on the risk-utility factors to establish a defect. With respect to above-ground swimming pools, for example, the plaintiff might seek to establish that pools are marketed primarily for recreational, not therapeutic

purposes; that because of their design, including their configuration, inadequate warnings, and the use of vinyl liners, injury is likely; that, without impairing the usefulness of the pool or pricing it out of the market, warnings against diving could be made more prominent and a liner less dangerous. It may not be necessary for the plaintiff to introduce evidence on all those alternatives. Conversely, the plaintiff may wish to offer proof on other matters relevant to the risk-utility analysis. It is not a foregone conclusion that plaintiff ultimately will prevail on a risk-utility analysis, but he should have an opportunity to prove his case. . . . [Id. at 305-306.]

In partial dissent, one justice chastised the majority for imposing "absolute liability":

The majority holds that the jury should have been permitted to decide whether the risks of above-ground swimming pools with vinyl bottoms exceed their usefulness despite adequate warnings and despite unavailability of any other design. The plaintiff had the burden of proving this proposition. Yet he adduced no evidence on many of the factors bearing on the risk-utility analysis. There was no evidence on the extent that these pools are used and enjoyed throughout the country; how many families obtain the recreational benefits of swimming and play during a summer; how many accidents occur in the same period of time; the nature of the injuries and how many result from diving. There was no evidence of the feasibility of risk spreading or of the availability of liability insurance or its cost. There was no evidence introduced to enable one to gauge the effect on the price of the product, with or without insurance. The liability exposures, particularly if today's decision is given retroactive effect, could be financially devastating.

There factors should be given some consideration when deciding the policy question of whether pool manufacturers and, in the final analysis, consumers should bear the costs of accidents arising out of the use of pools when no fault can be attributed to the manufacturer because of a flaw in the pool, availability of a better design, or inadequate warning. If this Court wishes to make absolute liability available in product cases and not leave such decisions to the Legislature, it should require that trial courts determine in the first instance as a matter of law what products should be subject to absolute liability. In that event the court would consider all relevant factors including those utilized in the risk-utility analysis. [Id. at 314.]

O'Brien has been effectively overruled by statute in New Jersey. It is clear that the drafters of the statute took dead aim at *O'Brien* when they provided that a product could not be found defective in design if "there was not a practical and technically feasible alternative design that would have prevented the harm without substantially impairing the reasonably anticipated or intended function of the product." N.J. Stat. Ann. §2A:58C-3(a)(1). The statute provides an exception from this provision when the product is (1) egregiously unsafe, (2) one whose dangers are unknown to the reasonable consumer, and (3) one that has little or no usefulness. (This exception, and the impetus behind it, will be discussed subsequently.) There is no doubt, however, that *O'Brien* on its facts is a dead letter. Another jurisdiction has imposed liability based on a risk-utility analysis of the value of the product to society. In Halphen v. Johns-Manville Sales Corp., 484 So. 2d 110 (La. 1986), the court concluded that an asbestos manufacturer could be held to a strict liability standard for a product that fails to meet risk-utility norms because the dangers created by its use, even if unforeseen at the time of manufacture, outweigh its utility. Only if a product passed the risk-utility test so that its social value outweighed its risk was the plaintiff required to prove an alternative design. *Halphen*, like *O'Brien*, was overridden by statute. La. Rev. Stat. Ann. §9:2800.56(1).

Perhaps because of anticipated legislative overrides, most courts do not entertain the possibility of product category liability. See, e.g., Graham v. R.J. Reynolds Tobacco Co., 2015 WL 1546522 (11th Cir. 2015) (the State of Florida "may not enforce a duty . . . premised on the theory that all cigarettes are inherently defective and that every cigarette sale is an inherently negligent act. . . . these specific, sweeping bases for state tort liability . . . frustrate the full purposes and objectives of Congress . . ."); S.F. v. Archer Daniels Midland Co., 594 Fed. App'x 11 (2d. Cir. 2014) (affirming dismissal of suit against manufacturer of high fructose corn syrup for allegedly causing diabetes because, under New York law, "a design-defect claim will not stand if the only alternative is an outright ban"); Fabiano v. Philip Morris Inc., 29 Misc. 3d 395, 909 N.Y.S.2d 314, 320 (Sup. Ct. N.Y. County 2010) (observing "the vast majority of courts have been markedly unreceptive to the call that they displace markets, legislatures, and governmental agencies by decreeing whole categories of products to be outlaws"). Notwithstanding such general reluctance, one may still find a court considering category liability on occasion. See, e.g., Union Carbide Corp. v. Aubin, 97 So. 3d 886 (Fla. Dist. Ct. App. 2012) (concluding that adequate evidence had been presented to allow jury to determine whether asbestos product was categorically unreasonable); Ruiz-Guzman v. Amvac Chem. Corp., 7 P.3d 795 (Wash. 2000) (entertaining the possibility that a pesticide may fail risk-utility balancing even absent proof of a RAD).

One doctrinal response courts use to deflect claims of categorical liability is primary assumption of the risk. Because the unavoidable risks inherent in categories of products are more often than not generally known and patently obvious, courts are able to say that users and consumers of such products assume, as a matter of law, the risks inherently associated with their use and consumption. In effect, primary assumption of risk is a no-duty rule that terminates the defendant's responsibility for the unavoidable risks inherent in product categories before getting to the question of defect. Thus, in Yoneda v. Tom, 133 P.3d 796 (Haw. 2006), the plaintiff was a golfer struck in the eye by a golf ball while leaving a restroom on the golf course. The Supreme Court of Hawaii affirmed a summary judgment in favor of the defendant golfer who hit the ball and in favor of the owner of the golf course for the unavoidable risks inherent in the sport of golf. But the high court remanded for trial of the plaintiff's claim that the course could have been designed differently to reduce the risks of being struck while exiting the restrooms. Many other jurisdictions also allow the primary assumption of risk defense in products liability. See, e.g., LePage v. E-One, Inc., 4 F. Supp. 3d 298 (D. Mass. 2014) (applying Rhode Island law); Garrison v. Novartis Pharm. Corp., 30 F. Supp. 3d 1325 (M.D. Ala. 2014) (applying Alabama law); Reott v. Asia Trend, Inc., 55 A.3d 1088 (Pa. 2012); Wangsness v. Builders Cashway, Inc., 779 N.W.2d 136 (S.D. 2010); Kane v. Landscape Structures, Inc., 709 S.E.2d 876 (Ga. Ct. App. 2011). In some states, this "inherent risk" defense has been codified by statute. See, e.g., Clark v. Brass Eagle, Inc., 866 So. 2d 456 (Miss. 2004) (paintball gun manufacturer not liable as a matter of law). But see Muller v. Jackson Hole Mountain Resort, 139 P.3d 1162 (Wyo. 2006) (statute providing defense regarding inherent risks of recreational activities does not apply to products used in such activities).

In McCarthy v. Olin Corp., 119 F.3d 148 (2d Cir. 1997) (applying New York law), a wrongful death action on behalf of victims who were killed in Colin Ferguson's highly publicized murderous shooting spree on the Long Island Railroad was brought against the manufacturer of the "Black Talon" bullets used by Ferguson. Black Talon ammunition incorporates a hollow point bullet that is designed to expand upon impact, exposing razor-sharp edges at a 90-degree angle to the bullet. The expansion dramatically increases the wounding power of the bullet. Plaintiffs argued that the bullets were defectively designed in that they caused more damage than would have been caused by an ordinary bullet. The claim was thus one for enhanced injury. See Chapter Three. The heart of plaintiffs' claim of design defect was that Black Talon bullets failed the risk-utility test, the governing test for defect in New York. In affirming the trial court's grant of defendant's motion to dismiss, the court said that "The purpose of the risk/utility analysis is to determine whether the risk of injury might have been reduced or avoided if the manufacturer had used a feasible alternative design. . . . However, the risk of injury to be balanced with the utility is a risk not intended as the primary function of the product. . . . There is no reason to search for an alternative safer design where the product's sole utility is to kill or maim. Accordingly we hold that appellants have failed to state a cause of action under New York strict products liability law." Id. at 155. Was the court right to view plaintiffs' case as a claim for product category liability? If so, which is the relevant product category: bullets or hollow point bullets?

Notwithstanding the overwhelming judicial rejection of product category liability, a debate continues in the law reviews as to its propriety.

James A. Henderson, Jr. & Aaron D. Twerski, Closing the American Products Liability Frontier: The Rejection of Liability Without Defect
66 N.Y.U. L. Rev. 1263 (1991)

Product-Category Liability: Some Initial Terminology

Before addressing the merits of the various product-category liability proposals, we should clarify certain issues of terminology that might seem confusing at first. Initially, one might argue that product-category liability would rest on a finding of defectiveness — the entire product category would be deemed defective either because it does not offer sufficient benefits to justify the injuries it causes or because it satisfies some other criterion. We prefer terminology that avoids reliance on defectiveness because we feel that legal terminology, whenever possible, should clarify what is happening in the litigation to which it refers. To stretch the term "defective" to include broad categories of products that are not defective in any traditional sense could mask the profound differences between this use of the term "defective" and its more traditional uses. Courts that have faced this issue appear to have sensed the possible confusion and have avoided using "defectiveness" terminology. . . .

The variable that determines whether one is dealing with a product category or merely a marginal design variation within a category is the degree of substitutability of the alternative suggested by the plaintiff and the product as designed by the defendant. In traditional, intracategory design litigation, the alternative design suggested or implicated by the plaintiff is a relatively close substitute for the product as designed by the defendant. Bicycles with slightly longer handlebars are close substitutes for bicycles with slightly shorter handlebars. Presumably, if plaintiffs succeeded with longer-handle bar claims, the new alternative design would resemble so closely the older design as to be nearly a perfect substitute, thus effectively driving the former variation, which alone would carry the burden of tort liability, from the new bicycle market. A few bicycle design purists might be willing to pay a substantial premium for the older, shorter-handled but less stable design. But intuitively, it seems likely that this demand would be so small that it would not justify the continued mass production of the earlier design.

In contrast, when a plaintiff attacks a bicycle design on the ground that a two wheeled cycle is inherently unsafe, the next best alternative — a tricycle — is not a very close substitute. Although a far better substitute for a bicycle than many other products, a tricycle is a much less suitable substitute for a bicycle than was the two-wheeled cycle with slightly longer handle bars. Indeed, a tricycle is so poor a substitute for a bicycle that if a court held that three wheels were minimally required to produce a safe cycle, it would be imposing liability not for how the defendant designed the bicycle but for having designed and distributed any sort of bicycle in the first place. Drawing on terminology currently in use, the court could be said to condemn bicycles for the "unavoidably unsafe" aspect that defines two-wheeled transportation: lateral instability at low speeds. In other words, the court would be condemning the product for the very design feature — two-wheeledness — that not only rendered it more dangerous but also made it desirable to a majority of its users and consumers.

Problems of Implementation Presented by Product-Category Liability

. . . For the traditional process of adjudication to work rationally and properly, the parties must use applicable legal doctrine to focus their claims so that they may insist upon a favorable outcome as a matter of right. As Professor Fuller explained, some problems are polycentric in nature. They consist of elements that are connected to one another as are the strands of a spider's web, so that a decision with regard to any element affects the decisions with regard to all the others. Such problems are not suited to judicial resolution because neither side can move from element to element in an orderly sequence. . . .

That risk-utility-based product-category liability cases would be unadjudicable can be seen by considering how the parties would attempt to argue a typical claim. For example, in connection with a claim that small, cheap handguns are unreasonably dangerous and should be subject to strict liability, how small is small? How cheap is cheap? For what range of accidents and adverse outcomes are distributors to be liable? Are suicides by handguns to be compensable? How are the parties to obtain relevant data on the social costs associated with small handguns, especially if they cannot agree on the relevant parameters of the problem? Presumably small handguns serve useful as well as wasteful social purposes: people collect them as hobbyists and possess them for protection, deriving pleasure and senses of well-being. How can a court quantify those utilities?

To be answered rationally, the question whether handguns of a particular size and monetary price are "good for society" would require extended legislative or administrative hearings and investigations. Even if courts attacked these problems incrementally, on a case-by-case basis, it is unrealistic to hope that courts could adjudicate their ways to intelligent, consistent solutions. Bearing in mind the magnitude of the stakes involved — imposing absolute liability might tax small handguns off the market — it is hardly surprising that most courts have refused to get involved.

Explicit Attempts to Establish Product-Category Liability

. . . Many plaintiffs have asked the courts to adopt a theory of product-category liability. Notwithstanding the plaintiff's success in *O'Brien*, courts overwhelmingly have turned plaintiffs away as a matter of law, offering a variety of reasons. Most of the reasons mirror both the policy and implementation problems identified earlier in our discussion of the theoretical and practical problems that would flow from the adoption of product-category liability. . . .

Several courts have noted that the list of products that would become subject to risk-utility attack is substantial. Alcohol, cigarettes, radar detectors, all-terrain vehicles, and high-speed automobiles are all products that arguably score high on the misery scale, and yet most are prominent fixtures in a free-market economy. Given the wide range of individual consumer behavior when making use of these products, judges understandably are loath to place the onus for injury on the manufacturer. Thus, one of the reasons that courts are hostile to the idea of product-category liability may be that they intuit that the list of product categories to which such an approach might apply is great and the implications for each product on the list enormous. Indeed, many judges appear to view the product-category liability derisively, describing it as "radical" and "delightfully nonsensical."[Footnotes omitted.]

The article called forth a response from Mark A. Geistfeld, Implementing Enterprise Liability: A Comment on Henderson and Twerski, 67 N.Y.U. L. Rev. 1157 (1992) and a rebuttal by Henderson and Twerski, The Unworkability of Court Made Enterprise Liability: A Reply to Geistfeld, 67 N.Y.U. L. Rev. 1174 (1992). The following excerpt is from another article responding to Henderson and Twerski.

Ellen Wertheimer, The Smoke Gets in Their Eyes: Product Category Liability and Alternative Feasible Designs in the Third Restatement
61 Tenn. L. Rev. 1429 (1994)

. . . Professors Henderson and Twerski seem to equate product category liability with liability without defect. This is only true, of course, if the concept of defect is defined as necessarily including the failure to use an alternative feasible design. If defect is defined in terms of failed risk-utility tests, then the test of defectiveness does not require an alternative feasible design. Because it requires the application of a risk-utility test, this definition does not constitute liability without defect.

Treating liability in the absence of an alternative feasible design as synonymous with liability without defect also falls into the common trap of using the concepts of "danger" and "defect" interchangeably. These terms do not mean the same thing; "dangerousness" represents a factual characteristic of a product, while "defectiveness" is a legal conclusion about that product. A dangerous product is not necessarily defective, it is only defective if its costs outweigh its benefits. In short, liability depends upon whether a product is defective, not whether it is dangerous. The argument that the definition of defect must require proof of an alternative feasible design to avoid this problem is grounded on the mistaken idea that danger and defect are synonymous.

Dangerous products exist that clearly pass the risk-utility test and are therefore not defective; automobiles are one example. Although automobiles must meet certain safety standards, there is no way to eliminate all the risks that they pose. Yet no one could seriously argue that their dangers outweigh their utility. Although the safest automobile remains dangerous, automobiles are not defective because their benefits outweigh their remaining costs. An automobile manufacturer cannot be held liable simply because a car has proved generically dangerous; there must be more to show that the car was defective.

Interestingly, it is difficult to distinguish product category liability cases from other design defect cases in automobile litigation. For example, in Dreisonstok v. Volkswagenwerk, A.G., the plaintiff argued that the design of a Volkswagen minibus was defective when compared with the design of a passenger car. Plaintiff contended that the minibus design was defective because it did not embody the level of crash-proofing possible for a passenger vehicle. This could be construed as either: (1) an argument that there was an alternative feasible design (passenger car) that should have been used instead, or (2) a challenge that minibuses as a product category are unavoidably unsafe and should not be manufactured at all. Given these two plausible interpretations, it is difficult to determine whether *Dreisonstok* was an alternative feasible design case or a product category liability case. The basic argument was that the minibus aspect of the design was defective, and that there was an alternative — the automobile. For plaintiff to prevail, however, requires the conclusion that minibuses are unavoidably unsafe because they are not cars.

My favorite example of a product which is dangerous, useless, and without alternative feasible design is the cigarette. If the Restatement (Third) requires proof of an alternative feasible design, cigarettes will be exempt from its coverage. Is this an appropriate result?

Lawsuits based on cigarette smoking have almost always been characterized as failure to warn cases. But a lawsuit against cigarette manufacturers for defective design need not involve failure to warn. In a lawsuit not brought on a failure to warn theory, the plaintiff would argue that cigarettes are defective under Section 402A because they fail the risk-utility test. Their defect lies in the fact that the dangers they embody outweigh any utility they might possess. Unfortunately, there is no alternative feasible design that would eliminate the dangers, but showing such an alternative feasible design was not required for liability under section 402A as originally written.

Current commentators reject the idea that cigarette manufacturers should be liable for their product. But they fail to make a convincing case for their position. On the contrary, a cigarette manufacturer's liability for its product would fulfill the purposes of strict products liability doctrine superbly.

Cigarettes cause untold injury and death, both to those who smoke and to those who are exposed to the smoke generated by others. This grotesque fact becomes even more appalling because manufacturers of cigarettes generate huge profits. The manufacturers, however, do not pay for the injuries their product causes. Strict products liability was designed to treat the injuries caused by products as a cost of doing business. Cigarette manufacturers thus receive a windfall because they collect profits on sales of their product, but do not pay its true costs. If cigarette manufacturers still turn a profit after properly being held liable for the true costs of their product, then presumably they will continue to make and sell cigarettes. If they do not continue to make a profit after paying the costs of their product, presumably they would halt production. Economists should rejoice in this result, because it represents the marketplace working to perfection. Products that make a profit will continue to be produced; those that do not make a profit, will not. If cigarette manufacturers are found liable for the injuries their product causes, they will raise their prices, and the costs will fall on smokers. . . .

Would Professor Wertheimer allow a jury to weigh the risk-utility of a minibus? Would it be irrational to conclude that the benefits of the minibus do not outweigh the rather substantial increased risk of harm to the driver and passengers when such vehicles are involved in collisions? And why shouldn't minibuses — or automobiles, for that matter — be made to pay the cost of accidents? Wouldn't the price of cars then reflect what she calls the "true costs" of the product?

The debate continues. Professor David Owen, after flirting with product category liability in The Graying of Products Liability Law: Paths Taken and Untaken in the New Restatement, 61 Tenn. L. Rev. 1241, 1253-1257 (1994), now seems to clearly reject it. See David G. Owen, Defectiveness Redefined: Exploding the Myth of "Strict" Products Liability, 1996 U. Ill. L. Rev. 743, 774-775 (1996) ("Generally, the proper focal point for the risk-utility balance is the particular safety feature of the alternative design proposed by the plaintiff that would have prevented or reduced the plaintiff's harm. Ordinarily, therefore, what are relevant are the *incremental* ('marginal') risks and benefits of adopting the particular design safety feature proposed by the plaintiff — those (that would have been) incurred in *moving* from the manufacturer's actual design to the plaintiff's hypothetical alternative design."). See also Richard C. Ausness, "Danger Is My Business": The Right to Manufacture Unsafe Products, 67 Ark. L. Rev. 827, 827 (2014); Neal S. Shechter, After Newtown: Reconsidering Kelley v. R.G. Industries and the Radical Idea of Product-Category Liability for Manufacturers of Unreasonably Dangerous Firearms, 102 Geo. L.J. 551, 552 (2014); Symposium on Generic Products Liability, 72 Chi.-Kent L. Rev. 1 et seq (1996); Harvey M. Grossman, Categorical Liability: Why the Gates Should be Kept Closed, 36 S. Tex. L. Rev. 385 (1995).

Giving in to pressures to allow for exceptions to the "no category liability" rule when products are egregiously dangerous, some state legislatures have built such exceptions into their statutes generally abolishing category liability. See the discussion of such statutes in the text immediately following *O'Brien v. Muskin Corp.*, supra. And the drafters of the Products Liability Restatement gave in to these same pressures and allowed for the possibility that courts might recognize such an exception on their own, as part of the common-law development of products liability law.

Restatement (Third) of Torts: Products Liability
(1998)

§2. CATEGORIES OF PRODUCT DEFECT

. . .

COMMENT:

. . .

e. Design defects: possibility of manifestly unreasonable design. Several courts have suggested that the designs of some products are so manifestly unreasonable, in that they have low social utility and high degree of danger, that liability should attach even absent proof of a reasonable alternative design. In large part the problem is one of how the range of relevant alternative designs is described. For example, a toy gun that shoots hard rubber pellets with sufficient velocity to cause injury to children could be found to be defectively designed within the rule of Subsection (b). Toy guns unlikely to cause injury would constitute reasonable alternatives to the dangerous toy. Thus, toy guns that project ping-pong balls, soft gelatin pellets, or water might be found to be reasonable alternative designs to a toy gun that shoots hard pellets. However, if the realism of the hard-pellet gun, and thus its capacity to cause injury, is sufficiently important to those who purchase and use such products to justify the court's limiting consideration to toy guns that achieve realism by shooting hard pellets, then no reasonable alternative will, by hypothesis, be available. In that instance, the design feature that defines which alternatives are relevant — the realism of the hard-pellet gun and thus its capacity to injure — is precisely the feature on which the user places value and of which the plaintiff complains. If a court were to adopt this characterization of the product, and deem the capacity to cause injury an egregiously unacceptable quality in a toy for use by children, it could conclude that liability should attach without proof of a reasonable alternative design. The court would declare the product design to be defective and not reasonably safe because the extremely high degree of danger posed by its use or consumption so substantially outweighs its negligible social utility that no rational, reasonable person, fully aware of the relevant facts, would choose to use, or to allow children to use, the product.

In McCarthy v. Olin Corp., 119 F.3d 148 (2d Cir. 1997), discussed supra, Judge Guido Calabresi dissented from the majority's dismissal of a categorical attack on "Black Talon" hollow-point bullets, suggesting that they might well fall within the exception in Comment *e*.

Parish v. Jumpking, Inc.
719 N.W.2d 540 (Iowa 2006)

LARSON, Justice.

James Parish was severely injured while using a trampoline manufactured by the defendant, Jumpking, Inc. Parish sued Jumpking on theories of defective design of the trampoline and negligence in failing to warn of the danger in using it. The defendant moved for summary judgment, which was granted, and the plaintiff appealed. We affirm.

I. *Facts and Prior Proceedings*

In June of 1999, Delbert Parish (the plaintiff's brother) and Shelley Tatro purchased a Jumpking fourteen-foot trampoline for use in their backyard. They set up the trampoline, and Delbert tried it out by attempting a somersault. He nearly fell off the trampoline, prompting Delbert and Shelley to purchase a "fun ring" — a netlike enclosure with one entry point onto the trampoline. While the plaintiff was visiting his brother on September 11, 1999, he attempted to do a back somersault on the trampoline, but he landed on his head and was rendered a quadriplegic. In August 2001 Parish filed suit, on his own behalf and on behalf of his minor son, against Jumpking, as designer and manufacturer of the trampoline and its enclosure.

II. The Issues

The district court entered summary judgment against the plaintiff on all claims, and he argues on appeal that this was error because there were genuine issues of material fact on his design-defect claim and on the adequacy of Jumpking's warnings. He also contends that the "open and obvious" defense is not applicable to a design-defect case, and in any event, there was an issue of material fact as to its application here. . . .

IV. The Defective Design Claim

In Wright v. Brooke Group Ltd., 652 N.W.2d 159 (Iowa 2002), we adopted sections 1 and 2 of the Restatement (Third) of Torts: Products Liability [hereinafter Restatement]. Section 2 of the Restatement recognizes three types of product defect:

> A product is defective when, at the time of sale or distribution, it contains a manufacturing defect, is defective in design, or is defective because of inadequate instructions or warnings. A product:
> . . .
> (b) is defective in design when the foreseeable risks of harm posed by the product could have been reduced or avoided by the adoption of a reasonable alternative design by the seller or other distributor, or a predecessor in the commercial chain of distribution, and the omission of the alternative design renders the product not reasonably safe[.]

The plaintiff's first argument is that the district court erred in granting summary judgment on his design-defect claim under section 2(b). Under a design-defect claim, a plaintiff is essentially arguing that, even though the product meets the manufacturer's design specifications, the specifications themselves create unreasonable risks. To succeed under section 2(b), a plaintiff must ordinarily show the existence of a reasonable alternative design, and that this design would, at a reasonable cost, have reduced the foreseeability of harm posed by the product. Restatement §2 cmt. d.

The Restatement recognizes exceptions to the requirement of a reasonable alternative design, but the plaintiff relies on only one: that the design was "manifestly unreasonable" under Restatement section 2(b) comment e. Under that comment,

> the designs of some products are so manifestly unreasonable, in that they have low social utility and high degree of danger, that liability should attach even absent proof of a reasonable alternative design.

The plaintiff concedes that he has not offered an alternative design; rather, he argues a trampoline is so inherently dangerous that a reasonable design alternative is not available. He contends there is no safe way to use a trampoline in a backyard, and it must be used only by properly trained and qualified participants under supervision.

The Restatement provides this illustration of a manifestly unreasonable product under comment e:

> ABC Co. manufactures novelty items. One item, an exploding cigar, is made to explode with a loud bang and the emission of smoke. Robert purchased the exploding cigar and presented it to his boss, Jack, at a birthday party arranged for him at the office. Jack lit the cigar. When it exploded, the heat from the explosion lit Jack's beard on fire causing

serious burns to his face. If a court were to recognize the rule identified in this Comment, the finder of fact might find ABC liable for the defective design of the exploding cigar even if no reasonable alternative design was available that would provide similar prank characteristics. The utility of the exploding cigar is so low and the risk of injury is so high as to warrant a conclusion that the cigar is defective and should not have been marketed at all.

Restatement §2(b) cmt. *e*, illus. 5.

Application of the "manifestly unreasonable" exception presents an issue of first impression in Iowa. However, the wording of section 2(b) and virtually all commentary on it suggest that this exception should be sparingly applied. In fact, such exceptions to the requirement of a reasonable alternative design were "grudgingly accepted by the Reporters," Keith C. Miller, Myth Surrenders to Reality: Design Defect Litigation in Iowa, 51 Drake L. Rev. 549, 564 (2003), suggesting that the drafters did not intend for there to be any exceptions to this requirement. One of the reporters to the Restatement agrees:

> [B]ear in mind that our comment *e* talks about extremely dangerous products with very low social utility. It substitutes for the qualitative problem in the general design area, a kind of quantitative solution. We admit that there may be times, and I think they'd be rare, probably non-existent, when a product might come to court, to you, that was so bad, so very outloud bad, so very antisocial, that it would tug against the very grain of the way you were raised.

James A. Henderson, Jr., The Habush Amendment: Section 2(b) comment *e*, 8-Fall Kan. J.L. & Pub. Pol'y 86, 86 (1998).

Suits involving common and widely distributed products are more likely than others to require the showing of a reasonable alternative. According to the Restatement,

> [c]ommon and widely distributed products such as alcoholic beverages, firearms, and above-ground swimming pools may be found to be defective only upon proof of [a reasonable alternative design]. If such products are [] sold without reasonable warnings as to their danger . . . then liability under §§1 and 2 may attach. Absent proof of defect under those Sections, however, courts have not imposed liability for categories of products that are generally available and widely consumed, even if they pose substantial risks of harm.

Restatement §2(b) cmt. *d*.

While comment *e* recognizes the possibility that egregiously dangerous products might be held defective for that reason alone, the Restatement has noted that "a clear majority of courts that have faced the issue have refused so to hold." Restatement §2, American Case Law and Commentary on Issues Related to Design-Based Liability, at 87. In this commentary, the Restatement discussed several cases imposing liability under comment *e* but observed that "[e]ach of these judicial attempts at imposing such liability have either been overturned or sharply curtailed by legislation." Id. at 89. . . .

In cases involving common and widely distributed products,

> courts generally have concluded that legislatures and administrative agencies can, more appropriately than courts, consider the desirability of commercial distribution of some categories of widely used and consumed, but nevertheless dangerous, products.

Restatement §2(b) cmt. *d.*

It is undisputed that trampolines are common and widely distributed products. In fact, the evidence showed approximately fourteen million people use them. Even data produced by the plaintiff in his resistance to summary judgment showed that in 2002 only 2.1% of trampolines were associated with injuries, and only one-half of one percent of jumpers were injured. The Consumer Product Safety Commission, based on 1997 and 1998 injury data, concluded trampolines ranked twelfth among recreational use products in terms of injuries. They rated below such common activities as basketball, bicycle riding, football, soccer, and skating.

The benefits of trampolining include use in cardiovascular workouts and other medical treatments, including "bouncing" therapy for children with cystic fibrosis. Trampolining obviously provides valuable exercise and entertainment.

We conclude that the plaintiff has failed to generate a genuine issue of fact sufficient to except this product from the alternative-design requirement of section 2(b), and the plaintiff's design-defect claim under that section must therefore be rejected.

[Judgment for defendant affirmed.]

In Lykins v. Fun Spot Trampolines, 172 Ohio App. 3d 226 (Ohio App. 2007), the plaintiff was a young woman who bounced off a backyard trampoline, landed on her back, and became a quadriplegic. She claimed that the defendants should have warned her of the risks accompanying her particular use of the trampoline. The trial court granted summary judgment for defendant trampoline sellers on the ground that the dangers of using trampolines are open and obvious. The appellate court reversed and remanded, holding that a jury could find that the particular dangers created by more than one person bouncing on the trampoline at the same time and the presence of more than 225 pounds on the trampoline were not obvious and that defendants may have breached their duty to warn.

Dawson v. Chrysler Corp.
630 F.2d 950 (3d Cir. 1980), *cert. denied*, 450 U.S. 959 (1981)

ADAMS, C.J.

This appeal from a jury verdict and entry of judgment in favor of the plaintiffs arises out of a New Jersey automobile accident in which a police officer was seriously injured. The legal questions in this diversity action, that are governed by New Jersey law, are relatively straight-forward. The public policy questions, however, which are beyond the competence of this Court to resolve and with which Congress ultimately must grapple, are complex and implicate national economic and social concerns. . . .

I.   *Factual Background*

On September 7, 1974, Richard F. Dawson, while in the employ of the Pennsauken Police Department, was seriously injured as a result of an automobile accident that occurred in Pennsauken, New Jersey. As Dawson was driving on a rain-soaked highway, responding to a burglar alarm, he lost control of his patrol car — a 1974 Dodge

Monaco. The car slid off the highway, over a curb, through a small sign, and into an unyielding steel pole that was fifteen inches in diameter. The car struck the pole in a backwards direction at a forty-five degree angle on the left side of the vehicle; the point of impact was the left rear wheel well. As a result of the force of the collision, the vehicle literally wrapped itself around the pole. The pole ripped through the body of the car and crushed Dawson between the seat and the "header" area of the roof, located just above the windshield. The so-called "secondary collision" of Dawson with the interior of the automobile dislocated Dawson's left hip and ruptured his fifth and sixth cervical vertebrae. As a result of the injuries, Dawson is now a quadriplegic. He has no control over his body from the neck down, and requires constant medical attention.

Dawson, his wife, and their son brought suit . . . against the Chrysler Corporation, the manufacturer of the vehicle in which Dawson was injured. . . . The plaintiffs' claims were based on theories of strict products liability and breach of implied warranty of fitness. They alleged that the patrol car was defective because it did not have a full, continuous steel frame extending through the door panels, and a cross-member running through the floor board between the posts located between the front and rear doors of the vehicle. Had the vehicle been so designed, the Dawsons alleged, it would have "bounced" off the pole following relatively slight penetration by the pole into the passenger space.

Expert testimony was introduced by the Dawsons to prove that the existing frame of the patrol car was unable to withstand side impacts at relatively low speed, and that the inadequacy of the frame permitted the pole to enter the passenger area and to injure Dawson. The same experts testified that the improvements in the design of the frame that the plaintiffs proposed were feasible and would have prevented Dawson from being injured as he was. According to plaintiffs' expert witnesses, a continuous frame and cross-member would have deflected the patrol car away from the pole after a minimal intrusion into the passenger area and, they declared, Dawson likely would have emerged from the accident with only a slight injury.

In response, Chrysler argued that it had no duty to produce a "crashproof" vehicle, and that, in any event, the patrol car was not defective. Expert testimony for Chrysler established that the design and construction of the 1974 Dodge Monaco complied with all federal vehicle safety standards, and that deformation of the body of the vehicle is desirable in most crashes because it absorbs the impact of the crash and decreases the rate of deceleration on the occupants of the vehicle. Thus, Chrysler's experts asserted that, for most types of automobile accidents, the design offered by the Dawsons would be less safe than the existing design. They also estimated that the steel parts that would be required in the model suggested by the Dawsons would have added between 200 and 250 pounds to the weight, and approximately $300 to the price of the vehicle. It was also established that the 1974 Dodge Monaco's unibody construction was stronger than comparable Ford and Chevrolet vehicles.

After all testimony had been introduced, Chrysler moved for a directed verdict, which the district judge denied. The jury thereupon returned a verdict in favor of the plaintiffs. In answers to a series of special interrogatories, the jurors concluded that (1) the body structure of the 1974 Dodge Monaco was defective and unreasonably dangerous; (2) Chrysler breached its implied warranty that the vehicle would be fit for use as a police car; (3) as a result of the defective design and the breach of warranty, Dawson sustained more severe injuries than he would have incurred had Chrysler used the alternative design proposed by Dawson's expert witnesses; (4) the defective design was the proximate cause of Dawson's enhanced injuries; and (5) Dawson's failure to use a seatbelt was not a proximate cause of his injuries. The jury awarded Mr. Dawson $2,064,863.19 for his expenses, disability, and pain and suffering, and granted Mrs. Dawson $60,000.00 for loss of consortium and loss of services. After the district court entered judgment, Chrysler moved for judgment notwithstanding the verdict or, alternatively for a new trial. The court denied both motions. The Dawsons then requested pre-judgment interest of eight percent per annum of the damages award, accruing from the time suit was instituted to the date of the judgment. The trial judge granted the request in the amounts of $388,012.53 for Mr. Dawson and $11,274.72 for Mrs. Dawson.

On appeal, Chrysler raises the following contentions: (1) It owed no duty to the Dawsons to manufacture an automobile that would withstand the type of collision that occurred here. (2) The evidence presented by the Dawsons was insufficient to establish that the patrol car was defective and unreasonably dangerous or that Chrysler breached an implied warranty of fitness. (3) The evidence did not sufficiently establish that Dawson's injuries in fact were caused by the allegedly defective design.

We affirm.

II.   Discussion

[The court concludes that strict liability applies, and that the defendant owed the plaintiff a duty to provide a reasonably crashworthy automobile. The court proceeds to the question of whether a jury could find for the plaintiff on the facts in this case.]

Chrysler maintains that, under these standards, the district court erred in submitting the case to the jury because the Dawsons failed, as a matter of law, to prove that the patrol car was defective. Specifically, it insists that the Dawsons did not present sufficient evidence from which the jury reasonably might infer that the alternative design that they proffered would be safer than the existing design, or that it would be cost effective, practical, or marketable. In short, Chrysler urges that the substitute design would be less socially beneficial than was the actual design of the patrol car. In support of its argument, Chrysler emphasizes that the design of the 1974 Dodge Monaco complied with all of the standards authorized by Congress in the National Traffic and Motor Vehicle Safety Act of 1966, Pub. L. 89-563, tit. I, §107, 80 Stat. 718, codified in 15 U.S.C. §1396 (1976), and set forth in accompanying regulations, 49 C.F.R. §571.1 (1979).

Compliance with the safety standards promulgated pursuant to the National Traffic and Motor Vehicle Safety Act, however, does not relieve Chrysler of liability in this action. For, in authorizing the Secretary of Transportation to enact these standards, Congress explicitly provided, "Compliance with any Federal motor vehicle safety standard issued under this subchapter does not exempt any person from any liability under common law." 15 U.S.C. §1397(c) (1976). Thus, consonant with this congressional directive, we must review Chrysler's appeal on the question of the existence of a defect under the common law of New Jersey that is set forth above.

Our examination of the record persuades us that the district court did not err in denying Chrysler's motion for judgment notwithstanding the verdict. The Dawsons demonstrated that the frame of the 1974 Dodge Monaco was noncontinuous — that is, it consisted of a front portion that extended from the front of the car to the middle of the front passenger seat, and a rear portion that ran from the middle of the rear passenger seat to the back end of the vehicle. Thus, there was a gap in the seventeen-inch side area of the frame between the front and rear seats. The plaintiffs also proved that, after colliding with the pole, the car slid along the left side portion of the rear frame until it reached the gap in the frame. At that point, the pole tore through the body of the vehicle into the passenger area and proceeded to push Dawson into the header area above the windshield.

Three experts — a design analyst, a mechanical engineer, and a biochemical engineer — also testified on behalf of the Dawsons. These witnesses had examined the patrol car and concluded that it was inadequate to withstand side impacts. They testified that there was an alternative design available which, had it been employed in the 1974 Monaco, would have prevented Dawson from sustaining serious injuries. The substitute design called for a continuous frame with an additional cross member running between the so-called B-posts — the vertical posts located at the side of the car between the front and rear seats. According to these witnesses, this design was known in the industry well before the accident and had been tested by a number of independent testing centers in 1969 and in 1973.

The mechanical engineer conducted a number of studies in order to ascertain the extent to which the alternative design would have withstood the crash. On the basis of these calculations, he testified that the pole would have penetrated only 9.9 inches into the passenger space, and thus would not have crushed Dawson. Instead, the engineer stated, the car would have deflected off the pole and back into the highway. Under these circumstances, according to the biochemical engineer, Dawson would have been able to "walk away from the accident" with but a bruised shoulder.

Also introduced by the Dawsons were reports of tests conducted for the United States Department of Transportation, which indicated that, in side collisions with a fixed pole at twenty-one miles per hour,[1] frame improvements similar to those proposed by the experts presented by the Dawsons reduced intrusion into the passenger area by fifty percent, from sixteen inches to eight inches. The study concluded that the improvements, "in conjunction with interior alterations, demonstrated a dramatic increase in occupant protection." There was no suggestion at trial that the alternative design recommended by the Dawsons would not comply with federal safety standards. On cross-examination, Chrysler's attorney did get the Dawsons' expert witnesses to acknowledge that the alternative design would add between 200 and 250 pounds to the vehicle and would cost an additional $300 per car. The Dawsons' experts also conceded that the heavier and more rigid an automobile, the less able it is to absorb energy upon impact with a fixed object, and therefore the major force of an accident might be transmitted to the passengers. Moreover, an expert for Chrysler testified that, even if the frame of the patrol car had been designed in conformity with the plaintiffs' proposals, Dawson would have sustained injuries equivalent to those he actually incurred. Chrysler's witness reasoned that Dawson was injured, not by the intrusion of the pole into the passenger space, but as a result of being thrown into the header area of the roof by the vehicle's initial contact with the pole — that is, prior to the impact of the pole against the driver's seat.

On the basis of the foregoing recitation of the evidence presented respectively by the Dawsons and by Chrysler, we conclude that the record is sufficient to sustain the jury's determination, in response to the interrogatory, that the design of the 1974 Monaco was defective. The jury was not required to ascertain that all of the factors enumerated by

---

1. Eyewitness as well as expert testimony was introduced to show that the speed of the car at the time of impact was between twenty-four and twenty-six miles per hour.

---

authors' dialogue 11

DOUG: Aaron and Jim, help me out with something — why is *Dawson* included in this section on category liability?

JIM: Funny you should ask, Doug, because *Dawson* is included here against my better judgment. *Dawson* is an interesting case, but not because it raises the issue of category liability. If I were to apply a label to the problem that *Dawson* poses, I would say that it presents the problem of *seriatim* liability. Suppose that Chrysler designs a car like the Dodge Monaco with a frame with less rigidity. In a side collision the plaintiff suffers enhanced injury and a jury finds that the frame should have been more rigid. If Chrysler conforms to the wishes of the jury and designs its car with a more rigid frame it will face lawsuits from plaintiffs who suffer enhanced injury in head-on collisions. Occupants of a car that has a less rigid frame are better off in head-on collisions with a frame that is deformable and thus takes the energy of the crash rather than passing it on to passengers. So Chrysler switches to a rigid frame after the first case and the next jury nails Chrysler for not having a deformable, less rigid frame. Chrysler ends up liable either way. That is the problem that the *Dawson* court talks about. I don't see this being a category liability case. It's a problem with any reasonableness issue presented on similar facts in different cases to successive juries in a "*seriatim*" fashion.

AARON: I don't disagree with you that the *Dawson* court is concerned with what you call the *seriatim* problem. But I see the court embracing category liability as well. Remember that the plaintiff's alternative design was one that would add 200-250 pounds of steel to the Dodge Monaco. That's one heck of a lot of steel and costs an additional $300 per vehicle. You must admit that redesigning a small economy car so that it becomes a mid-size sedan does raise category liability problems. Now, I'm not sure at what point you cross the line between marginal change to mega change, but I suspect that 250 pounds of steel is getting close. The majority does talk about the fact that American cars are in competition with the small foreign car market and that auto manufacturers have been attempting to reduce auto size to get better gas mileage. No, Jim, *Dawson* legitimately raises the category liability question.

JIM: Look, Aaron, *Dawson* is still a far cry from *O'Brien*, in which the New Jersey court held that above-ground swimming pools as a class may be declared

---

the New Jersey Supreme Court in [Cepeda v. Cumberland Engineering, Inc., 76 N.J. 152, 386 A.2d 816 (1978)] weighed in favor of the Dawsons in order to find the patrol car defective. Rather, it need only to have reasonably concluded, after balancing these factors, that, at the time Chrysler distributed the 1974 Monaco, the car was "not reasonably fit, suitable and safe for its intended or reasonably foreseeable purposes." [Suter v. San Angelo Foundry & Machine Co., 81 N.J. 150, 169, 406 A.2d 140, 149 (1979).] Moreover, our role in reviewing the record for purposes of determining

defective. But even if *Dawson* does not raise the problem of category liability it may raise an enterprise liability problem that is a first-cousin to category liability. You know economists would look at the *seriatim* problem and say that it is just not a real issue. Auto manufacturers will learn from experience that whether they make the frame of a car more rigid or less rigid they will be found liable by juries. They will then simply adopt the version they think is more cost-effective, insure against the residual accident/liability costs of not doing it the other way, and add those insurance costs to the price of the car.

AARON: Isn't that inevitable in a system that is not governed solely by administrative regulation? As long as fact finders, be they judge or jury, will be deciding factually similar cases *seriatim* we will get some of what you refer to as enterprise liability in the form of inconsistent jury verdicts case to case.

JIM: I agree. But the rules shouldn't encourage such verdict patterns, and commentators shouldn't ignore the fact that they are problematic. And if you think that it's essentially harmless to encourage inconsistent verdicts case to case you must have skipped that material on enterprise liability we set out at the beginning of this chapter explaining why our legal system cannot make manufacturers insurers of last resort. It is always possible to conjure up some design fix that would have avoided or lessened a plaintiff's enhanced injury. Auto manufacturers thus become liable for making cars (not for making defective cars). A liability system that does not utilize a sensibly defined concept of defect as the linchpin will eventually self-destruct because of adverse selection and moral hazard problems. I thought we did a good job of explaining those concepts earlier in the text.

AARON: My memory is not half as bad as you think. The argument as to why enterprise liability cannot be insured against is good. I buy it. However, liability is not imposed in all cases where an auto crashes and a plaintiff suffers enhanced injuries. Liability is imposed only when a jury decides that a reasonable alternative design could have been adopted. Admittedly, juries can make contradictory findings and that is troubling. But as long as the reasonable alternative designs that juries are advocating call for marginal changes we will not seriously threaten insurability.

JIM: Which leaves us where we started. *Dawson* presents a *seriatim* problem, not a category liability problem.

DOUG: Hmm, I'm starting to sense another *seriatim* problem developing.

---

whether a trial judge erred in denying a motion for a directed verdict or for judgment notwithstanding the verdict is necessarily a limited one. As we stated in [Huddell v. Levin, 537 F.2d 726 (3d Cir. 1976)], " 'The Seventh Amendment bars appellate review of facts found by a jury in actions at common law. . . . ' " 537 F.2d at 736 (quoting 9 C. Wright & A. Miller, Federal Practice and Procedure §2571, at 681 (1971)). Thus, we are admonished to review the record in this case in the light most favorable to the nonmoving party, the Dawsons, and to affirm the judgment of the district court denying the motions unless the record "is critically deficient of that minimum quantum of evidence from which a jury might reasonably afford relief." Denneny v. Siegel, 407 F.2d 433, 439 (3d Cir. 1969); accord, *Huddell*, 537 F.2d at 737. We hold that it is not. . . .

The remaining question in regard to the motion for judgment notwithstanding the verdict is whether the Dawsons presented sufficient evidence to permit the jury reasonably to conclude that the design defect was the proximate cause of Dawson's injuries. In this regard, Chrysler advances three arguments. First, it urges that the patrol car was substantially modified by Dawson's employer in such a way that the car, as sold by Chrysler, could not be said to have caused the injuries. Second, it maintains that Dawson's failure to wear a seat belt was, in fact, the proximate cause of his injuries.[2] Third, it claims that there was insufficient evidence that the defect caused Dawson to suffer more severe injuries than he would have incurred had the alternative design been employed — that is, had the patrol car not been defective.

Counsel for the Dawsons conceded that the patrol car had been modified by the addition of a tubular roll bar and a wire mesh screen that extended between the front and rear passenger areas in order to separate the police officer from suspects. Dawsons' expert witnesses testified, however, that this alteration neither compromised the structural integrity of the vehicle, nor in any way contributed to Dawson's injuries. In contrast, the expert witnesses for Chrysler testified merely that they were not certain whether the modifications affected Dawson's injuries. Under these circumstances, the jury's implicit conclusion that the alterations were not the proximate cause of Dawson's injuries is supported by the evidence.

The jury specifically found in interrogatory five that Dawson's failure to wear his seatbelt was not a proximate cause of his injuries. Chrysler presented expert testimony that Dawson was injured when he "ramped" up the seat back into the roof of the car — that is, as he slid upwards out of his seat along the back rest — following the vehicle's initial impact with the pole. It argues therefore that, if Dawson had been wearing a seatbelt, he would not have been thrown out of the seat and would not have smashed into the roof of the car. Chrysler maintains that the jury's verdict is inconsistent with this testimony.

In *Huddell*, we noted in reviewing on appeal a question regarding causation that "the credibility of opinion evidence is for the fact-finder." Here, the Dawsons presented expert witnesses who contradicted Chrysler's theory of causation. Observing initially that the patrol car was moving backwards at a forty-five degree angle at the time of impact, the witnesses opined that the force of the collision must have pushed Dawson's back and left shoulder against the rear of the seat. Under these circumstances, they concluded, he did not "ramp" up the seat into the roof, but remained in the seat until the pole entered the passenger space, collided with the rear of the seat, and pushed both the seat and Dawson into the ceiling. In other words, had the pole been prevented from crushing up against the rear of the driver's seat, Dawson would not have been thrown into the ceiling. This testimony was corroborated by a third expert, who stated that the nature of Dawson's dislocated hip indicated that he was not thrown from the seat as Chrysler's witnesses maintained. The jurors reasonably could have found the testimony offered by the Dawsons' witnesses to be more persuasive than

---

2. Dawson testified that, at the time of the accident, he was not wearing a seat belt, but that this was customary police practice in order to permit officers to enter and leave their vehicles as quickly as possible.

Chrysler's. Accordingly, Chrysler's contention that the jury's verdict is at odds with the evidence is without merit.

Chrysler's last argument regarding causation is that the plaintiffs failed to prove that Dawson's injuries were enhanced as a result of the design-defect in the patrol car. As with the other contentions, the record does not support this claim. The Dawsons presented expert testimony that the alternative design would have prevented the pole from intruding far enough into the passenger space to hit the front seat. And, as we have just observed, there was testimony that Dawson was not thrown into the ceiling of the car, but rather was crushed up against the roof as the pole forced the passenger seat into the roof. Had Dawson remained in his seat from gravity forces, and had the seat not been jammed against the roof, it is a reasonable inference that his cervical vertebrae would not have been ruptured. Indeed, the biochemical engineer who evaluated the accident and testified for the Dawsons concluded that, if the pole had not entered the patrol car and crushed Dawson, the officer would have suffered no more than a bruised shoulder. In view of this testimony, we cannot say that the jury's verdict on the question of proximate cause is unsupported by the record. . . .

III. Conclusion

Although we affirm the judgment of the district court, we do so with uneasiness regarding the consequences of our decision and of the decisions of other courts throughout the country in cases of this kind.

As we observed earlier, Congress, in enacting the National Traffic and Motor Vehicle Safety Act, provided that compliance with the Act does not exempt any person from liability under the common law of the state of injury. The effect of this provision is that the states are free, not only to create various standards of liability for automobile manufacturers with respect to design and structure, but also to delegate to the triers of fact in civil cases arising out of automobile accidents the power to determine whether a particular product conforms to such standards. In the present situation, for example, the New Jersey Supreme Court has instituted a strict liability standard for cases involving defective products, has defined the term "defective product" to mean any such item that is not "reasonably fit, suitable and safe for its intended or reasonably foreseeable purposes," and has left to the jury the task of determining whether the product at issue measures up to this standard.

The result of such arrangement is that while the jury found Chrysler liable for not producing a rigid enough vehicular frame, a factfinder in another case might well hold the manufacturer liable for producing a frame that is too rigid. Yet, as pointed out at trial, in certain types of accidents — head-on collisions — it is desirable to have a car designed to collapse upon impact because the deformation would absorb much of the shock of the collision, and divert the force of deceleration away from the vehicle's passengers. In effect, this permits individual juries applying varying laws in different jurisdictions to set nationwide automobile safety standards and to impose on automobile manufacturers conflicting requirements. It would be difficult for members of the industry to alter their design and production behavior in response to jury verdicts in such cases, because their response might well be at variance with what some other jury decides is a defective design. Under these circumstances, the law imposes on the industry the responsibility of insuring vast numbers of persons involved in automobile accidents.

Equally serious is the impact on other national social and economic goals of the existing case-by-case system of establishing automobile safety requirements. As we have become more dependent on foreign sources of energy, and as the price of that energy has increased, the attention of the federal government has been drawn to a search to find alternative supplies and the means of conserving energy. More recently, the domestic automobile industry has been struggling to compete with foreign manufacturers which have stressed smaller, more fuel-efficient cars. Yet, during this same period, Congress has permitted a system of regulation by ad hoc adjudications under which a jury can hold an automobile manufacturer culpable for not producing a car that is considerably heavier, and likely to have less fuel efficiency.

In sum, this appeal has brought to our attention an important conflict that implicates broad national concerns. Although it is important that society devise a proper system for compensating those injured in automobile collisions, it is not at all clear that the present arrangement of permitting individual juries, under varying standards of liability, to impose this obligation on manufacturers is fair or efficient. Inasmuch as it was the Congress that designed this system, and because Congress is the body best suited to evaluate and, if appropriate, to change that system, we decline today to do anything in this regard except to bring the problem to the attention of the legislative branch.

Bound as we are to adjudicate this appeal according to the substantive law of New Jersey, and because we find no basis in that law to overturn the jury's verdict, the judgment of the district court will be affirmed.

NOTE: CRASHWORTHINESS LITIGATION

In Chapter Two, we encountered cases dealing with comparative fault and other affirmative defenses in the context of claims that a plaintiff's injuries were enhanced because an auto had a defect. *Dawson* raises the question of such "crashworthiness" cases in their most common form. A huge body of case law deals with claims that autos were defectively designed and, as a result, either the driver or passengers suffered injuries that could have been avoided had a safer design been chosen. Crashworthiness litigation has become a subspecialty in the law of products liability. It is interesting to note that in the early days of products liability litigation, there was some controversy as to whether courts ought to recognize a cause of action for crashworthiness. An early case denying liability is Evans v. General Motors Corp., 359 F.2d 822 (7th Cir.) (applying Indiana law), *cert. denied*, 385 U.S. 836 (1966). But, beginning with Larsen v. General Motors Corp., 391 F.2d 495, 502 (8th Cir. 1968) (applying Minnesota law), crashworthiness liability was recognized as a theory of recovery when the court stated that a manufacturer had a duty to design an automobile "not only to provide a means of transportation, [but] to provide a safe means or as safe as is reasonably possible under the present state of the art." Since then, this genre of litigation has taken on tidal wave proportions. It is fair to say that today all states recognize crashworthiness liability.

Almost no aspect of automobile design has gone unchallenged. Cases have dealt with the design of child restraint systems, Lindner v. Ford Motor Co., 2014 WL 5334772 (9th Cir. 2014) (applying Nevada law); windshields, McCracken v. Ford Motor Co., 2010 WL 3010304 (3d Cir. 2010); door latches, Moisenko v. Volkswagenwerk Aktiengesellschaft, 1999 WL 1045075 (6th Cir. 1999) (applying Michigan law); cruise control, In re Ford Motor Co. Speed Control Deactivation Switch Products Liability Litigation, 2011 WL 2518776 (E.D. Mich. 2011); roof strength, Hyundai Motor Co. v. Rodriguez, 995 S.W.2d 661 (Tex. 1999); rear seatback, Zager v. Johnson Controls, Inc., 18 N.E.3d 533 (Ohio Ct. App. 2014); seat belts, Griffin v. Kia Motors Corp., 843 So. 2d 336 (Fla. Dist. Ct. App. 2003); strength of pillars, Wright v. Louisiana Power & Light Co., 752 So. 2d 919 (La. Ct. App. 1999); fuel tanks, Gerow v. Mitch Crawford Holiday Motors, 987 S.W.2d 359 (Mo. Ct. App. 1999); and gas caps, Tomasovic v. American Honda Motor Co., 525 N.E.2d 1111 (Ill. Ct. App. 1988). Some of the cases call for moderate changes in the design of the car. However, as *Dawson* demonstrates, plaintiffs have not been shy to ask for some rather significant changes in automobile design.

An issue raised in *Dawson* that troubles courts and commentators is the possibility that the alternative design that the plaintiff advances may pose greater risks to greater numbers of product users in other types of accidents, even if it would have saved the plaintiff in the actual accident before the court. Comment *f* to §2 of the Restatement (Third) of Torts: Products Liability (1998) addresses the issue:

> When evaluating the reasonableness of a design alternative, the overall safety of the product must be considered. It is not sufficient that the alternative design would have reduced or prevented the harm suffered by the plaintiff if it would also have introduced into the product other dangers of equal or greater magnitude.

In Potter v. Ford Motor Co., 213 S.W.3d 264 (Tenn. Ct. App. 2006), the plaintiff claimed that the front seat back of her Ford Escort automobile was defectively designed so that it collapsed during a rear-end collision, severing her spine and rendering her a paraplegic. The plaintiff was a 230-pound woman, and her reasonable alternative design involved a significant increase in the strength and stiffness of the seat back. The defendant's experts argued that the plaintiff's alternative design would be more dangerous to a majority of other occupants, including male and female adults of more average sizes and weights. The jury returned a plaintiff's verdict and Ford moved for JNOV. The Tennessee appellate court affirmed the trial court's denial of Ford's motion, holding that the question of whether the plaintiff's alternative design was more dangerous overall was proper for the jury to decide.

Another important issue that arises in crashworthiness litigation concerns causation and how to apportion plaintiff's injuries between the initial motor vehicle accident and the alleged failure of the vehicle to adequately protect plaintiff against harm. A leading case is Lahocki v. Contee Sand & Gravel Co., 398 A.2d 490 (Md. Ct. Spec. App. 1979), *reversed on other grounds*, General Motors Corp. v. Lahocki, 410 A.2d 1039 (Md. 1980), in which the court addressed a claim for injuries arising when plaintiff was thrown from a van manufactured by defendant after its roof detached during a one car collision. Defendant argued that plaintiff must establish via competent evidence precisely what extent of his injuries were attributable to a defect in the van, as opposed to other aspects of the collision for which defendant was not responsible. The court disagreed:

> The adoption of the concept of strict liability was intended to make it easier for injured parties to comply with the proof requirements of negligence actions. Since damages are a requisite element of proof in negligence actions, it would be contradictory to adopt, for public policy reasons, a concept to ease proof requirements of one aspect of negligence actions (liability), and then to erect an unreasonable and all but impossible barrier to recovery upon another aspect of proof (damages). To do so in this manner

---

authors' dialogue 12

AARON: The rules in *Lahocki* and Section 16 of the Restatement hold out a false promise to auto manufacturers, don't they?

JIM: In what way?

AARON: Well, think about it. In most cases involving increased harm — all of them, really — the manufacturer will want to argue under §16(a) that there was no enhancement at all; that the plaintiff's irreversible brain injury would have occurred even if the vehicle had been more crashworthy. They will argue that "in a horrific high-speed crash, nothing we could have done would have helped the plaintiff."

JIM: O.K. I'm with you so far.

AARON: Given the benefit of the doubt that §16(c) gives plaintiffs once they succeed in showing *some* enhancement under (a), manufacturers will tactically decide not to try to apportion under §16(b). They don't want to undercut their "no enhancement" argument under (a) by appearing to concede the issue in order to preserve their apportionment rights under (b). So they will litigate most (all) of these cases on an "all or nothing basis." And the plaintiff certainly won't raise the possibility of apportionment.

JIM: Come to think of it, that's exactly what the lawyers who opposed §16(c) argued: that it would turn all these crashworthiness cases into life-or-death struggles, leaving no middle ground of causal apportionment.

---

would be contrary even to our older traditional concepts of assigning burdens of proof of damages.

We find no fault with the underlying premise that a plaintiff must prove that his injuries were "enhanced" (i.e., caused) by the defect. Some evidence of enhancement (causation) is prerequisite to engendering a jury issue of assignable damages, just as some evidence of liability is a prerequisite to overcoming a motion for directed verdict. But the court below found, and we agree, that there was sufficient evidence to serve that purpose. The evidence ascribed the entire injury to the defect. The burden of persuading the jury by minimizing the degree of enhancement or causation is the defendant's responsibility. [Id. at 501 (internal quotations and citations omitted).]

The Products Liability Restatement follows the approach of *Lahocki*:

Restatement (Third) of Torts: Products Liability
(1998)

---

§16. Increased Harm Due to Product Defect

(a) When a product is defective at the time of sale and the defect is a substantial factor in increasing the plaintiff's harm beyond that which would have resulted from other causes, the product seller is subject to liability for the increased harm.

AARON: But isn't that more or less inevitably going to happen, whether or not §16(c) is the tiebreaker?

JIM: Not necessarily. If the plaintiff must prove how much enhancement occurred in order to recover anything, the plaintiff will have an incentive, not present given §16(c), to address the issue.

AARON: But that is very difficult to do in most cases. So under a "plaintiff must prove the extent of enhancement" approach, plaintiffs will go for the whole enchilada and try to prove *all* the injuries were caused by the defect.

JIM: Putting the enchilada issue to one side, if it's going to be all-or-nothing either way, why benefit the plaintiffs with §16(c)? Why not leave the burden on the plaintiff to prove 100 percent enhancement?

DOUG: Sorry to but in gentlemen, but there might be a third way here. A case in Utah [*Egbert*, supra] rejected both extremes, ruling that under a state tort reform statute abolishing joint and several liability, factfinders were *required* to apportion damages whenever plaintiff showed that a defect in defendant's product was a factor in causing plaintiff's harm. Apportionment had to occur *even if* neither side could satisfy a burden of proof in dividing up the injuries. The court even cited an earlier case stating that "arbitrary apportionment" might be appropriate in such circumstances.

AARON: Lawlessness! What's next? They'll have King Solomon threaten to split the car in half?

JIM: I'm with Aaron on this one. How could a self-respecting court sanction justice so candidly rough?

(b) If proof supports a determination of the harm that would have resulted from other causes in the absence of the product defect, the product seller's liability is limited to the increased harm attributable solely to the product defect.

(c) If proof does not support a determination under Subsection (b) of the harm that would have resulted in the absence of the product defect, the product seller is liable for all of the plaintiff's harm attributable to the defect and other causes.

(d) A seller of a defective product who is held liable for part of the harm suffered by the plaintiff under Subsection (b), or all of the harm suffered by the plaintiff under Subsection (c), is jointly and severally liable with other parties who bear legal responsibility for causing the harm, determined by applicable rules of joint and several liability.

In recent years, several American courts have explicitly adopted §16. See, e.g., Harsh v. Petroll, 887 A.2d 209, 215-216 (Pa. 2005) (applying §16(d)); Boryszewski v. Burke, 882 A.2d 410, 421-422 (N.J. Super. Ct. App. Div. 2005) (referring to court's adoption of §16(c) & (d)); Lally v. Volkswagen Aktiengesellschaft, 698 N.E.2d 28 (Mass. 1998) (citing to §16 in affirming verdicts and judgments for the defendant in an enhanced injury case); Jahn v. Hyundai Motor Co., 773 N.W.2d 550 (Iowa 2009) (adopting §16 and also recognizing that the comparative fault of the driver serves to reduce liability for enhanced injury damages as prescribed by Products Liability Restatement §16, comment *f*). Other state courts have adopted the substance reflected in §16 without citing to the Restatement. See, e.g., Nash v. General Motors Corp., 153 P.3d 73, 75 (Okla. App. 2006) (holding manufacturer liable for additional harm where a product defect increased the severity of the injury that would have occurred absent the defect).

Huddell, cited and rejected by *Lahocki*, supra, is the leading case contrary to the §16(c) approach, holding that the plaintiff takes nothing when causal apportionment is impossible. The *Huddell* approach remains in force in several states. See, e.g., Caiazzo v. Volkswagenwerk, A.G., 647 F.2d 241 (2d Cir. 1981) (applying New York law); Duran v. General Motors Corp., 688 P.2d 779 (N.M. Ct. App. 1983) (overruled on other grounds by Brooks v. Beech Aircraft Corp., 902 P.2d 54 (N.M. 1995)). An interesting middle ground can be found in Utah, where the state legislature has abolished joint and several liability by statute. In response to a certified question asking whether Utah accepts §16(b)-(d) of the Products Liability Restatement, the Utah Supreme Court determined that the legislative intent behind the state's tort reform statute required apportionment in every case, even if plaintiff is unable to establish a division of injury according to conventional evidentiary standards: "Under this rule of apportionment, in any enhanced-injury case, when a plaintiff provides evidence of a defect and evidence that the defect is a factor in enhancing the injury, the trial court shall instruct the jury that it must apportion fault between the defendant original tortfeasor and the defendant product seller." Egbert v. Nissan Motor Co., Ltd., 228 P.3d 737, 746 (Utah 2010).

E.   THE CONSUMER EXPECTATIONS STANDARD FOR DETERMINING DESIGN DEFECT

As observed in the previous discussions, design review based on feasible alternative/ risk-utility balancing seems very similar, if not identical, to negligence. This insight has not been lost on the commentators or the courts. Resisting wholesale reliance on risk-utility analysis, they argue that the economic test for liability gives inadequate attention to many of the forces that shape consumer attitudes toward product-related risk. Some of these observers have advocated an alternate test for defective design, one based on the disappointment of consumer expectations of product safety. An early advocate of the consumer expectations test was Professor Marshall Shapo. See A Representational Theory of Consumer Protection: Doctrine, Function and Legal Liability for Product Disappointment, 60 Va. L. Rev. 1109, 1370 (1974):

> Judgments of liability for consumer product disappointment should center initially and principally on the portrayal of the product which is made, caused to be made or permitted by the seller. This portrayal should be viewed in the context of the impression reasonably received by the consumer from representations or other communications made to him about the product by various means: through advertising, by the appearance of the product, and by the other ways in which the product projects an image on the mind of the consumer, including impressions created by widespread social agreement about the product's function. This judgment should take into consideration the result objectively determinable to have been sought by the seller, and the seller's apparent motivation in making or permitting the representation or communication.

1. Consumer Expectations as a Sword to Impose Liability

Heaton v. Ford Motor Co.
435 P.2d 806 (Or. 1967)

GOODWIN, J.

The plaintiff appeals a judgment entered after an involuntary nonsuit in a products-liability case involving a wheel on a Ford 4-wheel-drive pickup truck. The principal question is whether the plaintiff produced sufficient evidence to support his allegation that the wheel was dangerously defective.

Plaintiff purchased the truck new in July 1963 to use for hunting and other cross-country purposes as well as for driving upon paved highways. He drove the truck some 7,000 miles without noticing anything unusual about its performance. Prior to the day of the accident the truck had rarely been off the pavement, and plaintiff swore that it had never been subjected to unusual stress of any kind. On the day of the accident, however, the truck, while moving on a "black-top" highway at normal speed, hit a rock which plaintiff described as about five or six inches in diameter. The truck continued uneventfully for about 35 miles, when it left the road and tipped over.

After the accident, the rim of the wheel was found to be separated from the "spider." Witnesses described the "spider" as the interior portion of the wheel which is attached to the vehicle by the lug nuts. The twelve rivets connecting the rim to the spider appeared to have been sheared off. The spider, according to one witness, showed signs of having been dragged along the ground. There was also a large dent in the rim and a five-inch cut in the inner tube at a spot within the tire that was adjacent to the dent in the rim. Only three of the rivets which had held the rim on the spider were found after the accident. . . .

In the type of case in which there is no evidence, direct or circumstantial, available to prove exactly what sort of manufacturing flaw existed, or exactly how the design was deficient, the plaintiff may nonetheless be able to establish his right to recover, by proving that the product did not perform in keeping with the reasonable expectations of the user. When it is shown that a product failed to meet the reasonable expectations of the user the inference is that there was some sort of defect, a precise definition of which is unnecessary. If the product failed under conditions concerning which an average consumer of that product could have fairly definite expectations, then the jury would have a basis for making an informed judgment upon the existence of a defect. The case at bar, however, is not such a case. . . .

The court's function is to decide whether the evidence furnishes a sufficient basis for the jury to make an informed decision. If the record permits, the jury determines whether the product performed as an ordinary consumer would have expected. In the case at bar the record furnishes no basis for a jury to do anything but speculate.

Where the performance failure occurs under conditions with which the average person has experience, the facts of the accident alone may constitute a sufficient basis for the jury to decide whether the expectations of an ordinary consumer of the product were met. High-speed collisions with large rocks are not so common, however, that the average person would know from personal experience what to expect under the circumstances. Nor does anything in the record cast any light upon this issue. The jury would therefore be unequipped, either by general background or by facts supplied in the record, to decide whether this wheel failed to perform as safely as an ordinary consumer would have expected. To allow the jury to decide purely on its own intuition how strong a truck wheel should be would convert the concept of strict liability into the absolute liability of an insurer.

The argument has been made that the question of the ordinary consumer's expectations should be treated for jury purposes in the same way that the question of reasonable conduct in a negligence case is treated. But in deciding in a negligence case what is reasonable conduct, the jury is deciding in a context of "right and wrong" how someone *should* have behaved. In making this decision they are presumed to know the relevant factors. If not, such information is provided, as in a medical malpractice case where there is expert testimony as to the proper standards.

In the defective-product area, courts have already decided how strong products *should* be: they should be strong enough to perform as the ordinary consumer expects. In deciding what the reasonable consumer expects, the jury is not permitted to decide how strong products should be, nor even what consumers should expect, for this would in effect be the same thing. The jury is supposed to determine the basically factual question of what reasonable consumers do expect from the product. Where the jury has no experiential basis for knowing this, the record must supply such a basis. In the absence of either common experience or evidence, any verdict would, in effect, be the jury's opinion of how strong the product *should* be. Such an opinion by the jury would be formed without the benefit of data concerning the cost or feasibility of designing and building stronger products. Without reference to relevant factual data, the jury has no special qualifications for deciding what is reasonable. . . .

While the matter was never presented to the trial court, and thus requires no extended discussion in this appeal, the plaintiff has referred in this court to certain advertising published by the defendant, to reinforce the plaintiff's claim that a consumer would have expected the wheel in question to be engineered and manufactured in such a manner as to withstand the kind of force applied to it in this case. The plaintiff does not contend that the advertising constituted misrepresentation under Restatement (Second) of Torts §402B, but rather that the advertising in general tends to create expectations of strength and durability under Section 402A. A general impression of durability, however, does not help a customer to form an expectation about the breaking point of a wheel. A "rugged" Ford truck could be expected to negotiate rough terrain, including five-or-six-inch rocks, at appropriate off-the-road speeds, but it does not follow that a user could expect the same thing at highway speeds. If such expectations do exist, the record should contain evidence to support the inference that they do.

Affirmed.

O'CONNELL, J. (dissenting).

. . . It is plaintiff's position that the theory of strict liability should be deemed applicable whenever a person is injured as a result of exposing himself to a hazard in reasonable reliance upon the capabilities of a product as represented by the seller. The gist of plaintiff's argument is summed up as follows:

> . . . It is not unreasonable to suggest that the driver of a vehicle promoted as "solid,"
> "rugged" and "built like a truck" will subject that vehicle and its passengers to hazards

to which he would not subject a vehicle otherwise promoted. With specific reference to this case, it is not unreasonable to surmise that a driver of a vehicle so promoted who runs over a rock on the highway will not even consciously consider the possibility of stopping to check for damage because he takes it for granted that such an impact will not harm a vehicle which he has been conditioned to think of as "solid," "rugged," and "like a truck."

Plaintiff, then, is asking us to "take judicial notice of facts which form part of the common knowledge of people who possess average intelligence. . . ."

Apparently the majority opinion would hold that there was a failure of proof, irrespective of whether the question of strict liability is for the court or jury in a case of this kind. I disagree. If we had been presented with the same facts with the modification that plaintiff had struck a rock one inch in diameter rather than a five-inch rock, I am sure that the majority would have held that at least a jury question was made out. The beginning point of our reasoning would be that a manufacturer of automobiles must construct wheels of sufficient durability to withstand the impact of one-inch rocks, because one-inch rocks are not an uncommon obstacle on highways. A buyer could reasonably expect to have the wheel withstand such an impact and it would not be unreasonable for him to proceed on his journey after the impact. However, the buyer could not reasonably expect a wheel to remain safe after striking a rock two feet in diameter at seventy miles an hour. Somewhere along the continuum between one inch and two feet it will be necessary to draw a line. The line is drawn by deciding whether a manufacturer should be required to construct a wheel of such durability as to withstand the impact of a rock of the size in question. Whether the manufacturer has that duty in a particular case should depend, it seems to me, upon whether the manufacturer could reasonably foresee the likelihood that the hazard would be encountered by those using the product, and this would, of course, depend to some extent upon the representations made by the manufacturer with respect to the durability of the product.

The manufacturer's conduct must be measured against a standard of reasonableness, a standard similar to that employed in determining whether a defendant is negligent. Here, however, we do not measure defendant's conduct in terms of fault but simply upon the basis of its foreseeability. A jury is just as well equipped to judge the reasonableness of defendant's conduct on this score as it is when the inquiry is made as to defendant's negligence. The members of the jury draw upon their experiences and observations and set up some kind of a standard as a measure against which to appraise the defendant's conduct in the particular case. They would be justified in concluding that the wheel in this case was unreasonably dangerous according to the test stated in Restatement (Second) of Torts §402A, p.352 (1965), requiring a finding that "[t]he article sold must be dangerous to an extent beyond that which would be contemplated by the ordinary consumer who purchases it, with the ordinary knowledge common to the community as to its characteristics."

The majority apparently would require some evidence of what this community standard is. How is this to be done? Certainly this is not the type of question which calls for the testimony of an expert witness. Are we to call lay witnesses to testify what "would be contemplated by the ordinary consumer"? If that is required in the present case, it would be equally necessary in an ordinary negligence case to inform the jury of the community standard on such questions as the reasonableness of conduct in driving a car with respect to speed, lookout and control.

But we submit these questions of the reasonableness of defendant's conduct to the jury and, subject to the right of the court to decide as a matter of law that the standard was or was not met, we are willing to trust the jury's judgment as to the community standard and to appraise the defendant's conduct in light of it.

I believe that the question of defendant's liability is kept from the jury in the present case not because there is a lack of evidence upon which to sustain a verdict for plaintiff, but because the majority of the court, finding the imposition of strict liability a severe burden upon the seller, attempts to limit that burden by distorting the concept of the jury's function.

SLOAN, J., joins in this dissent.

In its penultimate paragraph, the majority opinion in *Heaton* implies that empirical proof of what consumers actually expect may be necessary when jurors' shared experiences are insufficient to fill the gap. Whether that is a fair reading of Justice Goodwin's opinion, the federal court of appeals in Valencia v. Crane Co., 132 Fed. App'x 171, 172 (9th Cir. 2005), interpreted a Washington State statute to require plaintiff, who relied in part on the consumer expectations standard, to "provide evidence that consumers expect hot chocolate to be served at a significantly lower temperature." Similarly, in Sexton v. Bell Helmets, Inc., 926 F.2d 331, 337 (4th Cir. 1991) (applying Kentucky law), the court refused to admit expert testimony on alternative design of a motorcycle helmet in part because plaintiff failed to produce evidence of consumer expectations: "There is no evidence in this case that purchasers of motorcycle helmets . . . expected a higher level of protection than that called for by the existing government and industry standards [or] expected more protection in helmets worn primarily by children than in helmets worn mainly by adults." Id. at 337.

One question under the consumer expectations test is whether the court is concerned with the presumed expectations of a hypothetical reasonable person or with the actual expectations of the plaintiff. The Supreme Court of California has made it clear that "the jury considers the expectations of a hypothetical reasonable consumer, rather than those of the particular plaintiff in the case." Campbell v. General Motors Corp., 649 P.2d 224, 233 n.6 (Cal. 1982). See also Redman v. John D. Bush & Co., 111 F.3d 1174, 1181 (4th Cir. 1997) ("[Plaintiff's] subjective expectations are insufficient to establish what degree of protection or deterrence society expects from a safe."); Brown v. Kia Motors Corp., 2010 WL 324440, at *4 (W.D. Pa. 2010). When the user/victim of a product is a minor, should the relevant expectations be those of a child? See Kelly v. Rival Mfg. Co., 704 F. Supp. 1039, 1043 (W.D. Okla. 1989) (crockpot fell on child in walker, imparting serious burns; liability "is not premised on the viewpoint of the minor child, but rather [is] based upon the contemplation of the parent consumer who purchased the product"); Calles v. Scripto-Tokai Corp., 864 N.E.2d 249, 257 (Ill. 2007) (unsupervised child ignited utility lighter; the adult purchaser's expectations control, not the child user's).

Potter v. Chicago Pneumatic Tool Co.
694 A.2d 1319 (Conn. 1997)

KATZ, Associate Justice.

This appeal arises from a products liability action brought by the plaintiffs against the defendants, Chicago Pneumatic Tool Company (Chicago Pneumatic), Stanley Works and Dresser Industries, Inc. (Dresser). The plaintiffs claim that they were injured in the course of their employment as shipyard workers at the General Dynamics Corporation Electric Boat facility (Electric Boat) in Groton as a result of using pneumatic hand tools manufactured by the defendants. Specifically, the plaintiffs allege that the tools were defectively designed because they exposed the plaintiffs to excessive vibration, and because the defendants failed to provide adequate warnings with respect to the potential danger presented by excessive vibration.

The defendants appeal from the judgment rendered on jury verdicts in favor of the plaintiffs, claiming [that] the interrogatories and accompanying instructions submitted to the jury were fundamentally prejudicial to the defendants [and that] the trial court should have rendered judgment for the defendants nothwithstanding the verdicts because there was insufficient evidence that the tools were defective in that the plaintiffs had presented no evidence of a feasible alternative design. . . .

The trial record reveals the following facts, which are undisputed for purposes of this appeal. The plaintiffs were employed at Electric Boat as "grinders," positions which required use of pneumatic hand tools to smooth welds and metal surfaces. In the course of their employment, the plaintiffs used various pneumatic hand tools, including chipping and grinding tools, which were manufactured and sold by the defendants. The plaintiff's use of the defendants' tools at Electric Boat spanned approximately twenty-five years, from the mid-1960s until 1987. The plaintiffs suffer from permanent vascular neurological impairment of their hands, which has caused blanching of their fingers, pain, numbness, tingling, reduction of grip strength, intolerance of cold and clumsiness from restricted blood flow. As a result, the plaintiffs have been unable to continue their employment as grinders and their performance of other activities has been restricted. The plaintiffs' symptoms are consistent with a diagnosis of hand arm vibration syndrome. Expert testimony confirmed that exposure to vibration is a significant contributing factor to the development of hand arm vibration syndrome, and that a clear relationship exists between the level of vibration exposure and the risk of developing the syndrome.

In addition to these undisputed facts, the following evidence, taken in favor of the jury's verdict, was presented. Ronald Guarneri, an industrial hygienist at Electric Boat, testified that he had conducted extensive testing of tools used at the shipyard in order to identify occupational hazards. This testing revealed that a large number of the defendants' tools violated the limits for vibration exposure established by the American National Standards Institute (institute), and exceeded the threshold limit promulgated by the American Conference of Governmental and Industrial Hygienists (conference).

Richard Alexander, a mechanical engineering professor at Texas A & M University, testified that because machinery vibration has harmful effects on machines and on people, engineers routinely research ways to reduce or to eliminate the amount of vibration that a machine produces when operated. Alexander discussed various methods available to control vibration, including isolation (the use of springs or mass to isolate vibration), dampening (adding weights to dampen vibrational effects), and balancing (adding weights to counterbalance machine imbalances that cause vibration). Alexander testified that each of these methods has been available to manufacturers for at least thirty-five years.

Alexander also stated that, in 1983, he had been engaged by another pneumatic tool manufacturer to perform testing of methods by which to reduce the level of vibration in its three horsepower vertical grinder. The vertical grinder had a live handle, which contained hardware for the air power, and a dead handle, which vibrated significantly more than the live handle because it weighed less. Alexander modified the design by inserting rubber isolation mounts between the handles and the housing, and by adding an aluminum rod to the dead handle to match the weight of the two handles. As a result of these modifications, which were published in 1987, Alexander achieved a threefold reduction in vibration levels. . . .

After a six week trial, the trial court rendered judgment on jury verdicts in favor of the plaintiffs. Finding that the defendants' tools had been defectively designed so as to render them unreasonably dangerous, the jury awarded the plaintiffs compensatory damages. The jury also concluded that the manufacturers had provided inadequate warnings. Because the plaintiffs failed to prove that adequate warnings would have prevented their injuries, the jury did not award damages on that claim. . . .

We first address the defendants' argument that the trial court improperly failed to render judgment for the defendants notwithstanding the verdicts because there was insufficient evidence for the jury to have found that the tools had been defectively designed. Specifically, the defendants claim that, in order to establish a prima facie design defect case, the plaintiffs were required to prove that there was a feasible alternative design available at the time that the defendants put their tools into the stream of commerce. We disagree.

[The court's summary of the history of strict products liability is omitted.]

Although courts have widely accepted the concept of strict tort liability, some of the specifics of strict tort liability remain in question. In particular, courts have sharply disagreed over the appropriate definition of defectiveness in design cases. As the Alaska Supreme Court has stated: "Design defects present the most perplexing problems in the field of strict products liability because there is no readily ascertainable external measure of defectiveness. While manufacturing flaws can be evaluated against the intended design of the product, no such objective standard exists in the design defect context." Caterpillar Tractor Co. v. Beck, 593 P.2d 871, 880 (Alaska 1979).

Section 402A imposes liability only for those defective products that are "unreasonably dangerous" to "the ordinary consumer who purchases it, with the ordinary knowledge common to the community as to its characteristics." 2 Restatement (Second), supra §402A, comment (i). Under this formulation, known as the "consumer expectation" test, a manufacturer is strictly liable for any condition not contemplated by the ultimate consumer that will be unreasonably dangerous to the consumer. . . .

Other jurisdictions apply only a risk-utility test in determining whether a manufacturer is liable for a design defect. . . .

This court has long held that in order to prevail in a design defect claim, "[t]he plaintiff must prove that the product is unreasonably dangerous." Id. We have derived our definition of "unreasonably dangerous" from comment (i) to §402A, which provides that "the article sold must be dangerous to an extent beyond that which would be contemplated by the ordinary consumer who purchases it, with the ordinary knowledge common to the community as to its characteristics." 2 Restatement (Second), supra,

§402A, comment (i). This "consumer expectation" standard is now well established in Connecticut strict products liability decisions.

The defendants propose that it is time for this court to abandon the consumer expectation standard and adopt the requirement that the plaintiff must prove the existence of a reasonable alternative design in order to prevail on a design defect claim. We decline to accept the defendants' invitation.

In support of their position, the defendants point to the second tentative draft of the Restatement (Third) of Torts: Products Liability (1995) (Draft Restatement [Third]), which provides that, as part of a plaintiff's prima facie case, the plaintiff must establish the availability of a reasonable alternative design. Specifically, §2(b) of the Draft Restatement (Third) provides: "[A] product is defective in design when the foreseeable risks of harm posed by the product could have been reduced or avoided by the adoption of a reasonable alternative design by the seller or other distributor, or a predecessor in the commercial chain of distribution, and the omission of the alternative design renders the product not reasonably safe." The reporters to the Draft Restatement (Third) state that "[v]ery substantial authority supports the proposition that [the] plaintiff must establish a reasonable alternative design in order for a product to be adjudged defective in design." Draft Restatement (Third), supra, §2, reporters' note to comment (c), p. 50.

We point out that this provision of the Draft Restatement (Third) has been a source of substantial controversy among commentators. See, e.g., John F. Vargo, "The Emperor's New Clothes: The American Law Institute Adorns a 'New Cloth' for Section 402A Products Liability Design Defects — A Survey of the States Reveals a Different Weave," 26 U. Mem. L. Rev. 493, 501 (1996) (challenging reporters' claim that Draft Restatement (Third)'s reasonable alternative design requirement constitutes "consensus" among jurisdictions). . . .

In our view, the feasible alternative design requirement imposes an undue burden on plaintiffs that might preclude otherwise valid claims from jury consideration. Such a rule would require plaintiffs to retain an expert witness even in cases in which lay jurors can infer a design defect from circumstantial evidence. Connecticut courts, however, have consistently stated that a jury may, under appropriate circumstances, infer a defect from the evidence without the necessity of expert testimony. . . .

Moreover, in some instances, a product may be in a defective condition unreasonably dangerous to the user even though no feasible alternative design is available. In such instances, the manufacturers may be strictly liable for a design defect notwithstanding the fact that there are no safer alternative designs in existence. See, e.g., O'Brien v. Muskin Corp. 94 N.J. 169, 184, 463 A.2d 298 (1983) ("other products, including some for which no alternative exists, are so dangerous and of such little use that . . . a manufacturer would bear the cost of liability of harm to others"). . . .

Although today we continue to adhere to our long-standing rule that a product's defectiveness is to be determined by the expectations of an ordinary consumer, we nevertheless recognize that there may be instances involving complex product designs in which an ordinary consumer may not be able to form expectations of safety. In such cases, a consumer's expectations may be viewed in light of various factors that balance the utility of the product's design with the magnitude of its risks. We find persuasive the reasoning of those jurisdictions that have modified their formulation of the consumer expectation test by incorporating risk-utility factors into the ordinary consumer expectation analysis. Thus, the modified consumer expectation test provides the jury with the product's risks and utility and then inquires whether a reasonable consumer would consider the product unreasonably dangerous. As the Supreme Court of Washington stated in Seattle-First National Bank v. Tabert, supra, at 154, 542 P.2d 774, "[i]n determining the reasonable expectations of the ordinary consumer, a number of factors must be considered. The relative cost of the product, the gravity of the potential harm from the claimed defect and the cost and feasibility of eliminating or minimizing the risk may be relevant in a particular case. In other instances the nature of the product or the nature of the claimed defect may make other factors relevant to the issue." Accordingly, under this modified formulation, the consumer expectation test would establish the product's risks and utility, and the inquiry would then be whether a reasonable consumer would consider the product design unreasonably dangerous.

In our view, the relevant factors that a jury may consider include, but are not limited to, the usefulness of the product, the likelihood and severity of the danger posed by the design, the feasibility of an alternative design, the financial cost of an improved design, the ability to reduce the product's danger without impairing its usefulness or making it too expensive, and the feasibility of spreading the loss by increasing the product's price. The availability of a feasible alternative design is a factor that the plaintiff may, rather than must, prove in order to establish that a product's risks outweigh its utility.

Furthermore, we emphasize that our adoption of a risk-utility balancing component to our consumer expectation test does not signal a retreat from strict tort liability. In weighing a product's risks against its utility, the focus of the jury should be on the product itself, and not on the conduct of the manufacturer.

Although today we adopt a modified formulation of the consumer expectation test, we emphasize that we do not require a plaintiff to present evidence relating to the product's risks and utility in every case. As the California Court of Appeals has stated: "There are certain kinds of accidents — even where fairly complex machinery is involved — [that] are so bizarre that the average juror, upon hearing the particulars, might reasonably think: 'Whatever the user may have expected from that contraption, it certainly wasn't that.' " Akers v. Kelley Co., 173 Cal. App. 3d 633, 651, 219 Cal. Rptr. 513 (1985). Accordingly, the ordinary consumer expectation test is appropriate when the everyday experience of the particular product's users permits the inference that the product did not meet minimum safety expectations. See Soule v. General Motors Corp., 8 Cal. 4th 548, 567, 882 P.2d 298, 34 Cal. Rptr. 2d 607 (1994).

Conversely, the jury should engage in the risk-utility balancing required by our modified consumer expectation test when the particular facts do not reasonably permit the inference that the product did not meet the safety expectations of the ordinary consumer. Furthermore, instructions based on the ordinary consumer expectation test would not be appropriate when, as a matter of law, there is insufficient evidence to support a jury verdict under that test. In such circumstances, the jury should be instructed solely on the modified consumer expectation test we have articulated today.

With these principles in mind, we now consider whether, in the present case, the trial court properly instructed the jury with respect to the definition of design defect for the purposes of strict tort liability. The trial court instructed the jury that a manufacturer may be strictly liable if the plaintiffs prove, among other elements, that the product in question was in a defective condition, unreasonably dangerous to the ultimate user. The court further instructed the jury that, in determining whether the tools were unreasonably dangerous, it may draw its conclusions based on the reasonable expectations of an ordinary user of the defendants' tools. Because there was sufficient evidence as a matter of law to support the determination that the tools were unreasonably dangerous based on the ordinary consumer expectation test, we conclude that this instruction was appropriately given to the jury. . . .

BERDON, J., concurring.

I write separately with respect to part I of the court's opinion regarding the test for determining whether a manufacturer is liable for a design defect. I would not depart from our long-standing rule that the consumer expectation test must be employed — that is, the product "must be dangerous to an extent beyond that which would be contemplated by the ordinary consumer who purchases it, with the ordinary knowledge common to the community as to its characteristics." 2 Restatement (Second), Torts, §402A, comment (i) (1965). Although the court today agrees that this test is to be applied to cases such as the present case, it adopts, by way of dicta, another test for "complex product designs."

I am concerned about the court adopting a risk-utility test for complex product designs — that is, a test where the trier of fact considers "the product's risks and utility and then inquires whether a reasonable consumer would consider the product unreasonably dangerous." Adopting such a test in a factual vacuum without the predicate facts to address its full implications can lead us down a dangerous path. More importantly, adopting such a risk-utility test for "complex product designs" sounds dangerously close to requiring proof of the existence of "a reasonable alternative design," a standard of proof that the court properly rejects today.

Finally because the court insists on addressing this issue that is not before us, I would at least sort out the burden of proof for the risk-utility test by adopting "a presumption that danger outweighs utility if the product fails under circumstances when the ordinary purchaser or user would not have so expected." W. Prosser & W. Keeton, Torts (5th ed. 1984) §99, p.702. Adoption of this presumption would lessen the concern that the risk-utility test undermines one of the reasons that strict tort liability was adopted — "the difficulty of discovering evidence necessary to show that danger outweighs benefits." Id.

Several courts (besides Connecticut) have embraced consumer expectations as the primary or exclusive test for defective design. See, e.g., Delaney v. Deere & Co., 999 P.2d 930, 946 (Kan. 2000) ("Kansas has adopted the consumer expectations test . . . as the standard for design defect"); Rahmig v. Mosley Mach. Co., Inc., 412 N.W.2d 56 (Neb. 1987) (pre-Products Liability Restatement case adopting the consumer-contemplation test and rejecting the need for plaintiff to establish a safer design); Braswell v. Cincinnati Inc., 731 F.3d 1081, 1089 (10th Cir. 2013) (given the lack of "any indication that the Oklahoma Supreme Court is inclined to adopt the risk-utility test, we will continue to apply the consumer expectations test to design defect cases such as this one"). Other courts, while expressing allegiance to the consumer expectations test, stop short of a full endorsement. See, e.g., Dart v. Wiebe Mfg., Inc., 709 P.2d 876 (Ariz. 1985) (consumer expectations test is adequate for manufacturing defects but will only "sometimes work well" in design cases as consumer will very often not know what to expect); Warner v. Fruehauf Trailer Co. v. Boston, 654 A.2d 1272, 1276 (D.C. 1995) ("In general, the plaintiff must 'show the risks, costs and benefits of the product in question and alternative designs,' " but the court implies in a footnote that consumer expectations test may be appropriate in some cases); McCathern v. Toyota Motor Co.,

---

authors' dialogue 13

DOUG: Aaron and Jim, there's no way to put this gently: *Potter* must have felt like a sucker punch to you.

JIM: It did, but say more before we give you our perspective on the case — it would be interesting to know how it looks to someone outside the process.

DOUG: Well, there you are as Reporters for the Products Liability Restatement, deep in the weeds of a lengthy drafting process that is still far from completion, when along comes the *Potter* court calling the project controversial and purporting to reject it, but then — to really add insult to injury — adopting a design defect standard that is functionally no different than the Restatements'.

AARON: You won't be surprised to learn that we agree with you. But, again, say a little more about this functional equivalence idea. That's exactly what we were arguing at the ALI about consumer expectations jurisdictions even before the *Potter* case came out.

DOUG: What the *Potter* court calls a "modified consumer expectation test" is just a res ipsa-like inference of defect in cases of obvious product failure along with standard risk-utility analysis for more complex product-caused accidents. In other words, it's sections 3 and 2(b) of the Restatement with the word "consumer" thrown in for window dressing.

JIM: That might be a tad too strong Doug. The *Potter* court does treat a reasonable alternative design as merely a factor in their risk-utility analysis, rather than a core requirement like the Restatement.

AARON: But that's a distinction without a difference given that successful design defect cases always rest on a RAD, even for jurisdictions like Connecticut that claim not to require one.

DOUG: And if the *Potter* court wanted to hold on to the narrow possibility that a product might fail risk-utility even when no reasonable alternative design is available, well that's exactly what the Restatement provides for in the comment regarding a "manifestly unreasonable design." So I'm really left scratching my head why the *Potter* court would claim to be distancing itself from the Restatement project when its actual holding is so simpatico with the Restatement framework.

JIM: Join the club.

---

23 P.3d 320, 331 (Or. 2001) (court held that Oregon statute mandates application of the consumer expectations test but held that if average consumer would not know what to expect then court may have to resort to risk-utility balancing).

Nevertheless, as Section C, supra, makes clear, a large majority of American courts reject consumer expectations as the primary or exclusive test for defective design, opting instead for some version of the risk-utility standard. Early judicial rejection of the consumer expectations test can be found in Turner v. General Motors Corp., 584 S.W.2d 844 (Tex. 1979). The plaintiff in that case suffered serious injuries when his 1969 Chevrolet Impala sedan overturned as he swerved to avoid a collision with a truck. The car rolled over once and the roof caved in at the driver's corner when it hit the ground. Although his seat belt was fastened, the plaintiff suffered a crushed vertebra, resulting in paralysis. The plaintiff alleged that the roof structure of the car was inadequately designed to withstand a rollover collision. The court in *Turner* used the occasion to indicate its dissatisfaction with the consumer expectations test. It reiterated the criticism that consumer expectations would hardly be anything more than the personal experiences of the jurors. A subsequent Texas court more squarely rejected the consumer expectations standard in favor of a reasonable alternative design requirement. See Caterpillar, Inc. v. Shears, 911 S.W.2d 379, 384 (Tex. 1995) ("[I]f there are no safer alternatives, a product is not unreasonably dangerous as a matter of law."). See also Evans v. Lorillard Tobacco Co., 990 N.E.2d 997 (Mass. 2013); Branham v. Ford Motor Co., 701 S.E.2d 5 (S.C. 2010); Wright v. Brooke Group, Ltd., 652 N.W.2d 159 (Iowa 2002); Bilotta v. Kelley Co., 346 N.W.2d 616 (Minn. 1984). In 2011, the state of Wisconsin, which had been a prominent jurisdiction defending the consumer expectations approach, passed legislation abandoning it in favor of the Products Liability Restatement model. Act of Jan. 27, 2011, sec. 31, §895.047 (1)(a) Wis. Sess. Laws 1, 6-7 (codified at Wis. Stat. §895.047(1)(a)).

Comment *g* to §2(b) of the Products Liability Restatement rejects the consumer expectations test as a stand-alone test for design defect:

> *g. Consumer expectations: general considerations.* Under Subsection (b), consumer expectations do not constitute an independent standard for judging the defectiveness of product designs. Courts frequently rely, in part, on consumer expectations when discussing liability based on other theories of liability. Some courts, for example, use the term "reasonable consumer expectations" as an equivalent of "proof of a reasonable, safer design alternative," since reasonable consumers have a right to expect product designs that conform to the reasonableness standard in Subsection (b). Other courts, allowing an inference of defect to be drawn when the incident is of a kind that ordinarily would occur as a result of product defect, observe that products that fail when put to their manifestly intended use disappoint reasonable consumer expectations. See §3. However, consumer expectations do not play a determinative role in determining defectiveness. . . . Consumer expectations, standing alone, do not take into account whether the proposed alternative design could be implemented at reasonable cost, or whether an alternative design would provide greater overall safety. Nevertheless, consumer expectations about product performance and the dangers attendant to product use affect how risks are perceived and relate to foreseeability and frequency of the risks of harm, both of which are relevant under Subsection (b). . . . Such expectations are often influenced by how products are portrayed and marketed and can have a significant impact on consumer behavior. Thus, although consumer expectations do not constitute an independent standard for judging the defectiveness of product designs, they may substantially influence or even be ultimately determinative on risk-utility balancing in judging whether the omission of a proposed alternative design renders the product not reasonably safe. . . .

As Comment *g* makes clear, part of the reason for rejecting consumer expectations as a stand-alone test for design defect is that the res ipsa-like inference of defect in §3 of the Products Liability Restatement works to accomplish the same function in all of the cases when consumer expectations are held to control the defectiveness determination. After all, both the *Heaton* and *Potter* courts stress that when product failure is of a complex nature such that ordinary consumers cannot be expected to have stable or well-formulated expectations regarding product capabilities, then the jury must be presented with more technical information regarding product risk and utility.

Despite accepting this characterization of the case law, one of the co-authors of this casebook proposed a variation of the consumer expectations test that aimed to give the test independent significance in light of the fact that some courts seem bent on retaining it. In an article entitled The Expectations of Consumers, 103 Colum. L. Rev. 1700, 1763 (2003), Professor Kysar argues:

> A great deal of human judgment and decisionmaking research focuses on the manner in which individuals perceive and process information regarding risks. As it turns out, the notion of "risk" for most individuals is not a purely actuarial concept involving probabilistic estimates of harm. Rather, according to proponents of the "psychometric paradigm" view of risk perception, risk is a complex, textured assessment of numerous variables that surround a given environmental, health, or safety hazard. In addition to the likelihood and severity of a harm, individuals also appear to care about a variety of qualitative attributes, such as whether a risk is voluntarily confronted by the victim, whether its potential harm is equitably distributed among the population, whether it poses a particularly dreaded form of death or illness, whether it threatens future generations, and whether the perceived source of the risk is believed to be a trustworthy actor. Such factors do not appear within the basic model of cost-benefit analysis, which tends to abstract away from qualitative characteristics in order to provide a uniform basis for assessing a wide range of health and safety risks. . . .
>
> The risk perception literature therefore suggests a possible independent role for consumer expectations analysis in products liability. Just as lay reactions to risk depart from those of experts, consumer expectations of product safety can be expected to depart from the standards that would be derived under a risk-utility test. Importantly, many of these departures cannot easily be dismissed as irrationalities that should be ignored in favor of more narrow instrumentalist balancing. Rather, . . . many aspects of consumer beliefs and behavior can be said to represent a "rival rationality" that is wider in scope and richer in detail than the stark logic of risk-utility analysis. . . .
>
> To be sure, application of the consumer expectations doctrine must not consist of the type of largely unguided, formless judgment that commentators to date have associated with it. Rather, juries should be charged with the task of determining specifically, as a factual matter, what level of safety the ordinary consumer does expect, taking into account the type of factors that cognitive psychologists and other observers of human judgment and decision making have identified as pertinent to public understanding and beliefs about risk. Expert testimony therefore should be admissible for those aspects of a product's design, manufacture, or marketing that raise issues relating to lay risk perception. More specifically, to survive a summary judgment motion, plaintiffs must demonstrate the existence of a triable question of fact concerning the extent to which consumer risk perceptions and safety expectations of the product in question differ in legitimate and significant ways from the standards derived under risk-utility analysis. In this manner, despite the longstanding complaint of products liability scholars that consumer expectations fail to provide a coherent and workable basis for design defect liability, and despite the failure of courts generally to articulate such a basis, the doctrine will provide an important complement to the spare instrumentalist balancing of risk-utility analysis.

Professors Henderson and Twerski offer a brief response in the same issue of the Columbia Law Review, arguing that the "reinvigorated" version of consumer expectations test "would be susceptible to result-oriented manipulation by litigants, would not guide manufacturers in making sensible design choices, would pressure courts to exceed the limits of their institutional competence, and would undermine the new Restatement's commitment to making products safer." James A. Henderson, Jr. &

Aaron D. Twerski, Consumer Expectations' Last Hope: A Response to Professor Kysar, 103 Colum. L. Rev. 1791, 1791 (2003).

Consider a hypothetical to illustrate an important difference between the "reinvigorated" consumer expectations approach and the Products Liability Restatement. Imagine two airbag designs, A and B. Design A saves 3,000 persons from death over a certain number of miles driven, but kills 100 persons who would have survived in the absence of the device. Airbag B also saves 3,000 persons and kills only 90. The 100 persons killed by airbag A are more or less equally divided between males and females; of the 90 persons killed by airbag B, a majority are females. (This result could occur due to differences in the average physical size of male and female victims.) P, a female, was riding in the right front seat of an automobile manufactured by M and equipped with airbag B. The airbag deployed in a minor accident, as it was designed to do, and killed P. P's death would not have occurred in the absence of an airbag. P's representative brings a wrongful death action against M, asserting that M should have adopted design A, which, compared with design B, would have improved P's chances of survival. An expert testifies, based on opinion polls, that a majority of consumers in the jurisdiction prefer design A, because of its gender neutrality, over design B, even though design A kills more people. Might P's representative recover from M under a consumer expectations approach that attempts to identify and guarantee consumer safety expectations, even when they depart from more technocratic risk-benefit assessments? Would P's representative lose as a matter of law under §2(b) of the Restatement? Recall comment f, §2, of the Products Liability Restatement. If so, which outcome in the action against M is preferable on these facts?

PROBLEM SIXTEEN

Sophie Wydler, a junior executive at the New California Savings Bank, was crossing the street while returning to her office from a lunch break when a commercial truck driven by Walter Sandhaus ran her down. Wydler brought suit against Sandhaus for negligent driving and against International Harvester (IH) for defectively designing the IH Model 404 that Sandhaus was driving at the time. The complaint alleged that the design of the truck prevented the driver from seeing pedestrian traffic immediately in front and to the right of the truck, and that the front-end profile of the vehicle should have been lowered to eliminate the blind spot. The case went to trial and experts on both sides testified regarding the benefits and disadvantages of the Model 404 design and those of the alternative design suggested by the plaintiff. Defendant's expert argued that the plaintiff's suggested alternative design would have required lowering the engine by at least three inches. Lowering the engine could not be accomplished without positioning the engine in close proximity to the gas tank. In that position, the high temperature from the heat of the engine would pose an unacceptable fire hazard. The gas tank could be repositioned, but only at the cost of creating other risks of accidental injury. The IH expert opined that drivers of heavy commercial trucks are experts who are well aware of the visibility problems that attend driving such large vehicles and know that their only way to compensate for the lack of visibility is by driving slowly with greater vigilance.

After the completion of the testimony, the court asked the parties to submit requests for instructions. The attorney representing the plaintiff submitted the following instruction to deal with the question of the defective design of the truck:

A product is dangerously defective when it is in a condition unreasonably dangerous to the user. Unreasonably dangerous in this context means dangerous to an extent beyond that which would be contemplated by the ordinary purchaser of this type of product in the community. In considering the expectations of an ordinary purchaser, you may consider the expectations of anyone who may reasonably be expected to be affected by the product, such as a pedestrian.

You are an associate with the law firm representing International Harvester. The senior partner handling the case asks you to draft a memorandum opposing plaintiff's requested instruction. He also wants you to suggest an alternative instruction that would be less prejudicial to the defendant and yet acceptable to the court. He wants you to support your alternative instruction with a memorandum. The Supreme Court of New California, the state in which all the events occurred, has cited with approval the decision of the Oregon court in *Heaton v. Ford Motor Co.*, supra.

THE UNIFORM COMMERCIAL CODE AND THE CONSUMER EXPECTATIONS TEST

In Chapter One we noted that in the early days of products liability law, strict liability actions for manufacturing defects were brought under Article 2 of the Uniform Commercial Code. Under the Code, every sale of goods is accompanied by an implied warranty of merchantability that the goods "are fit for the ordinary purposes for which such goods are used." The Code test for defect worked well for manufacturing defects. However, when plaintiffs sought to use the Code definition for defect in design cases involving personal injury, the question arose as to whether the risk-utility test for defect was to be engrafted into the Code or whether the Code mandated a consumer-expectations test. Most courts utilized whatever test for defect they used in a case brought in tort as the test for defect under the Code. One court, however, made it clear that if a plaintiff brings an action in implied warranty under Article 2, the case would be covered under the consumer expectation test. In Denny v. Ford Motor Co., 662 N.E.2d 730 (N.Y. 1995), the plaintiff, Nancy Denny, was severely injured when the Ford Bronco II (a utility vehicle designed for use on off-road and rugged terrain) she was driving rolled over. The rollover accident occurred when Denny slammed on her brakes in an effort to avoid a deer that had walked directly into her motor vehicle's path. She sued Ford, asserting claims of negligence, strict products liability, and breach of the implied warranty of merchantability.

Plaintiffs introduced evidence to show that small utility vehicles, like the Bronco, present a significantly higher risk of rollover accidents than do ordinary passenger automobiles. Ford countered that the design features of which plaintiff complained were necessary to the vehicle's off-road capabilities. The trial judge instructed the jury on both strict products liability and the implied warranty of merchantability. On the former, the jury was instructed on risk-utility balancing and to find for plaintiff only if the Bronco was not reasonably safe. On the latter, they were given a consumer expectations charge. Ford objected to the two charges, contending that the standard for design defect is the same whether the action is brought under tort or the Uniform Commercial Code. Interestingly, the jury found for the defendant under risk-utility standards, i.e., the Bronco was "reasonably safe," but found for the plaintiff on the grounds that the Bronco fell below consumer expectations. The case was originally tried in federal district court and went up on appeal to the Second Circuit. The Circuit certified to the New York Court of Appeals the question as to whether the standard for design defect under the Uniform Commercial Code was identical to or different from the risk-utility standard which governs New York products liability law.

The New York Court of Appeals decided that the implied warranty of merchantability of the U.C.C. (independent of tort) embodied a "consumer expectations" test that the court was not at liberty to disregard. The court observed:

> . . . As long as that legislative source of authority [the U.C.C.] exists, we are not free to merge the warranty cause of action with its tort-based sibling regardless of whether, as a matter of policy, the contract-based warranty claim may fairly be regarded as a historical relic that no longer has any independent substantive value. Rather, we must construe and apply this separate remedy in a manner that remains consistent with its *current* roots in contract law. . . . Id. at 736.

The Products Liability Restatement proposes a single test for defect whether the action is brought in tort or is based on the implied warranty of merchantability. Comment *n* to §2 contains the following:

> Similarly, a product defect claim satisfying the requisites of Subsections (a), (b) or (c), or other provisions in this Chapter, may be brought under the implied warranty of merchantability provisions of the Uniform Commercial Code. It is recognized that some courts have adopted a consumer expectations definition for design and failure-to-warn defects in implied warranty cases involving harm to persons or property. This Restatement contemplates that a well-coordinated body of law governing liability for harm to persons or property arising out of the sale of defective products requires a consistent definition of defect, and that the definition properly should come from tort law, whether the claim carries a tort label or one of implied warranty of merchantability.

2. Consumer Expectations as a Shield Against Liability

For almost two decades, Maryland utilized risk-utility balancing and required proof of a reasonable alternative design to make out a prima facie case of design defect. Then in what appeared to be an abrupt reversal in Halliday v. Sturm, Ruger & Co., 792 A.2d 1145 (Md. 2002), the Supreme Court embraced the consumer expectations test. Plaintiffs' decedent, a three-year-old boy, shot himself while playing with his father's handgun. The gun was sold with a lock box in which to store the gun, the magazine, and a padlock for the box. The instruction manual set forth multiple warnings about storing the handgun, with special cautionary instructions about storing the gun away from children. There were also warnings that ammunition should be stored separately from the firearm. The boy's father disregarded virtually every one of the warnings. Rather than putting the gun in the lock box, he placed it under his mattress and kept the loaded magazine on a bookshelf in the same room so that it was visible and accessible to his son. The child found the gun and the magazine. From watching television he knew how to load the magazine into the gun. While playing with the loaded handgun, he shot and killed himself.

Plaintiff alleged that the gun was defective and unreasonably dangerous, suggesting a host of alternative designs that would have substantially reduced the likelihood that a

---

authors' dialogue 14

JIM: Why did the court in *Halliday* have to adopt the consumer expectations test in order to deny recovery? It could have adopted the language in §2, Comment *g* of the Restatement that says that "although consumer expectations do not constitute an independent standard for judging the defectiveness of product designs, they may substantially influence or even be ultimately determinative on risk-utility balancing in judging whether the omission of a proposed alternative design renders the product defective."

AARON: I'm glad you mentioned that language from the Restatement. I never really understood what those words meant. If I'm not mistaken, that language came from the members during floor discussion at the Annual Meeting. We thought it would not cause mischief so we agreed to it. Now you're telling me that it has real meaning.

JIM: You're showing your age, Aaron. When we talked after the meeting and I objected to the language at the time, you said it could be interpreted to mean that in some cases consumer expectations so overwhelm the case that they resolve the risk-utility issue as a matter of law. Like there is an elephant in the living room. Sometimes you can't ignore the elephant.

AARON: Now that you mention it, I do recall saying something like that. But if I said it, I still don't see how it works in practice. In *Halliday* plaintiff suggested some very sensible alternative designs that would have prevented hundreds of accidental shootings of children every year. How does the consumer expectations test (elephant or no elephant) respond to that argument?

DOUG: It seems like proponents of the consumer expectations test could argue that *Halliday* was wrongly decided since consumers might expect that modern handguns, despite their inherent dangers, should come equipped with automatic safety features. They might also argue that the consumer expectations test should be available as an independent basis for product liability but

---

young child could fire the gun. After a lengthy discussion of earlier Maryland cases, the court concluded that it would not apply a risk-utility standard to handguns and would bar the action because the gun met consumer expectations. The court said:

> It is clear that under the consumer expectations test . . . no cause of action had been stated in this case. There was no malfunction of the gun; regrettably it worked exactly as it was designed and intended to work and as any ordinary consumer would have expected it to work. The gun is a lawful weapon and was lawfully sold. What caused this tragedy was the carelessness of [the] father in leaving the weapon and the magazine in places where the child was able to find them, in contravention not only of common sense but of multiple warnings given to him at the time of purchase.

not a defense in its own right when a reasonable alternative design is available.

JIM: After the Maryland court used the consumer expectation test in *Halliday* as a shield to protect against liability, I wondered what they would do when they faced a run-of-the-mill design defect case and had to decide whether the plaintiff could use the test as a sword to win a case without proving a reasonable alternative design. I predicted that they would rue the day that they turned their back on reasonable alternative design.

DOUG: The issue came up in Lloyd v. General Motors Corp., 275 F.R.D. 224 (D. Md. 2011). The plaintiffs argued that the consumer expectations test should be used in their class action regarding car seats that were prone to collapse during certain collisions. The court refused to apply the consumer expectations test in that case, finding instead that reasonable consumers would base their judgments on "inquiries that lie at the very heart of the risk-utility test," including safety tradeoffs and the cost-effectiveness and feasibility of alternative designs. The court distinguished *Halliday* on the grounds that its consumer expectations test applied to products designed to cause harm and their safety devices.

AARON: Even though the decision came from a federal district court, that case supports my prediction that Maryland courts will end up saying that consumers have a right to expect reasonably designed products and will end up turning their consumer expectations test into a risk-utility test. They have too many risk-utility cases in their published decisions. It's a shame that they felt pressured by a gun case to give voice to the consumer expectations test. The legislative history in Maryland is full of initiatives telling the courts that they don't want them fooling around with guns under standard products liability law. The Maryland court could simply have said that it wasn't going to face the reasonable alternative design issue in this case because the legislature did not want standard products law to govern guns. They came very close to actually saying that.

The court then noted that, given the controversy surrounding the risk-utility standard of the Products Liability Restatement and given the fact that the legislature had enacted its own standard for the sale and distribution of handguns, it would not adopt the risk-utility test for handguns.

Oddly, the *Halliday* court appeared to view its retention of the consumer expectations test as a blow in favor of consumer protection, even as the test's application in the particular case was arguably more protective of defendants' interests than would have been the Products Liability Restatement. Indeed, the court's strident pro-plaintiff rhetoric appears almost shockingly insensitive in light of the court's holding. Id. at 1154-55 (describing the reasonable alternative design approach proffered by plaintiff and adopted in the Products Liability Restatement as "an unwanted ascendancy of corporate interests under the guise of tort reform"). A similarly puzzling dissonance appeared in Wisconsin jurisprudence, prior to that state's legislative overriding of the consumer expectations test. In Horst v. Deere & Co., 769 N.W.2d 536 (Wis. 2009), a two-year-old whose feet were cut off by a lawnmower running in reverse was denied recovery on his products liability claim. One question presented by the case might have been whether it was unreasonable for the lawnmower manufacturer to allow users to override the blade cutoff mechanism and mow in reverse. Wisconsin's application of the consumer expectations test, however, prevented such a question from being considered because the risks were considered to be open and obvious: "At the end of the day . . . a lawn mower is a lawn mower–it is dangerous, and accidents happen." Id. at 554.

Legislation in several states has specifically referred to the consumer expectations test as a defense to a design defect claim. Although the legislation is not the equivalent of the "patent danger" rule, it does negate liability for dangers that are commonly known and are inherent to the product. N.J. Rev. Stat. §2A:58C-3 is illustrative:

a. In any product liability action against a manufacturer or seller for harm allegedly caused by a product that was designed in a defective manner, the manufacturer or seller shall not be liable if: . . .

   (2) The characteristics of the product are known to the ordinary consumer or user, and the harm was caused by an unsafe aspect of the product that is an inherent characteristic of the product and that would be recognized by the ordinary person who uses or consumes the product with the ordinary knowledge common to the class of persons for whom the product is intended, except that this paragraph shall not apply to industrial machinery or other equipment used in the workplace and it is not intended to apply to dangers posed by products such as machinery or equipment that can feasibly be eliminated without impairing the usefulness of the product. . . .

See also Ohio Rev. Code Ann. §2307.75(E). In McSwain v. Sunrise Medical, Inc., 689 F. Supp. 2d 835 (S.D. Miss. 2010), a similar statute from Mississippi was interpreted to preclude recovery by plaintiff against defendant manufacturer that failed to include anti-tip devices as standard equipment for its wheelchair. The court ruled that the risk of using a wheelchair without anti-tip protection was cognizable to plaintiff and ordinary consumers and therefore defendant was shielded from liability "[r]egardless of whether [plaintiff] has proved a feasible alternative design." Id. at 841.

F.   THE TWO-PRONG STANDARD FOR DETERMINING DESIGN DEFECT

Soule v. General Motors Corp.
882 P.2d 298 (Cal. 1994)

BAXTER, J.

Plaintiff's ankles were badly injured when her General Motors (GM) car collided with another vehicle. She sued GM, asserting that defects in her automobile allowed its left front wheel to break free, collapse rearward, and smash the floorboard into her feet.

GM denied any defect and claimed that the force of the collision itself was the sole cause of the injuries. Expert witnesses debated the issues at length. Plaintiff prevailed at trial, and the Court of Appeal affirmed the judgment. We granted review to resolve . . . [whether] a product's design [may] be found defective on grounds that the product's performance fell below the safety expectations of the ordinary consumer . . . if the question of how safely the product should have performed cannot be answered by the common experience of its users. . . .

Facts

On the early afternoon of January 16, 1984, plaintiff was driving her 1982 Camaro in the southbound center lane of Bolsa Chica Road, an arterial street in Westminster. There was a slight drizzle, the roadway was damp, and apparently plaintiff was not wearing her seat belt. A 1972 Datsun, approaching northbound, suddenly skidded into the path of plaintiff's car. The Datsun's left rear quarter struck plaintiff's Camaro in an area near the left front wheel. Estimates of the vehicles' combined closing speeds on impact vary from 30 to 70 miles per hour. The collision bent the Camaro's frame adjacent to the wheel and tore loose the bracket that attached the wheel assembly (specifically, the lower control arm) to the frame. As a result, the wheel collapsed rearward and inward. The wheel hit the underside of the "toe pan" — the slanted floorboard area beneath the pedals — causing the toe pan to crumple, or "deform," upward into the passenger compartment. Plaintiff received a fractured rib and relatively minor scalp and knee injuries. Her most severe injuries were fractures of both ankles, and the more serious of these was the compound compression fracture of her left ankle. This injury never healed properly. In order to relieve plaintiff's pain, an orthopedic surgeon fused the joint. As a permanent result, plaintiff cannot flex her left ankle. She walks with considerable difficulty, and her condition is expected to deteriorate.

After the accident, the Camaro was acquired by a salvage dealer, Noah Hipolito. Soon thereafter, plaintiff's son, Jeffrey Bishop, and her original attorney, Richard Hawkins, each inspected and photographed the car and its damaged floorboard area. The failed bracket assembly was retrieved. However, Hipolito later discarded the damaged toe pan, repaired the Camaro, and resold it. Thus, except for the bracket assembly, no part of the vehicle was retained as evidence.

Plaintiff sued GM for her ankle injuries, asserting a theory of strict tort liability for a defective product. She claimed the severe trauma to her ankles was not a natural consequence of the accident, but occurred when the collapse of the Camaro's wheel caused the toe pan to crush violently upward against her feet. Plaintiff attributed the wheel collapse to a manufacturing defect, the substandard quality of the weld attaching the lower control arm bracket to the frame. She also claimed that the placement of the bracket, and the configuration of the frame, were defective designs because they did not limit the wheel's rearward travel in the event the bracket should fail.

The available physical and circumstantial evidence left room for debate about the exact angle and force of the impact and the extent to which the toe pan had actually deformed. The issues of defect and causation were addressed through numerous experts produced by both sides in such areas as biomechanics, metallurgy, orthopedics, design engineering, and crash-test simulation.

Plaintiff submitted the results of crash tests, and also asserted the similarity of another real-world collision involving a 1987 Camaro driven by Dana Carr. According to plaintiff's experts, these examples indicated that Camaro accidents of similar direction and force do not generally produce wheel bracket assembly failure, extensive toe pan deformation, or severe ankle injuries such as those plaintiff had experienced. These experts opined that without the deformation of the toe pan in plaintiff's car, her accident could not have produced enough force to fracture her ankles.

A metallurgist testifying on plaintiff's behalf examined the failed bracket from her car. He concluded that its weld was particularly weak because of excess "porosity" caused by improper welding techniques. Plaintiff's experts also emphasized the alternative frame and bracket design used by the Ford Mustang of comparable model years. They asserted that the Mustang's design, unlike the Camaro's, provided protection against unlimited rearward travel of the wheel should a bracket assembly give way.

GM's metallurgist disputed the claims of excessive weakness or porosity in the bracket weld. Expert witnesses for GM also countered the assertions of defective design. GM asserted that the Camaro's bracket was overdesigned to withstand forces in excess of all expected uses. According to expert testimony adduced by GM, the Mustang's alternative frame and bracket configuration did not fit the Camaro's overall design goals and was not distinctly safer for all collision stresses to which the vehicle might be subjected. Indeed, one witness noted, at least one more recent Ford product had adopted the Camaro's design. . . .

The court instructed the jury that a manufacturer is liable for "enhanced" injuries caused by a manufacturing or design defect in its product while the product is being used in a foreseeable way. Over GM's objection, the court gave the standard design defect instruction without modification. . . . This instruction advised that a product is defective in design "if it fails to perform as safely as an ordinary consumer would expect when used in an intended *or* reasonably foreseeable manner or if there is a risk of danger inherent in the design which outweighs the benefit of the design." (Italics added.)

The jury was also told that in order to establish liability for a design defect under the "ordinary consumer expectations" standard, plaintiff must show (1) the manufacturer's product failed to perform as safely as an ordinary consumer would expect, (2) the defect existed when the product left the manufacturer's possession, (3) the defect was a "legal cause" of plaintiff's "enhanced injury," and (4) the product was used in a reasonably foreseeable manner. . . .

In a series of special findings, the jury determined that the Camaro contained a defect (of unspecified nature) which was a "legal cause" of plaintiff's "enhanced injury." . . . Plaintiff received an award of $1.65 million.

GM appealed. Among other things, it argued that the trial court erred by instructing on ordinary consumer expectations in a complex design-defect case, and by failing to give GM's special instruction on causation.

Following one line of authority, the Court of Appeal concluded that a jury may rely on expert assistance to determine what level of safe performance an ordinary consumer would expect under particular circumstances. Hence, the Court of Appeal ruled, there was no error in use of the ordinary consumer expectations standard for design defect in this case. . . .

Discussion

1.   Test for Design Defect

A manufacturer, distributor, or retailer is liable in tort if a defect in the manufacture or design of its product causes injury while the product is being used in a reasonably foreseeable way. Because traffic accidents are foreseeable, vehicle manufacturers must consider collision safety when they design and build their products. Thus, whatever the cause of an accident, a vehicle's producer is liable for specific collision injuries that would not have occurred but for a manufacturing or design defect in the vehicle. . . .

In Barker v. Lull Engineering Co., supra, 573 P.2d 443 (*Barker*), the operator of a high-lift loader sued its manufacturer for injuries he received when the loader toppled during a lift on sloping ground. The operator alleged various *design* defects which made the loader unsafe to use on a slope. [T]he court instructed that the operator could recover only if a defect in the loader's design made the machine " 'unreasonably dangerous for its intended use.' " [citation omitted] The operator appealed the defense verdict, citing the "unreasonably dangerous" instruction as prejudicial error.

The manufacturer responded that even if the "unreasonably dangerous" test was inappropriate for manufacturing defects, . . . it should be retained for design defects. . . .

The *Barker* court disagreed. It reasoned as follows: Our [earlier decisions] sought to avoid the danger that a jury would *deny* recovery, as the Restatement had intended, "so long as the product did not fall below the ordinary consumer's expectations as to [its] safety. . . .' " (*Barker*, supra, fn. omitted.) This danger was particularly acute in design defect cases, where a manufacturer might argue that because the item which caused injury was identical to others of the same product line, it must necessarily have satisfied ordinary consumer expectations. . . .

Despite these difficulties, *Barker* explained, it is possible to define a design defect, and the expectations of the ordinary consumer are relevant to that issue. At a minimum, said *Barker*, a product *is* defective in design if it *does* fail to perform as safely as an ordinary consumer would expect. This principle, *Barker* asserted, acknowledges the relationship between strict tort liability for a defective product and the common law doctrine of warranty, which holds that a product's presence on the market includes an implied representation " 'that it [will] safely do the jobs for which it was built.' " . . . " Under this [minimum] standard," *Barker* observed, "an injured plaintiff will frequently be able to demonstrate the defectiveness of the product *by resort to circumstantial evidence, even when the accident itself precludes identification of the specific defect at fault.*[Citations.]"

However, *Barker* asserted, the Restatement had erred in proposing that a violation of ordinary consumer expectations was *necessary* for recovery on this ground. "As Professor Wade has pointed out, . . . the expectations of the ordinary consumer cannot be viewed as the exclusive yardstick for evaluating design defectiveness because '[i]n many situations . . . *the consumer would not know what to expect*, because he would have *no idea* how safe the product could be made.' " (573 P.2d 443, quoting Wade, On the Nature of Strict Tort Liability for Products (1973) 44 Miss. L.J. 825, 829, italics added.)

Thus, *Barker* concluded, "a product may be found defective in design, even if it satisfies ordinary consumer expectations, if through hindsight the jury determines that the product's design embodies 'excessive preventable danger,' or, in other words, if the jury finds that the risk of danger inherent in the challenged design outweighs the benefits of such design. [Citations.]" . . . *Barker* held that under this latter standard, "a jury may consider, among other relevant factors, the gravity of the danger posed by the challenged design, the likelihood that such danger would occur, the mechanical feasibility of a safer alternative design, the financial cost of an improved design, and the adverse consequences to the product and to the consumer that would result from an alternative design. [Citations.]" (Id. at p. 431.) *Barker* also made clear that when the ultimate issue of design defect calls for a careful assessment of feasibility, practicality, risk, and benefit, the case should not be resolved simply on the basis of ordinary consumer expectations. As *Barker* observed, "past design defect decisions demonstrate that, as a practical matter, in many instances it is simply impossible to eliminate the balancing or weighing of competing considerations in determining whether a product is defectively designed or not. . . ."

An example, *Barker* noted, was the "crashworthiness" issue presented in Self v. General Motors Corp., [116 Cal. Rptr. 575 (Ct. App. 1974)]. The debate there was whether the explosion of a vehicle's fuel tank in an accident was due to a defect in design. This, in turn, entailed concerns about whether placement of the tank in a position less vulnerable to rear end collisions, even if technically feasible, "would have created a greater risk of injury in other, more common situations." (*Barker*, supra) Because this complex weighing of risks, benefits, and practical alternatives is "implicit" in so many design-defect determinations, *Barker* concluded, "an instruction which appears to preclude such a weighing process under all circumstances may mislead the jury." (Id.) . . .

Campbell v. General Motors Corp., (1982) 649 P.2d 224 (*Campbell*) provided additional strong hints about the proper use of the ordinary consumer expectations prong of *Barker*. Plaintiff Campbell, a bus passenger, was thrown from her seat and injured during a sharp turn. She sued GM, the manufacturer of the bus, alleging that the vehicle was defectively designed because there was no "grab bar" within easy reach of her seat. Campbell presented no expert testimony, but she submitted photographs of the interior of the bus, showing where safety bars and handles were located in relation to the seat she had occupied. At the conclusion of her case in chief, GM moved for nonsuit, arguing that her evidence of design defect and proximate cause was not sufficient. The trial court granted the motion, but we reversed. We emphasized that in order to establish a design defect under *Barker*'s ordinary consumer expectations test, it was enough for Campbell to show "the objective conditions of the product" so that the jurors could employ "[their] own sense of whether the product meets ordinary expectations as to its safety under the circumstances presented by the evidence. Since public transportation is a matter of common experience, no expert testimony was required to enable the jury to reach a decision on this part of the *Barker* inquiry." (*Campbell*, supra.)

"Indeed, it is difficult to conceive what testimony an 'expert' could provide. The thrust of the first *Barker* test is that the product must meet the safety expectations of the general public as represented by the ordinary consumer, not the industry or a government agency. '[O]ne can hardly imagine what credentials a witness must possess before he can be certified as an expert on the issue of *ordinary* consumer expectations.' " (*Campbell*, supra, 32 Cal. 3d at pp. 126-127, 184 Cal. Rptr. 891, 649 P.2d 224, quoting Schwartz, Foreword: Understanding Products Liability (1979) 67 Cal. L. Rev. 435, 480, italics added.)

Had we ended our discussion at this point, it would have been clear that a product violates ordinary consumer expectations only when the circumstances arouse such reasonable expectations based on common experience of the product's users. However, dictum in the next paragraph of *Campbell* injected ambiguity. We said, "The quantum of proof necessary to establish a prima facie case . . . under the first [i.e., ordinary consumer expectations] prong of *Barker* cannot be reduced to an easy formula. However, *if* the product is one within the common experience of ordinary consumers" (italics added), it will generally be enough for the injured plaintiff to show the circumstances of the accident and "the objective features of the product which are relevant to an evaluation of its safety. . . ." One might infer from this passage that the ordinary consumer expectations prong of *Barker* is not limited to product performance "within the common experience" of the product's ordinary consumers. . . .

In *Barker*, we offered two alternative ways to prove a design defect, each appropriate to its own circumstances. The purposes, behaviors, and dangers of certain products are commonly understood by those who ordinarily use them. By the same token, the ordinary users or consumers of a product may have reasonable, widely accepted minimum expectations about the circumstances under which it should perform safely. Consumers govern their own conduct by these expectations, and products on the market should conform to them.

In some cases, therefore, "ordinary knowledge . . . as to . . . [the product's] characteristics" (Rest. 2d Torts, supra, §402A, com. *i.*, p. 352) may permit an inference that the product did not perform as safely as it should. *If* the facts permit such a conclusion, and *if* the failure resulted from the product's design, a finding of defect is warranted without any further proof. The manufacturer may not defend a claim that a product's design failed to perform as safely as its ordinary consumers would expect by presenting expert evidence of the design's relative risks and benefits.[3]

However, as we noted in *Barker*, a complex product, even when it is being used as intended, may often cause injury in a way that does not engage its ordinary consumers' reasonable minimum assumptions about safe performance. For example, the ordinary consumer of an automobile simply has "no idea" how it should perform in all foreseeable situations, or how safe it should be made against all foreseeable hazards. (*Barker*, supra.)

An injured person is not foreclosed from proving a defect in the product's design simply because he cannot show that the reasonable minimum safety expectations of its ordinary consumers were violated. Under *Barker*'s alternative test, a product is still defective if its design embodies "excessive preventable danger" . . . that is, unless "the benefits of the . . . design outweigh the risk of danger inherent in such design" (id.). But this determination involves technical issues of feasibility, cost, practicality, risk, and benefit (id., at p. 431, 143 Cal. Rptr. 225, 573 P.2d 443) which are "impossible" to avoid. . . . In such cases, the jury *must* consider the manufacturer's evidence of competing design considerations . . . and the issue of design defect cannot fairly be resolved by standardless reference to the "expectations" of an "ordinary consumer."

As we have seen, the consumer expectations test is reserved for cases in which the *everyday experience* of the product's users permits a conclusion that the product's design violated *minimum* safety assumptions, and is thus defective *regardless of expert opinion about the merits of the design.* It follows that where the minimum safety of a product is within the common knowledge of lay jurors, expert witnesses may not be used to demonstrate what an ordinary consumer would or should expect. Use of expert testimony for that purpose would invade the jury's function (see Evid. Code, §801, subd. (a)), and would invite circumvention of the rule that the risks and benefits of a

---

3. For example, the ordinary consumers of modern automobiles may and do expect that such vehicles will be designed so as not to explode while idling at stoplights, experience sudden steering or brake failure as they leave the dealership, or roll over and catch fire in two-mile-per-hour collisions. If the plaintiff in a product liability action proved that a vehicle's design produced such a result, the jury could find forthwith that the car failed to perform as safely as its ordinary consumers would expect, and was therefore defective.

challenged design must be carefully balanced whenever the issue of design defect goes beyond the common experience of the product's users.[4]

By the same token, the jury may not be left free to find a violation of ordinary consumer expectations whenever it chooses. Unless the facts actually permit an inference that the product's performance did not meet the minimum safety expectations of its ordinary users, the jury must engage in the balancing of risks and benefits required by the second prong of *Barker.*

Accordingly, as *Barker* indicated, instructions are misleading and incorrect if they allow a jury to avoid this risk-benefit analysis in a case where it is required. Instructions based on the ordinary consumer expectations prong of *Barker* are not appropriate where, as a matter of law, the evidence would not support a jury verdict on that theory. Whenever that is so, the jury must be instructed solely on the alternative risk-benefit theory of design defect announced in *Barker.*[5]

GM suggests that the consumer expectations test is improper whenever "crashworthiness," a complex product, or technical questions of causation are at issue. Because the variety of potential product injuries is infinite, the line cannot be drawn as clearly as GM proposes. But the fundamental distinction is not impossible to define. The crucial question in each individual case is whether the circumstances of the product's failure permit an inference that the product's design performed below the legitimate, commonly accepted minimum safety assumptions of its ordinary consumers.[6]

GM argues at length that the consumer expectations test is an "unworkable, amorphic, fleeting standard" which should be entirely abolished as a basis for design defect. In GM's view, the test is deficient and unfair in several respects. First, it defies definition. Second, it focuses not on the objective condition of products, but on the subjective, unstable, and often unreasonable opinions of consumers. Third, it ignores the reality that ordinary consumers know little about how safe the complex products they use can or should be made. Fourth, it invites the jury to isolate the particular consumer, component, accident, and injury before it instead of considering whether the whole product fairly accommodates the competing expectations of all consumers in all situations (see Daly v. General Motors Corp., supra). Fifth, it eliminates the careful balancing of risks and benefits which is essential to any design issue. . . .

---

4. Plaintiff insists that manufacturers should be forced to design their products to meet the "objective" safety demands of a "hypothetical" reasonable consumer who is fully informed about what he or she should expect. Hence, plaintiff reasons, the jury may receive expert advice on "reasonable" safety expectations for the product. However, this function is better served by the risk-benefit prong of *Barker.* There, juries receive expert advice, apply clear guidelines, and decide accordingly whether the product's design is an acceptable compromise of competing considerations. . . .

5. Plaintiff urges that any limitation on use of the consumer expectations test contravenes [the purpose of Greenman v. Yuba Power Products, Inc., 377 P.2d 897 (Cal. 1963)] to aid hapless consumers. But we have consistently held that manufacturers are not insurers of their products; they are liable in tort only when "defects" in their products cause injury. (E.g., Daly v. General Motors Corp. (1978) 20 Cal. 3d 725, 733, 144 Cal. Rptr. 380, 575 P.2d 1162; [Cronin v. J.B.E. Olson Corp., 501 P.2d 1153 (Cal. 1972).] *Barker* properly articulated that a product's design is "defective" only if it violates the "ordinary" consumer's safety expectations, or if the manufacturer cannot show the design's benefits outweigh its risks. . . .

6. Contrary to GM's suggestion, ordinary consumer expectations are not irrelevant simply because expert testimony is required to prove that the product failed as marketed, or that a condition of the product as marketed was a "substantial," and therefore "legal," cause of injury. We simply hold that the consumer expectations test is appropriate only when the jury, fully appraised of the circumstances of the accident or injury, may conclude that the product's design failed to perform as safely as its ordinary consumers would expect.

We fully understand the dangers of improper use of the consumer expectations test. However, we cannot accept GM's insinuation that ordinary consumers lack any legitimate expectations about the minimum safety of the products they use. In particular circumstances, a product's design may perform so unsafely that the defect is apparent to the common reason, experience, and understanding of its ordinary consumers. In such cases, a lay jury is competent to make that determination. . . .

Applying our conclusions to the facts of this case, however, we agree that the instant jury should not have been instructed on ordinary consumer expectations. Plaintiff's theory of design defect was one of technical and mechanical detail. It sought to examine the precise behavior of several obscure components of her car under the complex circumstances of a particular accident. The collision's exact speed, angle, and point of impact were disputed. It seems settled, however, that plaintiff's Camaro received a substantial oblique blow near the left front wheel, and that the adjacent frame members and bracket assembly absorbed considerable inertial force.

An ordinary consumer of automobiles cannot reasonably expect that a car's frame, suspension, or interior will be designed to remain intact in any and all accidents. Nor would ordinary experience and understanding inform such a consumer how safely an automobile's design should perform under the esoteric circumstances of the collision at issue here. Indeed, both parties assumed that quite complicated design considerations were at issue, and that expert testimony was necessary to illuminate these matters. Therefore, injection of ordinary consumer expectations into the design defect equation was improper.

We are equally persuaded, however, that the error was harmless, because it is not reasonably probable defendant would have obtained a more favorable result in its absence. . . .

Here there were no instructions which specifically remedied the erroneous placement of the consumer expectations alternative before the jury. Moreover, plaintiff's counsel briefly reminded the jury that the instructions allowed it to find a design defect under either the consumer expectations or risk-benefit tests. However, the consumer expectations theory was never emphasized at any point. As previously noted, the case was tried on the assumption that the alleged design defect was a matter of technical debate. Virtually all the evidence and argument on design defect focused on expert evaluation of the strengths, shortcomings, risks, and benefits of the challenged design, as compared with a competitor's approach. . . .

Under these circumstances, we find it highly unlikely that a reasonable jury took that path. We see no reasonable probability that the jury disregarded the voluminous evidence on the risks and benefits of the Camaro's design, and instead rested its verdict on its independent assessment of what an ordinary consumer would expect. Accordingly, we conclude, the error in presenting that theory to the jury provides no basis for disturbing the trial judgment.[7]

---

7. In a separate argument, raised for the first time in GM's brief on the merits, both GM and the Council urge us to reconsider *Barker's* holding — embodied in the standard instruction received by this jury — that under the risk-benefit test, the manufacturer has the burden of proving that the utility of the challenged design outweighs its dangers. (*Barker*, supra. . . .) We explained in *Barker* that placement of the risk-benefit burden on the manufacturer is appropriate because the considerations which influenced the design of its product are "peculiarly within . . . [its] knowledge." (Id. . . .) Furthermore, we observed, the "fundamental policies" of *Greenman* dictate that a manufacturer who seeks to escape design defect liability on risk-benefit grounds "should bear the burden of persuading the trier of fact that its product should not be judged defective. . . ." (Id. . . .)

[Discussion of other issues omitted.]

Conclusion

The trial court erred when it instructed on the consumer expectations test for design defect. . . . However, [the] error [did not cause] actual prejudice. Accordingly, the judgment of the Court of Appeal, upholding the trial court judgment in favor of plaintiff, is affirmed.

Kennard, George, Werdegar and Boren, JJ., concur.

[Concurring opinions omitted.]

As the court in *Soule* noted, *Barker* refused to adopt the "unreasonably dangerous" test for defect because it feared that the Comment *i* (consumer expectations) interpretation of "unreasonably dangerous" would tag along with it. To impose liability only for dangers that are beyond the contemplation of the ordinary consumer might give new life to the patent danger rule. As explained earlier, the patent danger rule declares that any design-related hazard that is, or should be, obvious to a reasonable product user cannot be the basis of a valid claim of defective design. *Barker* made it clear that, in California at least, no formulation of defect that could lead courts to reimpose the patent danger rule was acceptable.

Developments post-*Soule* in California raise the question of whether the consumer expectations test will be read as narrowly as *Soule* suggests. In Bresnahan v. Chrysler Corp., 38 Cal. Rptr. 2d 446 (Cal. Ct. App. 1995), plaintiff was driving her 1988 Chrysler LeBaron when she was rear-ended at low speed by another car. When the collision occurred, the LeBaron's passive restraint air bag inflated, forcing plaintiff's left arm and hand upward. Her hand struck the LeBaron's overarching windshield, cracking it, and her elbow impacted the windshield's side pillar. Plaintiff suffered a fractured elbow, requiring extensive treatment. Plaintiff decided to try the case solely on the consumer expectations test and sought to exclude all evidence with regard to risk-utility factors. Defendant countered that under *Soule* a case dealing with the crashworthiness characteristics of an automobile could proceed only under the risk-utility theory. The trial court sided with the defendant. The court reversed on appeal, saying:

> We believe that, on the showing before us, an ordinary consumer would be capable of forming an expectation, one way or the other, about whether the design of the highly publicized and by now commonplace product of an air bag-equipped automobile satisfied

---

GM argues that *Barker* unfairly requires the manufacturer to "prove a negative" — i.e., the absence of a safer alternative design. The Council suggests our "peculiar knowledge" rationale is unrealistic under liberal modern discovery rules. We are not persuaded. *Barker* allows the evaluation of competing designs, but it does not require proof that the challenged design is the safest possible alternative. The manufacturer need only show that given the inherent complexities of design, the benefits of its chosen design outweigh the dangers. Moreover, modern discovery practice neither redresses the inherent technical imbalance between manufacturer and consumer nor dictates that the injured consumer should bear the primary burden of evaluating a design developed and chosen by the manufacturer. GM and the Council fail to convince us that *Barker* was incorrectly decided in this respect.

minimal safety expectations in causing that result (assuming that it was the cause). Plaintiff's theory here does not pose the consumer unawareness that attended the design defect claim in *Soule*. In contrast to *Soule's* complex and murky situation regarding the crashworthiness of wheel brackets and frames, ordinary experience may well advise a consumer what measure of safety to expect from her car's side windshield assembly and air bag in a minor rear-end collision.

. . . Chrysler cannot disqualify the consumer expectations test on the basis of asserted governmental conclusions that the benefits of air bags in high-speed collisions outweigh and justify the risk of injuries such as occurred here. Risk-benefit weighing is not a formal part of, nor may it serve as a "defense" to, the consumer expectations test. (*Soule*, supra, 8 Cal. 4th at p.566.) Chrysler's implicit suggestion that the favorableness to it of the risk-benefit test requires its use begs the question. [Id. at 451-52.]

Is the gist of this decision that plaintiff should recover even if Chrysler could establish that an alternative design would provide less overall safety than that provided by the design that caused the plaintiff's injury?

In a later case, Pruitt v. General Motors Corp., 86 Cal. Rptr. 2d 4 (Cal. Ct. App. 1999), on facts similar to *Bresnahan* — an air bag deployed in a low-impact collision, fracturing plaintiff's jaw — the trial court refused to give a consumer expectations design-defect instruction and the jury returned a verdict for the defendant. The court of appeals affirmed the judgment.

For other indications that California reads the consumer expectations test narrowly, see Stephen v. Ford Motor Co., 37 Cal. Rptr. 3d 9 (Cal. Ct. App. 2005) (consumer expectations test unsuitable to decide defect claims regarding a well-used tire's tread separation and an SUV's directional stability); Snyder v. Ortho-McNeil Pharmaceuticals, 2002 WL 1161208 (Cal. Ct. App. 2002) (consumer expectations test unsuitable for medical devices); McCabe v. American Honda Motor Co., 123 Cal. Rptr. 2d 303, n.7, (Cal. Ct. App. 2002) (consumer expectations test envisages an inquiry similar to that employed in res ipsa loquitur cases); Morson v. Superior Court, 109 Cal. Rptr. 2d 343 (Cal. Ct. App. 2001) (consumer expectations test not appropriate to decide whether design of latex gloves is defective).

Nevertheless, California courts continue to leave space for the consumer expectations test. See, e.g., Arnold v. Dow Chem. Co., 110 Cal. Rptr. 2d 722 (Cal. Ct. App. 2001) (insecticide "within the ordinary experience and understanding of the consumer"). One particularly capacious consumer expectations decision is Romine v. Johnson Controls, Inc., 224 Cal. App. 4th 990 (Cal. Ct. App. 2014), in which an injured driver brought suit against the designer and manufacturer of an automobile seat that collapsed when the driver was struck from behind in a collision. The collision immediately causing plaintiff's injury was actually only one in a series of chain collisions brought about when a third party driver slammed at high speed into a car stopped in traffic on a freeway exit ramp. Defendants argued that the circumstances surrounding the crash rendered it beyond the ken of ordinary consumers and that, accordingly, the trial court should not have instructed the jury to determine design defectiveness according to the consumer expectations test. The court disagreed:

The accident that caused plaintiff's injuries was not as complex as defendants claim. Although there were multiple vehicles and multiple collisions in the incident, there was a single collision that caused plaintiff's injuries — plaintiff was injured when the Altima rear-ended her Frontier. That another car first hit the Altima and that plaintiff's

---

authors' dialogue 15

DOUG: What do you fellows think about the *Romine* case?

JIM: Doug, you know our position on this issue. *Romine* is a terrible decision. First, consumers have no expectations as to how seats will behave in a high speed collision. Second, the court refused to allow the defendant to introduce risk/utility evidence as to whether the seat design was reasonable. If defendant was prepared to show that the design that would have met consumer expectations (i.e., would have prevented harm to the plaintiff in this collision) would have compromised overall safety for all collisions, then the court is in effect saying that consumers expect that manufacturers will design cars that are more dangerous than necessary. That is just plain ridiculous.

AARON: Not only is Jim right about the poor reasoning, but the California court relied on an Illinois decision and misstated the holding in that case. In *Mikolajczyk v. Ford Motor Co.*, infra, contrary to what the California court said, the Illinois court did not countenance giving a consumer expectation instruction when defendant introduced risk/utility evidence. The court reversed the trial court because it gave a "consumer expectation" instruction and did not give an instruction that told the jury that it was to consider consumer expectations and risk/utility factors. One of the reasons we so adamantly opposed the consumer expectation test as a stand alone test for defect was to prevent courts from ignoring safety considerations in deciding design liability. But Doug, you have written in defense of the consumer expectation test – do you find *Romine* acceptable?

DOUG: Not at all. I agree with you both that an unstructured consumer expectation test is unjustifiable and if we were writing from whole cloth I might say let's abandon the test altogether. But since some courts insist on retaining it, I've argued that they should beef up the test into something that's intellectually defensible. In order to make out a consumer expectations claim, a plaintiff should have to present expert testimony (through cognitive and social psychologists, behavioral economists, marketing experts, and the like) concerning the extent to which consumer risk perceptions differ in significant ways from the standards derived under risk-utility analysis. But I certainly won't defend the position of the *Romine* court that jurors should essentially be allowed to guess what consumers might expect about how a seat should function in a high speed collision.

JIM: For the first time in these dialogues we all seem to agree. Time to bring out the champagne.

Frontier hit the car in front of plaintiff, which in turn hit the car in front of it, after the Altima struck plaintiff's Frontier had no bearing on plaintiff's injuries. Defendants' own expert testified that plaintiff sustained her injuries during the rear-end impact on her car. Rear-end collisions are common and within the average consumer's ordinary experience. Consumers have expectations about whether a vehicle's driver's seat will collapse rearward in a rear-end collision, regardless of the speed of the collision. [Id. at 1004.]

Notably, the court in *Romine* also upheld the trial court's exclusion of defendants' proffered expert testimony regarding the risks and benefits of the challenged seat design. See id. at 1005. Finally, the court rejected the argument that plaintiff was required to demonstrate the content of consumer expectations through expert testimony or similarly targeted evidence:

> In this case, plaintiff provided evidence concerning her use of the product, the circumstances of the accident, and the objective features of her car seat that were relevant to an evaluation of its safety. . . . Plaintiff was not required to produce evidence in the form of advertising or marketing literature, vehicle manuals, or consumer test reports to demonstrate an ordinary consumer's expectations of how the seat in plaintiff's Frontier would perform if the vehicle was struck from behind. [Id. at 1005-1006.]

The two-prong approach has followers outside of California. See, e.g., In re Methyl Tertiary Butyl Ether (MTBE) Products Liab. Litig., 2015 WL 3763645 (S.D.N.Y. 2015) (applying Puerto Rico law); Tincher v. Omega Flex, Inc., 104 A.3d 328 (Pa. 2014); Jackson v. General Motors Corp., 60 S.W.3d 800 (Tenn. 2001); Acoba v. General Tire Co., 986 P.2d 288 (Haw. 1999); Knitz v. Minster Mach. Co., 432 N.E.2d 814 (Ohio), *cert. denied*, 459 U.S. 857 (1982); Caterpillar Tractor Co. v. Beck, 593 P.2d 871 (Alaska 1979). However, it appears that only California, Alaska, and Puerto Rico have coupled the two-step liability test with a shift to defendant of the burden of proof on the risk-utility issue. See *Soule*, supra, n.8; *Caterpillar*, supra, at 885-86; *MTBE*, supra at *4.

As in California, other jurisdictions applying the two-prong approach tend to reserve the consumer expectations test for relatively straightforward product failures. See, e.g., Brown v. Raymond Corp., 432 F.3d 640, 646 (6th Cir. 2005) (applying Tennessee law) (summary judgment for forklift manufacturer affirmed after plaintiff's expert's testimony was properly excluded under *Daubert*; "a forklift is a complex machine beyond the purview of the ordinary consumer and [the plaintiff] was therefore obligated to provide expert testimony [under the risk-utility prong of the test for design defect]''); In re Methyl Tertiary Butyl Ether (MTBE) Products Liability Litigation, 2015 WL 3763645 (S.D.N.Y. 2015) (applying Puerto Rico law) (because of the technical nature of the production of gasoline, including hazardous additives such as MTBE, design defect claim must be governed by risk-utility rather than consumer expectations test); Tillman v. C.R. Bard, Inc., 2015 WL 1456657, at *25 (M.D. Fla. 2015) ("Because this case pertains to a complex medical device, accessible to the consumer only through a physician, the Court finds that the consumer-expectation test is not applicable here.''). Given this narrow application of the consumer expectations test under the two-prong approach, the question again is raised whether consumer expectations really are playing a substantive role in design defect litigation any different from an inference of defect in res ipsa-like situations. Consider one final judicial attempt to expound upon the role of consumer expectations in design defect cases.

Authors' dialogue **16**

DOUG: Aaron and Jim, after all the fireworks, what's your take on the role that the consumer expectations test plays in design defect litigation?

AARON: Except for Kansas – the last remaining true believer – I believe that most of the cases that allow for liability under the consumer expectations test are cases that would be covered by Section 3 of the Products Liability Restatement which supports an inference of defect when the incident that caused the harm was of a kind that ordinarily occurs as a result of product defect. So my short answer is that I don't think that the consumer expectations test plays much of a role in design litigation.

JIM: I agree. Look at the cases that go to juries with both a risk-utility and consumer expectations instruction. Invariably the plaintiff has presented evidence of a reasonable alternative design. What courts are doing is allowing cases to go to a jury on dual instructions, thus giving the plaintiff two bites at the apple. Whether that is fair or not, we can debate. But, in any event, plaintiff has offered sufficient evidence of a reasonable alternative design so that the court is not prepared to direct a verdict for the defendant on that issue.

DOUG: But what if a jury comes back with a verdict for the defendant on risk-utility and for the plaintiff on consumer expectations? You can't say that consumer expectations is just window dressing.

AARON: I have two responses. First, those cases are few and far between. Now and then it happens. The *Denny* case in New York, supra, is an example. But there are not many other examples out there. Second, courts are prepared to allow the consumer expectation test's looser jury standard only once they are convinced that a practical alternative was probably available. Would courts be so free-wheeling with the consumer expectations instruction if they knew that a reasonable alternative design (even one ignored by a jury) was not in the picture? I think not.

JIM: The problem with your thesis, Aaron, is that you can't prove it. How is anyone to know what lurks in the minds of judges and jurors? But if I get you right, the consumer expectations test allows a jury that may be scared off by a risk-utility instruction as being too technical to do risk-utility justice but under a less rigid standard.

DOUG: It would be interesting if courts are using the consumer expectations test to encourage juries to assess the risks and benefits of particular products without feeling bogged down by technicalities. Courts could – and I think should – move further in that direction, using the consumer expectations test to incorporate risks that reflect public values but are not captured by the traditional risk-utility test. The tussle between technocracy and democracy is as American as apple pie and I think you see it reflected in the risk-utility/ consumer expectations debate.

Mikolajczyk v. Ford Motor Co.
901 N.E. 2d 329 (Ill. 2008)

Justice GARMAN delivered the judgment of the court, with opinion.

James Mikolajczyk died of injuries sustained when the Ford Escort he was driving was struck from behind by another vehicle. His widow, as special administrator of his estate, sued the other driver, claiming negligence, and Ford Motor Company and Mazda Motor Corporation, claiming defective design of the driver's seat. Summary judgment was entered against the other driver. The claims against the other two defendants proceeded to a jury trial in the circuit court of Cook County. The jury found defendants liable and awarded plaintiff $2 million in damages for loss of money, goods, and services, and $25 million for loss of society. . . .

Background

On February 2, 2000, William Timberlake shared two pints of gin with a friend before getting behind the wheel of his Cadillac. He was traveling approximately 60 miles per hour when he smashed into the rear of a 1996 Ford Escort that was stopped at a red light. The driver of the Escort, James Mikolajczyk, suffered severe, irreversible brain trauma and spent several days on life support before his death. His daughter, Elizabeth, then aged 10, who was asleep in the backseat at the time of the accident, suffered two broken legs. James was also survived by his wife, Connie, and son, Adam, then aged 14.

Plaintiff's negligence suit against defendant Timberlake resulted in the entry of summary judgment. Plaintiff's lawsuit against defendants Ford and Mazda alleged strict product liability premised on defective design of the driver's seat of the Escort. Specifically, she claimed that as a result of the defective design of the seat, it collapsed when the car was struck from behind, causing James to be propelled rearward and to strike his head on the backseat of the car. Plaintiff further alleged that the design of the seat was unreasonably dangerous and that the design defect proximately caused James's death. The Escort was manufactured by defendant Ford. The seat was designed by defendant Mazda; Ford has the authority to approve or disapprove the design. . . .

Before this court, defendants argue that the appellate court "turned back the evolution of Illinois law" by applying the "outdated" consumer-expectation test rather than the risk-utility test that, they assert, is now the exclusive test for defective design of a complex product. In the alternative, they argue that even if this court has not expressly adopted risk-utility as the exclusive test in such cases, it should do so now. In effect, they argue that the trial court applied the wrong substantive law to plaintiff's claim, raising this issue in the context of the trial court's refusal to give their non-IPI jury instruction. Defendants also argue that a new trial must be granted in any event because the jury instructions that were given did not correspond to the evidence presented at trial. . . .

In *Lamkin v. Towner*, . . . 563 N.E. 2d 449 (1990), this court reiterated its earlier adoption of section 402 A of the Restatement (Second) of Torts, observing that a product is "unreasonably dangerous" due to a defect in either manufacturing or design when it is " 'dangerous to an extent beyond that which would be contemplated by the ordinary consumer who purchases it, with the ordinary knowledge common to the community as to its characteristics.' " . . . quoting Restatement Second of Torts §402A, Comment *i*, at 352 (1965).

We further stated that in a strict product liability action, a claim of defective design may be proven in either of two ways. First, the plaintiff may introduce "evidence that the product failed to perform as safely as an ordinary consumer would expect when used in an intended or reasonably foreseeable manner." . . . This has come to be known as the consumer-expectation test. Second, the plaintiff may introduce "evidence that the product's design proximately caused his injury." If the defendant thereafter "fails to prove that on balance the benefits of the challenged design out-weigh the risk of danger inherent in such designs," the plaintiff will prevail. . . . This test, which added the balancing of risks and benefits to the alternative design and feasibility inquiries . . . has come to be known as the risk-utility or risk-benefit test.

Defendants argue that if we have not adopted the risk-utility test as the sole, exclusive test in design defect cases, we should do so now. They argue, in the alternative, that if we do not adopt the risk-utility test as the sole, exclusive test in all design defect cases, it should be the sole, exclusive test when the product is complex and the circumstances are not familiar to the ordinary consumer. This case, they insist, illustrates the need to restrict application of the consumer-expectation test to claims of defective manufacture or, at least, to design defects in simple products.

According to defendants, the consumer-expectation test evolved to evaluate claims of manufacturing defect where it is reasonable to believe that jurors, as ordinary consumers, can rely on their own experience and expectations to determine whether a manufacturing defect has rendered a product unreasonably dangerous. This, defendants assert, is a simple, straight-forward inquiry focused on one particular "unit" of the product and not on the product as a whole. Thus, there are no countervailing benefits to consider when a manufacturing defect is alleged.

The consumer-expectation test, defendants argue, does not make sense when a design defect is alleged because design decisions, by their very nature, involve considerations of the feasibility of alternative designs, cost, safety, and other factors with which the ordinary consumer is not familiar. In the context of the present case, defendants assert, the jurors could not have had reasonable expectations of their own regarding the proper degree of rigidity or flexibility in a car seat or how a seat should function in a wide range of potential accident conditions. According to defendants, the risk-utility test is specifically fashioned to evaluate this kind of claim and should be the sole measure of whether the product is unreasonably dangerous due to a design defect.

Plaintiff responds that defendants are proposing a "radical theory," adoption of which would overrule [existing Illinois case law]. . . .

The rule advocated by defendants is contained in section 2(b) of the Products Liability Restatement, which would allow a finding of design defect only "when the foreseeable risks of harm posed by the product could have been reduced or avoided by the adoption of a reasonable alternative design and the omission of the alternative design renders the product not reasonably safe." Restatement (Third) of Torts: Products Liability §2(b), at 14 (1998).

If we were to accept defendants' invitation to adopt section 2(b) of the Products Liability Restatement, we would indeed overrule precedent, because section 2(b) would redefine the elements of a product liability claim based on alleged defective design.

Under Illinois law, the elements of a claim of strict liability based on a defect in the product are: (1) a condition of the product as a result of manufacturing or design, (2) that made the product unreasonably dangerous, (3) and that existed at the time the product left the defendant's control, and (4) an injury to the plaintiff, (5) that was proximately cause by the condition. The plaintiff has the burden of proof on each element. See *Sollami*, 201 Ill. 2d at 7, 265 Ill. Dec. 177, 772 N.E.2d 215; *Suvada*, 31 Ill.2d at 623, 210 N.E.2d 182.

Section 2(b) of the Products Liability Restatement would alter the "unreasonably dangerous" element in design defect cases in two significant ways. First a plaintiff would be required to plead and prove the existence of a feasible alternative design in every case. Second, instead of proving that the defect rendered the product "unreasonably dangerous," the plaintiff would have the burden of proving that the product was "not reasonably safe." . . .

If a jury were to consider the two tests [consumer expectations and risk-utility] independently, there are four possible outcomes. First, the product could be found unreasonably dangerous under both tests and judgment would be for the plaintiff. . . .

Second, the product could be found not unreasonably dangerous under either test and judgment would be for the defendant. . . .

Third, the product could be found not unreasonably dangerous under the consumer-expectation test, but unreasonably dangerous under the risk-utility test. In such a case, judgment would be for the plaintiff. . . .

Defendants in the present case posit the fourth possible outcome when the two tests are applied independently. The product could be found unreasonably dangerous under the consumer-expectation test, but risk-utility analysis could reveal that an alternative is not available, or that available alternatives are not feasible, or that the benefits of the design outweigh its inherent risks. In such a case, defendants argue, the result of the risk-utility test should trump the result of the consumer-expectation test. Defendant argues that if the tests are treated as alternatives so that a plaintiff may prevail by meeting either test, the effect will be to impose absolute-not just strict liability. This will occur, defendants claim, because the consumer-expectation test will, at least where a complex product is involved, almost always lead to a finding of unreasonably dangerousness. As a result, defendants will be liable for all injuries in all circumstances, no matter how much the risk-utility balance weighs in favor of the challenged product design. . . .

The consumer-expectation test is a single-factor test and, therefore, narrow in scope. . . . The jury is asked to make a single determination: whether the product is unsafe when put to a use that is reasonably foreseeable considering its nature and function. . . . No evidence of ordinary consumer expectations is required, because the members of the jury may rely on their own experiences to determine what an ordinary consumer would expect.

The risk-utility test, in contrast, is a multifactor analysis and, therefore, much broader in scope. . . .

Although we have declined to adopt section 2 of the Products Liability Restatement as a statement of substantive law, we do find its formulation of the risk-utility test to be instructive. Under section 2(b), the risk-utility balance is to be determined based on consideration of a "broad range of factors," including the "magnitude and probability of the foreseeable risks of harm, the instructions and warnings accompanying the product, and the *nature and strength of consumer expectations regarding the product, including expectations arising from product portrayal and marketing*," as well as "the likely effects of the alternative design on production costs; the effects of the alternative design on product longevity, maintenance, repair, and esthetics; and the range of consumer choice among products." (Emphasis added.) Restatement (Third) of Torts: Products Liability §2, Comment *f*, at 23 (1998). . . .

Under this formulation, consumer expectations are included within the scope of the broader risk-utility test. In addition, the test refines the consumer-expectation factor by specifically allowing for advertising and marketing messages to be used to assess consumer expectations.

We adopt this formulation of risk-utility test and hold that when the evidence presented by either or both parties supports the application of this integrated test, an appropriate instruction is to be given at the request of either party. If, however, both parties' theories of the case are framed entirely in terms of consumer expectations, including those based on advertising and marketing messages, and/or whether the product was being put to a reasonably foreseeable use at the time of injury, the jury should be instructed only on the consumer-expectation test.

Adoption of this integrated test resolves the question of whether the answer to the risk-utility test "trumps" the answer to the consumer-expectation test because the latter is incorporated into the former and is but one factor among many for the jury to consider. This is consistent with our conclusion . . . that while a plaintiff might not prevail under the single-factor test, she might still prevail under the multifactor test. . . . See *Calles*, 224 Ill. 2d at 256, 309 Ill. Dec. 383, 864 N.E. 2d 249.

In sum, we hold that both the consumer-expectation test and the risk-utility test continue to have their place in our law of strict product liability based on design defect. Each party is entitled to choose its own method of proof, to present relevant evidence, and to request a corresponding jury instruction. If the evidence is sufficient to implicate the risk-utility test, the broader test, which incorporated the factor of consumer expectations, is to be applied by the finder of fact.

In the present case, the occupant of the car seat was killed when the car was struck from behind. Rear-end collisions are reasonably foreseeable and the ordinary consumer would likely expect that a seat would not collapse rearward in such an accident, allowing the occupant to sustain massive head injury. Thus, the jury concluded that the car seat was unreasonably dangerous because it proved "unsafe when put to a use that is reasonably foreseeable considering the nature and function of the product." If the evidence presented was sufficient to require the jury to engage in risk-utility analysis, this conclusion as to consumer expectations would be properly considered as one factor in the broader, integrated risk-utility analysis. . . .

Conclusion

In sum, we hold that both the consumer-expectation test and the risk utility test may be utilized in a strict liability design defect case to prove that the product is "unreasonably dangerous." Whether an instruction is required on either test or both tests will depend on the issues raised in the pleadings and the evidence presented at trial. When both tests are employed, consumer expectation is to be treated as one factor in the multifactor risk-utility analysis.

Because the trial court abused its discretion by refusing the tendered nonpattern instructions, the judgment of the appellate court, which affirmed in part and reversed in part the judgment of the circuit court, is reversed, the judgment of the circuit court is reversed, and the cause is remanded to the circuit court for a new trial.

Appellate court judgment reversed; circuit court judgment reversed; cause remanded.

In Aaron D. Twerski & James A. Henderson, Jr., Manufacturer's Liability for Defective Product Designs: The Triumph of Risk-Utility, 74 Brook. L. Rev. 1061, 1075-1077 (2009), two of the authors of this casebook make the following observations:

From a functional standpoint, it appears that the consumer expectations test is a dead letter in Illinois. In any case in which a plaintiff seeks to proceed solely under the consumer expectations test, a defendant need only counter with risk-utility evidence to cause the court to apply the factor set forth in section 2, comment *f*. Under that test, consumer expectations are but one factor among other risk-utility factors to be considered in deciding whether a product is unreasonably dangerous. Conversely, when a defendant defends on the ground that a product meets consumer expectations, perhaps because the risks are obvious, a plaintiff need only introduce risk-utility evidence for the court to apply risk-utility balancing. The only cases in which risk-utility balancing will not come into play are those in which a product fails to perform its manifestly intended function and in which defective design can be inferred from the fact of injury. There can be no rational risk-utility defense to a product that simply cannot do what it was designed to do. If the steering mechanism of a car fails when it is driven out of the dealership, one cannot say it was reasonably designed to fail in this manner. That contingency is, however, covered by section 3 of the Restatement, which allows a court to apply a res ipsa-like inference of defect when defect can easily be inferred from the mere occurrence of the accident. . . .

In any event, under the analysis in *Mikolajczyk* the reality is that, if risk-utility evidence is introduced by either side, the judge will give the case to the jury with a risk-utility instruction patterned after comment *f*. The defendant will argue that it correctly chose a cost-effective, reasonably safe design, and the plaintiff will insist that a reasonable alternative was available that could have been avoided or reduced the injury. Any plaintiff who shows up in court knowing full well that the defendant will introduce risk-utility evidence that supports the product design must be ready to counter with evidence that a reasonable alternative was available. The burden of proof on risk-utility, according to Illinois court, lies with the plaintiff. Reasonable alternative design is not an idea conjured up by the Restatement drafters. It lies at the very heart of risk-utility balancing.

In Show v. Ford Motor Co., 659 F.3d 584 (7th Cir. 2011), plaintiffs injured in a rollover accident argued that their 1993 Ford Explorer was defectively designed due to instability. Writing for a unanimous panel, Judge Easterbrook affirmed the trial judge's grant of summary judgment to defendant manufacturer:

Plaintiffs' argument that jurors should be able to rely on their own expectations as consumers reflects a belief that "expectations" are all that matters. Yet because under *Mikolajczyk* the consumer-expectations approach is just a means of getting at some issues that bear on the question whether a product is unreasonably dangerous, it is impossible to dispense with expert knowledge. . . .

Counsel for the plaintiffs repeat the mantra that cars "just don't roll over in low-speed collisions" unless defectively designed. How do they know that? The record doesn't tell us even why this car rolled over, let alone what cars usually do in particular kinds of collisions — or what design changes could reduce the rollover rate, by how much. . . .

Because consumer expectations are just one factor in the inquiry whether a product is unreasonably dangerous, a jury unassisted by expert testimony would have to rely on speculation. This record does not show whether 1993 Explorers are unduly (or unexpectedly) dangerous, because it lacks evidence about many issues, such as: (a) under what circumstances they roll over; (b) under what circumstances consumers expect them to do so; (c) whether it would be possible to reduce the rollover rate; and (d) whether a different and safer design would have averted this particular accident. All of these are subjects on which plaintiffs bear the burden of proof. [Id. at 587-588.]

PROBLEM SEVENTEEN

Jack Sittner was seriously injured when a three-wheel all-terrain vehicle (ATV) manufactured by ATV Inc. overturned as he was driving the ATV on his one-acre lawn. Sittner has sued ATV Inc. claiming that the design of the ATV was defective. At trial, he is prepared to introduce expert testimony that ATV Inc. could have adopted a mechanical suspension system and that such a design could have been adopted at reasonable cost. In deposing ATV's expert, Dr. Roger Cart, Sittner's attorney learns that Cart has developed statistics that compare the annual injury and fatality rates (adjusted for hours of participation) for ATVs with a host of other activities and products. He is prepared to testify that the risk of death in SCUBA diving is four times greater than ATV riding, and the risk of death is two and one-half times greater in football; deaths involving passenger cars are slightly greater, and deaths arising from motorcycling are substantially greater.

Sittner's attorney has filed a motion in limine to exclude Dr. Cart's comparative risk assessment. New California has adopted the *Barker-Soule* two-prong tests for defect. Plaintiff, however, retains the burden of proof on both of the tests. You are the trial judge faced with the decision of whether to grant the plaintiff's motion to exclude the comparative statistics. Would you exclude the testimony as to: (1) the consumer expectations test? (2) the risk-utility test? Or would you allow Dr. Cart to testify as to either or both of the issues?

G. SPECIAL DUTY PROBLEMS IN DESIGN LITIGATION

Having examined the standards for prosecuting a design defect case, we now examine a set of cases that raise the question of whether courts may decide that, for well-defined policy reasons, the issue of design defect should not be decided by the courts at all, but rather should be deferred to other decision-makers. For lack of a better word, we borrow from the duty terminology of tort law to describe the issues raised in this section.

1. *Whether and to What Extent Should Courts Explicitly Defer to Markets on a Case-by-Case Basis?*

Linegar v. Armour of America, Inc.
909 F.2d 1150 (8th Cir. 1990)

BOWMAN, Circuit Judge.

. . . Armour of America, Inc. (Armour) appeals a judgment based on a jury verdict in favor of the widow and children of Jimmy Linegar, a Missouri State Highway

Patrol trooper who was killed in the line of duty. The jury found that the bullet-resistant vest manufactured by Armour and worn by Linegar at the time of the murder was defectively designed, and it awarded his family $1.5 million in damages. We reverse.

On April 15, 1985, as part of a routine traffic check, Linegar stopped a van with Nevada license plates near Branson, Missouri. The van's driver produced an Oregon operator's license bearing the name Matthew Mark Samuels. Linegar ascertained from the Patrol dispatcher that the name was an alias for David Tate, for whom there was an outstanding warrant on a weapons charge. Linegar did not believe the driver matched the description the dispatcher gave him for Tate, so he decided to investigate further.

A fellow trooper, Allen Hines, who was working the spot check with Linegar, then approached the passenger's side of the van while Linegar approached the driver's side. After a moment of questioning, Linegar asked the driver to step out of the van. The driver, who was in fact David Tate, brandished an automatic weapon and fired at the troopers first from inside and then from outside the van. By the time Tate stopped firing, Hines had been wounded by three shots and Linegar, whose body had been penetrated by six bullets, lay dead or dying. None of the shots that hit the contour-style, concealable protective vest Linegar was wearing — there were five such shots — penetrated the vest or caused injury. The wounds Linegar suffered all were caused by shots that struck parts of his body not protected by the vest.

The Missouri State Highway Patrol issued the vest to Linegar when he joined the Patrol in 1981. The vest was one of a lot of various sizes of the same style vest the Patrol purchased in 1979 directly from Armour. The contour style was one of several different styles then on the market. It provided more protection to the sides of the body than the style featuring rectangular panels in front and back, but not as much protection as a wrap-around style. The front and back panels of the contour vest, held together with Velcro closures under the arms, did not meet at the sides of the wearer's body, leaving an area along the sides of the body under the arms exposed when the vest was worn. This feature of the vest was obvious to the Patrol when it selected this vest as standard issue for its troopers and could only have been obvious to any trooper who chose to wear it. The bullet that proved fatal to Linegar entered between his seventh and eighth ribs, approximately three-and-one-fourth inches down from his armpit, and pierced his heart.

The theory upon which Linegar's widow and children sought and won recovery from Armour was strict liability in tort based on a design defect in the vest. . . .

The parties agree that Missouri substantive law controls in this diversity case. Under Missouri products liability law, plaintiff potentially had available to her three theories of recovery: negligence, strict liability, and breach of warranty. . . .

To recover under a theory of strict liability in tort for defective design, Missouri law requires that a party prove the following elements:

(1) [the] defendant sold the product in the course of its business;
(2) the product was then in a defective condition unreasonably dangerous when put to a reasonably anticipated use;
(3) the product was used in a manner reasonably anticipated;
(4) [the] plaintiff was damaged as a direct result of such defective condition as existed when the product was sold. . . .

While there is some dispute between the parties over various of the elements, we predicate our reversal on the dearth of plaintiff's evidence of element (2). We conclude that, as a matter of law, the contour vest Trooper Linegar was wearing when he was murdered was not defective and unreasonably dangerous.

Under the Missouri law of strict liability in tort for defective design, before a plaintiff can recover from the seller or manufacturer he must show that "the design renders the product unreasonably dangerous." Nesselrode v. Executive Beechcraft, Inc., 707 S.W.2d 371, 377 (Mo. 1986) (en banc). Ordinarily, that will be a jury question, and "the concept of unreasonable danger, which is determinative of whether a product is defective in a design case, is presented to the jury as an ultimate issue without further definition," id. at 378, as it was here. In this case, however, there was simply no evidence that the vest's design made it unreasonably dangerous, and the District Court should have declared that, as a matter of law, the vest was not defective, and directed a verdict or granted judgment for Armour notwithstanding the verdict. See Racer v. Utterman, 629 S.W.2d 387, 394 (Mo. Ct. App. 1981) ("Unless a court can say as a matter of law that the product is not unreasonably dangerous the question is one for the jury"), cert. denied, 459 U.S. 803, 103 S. Ct. 26, 74 L. Ed. 2d 42 (1982).

The Missouri cases leave the meaning of the phrase "unreasonably dangerous" largely a matter of common sense, the court's or the jury's. The Missouri Supreme Court has stated, however, that a product is defectively designed if it "creates an unreasonable risk of danger to the consumer or user when put to normal use." Nesselrode, 707 S.W.2d at 375. Among the factors to be considered are "the conditions and circumstances that will foreseeably attend the use of the product." Jarrell v. Fort Worth Steel & Mfg. Co., 666 S.W.2d 828, 836 (Mo. Ct. App. 1984). The conditions under which a bullet-resistant vest will be called upon to perform its intended function most assuredly will be dangerous, indeed life-threatening, and Armour surely knew that. It defies logic, however, to suggest that Armour reasonably should have anticipated that anyone would wear its vest for protection of areas of the body that the vest obviously did not cover. . . .

We have no difficulty in concluding as a matter of law that the product at issue here was neither defective nor unreasonably dangerous. Trooper Linegar's protective vest performed precisely as expected and stopped all of the bullets that hit it. No part of the vest nor any malfunction of the vest caused Linegar's injuries. See [Richardson v. Holland, 741 S.W.2d 751, 754 (Mo. Ct. App. 1987)] ("The cases uniformly hold that the doctrine of strict liability under the doctrine of 402A is not applicable unless there is some malfunction due to an improper or inadequate design or defect in manufacturing"). The vest was designed to prevent the penetration of bullets where there was coverage, and it did so; the amount of coverage was the buyer's choice. The Missouri Highway Patrol could have chosen to buy, and Armour could have sold the Patrol, a vest with more coverage; no one contests that. But it is not the place of courts or juries to set specifications as to the parts of the body a bullet-resistant garment must cover. A manufacturer is not obliged to market only one version of a product, that being the very safest design possible. If that were so, automobile manufacturers could not offer consumers sports cars, convertibles, jeeps, or compact cars. All boaters would have to buy full life vests instead of choosing a ski belt or even a flotation cushion. Personal safety devices, in particular, require personal choices, and it is beyond the province of courts and juries to act as legislators and preordain those choices.

In this case, there obviously were trade-offs to be made. A contour vest like the one here in question permits the wearer more flexibility and mobility and allows better heat dissipation and sweat evaporation, and thus is more likely to be worn than a more confining vest. It is less expensive than styles of vests providing more complete coverage. If manufacturers like Armour are threatened with economically devastating litigation if they market any vest style except that offering maximum coverage, they may decide, since one can always argue that more coverage is possible, to get out of the business altogether. Or they may continue to market the vest style that, according to the latest lawsuit, affords the "best" coverage. Officers who find the "safest" style confining or uncomfortable will either wear it at risk to their mobility or opt not to wear it at all. *See* Transcript Vol. II at 333 (testimony of Missouri Highway Patrol Trooper Don Phillips that he continued to wear the Armour contour-style vest with his summer uniform, even though the Patrol had issued him a wrap-around vest). Law enforcement agencies trying to work within the confines of a budget may be forced to purchase fewer vests or none at all. How "safe" are those possibilities? "The core concern in strict tort liability law is safety." *Nesselrode*, 707 S.W.2d at 375. We are firmly convinced that to allow this verdict to stand would run counter to the law's purpose of promoting the development of safe and useful products, and would have an especially pernicious effect on the development and marketing of equipment designed to make the always-dangerous work of law enforcement Officers a little safer.

The death of Jimmy Linegar by the hand of a depraved killer was a tragic event. We keenly feel the loss that this young trooper's family has suffered, and our sympathies go out to them. But we cannot allow recovery from a blameless defendant on the basis of sympathy for the plaintiffs. To hold Armour liable for Linegar's death would cast it in the role of insurer for anyone shot while wearing an Armour vest, regardless of whether any shots penetrated the vest. That a manufacturer may be cast in such a role has been soundly rejected by courts applying Missouri law. . . .

The judgment of the District Court is reversed. The District Court shall enter a final judgment in favor of Armour.

Scarangella v. Thomas Built Buses, Inc.
717 N.E.2d 679 (N.Y. 1999)

Levine, J.

A school bus being operated in reverse by a co-employee struck and severely injured plaintiff Concetta Scarangella, a school bus driver for third-party defendant Huntington Coach Corp., Inc. The accident occurred in Huntington's bus parking yard on September 26, 1988. The vehicle was one of ten new school buses that defendant Thomas Built Buses, Inc., sold Huntington in 1988. At that time, Thomas offered buyers as an optional safety feature a back-up alarm that would automatically sound when a driver shifted the bus into reverse gear, but Huntington chose not to purchase this optional equipment.

After plaintiff and her husband commenced this action for negligence, breach of warranty and products liability, Thomas made a motion to preclude plaintiff from submitting to the jury her claim that the lack of a back-up alarm was a design defect. In support of its motion, Thomas submitted a memorandum of law and excerpts from the deposition of Huntington's President and Chief Operating Officer, Kevin Clifford.

According to Clifford's deposition testimony, Huntington owned and operated 190 school buses and had 300 employees. Clifford had worked for the company for over 30 years and had been a president of the New York State School Bus Owners Association. Clifford explained that he was aware that the backup alarms were available but made a considered decision not to purchase them. He opted against the alarm because "it screams" when a bus is put in reverse gear, and he intended to park the buses at a bus yard in the middle of a residential neighborhood where his company had been experiencing problems with neighbors concerning noise pollution. When the buses were being parked in the bus yard, there "had to be a tremendous amount of backing up," and Clifford believed it was unnecessary to equip all 100 buses in the lot with the "screaming" alarms. Instead, Clifford instructed the drivers to be cautious and to use the bus's ordinary horn before backing up.

In response to Thomas's motion, plaintiff proffered no specific evidence. She based her design defect claim entirely on the proposition that, because a school bus driver always has a substantial blind spot when operating the vehicle in reverse, a school bus must invariably be equipped with an automatically engaged back-up alarm. Supreme Court concluded that there was no triable issue of fact on this design defect claim. It thus granted defendant's motion to preclude plaintiff from presenting any evidence on the issue to the jury.

Plaintiff proceeded to trial on the theory that the bus was defectively designed because it did not have proper mirrors. At the conclusion of plaintiff's case, the Trial Judge directed a verdict for defendant and dismissed the complaint. The Appellate Division affirmed. . . .

A defectively designed product " 'is one which, at the time it leaves the seller's hands, is in a condition not reasonably contemplated by the ultimate consumer and is unreasonably dangerous for its intended use; that is one whose utility does not outweigh the danger inherent in its introduction into the stream of commerce' " (Voss v. Black & Decker Mfg. Co., 450 N.E.2d 204). A manufacturer can be held liable for selling a defectively designed product because the manufacturer "is in the superior position to discover any design defects and alter the design before making the product available to the public." . . .

In Voss, we identified seven non-exclusive factors to be considered in balancing the risks created by the product's design against its utility and cost. . . . As relevant here, these include the likelihood that the product will cause injury, the ability of the plaintiff to have avoided injury, the degree of awareness of the product's dangers which reasonably can be attributed to the plaintiff, the usefulness of the product to the consumer as designed as compared to a safer design and the functional and monetary cost of using the alternative design. . . . An additional pertinent factor that may be taken into account is "the likely effects of [liability for failure to adopt] the alternative design on . . . the range of consumer choice among products" (Restatement [Third] of Products Liability §2, comment f). Where a court, after considering the relevant facts and risk-utility factors, determines that the plaintiff has failed to make out a prima facie case of a design defect, the claim should not be submitted to the jury. . . .

Biss v. Tenneco, Inc. . . . , 409 N.Y.S.2d 874, lv. denied . . . , 416 N.Y.S.2d 1025, and Rainbow v. Elia Bldg. Co. . . . 436 N.Y.S.2d 480, aff'd. . . . 449 N.Y.S.2d 967, . . . applied New York's design defect jurisprudence to fact patterns in which the buyer of a product elected not to purchase an optional safety device to accompany it. Biss held that a manufacturer of a loader vehicle could not be found liable for negligent design where an employee of the purchaser was injured due to the absence of an optional roll-over protection structure the purchaser chose not to have included when the vehicle was acquired. The opinion reasoned that "defendants had fulfilled their duty to exercise reasonable skill and care in designing the product as a matter of law when they advised the purchaser that an appropriate safety structure . . . was available. . . . If knowledge of available safety options is brought home to the purchaser, the duty to exercise reasonable care in selecting those appropriate to the intended use rests upon him. He is the party in the best position to exercise an intelligent judgment to make the trade-off between cost and function, and it is he who should bear the responsibility if the decision on optional safety equipment presents an unreasonable risk to users'' (Biss v. Tenneco, Inc., supra . . .).

In Rainbow, plaintiff claimed that a motorcycle without an optional safety feature, side crash bars, was unreasonably dangerous. The plaintiff was ''an experienced motorcyclist [who] . . . had been a successful motorcycle racer for many years [and] . . . had removed crash bars mounted on a previously owned motorcycle.'' . . . The court dismissed plaintiff's complaint, holding that the buyer ''was in the best position to exercise an intelligent judgment in making the trade-off between cost and function and thus to decide whether crash bars were reasonably necessary on his motorcycle for his purposes'' (Id.).

In contrast, in Rosado v. Proctor & Schwartz. . . . 494 N.Y.S.2d 851 . . . a manufacturer who sold a textile machine with completely exposed massive gears, chains and pulleys, with no safety disconnect switches, could not escape responsibility for a user's injury by inserting boilerplate language in its sales contract that required the buyer to install any necessary safety devices. In contrast to the instant case, the manufacturer there did not give the buyer the choice of a machine that was already equipped with the safety equipment. We held that ''where, as here, the manufacturer is in the best position to know the dangers inherent in its product, and the dangers do not vary depending on jobsite, it is also in the best position to determine what safety devices should be employed. . . . To allow a manufacturer . . . which sells a product . . . with no safety devices, to shift the ultimate duty of care to others through boilerplate language in a sales contract, would erode the economic incentive manufacturers have to maintain safety and give sanction to the marketing of dangerous, stripped down, machines.'' . . .

We can thus distill some governing principles for cases where a plaintiff claims that a product without an optional safety feature is defectively designed because the equipment was not standard. The product is not defective where the evidence and reasonable inferences therefrom show that: (1) the buyer is thoroughly knowledgeable regarding the product and its use and is actually aware that the safety feature is available; (2) there exist normal circumstances of use in which the product is not unreasonably dangerous without the optional equipment; and (3) the buyer is in a position, given the range of uses of the product, to balance the benefits and the risks of not having the safety device in the specifically contemplated circumstances of the buyer's use of the product. In such a case, the buyer, not the manufacturer, is in the superior position to make the risk-utility assessment, and a well-considered decision by the buyer to dispense with the optional safety equipment will excuse the manufacturer from liability. When the factors are not present, there is no justification for departure from the accepted rationale imposing strict liability upon the manufacturer because it ''is in the superior position to discover any design defects.'' . . .

Applying the foregoing principles, plaintiff failed to make a prima facie showing that the lack of a back-up alarm on the bus that injured her was a design defect. First, Huntington was a highly knowledgeable consumer. Huntington and its management had owned and operated school buses serving a number of school districts for decades and certainly were aware that a bus driver had a blind spot when a bus was operated in reverse. It is also undisputed that when it purchased the bus, Huntington knew that the back-up alarm was available. The product was in the exact condition contemplated and selected by Huntington at the time of purchase.

Second, the uncontradicted evidence showed that, in the actual circumstances of the operation of the buses in reverse by Huntington, the risk of harm from the absence of a back-up alarm was not substantial. In his pre-trial deposition, Huntington's president indicated that the only significant incidence of operating buses in reverse was in positioning buses in and backing them out of the yard. Plaintiff submitted no evidence regarding Huntington buses backing up under any other circumstances, e.g., while transporting children to and from school or outside the parking yard. Indeed, at the trial plaintiff herself testified that, because of the blind spot, Huntington drivers were instructed as part of their training not to operate buses in reverse except in the yard. Drivers were also instructed to exercise caution and sound their regular horns when backing up.

Thus, the individuals at risk from the absence of back-up alarm equipment on Huntington buses were almost exclusively its drivers and other employees at its parking yard. It was readily inferable from the only evidence submitted on the motion that these persons at risk, including plaintiff, were fully aware of a bus driver's blind spot in backing up a bus and the resultant hazard, and could be expected to exercise special care whenever positioned in proximity to the rear of any bus that was idling or moving in reverse in the yard. Again, plaintiff made no factual showing to the contrary that school children, other pedestrians or occupants of other vehicles were exposed to any hazards of the operation of Huntington buses in reverse, without back-up alarms.

Third, Huntington was in a position to balance the benefits and the dangers of not having the safety device, given the contemplated use of the bus. After weighing the risks against the costs, Huntington made a considered decision not to buy the backup alarm. Only Huntington knew how it would instruct and train its drivers and when and how the buses would be operated in reverse. Huntington and not Thomas was in a position to assess the efficacy of alternative safety measures in its operational rules and training of drivers. The buyer had the ability to understand and weigh the significance of costs associated with noise pollution and neighborhood relations, given the particular suburban location of the parking lot, against the anticipated, foreseeable risks of operating buses in a parking lot without a back-up alarm device or safeguard.

As shown above, plaintiff was confronted with proof that brought this case within the Biss-Rainbow three-factor analysis of the sophisticated consumer's knowledge of the safety feature, the existence of reasonably safe circumstances of normal use and the superior vantage point of the buyer in risk-utility balancing with respect to its own individualized use of the product. Plaintiff failed to submit, in opposition to the preclusion motion, any proof negating any of these three factors. Indeed, she failed to make out a prima facie case with evidence regarding other relevant considerations generally applicable in design defect cases, e.g., the ability of the plaintiff to have avoided injury, the plaintiff's degree of awareness of the potential danger, the cost of the back-up alarm or the effect of liability on the range of consumer choice (see Restatement [Third] of Products Liability, op. cit., §2, comment *f*, illustrations 9 and 10). Thus, plaintiff created no triable issues for the jury in connection with her claim that the absence of a back-up alarm was a design defect, and preclusion was warranted here.

Accordingly, the order of the Appellate Division should be affirmed, with costs.

_____

In Passante v. Agway Consumer Prods., Inc., 12 N.Y. 3d 372 (N.Y. 2009), the plaintiff was using a dock leveler — a piece of equipment designed to bridge the gap between a loading dock and a tractor trailer — when the trailer suddenly pulled away and the leveler lip on which he was standing collapsed, causing injury. The defendants moved for summary judgment, arguing that the plaintiff's employer knew of the dangers resulting from unscheduled departures of tractor trailers and of safety measures that would prevent risks of harm — including equipment manufactured and sold by the defendants that would restrain the trailer and audibly alert the operator when it was safe to enter the trailer. The plaintiff alleged that the equipment was unsafe under normal use because the operator was required to use his body weight to "walk down" the leveler until it rested on the trailer, and neither the injured plaintiff nor his heavier co-worker were able to do this without standing on the lip of the leveler, which they knew would collapse when the support of the trailer was removed. The trial court denied the defendants' motion. The Appellate Division reversed and dismissed the plaintiff's claim in its entirety. With a view to *Scarangella*, the New York Court of Appeals stated that although the plaintiff's employer was a highly knowledgeable consumer, the defendants did not deserve judgment as a matter of law on the issue of whether there existed normal circumstances under which the product is not unreasonably dangerous without the optional safety equipment. The dissent decried this as the "evisceration of *Scarangella*," stating that here the buyer knew the relevant facts and was in a position to balance the risks and benefits. The result of the majority decision, the dissent insisted, would be "an increase in cost — in the cost of liability insurance, and in the cost of safety features that buyers will no longer have the option to refuse." Id. For a recent case discussing the application of *Scarangella* in light of *Passante*, see Campbell v. NACCO Materials Handling Grp., Inc., 2011 WL 5187930, at *7-9 (W.D.N.Y. 2011) *report and recommendation adopted as modified*, 2011 WL 5240292 (W.D.N.Y. 2011).

In the majority of cases alleging design defect, courts do not hesitate to review manufacturers' design decisions even when consumers are quite aware of the dangers associated with the risks attendant to the use of the product. (The patent-danger rule is, after all, quite dead, is it not?) If a reasonable alternative design was available at time of sale that would have protected the consumer, failure to adopt such an alternative design may be found to render a product not reasonably safe. You will recall that sellers cannot automatically purge themselves from liability by offering extensive warnings of product-related risks. See Uniroyal Goodrich Tire, supra. Risk-utility balancing requires that reasonable designs be adopted to avoid risks even though consumers decide to purchase the product with full knowledge of the attendant dangers, and courts tend to let juries sort the cases out.

Thus, one cannot simply ring the bell of "consumer choice" and expect the courts to defer to the market. What, then, is so special about *Linegar* and *Scarangella*? In both cases plausible reasonable alternative designs were offered by the plaintiff that would have avoided the plaintiffs' injuries. And in both cases the appellate court said that there was no liability as a matter of law because the court wanted to maximize consumer choice. *Linegar* might be explained on the ground that the plaintiff sought to impose category liability on open-sided vests. In any event, *Scarangella* was clearly a RAD-based claim, was it not?

There is no easy answer as to when paternalism ends and consumer choice takes over. Perhaps we may invoke Justice Stewart's famous definition of obscenity: "I can't define it but I know it when I see it." At some point in the continuum, the role of consumer choice is of such a magnitude that it cannot be ignored. To a significant degree the hostility of courts to category liability stems from their unwillingness to deny consumers the right to purchase products that would otherwise become unavailable if we were to impose a tort tax on products for all injuries arising from their use. Consider the following illustration taken from the Products Liability Restatement §2, comment *f*:

ILLUSTRATION:

9. John was driving a compact automobile manufactured by the ABC Auto Company when he lost control and collided with a tree. John suffered serious injuries. John brings a products-liability claim against ABC, arguing that the design of his car is defective in that it does not offer the same level of crashworthiness as does a full-size automobile. John's experts admit that reducing the size of an automobile unavoidably increases the risk of injuries to occupants in collisions. John can identify no specific feature of the ABC automobile that could have been designed differently so as to be safer without increasing its size and substantially reducing its desirable characteristics of lower cost and lower fuel economy. John has not established a defect within the meaning of Subsection (b) [the section requiring a reasonable alternative design]. Although ABC's design is less safe than larger vehicles, the only way to make it safer, on John's own proof, is to make it larger, and the costs of doing that are unacceptably great. Moreover, eliminating smaller automobiles from the market would unduly restrict the range of consumer choice among automobile designs. Thus, the ABC design is not, by reason of its being smaller than other automobiles, "not reasonably safe." Given that the risks and benefits associated with relative automobile size are generally known, decisions regarding which sizes to purchase and use should be left to purchasers and users in the market.

However, when courts detect that consumers are vulnerable because their choices are limited or impaired, they will provide the necessary protection. Celmer v. Jumpking, Inc., 2006 U.S. Dist. LEXIS 34104, *15-16 (D. Md. 2006) (denying trampoline maker's motion for summary judgment after discussing obviousness of risk and possible alternative designs). Thus, when employees are required to work on machines without reasonably available safety features that should protect them from their own inadvertence, inattention, or ignorance, courts may impose liability no matter how clearly visible the danger. See, e.g., Jurado v. Western Gear Works, 619 A.2d 1312 (N.J. 1993) (failure to install guard at nip point of collating machine); Micallef v. Miehle Co., 348 N.E.2d 571 (N.Y. 1976) (plaintiff injured when he sought to remove a blemish from a high speed press while in operation; injury could have been avoided by a guard that would have prevented employee's hand from getting caught between the cylinder and the ink-form roller). Note that the fact that the plaintiff is an employee does not guarantee that the court will step in to second-guess the market. In both *Linegar* and *Scarangella* the plaintiffs were employees for whom the employer chose the less safe alternative. So once again we pose the question: How does one differentiate *Linegar* and *Scarangella* from the huge body of case law that imposes liability on a manufacturer for failing to adopt safer alternative designs that would prevent harm to employees from even the most obvious of dangers? This problem is explored in James A. Henderson & Aaron D. Twerski, Optional Safety Devices:

Delegating Product Design Responsibility to the Market, 45 Arizona St. L.J. 1399 (2013).

2. Whether and to What Extent Should Courts Defer to Safety Statutes or Administrative Regulations?

Restatement (Third) of Torts: Products Liability
(1998)

---

§4. NONCOMPLIANCE AND COMPLIANCE WITH PRODUCT SAFETY STATUTES OR REGULATIONS

In connection with liability for defective design or inadequate instructions or warnings:

(a) a product's noncompliance with an applicable product safety statute or administrative regulation renders the product defective with respect to the risks sought to be reduced by the statute or regulation; and

(b) a product's compliance with an applicable product safety statute or administrative regulation is properly considered in determining whether the product is defective with respect to the risks sought to be reduced by the statute or regulation, but such compliance does not preclude as a matter of law a finding of product defect.

COMMENT:

. . .

d. Noncompliance with product safety statute or administrative regulation. . . . In contrast to Subsection (a), the parallel common-law rule governing noncompliance with safety statutes or regulations in negligence actions not involving product liability claims recognizes that noncompliance with an applicable safety statute or regulation does not constitute failure to use due care when the defendant establishes a justification or excuse for the violation. For example, if noncompliance with an administrative regulation under conditions of emergency or temporary impossibility would not constitute a violation in a direct enforcement proceeding, noncompliance alone does not prove negligence. In connection with the adequacy of product designs and warnings, however, design and marketing decisions are made before distribution to users and consumers. The product seller therefore has the option of deferring sale until statutory or regulatory compliance is achieved. Consequently, justification or excuse of the sort anticipated in connection with negligence claims generally does not apply in connection with failure to comply with statutes or regulations governing product design or warnings.

e. Compliance with product safety or administrative regulation. . . . Subsection (b) addresses the effects of compliance with a federal statute or regulation to be non-preemptive. It addresses the question, under state law, of the effect that compliance with product safety statutes or regulations — federal or state — should have on the issue of product defectiveness. Subsection (b) reflects the traditional view that the standards set by most product safety statutes or regulations generally are only minimum standards. Thus, most product safety statutes or regulations establish a

authors' dialogue 17

AARON: Jim and Doug, why has there been so much resistance to compliance with administrative regulation as a defense? We have some pretty good federal administrative agencies — the FDA, NHTSA, and the EPA. They do a decent job. Probably as good as the courts do. And we would save all the wear and tear of trying to develop standards on a case-by-case basis.

DOUG: Hmm, I'm not sure I agree those agencies do a decent job. But even if they are performing okay now, maybe it's because they have more leverage with industry due to the background threat of tort liability. Would they still be able to demand tough safety standards if industry knew that regulations would come with the added bonus of tort immunity?

JIM: Doug, you've just jogged my memory. Aaron, you remember way back when in the 1980s, before we became partners we used to run into each other in legislative hearings in Washington. Every year there was another industry-sponsored bill. I don't know if you recall but one such bill would have made administrative regulation binding on the courts if the administrative standard was issued from an agency that was adjudged to be competent.

AARON: Ah, those were the good old days. If my memory serves me right that's when you got the reputation among plaintiffs' lawyers as being somewhere to the right of Atilla the Hun.

JIM: Hey, that's not fair. I never testified in favor of provisions that I thought were unfairly loaded on the side of industry. In any event you're not one to talk. It's like the pot calling the kettle black. But back to the subject, that bill went nowhere. Agency representatives told the congressional committee that the last thing they needed was for courts to pass on the competence of what their agencies were doing.

AARON: Okay, that was a nutty idea. But what about the statutes creating a rebuttable presumption that a product that meets agency standards is not defective? That isn't crazy.

floor of safety below which product sellers fall only at their peril, but they leave open the question of whether a higher standard of product safety should be applied. This is the general rule, applicable in most cases.

Occasionally, after reviewing relevant circumstances, a court may properly conclude that a particular product safety standard set by statute or regulation adequately serves the objectives of tort law and therefore that the product that complies with the standard is not defective as a matter of law. Such a conclusion may be appropriate when the safety statute or regulation was promulgated recently, thus supplying currency to the standard therein established; when the specific standard addresses the very issue of product design or warning presented in the case before the court; and when the court is confident that the deliberative process by which the safety standard was established was full, fair, and thorough and reflected substantial expertise. Conversely,

DOUG: It's not crazy. But would it actually change anything? It leaves plaintiffs where they were before, with the burden of coming forward with a reasonable alternative design.

JIM: The only thing that will work is something with teeth like the complete immunity from lawsuits that defendants gain through federal preemption. Short of that a court might require plaintiff to prove defect by clear and convincing evidence if the product meets relevant federal standards.

DOUG: That kind of proposal is DOA. Either it doesn't really add anything or, if it does, it puts too much power in the hands of federal agencies whose policies and standards change based on which party controls the White House. (Or, if you're really cynical, agencies whose policies and standards are controlled by the big industries that control both parties regardless of which one holds the White House).

AARON: What might work is the two-step process that our good friend Hans Linde, the former Chief Justice of the Supreme Court of Oregon, once suggested in Wilson v. Piper Aircraft [579 P.2d 1287 (Or. 1978)]. First, courts should determine that the administrative agency utilizes the same legal standard for regulation as the courts use in deciding whether a product is defective. Second, courts should examine whether, in fact, the agency utilizing the standard did a thorough job of applying the standard in the specific instance.

JIM: It's an interesting idea. But like Michelangelo's horse, it won't fly. Can you imagine a court hearing evidence concerning how an agency standard was developed? We would be subpoenaing half the bureaucrats in Washington to testify in the fifty states. Who would run the federal government?

AARON: Not a half-bad idea. They would probably do less damage if they were away from their desks testifying in products liability cases in Boise, Idaho.

DOUG: Wait, Aaron, what happened to your view that we have some "pretty good federal administrative agencies"?

---

when the deliberative process that led to the safety standard with which the defendant's product complies was tainted by the supplying of false information to, or the withholding of necessary and valid information from, the agency that promulgated the standard or certified or approved the product, compliance with regulation is entitled to little or no weight.

Section 4(a) reflects the common law rule that violation of a statute is negligence per se. In a similar fashion, violation of statute or administrative regulation constitutes defect per se. See, e.g., S.L.M. ex rel. Musick v. Dorel Juvenile Group, Inc., 514 Fed. App'x 389 (4th Cir. 2013); Harned v. Dura Corp., 665 P.2d 5, 12-13 (Alaska 1983); Toole v. Richardson-Merrell, Inc., 60 Cal. Rptr. 398, 409 (Cal. Ct. App. 1967). See generally Malcolm Wheeler, The Use of Criminal Statutes to Regulate Product Safety, 13 J. Legal Stud. 593 (1984).

A more difficult question is whether a court should treat a manufacturer's compliance with a governmental regulation as conclusive that a product design is nondefective as a matter of law, at least regarding the risk that the regulation aims to reduce or eliminate. The clear majority rule is reflected in Restatement §4(b) . . . compliance comes in as proof, but is not conclusive. See, e.g., Rader v. Teva Parental Medicines, Inc., 795 F. Supp. 2d 1143, 1149 (D. Nev. 2011) ("[T]he court does not find that evidence of compliance is a bar to recovery under strict products liability."); Beatty v. Trailmaster Prods. Inc., 625 A.2d 1005, 1014 (Md. 1993); Soproni v. Polygon Apartment Partners, 971 P.2d 500, 505 (Wash. 1999). Several states treat compliance with statute as a presumption of nondefectiveness. For example, in Schultz v. Ford Motor Co., 857 N.E.2d 977 (Ind. 2006), the Supreme Court of Indiana held that the presumption of nondefectiveness required the jury to weigh the presumption against the plaintiff's evidence and return a verdict for the defendant unless the plaintiff carried its burden of persuasion. See also Colo. Rev. Stat. §13-21-403 (2014); Kan. Stat. Ann. §60-3304 (2014); Utah Code Ann. §78B-6-703(2). Query: Does a presumption leave the plaintiff where she would have been in the absence of a presumption?

In any event, the question remains whether a common law court will adopt the governmental design standard not only as a minimum standard but as the appropriate standard for design defect litigation. Section 4, Comment *e* of the Products Liability Restatement, set forth above, suggests that in some cases a court should treat compliance with a statute as dispositive on the issue of design defect even absent a presumption statute. Some courts concur. See, e.g., Lorenz v. Celotex Corp., 896 F.2d 148 (5th Cir.) (applying Texas law), *reh'g denied*, 901 F.2d 1110 (5th Cir. 1990) (compliance with safety regulation constitutes strong and substantial evidence of lack of defect); Dentson v. Eddins & Lee Bus Sales, 491 So. 2d 942, 944 (Ala. 1986) ("[I]n this context, involving school transportation, an area traditionally reserved for the legislature, we find that the legislature's pronouncement is conclusive: a school bus in Alabama may not be found defective . . . because it is not equipped with passenger seat belts."); Ramirez v. Plough, Inc., 863 P.2d 167, 176 (Cal. 1993) ("Lacking the procedure and the resources to conduct the relevant inquiries, we conclude that the prudent course is to adopt for tort purposes the existing legislative and administrative standard of care on this issue."). See generally Richard Ausness, The Case for a "Strong" Regulatory Compliance Defense, 55 Md. L. Rev. 1210 (1996); Ashley W. Warren, Compliance with Governmental Regulatory Standards: Is It Enough to Immunize a Defendant from Tort Liability?, 49 Baylor L. Rev. 763 (1997).

3. Beyond the Pale: High Profile No-Duty Cases

In the previous sections, we examined certain cases in which the courts decided not to impose a duty on a manufacturer to make a product reasonably safe. The decision to allow the market to choose between two types of bullet-proof vests, for instance, is viewed as one based on the lack of a duty on the manufacturer to impose the same vest design on all vest users.

On occasion we run into a no-duty rule that is very broad in its scope. They pronounce to the world that a court is unwilling to enter the thicket of a certain class of litigation. Consider the following two cases.

Hamilton v. Beretta U.S.A. Corp.
750 N.E.2d 1055 (N.Y. 2001)

WESLEY, J.

In January 1995 plaintiffs — relatives of people killed by handguns — sued 49 handgun manufacturers in Federal court alleging negligent marketing, design defect, ultra-hazardous activity and fraud. A number of defendants jointly moved for summary judgment. The United States District Court for the Eastern District of New York (Weinstein, J.), dismissed the product liability and fraud causes of action, but retained plaintiffs' negligent marketing claim (*see*, Hamilton v. Accu-Tek, 935 F. Supp. 1307, 1315). Other parties intervened, including plaintiff Stephen Fox, who was shot by a friend and permanently disabled. The gun was never found; the shooter had no recollection of how he obtained it. Other evidence, however, indicated that he had purchased the gun out of the trunk of a car from a seller who said it came from the "south." Eventually, seven plaintiffs went to trial against 25 of the manufacturers.

Plaintiffs asserted that defendants distributed their products negligently so as to create and bolster an illegal, underground market in handguns, one that furnished weapons to minors and criminals involved in the shootings that precipitated this lawsuit. Because only one of the guns was recovered, plaintiffs were permitted over defense objections to proceed on a market share theory of liability against all the manufacturers, asserting that they were severally liable for failing to implement safe marketing and distribution procedures, and that this failure sent a high volume of guns into the underground market.

After a four-week trial, the jury returned a special verdict finding 15 of the 25 defendants failed to use reasonable care in the distribution of their guns. Of those 15, nine were found to have proximately caused the deaths of the decedents of two plaintiffs, but no damages were awarded. The jury awarded damages against three defendants — American Arms, Beretta U.S.A. and Taurus International Manufacturing — upon a finding that they proximately caused the injuries suffered by Fox and his mother (in the amounts of $3.95 million and $50,000, respectively). Liability was apportioned among each of the three defendants according to their share of the national handgun market: for American Arms, 0.23% ($9,000); for Beretta, 6.03% ($241,000); and for Taurus, 6.80% ($272,000).

Defendants unsuccessfully moved for judgment as a matter of law pursuant to Federal Rules of Civil Procedure rule 50(b). The District Court articulated several theories for imposing a duty on defendants "to take reasonable steps available at the point of . . . sale to primary distributors to reduce the possibility that these instruments will fall into the hands of those likely to misuse them" (Hamilton v. Accu-Tek, 62 F. Supp. 2d 802, 825). The court noted that defendants, as with all manufacturers, had the unique ability to detect and guard against any foreseeable risks associated with their products, and that ability created a special "protective relationship" between the manufacturers and potential victims of gun violence (id., at 821). It further pointed out that the relationship of handgun manufacturers with their downstream distributors and retailers gave them the authority and ability to control the latter's conduct for the protection of prospective crime victims. Relying on Hymowitz v. Eli Lilly & Co. (73 N.Y.2d 487, *cert. denied* 493 U.S. 944), the District Court held that apportionment of liability among defendants on a market share basis was appropriate and that plaintiffs need not connect Fox's shooting to the negligence of a particular manufacturer.

On appeal, the Second Circuit certified the following questions to us:

"(1) Whether the defendants owed plaintiffs a duty to exercise reasonable care in the marketing and distribution of the handguns they manufacture?"

"(2) Whether liability in this case may be apportioned on a market share basis, and if so, how?"

We accepted certification and now answer both questions in the negative.

Parties' Arguments

Plaintiffs argue that defendant-manufacturers have a duty to exercise reasonable care in the marketing and distribution of their guns based upon four factors: (1) defendants' ability to exercise control over the marketing and distribution of their guns, (2) defendants' general knowledge that large numbers of their guns enter the illegal market and are used in crime, (3) New York's policy of strict regulation of firearms and (4) the uniquely lethal nature of defendants' products.

According to plaintiffs, handguns move into the underground market in New York through several well-known and documented means including straw purchases (a friend, relative or accomplice acts as purchaser of the weapon for another), sales at gun shows, misuse of Federal firearms licenses and sales by non-stocking dealers (i.e., those operating informal businesses without a retail storefront). Plaintiffs further assert that gun manufacturers have oversaturated markets in states with weak gun control laws (primarily in the Southeast), knowing those "excess guns" will make their way into the hands of criminals in states with stricter laws such as New York, thus "profiting" from indiscriminate sales in weak gun states. Plaintiffs contend that defendants control their distributors' conduct with respect to pricing, advertising and display, yet refuse to institute practices such as requiring distribution contracts that limit sales to stocking gun dealers, training salespeople in safe sales practices (including how to recognize straw purchasers), establishing electronic monitoring of their products, limiting the number of distributors, limiting multiple purchases and franchising their retail outlets.

Defendants counter that they do not owe a duty to members of the public to protect them from the criminal acquisition and misuse of their handguns. Defendants assert that such a duty—potentially exposing them to limitless liability—should not be imposed on them for acts and omissions of numerous and remote third parties over which they have no control. Further, they contend that, in light of the comprehensive statutory and regulatory scheme governing the distribution and sale of firearms, any fundamental changes in the industry should be left to the appropriate legislative and regulatory bodies.

The Duty Equation

The threshold question in any negligence action is: does defendant owe a legally recognized duty of care to plaintiff? Courts traditionally "fix the duty point by balancing factors, including the reasonable expectations of parties and society generally, the proliferation of claims, the likelihood of unlimited or insurer-like liability, disproportionate risk and reparation allocation, and public policies affecting the expansion or limitation of new channels of liability" (Palka v. Servicemaster Mgt. Servs. Corp., 83 N.Y.2d 579, 586). Thus, in determining whether a duty exists, "courts must be mindful of the precedential, and consequential, future effects of their rulings, and 'limit the legal consequences of wrongs to a controllable degree' " (Lauer v. City of New York, 95 N.Y.2d 95, 100 [quoting Tobin v. Grossman, 24 N.Y.2d 609, 619]).

Foreseeability alone does not define duty — it merely determines the scope of the duty once it is determined to exist (*see*, Eiseman v. State of New York, 70 N.Y.2d 175, 187). The injured party must show that a defendant owed not merely a general duty to society but a specific duty to him or her, for ''[w]ithout a duty running directly to the injured person there can be no liability in damages, however careless the conduct or foreseeable the harm'' (*Lauer*, supra, at 100). That is required in order to avoid subjecting an actor ''to limitless liability to an indeterminate class of persons conceivably injured by any negligence in that act'' (*Eiseman*, supra, at 188). Moreover, any extension of the scope of duty must be tailored to reflect accurately the extent that its social benefits outweigh its costs.

The District Court imposed a duty on gun manufacturers ''to take reasonable steps available at the point of . . . sale to primary distributors to reduce the possibility that these instruments will fall into the hands of those likely to misuse them'' (Hamilton v. Accu-Tek, supra, 62 F. Supp. 2d, at 825). We have been cautious, however, in extending liability to defendants for their failure to control the conduct of others. ''A defendant generally has no duty to control the conduct of third persons so as to prevent them from harming others, even where as a practical matter defendant can exercise such control'' (D'Amico v. Christie, 71 N.Y.2d 76, 88). This judicial resistance to the expansion of duty grows out of practical concerns both about potentially limitless liability and about the unfairness of imposing liability for the acts of another.

A duty may arise, however, where there is a relationship either between defendant and a third-person tortfeasor that encompasses defendant's actual control of the third person's actions, or between defendant and plaintiff that requires defendant to protect plaintiff from the conduct of others. Examples of these relationships include master and servant, parent and child, and common carriers and their passengers.

The key in each is that the defendant's relationship with either the tortfeasor or the plaintiff places the defendant in the best position to protect against the risk of harm. In addition, the specter of limitless liability is not present because the class of potential plaintiffs to whom the duty is owed is circumscribed by the relationship. We have, for instance, recognized that landowners have a duty to protect tenants, patrons or invitees from foreseeable harm caused by the criminal conduct of others while they are on the premises. However, this duty does not extend beyond that limited class of plaintiffs to members of the community at large (*see*, Waters v. New York City Hous. Auth., 69 N.Y.2d, 225, 228-231). In *Waters*, for example, we held that the owner of a housing project who failed to keep the building's door locks in good repair did not owe a duty to a passerby to protect her from being dragged off the street into the building and assaulted. The Court concluded that imposing such a duty on landowners would do little to minimize crime, and the social benefits to be gained did ''not warrant the extension of the landowner's duty to maintain secure premises to the millions of individuals who use the sidewalks of New York City each day and are thereby exposed to the dangers of street crime'' (id., at 230).

Similar rationale is relevant here. The pool of possible plaintiffs is very large — potentially, any of the thousands of victims of gun violence. Further, the connection between defendants, the criminal wrongdoers and plaintiffs is remote, running through several links in a chain consisting of at least the manufacturer, the federally licensed distributor or wholesaler, and the first retailer. The chain most often includes numerous subsequent legal purchasers or even a thief. Such broad liability, potentially encompassing all gunshot crime victims, should not be imposed without a more tangible showing that defendants were a direct link in the causal chain that resulted in plaintiffs' injuries, and that defendants were realistically in a position to prevent the wrongs. Giving plaintiffs' evidence the benefit of every favorable inference, they have not shown that the gun used to harm plaintiff Fox came from a source amenable to the exercise of any duty of care that plaintiffs would impose upon defendant manufacturers. . . .

In sum, analysis of this State's longstanding precedents demonstrates that defendants — given the evidence presented here — did not owe plaintiffs the duty they claim; we therefore answer the first certified question in the negative.

[The court's discussion of market share liability, in which it determines that handgun violence provides an inapposite context for application of the doctrine, is omitted.]

This case challenges us to rethink traditional notions of duty, liability and causation. Tort law is ever changing; it is a reflection of the complexity and vitality of daily life. Although plaintiffs have presented us with a novel theory — negligent marketing of a potentially lethal yet legal product, based upon the acts not of one manufacturer, but of an industry — we are unconvinced that, on the record before us, the duty plaintiffs wish to impose is either reasonable or circumscribed. Nor does the market share theory of liability accurately measure defendants' conduct. Whether, in a different case, a duty may arise remains a question for the future.

Accordingly, both certified questions should be answered in the negative.

In re September 11 Litigation
280 F. Supp. 2d 279 (S.D.N.Y. 2003)

ALVIN K. HELLERSTEIN, U.S. District Judge . . .

[Discussion of claims against defendants other than Boeing is omitted]

Some of those who were injured and the successors of those who died in the Pentagon, in American Airlines flight 77 which crashed into the Pentagon, and in United Air Lines flight 93 which crashed into the Shanksville, Pennsylvania field, claim the right to recover against Boeing, the manufacturer of the two "757" jets flown by United and American. Plaintiffs allege that Boeing manufactured inadequate and defective cockpit doors, and thus made it possible for the hijackers to invade the cockpits and take over the aircraft. Boeing moves to dismiss the lawsuits. . . .

Boeing argues that its design of the cockpit was not unreasonably dangerous in relation to reasonably foreseeable risks, and that the risk of death to passengers and ground victims caused by a terrorist hijacking was not reasonably foreseeable. The record at this point does not support Boeing's argument. There have been many efforts by terrorists to hijack airplanes, and too many have been successful. The practice of terrorists to blow themselves up in order to kill as many people as possible has also been prevalent. Although there have been no incidents before the ones of September 11, 2001 where terrorists combined both an airplane hijacking and a suicidal explosion, I am not able to say that the risk of crashes was not reasonably foreseeable to an airplane manufacturer. Plaintiffs have alleged that it was reasonably foreseeable that a failure to design a secure cockpit could contribute to a breaking and entering into, and a take-over of, a cockpit by hijackers or other unauthorized individuals, substantially increasing the risk of injury and death to people and damage to property. I hold that the allegation is sufficient to establish Boeing's duty. . . .

Boeing next argues that its design of the cockpit doors on its "757" passenger aircraft, even if held to constitute an "unreasonably dangerous condition," was not the proximate cause of plaintiffs' injuries. Boeing argues that the criminal acts of the terrorists in hijacking the airplanes and using the airplanes as weapons of mass destruction constituted an "efficient intervening cause" which broke the "natural and continuous sequence" of events flowing from Boeing's allegedly inadequate design. *See* Sugarland Run Homeowners Ass'n v. Halfmann, 535 S.E.2d 469, 472 (Va. 2000) (a "proximate cause of an event is that 'act or omission which, in natural and continuous sequence, unbroken by an efficient intervening cause, produces the event, and without which that event would not have occurred,' " quoting Beale v. Jones, 171 S.E.2d 851, 853 (Va. 1970)). Plaintiffs have the burden to prove proximate cause and, generally, the issue is a question of fact to be resolved by a jury. *Sugarland*, 535 S.E.2d at 472. However, when reasonable people cannot differ, the issue becomes a question of law for the court. Id.

The record at this point does not support Boeing's argument that the invasion and take-over of the cockpit by the terrorists must, as a matter of law, be held to constitute an "efficient intervening act" that breaks the "natural and continuous sequence" flowing from Boeing's allegedly inadequate design. Plaintiffs allege that Boeing should have designed its cockpit door to prevent hijackers from invading the cockpit, that acts of terrorism, including hijackings of airplanes, were reasonably foreseeable, and that the lives of passengers, crew and ground victims would be imminently in danger from such hijackings. Virginia law does not require Boeing to have foreseen precisely how the injuries suffered on September 11, 2001 would be caused, as long as Boeing could reasonably have foreseen that "some injury" from its negligence "might probably result." *See* Blondel v. Hays, 403 S.E.2d 340, 344 (Va. 1991) ("[A] reasonably prudent [person] ought under the circumstances to have foreseen that some injury might probably result from that negligence"). Given the critical nature of the cockpit area, and the inherent danger of crash when a plane is in flight, one cannot say that Boeing could not reasonably have foreseen the risk flowing from an inadequately constructed cockpit door. . . .

[T]he danger that a plane could crash if unauthorized individuals invaded and took over the cockpit was the very risk that Boeing should reasonably have foreseen. "Privacy" within a cockpit means very little if the door intended to provide security is not designed to keep out potential intruders.

[In] Gaines-Tabb v. ICI Explosives USA, Inc., 160 F.3d 613 (10th Cir. 1998), . . . the courts of appeals . . . addressed the question of causation and held that defendants' actions or inactions were not the "legal proximate cause" of the injuries suffered by the victims of the 1993 World Trade Center and 1995 Oklahoma City bombings. They ruled that the manufacturers of the fertilizer products utilized in the attacks, having made lawful and economically and socially useful fertilizer products, did not have to anticipate that criminals would misappropriate ingredients, mix them with others, and make bombs to bring down a building. The bomb-making by the terrorists were found to be superseding and intervening events and were not natural or probable consequences of any design defect in defendants' products. *See* [Port Auth. of N.Y. & N.J. v. Arcadian Corp., 189 F.3d 305, 318 (3d Cir. 1999)]; *Gaines-Tabb*, 160 F.3d at 621.

In re Korean Air Lines Disaster of September 1, 1983, No. 83-3442, 1985 U.S. Dist. LEXIS 17211 (D.D.C. 1985), involved lawsuits by the legal successors of passengers who died when Korean Airlines passenger flight 007 was shot down by Russian fighter planes. The passenger plane had flown off course and over a sensitive military zone in Russia. Russian fighter pilots intercepted the plane and, instead of following international protocol for causing the plane to return to international routes over the high seas or to land at a selected landing field, shot it down. Plaintiffs sued Boeing, the manufacturer of the airplane, alleging that a product defect in its navigation systems caused it to fly off course and over Soviet territory, and that Boeing's improper and unsafe design was therefore the proximate cause of plaintiffs' damages. The court dismissed the complaint, holding that Boeing could not foresee that the Soviet Union would destroy an intruding aircraft in violation of international conventions, and had no ability to guard against such conduct. *See id.* at *17-20. The court held, consequently, that Boeing did not owe a duty to passengers with respect to such risks, and that the actions of the Russian pilots were independent and supervening causes that broke the chain of causation.

These three cases do not offer Boeing much support in its motion. In each, the acts of the third-parties were held to be superseding causes because they were not reasonably foreseeable to the product manufacturer. In *Gaines-Tabb* and *Arcadian*, the courts of appeals held that the fertilizer manufacturers could not reasonably foresee that terrorists would mix their products with other ingredients to create explosives to cause buildings to collapse and occupants to be killed. In *KAL*, the court held that the manufacturer of airplane navigational systems could not reasonably foresee that a passenger aircraft that strayed off course would be shot down by hostile military forces in violation of international conventions. In the cases before me, however, plaintiffs allege that Boeing could reasonably have foreseen that terrorists would try to invade the cockpits of airplanes, and that easy success on their part, because cockpit doors were not designed to prevent easy opening, would be imminently dangerous to passengers, crew and ground victims. Plaintiffs' allegations that duty and proximate cause existed cannot be dismissed as a matter of law on the basis of the record now before me.

[The court found that the case could not be dismissed under Pennsylvania law for reasons similar to those set forth above under Virginia law.]

Do you agree with Judge Hellerstein? Bear in mind that he is ruling on the pleadings. Once the plaintiff gets past the duty issue and reaches trial, is there any way that Boeing can hope to stop the steamroller? In 2015, a Germanwings Airbus A320 crashed, killing all 150 people on board. Investigations into the crash determined that the co-pilot of the plane, later understood to be suffering from mental illness, locked the pilot out of the fortified cockpit when the pilot had left to use the restroom. The co-pilot then intentionally flew the plane into a mountainside. See Jad Mouawad & Christopher Drew, Post-Sept. 11, Cockpits are Built to Protect from Outside Threats, N.Y. Times, March 26, 2015.

H.   SPECIAL PROBLEMS OF MISUSE, ALTERATION, AND MODIFICATION

In this section we shall attempt to straighten out the mess that courts and legislatures have created in product design cases by treating the issues of product use (foreseeable and unforeseeable), misuse, abuse, alteration, and modification as affirmative defenses. The issues need to be clarified once and for all. They are not difficult to understand, and absolutely nothing is gained by continuing to treat them as separate sources of concern.

Much of the confusion up until now stems from the fact that the manufacturer's duty to adopt reasonable product designs includes the duty to foresee and guard against a certain amount of foolish behavior on the part of users and consumers. For example, in Cevallos v. Toys "R" Us, Inc., 2010 U.S. Dist. LEXIS 17336 (N.D. Tex. 2010), a pallet return system allegedly failed, causing a huge pile of wooden pallets to fall on, and kill, the plaintiff's decedent. Evidence showed that forklifts used at the worksite may have damaged the return system, causing it to fail. The district court denied the manufacturer's motion for summary judgment, reasoning that if the jury were to find the forklift interaction to be foreseeable, the pallet return system could be defectively designed for failing to prevent the system's failure.

In Horn v. Fadal Machine Centers, 972 So. 2d 63 (Ala. 2007), the plaintiff's decedent died from injuries suffered while using an industrial milling machine. Someone had disabled an interlock device that would have prevented the accident, but the plaintiff's experts showed how that sort of modification and misuse could have been avoided by a safer design. Because the risks were obvious and relevant warnings were posted on the machine, the trial court granted summary judgment for the defendant manufacturer. The Supreme Court of Alabama reversed and remanded, holding that the question whether the defendant breached its duty to provide reasonable safeguards against injury was for the jury. The notion that a manufacturer owes the duty reasonably to foresee product misuse and design against it was one of the points emphasized at the beginning of this chapter, when we first embarked on our study of liability for defective product designs. Thus, whenever a court decides as a matter of law that a design resulting in injury is not defective, it is possible to talk in terms of the user's "misuse" of the product. However, we would prefer instead to stick with the traditional, tried-and-true terminology from first-year Torts. On the liability side, every design case presents three basic issues: (1) duty/breach; (2) proximate causation; and (3) contributory fault. Comment *a* to §17 of the Products Liability Restatement explains how these issues play out in products liability actions:

> Certain forms of consumer behavior — product misuse and product alteration or modification — have been the subject of much confusion and misunderstanding. Early decisions treated product misuse, alteration, and modification, whether by the plaintiff or a third party, as a total bar to recovery against a product seller. Today misuse, alteration, and modification relate to one of three issues in a products liability action. In some cases, misuse, alteration, and modification are important in determining whether the product is defective. In others, they are relevant to the issue of legal cause. Finally, when the plaintiff misuses, alters, or modifies the product, such conduct may constitute contributory fault and reduce the plaintiff's recovery under the rules of comparative responsibility. See Comment *c*.

We advise the student, when confronted with a design case, to work through each of these issues, resolving the first before going on to the second, and the second before the third. The behavior of the user or consumer will be relevant in connection with all three issues, but in different ways.

In connection with the duty/breach issue, there is general agreement that the burden is on the plaintiff to make his case that the design is defective for failing adequately to protect the victim. Thus, for example, in Newman v. Utility Trailer & Equip. Co., 564 P.2d 674, 676-677 (Or. 1977) (en banc), the court properly observed:

It is obvious that trial courts are experiencing difficulty in distinguishing foreseeability of use from foreseeability of the risk of harm. Before a manufacturer or other seller is strictly liable for injury inflicted by a product, the product must have been put to a foreseeable use. As an example: if a shovel is used to prop open a heavy door, but, because of the way the shovel was designed, it is inadequate to the task and the door swings shut and crushes the user's hand, no responsibility for the injury results by reason of the shovel's not being designed to prop open doors since it was not reasonably foreseeable by the manufacturer or seller that it would be so used.

See also Ferguson v. Winkler & Co., 79 F.3d 1221 (D.C. Cir.), *cert. denied*, 519 U.S. 949 (1996).

With respect to the second issue, proximate cause, most believe the burden is also on the plaintiff to prove that the defect in design was a but-for and proximate cause of plaintiff's harm. See, for example, Hughes v. Magic Chef, Inc., 288 N.W.2d 542 (Iowa 1980), in which defendant manufactured a stove that exploded when the oven's pilot light failed to ignite, causing a pocket of propane to form in the oven. The gas pocket was later ignited by the stove-top's pilot light. Affirming verdict and judgment for defendant, the court said, "[T]he burden is on the plaintiff to prove that the legal cause of the injury was a product defect which rendered the product unreasonably dangerous in a reasonably foreseeable use." Id. at 546. But the issue is not free from controversy. Ellsworth v. Sherrie Lingerie, Inc., 495 A.2d 348 (Md. 1985), agrees with *Hughes* and sets forth both the cases supporting the view that misuse should be considered in deciding whether plaintiff has made out a prima facie case and those holding that misuse is an affirmative defense.

With respect to the third issue, contributory fault, everyone agrees that the defendant bears the burden of making out the affirmative defense. Another important difference between the first two issues (duty/breach and proximate cause) and the third (contributory fault) is that the first two dispose of the plaintiff's claim on an all-or-nothing basis, but the third does not. Thus, if the defendant owed or breached no duty, or if the breach did not proximately cause the plaintiff's harm, the plaintiff gets nothing. But under comparative fault, even if the defendant succeeds in showing that the plaintiff was at fault, the plaintiff may get something under the comparative fault rules that apply in many jurisdictions. In most states, plaintiff's fault reduces, but does not eliminate, plaintiff's recovery.

The important point here is that misuse, abuse, alteration, and modification are not discrete problems and should be analyzed under one of the three legitimate issues described above. Having said that, one further point remains. Despite our admonitions, many courts, commentators, and legislatures insist on talking as though misuse, et al., have lives of their own. Our advice? When treating these concepts as independently significant helps your client, do not look a gift horse in the mouth. On the other hand, when giving "misuse" independent significance hurts your client, scream "let's get back to the basics!" at the top of your lungs.

With regard to proximate cause in design defect cases, we note that it will be rare that a defendant will be entitled to a directed verdict on the grounds that product misuse, alteration, or modification were outside the scope of foreseeable risk. Since safety features exist to protect against a broad range of foolish and even reckless uses, it will be for the jury to determine whether the user's conduct was foreseeable. On the other hand, in Morguson v. 3M Co., 857 So. 2d 796 (Ala. 2003), the court upheld summary judgment for defendant medical device manufacturers, ruling that it was unforeseeable as matter of law that a medical technician assisting with bypass surgery would: (1) fail to check the vent tubing direction in a heart-lung machine as required by a pre-bypass safety checklist; (2) falsify the safety checklist to claim that he had checked the direction of the vent tubing; and (3) lie to the surgeon about having checked the direction of the vent tubing after being asked directly to do so. The plaintiff in *Morguson* contended that her experts were prepared to proffer a reasonable alternative design of a perfusion pump that would have prevented Mr. Morguson's death by eliminating the danger of human error. Admittedly, the human error in this case was egregious — perhaps even willful — but why should that make a difference?

In Jurado v. Western Gear Works, 619 A.2d 1312 (N.J. 1993), the court suggested that in some design defect cases a finding of defective design might preclude any argument that the defect was not the proximate cause of the injury. In that case plaintiff, an employee, working in the vicinity of a high speed printing press slipped and fell. When he extended his right hand to break his fall his hand came in contact with the running machine at its nip point causing serious personal injury. The plaintiff's expert testified that there should have been a guard around the nip point to prevent accidents of this type. The court opined:

> In some situations, however, the issue of proximate cause is predetermined by the finding that the product is defective solely because of the manufacturer's failure to protect against a foreseeable misuse. As Professor Aaron D. Twerski explains:
>
>> If a court determines that a design defect exists [solely] because the manufacturer has failed to include [] safety devices, there is no proximate cause question of any moment left to consider. The very reason for declaring the design defective was to prevent this kind of foreseeable misuse. Proximate cause could not, in such a case, present an obstacle on the grounds of misuse. To do so would negate the very reason for declaring the design defective in the first instance.
>
> [The Many Faces of Misuse: An Inquiry Into the Emerging Doctrine of Comparative Causation, 29 Mercer L. Rev. 403, 421 (1978).]
>
> In sum, when misuse is an issue in a design-defect case, the jury should first determine whether the plaintiff used the product for an objectively foreseeable purpose. If the jury finds that the plaintiff's purpose was not foreseeable, the defendant did not breach any duty owed to the plaintiff. If, however, the jury finds that the plaintiff's purpose was foreseeable, it must then decide whether the product was defective. . . .
>
> If the jury finds that the product is defective, it must then decide whether the misuse proximately caused the injury. In cases in which the product is defective solely because of a foreseeable misuse, the determination of defect predetermines the issue of proximate cause. In other cases, however, where a product is defective for reasons other than the particular misuse, the jury must separately determine proximate cause. Id. 619 A. 2d at 1319.

One class of cases in which courts have refused to impose liability (either on proximate cause or no-duty grounds) involves alteration or modification of safe products. The New York Court of Appeals faced this issue in Robinson v. Reed-Prentice

Div. of Package Mach. Co., 403 N.E.2d 440 (N.Y. 1980). In that case an employee of Plastic Jewel Parts Co. suffered severe injuries when his hand was caught between the molds of a plastic molding machine. The plaintiff sued Reed-Prentice, the manufacturer of the machine. Reed-Prentice had sold the machine to the plaintiff's employer with a safety gate in place that would have prevented injury to employees. However, the machine as sold to Jewel did not comport with the buyer's production needs. The Court of Appeals summarized the record as follows:

Plastic Jewel purchased the machine in order to mold beads directly onto a nylon cord. The cord was stored in spools at the back of the machine and fed through the mold where the beads were molded around it. After each molding cycle, the beads were pulled out of the mold and the nylon cord was reset in the mold for the next cycle. To allow the beads to be molded on a continuous line, Plastic Jewel determined that it was necessary to cut a hole of approximately 6 by 14 inches in the Plexiglas portion of the safety gate. The machine, as designed, contracted for and delivered, made no provision for such an aperture. At the end of each cycle, the now corded beads would be pulled through the opening in the gate, the nylon cord would be restrung, and the next cycle would be started by opening and then closing the safety gate without breaking the continuous line of beads. While modification of the safety gate served Plastic Jewel's production needs, it also destroyed the practical utility of the safety features incorporated into the design of the machine for it permitted access into the molding area while the interlocking circuits were completed. Although the record is unclear on this point, plaintiff's hand somehow went through the opening cut into the safety gate and was drawn into the molding area while the interlocks were engaged. The machine went through the molding cycle, causing plaintiff serious injury.

The record contains evidence that Reed-Prentice knew, or should have known, the particular safety gate designed for the machine made it impossible to manufacture beads on strings. During the period immediately prior to the purchase of the machine, Reed-Prentice representatives visited the Plastic Jewel plant and observed two identical machines with holes cut in the Plexiglas portion of their safety gates. At that meeting, Plastic Jewel's plant manager discussed the problem with a Reed-Prentice salesman and asked whether a safety gate compatible with its product needs could be designed. Moreover, a letter sent by Reed-Prentice to Plastic Jewel establishes that the manufacturer knew precisely what its customer was doing to the safety gate and refused to modify its design. However, the letter pointed out that the purchaser had "completely flaunted the safeties built into this machine by removing part of the safety window," and that it had not "held up your end of the purchase when you use the machine differently from its design" and the manufacturer stated "[a]s concerns changes, we will make none in our safety setup or design of safety gates." At trial, plaintiff's expert indicated that there were two modifications to the safety gate which could have been made that would have made it possible to mold beads on a string without rendering the machine unreasonably dangerous. Neither of these modifications were made, or even contemplated, by Reed-Prentice. [Id. at 477-478.]

In absolving the manufacturer from liability as a matter of law, the court said:

The manufacturer's duty, however, does not extend to designing a product that is impossible to abuse or one whose safety features may not be circumvented. A manufacturer need not incorporate safety features into its product so as to guarantee that no harm will come to every user no matter how careless or even reckless. Nor must he trace his product through every link in the chain of distribution to insure that users will not adapt the product to suit their own unique purposes. The duty of a manufacturer, therefore, is not an open-ended one. It extends to the design and manufacture of a finished product which is safe at the time of sale. Material alterations at the hands of a third party which work a substantial change in the condition in which the product was sold by destroying the functional utility of a key safety feature, however foreseeable that modification may have been, are not within the ambit of a manufacturer's responsibility. Acceptance of plaintiff's concept of duty would expand the scope of a manufacturer's duty beyond all reasonable bounds and would be tantamount to imposing absolute liability on manufacturers for all product-related injuries. [Id. at 444.]

It is not clear why a manufacturer who has full knowledge that its product is being used by employees in a dangerous fashion does not have a duty to supply the needed safety device. Judge Fuchsberg had this to say in dissent:

Plastic Jewel had made frequent but unavailing entreaties of the manufacturer and its sales and service personnel seeking some modification of the machine that would eliminate the need for piercing the safety gate. As expert testimony revealed, the machine could easily have been made safe for the anticipated use by either of at least two simple modifications. One, at a cost of only $200, would be the installation of "dual hand controls," which would cause the machine to stop unless both of the operator's hands were safely occupied pressing buttons spaced widely apart. The second, at a cost of $400 to $500, would, by conversion of the horizontal gate to a vertical one, allow for the extrusion of the product without a dangerously wide aperture.

This array of facts proved the allegations that Reed-Prentice had been negligent "in selling and distributing a machine which [it] knew or should have known to be dangerous, defective and unsafe" as well as "in failing to affix proper and adequate warnings of the dangers." The law of negligence therefore required no extension to permit a finding of liability. . . . [Id. at 445.]

In Lopez v. Precision Papers Inc., 484 N.Y.S.2d 585 (N.Y. App. Div. 1985), *aff'd*, 492 N.E.2d 1214 (N.Y. 1986), the plaintiff was rendered a paraplegic due to an injury he suffered when a large roll of paper fell from a wooden pallet on a forklift machine he was operating within a warehouse. The plaintiff alleged that the forklift was defectively designed because (a) it relied on a nonwelded, easily removable safety canopy; and (b) it lacked a gauge that would have indicated the weight of the load being raised or its attendant hazards to the vehicle and the driver. The trial court, citing *Robinson*, held that the manufacturer should not be liable due to the fact that the removable overhead safety canopy had been removed by the plaintiff's employer. On appeal, the intermediate court reversed, holding:

In *Robinson*, the modification was so substantial that it permanently destroyed the functional utility of a safety gate. Under no view of the facts could one conclude that that modification was intended either for versatility of functioning or for ease of cleaning. We believe that *Robinson* represents a sensible limitation on the scope of manufacturer liability lest a manufacturer be made an insurer against all injuries that might arise from the use or misuse of a product.

The facts here simply do not approach those of *Robinson*. . . . Because of the ease with which the overhead guard could be removed and the forklift's added versatility when operated without the guard, there is a legitimate jury question as to the scope of the forklift's intended purpose. . . . In short, the jury must ascertain whether in light of these factors, the manufacturer, given its resources and expertise, breached its duty by placing a product on the market that is not reasonably safe. [Id. at 587.]

Courts continue to apply *Robinson* to shield manufacturers in cases dealing with product alterations. See, e.g., State Farm Fire & Cas. Co. v. Nutone, Inc., 2010 WL 3154853, at *9 (E.D.N.Y. Aug. 9, 2010), *aff'd*, 426 F. App'x 8 (2d Cir. 2011) (using the defense to block liability for a bathroom fan that caused a house fire); Wick v. Wabash Holding Corp., 801 F. Supp. 2d 93, 105 (W.D.N.Y. 2011) ("substantial modification" of wood moulding machine precludes strict liability); Islam v. Modern Tour, Inc., 2004 U.S. Dist. LEXIS 19768, *11-12 (S.D.N.Y. 2004) (removal of safety guard and foot pedal constituted alteration); Birriel v. F.L. Smithe Mach. Co., 99 A.D.3d 480 (N.Y. App. Div. 2012) (no manufacturer liability for envelope-making machine that was "substantially materially altered post manufacture"); Sheikh v. Chem-Tainer Indus., 816 N.Y.S.2d 701 (N.Y. Sup. Ct. 2006) (hiding warning labels did not constitute a product modification). But note that *Lopez* provides an exception to the rule where a manufacturer purposely designs a product to permit use without safety features. See Gaudette v. Saint-Gobain Performance Plastics Corp., 2014 WL 1311530, at *13 (N.D.N.Y. Mar. 28, 2014) (finding that "a reasonable jury could conclude" that the allegedly defective forklift was manufactured to allow use without safety device); Gunn v. Hytrol Conveyor Co., 2013 WL 2249241, at *10 (E.D.N.Y. May 22, 2013), *reconsideration granted in part* (July 12, 2013) (finding "triable issue of fact as to whether [defendant] purposefully manufactured the subject conveyor belt so as to permit use without the dust pan covers").

I. FEDERAL PREEMPTION OF DESIGN DEFECT CLAIMS

The most potent defense to a products liability claim based on either failure to warn or defective design is that the federal government has preempted the right of state courts and legislatures to independently set standards for warning or design. When this happens, the plaintiff loses even if she has a perfectly valid claim under state law. By reason of its potency and potentially sweeping effects, preemption has become a very hot topic. Preemption should be distinguished from the defense under state law of compliance with a safety standard. As we have noted earlier, most states treat compliance with a relevant regulation or statute as a circumstance that a factfinder may take into consideration in deciding whether a product is defective, but that does not bar a finding of product defect. When, however, a court finds federal preemption, the supremacy clause of the United States Constitution mandates that the federal standard govern the litigation. If the defendant has complied with that federal standard, the plaintiff cannot press her state law claim.

For almost a century the United States Supreme Court has recognized three circumstances that warrant federal preemption. First, Congress may have expressly preempted state tort claims. Where the Court divines such congressional intent from explicit statutory language, the task of the Court is relatively easy. Second, even in absence of explicit statutory language, the Court may find that the federal government has so pervasively occupied a field that Congress has left no room for state law to operate. Finally, situations arise where it is impossible for a private party to comply with both state and federal mandates. When this occurs, state law must give way to federal law. See English v. General Electric, 496 U.S. 72, 78-79 (1990).

The problem in the preemption area has been trying to predict whether the Supreme Court will decide that a given statute or administrative law rule fits into one of the three categories described above. Any given Supreme Court preemption decision can make sense within its own factual context, but reading them together is a maddening experience. One senses that a Ouija board would be of greater assistance than access to the most learned constitutional scholar in attempting to predict how the Supreme Court will rule in a pending case. See, e.g., Mary J. Davis, On Restating Products Liability Preemption, 74 Brook. L. Rev. 759, 780 (2009) (arguing that "preemption doctrine is out of balance, uncertain and unwieldy in application"). Congress has contributed to the confusion in drafting preemption clauses that leave one scratching one's head as to Congressional intent. In several instances a statute contains a preemption clause giving primacy to the administrative rule and then sets forth a "savings" clause that allows a plaintiff to bring a tort cause of action utilizing a standard for liability greater than that set forth in the administrative rule. Trying to read preemption and saving clauses together has been no easy task. Congress quite clearly has sought to placate both industry and consumers by speaking out of both sides of its mouth. The job of making sense out of these seemingly contradictory clauses is left to the United States Supreme Court, which does not have to face the wrath of political constituencies.

One prominent context in which the Supreme Court has developed its preemption jurisprudence concerns standards promulgated by the National Highway and Traffic and Safety Administration (NHTSA). Such standards are often claimed by automakers to preempt claims under state tort law that question design choices approved under federal standards. For instance, although today air bags are mandatory equipment on all new cars, there was a period of time when NHTSA allowed auto manufacturers the right to "phase in" air bags so long as they chose to install other approved passive restraint devices that would protect drivers and passengers in the event of a collision. Courts split sharply as to whether NHTSA regulations preempted common law design defect actions for cars manufactured in the "phase in" era that were not equipped with air bags.

In a highly controversial decision, the Court found in favor of federal preemption. See Geier v. American Honda Motor Co., 529 U.S. 861 (2000). Justice Breyer, writing for the majority, first noted that, although the National Traffic and Motor Vehicle Safety Act of 1966 (the "Safety Act") includes an express preemption provision, the Safety Act could not be read to expressly preempt a defective design claim under state common law because the Act also contains a savings clause stating that compliance with a federal safety standard "does not exempt any person from any liability under common law." Id. at 868 (quoting 15 U.S.C. §1397(k) (1988 ed.). Despite this holding, Justice Breyer's opinion then went on to determine that state common law claims were impliedly preempted insofar as they "stood as an obstacle" to federal standards promulgated under the Safety Act. In particular, because the federal airbag "phase in" program sought to preserve choice and flexibility for automobile manufacturers for a period of time as they incorporated airbags and other passive restraint devices into their product lines, allowing design defect claims to go forward premised on the absence of airbags would undermine the objectives of the federal program:

---

authors' dialogue 18

AARON: Jim, believe it or not I think that I can make some sense out of the preemption decisions of the United States Supreme Court.

JIM: You may be the first in the universe to do so. I'm all ears.

AARON: Think about it. The cases require that the oversight of the administrative agency over the particular rule or standard under examination be thorough and comprehensive. When the courts are satisfied that the agency has done its own risk/utility balancing, it won't second-guess the result.

JIM: Nice try, Aaron. But if that be the common thread among the cases, then how do you explain a case like *Wyeth v. Levine* (Chapter Five, infra), in which the court said that to make out a "conflict preemption" defense the defendant must prove that it is "impossible" to comply with both the agency rule and the state common law standard. Even if the agency has done an admirable job in setting the standard and performed a responsible risk/utility balancing, there remains some possibility that the agency might have considered a higher standard so the preemption defense goes down the drain.

AARON: Jim, you confuse the evidence necessary to convince the court that the administrative standard is truly a ceiling with the principle that when a court is truly convinced that an agency has set a ceiling in adopting a well-thought-through standard the Court will preempt.

JIM: Won't this approach force the courts to evaluate the performance level of various administrative agencies? That would seem to be a nightmare. We like the FDA but don't like the Consumer Product Safety Commission. Please save

---

In effect, petitioners' tort action depends upon its claim that manufacturers had a duty to install an airbag when they manufactured the 1987 Honda Accord. Such a state law — *i.e.*, a rule of state tort law imposing such a duty — by its terms would have required manufacturers of all similar cars to install airbags rather than other passive restraint systems, such as automatic belts or passive interiors. It thereby would have presented an obstacle to the variety and mix of devices that the federal regulation sought. It would have required all manufacturers to have installed airbags in respect to . . . their 1987 new car fleet, even though [the federal "phase in" program] at that time required only that 10% of a manufacturer's nationwide fleet be equipped with any passive restraint device at all. It thereby also would have stood as an obstacle to the gradual passive restraint phase-in that the federal regulation deliberately imposed. . . . Because the rule of law for which petitioners contend would have stood "as an obstacle to the accomplishment and execution of" the important means-related federal objectives that we have just discussed, it is pre-empted. . . . [Id. at 881.]

Justice Stevens dissented in an opinion joined by Justices Souter, Thomas, and Ginsburg, arguing that "neither the text of the statute nor the text of the regulation contains any indication of an intent to pre-empt petitioners' cause of action." Id. at 912-913.

me. Wouldn't we be better off to let the defendant at the trial level introduce the evidence of compliance with administrative standards and let juries decide whether the standard is reasonable? Plaintiffs will be free to slug it out and attempt to prove that a higher or more consumer friendly standard should have been adopted.

DOUG: But Jim, under your own logic, courts are still, in effect, evaluating the performance level of administrative agencies when juries decide whether the standard they set is reasonable. Surely agencies should not be immune from democratic review.

AARON: You know, if I had some confidence that trial judges would direct verdicts for defendants when the evidence is convincing that the administrative standard is reasonable, then I might agree with Jim. However, I have no such confidence, and I am left with the reality that standards adopted by a federal agency after years of study will be set aside by a jury who has sympathy for an injured plaintiff. At some point there must be some agency that can speak with one voice for the entire nation. Healthy federalism and respect for state tort law must give way to national interests.

DOUG: Nationalism means consolidated power which spawns a "who-will-watch-the-watchmen" problem. It is for injured plaintiffs, sympathetic or otherwise, that these agencies promulgate rules in the first place. Agencies are especially prone to capture and compromise and should not be given special deference by common law courts. Sometimes the sympathetic plaintiff *was* injured as a result of the agency's improper standard and juries should not hesitate, for fear of hampering national interests, to find for the plaintiff in such scenarios. Indeed, agencies promulgate rules and standards in the shadow of litigation. Such is the nature of our adversarial system.

In the aftermath of *Geier*, several commentators expressed concern that the Court had effectively abandoned the traditional presumption against preemption, resulting in an unwarranted extension of the doctrine. See, e.g., Mary J. Davis, Unmasking the Presumption in Favor of Preemption, 53 S.C. L. Rev. 967, 1008-1012 (2002) (characterizing *Geier* as a "seismic shift" in the Court's preemption analysis that improperly drifts away from any meaningful assessment of congressional intent); Susan Reaker-Jordan, A Study in Judicial Sleight of Hand: Did Geier v. American Honda Motor Co. Eradicate the Presumption Against Preemption?, 17 B.Y.U. J. Pub. L. 1 (2002) (criticizing the Court for muddying up its preemption jurisprudence and for enabling the preemption doctrine to more easily trump state law); The Supreme Court 1999 Term: Leading Cases, Federal Preemption of State Law, 114 Harv. L. Rev. 339 (2000) (reading *Geier* as "signal[ing] the Court's subtle drift away from the presumption against preemption in favor of a more functional federal law preference rule").

However, *Geier*'s reach was subsequently limited in Williamson v. Mazda Motor of America, Inc., 562 U.S. 323 (2011). Justice Breyer, again writing for the majority, held that a federal standard giving auto manufacturers the choice of installing either simple lap belts or lap/shoulder belts on rear inner seats did not preempt state common law claims alleging that the manufacturer should have installed a lap/shoulder belt. In contrast to *Geier*, the Court concluded that providing manufacturers with this seatbelt choice was not a significant objective of the federal regulation. Consequently, the regulation did not preempt the state tort suit.

Even when Congress does attempt to draft a detailed preemption provision, the results often lead to confusion. In Bruesewitz v. Wyeth LLC, 562 U.S. 223 (2011), the Court construed an express preemption provision of the National Childhood Vaccine Injury Act (NCVIA), a statute that creates a no-fault compensation scheme, funded by an excise tax on vaccines, for individuals who suffer harmful side effects of vaccines. The NCVIA provides:

> No vaccine manufacturer shall be liable in a civil action for damages arising from a vaccine-related injury or death associated with the administration of a vaccine after October 1, 1988, if the injury or death resulted from side effects that were unavoidable even though the vaccine was properly prepared and was accompanied by proper directions and warnings. [42 U.S.C. §300aa-22(b)(1).]

Plaintiffs in *Bruesewitz* were parents of a seven-month-old girl who was given the diphtheria, tetanus, and pertussis vaccine and suffered seizures resulting in permanent disability. Her parents brought a claim for design defect, alleging that defendant manufacturer knew of a safer alternative vaccine design and failed to produce it. In an opinion authored by Justice Scalia, the Court determined that design defect claims were expressly preempted by the NCVIA despite the fact that the provision seems to speak only to manufacturing and warning defect claims. Any other result, Justice Scalia argued, would frustrate the statute's purpose of encouraging vaccine manufacture by shielding makers from liability. Is it possible to interpret the specific NCVIA preemption language as only blocking product category design claims, rather than ones rooted in the reasonable alternative design test?

The Supreme Court's most recent significant products liability preemption decision offers a fitting conclusion to this chapter. As you read the following decision, consider how the unusual design defect standard at issue in the case — New Hampshire's embrace of a risk-utility test without a requirement that plaintiff demonstrate reasonable alternative design — affects the justices' interpretation of the aim and impact of state products liability law. Notice also how the federal regulatory scheme for generic drugs forces the Court to consider the interplay between design defect and warning defect claims, a topic considered in Section C.5 of this chapter and also taken up in the next chapter on inadequate warnings.

Mutual Pharmaceutical Co., Inc. v. Bartlett
133 S. Ct. 2466 (2013)

Justice ALITO delivered the opinion of the Court.

We must decide whether federal law pre-empts the New Hampshire design-defect claim under which respondent Karen Bartlett recovered damages from petitioner Mutual Pharmaceutical, the manufacturer of sulindac, a generic nonsteroidal anti-inflammatory drug (NSAID). New Hampshire law imposes a duty on manufacturers to ensure that the drugs they market are not unreasonably unsafe, and a drug's safety is evaluated by reference to both its chemical properties and the adequacy of its warnings. Because Mutual was unable to change sulindac's composition as a matter of both federal law and basic chemistry, New Hampshire's design-defect cause of action effectively required Mutual to change sulindac's labeling to provide stronger warnings. But, as this Court recognized just two Terms ago in *PLIVA, Inc. v. Mensing,* 564 U.S. ___, 131 S. Ct. 2567, 180 L. Ed. 2d 580 (2011), federal law prohibits generic drug manufacturers from independently changing their drugs' labels. Accordingly, state law imposed a duty on Mutual *not* to comply with federal law. Under the Supremacy Clause, state laws that require a private party to violate federal law are pre-empted and, thus, are "without effect." *Maryland v. Louisiana,* 451 U.S. 725, 746, 101 S. Ct. 2114, 68 L. Ed. 2d 576 (1981).

The Court of Appeals' solution — that Mutual should simply have pulled sulindac from the market in order to comply with both state and federal law — is no solution. Rather, adopting the Court of Appeals' stop-selling rationale would render impossibility pre-emption a dead letter and work a revolution in this Court's pre-emption case law.

Accordingly, we hold that state-law design-defect claims that turn on the adequacy of a drug's warnings are pre-empted by federal law under *PLIVA*. We thus reverse the decision of the Court of Appeals below.

I

Under the Federal Food, Drug, and Cosmetic Act (FDCA), ch. 675, 52 Stat. 1040, as amended, 21 U.S.C. §301 *et seq.,* drug manufacturers must gain approval from the United States Food and Drug Administration (FDA) before marketing any drug in interstate commerce. §355(a). In the case of a new brand-name drug, FDA approval can be secured only by submitting a new-drug application (NDA). An NDA is a compilation of materials that must include "full reports of [all clinical] investigations," §355(b)(1)(A), relevant nonclinical studies, and "any other data or information relevant to an evaluation of the safety and effectiveness of the drug product obtained or otherwise received by the applicant from any source," 21 C.F.R. §§314.50(d)(2) and (5)(iv) (2012). The NDA must also include "the labeling proposed to be used for such drug," 21 U.S.C. §355(b)(1)(F); 21 C.F.R. §314.50(c)(2)(i), and "a discussion of why the [drug's] benefits exceed the risks under the conditions stated in the labeling," 21 C.F.R. §314.50(d)(5)(viii); §314.50(c)(2)(ix). The FDA may approve an NDA only if it determines that the drug in question is "safe for use" under "the conditions of use prescribed, recommended, or suggested in the proposed labeling thereof." 21 U.S.C. §355(d). In order for the FDA to consider a drug safe, the drug's "probable therapeutic benefits must outweigh its risk of harm." *FDA v. Brown & Williamson Tobacco Corp.,* 529 U.S. 120, 140, 120 S. Ct. 1291, 146 L. Ed. 2d 121 (2000). . . .

In order to provide a swifter route for approval of generic drugs, Congress passed the Drug Price Competition and Patent Term Restoration Act of 1984, 98 Stat. 1585, popularly known as the "Hatch–Waxman Act." Under Hatch–Waxman, a generic drug may be approved without the same level of clinical testing required for approval of a new brand-name drug, provided the generic drug is identical to the already-approved brand-name drug in several key respects.

First, the proposed generic drug must be chemically equivalent to the approved brand-name drug: it must have the same "active ingredient" or "active ingredients," "route of administration," "dosage form," and "strength" as its brand-name counterpart. 21 U.S.C. §§355(j)(2)(A)(ii) and (iii). Second, a proposed generic must be "bioequivalent" to an approved brand-name drug. §355(j)(2)(A)(iv). That is, it must have the same "rate and extent of absorption" as the brand-name drug. §355(j)(8)(B). Third, the generic drug manufacturer must show that "the labeling proposed for the new drug is the same as the labeling approved for the [approved brand-name] drug." §355(j)(2)(A)(v). . . .

II

In 1978, the FDA approved a nonsteroidal anti-inflammatory pain reliever called "sulindac" under the brand name Clinoril. When Clinoril's patent expired, the FDA approved several generic sulindacs, including one manufactured by Mutual Pharmaceutical. . . .

In December 2004, respondent Karen L. Bartlett was prescribed Clinoril for shoulder pain. Her pharmacist dispensed a generic form of sulindac, which was manufactured by petitioner Mutual Pharmaceutical. Respondent soon developed an acute case of toxic epidermal necrolysis. The results were horrific. Sixty to sixty-five percent of the surface of respondent's body deteriorated, was burned off, or turned into an open wound. She spent months in a medically induced coma, underwent 12 eye surgeries, and was tube-fed for a year. She is now severely disfigured, has a number of physical disabilities, and is nearly blind.

At the time respondent was prescribed sulindac, the drug's label did not specifically refer to Stevens–Johnson Syndrome or toxic epidermal necrolysis, but did warn that the drug could cause "severe skin reactions" and "[f]atalities." . . . However, Stevens–Johnson Syndrome and toxic epidermal necrolysis were listed as potential adverse reactions on the drug's package insert. . . . In 2005 — once respondent was already suffering from toxic epidermal necrolysis — the FDA completed a "comprehensive review of the risks and benefits, [including the risk of toxic epidermal necrolysis], of all approved NSAID products." . . . As a result of that review, the FDA recommended changes to the labeling of all NSAIDs, including sulindac, to more explicitly warn against toxic epidermal necrolysis. . . .

Respondent sued Mutual in New Hampshire state court, and Mutual removed the case to federal court. Respondent initially asserted both failure-to-warn and design-defect claims, but the District Court dismissed her failure-to-warn claim based on her doctor's "admi[ssion] that he had not read the box label or insert." . . . After a 2–week trial on respondent's design-defect claim, a jury found Mutual liable and awarded respondent over $21 million in damages.

The Court of Appeals affirmed. . . . As relevant, it found that neither the FDCA nor the FDA's regulations pre-empted respondent's design-defect claims. It distinguished *PLIVA, Inc. v. Mensing,* 564 U.S. ___, 131 S. Ct. 2567 — in which the Court held that failure-to-warn claims against generic manufacturers are pre-empted by the FDCA's prohibition on changes to generic drug labels — by arguing that generic manufacturers facing design-defect claims could simply "choose not to make the drug at all" and thus comply with both federal and state law. . . . We granted certiorari.

III

. . . Even in the absence of an express pre-emption provision, the Court has found state law to be impliedly pre-empted where it is "impossible for a private party to comply with both state and federal requirements." *English v. General Elec. Co.,* 496 U.S. 72, 79, 110 S. Ct. 2270, 110 L. Ed. 2d 65 (1990). See also *Florida Lime & Avocado Growers, Inc.* v. *Paul,* 373 U.S. 132, 142-143, 83 S. Ct. 1210, 10 L. Ed. 2d 248 (1963) ("A holding of federal exclusion of state law is inescapable and requires no inquiry into congressional design where compliance with both federal and state regulations is a physical impossibility for one engaged in interstate commerce").

In the instant case, it was impossible for Mutual to comply with both its state-law duty to strengthen the warnings on sulindac's label and its federal-law duty not to alter sulindac's label. Accordingly, the state law is pre-empted.

A

. . . Respondent is correct that New Hampshire has adopted the doctrine of strict liability in tort as set forth in Section 402A of the Restatement (Second) of Torts. See 2 Restatement (Second) of Torts §402A (1963 and 1964) (hereinafter Restatement 2d). See *Buttrick v. Arthur Lessard & Sons, Inc.,* 110 N.H. 36, 37-39, 260 A.2d 111, 112-113 (1969). Under the Restatement — and consequently, under New Hampshire tort law — "[o]ne who sells any product in a defective condition unreasonably dangerous to the user or consumer or to his property is subject to liability for physical harm thereby caused" even though he "has exercised all possible care in the preparation and sale of the product." Restatement 2d §402A, at 347-348.

But respondent's argument conflates what we will call a "strict-liability" regime (in which liability does not depend on negligence, but still signals the breach of a duty) with what we will call an "absolute-liability" regime (in which liability does not reflect the breach of any duties at all, but merely serves to spread risk). New Hampshire has adopted the former, not the latter. Indeed, the New Hampshire Supreme Court has consistently held that the manufacturer of a product has a "duty to design his product reasonably safely for the uses which he can foresee." *Thibault v. Sears, Roebuck & Co.,* 118 N.H. 802, 809, 395 A.2d 843, 847 (1978). . . . Accordingly, respondent is incorrect in arguing that New Hampshire's strict-liability system "imposes no substantive duties on manufacturers." Brief for Respondent 19.[8]

B

. . . New Hampshire requires manufacturers to ensure that the products they design, manufacture, and sell are not "unreasonably dangerous." The New Hampshire Supreme Court has recognized that this duty can be satisfied either by changing a drug's design or by changing its labeling. Since Mutual did not have the option of

---

8. We can thus save for another day the question whether a true absolute-liability state-law system could give rise to impossibility pre-emption. As we have noted, most common-law causes of action for negligence and strict liability do not exist merely to spread risk, but rather impose affirmative duties. See *Riegel v. Medtronic, Inc.,* 552 U.S. 312, 323-324, 128 S. Ct. 999, 169 L. Ed. 2d 892 (2008) ("In [*Medtronic, Inc. v. Lohr,* 518 U.S. 470, 116 S. Ct. 2240, 135 L. Ed. 2d 700 (1996)], five Justices concluded that common-law causes of action for negligence and strict liability do impose 'requirement[s]' and would be pre-empted by federal requirements specific to a medical device. . . . We adhere to that view"); *id.,* at 324, 128 S. Ct. 999 ("Absent other indication, reference to a State's 'requirements' includes its common-law duties. As the plurality opinion said in *Cipollone* [*v. Liggett Group,* 505 U.S. 504, 522, 112 S. Ct. 2608, 120 L. Ed. 2d 407 (1992)], common-law liability is 'premised on the existence of a legal duty,' and a tort judgment therefore establishes that the defendant has violated a state-law obligation").

changing sulindac's design, New Hampshire law ultimately required it to change sulindac's labeling. . . .

While the set of factors to be considered is ultimately an open one, the New Hampshire Supreme Court has repeatedly identified three factors as germane to the risk-utility inquiry: "the usefulness and desirability of the product to the public as a whole, whether the risk of danger could have been reduced without significantly affecting either the product's effectiveness or manufacturing cost, and the presence and efficacy of a warning to avoid an unreasonable risk of harm from hidden dangers or from foreseeable uses." *Vautour, supra,* at 154, 784 A.2d, at 1182. . . .

Given the impossibility of redesigning sulindac, the only way for Mutual to ameliorate the drug's "risk-utility" profile — and thus to escape liability — was to strengthen "the presence and efficacy of [sulindac's] warning" in such a way that the warning "avoid[ed] an unreasonable risk of harm from hidden dangers or from foreseeable uses." *Vautour, supra,* at 154, 784 A.2d, at 1182. . . . Thus, New Hampshire's design-defect cause of action imposed a duty on Mutual to strengthen sulindac's warnings. . . . In holding Mutual liable, the jury determined that Mutual had breached that duty.

C

The duty imposed by federal law is far more readily apparent. As *PLIVA* made clear, federal law prevents generic drug manufacturers from changing their labels. See 564 U.S., at ____, 131 S. Ct., at 2577 ("Federal drug regulations, as interpreted by the FDA, prevented the Manufacturers from independently changing their generic drugs' safety labels"). See also 21 U.S.C. §355(j)(2)(A)(v) ("[T]he labeling proposed for the new drug is the same as the labeling approved for the [approved brand-name] drug"); 21 C.F.R. §§314.94(a)(8)(iii), 314.150(b)(10) (approval for a generic drug may be withdrawn if the generic drug's label "is no longer consistent with that for [the brand-name] drug"). Thus, federal law prohibited Mutual from taking the remedial action required to avoid liability under New Hampshire law.

D

When federal law forbids an action that state law requires, the state law is "without effect." *Maryland,* 451 U.S., at 746, 101 S. Ct. 2114. Because it is impossible for Mutual and other similarly situated manufacturers to comply with both state and federal law,[9]

---

9. Justice Breyer argues that it is not "literally impossible" for Mutual to comply with both state and federal law because it could escape liability "either by not doing business in the relevant State or by paying the state penalty, say damages, for failing to comply with, as here, a state-law tort standard." . . . . But, as discussed below . . . , — leaving aside the rare case in which state or federal law actually requires a product to be pulled from the market — our pre-emption cases presume that a manufacturer's ability to stop selling does not turn impossibility into possibility. See, *e.g., Florida Lime & Avocado Growers, Inc. v. Paul,* 373 U.S. 132, 143, 83 S. Ct. 1210, 10 L. Ed. 2d 248 (1963) (There would be "impossibility of dual compliance" where "federal orders forbade the picking and marketing of any avocado testing more than 7% oil, while the California test excluded from the State any avocado measuring less than 8% oil content"). And, of course, *PLIVA, Inc. v. Mensing,* 564 U.S. ____, 131 S. Ct. 2567, 180 L. Ed. 2d 580 (2011), forecloses any argument that impossibility is defeated by the prospect that a manufacturer could "pa[y] the state penalty" for violating a state-law duty; that prospect would have defeated impossibility in *PLIVA* as well. See *id.,* at ____, 131 S. Ct., at 2578 ("[I]t was impossible for the Manufacturers to comply with both their state-law duty to change the label and their federal law duty to keep the label the same"). To hold otherwise would render impossibility pre-emption "all but meaningless." *Id.,* at ____, 131 S. Ct., at 2579.

New Hampshire's warning-based design-defect cause of action is pre-empted with respect to FDA-approved drugs sold in interstate commerce.[10]

IV

The Court of Appeals reasoned that Mutual could escape the impossibility of complying with both its federal- and state-law duties by "choos[ing] not to make [sulindac] at all." . . . We reject this "stop-selling" rationale as incompatible with our pre-emption jurisprudence. Our pre-emption cases presume that an actor seeking to satisfy both his federal- and state-law obligations is not required to cease acting altogether in order to avoid liability. Indeed, if the option of ceasing to act defeated a claim of impossibility, impossibility pre-emption would be "all but meaningless." 564 U.S., at ___, 131 S. Ct., at 2579. . . .

V

. . . The dissent accuses us of incorrectly assuming "that federal law gives pharmaceutical companies a right to sell a federally approved drug free from common-law liability," . . . but we make no such assumption. Rather, as discussed at length above . . . , we hold that state-law design-defect claims like New Hampshire's that place a duty on manufacturers to render a drug safer by either altering its composition or altering its labeling are in conflict with federal laws that prohibit manufacturers from unilaterally altering drug composition or labeling. The dissent is quite correct that federal law establishes no safe-harbor for drug companies — but it does prevent them from taking certain remedial measures. Where state law imposes a duty to take such remedial measures, it "actual[ly] conflict[s] with federal law" by making it "'impossible for a private party to comply with both state and federal requirements.'" *Freightliner Corp. v. Myrick,* 514 U.S. 280, 287, 115 S. Ct. 1483, 131 L. Ed. 2d 385 (1995) (quoting *English,* 496 U.S., at 78-79, 110 S. Ct. 2270). The dissent seems to acknowledge that point when it concedes that, "if federal law requires a particular product label to include a complete list of ingredients while state law specifically forbids that labeling practice, there is little question that state law 'must yield.'" . . . (quoting *Felder v. Casey,* 487 U.S. 131, 138, 108 S. Ct. 2302, 101 L. Ed. 2d 123 (1988)). What the dissent does not see is that *that is this case*: Federal law requires a very specific label for sulindac, and state law forbids the use of that label. . . .

---

10. We do not address state design-defect claims that parallel the federal misbranding statute. The misbranding statute requires a manufacturer to pull even an FDA-approved drug from the market when it is "dangerous to health" even if "used in the dosage or manner, or with the frequency or duration prescribed, recommended, or suggested in the labeling thereof." 21 U.S.C. §352(j); cf. *Bates v. Dow Agrosciences LLC,* 544 U.S. 431, 447, 125 S. Ct. 1788, 161 L. Ed. 2d 687 (2005) (state-law pesticide labeling requirement not pre-empted under express pre-emption provision, provided it was "equivalent to, and fully consistent with, [federal] misbranding provisions"). The parties and the Government appear to agree that a drug is misbranded under federal law only when liability is based on new and scientifically significant information that was not before the FDA. Because the jury was not asked to find whether new evidence concerning sulindac that had not been made available to the FDA rendered sulindac so dangerous as to be misbranded under the federal misbranding statute, the misbranding provision is not applicable here. Cf. 760 F. Supp. 2d 220, 233 (D.N.H. 2011) (most of respondent's experts' testimony was "drawn directly from the medical literature or published FDA analyses").

Finally, the dissent laments that we have ignored "Congress' explicit efforts to preserve state common-law liability." . . . We have not. Suffice to say, the Court would welcome Congress' "explicit" resolution of the difficult pre-emption questions that arise in the prescription drug context. That issue has repeatedly vexed the Court — and produced widely divergent views — in recent years. See, *e.g., Wyeth v. Levine*, 555 U.S. 555, 129 S. Ct. 1187, 173 L. Ed. 2d 51 (2009); *PLIVA*, 564 U.S. ___, 131 S. Ct. 2567. As the dissent concedes, however, the FDCA's treatment of prescription drugs includes neither an express pre-emption clause (as in the vaccine context, 42 U.S.C. §300aa-22(b)(1)), nor an express non-pre-emption clause (as in the over-the-counter drug context, 21 U.S.C. §§379r(e), 379s(d)). In the absence of that sort of "explicit" expression of congressional intent, we are left to divine Congress' will from the duties the statute imposes. That federal law forbids Mutual to take actions required of it by state tort law evinces an intent to pre-empt. . . .

This case arises out of tragic circumstances. A combination of factors combined to produce the rare and devastating injuries that respondent suffered: the FDA's decision to approve the sale of sulindac and the warnings that accompanied the drug at the time it was prescribed, the decision by respondent's physician to prescribe sulindac despite its known risks, and Congress' decision to regulate the manufacture and sale of generic drugs in a way that reduces their cost to patients but leaves generic drug manufacturers incapable of modifying either the drugs' compositions or their warnings. Respondent's situation is tragic and evokes deep sympathy, but a straightforward application of pre-emption law requires that the judgment below be reversed.

It is so ordered.

Justice BREYER, with whom Justice KAGAN joins, dissenting.

. . . Without giving the agency's views special weight, I would conclude that it is not impossible for petitioner to comply with both state and federal regulatory schemes and that the federal regulatory scheme does not pre-empt state common law (read as potentially requiring petitioner to pay damages or leave the market). As two former FDA Commissioners tell us, the FDA has long believed that state tort litigation can "supplemen[t] the agency's regulatory and enforcement activities." Brief for Donald Kennedy et al. as *Amici Curiae* 5. See also *Wyeth, supra,* at 578, 129 S. Ct. 1187 ("In keeping with Congress' decision not to pre-empt common-law tort suits, it appears that the FDA traditionally regarded state law as a complementary form of drug regulation"). . . .

Furthermore, I have found no convincing reason to believe that removing this particular drug from New Hampshire's market, or requiring damage payments for it there, would be so harmful that it would seriously undercut the purposes of the federal statutory scheme. . . .

For these reasons, I respectfully dissent.

Justice SOTOMAYOR, with whom Justice GINSBURG joins, dissenting.

In *PLIVA, Inc. v. Mensing,* 564 U.S. ___, 131 S. Ct. 2567, 180 L. Ed. 2d 580 (2011), this Court expanded the scope of impossibility pre-emption to immunize generic drug manufacturers from state-law failure-to-warn claims. Today, the Court unnecessarily and unwisely extends its holding in *Mensing* to pre-empt New Hampshire's law governing design-defects with respect to generic drugs. . . .

Of greater consequence, the Court appears to justify its revision of respondent Karen Bartlett's state-law claim through an implicit and undefended assumption that federal law gives pharmaceutical companies a right to sell a federally approved drug free from common-law liability. . . .

[S]tate common law provides injured consumers like Karen Bartlett with an opportunity to seek redress that is not available under federal law. "[U]nlike most administrative and legislative regulations," common-law claims "necessarily perform an important remedial role in compensating accident victims." *Sprietsma v. Mercury Marine,* 537 U.S. 51, 64, 123 S. Ct. 518, 154 L. Ed. 2d 466 (2002). While the Court has not always been consistent on this issue, it has repeatedly cautioned against reading federal statutes to "remove all means of judicial recourse for those injured" when Congress did not provide a federal remedy. *Silkwood v. Kerr–McGee Corp.,* 464 U.S. 238, 251, 104 S. Ct. 615, 78 L. Ed. 2d 443 (1984); see *e.g., Bates,* 544 U.S., at 449, 125 S. Ct. 1788; *Lohr,* 518 U.S., at 487, 116 S. Ct. 2240 (plurality opinion). And in fact, the legislative history of the FDCA suggests that Congress chose not to create a federal cause of action for damages precisely because it believed that state tort law would allow injured consumers to obtain compensation. See *Levine,* 555 U.S., at 574-575, and n. 7, 129 S. Ct. 1187. . . .

The design-defect claim that was applied to Mutual subjects the manufacturer of an unreasonably dangerous product to liability, but it does not require that manufacturer to take any specific action that is forbidden by federal law. Specifically, and contrary to the majority . . . , New Hampshire's design-defect law did not require Mutual to change its warning label. A drug's warning label is just one factor in a nonexclusive list for evaluating whether a drug is unreasonably dangerous, see *Vautour,* 147 N.H., at 156, 784 A.2d, at 1183, and an adequate label is therefore neither a necessary nor a sufficient condition for avoiding design-defect liability. Likewise, New Hampshire law imposed no duty on Mutual to change sulindac's chemical composition. The New Hampshire Supreme Court has held that proof of an alternative feasible design is not an element of a design-defect claim, see *Kelleher v. Marvin Lumber & Cedar Co.,* 152 N.H. 813, 831, 891 A.2d 477, 492 (2006), and as the majority recognizes . . . sulindac was not realistically capable of being redesigned anyway because it is a single-molecule drug.[11] . . .

The fact that imposing strict liability for injuries caused by a defective drug design might make a drug manufacturer want to change its label or design (or both) does not mean the manufacturer was actually required by state law to take either action. And absent such a legal obligation, the majority's impossibility argument does not get off the ground, because there was no state requirement that it was physically impossible for Mutual to comply with while also following federal law. . . . New Hampshire's design-defect law did not require Mutual to do anything other than to compensate consumers who were injured by an unreasonably dangerous drug. . . .

A manufacturer of a drug that is unreasonably dangerous under New Hampshire law has multiple options: It can change the drug's design or label in an effort to alter its risk-benefit profile, remove the drug from the market, or pay compensation as a cost of doing business. If federal law or the drug's chemical properties take the redesign option off the table, then that does not mean the manufacturer suddenly has a legal obligation under state law to improve the drug's label. Indeed, such a view of state law makes very little sense here because even if Mutual had strengthened its label to fully account for

---

11. Because of this feature of New Hampshire law, it is unnecessary to consider whether the preemption analysis would differ in a jurisdiction that required proof of a feasible alternative design as an element of liability.

sulindac's risks, the company might still have faced liability for having a defective design. See *Thibault,* 118 N.H., at 808, 395 A.2d, at 847 (explaining that strict liability "may attach even though . . . there was an adequate warning"). When a manufacturer cannot change the label or when doing so would not make the drug safe, the manufacturer may still choose between exiting the market or continuing to sell while knowing it may have to pay compensation to consumers injured by its product.[12] . . .

The majority derides any suggestion that Mutual's ability to "stop selling" sulindac is relevant to the validity of its impossibility pre-emption defense. . . . But the majority's argument is built on the mistaken premise that Mutual is legally obligated by New Hampshire's design-defect law to modify its label in a way that federal law forbids. It is not. . . . For that reason, rejecting impossibility pre-emption here would not render the doctrine "a dead letter" or "'all but meaningless.'" . . . On the other hand, it is the majority that "work[s] a revolution in this Court's [impossibility] pre-emption case law," . . . by inferring a state-law requirement from the steps a manufacturer might wish to take to avoid or mitigate its exposure to liability. . . .

In taking the approach it does, the majority replaces careful assessment of regulatory structure with an *ipse dixit* that pharmaceutical companies must have a way to "escape liability," . . . while continuing to sell a drug that received FDA approval. As a result, the majority effectively makes a highly contested policy judgment about the relationship between FDA review and state tort law — treating the FDA as the sole guardian of drug safety — without defending its judgment and without considering whether that is the policy judgment that Congress made.[13] . . .

The most troubling aspect of the majority's decision to once again expand the scope of this Court's traditionally narrow impossibility pre-emption doctrine is what it implies about the relationship between federal premarket review and state common-law remedies more generally. Central to the majority's holding is an assumption that manufacturers must have a way to avoid state-law liability while keeping particular products in commerce. . . . This assumption, it seems, will always create an automatic conflict between a federal premarket review requirement and state-law design-defect liability because premarket review, by definition, prevents manufacturers from unilaterally changing their products' designs.[14] That is true, for example, of the designs (*i.e.,* the chemical composition) of brand-name drugs under the FDCA no less than it is for generic drugs. . . . The majority's reasoning thus "has the 'perverse effect' of

---

12. The majority's suggestion that a manufacturer's option of continuing to sell while paying compensation is akin to violating a statutory mandate and then suffering the consequence (such as paying a fine) is flawed. . . . In that scenario, the manufacturer would have violated the law, and the fact that the law is enforced through monetary sanctions (rather than through an injunction or imprisonment) would not change that. Here, no matter how many times the majority insists otherwise . . . , a manufacturer who sells a drug whose design is found unreasonably dangerous based on a balance of factors has not violated a state law requiring it to change its label. In both cases, the manufacturer may owe money. But only in the former will it have failed to follow the law. Cf. *National Federation of Independent Business v. Sebelius,* 567 U.S. ____, ____, 132 S. Ct. 2566, 2593-2594, 183 L. Ed. 2d 450 (2012) (recognizing that a condition that triggers a tax is not necessarily a "legal command" to take a certain action).

13. Defending a policy judgment that treats the FDA as the exclusive guarantor of drug safety would be no easy task in light of evidence that resource constraints and gaps in legal authority, among other factors, limit the agency's ability to safeguard public health. See Kessler & Vladeck, A Critical Examination of the FDA's Efforts to Preempt Failure-to-Warn Claims, 96 Geo. L.J. 461, 483-495 (2008); see also *Wyeth v. Levine,* 555 U.S. 555, 578-579, and n. 11, 129 S. Ct. 1187, 173 L. Ed. 2d 51 (2009).

14. Or at least it creates an automatic conflict with the caveat that design-defect claims that parallel a federal duty for manufacturers to withdraw a product might not be pre-empted. . . .

granting broad immunity 'to an entire industry that, in the judgment of Congress, needed more stringent regulation.'" *Riegel,* 552 U.S., at 338, 128 S. Ct. 999 (GINSBURG, J., dissenting) (quoting *Lohr,* 518 U.S., at 487, 116 S. Ct. 2240 (plurality opinion)). . . .

The Court recognizes that "[t]his case arises out of tragic circumstances." . . . And I do not doubt that Members of the majority personally feel sympathy for Karen Bartlett. But the Court's solemn affirmation that it merely discharges its duty to "follo[w] the law," . . . , and gives effect to Congress' policy judgment, rather than its own, is hard to accept. By once again expanding the scope of impossibility pre-emption, the Court turns Congress' intent on its head and arrives at a holding that is irreconcilable with our precedents. As a result, the Court has left a seriously injured consumer without any remedy despite Congress' explicit efforts to preserve state common-law liability.

I respectfully dissent.

CHAPTER FIVE

Liability for Failure to Warn

This chapter focuses on the issues presented when a products liability plaintiff claims that the defendant distributor or a predecessor in the chain of distribution failed to adequately instruct or warn of product-related risks. Instructions and warnings serve two functions. They reduce risks of harm by helping users and consumers to behave more carefully, and they enable users and consumers to make informed decisions regarding whether to encounter risks that cannot be eliminated by careful use and consumption. Regarding what might be termed the "risk-reduction" function, warnings are similar to safety features in designs; they lower product risks by allowing users and consumers to interact with products more safely than if they remained ignorant of hidden product risks. (In some cases, persons other than users and consumers are in positions to reduce the relevant risks.)

The cases and problems in this chapter presented in connection with the risk-reduction function assume that the addressees of warnings have opportunities to alter their modes of product use and consumption to reduce risks of injury. This chapter also considers instances in which this assumption is not warranted — instances in which the only risk-avoidance method open to the user and consumer is the decision not to use the product in the first instance. In those "informed choice" cases, which typically involve consumables such as prescription drugs and cosmetics, once the choice to use or consume is made, the user or consumer can do little or nothing to reduce the risk of injury. Should the analysis of the warning's adequacy and the defendant's liability be the same in each type of failure-to-warn case?

Quite a few failure-to-warn cases implicitly or explicitly involve concerns about potential defects in design as well. Remember from the last chapter that, as provided in Comment *l* to §2 of the Products Liability Restatement, warnings cannot by themselves absolve the manufacturer of all responsibility for its products' safety, nor can they necessarily serve as a substitute for a safer design. In products liability cases that implicate both warning and design, courts must consider the complex interaction between the two in order to determine where a product defect may lie and where reasonable, safer alternatives were possible. As you read this chapter, consider whether these issues may be so closely intertwined that courts cannot discuss warning defects without also bringing a product's design into question.

In connection with the cases to be considered in this chapter, a distinction may be drawn between instructions and warnings. Instructions tell product users what they should do to reduce the risks of injury. "Wear insulated gloves to protect your hands." Warnings describe risks that would not otherwise be obvious to persons of average intelligence and experience. "Caution! The top of this product becomes very hot!" Often, product suppliers will be required to provide both sorts of information.

Sometimes only the warning is necessary, as when what to do about the risk is obvious. Less frequently, only instructions are required, as when the risk is obvious but an effective risk-avoidance technique is not.

Legal doctrine governing failure to warn is confusing. Plaintiffs often proceed under both negligence and strict liability theories. Negligence focuses on the conduct of the defendant, while strict liability focuses on the defective product irrespective of the conduct of the defendant. Courts have faced considerable difficulty in applying this theoretical distinction to failure-to-warn actions. It is relatively simple to talk about a hairline crack in a soda bottle as a product defect, separate and apart from the conduct of the defendant. However, "failure to warn" implies that someone "failed" to do something he was supposed to do. This characterization translates easily into the language of negligence. It is harder to fit "failure to warn" under the rubric of strict liability. For example, in Hauenstein v. Loctite Corp., 347 N.W.2d 272, 274 (Minn. 1984), the court noted that in a failure-to-warn action brought against the manufacturer, "if the failure to warn is not negligent, the product is not 'defective' and there is no strict liability." Pay attention to the different ways in which courts in different states and over time use negligence and strict liability to describe the defendant's liability for an alleged warning defect.

One more preliminary observation remains. Some judges (and commentators) succumb to the temptation to assume that instructions and warnings are "free." That is, they take the view that while modifying a design to make it safer may (and usually does) have serious cost implications, the costs of adding a few words of warning are almost nil. In some cases this assumption is obviously false; if a manual of instructions and warnings is required, such a manual costs money to prepare and distribute. But if all that is missing is a simple "This product can explode and injure you if you drop it" in an existing manual of instructions and warnings, the marginal monetary costs of adding such a warning seem to approach zero. On that view, no appreciable risk would seem too small not to be warned against, given the very low monetary costs of doing so. But are there not other, nonmonetary costs associated with warning about all risks, however small? Could not each additional warning involve a "cost" insofar as it diminishes the importance of its neighbors and raises concerns–perhaps unwarranted–about the overall dangerousness of the product? What about the cost to the end-users and intermediaries who must locate, read, understand, and act upon the warnings, as well as in some cases convey them to others? More broadly, how should we weigh the costs associated with creating and implementing effective warnings against the costs of developing a potentially safer design? Think about these questions as you consider the materials that follow.

A.   THE BASIC DUTY TO WARN AT TIME OF SALE

When we speak of "the basic duty," we refer to those circumstances in which the central issue is whether or not some instruction or warning should have been forthcoming. Thus, in the cases and problems in this section, the defendants typically have said little or nothing about the relevant risks, and argue that they owed no duty to speak up at all. The next section of this chapter will address the question of what must be warned about, and by what means, once a court imposes a duty to warn.

1. The General Rule Governing Failure to Warn

Restatement (Third) of Torts: Products Liability
(1998)

---

§2. CATEGORIES OF PRODUCT DEFECT

A product is defective when, at the time of sale or distribution, it contains a manufacturing defect, is defective in design, or is defective because of inadequate instructions or warnings. A product: . . .

> (c) is defective because of inadequate instructions or warnings when the <u>foreseeable risks of harm</u> posed by the product could have been reduced or avoided by the provision of <u>reasonable instructions</u> or warnings by the seller or other distributor, or a predecessor in the commercial chain of distribution, and the omission of the instructions or warnings renders the product not reasonably safe.

COMMENT:

i. Inadequate instructions or warnings. Commercial product sellers must provide reasonable instructions and warnings about risks of injury posed by products. Instructions inform persons how to use and consume products safely. Warnings alert users and consumers to the existence and nature of product risks so that they can prevent harm either by appropriate conduct during use or consumption or by choosing not to use or consume. In most instances the instructions and warnings will originate with the manufacturer, but sellers down the chain of distribution must warn when doing so is feasible and reasonably necessary. In any event, sellers down the chain are liable if the instructions and warnings provided by predecessors in the chain are inadequate. See Comment o. Under prevailing rules concerning allocation of burdens of proof, plaintiff must prove that adequate instructions or warnings were not provided. Subsection (c) adopts a reasonableness test for judging the adequacy of product instructions and warnings. It thus parallels Subsection (b), which adopts a similar standard for judging the safety of product designs. . . .

Section 1 of the Products Liability Restatement subjects all sellers and other commercial distributors of products to liability for harm caused by product defects. Thus, all commercial actors who are "sellers or other distributors" owe duties to warn of nonobvious product risks. The interesting basic duty questions arise in connection with commercial actors who fall close to the boundaries. For example, suppose that a homeowner has a problem with a washer/dryer and calls a repairman who does not sell products. While working on the problem, the repairman notices something dangerously defective with the appliance — something having nothing to do with the problem he was called to repair. If he says nothing, is he liable for harm subsequently caused by the defect? Observe that the repairer is clearly not a seller of the washer/dryer. But repairers owe duties of reasonable care. The issue is one of basic policy — should repairers owe duties to warn of dangers that they have not been called upon to fix? Generally, courts have answered that question in the negative. See, e.g., Menz v. New

Holland North America, Inc., 440 F.3d 1002, 1005 (8th Cir. 2006) ("We found no jurisdiction which has expanded a repairer's duty to include the duty to warn of general dangers associated with a product unrelated to the specific repair work performed.").

A related question is whether nonmanufacturing sellers—wholesalers and retailers—owe duties to warn of the dangers their products create. Clearly they are strictly liable as commercial sellers of products when the manufacturers fail to warn. But do they owe independent duties to supply their own warnings even if the manufacturers' warnings are adequate? See M. Stuart Madden, The Duty to Warn in Products Liability: Its Contours and Criticism, 89 W. Va. L. Rev. 221, 235 (1987) (reviewing relevant case law and Restatement provisions and concluding that "the seller or the distributor of a product manufactured by another must, under negligence principles, give a warning only when it knows or has reason to know of product-related hazards").

Olson v. Prosoco, Inc.
522 N.W.2d 284 (Iowa 1994)

Snell, Justice.

I. Facts

David Olson is a bricklayer foreman employed by Seedorf Masonry Company (Seedorf). Late on the afternoon of December 15, 1988, Olson spotted a fifteen gallon drum of mortar cleaner sitting on the ground. To prevent the cleaner drum from freezing to the ground, he picked it up and moved it onto a nearby pallet. When Olson dropped the drum on the pallet, the bung closure popped out of the drum, splashing hydrochloric acid based cleaner into his right eye. Despite extensive medical care, Olson eventually lost sight in his right eye. In April 1990 doctors fitted Olson with an artificial eye.

The mortar cleaner, called "Sure Klean 600," is manufactured and packaged by Prosoco. The fifteen gallon drum into which Prosoco packages the cleaner is manufactured by Delta Drum Corporation (Delta Drum). The bung closures used in the fifteen gallon drums are manufactured by Rieke Corporation (Rieke). Olson initially named Rieke and Delta Drum in this lawsuit. Rieke and Delta Drum settled their cases with Olson. Olson sued Prosoco under several theories of strict liability and negligence. Prosoco requested and received a state-of-the-art defense jury instruction with regard to Olson's strict liability and negligence theories. The jury found Prosoco one-hundred percent at fault for Olson's injuries under both theories.

II.   Strict Liability and Negligence Claims . . .

Prosoco contends the submission of instructions on both strict liability and negligence theories was duplicative and confusing, resulting in prejudicial error. . . .

Olson contends the submission of a strict liability instruction does not preclude liability based on a negligence theory. He stresses that our decision in Hillrichs was limited strictly to the facts of that case and claims that in the case at bar the strict liability and negligence instructions submitted do not depend on the same elements of proof. . . .

Generally, there are two competing views regarding the failure to warn/strict liability question. The first is that there is little, if any, difference between strict liability and negligence in failure to warn cases. Opposing this view are cases that apply varying forms of a strict liability analysis in failure to warn cases. Some jurisdictions impose strict liability by imputing knowledge of a product's propensity to injure as it did to a defendant-manufacturer, and then asking the jury: With such knowledge would the defendant have been negligent in selling the product without a warning?

Other jurisdictions apply strict liability by requiring plaintiffs to prove defendants knew or should have known of the danger. . . . A different analysis is made in some cases to distinguish strict liability from negligence concepts in failure to warn cases on the ground that in negligence the focus is on the defendant's conduct, while in strict liability, the focus is on the condition of the product.

After reviewing the authorities and comments on the failure to warn question, we believe any posited distinction between strict liability and negligence principles is illusory. We fail to see any distinction between negligence and strict liability in the analyses of those jurisdictions injecting a knowledge requirement into their strict liability/failure to warn equation. The standard applied by these "strict liability" jurisdictions is exactly the same in practice as holding defendants to an expert standard of care under a negligence theory. The burden on plaintiffs is the same. They must prove a defendant knew or should have known of potential risks associated with the use of its product, yet failed to provide adequate directions or warnings to users. With regard to those jurisdictions imputing to defendants knowledge of its product's propensity to injure as it did, we have refused in the past to impose a duty upon manufacturers to warn of unknowable dangers.

We also find the product/conduct distinction made by several jurisdictions to justify maintaining a strict liability/failure to warn theory of little practical significance. See, e.g., Anderson, 281 Cal. Rptr. at 537, 810 P.2d at 558. According to courts taking stock in this distinction, under a strict liability theory the focus is on the unreasonably dangerous condition of the product. In contrast, these courts hold the question in negligence cases is whether the defendant's conduct breached a duty to exercise reasonable care. In practice, the courts basing the application of a strict liability theory on this distinction cannot help but slip back into the type of analyses virtually identical to those employed in negligence cases. Inevitably the conduct of the defendant in a failure to warn case becomes the issue. . . .

Maintaining the distinction to justify submission of failure to warn claims under both strict liability and negligence theories is a vain effort. We hold it was error to submit instructions regarding Prosoco's failure to warn under both negligence and strict liability theories. . . . Both instructions essentially required the jury to determine whether Prosoco negligently failed to warn users of the dangers in moving or using Sure Klean 600 in fifteen gallon containers.

We believe that the correct submission of instructions regarding a failure to warn claim for damages is under a theory of negligence and the claim should not be submitted as a theory of strict liability. In testing the defendant's liability for negligence in failing to warn, the defendant should be held to the standard of care of an expert in its field. The relevant inquiry therefore is whether the reasonable manufacturer knew or should have known of the danger, in light of the generally recognized and prevailing best scientific knowledge, yet failed to provide adequate warning to users or consumers. . . .

In reviewing the instructions given on the theory of negligence, we find that the claim of failure to warn as submitted substantially invoked this standard. Special verdict form No. 1 found Prosoco one-hundred percent liable on the claim of negligence. Also submitted by a special verdict form was the claim of strict liability under which the jury found Prosoco one-hundred percent at fault.

We have reversed and remanded cases where a general verdict of liability resulted from the submission of two theories, one of which contained an error in the instructions. . . . In these situations, we were unable to determine that the verdict resulted from a theory that was free of error. . . . However, in the case at bar, the special verdicts are sufficiently insulated from each other to stand on their own. We do not believe the error in submitting a failure to warn instruction as part of the strict liability claim had any prejudicial effect on the jury's consideration of the same issue contained in the negligence claim. . . .

We have considered all of the arguments and issues raised by Prosoco in this appeal. No reversible error has occurred. The judgment entered by the trial court is affirmed.

Affirmed.

Other jurisdictions preserve the distinction rejected in *Olson*, allowing parties to argue and submit failure-to-warn claims under both negligence and strict liability. See, e.g., Butz v. Werner, 438 N.W.2d 509, 515 (N.D. 1989). Might juries become confused when considering potentially overlapping theories of liability in failure-to-warn claims? See Walter W. Steele, Jr. & Elizabeth G. Thornburg, Jury Instructions: A Persistent Failure to Communicate, 67 N.C. L. Rev. 77, 99 (1988) (reporting that jury understanding of complex instructions is low and that such confusion is commonly believed to benefit plaintiffs, although empirical studies have not demonstrated such a one-sided effect). In jurisdictions that follow *Olson* in considering failure-to-warn claims under strict liability and negligent equivalent, inconsistent jury verdicts in response to instructions on both negligence and strict liability will lead courts to order new trials. Cf. Chapter Four, supra. Minnesota has adopted a hybrid approach to avoid the risk of inconsistent verdicts, in which plaintiffs may argue failure-to-warn claims under both negligence and strict liability but may only submit one theory to the jury. Hauenstein v. Loctite Corp., 347 N.W.2d 272, 275 (Minn. 1984).

2. *No Duty to Warn of Unknowable Risks*

One context in which courts have found a more meaningful distinction between strict liability and negligence theories in failure-to-warn cases concerns unknowable risks. You may recall the discussion in Chapter Four, supra, of the subject of unknowable risks in the context of liability for defective designs. There, we concluded that the potential exposure of product sellers to liability was not very significant because almost all of the risks generically associated with product designs are widely known and understood by experts. The one significant product area in which entire industries may be unavoidably ignorant of product-related risks involves toxic substances. But inherently risky toxic substances do not give rise to viable claims for defective design. Reasonable alternative designs are not typically available, and as we saw in Chapter Four, courts refuse to impose category liability. So as a practical matter, the issue of liability for unknowable risks arises only in connection with alleged failures by manufacturers to warn of risks presented by products consisting of, or containing, toxic substances.

Anderson v. Owens-Corning Fiberglas Corp., 810 P.2d 549 (Cal. 1991) (en banc), was the case whose approach to distinguishing failure-to-warn claims based in strict liability and negligence was rejected in *Olson*, supra. In *Anderson*, the Supreme Court of California reviewed a failure-to-warn claim against a manufacturer of asbestos-containing insulation. The high court held that the claim sounded in strict liability, not negligence, but that the plaintiff was required to prove that the defendant knew or reasonably should have known at the time of sale that asbestos caused lung injuries. The court explained its holding:

> We therefore reject the contention that every reference to a feature shared with theories of negligence [such as knowability of risk] can serve to defeat limitations on the doctrine of strict liability. Furthermore, despite its roots in negligence, failure to warn in strict liability differs markedly from failure to warn in the negligence context. Negligence law in a failure-to-warn case requires a plaintiff to prove that a manufacturer or distributor did not warn of a particular risk for reasons which fell below the acceptable standard of care, i.e., what a reasonably prudent manufacturer would have known and warned about. Strict liability is not concerned with the standard of due care or the reasonableness of a manufacturer's conduct. The rules of strict liability require a plaintiff to prove only that the defendant did not adequately warn of a particular risk that was known or knowable in light of the generally recognized and prevailing best scientific and medical knowledge available at the time of manufacture and distribution. Thus, in strict liability, as opposed to negligence, the reasonableness of the defendant's failure to warn is immaterial.
>
> Stated another way, a reasonably prudent manufacturer might reasonably decide that the risk of harm was such as not to require a warning as, for example, if the manufacturer's own testing showed a result contrary to that of others in the scientific community. Such a manufacturer might escape liability under negligence principles. In contrast, under strict liability principles the manufacturer has no such leeway; the manufacturer is liable if it failed to give warning of dangers that were known to the scientific community at the time it manufactured or distributed the product. . . . [Id. at 558-59.]

Is the court successful in retaining strict liability but adding a significant element of fault-based liability? Consider an alternative articulation that draws a sharper distinction between knowability in the two theories: "In a strict-liability case, the defendant is assumed to know of the dangerous propensity of the product, whereas in a negligence case, the plaintiff must prove that the defendant knew or should have known of the danger." Becker v. Baron Bros. Coliseum Auto Parts, Inc., 649 A.2d 613, 616 (N.J. 1994) (quotations omitted) (proceeding to reject a purely strict-liability approach to failure-to-warn claims). What policy problems might be created by a legal regime that preserves a more orthodox conception of strict liability for failure-to-warn claims?

In Carlin v. Superior Court, 920 P.2d 1347 (Cal. 1996), the Supreme Court of California faced the question of whether *Anderson* requires the application of strict liability in a case against a prescription drug manufacturer for its alleged failure to warn physicians of the risks associated with its drug. The defendant urged that the strict-liability approach outlined in *Anderson*, even if liability for unknowable risks was not part of it, would expose drug manufacturers to crushing liability that would inhibit new drug development. The Supreme Court rejected defendant's argument and, with three separate dissenting opinions, held that *Anderson* required strict liability in that context as well as all others. To refute the defendant's claim that the strict-liability standard would reduce innovation, the majority concluded that "requiring manufacturers to internalize the costs of failing to determine such risks may instead *increase* the level of research into safe and effective drugs." Id. at 1354 (Emphasis in original.) Does the court strike the right balance between protecting safety and encouraging innovation, and should this same analysis apply to development of potentially lifesaving products?

Not all courts agree with California that the plaintiff must prove that the relevant risks were knowable at time of sale. The leading decision allowing triers of fact to find defendants liable for failing to warn of risks that were scientifically unknowable at the time the defendant distributed the product is Beshada v. Johns-Manville Prod. Corp., 447 A.2d 539 (N.J. 1982). The court concluded that imposing such liability was consistent with the "liability without fault" aspects of strict liability. It would also help to achieve the major goals of strict liability: risk spreading, accident avoidance, and simplification of proof at trial. Regarding the accident avoidance goal, the court observed that "[b]y imposing on manufacturers the costs of failure to discover hazards, we create an incentive for them to invest more actively in safety research." Id. at 548. In imposing strict liability, the court also displayed a concern for basic fairness: "The burden of illness from dangerous products such as asbestos should be placed upon those who profit from its production and, more generally, upon society at large, which reaps the benefits of the various products our economy manufactures. That burden should not be imposed exclusively on the innocent victim." Id. at 549. Do these goals and values outweigh the concerns expressed in Anderson of stifling innovation and raising consumer prices by making the manufacturer bear the costs of unknowable risks from its products?

The New Jersey Supreme Court addressed the question of whether the holding in Beshada applied in prescription drug cases and held that it did not. See Feldman v. Lederle Laboratories, 479 A.2d 374 (N.J. 1984). The court first concluded that strict liability applied to drug manufacturers, and then proceeded to the question of whether Beshada applied:

> If Beshada were deemed to hold generally or in all cases, particularly with respect to a situation like the present one involving drugs vital to health, that in a warning context knowledge of the unknowable is irrelevant in determining the applicability of strict liability, we would not agree. Many commentators have criticized this aspect of the Beshada reasoning and the public policies on which it is based. The rationale of Beshada is not applicable to this case. We do not overrule Beshada, but restrict Beshada to the circumstances giving rise to its holding. We note, in passing, that, although not argued and determined in Beshada, there were or may have been data and other information generally available, aside from scientific knowledge, that arguably could have alerted the manufacturer at an early stage in the distribution of its product to the dangers associated with its use.
>
> In strict liability warning cases, unlike negligence cases, however, the defendant should properly bear the burden of proving that the information was not reasonably available or obtainable and that it therefore lacked actual or constructive knowledge of the defect. The defendant is in a superior position to know the technological material or data in the particular field or specialty. The defendant is the expert, often performing self-testing. It is the defendant that injected the product in the stream of commerce for its economic gain. As a matter of policy the burden of proving the status of knowledge in the field at the time of distribution is properly placed on the defendant. [Id. at 387-88.]

As the excerpt from Feldman, above, indicates, most courts and commentators have rejected the proposition that product sellers should be strictly liable for harm caused by risks that were unknowable and unforeseeable at the time of sale. Comment m to §2 of the Products Liability Restatement reflects the clear majority position on this issue and also rejects the shifting of the burden of proof adopted by the Feldman court. For a rare exception holding manufacturers to time-of-trial knowledge of risks that were unknowable at the time of original sale, see Sternhagen v. Dow Co., 935 P.2d 1139, 1142-46 (Mont. 1997) (rejecting a "state of the art" defense to failure-to-warn causes of action as contrary to strict products liability, despite recognition of the principles of the Restatement (Third) of Torts: Products Liability, and instead applying "imputation of knowledge doctrine" whereby the manufacturer is deemed to have knowledge of a "product's undiscovered or undiscoverable dangers" as "more consistent with existing Montana law" because such doctrine "reinforces" the courts' "commitment to provide maximum protection for consumers, while still assuring 'an appropriate limitation to a manufacturer's liability'").

Like courts, the majority of commentators have argued against imputing time-of-trial knowledge to a product seller. See, e.g., Ellen Wertheimer, Unknowable Dangers and the Death of Strict Products Liability: The Empire Strikes Back, 60 U. Cin. L. Rev. 1183 (1992); James A. Henderson, Jr., Coping with the Time Dimension in Products Liability, 69 Calif. L. Rev. 919 (1981). Those who favor at least a limited degree of hindsight evaluation of products' risks and benefits respond that having plaintiffs bear all risks from unknowable dangers may not lead to the most efficient outcomes; imposing manufacturer liability for unknowable dangers may further encourage research and development of innovative safety measures; and imputing such knowledge may lead to more efficient trials. See Gary T. Schwartz, Foreword: Understanding Products Liability, 67 Calif. L. Rev. 435, 482-88 (1979); Guido Calabresi, Concerning Cause and the Law of Torts, 43 U. Chi. L. Rev. 69, 93 (1975).

LIABILITY INSURANCE AND LONG-TAIL, UNKNOWABLE RISKS

Beshada and the asbestos liability litigation of which it is part present two important issues involving liability insurance. First, can manufacturers adequately insure against risks that are unknown at the time the products are distributed? Second, regarding liability insurance actually in place (whether or not it is adequate), as of what time does the plaintiff's "bodily injury" (the insured-against event) occur for purposes of determining which of several insurance policies covers the liability in question?

Regarding the first of these issues, a number of commentators have argued that manufacturers cannot, by hypothesis, insure against risks no one knows exist. As a consequence, when liability is later imposed strictly, based on hindsight, all they can do is charge the losses against earnings or capital, or go out of business. Either way, inefficiencies result. For a contrary perspective, see Joseph A. Page, Generic Product Risks: The Case against Comment k and for Strict Liability, 58 N.Y.U. L. Rev. 853 (1983).

Regarding the issue of which liability policy should cover a risk that took twenty or thirty years (from first distribution to full manifestation of plaintiff's injury) to materialize, courts have disagreed. The problem in these cases stems from the fact that typically a number of different insurers wrote liability coverage over the relevant period and the policy language is ambiguous. Some courts have held that insurers who wrote liability coverage during the period of plaintiff's exposure should be "on the risk." See, e.g., Insurance Co. of N. Am. v. Forty-Eight Insulations, Inc., 633 F.2d 1212 (6th Cir. 1980), *cert. denied*, 454 U.S. 1109 (1981). Other courts have held that it should be insurers under policies in effect when the plaintiff first manifests his injury. See, e.g., Eagle-Picher Indus., Inc. v. Liberty Mutual Ins. Co., 682 F.2d 12 (6th Cir. 1982), *cert. denied*, 460 U.S. 1028 (1983). And still others have held that insurers at both points in time are liable under their policies. See, e.g., Keene Corp. v. Insurance Co. of N. Am., 667 F.2d 1034 (D.C. Cir. 1981), *cert. denied*, 455 U.S. 1007 (1982).

3. *No Duty to Warn of Obvious or Generally Known Risks*

Contrast the problems outlined supra regarding unknowable dangers with the issues that arise in cases involving what courts believe to be obvious and generally known risks. While many cases involving unknowable dangers ask what the defendant should have known, cases involving obvious risks ask whether the defendant had a duty to disclose what it did know. Manufacturers and courts must balance the desire to warn users of all possible risks associated with the product against the diluted importance each particular warning will have as the collective list grows in length. Cognitive research shows that a proliferation of product warnings can lead to "wear-out," in which consumers tune out messages that are repeated too often. See Christine Jolls & Cass R. Sunstein, Debasing Through Law, 35 J. Legal Stud. 199, 212 (2006). The general rule regarding obvious, generally known risks is set forth in the following Comment and Illustration to §2(c) of the Products Liability Restatement:

> *j. Warnings: obvious and generally known risks.* In general, a product seller is not subject to liability for failing to warn or instruct regarding risks and risk-avoidance measures that should be obvious to, or generally known by, foreseeable product users. When a risk is obvious or generally known, the prospective addressee of a warning will or should already know of its existence. Warning of an obvious or generally known risk in most instances will not provide an effective additional measure of safety. Furthermore, warnings that deal with obvious or generally known risks may be ignored by users and consumers and may diminish the significance of warnings about non-obvious, not-generally-known risks. Thus, requiring warnings of obvious or generally known risks could reduce the efficacy of warnings generally. When reasonable minds may differ as to whether the risk was obvious or generally known, the issue is to be decided by the trier of fact. The obviousness of risk may bear on the issue of design defect rather than failure to warn.

ILLUSTRATIONS:

12. XYZ Ladder Co. manufactures kitchen step ladders for home use. Sid used an XYZ ladder to post a sign above the door of his home office, unaware that his five-year-old son was playing in the office. While Sid was standing on the ladder, his son suddenly opened the door, which struck the ladder. Sid fell off the ladder and suffered a fractured hip. There were no warnings on the ladder, nor in the instruction booklet that came with it, not to use the ladder in front of an unlocked door. The danger should be obvious to foreseeable product users. No reasonable trier of fact would find XYZ liable for failing to warn about it and the court should rule for XYZ as a matter of law.

Jamieson v. Woodward & Lothrop
247 F.2d 23 (D.C. Cir.), *cert. denied*, 355 U.S. 855 (1957)

PRETTYMAN, Cir. J.

Appellant, Mrs. Marguerite Jamieson, bought . . . an elastic exerciser manufactured by Helena Rubinstein, Inc., which she had seen advertised in a magazine. She bought by brand name, "Lithe-Line," and no special instructions as to use were given her by the vendor's salesperson. While she was using the exerciser she suffered a sudden unconsciousness, and although she testified she did not know what happened it appears to be a reasonable inference that the exerciser slipped and struck her in the eye. She sued . . . Helena Rubinstein, Inc., for negligence. The defendant answered. . . . The District Court, on the basis of the complaint, the answers, the deposition, and the exhibits, granted summary judgment for the defendant. This appeal followed. . . .

The court is divided in its view of the judgment in favor of the manufacturer, Helena Rubinstein, Inc. A majority agree with the District Court, and so the judgment will be affirmed.

The theory of the plaintiff as to the manufacturer, as set forth in her complaint, was that the exerciser was inherently dangerous and that the manufacturer had failed to warn or otherwise protect her against such danger. In answer to an interrogation she said that when the solid rubber rope is subjected to stress, as in an exercise, great potential striking power is created; that the rope "can depart from the instep" in the course of an exercise; and that no safety or protective device was provided and no warning given.

The exerciser in question was an ordinary rubber rope, about the thickness of a large lead pencil, about forty inches long, with loops on the ends. It had no imperfections or defects whatsoever and no added gadgets. It never broke or went awry. It was a simple elastic exerciser. With the rope came a set of "Instructions." These consisted of a series of eight silhouette sketches of exercises to be done with the rope, with a summary description of each exercise. There were no instructions as to how to operate the device; there was no device to operate, the article in question being merely a rubber rope. In appearance it resembled a child's skipping rope.

In the course of her program Mrs. Jamieson began one of the most normal and natural of exercises. She lay down on the floor, put the rope under her feet, held on to the handles, and, with knees stiff, raised her feet straight up, intending then to lower them and so, alternately raising and lowering them, to give her body muscles a workout. Apparently the rope slipped off the soles of her feet and hit her in the eye. She suffered a serious injury.

The unfortunate event was an accident, we think — an event so natural that responsibility for it is by common consent not ascribed to fault. Of course one is truly sorry for the unfortunate victim of a chance accident, but the premise of pecuniary liability for tort is not the fact of injury but is negligence. . . .

There are on the market vast numbers of products as to which the law holds the manufacturer to a duty to warn of foreseeable dangers or to provide safeguards against such dangers. But there are also on the market vast numbers of potentially dangerous products as to which the manufacturer owes no duty of warning or other protection. The law does not require that an article be accident-proof or incapable of doing harm. It would be totally unreasonable to require that a manufacturer warn or protect against every injury which may ensue from mishap in the use of his product. Almost every physical object can be inherently dangerous or potentially dangerous in a sense. A lead pencil can stab a man to the heart or puncture his jugular vein, and due to that potentiality it is an "inherently dangerous" object; but, if a person accidentally slips and falls on a pencil-point in his pocket, the manufacturer of the pencil is not liable for the injury. He has no obligation . . . to issue a warning with its sale. A tack, a hammer, a pane of glass, a chair, a rug, a rubber band, and myriads of other objects are truly "inherently dangerous," because they might slip. They cause accidents and injury even more often, we expect, than do rubber exercisers. But the doctrines fashioned by the law for inherently dangerous objects do not encompass these things. A hammer is not . . . defective . . . because it may hurt the user if it slips. A manufacturer cannot manufacture a knife that will not cut or a hammer that will not mash a thumb or a stove that will not burn a finger. The law does not require him to warn of such common dangers. On the other end of the spectrum of practicalities, a manufacturer . . . might be liable for failure to provide . . . an emphatic warning to users of an electric power saw, but he would not be liable if he failed so to provide in respect to a kitchen knife. . . .

The case at bar falls within the category just described. The only "dangerous condition" was that a rubber rope is elastic and when stretched will, when released, return to its original length with some degree of force. Small boys know that fact and fashion slingshots upon the principle. Surely every adult knows that, if an elastic band, whether it be an office rubber band or a rubber rope exerciser, is stretched and one's hold on it slips, the elastic snaps back. There was no duty on the manufacturer to warn of that simple fact. . . .

Since the rope in the case at bar was without defect or accessory gadgets and did not break or fail in any manner, no fault, and surely no negligence, can be ascribed to the manufacturer merely because it slipped off the lady's foot while in perfectly normal use. It would be erroneous to hold that the manufacturer may be liable for damages if he fails to warn users that a rope such as this might slip off a foot or out of a hand. When all the discussion of involved legal principles has been concluded, the case remains as simple as it was in the beginning: A lady was doing a simple exercise with a simple rubber rope, and it slipped off her foot and hit her in the eye. That is the whole of it. And the question is equally simple: Was the manufacturer therefore negligent? We think it was not. To hold otherwise would go beyond any reasonable dictates of justice in fixing the liabilities of manufacturers of products sold on the market.

Affirmed.

WASHINGTON, Cir. J. (dissenting), with whom EDGERTON, C.J., and BAZELON and FAHY, Cir. JJ., join.

I would reverse as to defendant Rubinstein.

Mrs. Jamieson bought the Lithe-Line, manufactured and marketed by this defendant, for the purpose of reducing her abdomen. Instructions for its use were packed in the container with the Lithe-Line. On the afternoon of the day the device was delivered to her home in nearby Virginia, plaintiff said, she read the instructions through, did two of the exercises there described and recommended "to get the feel of the rubber hose," and then proceeded to the "Tummy Flattener" exercise, the particular exercise "that was supposed to reduce" the abdomen. She followed the recommended procedure contained in the instruction booklet and, while so doing, the Lithe-Line slipped off her feet and struck her across the eyes, knocking her unconscious and causing a detached retina and permanent partial loss of vision in the left eye. The injury occurred while she was performing the exercise exactly as the manufacturer had directed and recommended, without any deviation from the instructions and without fault on her part, so far as the record before us shows. Her suit is based, not on the theory that the manufacturer put on the market an exerciser in itself inherently dangerous, as the majority appears to believe, but on the premise that the exerciser *when used as directed* by the manufacturer became dangerous and that the manufacturer owed a duty to warn . . . her against such danger. In other words, her theory is that the use of the Lithe-Line in the Tummy Flattener exercise as directed by the manufacturer created an unreasonable risk of injury which gave rise to a duty toward users of the device. That theory of liability finds abundant support not only in the decisions of the Virginia courts, which govern here, but also in the general law of negligence. . . .

The Lithe-Line was marketed for a particular class of persons — overweight women who desired to reduce or "streamline" parts of their body. It was not marketed for individuals who could be expected to have any special training or experience. The tendency of expanded rubber to contract to its original length, when released, is undoubtedly commonly known and was known by Mrs. Jamieson, according to her deposition. But the fact that she understood this hardly justifies the legal conclusion that she or any other user of the Lithe-Line would understand, without some tests, training or experience, that rubber of the type and consistency used in the Lithe-Line, when stretched in the Tummy Flattener exercise as directed, would or could recoil and strike the face of the user, with the impact alleged to have occurred. . . .

. . . [R]easonable minds could differ as to whether the manufacturer could justifiably expect that prospective users would remain fully aware of the danger after reading his advertising claims, even assuming for purposes of argument that they might otherwise be reasonably expected to recognize and appreciate it. The leaflet of instructions furnished with the Lithe-Line stated inter alia:

> Lithe-Line — easily the best turn done to the body beautiful since the curve was invented. For, given enough of this ingenious little elastic rope it is possible for *any* body to prune the hips, sleek the legs, carve the waistline. . . . And do it pleasantly! As a cat does it — with the same grace-giving movements. . . . You'll have great fun, besides, pulling and stretching, bending and twisting. . . . A real workout is yours, too, against the tenacity of the Lithe-Line. You'll marvel at the supple way your body responds with new lines of rhythm and beauty as you stretch yourself into shape and gain the grace and poise that you've coveted all your life!

The atmosphere created by such statements, especially the representation that it is possible for "*any* body" to reduce with it, directed at weight-conscious women such as the plaintiff, can reasonably be expected to dispel any suspicion of danger and to "lull the user . . . into a false sense of security," and this "might also reasonably have been foreseen by the defendant." . . .

Thus, I must disagree strongly with the majority view. I think that the evidence adduced thus far — the device itself plus the directions and the plaintiff's testimony on deposition that she was injured as she used the device precisely as directed — indicate at the very least that there may be liability and that the plaintiff is entitled to an opportunity to present her evidence. This is not to say, of course, that if evidence were received the plaintiff would necessarily prevail. It would be a question for the trier of fact on all the evidence to resolve the factual issues bearing on the manufacturer's alleged negligence and the affirmative defenses, if any, which might be pleaded. . . .

———————————

Whether or not the application of the "no duty to warn of obvious dangers" rule to the particular facts in *Jamieson* was correct, the rule itself is solidly embedded in the caselaw. See, e.g., Hodges v. Summer Fun Rentals, Inc., 203 Fed. App'x 89, 92 (9th Cir. 2006) (risks of jumping boat wakes while riding a personal watercraft are obvious; requiring lessor to warn about wakes being different sizes would be like "requiring the lessor of a building to tell the lessee to walk slowly going down stairs and to keep a safe distance from others"); Hutton v. Globe Hoist Co., 158 F. Supp. 2d 371 (S.D.N.Y. 2001) (the danger of car falling from hydraulic lift in auto repair shop was obvious as a matter of law and knowing to run in the direction opposite the fall was even more obvious); Abney v. Crosman Corp., 919 So. 2d 289 (Ala. 2005) (risks of injury or death from air gun were open and obvious; manufacturer owed no duty to warn); Weiner v. American Honda Motor Co., 718 A.2d 305 (Pa. Super. Ct. 1998) (auto manufacturer had no duty to warn of the open and obvious danger that a 180-pound industrial gas canister placed in a hatchback's cargo compartment unrestrained would catapult forward during a head-on collision and injure plaintiff sitting in the front seat); Roland v. Daimler-Chrysler Corp., 33 S.W.3d 468 (Tex. App. 2001) (holding that manufacturer of pickup truck had no duty to warn of danger of ejection posed by riding in open bed); Kessel v. Stansfield Vending, Inc., 714 N.W.2d 206 (Wis. Ct. App. 2006) (no duty to warn that steaming hot water from dispenser in hospital could cause burn injuries).

Some states have codified the "no duty to warn of obvious risks" rule by statute. See, e.g., Tennessee Code §29-28-105(d) ("A product is not unreasonably dangerous because of a failure to adequately warn of a danger or hazard that is apparent to the ordinary user."). Consider the following decision by the Supreme Court of Michigan.

Greene v. A.P. Products, Ltd.
717 N.W.2d 855 (Mich. 2006)

BEFORE THE ENTIRE BENCH

CORRIGAN, J.

In this case we consider the scope of a manufacturer's or seller's duty to warn of product risks under MCL 600.2948(2). We conclude that the statute imposes a duty to warn that extends only to material risks not obvious to a reasonably prudent product user, and to material risks that are not, or should not be, a matter of common knowledge to persons in the same or a similar position as the person who suffered the injury in question. Because the material risk associated with ingesting and inhaling Wonder 8 Hair Oil, as occurred here, would have been obvious to a reasonably prudent product user, the failure to warn against the risk is not actionable. The Court of Appeals misunderstood this duty and held that a duty also existed to warn of the kind of injuries that were suffered. . . . Because no warning was required, [this] holding was in error. Accordingly, we reverse the judgment of the Court of Appeals and reinstate the trial court's order granting summary disposition to all defendants.

I.   Underlying Facts and Procedural History

In April 1999, plaintiff purchased a spray bottle of African Pride Ginseng Miracle Wonder 8 Oil, Hair and Body Mist-Captivate (Wonder 8 Hair Oil) from defendant Pro Care Beauty Supply, which is currently known as Super 7 Beauty Supply, Inc. Defendant A.P. Products, which was subsequently acquired by Revlon Consumer

Products Corporation, packaged and labeled Wonder 8 Hair Oil. Wonder 8 Hair Oil was marketed principally to African-Americans as a new type of spray-on body and hair moisturizer containing eight natural oils. Plaintiff decided to try the oil after reading the ingredients on the label, some of which were familiar to her and some of which were not. Although the bottle's label cautioned the user never to spray the oil near sparks or an open flame, it did not warn that the hair oil should be kept out of reach of children or that it was potentially harmful or fatal if swallowed. Plaintiff's 11-month-old son, Keimer Easley, had been left unattended. Somehow he obtained the bottle of hair oil, which had been left within his reach. He ingested and inhaled the hair oil. The child died about one month later from multisystem organ failure secondary to chemical pneumonitis, secondary to hydrocarbon ingestion. In other words, the mineral oil clogged the child's lungs, causing inflammatory respiratory failure.

Plaintiff filed this products-liability action, alleging that defendants breached their duty to warn that the product could be harmful if ingested and that it should be kept out of reach of small children. . . .

Defendants moved for summary disposition. A.P. Products and Revlon argued that they had no duty to warn because the material risks associated with ingesting Wonder 8 Hair Oil were obvious to a reasonably prudent product user. They further argued that the lack of warning was not the proximate cause of the injury and that the product had been misused in a way that was not reasonably foreseeable. Super 7 Beauty Supply argued that plaintiff failed to establish that it, as a nonmanufacturing seller, . . . was independently negligent. . . .

The trial court granted defendants' motions for summary disposition. The Court of Appeals reversed and remanded, concluding that the questions whether the Wonder 8 Hair Oil required a warning label . . . and whether plaintiff established proximate cause should have been submitted to a jury.

Defendants sought leave to appeal in this Court. We granted defendants' applications for leave to appeal. . . .

III.   Analysis

Before 1995, a manufacturer's or seller's duty to warn of material risks in a products-liability action was governed by common-law principles. Tort reform legislation enacted in 1995, however, displaced the common law. MCL 600.2948, in chapter 29 of the Revised Judicature Act, now governs a defendant's duty to warn of an obvious danger in a products-liability action. It states, in relevant part:

> A defendant is not liable for failure to warn of a material risk that is or should be obvious to a reasonably prudent product user or a material risk that is or should be a matter of common knowledge to persons in the same or similar position as the person upon whose injury or death the claim is based in a product liability action.

Under the plain language of MCL 600.2948(2), a manufacturer has no duty to warn of a material risk associated with the use of a product if the risk: (1) is obvious, or should be obvious, to a reasonably prudent product user, or (2) is or should be a matter of common knowledge to a person in the same or a similar position as the person upon whose injury or death the claim is based. Accordingly, this statute, by looking to the reasonably prudent product user, or persons in the same or a similar position as the injured person,[1] establishes an objective standard.

[Based on general principles of statutory interpretation, we] conclude that a "material risk" is an important or significant exposure to the chance of injury or loss.

Finally, regarding the meaning of the statute, we conclude that the Legislature has imposed no duty to warn beyond obvious material risks. The statute does not impose a duty to warn of a specific type of injury that could result from a risk. The Court of Appeals, however, mistakenly held that warnings must cover not only material risks, as described, but must also cover potential injuries that could result.

While the Court of Appeals properly applied an objective standard in determining the suitability of the warning, it stated that it could not conclude that "as a matter of law, *the risk of death* from the ingestion of Wonder 8 Hair Oil would be obvious to a reasonably prudent product user and be a matter of common knowledge, especially considering the lack of *any* relevant warning." 264 Mich. App. at 401, 691 N.W.2d 38 (first emphasis added). The Court of Appeals thus required that the warning indicate specific injuries a product user could incur. Yet, as we have stated, the statute does not require that a warning address possible injuries that might occur.

Here, tragically, plaintiff's 11-month-old son died after ingesting and inhaling Wonder 8 Hair Oil. Under the law, however, defendants owed no duty to warn of specific injuries or losses, no matter how severe, if it is or should have been obvious to a reasonably prudent product user that ingesting or inhaling Wonder 8 Hair Oil involved a material risk. We conclude that it is obvious to a reasonably prudent product user that a material risk is involved with ingesting and inhaling Wonder 8 Hair Oil.

The product, as plaintiff concedes, was not marketed as safe for human consumption or ingestion. Rather, the label clearly states that the product is intended for use as a hair and body oil. Although subjective awareness is not the standard, we find it noteworthy that plaintiff herself demonstrated an understanding that Wonder 8 Hair Oil posed a material risk if ingested. We believe it would also be obvious to a reasonably prudent user that ingestion and inhalation of the product poses a material risk. The ingredient label's inclusion of eight natural oils has no bearing on our conclusion. Many, if not all, oils are natural. It should be obvious to a reasonably prudent product user that many oils, although natural, pose a material risk if ingested or inhaled. For instance, the reasonably prudent product user would know that breathing oil would be harmful. A reasonably prudent product user would also know that ingesting such things as crude oil or linseed oil poses a material risk although such oils are natural and pose no immediate danger from contact with hair or skin. In fact, paraffin oil is listed as one of the ingredients in Wonder 8 Hair Oil. It should be obvious to a reasonably prudent product user that ingesting paraffin oil poses a material risk since paraffin is commonly associated with such things as wax.

Additionally, the product label on Wonder 8 Hair Oil does not state that it contains *only* natural oils. Indeed, it lists numerous other ingredients, many of which would be unfamiliar to the average product user, such as isopropryl myristate, fragrance, and azulene. Given such unfamiliar ingredients, a reasonably prudent product user would be, or should be, loath to ingest it.

---

1. Because it would not be a matter of common knowledge to a person in the same or a similar position as plaintiff's son, an 11-month-old, that a material risk is involved with ingesting Wonder 8 Hair Oil, the only issue in this case is whether it would be obvious to a reasonably prudent product user that a material risk is involved with ingesting Wonder 8 Hair Oil.

Accordingly, we hold that defendants owed no duty to warn plaintiff that her son's ingestion and inhalation of the Wonder 8 Hair Oil posed a material risk. Moreover, defendants owed no duty to warn of the potential injuries that could arise from ingesting and inhaling the product. . . .

IV.   *Response to Justice Cavanagh's Dissent*

The crux of Justice Cavanagh's dissent is that we erroneously conclude that the obviousness of *one* risk means the obviousness of *all* risks. This contention, however, is a gross mischaracterization of our holding and can be found nowhere in our opinion. Rather, we hold that a defendant has no duty to warn of a material risk that is or should be obvious to a reasonably prudent product user. We further hold that the material risk associated with the ingestion and inhalation of hair oil is or should be obvious to a reasonably prudent product user. This conclusion is entirely consistent with the plain language of the statute and focuses on the obviousness of the material risk in question. It does not charge Michigan consumers with "knowledge of hidden dangers" as suggested by Justice Cavanagh.

Justice Cavanagh also contends that we fail to identify the material risk in question and mislabel the risk as "ingesting or inhaling" the hair oil. Contrary to his contention, we have clearly identified the material risk in this case. To the contrary, Justice Cavanagh has mislabeled the risk as the "consequence" that results from the misuse of the product.

The material risk in this case is neither the misuse of the product (the inhalation or ingestion) nor the consequence of the misuse (injury or death). Rather the material risk is the important or significant exposure to the chance of loss or injury stemming from certain behavior, in this case, the ingestion and inhalation of hair oil. In simple terms, the material risk is the chance that injury could result from drinking or inhaling hair oil. Because a reasonable person knows or should know that ingesting or inhaling hair oil would expose that person to the chance of injury or loss, a defendant has no duty to warn that ingesting or inhaling hair oil could result in exposure to injury or loss. Furthermore, the statute does not require that a person be aware of the worst injury or loss (death) that could possibly result from the misuse of the product. Rather, under the plain language of the statute, it need only be obvious to a reasonably prudent product user that a chance exists that he or she might suffer an injury or loss if they drink or inhale hair oil. . . .

V.   *Conclusion*

We conclude that the Court of Appeals erroneously reversed the trial court's grant of summary disposition to defendants A.P. Products and Revlon. The material risk of harm associated with ingesting and inhaling Wonder 8 Hair Oil is obvious to a reasonably prudent product user. Defendants thus owed no duty to warn plaintiff of that harm.

CAVANAGH, J. (dissenting).

Michigan consumers beware: If you know or should know that there is *any* material risk from using or accidentally misusing the product you buy, then the manufacturer of that product now has no duty to warn you of any risk at all, even when the potential harm you knew of is not the harm you ultimately suffer. Stated differently, if you know or should know that if, for example, you accidentally drink or inhale a product, you may become ill, then you are charged with knowing that if you accidentally drink or inhale that product, you could die. And the manufacturer need not warn you of *either* of those risks—illness or death. According to the majority, the obviousness of any material risk, such as that of illness, is identical to and has the same effect on your behavior as the obviousness of all risks, including death.

To cut right to the core of the majority's faulty reasoning, the majority completely misreads MCL 600.2948(2), and, in doing so, reaches the erroneous conclusion that obviousness of *one* risk means obviousness of *all* risks. . . .

[In reaching its conclusion] the majority rewrites the statute and, consequently, fails to effectuate the protections the Legislature intended. Had the Legislature intended what the majority holds, it would have written the statute as follows: "A defendant is not liable for failure to warn of *any* material risk when *a* material risk should be obvious to a reasonably prudent product user. . . ." Or it would have stated, "A defendant need not warn about *all* material risks if *one* material risk should be obvious to a reasonably prudent product user. . . ." Plainly, it did not write the statute that way, and the majority errs by ignoring the unambiguous language. . . .

KELLY, J. (dissenting).

. . .

The majority dismisses the product label's inclusion of "eight natural oils" and simply asserts that "[i]t should be obvious to a reasonably prudent product user that many oils, although natural, pose a material risk if ingested or inhaled." It also concludes that, "[g]iven such unfamiliar ingredients, a reasonably prudent product user would be, or should be, loath to ingest it."

I disagree. The vast majority of the ingredients listed on the label are seemingly edible food products. They include avocado oil, coconut oil, and wheat germ oil. Also, the label contains a number of safely ingestible herbs: rosemary, sage, angelica root, licorice root, Job's tears, cedar, clove, lemon balm, and chamomile. In addition, the product label announces that it contains Vitamins E, A, and D. None of these ingredients alerts a reasonably prudent product user to the fatal result of ingesting them. On the contrary, they seem harmless and inviting. . . .

Conclusion

Here, the majority improperly holds as a matter of law that Wonder 8 Hair Oil's material fatal risk was open and obvious. It finds that all reasonable users of this product should be aware that swallowing or inhaling it can result in death. Like the Court of Appeals, I do not believe that is true. The question whether the material risk is open and obvious is for the jury to decide.

I would reverse the trial court's grant of summary disposition to defendants and remand the case to the trial court for further proceedings.

When reasonable persons can differ as to the obviousness of the danger, the issue is for the trier of fact. See, e.g., Stanley v. Aeroquip Corp., 181 F.3d 103 (6th Cir. 1999); Osontoski v. Wal-Mart Stores, Inc., 143 F.3d 1027 (6th Cir. 1998); Lagano v. Chrysler Corp., 141 F.3d 1151 (2d Cir. 1998).

A relevant factor in determining the obviousness of the risk is the expertise of the class of users for whom the product is intended. In Antcliff v. State Employees Credit Union, 327 N.W.2d 814 (Mich. 1982), the plaintiff was seriously and permanently injured when the support system of a powered scaffold on which he was standing unexpectedly gave way and fell to the ground. Plaintiff's safety line apparently failed, and he fell with the scaffold. Plaintiff and a co-worker personally designed the support system and rigged the scaffold. The scaffold was manufactured and sold by the defendant to the plaintiff's employer. The plaintiff claimed that the defendant owed a duty to provide warnings and instructions concerning how the scaffold should be set up, and that failure to provide such warnings caused the accident. The Michigan high court affirmed the lower court's denial of this claim as a matter of law, on the ground that defendant owed no duty to warn knowledgeable, experienced users:

> [P]laintiff and his co-worker were both journeyman painters. In view of their knowledge and experience as riggers, we feel constrained to charge them with full appreciation of the danger of inadequately supporting the scaffold on which they worked. As a result, the circumstances here (a non-defective product lacking in dangerous propensities and a known or obvious product-connected danger) do not support application of the policy which would require [the defendant] to provide instructions for the safe rigging of its product.
>
> Moreover, the contrary conclusion would lead to demonstrably unfair and unintended results. There are countless skilled operations, such as the rigging of scaffolding, which involve otherwise non-dangerous products in potentially dangerous situations. A manufacturer of such a product should be able to presume mastery of the basic operation. The more so when, as here, the manufacturer affirmatively and successfully limits the market of its product to professionals. In such a case, the manufacturer should not be burdened with the often difficult task of providing instructions on how to properly perform the basic operation. [Id. at 821.]

See also Carrell v. Nat'l Cord & Braid Corp., 852 N.E.2d 100, 104 (Mass. 2006) ("[W]e explicitly adopt the 'sophisticated user doctrine' as an affirmative defense in product liability actions.") (footnote omitted).

How should courts react when it is not so clear that the class of users knew of the risks, but it is clear that the individual plaintiff knew? Should such a case be dealt with under the heading of "duty," as in *Antcliff*, or under some other heading, such as "proximate causation," or "assumption of the risk?" In Wick v. Wabash Holding Corp., 801 F. Supp. 2d 93, 106 (W.D.N.Y. 2011), the court observed that "[n]o duty to warn arises when the injured party is already aware of the specific hazard. . . . Under such circumstances, 'the failure to warn was therefore not a cause of the harm'" (quoting Burke v. Spartanics, Ltd., 252 F.3d 131, 139 (2d Cir. 2001)).

Some courts use terminology other than "duty" and "proximate cause" to deny plaintiff's recovery. For example, in Raimbeault v. Takeuchi, 772 A.2d 1056 (R.I. 2001), the Supreme Court of Rhode Island spoke in terms of "assumption of the risk" to arrive at a similar result. In affirming judgment for the defendant, the court noted that ample testimony from the plaintiff at trial, which showed that plaintiff had five years of experience with the excavator that caused his injuries, indicated his awareness of the risks involved in using an earth-mover with a rotating cab on an embankment.

Alcoholic beverages have generated cases in which the obviousness of the risks has been the subject of controversy. The general rule is that the risks of excessive drinking are obvious. See, e.g., Cook v. MillerCoors, LLC, 872 F. Supp. 2d 1346 (M.D. Fla.

2012) (holding that the risks of consuming excessive amounts of an alcoholic beverage are reasonably obvious even though the beverage in question was also marketed as an energy drink); Maguire v. Pabst Brewing Co., 387 N.W.2d 565 (Iowa 1986) (holding that the defendant had no duty to warn of the dangers of drinking beer prior to driving automobile); Brown Forman Corp. v. Brune, 893 S.W.2d 640 (Tex. App. 1994) (holding that the defendant had no duty to warn of the dangers of rapidly consuming a large quantity of tequila). But there have been rare exceptions. For instance, in Hon v. Stroh Brewery Co., 835 F.2d 510 (3d Cir. 1987), the plaintiff's husband died from pancreatitis at the age of 26. Medical experts supported the plaintiff's claim that relatively moderate consumption of beer distributed by the defendant — two or three cans per night on an average of four nights a week for a period of six years — caused his fatal disease. The district court granted summary judgment for the defendant, relying on the general rule that the risks of drinking alcohol are widely known. The court of appeals reversed, concluding:

> [The medical] affidavits provide evidence tending to show that beer in the quantity and manner [decedent] consumed it can have fatal consequences. Nothing in the record suggests that [decedent] was aware of this fact, however. Moreover [one medical] affidavit tends to show that the general public is unaware that consumption at this level and in this manner can have any serious adverse effects. There is no evidence in the record that the public appreciates any hazard that may be associated with this kind of consumption. [Id. at 514.]

Did this case involve risk reduction, informed choice, or both?

The Federal Alcoholic Beverage Labeling Act of 1988, 27 U.S.C.A. §215 et seq., contains the following provisions:

> Section 215(a). Statement required on container. On and after the expiration of the 12-month period following the date of enactment of this title, it shall be unlawful for any person to manufacture, import, or bottle for sale or distribution in the United States any alcoholic beverage unless the container of such beverage bears the following statement:
>
> **GOVERNMENT WARNING:** (1) According to the Surgeon General, women should not drink alcoholic beverages during pregnancy because of the risk of birth defects. (2) Consumption of alcoholic beverages impairs your ability to drive a car or operate machinery, and may cause health problems.
>
> Section 216. No statement relating to alcoholic beverages and health, other than the statement required by section 215 of this title, shall be required under State law to be placed on any container of an alcoholic beverage, or on any box, carton, or other package, irrespective of the material from which made, that contains such a container.

What effect should this statute have on claims such as the one in *Hon,* supra, that accrue after the effective date of the statute?

Not all legislatively or administratively imposed product warnings take the form of bare factual information such as the foregoing Surgeon General's warning. In 2009, Congress authorized the Food & Drug Administration (FDA) to develop and impose nine new warnings for tobacco products. The FDA finalized the required warnings, some of which included graphic images of smokers ravaged by illnesses attributed to their smoking habit. Several tobacco companies challenged the mandate as an unconstitutional compulsion of speech. The D.C. Circuit Court of Appeals agreed in R.J.

Reynolds Tobacco Co. v. U.S. Food & Drug Admin., 696 F.3d 1205 (D.C. Cir. 2012), holding that the FDA did not provide substantial evidence that graphic warnings on cigarette advertising would directly advance its substantial interest in reducing smoking rates to a material degree. Rather than press its case before the Supreme Court, the FDA withdrew its graphic warning rule in 2013. See Nathan Cortez, Do Graphic Tobacco Warnings Violate the First Amendment?, 64 Hastings L.J. 1467,1486 (2013).

PROBLEM EIGHTEEN

A senior partner in the law firm in which you are an associate has asked for input in a products case he is handling on behalf of Starbrite Pools, Inc., a major manufacturer of above-ground swimming pools. The plaintiff is Jack Parent, age 19, who broke his neck in a diving accident nine months ago in one of Starbrite's pools. The complaint is lengthy and complicated, and contains a number of different claims. The partner wants your assistance in connection with the failure-to-warn claim. The plaintiff alleges that nine months ago he was visiting the home of neighbors, Ed and Alice Bancroft, who had invited him and his younger sisters over for an afternoon swim in their backyard swimming pool. The Bancrofts had bought the pool four years earlier from a Starbrite retail outlet, and had paid Starbrite personnel to set up the pool in their backyard. The pool was oval-shaped, 12 feet by 24 feet, and uniformly four feet in depth. Ed Bancroft had built a sturdy wooden deck level with the top of the side of the pool closest to the house, on which the Bancrofts had placed lawn furniture. The vinyl liner of the pool indicated, in four-inch contrasting lettering facing inwards just below the top of the side of the pool and just above the water level, that the water was three and one-half feet deep. The lettering read "3 feet deep" and ran, at one-foot intervals, around the entire inner circumference of the pool.

The plaintiff and his family had just moved into the neighborhood, and had never used the pool before that day. When he and his sisters arrived at the Bancroft's house dressed in their bathing suits, they went immediately to the pool area, walked up steps to the poolside wooden deck, and took off their shoes and outer garments preparatory to going swimming. His two sisters entered the pool by sitting on the decking at the edge and sliding feet first into the water. Jack dove head-first into the water, struck his head on the unyielding pool bottom, and broke his neck. He was rendered a quadriplegic, a permanent condition.

The complaint claims that Starbrite should have warned swimmers not to dive into the pool and that doing so would likely lead to severe and permanent injury, including quadriplegia. The complaint does not allege specifically what Starbrite should have said, or how it should have said it to people using the pool. It simply asserts that the failure to provide any warning at all rendered the pool defective and that the failure-to-warn defect proximately caused the plaintiff's injuries.

The partner explains that the lawyers representing the plaintiff are experienced trial lawyers and will argue effectively for their client. It appears that they have lined up an expert witness, a qualified cognitive psychologist, whom the partner has seen in action before. She will testify that an adequate warning in this case could have served as a "prompt," reminding swimmers such as Jack Parent of the danger of diving that, while understood abstractly, tends to get suppressed from consciousness in the excitement of the moment. Also, the expert will almost certainly rely on the "optimism bias" in her testimony — a built-in tendency for otherwise rational people to assume that "it can't happen to me." Vivid, even shocking, warnings can bring reality home to such actors, penetrating and offsetting the otherwise potentially disastrous effects of this cognitive bias.

The partner wants your "take" on the plaintiff's failure-to-warn claim. In responding to his query, you are to assume that the high court of your state recognizes §2(c) and comment *j* of the Products Liability Restatement, supra, as accurate statements of the relevant law. Should the plaintiff be required to propose specifically what the warning should have been? Can we fashion an argument that any feasible warning would not have made a difference? How can we counter, or exclude entirely, plaintiff's expert? Do you think the plaintiff will reach the jury with his failure-to-warn claim?

TO SPEAK OR NOT TO SPEAK; "DIGGING YOUR OWN GRAVE WITH THE BEST OF INTENTIONS"

Imagine that you are general counsel to a medium-sized manufacturer of a product whose risks are pretty obvious to the average user but arguably are not obvious to a subset of foreseeable (though by no means typical) users who for various reasons do not appreciate the risks (e.g., they are particularly young or particularly old, they are non-English speakers, they are unfamiliar with advanced technology, they suffer a learning disability). The question is whether you will advise the manufacturer to warn this unaware minority of users, assuming that the warning could be attached to the product and would likely reach those users. Or rather, the question is what considerations you should weigh in deciding what is the best advice to render. The marketing people tell you they don't like warnings. "Most of our users don't need them, and they hurt our product image," they insist. But if the savings in liability would be significant, the CEO indicates that he will use them. How would you set about to assess the value to the company of going ahead and warning about fairly obvious risks?

The purpose of this note is to raise the possibility that supplying a warning in such a context might increase, rather than decrease, the company's exposure to liability. Without any warning, you will be able to argue on behalf of the client that the risk is obvious and no reasonable person would seriously consider warning of it. You may lose the argument, but at least it can be made with a straight face. But once some kind of warning is provided, the "no duty" argument is more difficult to make — the warning itself works as an admission by the company, in effect, that an underlying duty to warn was owed. You may still argue that the warning was sufficient, of course. But the question of whether an admitted duty to warn was breached sounds like a question of fact for the jury. Although there is of course the possibility that the warning will work as intended and avoid some amount of harm that would have otherwise occurred, you might actually increase your overall exposure to liability by warning rather than choosing not to warn. And if you try to make the warning against low-level risks strong enough to be impervious to attack, the gripes of the marketing people will be (even if they were not before) well grounded.

A case presenting the possibility of a manufacturer incurring such self-inflicted wounds is May v. Dafoe, 611 P.2d 1275 (Wash. Ct. App.), *review denied*, 93 Wash. 2d 1030 (1980). An incubator manufacturer went ahead and warned its users (medical personnel) against administering too-high concentrations of oxygen to premature infants (too much oxygen can cause blindness), even though it insisted that it owed no duty to warn doctors about the current state of medical research. The plaintiff argued that the doctor who administered oxygen to the injured infant misunderstood, and assumed that if lower concentrations were used, the duration of use did not matter. In fact, duration mattered as much as concentration, and the baby was blinded. The court of appeals affirmed a directed verdict for the defendant-manufacturer, reiterating the view that manufacturers owe no duty to warn doctors about the current state of medical research, but only about the design, engineering, and functional dangers associated with their products.

The defendant in *May* escaped the fate of having dug its own grave. But should it have escaped? And will the next such defendant be so fortunate, regardless of the merits of the plaintiff's case?

PROBLEM NINETEEN

The vice president in charge of marketing for a medium-sized television antenna manufacturer in your area seeks your advice concerning the instructions and/or warnings that should accompany his company's products. More particularly, he is concerned with what he refers to as a "rash of incidents" in recent months involving injuries and deaths caused when persons (typically unskilled "do-it-yourselfers") allow the antennae to come in contact with uninsulated power lines while installing the antennae on rooftops and other high places. A few of these accidents have involved his own products; a greater number have involved products manufactured and distributed by others. "You would think that the risks were obvious," he says. "But something must be breaking down. Should we include in our packaging, for the first time, warnings about the risks of power lines? No one else does it. But should we be the first?" Making reasonable assumptions where necessary, advise him on this matter.

4. Informed-Choice Warnings

The terminology of "informed choice" bothers some people. See Authors' Dialogue 19, infra. Obviously, a product user or consumer's threshold decision not to use or consume the product in the first instance has risk-reduction implications, but these materials reserve the phrase "risk reduction warnings" for situations in which adequately informed users and consumers can "have their cake and eat it too" — situations in which, when adequate instructions and warnings are given, they can go ahead and derive the benefits from use or consumption and yet reduce or avoid the risks of which the instructions and warnings inform them. In contrast, the phrase "informed choice" connotes an "eat the cake or don't eat it" situation. As with all legal distinctions, this one gives way under pressure. Even in a classic case of the product user being able to use the product more safely thanks to clear warnings, the user may also decide to reduce his level of usage to reduce the residual risks of injury. And even when the warning says "One out of one million people who take this drug become blind as a result," the consumer who chooses to go ahead and take it can be on the lookout for early symptoms that might reduce the severity of his injury if he turns out (inescapably, once he decides to consume) to be one of the unlucky few. Still products liability observers have come to agree that informed choice deserves to be distinguished as a separate category of warning defect liability from risk reduction.

The earliest case recognizing a products liability informed-choice cause of action is Davis v. Wyeth Laboratories, Inc., 399 F.2d 121 (9th Cir. 1968). In that case, the defendant manufacturer sold polio vaccine without warning of the risk that one person in a million would contract polio from taking the vaccine. The court held that the manufacturer had a duty to warn the consumer of the risks involved and that the failure to meet this duty rendered the drug "unfit" and "unreasonably dangerous" within the meaning of §402A of the Second Restatement. The court stated:

> In such cases, then, the drug is fit and its danger is reasonable only if the balance is struck in favor of its use. Where the risk is otherwise known to the consumer, no problem is presented, since a choice is available. Where not known, however, the drug can properly be marketed only in such fashion as to permit the striking of the balance; that is, by full disclosure of the existence and extent of the risk involved. . . .
>
> There will, of course, be cases where the personal risk, although existent and known, is so trifling in comparison with the advantage to be gained as to be de minimis. Appellee so characterizes this case. It would approach the problem from a purely statistical point of view; less than one out of a million is just not unreasonable. This approach we reject. When, in a particular case, the risk qualitatively (e.g., of death or major disability) as well as quantitatively, on balance with the end sought to be achieved, is such as to call for a true choice judgment, medical or professional, the warning must be given. [Id. at 129-30.]

Two scholars (including one of the authors of this casebook) have argued that causation is too difficult to prove in informed-choice cases, especially in prescription drug cases. See Margaret A. Berger & Aaron D. Twerski, Uncertainty and Informed Choice: Unmasking *Daubert*, 104 Mich. L. Rev. 257 (2005). They "advocate a cause of action for negligent infliction of emotional distress when plaintiff is deprived of an informed choice about [a] material risk even if causation of the actual physical injury cannot be established with the certainty demanded by traditional causation norms." Id. at 285. Professors Berger and Twerski explain that, currently, drug manufacturers are able to escape liability after postponing issuing warnings of harmful side effects despite initial studies claiming a correlative/causative relationship. Even if those studies are later shown to be inconclusive, many of those patients, they say, would surely choose to forgo the treatment if the patients were informed of even minor possibilities of harmful side effects. A challenging response from Professor David Berstein asserts that the Berger-Twerski proposal would have numerous negative effects, including opening the floodgates of litigation, encouraging unreliable testimony, requiring too much expertise from juries, and reducing the effectiveness of warnings by causing a proliferation of warnings about all conceivable side effects. See David E. Berstein, Learning the Wrong Lessons from "An American Tragedy": A Critique of Berger-Twerski Informed Choice Proposal, 104 Mich. L. Rev. 1961 (2006). Professors Berger and Twerski respond in Margaret A. Berger & Aaron D. Twerski, From the Wrong End of the Telescope: A Response to Professor David Berstein, 104 Mich. L. Rev. 1983 (2006).

The informed-choice theory was extended beyond prescription drugs to impose liability against asbestos manufacturers in favor of industrial insulation workers who suffered asbestosis and mesothelioma after exposure over a thirty-year period to insulation products containing asbestos. In Borel v. Fiberboard Paper Products Corp., 493 F.2d 1076, 1088 (5th Cir. 1973), *cert. denied*, 419 U.S. 869 (1974), the court held that under §402A "a seller has a responsibility to inform users and consumers of dangers which the seller either knows or should know at the time the product is sold. The requirement that the danger be reasonably foreseeable, or scientifically discoverable, is an important limitation of the seller's liability." The court acknowledged that the "requirement of foreseeability coincides with the standard of due care in negligence cases in that a seller must exercise reasonable care and foresight to discover a danger in his product and to warn users and consumers of that danger." Id.

The court went on to note that the utility of insulation products containing asbestos may outweigh the known foreseeable risk to insulation workers and thus justify their marketing. But it reasoned that the failure to give adequate warnings may render the products unreasonably dangerous:

> The rationale for this rule is that the user or consumer is entitled to make his own choice as to whether the product's utility or benefits justify exposing himself to the risk of harm. Thus, a true choice situation arises, and a duty to warn attaches, whenever a reasonable man would want to be informed of the risk in order to decide whether to expose himself to it. [Id. at 1089.]

Comment *i* to §2 of the Products Liability Restatement agrees with the thrust of these cases. It provides:

> (i) Inadequate Instructions or Warnings . . .
> In addition to alerting users and consumers to the existence and nature of product risks so that they can, by appropriate conduct during use or consumption, reduce the risk of harm, warnings also may be needed to inform users and consumers of nonobvious and not generally known risks that unavoidably inhere in using or consuming the product. Such warnings allow the user or consumer to avoid the risk warned against by making an informed decision not to purchase or use the product at all and hence not to encounter the risk. In this context, warnings must be provided for inherent risks that reasonably foreseeable product users and consumers would reasonably deem material or significant in deciding whether to use or consume the product. Whether or not many persons would, when warned, nonetheless decide to use or consume the product, warnings are required to protect the interests of those reasonably foreseeable users or consumers who would, based on their own reasonable assessments of the risks and benefits, decline product use or consumption. When such warnings are necessary, their omission renders the product not reasonably safe at time of sale. Notwithstanding the defective condition of the product in the absence of adequate warnings, if a particular user or consumer would have decided to use or consume even if warned, the lack of warnings is not a legal cause of that plaintiff's harm. Judicial decisions supporting the duty to provide warnings for informed decision-making have arisen almost exclusively with regard to those toxic agents and pharmaceutical products with respect to which courts have recognized a distinctive need to provide risk information so that recipients of the information can decide whether they wish to purchase or utilize the product. . . .

See, e.g., Edwards v. Hop Sin, Inc., 140 S.W.3d 13 (Ky. Ct. App. 2003) (citing Comment *i* and remanding to trial court on whether restaurant was liable for failure to warn of bacteria in raw oyster).

In Watkins v. Ford Motor Co., 190 F.3d 1213 (11th Cir. 1999), the plaintiff claimed that the defendant failed to warn adequately of the risks of rollover in a Ford Bronco II. Ford argued that no driver could have prevented the emergency situation that led to the rollover that injured the plaintiff. Quoting Comment *i*, supra, the court held that a warning might have led the plaintiff not to take the risk in the first instance. Id. at 1219.

PROBLEM TWENTY

You just received the following memorandum from a partner in the law firm in which you are an associate:

Memorandum

To: Associate
From: Barb Fischel
Subject: Applicability of strict liability in *Borel*-type cases

I am working on a case in which our client, Jeffrey Polsby, is dying from liver cancer that we maintain was caused by his exposure to chemical solvents at his workplace over a period of 17 years. We claim that the defendant solvent manufacturer failed adequately to warn our client of the cancer risks associated with long-term exposure to its product. The case is fairly close to *Borel* on its facts, and I think we will reach the jury on our failure-to-warn count against the manufacturer.

One aspect of the case bothers me, however, and I would like your reactions to it. Our case on behalf of Mr. Polsby is weaker than *Borel* in one respect — the manufacturer in our case did supply the employer with warning signs that the employer posted in the shop where Polsby worked. The signs told the workers that continued exposure to the solvent could cause serious liver damage, and instructed them to wear latex gloves while using the solvent and to avoid direct contact with the skin. We insist that the warnings were inadequate (no mention of cancer, foreseeable that workers would ignore signs when no symptoms had appeared after years of exposure, etc.), but we could lose on this issue. What bothers me is why the manufacturer should get off the hook even if the warnings are found to be adequate.

Our investigation into the background data reveals that approximately one out of 20,000 or so workers will develop liver cancer (a greater-than-normal cancer rate) from long-term exposure (eight years or longer) to the solvent, notwithstanding efforts to avoid direct contact. Suppose that the manufacturer had spelled that fact out in grisly detail in its warnings: "You have a one in 20,000 chance of getting liver cancer if you choose to continue to work with this product, compared with a one in 200,000 chance in the general population not exposed to the product. Thus, your chances of getting liver cancer, while still remote, will be ten times greater than would otherwise be the case if you were not exposed to this product." Let us assume that such a warning, posted on the worker's first day of exposure to the solvent, would meet the test set forth in Borel v. Fibreboard. My question is why that should get the manufacturer off the liability hook. Imagine that the worker had gone into a new car dealership and bought a new automobile. If a sign were posted on the windshield: "Warning! There is a 1/20,000 chance that this vehicle contains a latent defect that will cause a harmful accident!" Would that get the manufacturer off the hook if a defect caused a harmful accident? Of course not — Henningsen v. Bloomfield Motors taught us that much before I went to law school. So why should a "1/20,000 warning" about liver cancer be treated differently?

Putting the question a little differently, if *Henningsen* teaches us that consumers are not in a position to understand and act intelligently in reaction to warnings about remote risks of defect-caused injury, why should the manufacturer in our chemical solvent case be allowed to escape liability on that basis? If you think there is something to my argument that *Borel*'s reliance on the idea of "consumer choice" is misplaced, then I am inclined to want to include it in my trial brief, in case we can't sell the judge and jury on our view of the facts.

Respond to the partner's memorandum.

Now, for an eye-opener. In the following case, Judge Guido Calabresi potentially moved informed choice theory into an entirely new sphere.

Liriano v. Hobart Corp.
170 F.3d 264 (2d Cir. 1999)

CALABRESI, Circuit Judge:

In Liriano v. Hobart Corp., 132 F.3d 124 (2d Cir. 1998) ("Liriano I"), we certified to the New York Court of Appeals the question of whether a manufacturer can be liable under a failure-to-warn theory in a case in which the substantial modification defense would preclude liability under a design defect theory. We also certified the question of whether, if failure-to-warn liability could exist, it would nonetheless be unavailable as a matter of law on the facts of the present case. The New York Court of Appeals answered the first question in the affirmative and declined to answer the second. See Liriano v. Hobart Corp., 700 N.E.2d 303 (1998) ("Liriano II"). Consequently, we now address the second question ourselves, and we find it to be a close one. Viewing the facts, as we must, in the light most favorable to the plaintiff, we resolve that question in the negative. We also find that all other claims the appellants have raised on appeal lack merit. We therefore affirm the decision of the district court granting judgment and damages for the plaintiff. . . .

Background

[The following recitation of the facts is taken from "Liriano I."]

Luis Liriano, a seventeen-year-old employee in the meat department at Super Associated grocery store ("Super"), was injured on the job in September 1993 when he was feeding meat into a commercial meat grinder whose safety guard had been removed. His hand was caught in the "worm" that grinds the meat; as a result, his right hand and lower forearm were amputated.

The meat grinder was manufactured and sold in 1961 by Hobart Corporation ("Hobart"). At the time of the sale, it had an affixed safety guard that prevented the user's hands from coming into contact with the feeding tube and the grinding "worm." No warnings were placed on the machine or otherwise given to indicate that it was dangerous to operate the machine without the safety guard in place. Subsequently, Hobart became aware that a significant number of purchasers of its meat grinders had removed the safety guards. And in 1962, Hobart began issuing warnings on its meat grinders concerning removal of the safety guard.

There is no dispute that, when Super acquired the grinder, the safety guard was intact. It is also not contested that, at the time of Liriano's accident, the safety guard had been removed. There is likewise no doubt that Hobart actually knew, before the accident, that removals of this sort were occurring and that use of the machine without the safety guard was highly dangerous. And Super does not question that the removal of the guard took place while the grinder was in its possession.

Liriano sued Hobart under several theories, including failure to warn. Hobart brought a third-party claim against Super. The United States District Court . . . dismissed all of Liriano's claims except the one based on failure to warn, and the jury returned a verdict for Liriano on that claim. It attributed five percent of the liability to Hobart and ninety-five percent to Super. The district court then held a partial retrial limited to the issue of whether and to what extent Liriano was responsible for his own injury. On that retrial, the jury assigned Liriano one-third of the fault. . . .

Hobart and Super appealed, arguing (1) that as a matter of law, there was no duty to warn, and (2) that even if there had been a duty to warn, the evidence presented was not sufficient to allow the failure-to-warn claim to reach the jury. . . . We certified questions (1) and (2) to the New York Court of Appeals. That Court answered question (1) in Liriano's favor, saying that there can indeed be a duty to warn in a case like this one. The Court of Appeals, however, declined to answer question (2). . . .

Discussion

A. Sufficiency of the Evidence

Hobart makes two arguments challenging the sufficiency of the evidence. The first concerns the obviousness of the danger that Liriano faced, and the second impugns the causal relationship between Hobart's negligence and Liriano's injury. Each of these arguments implicates issues long debated in the law of torts. With respect to the asserted clarity of the danger, the question is when a danger is so obvious that a court can determine, as a matter of law, that no additional warning is required. With respect to causation, the issue is whether a jury may infer that a defendant's particular negligence was the cause-in-fact of a plaintiff's actual injury from the general fact that negligence like the defendant's tends to cause injuries like the plaintiff's. . . .

(1) Obviousness

The courts of New York have several times . . . ruled that judges should be very wary of taking the issue of liability away from juries, even in situations where the relevant dangers might seem obvious, and especially when the cases in question turn on particularized facts. See, e.g., . . . Cabri v. Long Island R.R. Co., 306 N.Y. 765, 118 N.E.2d 475 (1954) (holding that the danger of crossing railroad tracks is not so obvious as to prevent the issue of contributory negligence from reaching the jury). . . .

But the . . . tendency of the New York Court of Appeals to permit issues of obviousness to go to the jury do not fully dispose of the question before us. . . . And it is not surprising that there have been situations in which New York state courts have deemed dangers to be sufficiently clear so that warnings were, as a matter of law, not necessary. See, e.g., Dickerson v. George J. Meyer Mfg., . . . 669 N.Y.S.2d 1001, 1002 (4th Dep't 1998) (holding that there is no duty to warn of the danger of closely examining the mechanical workings of a machine while the machine is operating); Pigliavento v. Tyler Equip. Corp., . . . 669 N.Y.S.2d 747, 749 (3d Dep't 1998) (holding that there is no duty to warn of the danger of falling from an unguarded platform on a concrete mixer truck); Carvis v. Mele, . . . 521 N.Y.S.2d 260, 261 (2d Dep't 1987) (holding that there is no duty to warn of the danger of diving headfirst into an above-ground swimming pool only four feet deep).

If the question before us were, therefore, simply whether meat grinders are sufficiently known to be dangerous so that manufacturers would be justified in believing that further warnings were not needed, we might be in doubt. On one hand, . . . most New Yorkers would probably appreciate the danger of meat grinders [without warning]. Any additional warning might seem superfluous. On the other hand, Liriano was only seventeen years old at the time of his injury and had only recently immigrated to the United States. He had been on the job at Super for only one week. He had never been given instructions about how to use the meat grinder, and he had used the meat grinder only two or three times. And, as Judge Scheindlin noted, the mechanism that injured Liriano would not have been visible to someone who was operating the grinder. It could be argued that such a combination of facts was not so unlikely that a court should say, as a matter of law, that the defendant could not have foreseen them or, if aware of them, need not have guarded against them by issuing a warning. That argument would draw strength from the Court of Appeals' direction that the question of whether a warning was needed must be asked in terms of the information available to the injured party rather than the injured party's employer, 700 N.E.2d at 308, and its added comment that "in cases where reasonable minds might disagree as to the extent of the plaintiff's knowledge of the hazard, the question is one for the jury." Id.

Nevertheless, it remains the fact that meat grinders are widely known to be dangerous. Given that the position of the New York courts on the specific question before us is anything but obvious, we might well be of two minds as to whether a failure to warn that meat grinders are dangerous would be enough to raise a jury issue.

But to state the issue that way would be to misunderstand the complex functions of warnings. As two distinguished torts scholars have pointed out, a warning can do more than exhort its audience to be careful. It can also affect what activities the people warned choose to engage in. See James A. Henderson, Jr., and Aaron D. Twerski, Doctrinal Collapse in Products Liability: The Empty Shell of Failure to Warn, 65 N.Y.U. L. Rev. 265, 285 (1990). And where the function of a warning is to assist the reader in making choices, the value of the warning can lie as much in making known the existence of alternatives as in communicating the fact that a particular choice is dangerous. It follows that the duty to warn is not necessarily obviated merely because a danger is clear.

To be more concrete, a warning can convey at least two types of messages. One states that a particular place, object, or activity is dangerous. Another explains that people need not risk the danger posed by such a place, object, or activity in order to achieve the purpose for which they might have taken that risk. Thus, a highway sign that says "Danger — Steep Grade" says less than a sign that says "Steep Grade Ahead — Follow Suggested Detour to Avoid Dangerous Areas."

If the hills or mountains responsible for the steep grade are plainly visible, the first sign merely states what a reasonable person would know without having to be warned. The second sign tells drivers what they might not have otherwise known: that there is another road that is flatter and less hazardous. A driver who believes the road through the mountainous area to be the only way to reach her destination might well choose to drive on that road despite the steep grades, but a driver who knows herself to have an alternative might not, even though her understanding of the risks posed by the steep grade is exactly the same as those of the first driver. Accordingly, a certain level of obviousness as to the grade of a road might, in principle, eliminate the reason for posting a sign of the first variety. But no matter how patently steep the road, the second kind of sign might still have a beneficial effect. As a result, the duty to post a sign of the second variety may persist even when the danger of the road is obvious and a sign of the first type would not be warranted.

One who grinds meat, like one who drives on a steep road, can benefit not only from being told that his activity is dangerous, but from being told of a safer way. As we have said, one can argue about whether the risk involved in grinding meat is sufficiently obvious that a responsible person would fail to warn of that risk, believing reasonably that it would convey no helpful information. But if it is also the case — as it is — that the risk posed by meat grinders can feasibly be reduced by attaching a safety guard, we have a different question. Given that attaching guards is feasible, does reasonable care require that meat workers be informed that they need not accept the risks of using unguarded grinders? Even if most ordinary users may — as a matter of law — know of the risk of using a guardless meat grinder, it does not follow that a sufficient number of them will — as a matter of law — also know that protective guards are available, that using them is a realistic possibility, and that they may ask that such guards be used. It is precisely these last pieces of information that a reasonable manufacturer may have a duty to convey even if the danger of using a grinder were itself deemed obvious.

Consequently, the instant case does not require us to decide the difficult question of whether New York would consider the risk posed by meat grinders to be obvious as a matter of law. A jury could reasonably find that there exist people who are employed as meat grinders and who do not know (a) that it is feasible to reduce the risk with safety guards, (b) that such guards are made available with the grinders, and (c) that the grinders should be used only with the guards. Moreover, a jury can also reasonably find that there are enough such people, and that warning them is sufficiently inexpensive, that a reasonable manufacturer would inform them that safety guards exist and that the grinder is meant to be used only with such guards. Thus, even if New York would consider the danger of meat grinders to be obvious as a matter of law, that obviousness does not substitute for the warning that a jury could, and indeed did, find that Hobart had a duty to provide. It follows that we cannot say, as a matter of law, that Hobart had no duty to warn Liriano in the present case. We therefore decline to adopt appellants' argument that the issue of negligence was for the court only and that the jury was not entitled, on the evidence, to return a verdict for Liriano.

(2) Causation

On rebriefing following the Court of Appeals decision, Hobart has made another argument as to why the jury should not have been allowed to find for the plaintiff. In this argument, Hobart raises the issue of causation. It maintains that Liriano "failed to present any evidence that Hobart's failure to place a warning [on the machine] was causally related to his injury." Whether or not there had been a warning, Hobart says, Liriano might well have operated the machine as he did and suffered the injuries that he suffered. Liriano introduced no evidence, Hobart notes, suggesting either that he would have refused to grind meat had the machine borne a warning or that a warning would have persuaded Super not to direct its employees to use the grinder without the safety attachment.

Hobart's argument about causation follows logically from the notion that its duty to warn in this case merely required Hobart to inform Liriano that a guard was available and that he should not use an unguarded grinder. The contention is tightly reasoned, but it rests on a false premise. It assumes that the burden was on Liriano to introduce additional evidence showing that the failure to warn was a but-for cause of his injury, even after he had shown that Hobart's wrong greatly increased the likelihood of the harm that occurred. But Liriano does not bear that burden. When a defendant's negligent act is deemed wrongful precisely because it has a strong propensity to cause the type of injury that ensued, that very causal tendency is evidence enough to establish a *prima facie* case of cause-in-fact. The burden then shifts to the defendant to come forward with evidence that its negligence was *not* such a but-for cause. . . .

The district court did not err. We affirm its decision in all respects.

For a holding directly contrary to *Liriano,* see Chaney v. Hobart International, Inc., 54 F. Supp. 2d 677 (E.D. La. 1999). On facts almost identical to *Liriano* the Louisiana federal district court granted defendant's motion for summary judgment on plaintiff's claim that adequate warning was not provided about the dangers of using the meat grinder without a feed pan in place. The court reasoned that "[a]s dangerous as the meat grinder may have been without a feed pan guard, it was clearly 'not dangerous to an extent beyond that which would be contemplated by the ordinary consumer.' The possibility of injury is glaring."

For a thoughtful analysis of *Liriano* and the informed-choice approach to duty to warn, see Robert G. Knaier, Note, An Informed-Choice Duty to Instruct? *Liriano*, *Burke*, and the Practical Limits of Subtle Jurisprudence, 88 Cornell L. Rev. 814 (2003), in which the author argues that *Liriano* recognized a subtle, but coherent, duty to warn. He cautions, however, that *Liriano* threatens to undermine practical limitations on liability by enabling nearly every well-pled failure to warn claim to reach the jury. For a sharp critique of *Liriano,* see Hildy Bowbeer & David S. Killorian, *Liriano v. Hobart Corporation*: Obvious Dangers, The Duty to Warn of Safe Alternatives and the Heeding Presumption, 65 Brook. L. Rev. 717 (1999).

authors' dialogue 19

JIM: This "informed choice" terminology bothers me. I agree it captures the "threshold decision to use or consume" aspects of these cases, but that bit of clarity comes at a high price. "Informed choice" sounds too much like "informed consent" from medical malpractice.

AARON: What's wrong with that? The two situations are quite analogous, I think.

JIM: No, they're not. Informed consent in malpractice conjures notions of the patient consenting to physical contacts that would otherwise constitute highly offensive invasions of the patient's personal dignity. It has the feel of battery law about it. Personal sovereignty is at issue.

DOUG: You're talking ancient history, Jim. In medical malpractice, informed consent in most states no longer involves battery. It's now part of the law of negligence — much less personal and moralistic.

JIM: Reasonableness may be the test for what a doctor must tell the patient, but from there on it has the look and feel of battery. If the doc doesn't get informed consent, the doc is strictly liable for bad outcomes. But let's not rehash malpractice law. In the products setting, the personal invasion implications of "informed choice" can lead to remarkably wrong-headed conclusions.

AARON: Give us an example, Jim. That might be more, well, informative.

JIM: *Liriano* is the poster-child. When Judge Calabresi invokes the idea of informed choice on behalf of the young worker, he transforms the case into an invasion of the plaintiff's personal dignity. All of a sudden, instead of being concerned with whether a warning would've saved the kid's arm, it becomes a matter of punishing the manufacturer for not having treated him with sufficient respect to tell him that an alternative — the safety guard — was theoretically available. Even if the kid couldn't do anything about it, the manufacturer became implicated in the employer's exploitation of immigrant laborers.

DOUG: Even if your diagnosis is accurate, I'm not sure that's so bad in that case. By keeping the manufacturer on the hook, even by using the "pixie dust" of informed choice, almost all of the liability ended up, via contribution, where it belonged — in the employer's lap.

JIM: That last point gives me some comfort. But using informed choice that way is bound to cause mischief down the road, don't you agree?

AARON: Let us think about it before we make an informed choice whether to use or consume your conclusions.

5. *Who Must Warn Whom?*

In some cases it is clear that a manufacturer has a duty to warn about dangers associated with the use of its product. However, the question to whom the warning should be directed is unclear. Must the manufacturer find a way to communicate with the ultimate consumer?

Persons v. Salomon North America, Inc., 265 Cal. Rptr. 773 (Cal. Ct. App. 1990) is a leading case. A skier suffered leg injuries when her ski bindings failed to release during a fall. She joined a number of defendants, including the bindings manufacturer and the ski shop where she had rented the skis with the defendant's bindings attached. The plaintiff claimed that the manufacturer had not warned her directly (it had warned the ski shop) that the bindings were incompatible with her boots, causing their failure to release. The only claim that went to trial was against the binding manufacturer; the jury returned a verdict for defendant. On appeal, the plaintiff argued that the trial court erred in denying her motion for summary judgment — the defendant owed her a duty to warn and supplied no warning to her. The court of appeals affirmed the judgment for defendant, concluding:

> The evidence establishes that Salomon 444 bindings do not pose a danger unless used with nonstandard or untreated thermoplastic boots. Once it has distributed its bindings to rental shops such as Cornice, Salomon has no practical way, other than warning and educating the rental shops of the danger, to control its product to see that the bindings are not used with untreated thermoplastic boots. Moreover, issuance of an effective warning depends upon proper identification of the skier's boot. Salomon cannot be expected to know the identity of the ultimate user of its rental bindings much less the type of boot the consumer is using. However, the ski shop technician has direct contact with each customer and has the ability, applying Salomon's technical manual and seminar training, to identify a customer's boot, assess its compatibility with Salomon bindings, lubricate the boot if necessary and set a safe release level.
>
> Having provided a warning to Salomon dealers, defendant had a reasonable basis to believe Cornice would pass along the product warning and was justified in relying upon Cornice to perform its independent duty to warn as required by law. . . . [Id. at 779.]

In Gonzalez v. Volvo of Am. Corp., 752 F.2d 295 (7th Cir. 1985), plaintiffs were injured when their Volvo station wagon ran off the road and overturned while pulling a U-Haul trailer. The plaintiffs claimed that a mismatch of the trailer hitch and the bumper caused the accident, and that defendant Volvo should have warned them about the risks. The court found for defendant Volvo as a matter of law because of a lack of foreseeability as well as the duties of the intermediary:

> We acknowledge that Section 402A imposed upon Volvo a duty to provide plaintiffs with a reasonably safe station wagon. In our opinion, however, this duty did not extend to a requirement to warn them that a particular trailer hitch was unsafe to use, particularly when it was installed as appropriate by a company engaged in the business of renting trailers. The intervention of a professional such as U-Haul is the rule and not the exception when consumers rent trailer hitches. It was the duty of such professionals and not the duty of defendant-appellant to select an appropriate hitch for plaintiffs. [Id. at 300.]

Consider another type of case where the primary user of the product may not be the person at the greatest risk of harm. In Patch v. Hillerich & Bradsby Co., 257 P.3d 383 (Mont. 2011), a high-school pitcher was fatally struck in the head by a baseball hit with defendant's aluminum bat. The child's family sued the bat manufacturer for an alleged design defect and for failure to warn of the enhanced risk of high-velocity batted balls associated with the aluminum bat's use. The trial court granted the defendant's summary judgment motion on the design defect claim but allowed the failure-to-warn claim to go to a jury, which awarded the plaintiffs $850,000. The Montana Supreme Court affirmed finding that bystanders, as well as the primary purchaser and user of the product (the batter), could raise a valid failure-to-warn claim when they were subject to the product's risks. The Court noted that allowing bystanders' claims comported with the "realities of the game of baseball." Id. at 388. The Court rejected the defendant's claim that providing such a warning would be "unworkable," explaining that the "workability" of a warning is a jury question and that placing warnings directly on the bat is not the only way to inform the public of the risks associated with a product.

Courts differ regarding whether manufacturers of component parts owe a duty to warn ultimate users of risks associated with the products in which their components are foreseeably incorporated. The general subject of component manufacturers' liability is taken up in Section A of Chapter Seven., infra. But it is useful in this "who/whom" context to consider the question of the component manufacturer's duty to warn ultimate users and consumers. Thus, in Maake v. Ross Operating Valve Co., 717 P.2d 923 (Ariz. Ct. App. 1985), the court recognized such a duty. Defendant manufactured palm buttons and pneumatic valves that had been installed in a sixty-year-old power press. Defendant was aware that its palm buttons and pneumatic valves are installed on power presses. Plaintiff suffered injury when the press cycled unexpectedly. Defendant had placed no warning, aimed at operators, on the safety devices that such cycling might occur. The court held that a jury might find defendant liable for failure to warn.

Whether a bulk supplier has a duty to warn all foreseeable users of the risks associated with a bulk product's ultimate use also implicates a "who/whom" problem. In Hoffman v. Houghton Chemical Corp., 751 N.E.2d 848 (Mass. 2001), the Supreme Judicial Court of Massachusetts affirmed judgment in favor of the defendant, a bulk supplier of toluene, a highly volatile and flammable chemical allegedly involved in an explosion that killed two workers and injured several others at an ink plant. The court adopted the "bulk supplier doctrine" as an affirmative defense in products liability actions, reasoning that the nature of bulk products requires separate consideration and that the bulk suppliers should be able to rely on the intermediary's own obligation to provide safety measures for end users. The court justified its holding as follows:

> Under the bulk supplier doctrine, the bulk supplier is by no means absolved of its duty either to supply adequate warnings to the intermediary or to ensure that its reliance on the intermediary is reasonable, but it is permitted to discharge its duty to warn in a practical and responsible way that equitably balances the realities of its business with the need for consumer safety. [Id. at 857.]

See also Gray v. Badger Mining Corp., 676 N.W.2d 268 (Minn. 2004) (holding that the duty of a supplier of sand to warn of the hazards of silica dust depended on the sophistication of the purchaser and purchaser's employees and on whether the bulk supplier had in fact adequately warned the purchaser; the level of sophistication and presence of an adequate warning were questions of fact for the jury to decide).

An underlying question in the foregoing materials is whether the manufacturer's duty to warn includes a duty to warn any and all persons who are in a position to act effectively on the information. Comment *i* to §2(c) of the Products Liability Restatement summarizes the case law as follows:

> Depending on the circumstances, Subsection (c) may require that instructions and warnings be given not only to purchasers, users, and consumers, but also to others who a reasonable seller should know will be in a position to reduce or avoid the risk of harm. There is no general rule as to whether one supplying a product for the use of others through an intermediary has a duty to warn the ultimate product user directly or may rely on the intermediary to relay warnings. The standard is one of reasonableness in the circumstances. Among the factors to be considered are the gravity of the risks posed by the product, the likelihood that the intermediary will convey the information to the ultimate user, and the feasibility and effectiveness of giving a warning directly to the user. Thus, when the purchaser of machinery is the owner of a workplace who provides the machinery to employees for their use, and there is reason to doubt that the employer will pass warnings on to employees, the seller is required to reach the employees directly with necessary instructions and warnings if doing so is reasonably feasible.

B. THE SUFFICIENCY OF THE DEFENDANT'S WARNING

Obviously, the question of whether the warnings accompanying the product are adequate blurs over into the question raised in Section A, supra, concerning the extent of the defendant seller's duty to warn. All of the cases in this Section B could, for example, be said to raise the issue of whether the defendant owed a duty to provide more specific, or more forceful, warnings. No great mischief is done when the concepts of duty and sufficiency are mingled together in this way. But strictly speaking, these cases present the separate issues of duty, on the one hand, and breach, on the other. Why would a defendant prefer to talk in "duty" terms? Could it have something to do with the tradition that holds that questions of duty are questions of law, for the judge, and questions of breach are questions of fact, for the jury? In any event, when the manufacturer supplies warnings with the product that causes harm, the defendant usually concedes the basic duty issue and argues that the instructions and warnings provided were adequate. The defendant in such a case is theoretically free to argue that no duty was owed in the first instance, but the fact that a warning was actually given usually makes the "no duty whatever" argument more difficult.

Moore v. Ford Motor Company
332 S.W.3d 749 (Mo. 2011) (en banc)

STITH, Judge.

I. FACTUAL AND PROCEDURAL BACKGROUND

In April 2005, [Jeanne and Monty Moore] purchased a 2002 Ford Explorer. On November 1, 2005, the day of the collision, Ms. Moore was 6 feet tall and weighed approximately 300 pounds. She was stopped to make a left turn in the Explorer when she was hit from behind by another vehicle. At impact, the driver's seat collapsed backward and Ms. Moore's head and shoulders hit the back seat, fracturing her T9 vertebra. The injury rendered Ms. Moore a paraplegic.

Ms. Moore and her husband sued Ford under theories of negligent failure to warn, strict liability failure to warn, negligent design and strict liability design defect. The Moores' counsel explained their failure to warn claims during his opening statement as follows:

> The third reason we've sued Ford arises from simple common sense. *Nowhere in the owner's manual or on the on-product labels did Ford tell people who might use the Explorer that it intended the front seats to collapse in a rear impact.* That's information we contend in this trial that people are entitled to know before they sit in those front seats. Just as important, I think, that's information we contend in this case that people are entitled to know before they put their children or loved ones behind these seats. None of that information was given to consumers by Ford. *If Jeanne and Monty would have been warned by Ford or instructed by Ford that the seats in the 2002 Explorer were intended to collapse in a rear impact, they may never have bought their car and we wouldn't be here* (emphasis added).

At trial, Ms. Moore testified that she paid attention to weight warnings when she purchased products because of her size and because her husband and son were both tall and heavy. Ms. Moore testified that she routinely read warnings, instructions and manuals if they involved something in which she was interested. Ms. Moore further testified that, after she purchased the vehicle but prior to the wreck, she looked through the owner's manual for information about other matters and, in doing so, saw no listing of maximum weight limits for the front seats. Ms. Moore also testified that she saw no warnings that the seats of the Explorer might collapse backward in a rear-end impact. In her words, she "figured that, you know, if you had that you would go forward." Ms. Moore further testified, without objection, that she would not have bought the Explorer had she known that the seats were not designed for people of her size. . . .

At the close of the Moores' case, Ford moved for a directed verdict on all counts. In opposing this motion, the Moores further articulated why they had made a case on their failure to warn claims:

> The subject Explorer is devoid of *any warning whatsoever* telling its customers like Jeanne that *the seat in the Explorer is dangerously susceptible to breaking and collapsing in a mild to moderate impact when holding an occupant of Mrs. Moore's size and weight, or that this condition leads to a loss of restraint that can allow an occupant to strike the rear seat causing spinal cord injuries and paralysis.* (emphasis added).

The trial court granted the motion for directed verdict on the Moores' failure to warn claims. . . . After opinion by the court of appeals, this Court accepted transfer. . . .

III. THE TRIAL COURT ERRED IN DIRECTING A VERDICT ON THE FAILURE TO WARN CLAIMS

A. Failure to Warn of Higher Risk when Seats Used by Overweight Persons.

The Moores contend that they made a submissible case of strict liability for failure to warn in that the Explorer lacked any warnings that the front seats could collapse in rear impacts and were not tested or designed to perform with occupants of Ms. Moore's size.

The elements of a cause of action for strict liability failure to warn are: (1) the defendant sold the product in question in the course of its business; (2) the product was unreasonably dangerous at the time of sale when used as reasonably anticipated without knowledge of its characteristics; (3) the defendant did not give adequate warning of the danger; (4) the product was used in a reasonably anticipated manner; and (5) the plaintiff was damaged as a direct result of the product being sold without an adequate warning. . . .

There is no dispute that the Moores presented substantial evidence with respect to the first and fourth elements in that (1) Ford stipulated that it designed, manufactured and sold the Explorer involved in this case, and (4) there is no dispute that by driving the car, Ms. Moore was using the Explorer in a reasonably anticipated manner at the time of the accident. There also is no dispute that no warnings were given as to whether the seats were designed for a person of Ms. Moore's size or that they were designed to collapse backward in rear-impact collisions. Ford strongly disputes, however, that the Moores adduced sufficient evidence that the Explorer was unreasonably dangerous when used as reasonably anticipated without knowledge of its characteristics.

. . . [M]any products that otherwise might be dangerous can be used safely if adequate instructions for use are given and if warnings of dangers are adequate. Failure to warn claims are concerned with how a lack of warning about a product, and the user's resultant lack of knowledge about the product's dangers or safe use, may give rise to an unreasonable danger to the consumer. In such a case, it would not be inconsistent for a jury to find that a product's design is not unreasonably dangerous in itself but that, without an accompanying warning imparting knowledge of the product's dangerous characteristics or safe use, the otherwise non-defective product is unreasonably dangerous. . . .

Viewing the evidence in the light most favorable to the Moores and drawing all inferences in their favor, they adduced sufficient evidence for the jury to find that the Explorer was unreasonably dangerous without a warning imparting knowledge of its characteristics despite the finding that the design of the seats themselves was not defective. Louis D'Aulerio, one of the Moores' experts, testified that pull testing he conducted showed that the point of failure for a 2002 Explorer seat is 16,870 inch pounds. Mr. D'Aulerio then calculated the forces that were generated on Ms. Moore's seat in the wreck given the change in velocity, sustained "g-forces" and her weight. Mr. D'Aulerio testified that although the change in velocity for the collision was as low as 12.8 miles per hour, due to Ms. Moore's weight and other calculations, the Explorer seat endured forces of 15,800 to 19,000 inch pounds. Mr. D'Aulerio testified that this calculation showed that, in rear-end collisions at mild to moderate speeds — 12.8 to 17.2 miles per hour change in velocity — given Ms. Moore's weight, the forces in the crash exceeded the seat's capability. The jury was entitled to consider whether the Explorer seat was rendered unreasonably dangerous when not accompanied with a warning of its greater potential to collapse under the circumstances of a low to moderate rear-end collision while carrying a person of Ms. Moore's weight.

Ford argues that the type of danger presented by its seats is not amenable to a simple warning because the seat is safe for use by people of Ms. Moore's weight in normal driving conditions and in most accidents, other designs present other dangers, and the risk of danger varies with the type and speed of accident. Ford argues that because the Moores never state precisely what an appropriate warning would have said, such a warning could not realistically be made; the Moores, therefore, failed to make their case of failure to warn. This Court disagrees.

Ford does not cite any Missouri law placing the burden on the plaintiff to propose the wording of an adequate warning to make a submissible case.[2] While both Ford and the dissenting opinion note that Indiana apparently does place this burden on plaintiff, Indiana appears to be unique in this regard. . . . Indeed, Washington specifically provides that the plaintiff in a failure to warn case need not "prove the exact wording of an adequate warning." Ayers v. Johnson & Johnson Baby Products Co., 59 Wash.App. 287, 797 P.2d 527, 531 (1990). The other cases cited by the dissent do not concern whether a plaintiff must propose specific alternative language for a warning, much less require plaintiff to do so, but rather discuss generally the types of issues that may be relevant in a failure to warn case, including the feasibility of giving a warning about the danger at issue. . . .

The broad principles the dissent cites concerning relevance and feasibility do not address Ford's real difficulty here, which seems to be in how to phrase its warning. But Ford has not cited any authority that the difficulty of phrasing an adequate warning excuses the failure to give any warning. While the warning alleged to be needed here may take some thought to construct, in the absence of a showing that giving a warning simply would not be technically feasible, any remaining difficulty Ford might have in formulating the precise wording to use in the warning does not negate its need to warn but rather emphasizes the need to do so carefully.[3]

VII. CONCLUSION

For the reasons set out above, the directed verdict for Ford on the Moores' . . . failure to warn claims is reversed. In all other respects, the judgment is affirmed. The cause is remanded.

TEITELMAN, WOLFF and BRECKENRIDGE, JJ., concur. PRICE, C.J., dissents in separate opinion filed. FISCHER, J., concurs in opinion of PRICE, C.J. RUSSELL, J., not participating.

WILLIAM RAY PRICE, JR., Chief Justice[, dissenting].

In this case a six foot tall, three hundred pound woman, Ms. Moore, was driving a 2002 Ford Explorer. The Ford was struck from behind by another vehicle, causing Ms.

---

2. Of course, prudence and good lawyering may dictate that a plaintiff do so. In their response to Ford's motion for directed verdict, the Moores did explain the basic structure of what they believed to be an adequate warning. The Moores argued that Ford should have told "its customers . . . that the seat in the Explorer is dangerously susceptible to breaking and collapsing in a mild to moderate impact when holding an occupant of Ms. Moore's size and weight, or that this condition leads to a loss of restraint that can allow an occupant to strike the rear seat causing spinal cord injuries and paralysis."

3. Moreover, this Court's holding will not lead to a requirement that Ford must provide detailed warnings about how each part of the car will behave for persons of all different weights, sizes and shapes. The Court holds only that where, as here, the evidence shows that Ford knew its design meant that its seats were more likely to collapse backward in rear-end collisions when used by persons of more than normal weight, subjecting them to the risk of serious injuries such as those sustained by Ms. Moore, a jury could find that it had a duty to warn the consumer of that increased risk so the consumer could make an informed choice whether to use the seats despite that danger. Only if a comparable showing were made that other features rendered the product unreasonably dangerous in the absence of an adequate warning would a failure to warn claim be submissible as to other features of a vehicle, as that is the standard for recovery under Missouri law.

Moore's seat to collapse backward, despite the seat being one of the more secure in the industry. The collapse resulted in the fracture of Ms. Moore's T9 vertebra. . . .

Notwithstanding the failure of the plaintiffs to offer any evidence of a feasible, adequate warning that would have avoided the injury, the majority reverses the trial court's directed verdict ruling. I respectfully dissent and would affirm the trial courts ruling with respect to the failure to warn claims. . . .

To make a submissible failure to warn case in Indiana, a plaintiff must offer some evidence of the content or placement of a warning that would have prevented the danger posed by the product in question. Nissen Trampoline Co. v. Terre Haute First Nat'l Bank, 265 Ind. 457, 358 N.E.2d 974, 978 (1976); Morgen v. Ford Motor Co., 797 N.E.2d 1146, 1152 (Ind. 2003). Such evidence is "indispensable to a rational conclusion that the product was defective and unreasonably dangerous to the user without warnings, and to a rational conclusion that such unreasonably dangerous condition was the proximate cause of the accident and injury." Nissen Trampoline, 358 N.E.2d at 978. Failure to offer evidence of this nature imposes upon courts the onerous duty of hypothesizing warnings that would alter a plaintiff's behavior or, as is the case here, they may choose to ignore the inquiry altogether. Id.

Other jurisdictions also require plaintiffs to offer evidence as to what specific warnings would have been sufficient to avoid injury in order to establish a prima facie case for failure to warn. . . . To require anything less invites not only a roving jury instruction, but the danger of subjecting a manufacturer to liability for failing to do the impossible. . . .

Despite the fact that the seat in question was one of the safest in the industry, the Moores argue that when people of a particular size are traveling at a particular speed the seat may fail. Thus, a hypothetical warning, as to the likelihood that the seats might collapse, must be in the form of a sliding-scale, varying among a myriad of factors, including weight of occupants, height of occupants and the velocity of impact. Tellingly, the Moores failed to offer any evidence as to the wording of this problematic warning, its feasibility or where it might have been placed. . . .

Because the Moores failed to offer any evidence as to what a feasible, adequate warning might say or where it might be placed, they did not make a submissible case. . . .

Observe that the plaintiffs in *Moore* attacked the defendant's warning as inadequate without offering a reasonable alternative warning (RAW). Most plaintiffs employ this same tactic. But not all plaintiffs do. Thus, in Nilson v. Hershey Entm't & Resorts Co., 649 F. Supp. 2d 378 (M.D. Pa. 2009), the plaintiffs' expert offered a RAW. The plaintiffs were parents of a boy who at age eleven lost hearing in his left ear shortly after riding a roller coaster at the defendant's amusement park. The plaintiffs alleged that the warnings the park posted on the roller coaster — essentially that the ride involved "speed changes and unexpected forces" — did not adequately advise the riders of the potential dangers involved in the ride. The plaintiffs' expert proposed an alternative warning that would more specifically alert riders that the physical stresses they would experience on the ride would be severe: "WARNING!!! THIS IS A HIGH SPEED RIDE WITH RAPID JOLTS IN SHARP TURNS AND HARD DIPS. DO NOT RIDE UNLESS YOU ARE PREPARED FOR THE MOST SEVERE LEVEL OF PHYSICAL IMPACT AND THRILL." Id. at 388. The trial court, in ruling against the plaintiffs as a matter of law, did not see "any informative significant difference in Plaintiffs' expert's suggested alternative warning and the warning actually on the [roller coaster]." Id. Why didn't the expert propose a warning that riding the defendant's roller coaster could lead to hearing loss?

Two of the authors have recently argued that the proposal of a RAW should be seen as a necessary element of the plaintiff's prima facie case:

> We come to our proposal informed by lessons learned from our experience as reporters for the Restatement (Third). In recommending the appropriate test for determining design defect in that project, we followed the majority position that imposes upon the plaintiff the burden of proving a RAD rather than the minority position that allows the plaintiff to recover by merely showing that the product's design disappoints consumer expectations. We, like most courts, reject the latter test as standardless, collapsing defect and causation into a single issue that a jury is permitted to resolve intuitively based on amorphous consumer expectations. In like fashion, allowing the plaintiff to allege failure to warn without specifically setting forth the relevant details — the medium and, if written, the text, placement, color, and size of the proposed warning — condones a cause of action without any standard and allows a jury to intuit causation without being required to test its finding against what a real-world warning would have said. . . . [Aaron D. Twerski & James A. Henderson, Jr., Fixing Failure to Warn, 90 Ind. L.J. 237, 254 (2015).]

If "prudence and good lawyering may dictate that a plaintiff [submit a RAW]," as the *Moore* court indicated in footnote 2, above, why do plaintiffs' lawyers object to a formal requirement of the RAW as a doctrinal matter? If you think a plaintiff must supply a RAW to maintain a successful a failure-to-warn claim, is the plaintiff required to supply expert testimony supporting the RAW's adequacy? For a subsequent interpretation of the rule in Indiana addressing this question, see Cook v. Ford Motor Co., 913 N.E.2d 311, 327 n.9 (Ind. Ct. App. 2009), which explained that "[a]lthough evidence of an alternate adequate may be required, an expert is not necessarily the sole source of such evidence."

The Eleventh Circuit ruled on the adequacy of a warning supplied with a cordless telephone. The handset of the phone had a switch that, in the "standby" position, allowed the phone to ring. To talk on the phone, the user had to push the switch to the "talk" position. The use of the phone, including the switch, was explained in the instruction manual, which the plaintiff said she read: "CAUTION — LOUD RING. Move switch to talk position before holding receiver to ear." The first time plaintiff answered the phone after it was installed, she forgot to push the switch to "talk." As she put the receiver to her ear, it rang again and permanently impaired her hearing. The district court granted summary judgment for the defendant-manufacturer, holding that the warning on the headset was adequate as a matter of law. The court of appeals reversed and sent the case back for trial on the question of whether Uniden had used adequate means to convey the warning. See Watson v. Uniden Corp. of Am., 775 F.2d 1514 (11th Cir. 1985). Might this have been a design case "in disguise?"

In Mattis v. Carlon Electrical Products, 295 F.3d 856 (8th Cir. 2002), a 25-year-old apprentice electrician read the safety warnings on the label of a can of glue before using the product. He opened and closed the can at least ten to twelve times throughout the workday. The plaintiff worked one more day, using the glue, before he was admitted to the hospital and diagnosed with reactive airways dysfunction syndrome (RADS). The court of appeals affirmed a jury verdict in favor of the plaintiff, stating that "although the label stated 'vapor harmful,' this warning was followed by the statements, 'may irritate eyes and skin' and 'vapors may cause flash fires.' The label does not make it clear that *inhalation* of the vapors is harmful." Id. at 862. See also Mathis v. Harrell Co., 828 So. 2d 248 (Ala. 2002) (reversing summary judgment for defendants based on an expert's statement that the warning on a piece of farm machinery was inadequate because it failed to identify the risk and likelihood of injury associated with attempting to open the hydraulic-cylinder latch manually and failed to state the consequences of not following the instruction).

Comment *i* to §2(c) of the Products Liability Restatement supplies the following summary of how courts should approach the task of evaluating the sufficiency of product warnings and weighing competing desires for completeness and conciseness:

> In evaluating the adequacy of product warnings and instructions, courts must be sensitive to many factors. It is impossible to identify anything approaching a perfect level of detail that should be communicated in product disclosures. For example, educated or experienced product users and consumers may benefit from inclusion of more information about the full spectrum of product risks, whereas less-educated or unskilled users may benefit from more concise warnings and instructions stressing only the most crucial risks and safe-handling practices. In some contexts, products intended for special categories of users, such as children, may require more vivid and unambiguous warnings. In some cases, excessive detail may detract from the ability of typical users and consumers to focus on the important aspects of the warnings, whereas in others reasonably full disclosure will be necessary to enable informed, efficient choices by product users. Product warnings and instructions can rarely communicate all potentially relevant information, and the ability of a plaintiff to imagine a hypothetical better warning in the aftermath of an accident does not establish that the warning actually accompanying the product was inadequate. No easy guideline exists for courts to adopt in assessing the adequacy of product warnings and instructions. In making their assessments, courts must focus on various factors, such as content and comprehensibility, intensity of expression, and the characteristics of expected user groups. . . .

PROBLEM TWENTY-ONE

A senior partner in the litigation department of the law firm in which you are an associate has sought your help in a case recently brought to her. The clients, Mr. and Mrs. Ronald Kritzik and their daughter Kathy, want to bring an action in tort based on injuries suffered by Kathy after she began to wear contact lenses. The clients have related the following events: Kathy, a 16-year-old girl, had been pestering her parents for months to let her get contact lenses to replace her glasses. Early last December, they arranged for an appointment with Dr. Richard Quell, a local optometrist, who advertised his services in the Yellow Pages and in the local newspaper. They told Kathy that the contact lenses were to be her Christmas present.

Dr. Quell examined Kathy and decided that because she suffered from astigmatism, she would be better off with hard contact lenses than with the more popular soft lenses. Hard lenses provide a kind of "encasement" that prevents the distortion in vision that can sometimes occur with soft lenses. Dr. Quell fitted Kathy with the lenses in the early afternoon of December 24. She felt comfortable wearing her new lenses, and was delighted by the improvement in her looks once rid of what she considered rather ugly-looking glasses. Dr. Quell told Kathy that for the first week she was to wear her lenses for no more than four hours per day. He told her that more than four hours' use could cause "real trouble." After fitting Kathy with the lenses, Dr. Quell had her sit in the waiting room for 15 minutes. He then examined Kathy once again and found that the fit was excellent. As Kathy was leaving, Dr. Quell said, "Remember, Kathy — no more than four hours a day. You don't want to hurt those pretty eyes of yours."

That same evening, Kathy went to a Christmas Eve party. Four hours had already passed but she was feeling "great." She hardly felt that she was wearing the lenses. The party lasted until 2:00 A.M. and Kathy did not remove the lenses until 4:00 A.M., when she went to bed. According to Kathy, at no time up to that point did her eyes bother her in any way. When she awoke at 10:00 A.M. on Christmas morning, she felt a burning sensation in both eyes. Mrs. Kritzik called Dr. Quell and told him what had happened. He saw Kathy immediately. Fifteen hours of continuous wear had caused ulcerated corneas. When Dr. Quell discovered the ulcerations, he was furious. "Kathy," he said, "why didn't you listen to directions? Twice I told you to remove the lenses after four hours." Kathy, somewhat ashamed of herself, replied, "I guess that I thought it was just doctor talk. My eyes weren't irritated or tearing or anything." Then she thought for a few seconds and with a half-smile remarked, "You know, when I left for the party at eight and I thought to myself, should I take the lenses out like you said, I had this crazy thought. 'What the heck, I already broke curfew; que será, será.' " Dr. Quell shook his head in disbelief. "Kathy, overwearing hard lenses for three or four hours isn't likely to cause trouble. But every hour after that, the lenses eat away at the cornea. I hope to God this is reversible." The next several weeks were hell. The pain resulting from the ulcerated corneas was excruciating. Although the ulcers eventually healed, residual scarring may permanently affect her vision.

The lenses worn by Kathy were manufactured by Seenco, Inc. They came with an instruction booklet entitled "How to Care for Your Contact Lenses." Kathy had read the booklet carefully when she got her lenses. A box in the booklet, outlined in bright red, contained the following message:

> Instructions for wearing these lenses will be given to you by your physician or optometrist. Failure to follow the instructions carefully may result in irritation to the eyes and could cause serious complications, including impairment of vision.

The senior partner is concerned that the case may be too "thin" and may be dismissed on a motion for summary judgment or a motion for directed verdict. She has asked you to assess the likelihood of getting to a jury. Indicate any further information that should be obtained.

Recall from Chapter Four that the reasonable alternative design standard in design litigation lends itself to a fairly robust motions practice, in which judges are able to play a meaningful role in deciding which design claims should, and which should not, reach the jury. Indeed, that is one of the reasons why plaintiffs' lawyers favor the consumer expectations test for defective design — the vagueness of the expectations test sends almost all design claims, at least the ones that do not involve obvious risks, to the jury. In connection with failure to warn, it is more difficult for courts to rule as a matter of law on plaintiffs' claims even if they adopt the Restatement's standard for warnings defects. Accordingly Comment *i* to §2 of the Products Liability Restatement observes that, while the liability standard for warnings in Subsection (c) is formulated in essentially identical terms as the standard for defective designs in Subsection (b), (see p. 311, supra, for the parallel language), "the defectiveness concept is more difficult to apply in the warnings context." Even as courts devote significant attention to the precise wording of jury instructions in failure-to-warn cases — see, e.g., Lewis v. Sea Ray Boats, Inc., 65 P.3d 245 (Nev. 2003) — the question remains whether a judge's instructions to the jury really matter in affecting outcomes.

James A. Henderson, Jr. & Aaron D. Twerski, Doctrinal Collapse in Products Liability: The Empty Shell of Failure to Warn
65 N.Y.U. L. Rev. 265, 292-294 (1990)

We use the phrase "preliminary risk-utility screening" to refer to a court's initial assessment of the relative proximity or remoteness of a product-related risk, measured by the probability of injury that a reasonable defendant would have perceived at the time she acted. To understand how this preliminary screening process affects judicial decisionmaking in failure-to-warn cases, we will first consider in the defective-design context how it helps courts decide which cases should not reach the jury. This comparison is important because it highlights the potential ability of preliminary screening to serve as an independent test of the validity of plaintiffs' failure-to-warn claims.

When a judge's initial assessment of a design claim reveals that, at the time the defendant acted, the risk of plaintiff's injury was quite remote, a distinctive train of logic is set in motion. The judge knows that design changes have risk-utility implications extending beyond the category of user and consumer represented by the plaintiff. Any design change will have to be weighed against the possible increased cost it will impose on the manufacturer, and against the new potential risks it will pose for the consumer. Design changes, in other words, come in "chunks," and the chunks tend to come in minimum sizes. The risk of injury, therefore, must exceed some instinctive, judicially-measured threshold of significance before a costly design change is evaluated under full-blown risk-utility balancing.

While every design change suggested by an injured plaintiff need not require a complete product overhaul, even the smallest chunk of alternative design entails at least some degree of modification. An analogy to writing and editing a paper helps to illustrate this point. Introducing a new idea toward the end of a nearly completed paper will almost inevitably require revisions at various earlier stages in order to maintain the argument and logic of the piece. When the benefits to be gained by making this late addition are minimal, the writer may intuitively decide that it is simply not worth the effort to add the new section if doing so would require reorganizing and rewriting significant portions of the paper. Likewise, in design litigation, judges frequently determine at the outset that an improved design which might have protected the plaintiff would nonetheless require such costly and elaborate alterations that the change simply does not merit a more careful analysis under full-blown risk-utility balancing. Judges can, and often do, wait to intervene until more substantial risk-utility data are before them, much as an editor might wait to abandon a proposed addition to a text until she had carefully reviewed the entire piece. But when the relevant risks are remote, those data (which, after all, are costly to obtain) may not be required in order to reach, at the outset of the analysis, a principled decision not to impose the change.

In contrast to suggested alternatives in design cases, suggested alternatives in failure-to-warn cases appear to be easily compartmentalized. Like additional memory chips which are used to expand the capacity of a computer, warnings would seem to be added easily without requiring adjustments to the rest of the machine. When a risk is perceived in the context of an alternative design, it can be addressed only by a design change which unavoidably affects other related risks and utilities and thereby generates a not insignificant minimum threshold of avoidance costs. But when a risk is perceived in the context of failure to warn, a tailor-made remedy seems to be automatically available, precisely limited to the category of users and consumers represented by the plaintiff. The plaintiff argues that the manufacturer should share the information, however remote the risks it describes, with users and consumers.[4] The relative remoteness of the risk may create problems for the failure-to-warn plaintiff when the court reaches the full-blown risk-utility stage of the analysis — eliminating remote risks cannot justify much in the way of avoidance costs. The remoteness of the risk may also create problems with causation — would telling the plaintiff about a remote risk have done any good? . . . But at the preliminary screening stage, the remoteness of the perceived risk will rarely provide the court in a failure-to-warn case with an independent means of taking the plaintiff's claim from the jury. This difficulty will occur because the plaintiff who claims that the manufacturer failed to warn, unlike the plaintiff claiming defective design, will be able to tailor his suggested alternative course of conduct precisely to the facts of his case in terms that have no immediately obvious consequences for other aspects of production, marketing, and distribution. All the defendant must do, contends the plaintiff, is add slightly to his warnings. On its face, the failure-to-warn claim is so modestly self-contained that, even when the risk is remote, it nevertheless fails to trigger the preliminary risk-utility screening which courts give to design-defect claims because the apparent unobtrusiveness of the plaintiff's request automatically counterbalances the remoteness of the risk. Thus, the relative unlikelihood of injury viewed ex ante loses its independent capacity to serve as a basis for taking the failure-to-warn case from the jury.

Occasionally, courts explicitly recognize that, contrary to loose talk in other opinions, warnings are not free. An example is Cotton v. Buckeye Gas Products, Co., 840 F.2d 935 (D.C. Cir. 1988), in which the plaintiff was injured when a fire broke out due to mishandled gas cylinders. The plaintiff claimed that the defendant should have provided more adequate warnings of the risks associated with leaving the valves open on used but not empty cylinders. At trial the court granted defendant's motion for J.N.O.V. after a verdict was returned for the plaintiff. The court of appeals held that additional warnings were not required because the warnings given were adequate. The employer had sufficient knowledge of the relevant risks, and the plaintiff would not have heeded them anyway. The opinion contains the following observations:

---

4. In addition to arguments based on cost, plaintiffs frequently succeed at trial in characterizing risks previously considered unknowable as "knowable from the outset" by a reasonable observer. Simply stated, it is extremely difficult for a court to dismiss as a matter of law a failure-to-warn claim on remoteness grounds when the plaintiff has introduced evidence that the risk actually materialized in the form of the plaintiff's injury. Because the product did, in fact, cause the injury, a court is sorely tempted to permit the inference to be drawn that a reasonable product distributor should have foreseen the risk of injury and should have warned against it. Thus the plaintiff will argue that at least some additional information was obtainable and should have been shared with him in the form of a warning, even if information sufficient to justify massive redesign or withholding of the product from the market was not.

Failure-to-warn cases have the curious property that when the episode is examined in hindsight, it appears as though addition of warnings keyed to a particular accident would be virtually cost free. What could be simpler than for the manufacturer to add the few simple items noted above [what the plaintiff claimed should have been said in addition to what was said]. The primary cost is, in fact, the increase in time and effort required for the user to grasp the message. The inclusion of each extra item dilutes the punch of every other item. Given short attention spans, items crowd each other out; they get lost in fine print. Here in fact Buckeye responded to the information-cost problem with a dual approach: a brief message on the canisters themselves and a more detailed one in the . . . - pamphlet delivered to [the employer] and posted on the bulletin board at the construction site where [the plaintiff] was employed.

Plaintiff's analysis completely disregards the problem of information costs. He asserts that "it would have been neither difficult nor costly for Buckeye to have purchased or created for attachment to its propane cylinders a clearer, more explicit label, such as the alternatives introduced at trial, warning of propane's dangers and instructing how to avoid them." But he offers no reason to suppose that any alternative package of warnings was preferable. He discounts altogether the warnings in the pamphlet, without even considering what the canister warning would look like if Buckeye had supplemented that not only with the special items he is personally interested in — in hindsight — but also with all other equally valuable items (i.e., "equally" in terms of the scope and probability of the danger likely to be averted and the incremental impact of the information on user conduct). If every foreseeable possibility must be covered, "the list of foolish practices warned against would be so long, it would fill a volume." Unlike plaintiff, we must review the record in light of these obvious information costs. [Id. at 937-38.]

The court goes on to review the actual warning given compared with the warning proposed by the plaintiff, and concludes that the warning was adequate as a matter of law.

For the reasons developed in the Henderson-Twerski excerpt and Cotton v. Buckeye Gas, supra, courts rule for defendants as a matter of law only rarely in failure-to-warn litigation when the issue is the sufficiency of warnings actually given. But it does happen. Thus, in Jack v. Alberto-Culver USA, Inc., 949 So. 2d 1256 (La. 2007), the plaintiff alleged that defendant's hair product caused an abscess on her scalp and that the defendant manufacturer should have warned her to perform a scalp test before using the product. The trial court found for the plaintiff, and the intermediate court affirmed. The Supreme Court of Louisiana reversed and entered judgment for the defendant, concluding that "although they did not include an instruction to perform a 'scalp test,' the 18 warnings and instructions given by Alberto-Culver in this case clearly satisfy the requirements of [the Louisiana Products Liability Act." Id at 1259, n.5. See also Carr v. Gillis Associated Indus., 227 Fed. App'x 172 (3d Cir. 2007) (applying Pennsylvania law) (affirming summary judgment for ladder manufacturer and explaining that warnings were not required to advise weekly inspections as a matter of law).

<h2 style="text-align:center">Broussard v. Continental Oil Co.</h2>

433 So. 2d 354 (La. Ct. App.), cert. denied, 440 So. 2d 726 (La. 1983)

STOKER, J.

This is a personal injury suit by Mildredge T. Broussard against Black & Decker (U.S.), Inc. and The Home Insurance Company. Plaintiff-appellant (Broussard) was badly burned in an explosion of natural gas sparked by a Black & Decker hand drill. Broussard was using the drill while working at a Continental Oil Company (Conoco) plant at Grand Chenier, Louisiana. . . .

The verdict of the jury at trial was that Black & Decker was not at fault for failure to adequately warn in connection with the accident. . . .

Background Facts

Plaintiff was directly employed by Crain Brothers Construction Company, and the trial court found he was the statutory employee of Conoco. On the day of the accident, plaintiff and four other men, including Sanders Miller, were in the process of building a sump box enclosure at the end of a natural gas vent line (pipe) at the Grand Chenier plant. Plaintiff was a carpenter's helper and Miller was a carpenter. Upon arriving at the site, both men noticed that natural gas could be heard and smelled coming from the vent line. Miller immediately notified Conoco's relief plant foreman about the escaping gas and asked if it could be shut off. The foreman refused to do so because the whole plant would have had to be shut down to prevent the gas from being vented at the location of the sump box. After Miller requested a shut down a second time, the foreman talked to Mr. Leeman, another Conoco employee and the plant supervisor. Miller was again told nothing could be done.

Miller testified that he recognized the danger of working around the flammable natural gas. The workers took what precautions they could to minimize the risk of igniting the natural gas fumes. Cigarettes, cigarette lighters and matches were left in the work vehicles. The vehicles were parked some distance away from the site. A gasoline powered electricity generator was placed at the end of two 50-foot extension cords. Miller warned the plaintiff to be careful not to cause a spark while hammering, especially when the fumes were heavy.

The explosion occurred as plaintiff was standing inside a plywood box loosely held together and being constructed as a concrete form. He was positioned inside the form to drill holes in its sides through which rods were to be inserted. It is not seriously contested that sparks from the drill plaintiff was using ignited the natural gas fumes coming from the vent line. Such sparks are normally emitted from this and similar type drills when the "brushes" inside the armature of the drill contact and slide along the inside surface of the rapidly spinning cylinder in which the brushes sit. There is no evidence, nor is the issue before this Court, that the design which allows the creation and emission of these sparks constitutes a design defect. Rather, the issues relate to the failure to warn on the part of the defendant manufacturer of the hazard of explosion.

Both the plaintiff Broussard and Sanders Miller testified that they were unaware at the time of the accident that sparks from electrical power drills could ignite gaseous atmospheres. Allen Nunez, the relief foreman, likewise testified that neither he nor anyone at the Conoco plant knew of the potential of explosion in a like situation before the accident occurred. However, a warning that would have informed the users of the drill of the precise cause and effect encountered appears in [item 18 in] the owner's manual. Black & Decker claim that a copy of this manual is placed in every box containing one of their drills as it leaves the manufacturer's control. . . .

Did Black & Decker Fail to Provide Adequate Warning?

With reference to adequacy of warning of the danger from the emission of sparks, Black & Decker contends item eighteen in the owner's manual was sufficient. Plaintiff Broussard contends that it was not. Broussard contends that Black & Decker was guilty of fault in not putting the warning on the drill itself. Item eighteen reads as follows:

18. DO NOT OPERATE portable electric tools in gaseous or explosive atmospheres. Motors in these tools normally spark, and the sparks might ignite fumes.

The warning set forth in these words is adequate; the question is whether it was sufficient to put it in the owner's manual or whether it was unreasonable under the circumstances not to put this warning on the drill itself. . . . [T]here was a warning on the drill which read, "CAUTION: For Safe Operation See Owner's Manual."

We are confronted here with the application of absolute liability of a manufacturer. The product, the drill, does not contain a defect in the ordinary sense of design or manufacturing defect, but ordinary use of the drill is dangerous under the factual circumstances which were present in this case, i.e., use in the presence of natural gas fumes. Unreasonable risk is a requirement of strict liability just as it is in negligence.

The judicial process involved in deciding whether a risk is unreasonable in strict liability is similar to that employed in determining whether a risk is unreasonable in a traditional negligence problem and in deciding the scope of duty or legal cause under the duty risk analysis. . . .

In approaching our decision in this case we accept at face value the assertions of Broussard and Sanders Miller that they were unaware that the drill in question would emit sparks when in operation. . . .

The questions before us are:

1. Was adequate warning given through the general caution on Black & Decker's drill directing users to consult the owner's manual for safe operation?
2. If the general warning was not adequate, was it unreasonable for Black & Decker not to place on the drill itself the warning contained in item 18 of its safety rules contained in the owner's manual?

These questions must be tested together as they rest on the same practical considerations.

Plaintiff's own expert witness unwittingly pointed up the difficulty in putting warnings on the drill itself. This expert demonstrated the use of warnings through symbols as opposed to words. The expert devised a series of symbols of his own creation based on international symbols which he suggested could have been placed on the drill itself. The symbols purportedly represent ten of the eighteen warnings Black & Decker set forth in the owner's manual. . . .

While we think the use of symbols as suggested by plaintiff's expert merits no consideration, we note that the expert deemed at least ten of the warnings represented by the symbols were worthy of being noted on the drill. The fact that numerous risks other than sparking explosions or fires merit notice is a significant factor. The suggested use of symbols is also significant because the reason for it is the recognition that the space on the drill is not large enough to contain extensive warnings and cautions in words. This factor will be discussed later, but at this point we will state our opinion relative to the efficacy [of] symbols in lieu of words. . . .

We think counsel for plaintiff recognized lack of merit in the suggested use of symbols. On plaintiff's behalf Exhibit P-17 was introduced in evidence. On the side of this exhibit a label measuring approximately 25/8 inches by 13/4 inches was affixed on which the following words were typed:

SAFETY RULES
• Don't abuse cord
• Wear proper apparel
• Don't use in damp areas
• Use proper extension cords outdoors
• Don't touch metal parts when drilling near any electrical wiring
• Remove tightening key
• Unplug to change bits
• Use safety glasses
• Avoid gaseous areas
• Secure work
SEE MANUAL FOR COMPLETE TEXTS

The whole of the above quoted material is typed in small letter characters in a slantwise or diagonal fashion on the label in order to fit. It will be noted that the only reference to the risk of igniting gas from emission of sparks is contained in the three words, "Avoid gaseous areas."

We are not impressed with plaintiff's Exhibit P-17. The most important failing of the exhibit is that the mere words, "Avoid gaseous areas" does not meet the test of [adequacy] because it does not explain or point out the precise risk of injury posed by use in gaseous areas. Moreover, this exhibit graphically illustrates the problem of attempting to put multiple warnings on a hand drill of the size and nature involved.

Defendant considers that more than ten warnings should be given. Nevertheless, if only ten are selected, deficiencies in any scheme for putting them all on the drill become apparent. As a practical matter, the effect of putting at least ten warnings on the drill would decrease the effectiveness of all of the warnings. A consumer would have a tendency to read none of the warnings if the surface of the drill became cluttered with the warnings. Unless we should elevate the one hazard of sparking to premier importance above all others, we fear that an effort to tell all about each hazard is not practical either from the point of view of availability of space or of effectiveness. We decline to say that one risk is more worthy of warning than another.

With the merits and demerits of the arguments urged by the parties in mind, we now decide whether Black & Decker exposed plaintiff to unreasonable risk. . . . We conclude that defendant acted reasonably toward plaintiff and all persons who might use its hand drill. In view of the numerous risks which a manufacturer of a hand drill must explicitly describe, the most practical and effective thing which the manufacturer could do is to direct the user to the owner's manual as Black & Decker did.

For the reasons we have given we hold that the jury's finding of no fault on the part of Black & Decker was correct. . . .

Decree

For the reasons assigned, the judgment of the trial court is affirmed. All costs of this appeal are to be paid by plaintiff.

Affirmed.

One problem that occurs in warnings cases involves the difficulty of informing persons who are not literate or who do not read English. In Campos v. Firestone Tire & Rubber Co., 485 A.2d 305 (N.J. 1984), plaintiff was born and reared in Portugal, and did not read English. He was injured while installing a new truck tire on a three-piece rim assembly manufactured by defendant. An adequate warning in English was supplied and prominently posted at the workplace. Plaintiff's expert argued that defendant should have produced a graphic or symbolic warning against inserting one's hand in the assembly during tire inflation—a sign containing a picture of a hand inside the assembly, with a red diagonal line through it, similar to international road signs. The high court concluded that a jury could find that defendant breached its duty to warn, and remanded the case for a new trial. However, in Torres-Rios v. LPS Laboratories, Inc., 152 F.3d 11 (1st Cir. 1998), a prominent display of a flame symbol on a drum containing flammable electrical contact cleaner was held to be an adequate warning as a matter of law in the absence of federal requirements to provide warnings in Spanish, even though the product was sold in Puerto Rico where the dominant language is Spanish. For an argument that in certain situations manufacturers should bear a duty in the United States to provide warnings in Spanish, see Keith Sealing, Peligro!: Failure to Warn of a Product's Inherent Risk in Spanish Should Constitute a Product Defect, 11 Temp. Pol. & Civ. Rts. L. Rev. 153, 154 (2001). See also Martinez v. Triad Controls, Inc., 593 F. Supp. 2d 741, 764-65 (E.D. Pa. 2009) (presenting but declining to adopt Professor Sealing's analytical framework in that particular case). On the subject of foreign language warnings generally, see S. Mark Mitchell, Note, A Manufacturer's Duty to Warn in a Modern Day Tower of Babel, 29 Ga. J. Int'l & Comp. L. 573 (2001).

C. POST-SALE WARNINGS

Although the time-of-sale duty to warn is long-established, the product seller's post-sale duty to warn is of more recent vintage.

Restatement (Third) of Torts: Products Liability
(1998)

---

§10. LIABILITY OF COMMERCIAL PRODUCT SELLER OR DISTRIBUTOR FOR HARM CAUSED BY POST-SALE FAILURE TO WARN

(a) One engaged in the business of selling or otherwise distributing products is subject to liability for harm to persons or property caused by the seller's failure to provide a warning after the time of sale or distribution of a product if a reasonable person in the seller's position would provide such a warning.

(b) A reasonable person in the seller's position would provide a warning after the time of sale if:

(1) the seller knows or reasonably should know that the product poses a substantial risk of harm to persons or property; and

(2) those to whom a warning might be provided can be identified and can reasonably be assumed to be unaware of the risk of harm; and

(3) a warning can be effectively communicated to and acted on by those to whom a warning might be provided; and

(4) the risk of harm is sufficiently great to justify the burden of providing a warning.

COMMENT:

a. Rationale. Judicial recognition of the seller's duty to warn of a product-related risk after the time of sale, whether or not the product is defective at the time of original sale within the meaning of other Sections of this Restatement, is relatively new. Nonetheless, a growing body of decisional and statutory law imposes such a duty. Courts recognize that warnings about risks discovered after sale are sometimes necessary to prevent significant harm to persons and property. Nevertheless, an unbounded post-sale duty to warn would impose unacceptable burdens on product sellers. The costs of identifying and communicating with product users years after sale are often daunting. Furthermore, as product designs are developed and improved over time, many risks are reduced or avoided by subsequent design changes. If every post-sale improvement in a product design were to give rise to a duty to warn users of the risks of continuing to use the existing design, the burden on product sellers would be unacceptably great.

As with all rules that raise the question whether a duty exists, courts must make the threshold decisions that, in particular cases, triers of fact could reasonably find that product sellers can practically and effectively discharge such an obligation and that the risks of harm are sufficiently great to justify what is typically a substantial post-sale undertaking. In deciding whether a claim based on breach of a post-sale duty to warn should reach the trier of fact, the court must determine whether the requirements in Subsection (b)(1) through (4) are supported by proof. The legal standard is whether a reasonable person would provide a post-sale warning. In light of the serious potential for overburdening sellers in this regard, the court should carefully examine the circumstances for and against imposing a duty to provide a post-sale warning in a particular case. . . .

j. Distinguishing post-sale failures to warn from defects existing at the time of sale. When a product is defective at the time of sale liability can be established without reference to a post-sale duty to warn. A seller who discovers after sale that its product was defective at the time of sale within the meaning of this Restatement cannot generally absolve itself of liability by issuing a post-sale warning. As long as the original defect is causally related to the harm suffered by the plaintiff, a prima facie case under this Restatement can be established notwithstanding reasonable post-sale efforts to warn. Of course, even when a product is defective at the time of sale a seller may have an independent obligation to issue a post-sale warning based on the rule stated in this Section. Thus, a plaintiff may seek recovery based on both a time-of-sale defect and a post-sale failure to warn. . . .

Lovick v. Wil-Rich
588 N.W.2d 688 (Iowa 1999)

CADY, JUSTICE.

The manufacturer of a farm cultivator appeals from a judgment entered by the district court in favor of the product user in this product liability action. We conclude the district court failed to fully instruct the jury on the negligence claim based upon a post-sale duty to warn, and this incomplete instruction constituted prejudicial error. We affirm in part, reverse in part, and remand for a new trial.

I. Background Facts and Proceedings

On May 20, 1993, Leo Lovick set out to cultivate a field preparatory to spring planting. He was an experienced farmer. The land was owned by Paul Rotgers and Lovick was using his cultivator.

Lovick pulled the cultivator to the field with a tractor. The wings of the cultivator were in the upright, vertical position to accommodate its transportation. Once in the field, Lovick attempted to unfold or lower the wings into position to begin cultivation.

The wings of the cultivator folded and unfolded by the operation of two hydraulic cylinders, which also held the wings in its vertical position. Additionally, the wings were secured in the upright position by a metal pin manually inserted under each wing, near the rear of the implement. The pins were designed to hold the wing in the vertical position in the event of hydraulic or mechanical failure.

Lovick positioned himself under the left wing of the cultivator to remove the first pin. The wing immediately fell when the pin was removed. Lovick was severely injured. Later investigation revealed the wing fell when Lovick removed the pin because the linkage attaching the cylinder to the wing had broken. Consequently, the pin was the only device holding the wing in its upright position at the time it was removed.

Wil-Rich first introduced the vertical fold model cultivator into the market in 1971. Since that time it has manufactured approximately 35,000 units. The cultivator which injured Lovick was manufactured and sold by Wil-Rich in 1981. Rotgers purchased the cultivator in "the late 80's." He was at least the second owner. The cultivator contained a warning sign which cautioned the operator to remove the pin prior to lowering the wings. Wil-Rich placed the warning on the cultivator because it believed hydraulic pressure against the wing pins could break the hydraulic cylinder. The operator's manual further warned against going under the wings to remove the pins.

In 1983, Wil-Rich received a report that a wing of one of its cultivators had fallen and injured the operator. Since that time, it received eight other such reports. In 1988, Wil-Rich began to affix a warning label to the cultivators it manufactured to caution operators of the danger of going under the wing to remove the pin. Wil-Rich added this warning in response to the reports of operators injured by a falling cultivator wing, as well as changes in engineering standards.

In 1994, Wil-Rich began a campaign to notify current owners of its cultivators of the danger of falling wings. It also made a backup safety-latch kit available for installation on the wings.

Lovick instituted a strict liability and negligence action against Wil-Rich. He sought compensatory and punitive damages. At trial, Lovick successfully introduced evidence that Deere & Company, a competitor of Wil-Rich, instituted a safety program in 1983 for its similarly designed cultivator after learning of instances of the wing falling on the operator. The Deere & Company program included efforts to locate the cultivator owners, and equip the existing cultivators with a wing safety latch and an upgraded warning label. Lovick also introduced evidence of the nine other accidents involving the wing of a Wil-Rich cultivator falling on an operator.

Wil-Rich investigated the prior accidents as the information became available. It also became aware of the Deere & Company post-sale warning program in 1987, but did not institute its post-sale warning program prior to 1994 essentially due to the practical difficulties of identifying and locating the owners and users of previously sold cultivators.

The trial court submitted the case to the jury on the strict liability theory of defective design and the negligence claim of breach of a post-sale duty to warn. It also submitted punitive damages on the negligence claim. The jury returned a verdict in the amount of $2,057,000. The verdict included $500,000 in punitive damages and $400,000 in loss of consortium to Lovick's wife. . . .

III.   Post-Sale Duty to Warn

We first address the issue of whether the trial court erred in instructing the jury on the duty of Wil-Rich to warn. Wil-Rich claimed it had no duty to warn following the sale. It further claimed the instruction given by the district court was too vague to permit the jury to understand the scope of the duty or to properly determine whether it was breached.

A.   Existence of Duty . . .

The body of law we have developed concerning a manufacturer's duty to warn has been predicated on warning of inadequacies at the time of manufacture and sale. A growing number of jurisdictions, however, have now expanded this duty to require warnings after the sale when the product later reveals a defect not known at the time of sale. See 3, American Law of Products Liability §32:79 (3d ed. 1998). . . .

Iowa unceremoniously joined this growing trend in 1986 when our legislature enacted the products liability state-of-the-art defense statute. In establishing the state-of-the-art defense in products liability actions, our legislature added:

> Nothing contained in this section shall diminish the duty of an assembler, designer, supplier of specifications, distributor, manufacturer or seller to warn concerning subsequently acquired knowledge of a defect or dangerous condition that would render the product unreasonably dangerous for its foreseeable use or diminish the liability for failure to so warn.

Iowa Code §668.12 (1987). Although no statutory or judicial post-sale duty to warn had been recognized in Iowa prior to the statute, section 668.12 clearly established our legislature's understanding of the duty. We previously recognized this statutory post-sale duty, but have not had the occasion to begin to consider its specific application or parameters. This case presents such an occasion.

The district court recognized the existence of a post-sale duty to warn but only submitted a general reasonableness standard of care instruction to the jury. WilRich claims the instruction was legally insufficient because the duty to warn is not absolute and the instruction did not identify the important factors to consider in determining whether the duty would be breached in a particular case. It requested an instruction which told the jury it was required to give a warning if it knew the cultivator posed a substantial risk of harm, the operator could be identified and would be unaware of the harm, a warning could be effectively communicated and acted upon, and the risk of harm was great enough to justify imposing a duty.

We acknowledge a post-sale duty to warn is compatible with the traditional point-of-sale duty to warn. See Frumer & Friedman, 1 Products Liability §2.22(2) (1991). It serves the same underlying purpose to reduce the chance of injury by equalizing the asymmetry of information between the parties. It is understandable that our legislature wanted to join the growing list of jurisdictions which recognize this post-sale duty. Yet, there are some distinctions which are important to recognize in considering the scope and nature of the post-sale duty.

Foremost, the burden of a manufacturer to warn product users can radically change after the sale has occurred and the manufacturer no longer has control over the product. Warning labels can be easily placed on products the manufacturer still controls. However, once the product is sold, a variety of circumstances can impede, if not make impossible, the ability of a manufacturer to warn users. Thus, while the rationale for post-sale and point-of-sale duties to warn are nearly identical, the parameters of those duties must be separately identified.

Most states which have considered the parameters of the post-sale duty to warn have developed various factors to guide its implementation. The American Law Institute recently distilled some of these factors from these decisions in the adoption of the post-sale duty to warn in the Restatement (Third) of Torts: Products Liability §10 (1998). The Restatement uses the reasonable person test to determine liability for the failure to warn following the sale, and articulates four factors to guide the determination of the reasonableness of the seller's conduct.

[The opinion sets out the text of §10, supra.]

We agree negligence is the appropriate theory to resolve post-sale failure to warn product liability claims. This theory of recovery is consistent with our approach to our prior cases involving the duty to warn at the point of sale. See Olson v. Prosoco, Inc., 522 N.W.2d 284, 288-90 (Iowa 1994). It recognizes the analytical merger of strict liability and negligence in determining liability for failure to warn, and we perceive no reason to resurrect the former distinction in post-sale failure to warn claims. The fighting question is whether it is necessary to articulate the various factors to consider in analyzing the reasonableness of a manufacturer's conduct once it acquires knowledge of a defect in a product following the sale.

B. Post-Sale Warning Jury Instruction . . .

Although we recognize a post-sale duty to warn, we have identified potential circumstances faced by manufacturers after the sale of a product not present prior to the sale. The jury instruction given in this case, however, failed to inform the jury of these circumstances, or how they might impact the reasonableness of a manufacturer's conduct. Instead, the jury was told that if Wil-Rich subsequently learned its product is defective and unreasonably dangerous, it had a duty to warn those it knows or reasonably should know will be affected by the use of the product. This is essentially the same standard applied to a point-of-sale warning claim. We believe this standard is insufficient to guide the jury.

The duty to warn analysis at the point-of-sale essentially focuses on the foreseeability of a defective product. This standard does not, however, identify the special burdens which may exist for manufacturers to discharge this duty. Thus, if used in a post-sale case, it restricts the jury's considerations to the danger of the product and the manufacturer's foreseeability of the danger. It excludes numerous critical factors identified by the Restatement. The jury is not told to consider the manufacturer's ability to identify users, the likelihood the risk of harm is unknown, the ability to effectively communicate a warning, and any other burden in providing a warning compared to the risk of harm. These factors are critical to understanding the reasonableness of the conduct.

Factors

We believe the post-sale failure to warn instruction must be more specific than the point of sale failure to warn instruction and inform the jury to consider those factors which make it burdensome or impractical for a manufacturer to provide a warning in determining the reasonableness of its conduct. It is prejudicial error to fail to do so. Accordingly, we adopt the Restatement (Third) of Torts: Products Liability §10, including the need to articulate the relevant factors to consider in determining the reasonableness of providing a warning after the sale.

We recognize the comments to the Restatement refer to the need for the court to consider the four factors in deciding whether a post-sale breach of duty to warn claim should reach the jury. See Restatement (Third) of Torts: Products Liability §10 cmt. *a.* Clearly, the particular circumstances of a case may permit a trial court to utilize the factors to determine as a matter of law no duty existed. Normally, however, the jury determines whether a warning of a product danger should have been given. Thus, if the trial court finds sufficient proof to impose a duty, the Restatement factors must be further utilized so the jury can understand the extent of the duty and properly perform its function in deciding the reasonableness of the conduct.

Our decision today confirms the existence of a post-sale duty for manufacturers to warn when it is reasonable to do so. The trial court may determine no duty existed in a particular case as a matter of law. Otherwise, the trial court should instruct the jury to determine whether it was reasonable to provide a warning by using the four Restatement factors.

We recognize the Restatement approach gives rise to other issues, but they are not before us at this time. We hold trial courts must incorporate the Restatement factors in instructing the jury on the duty to warn following the sale. . . .

V. Conclusion

[The Court affirmed the judgment for compensatory damages in favor of the plaintiff based on a claim that the cultivator was defectively designed. The Court's discussion of design defect is omitted from the opinion. Plaintiff's claim for punitive damages was predicated on the negligent post-sale failure to warn claim. Since the court concluded that the instruction on post-sale failure to warn was erroneous, it reversed the finding of punitive damages and ordered a new trial on post-sale failure to warn and punitive damages.]

AFFIRMED IN PART, REVERSED IN PART, AND REMANDED FOR NEW TRIAL

Did the Iowa court correctly apply the Restatement test? Must all four factors in §10(b) be established for a post-sale duty to be owed? Or are they to be considered and weighed in whatever fashion that the court deems appropriate in each case? For a recent decision perhaps attempting to split this difference, see Jones v. Bowie Industries, Inc., 282 P.3d 316, 335 (Alaska 2012), which explained that

> [t]he [Products Liability] Restatement [§10(b)] sets out four factors to balance in determining whether a reasonable person in the seller's position would provide a post-sale warning. It contemplates that a court will make an initial determination that some evidence has been introduced to support each factor before instructing a jury on the question [of whether the seller breached a post-sale duty to warn]. [Citations omitted.]

In Daniel v. Coleman Co., 599 F.3d 1045 (9th Cir. 2010), both the plaintiff's husband and her father died of carbon monoxide poisoning after they and a friend (who survived) used a propane heater to warm a camper before sleeping there during the night. The plaintiff brought claims of design defect and failure to warn against the defendant manufacturer. She also alleged the defendant had a post-sale duty to notify consumers of the risk of carbon monoxide poisoning — in addition to the warnings the defendant had already posted on the heater — because a number of similar accidents involving the same heater had occurred after manufacture. The trial court refused to give a jury instruction on post-sale duty to warn but allowed her claims on design defect and failure to warn to go to the jury, who returned verdicts favorable to the defendant on both claims. The court of appeals affirmed the trial court's holding that the defendant owed no post-sale duty under Washington law, stating that any newly perceived risk arising from the other, similar accidents was accounted for by the warnings already on the heater.

Judicial support for the post-sale duty to warn is strong. See, e.g., Brown v. Crown Equip. Corp., 554 F.3d 34 (1st Cir. 2009); Stanger v. Smith & Nephew, Inc., 401 F. Supp. 2d 974, 982 (E.D. Mo. 2005). But there are some holdouts. See, e.g., McLennan v. American Eurocopter Corp., 245 F.3d 403 (5th Cir. 2001) (applying Texas law); Cameron v. DaimlerChrysler, Corp., 2005 U.S. Dist. LEXIS 24361 (E.D. Ky. 2005); Modelski v. Navistar Int'l Transp. Corp., 707 N.E.2d 239 (Ill. App. Ct. 1999). Other courts impose a post-sale duty to warn only if the product was defective from the time of manufacture and the manufacturer had notice of the defect. DeSantis v. Frick Co., 745 A.2d 624 (Pa. Super. Ct. 1999), *appeal granted*, 785 A.2d 89 (Pa. 2000), *appeal dismissed as improvidently granted*, 778 A.2d 619 (Pa. 2001); cf. Jones v. Cooper Tire & Rubber Co., 2004 U.S. Dist. LEXIS 4352, *7 (E.D. Pa. 2004) ("Virginia courts have concluded that 'though the duty to warn clearly is continuous from the date of manufacture/sale, it requires the manufacturer to warn only about dangerous conditions it knew about, or in the exercise of reasonable care should have known about, at the time.'"); Jablonski v. Ford Motor Co., 955 N.E.2d 1138, 1161 (Ill. 2011) ("Illinois has 'reject[ed] the imposition of any post-sale duty to warn if the product was not defective at the time of sale.'").

An interesting application of the post-sale duty to warn occurs in the context of plaintiffs' efforts to circumvent statutes of repose. Many jurisdictions have enacted time bars to tort liability that begin to run at the time of original sale by the last member of the vertical chain of product distribution. In contrast to statutes of limitations, which run from the time the plaintiff knows or has reason to know he has been injured by the product, and thus always give the diligent plaintiff time to file a claim, statutes of repose can bar claims before the plaintiff even suffers injury. The harshness of statutes of repose has led some plaintiffs to argue that, in addition to whatever defects may have existed at the time of original sale, claims for which are barred by an applicable statute of repose, the defendant manufacturer also breached a post-sale duty to warn, claims for which are not time-barred because the period of repose has not yet run. Were courts to recognize such post-sale warning claims indiscriminately, statutes of repose could be circumvented in every instance involving original design or warning defects.

On the other hand, for courts automatically to hold such post-sale warnings claims to be time-barred after the running of the period of repose would undermine the manufacturer's incentives to provide timely warnings. Outcomes depend, of course, on the wording of the repose statute involved in a particular case. When the defect existed at the time of original sale, courts tend to hold that the claim based on the post-sale duty merges with the claim based on original defect, and is therefore time-barred. See, e.g., Land v. Yamaha Motor Corp., U.S.A., 272 F.3d 514 (7th Cir. 2001) (applying Indiana law); Quiray v. Heidelberg, USA, 2006 U.S. Dist. LEXIS 55191 (D. Or. 2006); Saporito v. Cincinnati Inc., 2004 Tex. App. LEXIS 1206 (2004). But when the post-sale duty is based on new information that became available after the time of original sale, the post-sale breach is deemed to be independent of the original defect and the failure to warn claim is not time-barred. See, e.g., Hunter v. Werner Co., 574 S.E.2d 426 (Ga. Ct. App. 2002).

An obligation somewhat related to the post-sale duty to warn is the duty to recall. Much like the post-sale duty to warn, this duty entails an informational component in that recall notice certainly may warn users of the dangers posed by a given product. However, beyond this, the duty to recall also encompasses a duty to retrieve the product and physically correct some feature of the recalled product or, if correction is not feasible, to remove the product from the stream of commerce. Generally the duty to recall is fairly circumscribed. As the Restatement (Third) of Torts: Products Liability §11 explains, courts have refused to recognize a common law duty to recall products. See, e.g., Murray v. Gen. Motors, L.L.C., 478 Fed. App'x 175, 182 (5th Cir. 2012) (holding that under Mississippi law a car dealership does not have a post-sale duty to notify a buyer about manufacturer recalls); Stanger v. Smith & Nephew, Inc., 401 F. Supp. 2d 974, 982 (E.D. Mo. 2005) (holding that "absent a mandated recall by a governmental agency," no duty to recall exists under Missouri law). As the Restatement notes, a duty to recall arises only when a governmental directive issued pursuant to a statute or administrative regulation specifically requires that a product seller or distributor recall a product line or when a seller or distributor voluntarily undertakes to recall a product. In the latter case, the seller or distributor may be liable if it fails to exercise a reasonable degree of care. See, e.g., Silver v. Bad Boy Enterprises., LLC, 907 F. Supp. 2d 1351, 1356-57 (M.D. Ga. 2012).

More recent cases seems to be stretching the idea of when a retailer "voluntarily undertakes" to notify its customers regarding product recalls. See, e.g., Nationwide Prop. & Cas. Ins. Co. v. Gen. Motors, LLC, — F. Supp. 3d —, 2015 WL 1281751 (S.D. Tex. 2015) (holding that dealer conducting a multi-point inspection has a duty to ensure no outstanding recalls concern plaintiff's vehicle); Hensley-Maclean v. Safeway, Inc., 2014 WL 1364906 (N.D. Cal.) (holding that supermarket retailer could have a duty under California law to notify customers of food product recalls in light of retailer's use of a customer loyalty card that enables extensive purchase tracking information). In some ways, then, the duty to conduct a recall is analogous to the duty to rescue: the duty to exercise reasonable care is only imposed once the recall or rescue is undertaken — no freestanding duty exists. As Comment *a* of the Restatement asserts, a duty to recall imposes significant burdens on manufacturers, and as such, imposition of such a duty may best be left to government agencies that have the data-gathering capacity to best determine when the benefits of a recall justify its burdens.

Many recent high-profile recall cases involved the National Highway Traffic Safety Administration (NHTSA). The Secretary of the U.S. Department of Transportation is authorized under 49 U.S.C.A. §30118 to compel manufacturers to recall a product and notify all owners, purchasers, and dealers of the product's defect. A 2014 controversy involving faulty ignition switches and other defects in vehicles produced by General Motors, which led to at least thirty deaths, exposed potential drawbacks in relying on a central authority to monitor an entire industry for defects meriting a recall. In a congressional investigation into why the eventual recall was delayed, NHTSA claimed that General Motors failed to disclose information about the defects for years after the company's engineers first became aware of the problem. An initiative within NHTSA to open an investigation in 2007 into the same defects that led to the eventual recalls in 2014 was blocked internally for lack of sufficient information to justify ordering a recall. Indeed, much of the engineering information that led to the recall was only discovered during a products liability lawsuit against General Motors filed in June 2011 on behalf of a woman who died in an automobile accident. See Melton v. Gen. Motors LLC, U.S. Dist. LEXIS 97693 (M.D. Ga. 2014). Should the problems exposed by the General Motors recall controversy force a reexamination of the roles of public regulation and private litigation in exposing and addressing potential post-sale safety issues, or should the controversy be regarded as an aberration in which the public recall system did not work as intended? For an unsuccessful attempt to perform a NHTSA function through a private lawsuit, see Silvas v. General Motors, LLC, U.S. Dist. LEXIS 52979 (S.D. Tex. 2014), which denied the plaintiff's motion to compel General Motors to send a "Park It Now" alert to all 2.6 million owners of potentially defective vehicles because such an injunction falls within NHTSA's primary jurisdiction.

D. SPECIAL PROBLEMS WITH CAUSATION

1. *Would the Product User/Consumer Have Heeded an Adequate Warning?*

The issue of but-for-the-defect causation pursued in Section C of Chapter Three is especially difficult in the context of failure to warn. Under every approach taken in every jurisdiction, the plaintiff must show that the defendant's failure to warn was an actual and proximate cause of the plaintiff's injury. To do that, the plaintiff must show that, if an adequate instruction or warning had been given, the addressee (typically the product user or consumer) would have acted differently in a manner that would have reduced or avoided the plaintiff's injury. For example, in Gray v. Cannon, 807 So. 2d 924 (La. Ct. App. 2002), an automobile passenger was injured in an accident allegedly caused by a tire blow-out. The plaintiff claimed, inter alia, that the manufacturer should have warned the driver not to drive on tires with low air pressure. The tire in question had a slow leak that caused it to overheat and fail catastrophically. In affirming summary judgment for the tire manufacturer, the court noted that the tires "seemed fine" to the parties involved in the accident. Thus, any failure to warn against driving on an underinflated tire was not a cause of the plaintiffs' harm: "an absence of warnings, unless it is coupled with the knowledge that *would have* called the warnings into play, was not 'reasonably connected' to the accident caused by the tire's eventual rupture." Id. at 929. The "what if" inquiries that the causation issue presents in failure-to-warn cases are among the most difficult that courts confront.

The Washington Court of Appeals confronted these difficulties in Ayers v. Johnson & Johnson Baby Products Co., 797 P.2d 527 (Wash. Ct. App. 1990), involving a 15-month-old toddler who aspirated (breathed in) baby oil and suffered irreversible brain injury. The trial court set aside a $2,500,000 verdict in favor of the child and his family, in part on the ground that a more adequate warning by the defendant would not have done any good. The family had kept the baby oil on a high shelf along with other products they did not want the toddler to reach. The child's teen-aged sister had transferred some of the oil into a small bottle which she kept in her purse to use after high school gym class. On the day of the accident the sister inadvertently left her purse on the floor in their home. The toddler found the purse, opened the small bottle and began to drink its contents. At that moment the child's mother entered the room, discovered the child drinking the contents, and yelled at him to stop. Responding reflexively, the boy gasped and inhaled the oil into his lungs, where it prevented his lungs from functioning properly. When the mother discovered he had been drinking baby oil her concerns were alleviated and she took no further steps to check for difficulties. Hours later, she discovered the child had suffered brain damage from oxygen deprivation.

The plaintiffs claimed that Johnson & Johnson should have warned of the risks of aspiration and the very great harm that could result if aspiration should occur. In reversing the JNOV entered below, the appellate court reasoned:

> Family members testified that house rules required that anything known to be dangerous be kept high out of reach of the twin baby boys. Mrs. Ayers testified that she was a label reader and that had she known of the risks of aspiration, everyone else in the family would have known also. Laurie Ayers, who left the purse containing the baby oil on the floor, testified that Mrs. Ayers told all the family members to keep items known to be dangerous away from the boys. Laurie said that, never having been told of any risks associated with baby oil, she thought it was "no big deal" when she left her purse on the floor because there was nothing in it that could be harmful.
>
> Mr. Ayers also testified that products known to be dangerous were kept up on a top shelf out of reach. He testified further that had the product carried a warning of the risks, they would not have had it in the house.
>
> An appropriate inference from all this is that because the product was without a warning, the family members did not know it was dangerous and so did not treat it as such. The family members' testimony shows that they did not know of the particular harm that could result from aspirating mineral oil. . . . [Id. at 530-31.]

One judge dissented in *Ayers* on the ground that but-for causation had not been established and intervening events had broken the chain of causation tying the warning's adequacy to the child's harm. The Supreme Court of Washington, sitting en banc, unanimously affirmed the decision of the Court of Appeals, in an opinion closely tracking that of the intermediate court. Ayers v. Johnson & Johnson Baby Prods. Co., 818 P.2d 1337 (Wash. 1991) (en banc).

Would it have made a difference in the court's reaction in *Ayers* if the oil that the child aspirated had been a hair conditioning product that contained a number of ingredients that a reasonable person would be loath to ingest? You will recall that the majority of the Supreme Court of Michigan thought so in Greene v. A.P. Products, Ltd., 717 N.W.2d 855 (Mich. 2006), included in full near the beginning of this chapter. The court in *Greene* ruled for defendant as a matter of law on the ground that the risks of injury from allowing an 11-month-old toddler to ingest hair conditioning oil were obvious. You will also recall that one of the dissents in that case emphasized that the hair oil's main ingredients appeared nontoxic, suggesting they were safe to ingest. The susceptibility of infants to suffer injury at the hands of apparently innocuous household products knows no bounds. Thus, in Fraust v. Swift & Co., 610 F. Supp. 711 (W.D. Pa. 1985), the district court denied the defendant's motion for summary judgment, ruling that the mother of a 16-month-old infant might not have known of the risk of feeding him a peanut butter sandwich. The child choked on the peanut butter and suffered severe brain damage. A jury might find that the defendant-manufacturer breached its duty to warn of hidden dangers and that the breach proximately caused the injuries. And in Emery v. Federated Foods, Inc., 863 P.2d 426 (Mont. 1993), a two-and-one-half-year-old toddler choked on a marshmallow in the kitchen of his home, suffering brain injuries. The Supreme Court of Montana reversed summary judgment for the defendant, holding that genuine issues of fact were presented regarding whether a warning should have been given that young children might choke on marshmallows and, if warnings had been given, the child's mother would have been able to prevent the injury. The dissent took a different view: "The net result of the majority opinion may well be that warnings must be placed on nearly every food item available to the public if the provider is to avoid litigation for a claim of products liability — an interesting challenge for the providers of edible items." Id. at 434.

Obviously, the but-for causation issue looms large in these "child ingestion" cases. Even if warnings had been given, would the warnings have made any difference? As in *Ayers,* supra, the parents swear on a Bible, no doubt sincerely, that "if we had only known, we would have saved our baby!" But if all foods came with warnings in big red letters: "Babies may choke on this and suffer brain damage," would parents keep *everything* in the house locked away where older siblings could not get them and give them to the toddlers? The plaintiffs in Cook v. Ford Motor Co., 913 N.E.2d 311 (Ind. Ct. App. 2009), mentioned in the discussion of Indiana's RAW requirement, supra, claimed that the defendant insufficiently warned them regarding the dangers that air-bags posed to children. Their eight-year-old daughter, who had unbuckled her seat belt and was riding unrestrained in the front passenger seat, suffered severe brain injuries from the passenger-side airbag, which deployed after a low-speed rear-end collision. The plaintiffs contended that the warnings on the vehicle and in the driver's manual — which stated that the passenger side airbag should be activated unless the operator was using a rear-facing child safety seat — did not adequately warn them of the dangers the airbag posed to *all* children in the front seat, not just those in a rear-facing child safety seat. The father testified at trial that he buckled his daughter into the passenger seat when he placed her in the car and that, although he had not read all the warnings contained in the manual, even if he had he would not have altered his behavior because they did not contradict his belief that the front seat was safer because it was equipped with an airbag. The defendant manufacturer argued that the airbag instructions were not a proximate cause of the girl's injuries because her unbuckling her seat belt was an intervening cause. The defendant also argued that, had the plaintiff followed the vehicle's other instructions — which told operators that the back seat is safer for children and instructed all passengers to wear seat belts — their daughter would not have been injured. The Indiana Court of Appeals, reversing the trial court's summary judgment for defendant, held that there were genuine issues of material fact concerning whether the girl's actions were sufficient to break the chain of causation and whether the plaintiffs would have altered their behavior if they had been warned more directly about the danger the airbags posed to all children riding in the front seat.

In response to the obvious difficulties of trying to answer the but-for questions in these cases, courts began to hold that when a product is sold without a warning, a rebuttable presumption arises that the consumer would have read any warning provided by the manufacturer and acted so as to minimize the risks. In an influential early decision, the Texas high court affirmed an alternative holding of the trial court giving the plaintiff a new trial on what, without a presumption, would have been very weak evidence of causation. See Technical Chem. Co. v. Jacobs, 480 S.W.2d 602 (Tex. 1972). The court explained:

> It has been suggested that the law should supply the presumption that an adequate warning would have been read. "Where warning is given, the seller may reasonably assume that it will be read and heeded." Restatement (Second) of Torts §402A, Comment *j* (1965). Such a presumption works in favor of the manufacturer when an adequate warning is present. Where there is no warning, as in this case, however, the presumption that the user would have read an adequate warning works in favor of the plaintiff user. In other words, the presumption is that Jacobs would have read an adequate warning. The presumption may, however, be rebutted if the manufacturer comes forward with contrary evidence that the presumed fact did not exist. Depending upon the individual facts, this may be accomplished by the manufacturer's producing evidence that the user was blind, illiterate, intoxicated at the time of the use, irresponsible or lax in judgment or by some other circumstance tending to show that the improper use was or would have been made regardless of the warning. [Id. at 606.]

Notice that the quoted language from Comment *j* of the Second Restatement may have been intended to shield manufacturers from any liability for product-caused harms when adequate warnings are given, rather than to create a presumption of causation when inadequate warnings are delivered. Nevertheless, the trend in favor of applying a heeding presumption in warnings cases has been substantial. See, e.g., Tenbarge v. Ames Taping Tool Sys. Inc., 190 F.3d 862 (8th Cir. 1999); Reyes v. Wyeth Labs., 498 F.2d 1264 (5th Cir.), *cert. denied*, 419 U.S. 1096 (1974); Nissen Trampoline Co. v. Terre Haute First Nat'l Bank, 332 N.E.2d 820 (Ind. Ct. App. 1975), *rev'd on other grounds*, 358 N.E.2d 974 (Ind. 1976); Cunningham v. Charles Pfizer & Co., Inc., 532 P.2d 1377 (Okla. 1974). In 1998, the Third Circuit predicted that Pennsylvania would adopt a heeding presumption in failure-to-warn cases. Pavlik v. Lane Ltd./Tobacco Exporters Int'l, 135 F.3d 876, 883 (3d Cir. 1998). Although Pennsylvania's high court has not yet decided this issue, the lower courts have adopted a heeding presumption with increasing consistency. See, e.g., Maya v. Johnson & Johnson, 97 A.3d 1203 (Pa. Super. Ct. 2014) (deciding that the trial court erred in failing to instruct the jury on the heeding presumption in a case involving Children's Motrin).

Other courts continue to place the traditional burden on the plaintiff to establish causation in failure-to-warn cases. See, e.g., Wilson v. Bradlees of New England, 250 F.3d 10 (1st Cir. 2001) (refusing to recognize the heeding presumption in suit based on diversity jurisdiction where New Hampshire has not adopted the "read and heed" presumption); Rivera v. Philip Morris, Inc., 209 P.3d 271, 276 (Nev. 2009) ("A heeding presumption, which [plaintiff] seeks this court to adopt, departs from well-settled and established Nevada law."); Hiner v. Bridgestone/Firestone, Inc., 978 P.2d 505 (Wash. 1999) (failure to warn that installation of snow tires on front wheels only can cause mishandling was not cause-in-fact of accident since plaintiff had not examined tires for any warnings imprinted on the tire and had not read the instruction manual); Riley v. American Honda Motor Co., 856 P.2d 196 (Mont. 1993) (a heeding presumption is unwarranted since warnings often go unread and even when read are ignored).

How much evidence should be sufficient to rebut the presumption that, if a warning had been given, the plaintiff would have heeded it? And what happens to the presumption when the defendant introduces sufficient rebuttal evidence? In Golonka v. General Motors Corp., 65 P.3d 956 (Ariz. Ct. App. 2003), the court summarized the law in Arizona as follows:

[T]he heeding presumption serves to shift the burden of production [on causation] to the manufacturer. The manufacturer meets this burden by introducing evidence that would permit reasonable minds to conclude that the injured party would not have heeded an adequate warning. The court determines whether the manufacturer has rebutted the presumption and, if so, the presumption is destroyed, the existence or non-existence of the presumed fact must be determined as if the presumption had never operated in the case, and the jury is never told of the presumption. However, the jury may still draw reasonable inferences from the facts originally giving rise to the presumption.

In Waterhouse v. R.J. Reynolds Tobacco Co., 162 Fed. App'x 231 (4th Cir. 2006), the plaintiff claimed that the cigarette manufacturer had failed to warn him of the risks of smoking, a habit that plaintiff began in 1947. Defendant introduced proof that the plaintiff had been warned of the risks by family, friends, athletic coaches, medical advisers, and others for years, and that the general public knew full well that smoking was hazardous. Plaintiff argued that he did not understand the *real* dangers. Affirming summary judgment for the defendant based on Maryland law, the court of appeals concluded "that, by [the plaintiff's] own admissions, the presumption that [the plaintiff] would have read and heeded an adequate warning if it had been given, had been rebutted." Id. at 234. The strength of the defendant's rebuttal evidence will determine whether the question of causation goes to the jury or can be resolved as a matter of law. See Bachtel v. TASER Int'l, Inc., 747 F.3d 965 (8th Cir. 2014). In *Bachtel*, a police officer's use of a taser led to the death of a detainee. The deceased's mother sued the taser manufacturer. Because officers customarily received instructions on the use of such products from superiors rather than the manufacturer's packaging information and the particular officer who used the taser had not read the manufacturer's warnings, the court found no causation as a matter of law for plaintiff's failure-to-warn claim. The court also suggested that to sustain the heeding presumption, plaintiff should have presented expert testimony as to "the effect of a warning on a police officer in the field." Id. at 970. Does imposing this evidentiary requirement of expert testimony effectively remove the heeding presumption in this case?

Establishing that the plaintiff failed to read the warning provided does not automatically prove that the defendant's warning was adequate. In Bryant v. BGHA, Inc., 9 F. Supp. 3d 1374 (M.D. Ga. 2014), the plaintiff sued under a failure-to-warn theory after falling while descending a hunting stand without securing the provided ratchet straps. Paper instructions packaged along with the stand stated in bold, capitalized text that "vital ratchet straps are included and necessary for the . . . [hunting stand]. Do not attempt to use these ladderstands without all vital ratchet straps secured." Id. at 1381. The court ruled that the plaintiff's admission that he did not read the warnings provided with the stand precluded recovery on the theory that the defendant failed "to provide adequate warning of the product's potential risk." Id. at 1395. However, the court held that the plaintiff could still seek to challenge "the adequacy of the efforts of the manufacturer or seller to communicate the dangers of the product to the buyer or user." In fact, the plaintiff's failure to read the warning could provide important "circumstantial evidence" that the defendant failed to communicate its warnings adequately, which raised a question of fact for the jury. Id. *Bryant* seems to show that defeating the heeding presumption does not necessarily bar plaintiff's failure-to-warn claim, but can raise and even contribute to a different theory of recovery under failure-to-warn.

2. If the User/Consumer Had Heeded the Warning, Would the Plaintiff's Harm Have Been Reduced/Avoided?

An underlying premise in all of the talk in Section 1 about users/consumers heeding warnings is that, if the warning had been heeded, the plaintiff would not have been harmed or would have been harmed less severely. This but-for-the-defect aspect of causation is evident in the cases considered thus far, but it is not always so clear. Thus, in Gigus v. Giles & Ransome, Inc., 868 A.2d 459 (Pa. Super. Ct. 2005), the plaintiff suffered injury while operating an excavator when a steel fragment chipped off the excavator's hammer tool point and struck plaintiff. At the time of the accident, the plaintiff did not have a safety glass shield properly in place. She claimed that the shield was defectively weak and would not have prevented her injury even if she had placed it properly. The plaintiff also argued that the manufacturer should have warned her more forcefully to put the safety shield in place. The trial court granted summary judgment for the defendant sellers, holding that plaintiff had failed to prove the shield design was inadequate and had failed to show that defendants' forceful warnings were inadequate. The intermediate court of appeals affirmed on both counts. But what if the appellate court had affirmed on the design count — no safety shield strong enough to prevent plaintiff's injury was feasible — but had held that the defendant's warnings about using the shield could be found by a jury to be insufficiently urgent? Would not the defendant be able to argue persuasively that, even if the plaintiff had heeded stronger warnings, it would not have prevented her injuries? If this observation is correct, the plaintiff would have failed to prove that the defendant's failure to warn was a but-for cause of her injuries, even if the plaintiff established that she would have heeded a stronger warning to put the safety shield in place. (Query whether plaintiff could argue that she is still entitled to that stronger warning on the "informed choice" notion of a manufacturer's warning duty).

A federal court of appeals reached a conclusion similar to the one suggested above in Koken v. Black & Veatch Construction, Inc., 426 F.3d 39 (1st Cir. 2005), in which a fire blanket proved to be inadequate to contain red-hot cuttings from a torch-cutting operation, resulting in substantial fire losses. The plaintiff argued that the defendant blanket manufacturer should have warned that the blanket was inadequate to achieve "horizontal capture of concentrated splatter or red-hot cut pieces," and that such a warning would have been heeded. The court of appeals affirmed summary judgment for defendants, concluding:

> The problem is that even after applying the [heeding] presumption to the facts of this case, there is still no evidence of causation in fact. The presumption that a warning would be heeded would readily support a finding that, had Austin been engaged in "horizontal capture of concentrated spatter or red-hot cut pieces," he would have desisted. The crucial evidence lacking is any evidence that this was horizontal capture of *concentrated* spatter or *red-hot* cut pieces. B & V's counsel conceded at oral argument that "there is no testimony that particularly says this is concentrated spatter . . . the only thing in the record is that there is molten slag that is generated from a cutting application." Without testimony that the blanket was being used to horizontally capture concentrated spatter or red-hot cut pieces, or that molten slag is the equivalent of concentrated spatter, the legal presumption that a warning against such use would have been heeded is of no aid to appellants. Appellants thus fail to meet their burden of producing evidence sufficient to prove causation in fact under this proposed warning [Id. at 50.]

For an original approach to the problem of causation in failure-to-warn law, see Aaron D. Twerski & Neil B. Cohen, Resolving the Dilemma of Non-Justiciable Causation in Failure-to-Warn Litigation, 84 S. Cal. L. Rev. 125 (2010).

3. What If the Defendant's Failure to Warn Causes Plaintiff to Suffer Harm from Another Product?

Powell v. Standard Brands Paint Co.
212 Cal. Rptr. 395 (Cal. Ct. App. 1985)

SIMS, J.

Plaintiffs Bruce Powell and Dale Mereness appeal from a summary judgment granted in favor of defendant Standard Brands Paint Company (Standard Brands) in an action for personal injuries. We affirm.

Factual and Procedural Background

As relevant to this appeal, the complaint prepared by plaintiffs' attorneys stated that defendant Standard Brands and other defendants were the suppliers or manufacturers "of certain equipment and cleaning solvents, specifically being, but not limited to a buffer and/or thinner referred to herein." The complaint further alleged that Standard Brands and other defendants "negligently and carelessly operated, controlled, warned, supplied, maintained, managed, designed, manufactured, or modified said buffer and/or thinner which proximately caused the injuries and damages to plaintiff as herein described." Paragraph X of the complaint pleaded in pertinent part, "That on or about June 10, 1982, . . . *while plaintiff was stripping a tile floor with said buffer* and *thinner*, an explosion occurred due to the negligence of the defendants, and each of them, proximately causing the hereinafter described injuries and damages to plaintiff." (Italics added.)

---

authors' dialogue 20

AARON: I don't like the heeding presumption. It's a huge embarrassment.

JIM: Don't mince words, Aaron; tell us how you really feel.

AARON: Failure-to-warn claims are difficult enough for defendants. It's essentially a rhetorical tort. Unlike design, there's no technology involved. All the plaintiff needs to do is cook up a story with his lawyer about something that wasn't obvious that they should have told him, and he's getting to the jury. Informed choice makes it even easier. "Many people wouldn't have cared, but I do — I'm special." But-for causation is, or was, the defendant's only hope. "Even if we should have told you, it wouldn't have made any difference, for crying out loud." But now many states put the burden on defendant to prove it wouldn't have mattered. Every warnings claim has clear sailing to the jury.

DOUG: That is a slight exaggeration, Aaron, but I get your point. On the other hand, without a presumption, wouldn't every warning claim fail to leave harbor? Unlike design defect cases where it's relatively straightforward to imagine how an event would have unfolded with a different product design, warning cases require a very uncertain and artificial counterfactual: How would plaintiff have behaved if defendant provided a better warning? That's pure psychological speculation.

JIM: Now I think you are both exaggerating. Aaron, don't you at least agree that when the person who should have been warned is dead, or otherwise unavailable to testify, there should be a presumption?

AARON: Yes, but we don't need a formal presumption. Circumstantial proof and common sense should be enough in those cases to avoid unfairness to the plaintiff. But an across-the-board presumption is overkill. The *Ayers* case

---

As relevant here, plaintiff sought recovery for damages on theories of negligence and strict liability.

In moving for summary judgment, Standard Brands competently showed that plaintiffs commenced work on June 9, 1982, using lacquer thinner supplied by Standard Brands to remove sealer from ceramic tile. They worked without incident throughout the evening until they had used up the Standard Brands lacquer thinner. However, plaintiffs were unable to finish the job on June 9. The following day, June 10, plaintiffs' employer ordered two five-gallon containers of lacquer thinner from codefendant Harris Automotive (Harris). This lacquer thinner was manufactured by codefendant Grow Chemical Coatings Company (Grow).[5] Working in an area approximately 25-50

---

5. The declarations submitted on the motion for summary judgment do not indicate whether the Grow thinner contained warnings. . . . Plaintiffs' complaint alleged that defendants Grow and Harris wrongfully failed to warn of risks of their product. The burden was on defendant Standard Brands to refute those pleaded allegations by competent evidence. It did not do so. For present purposes, we must assume the unchallenged allegations of the complaint control and that the Grow lacquer thinner contained inadequate warnings.

(pp. 366-367, supra) is a good example of what I'm talking about. Even if Johnson & Johnson had told that family all about the dangers of aspiration of baby oil, the same thing would've happened. The dissent was clearly right in that case.

DOUG: I'm glad you mentioned *Ayers.* I read the majority as saying that when a tragedy like that occurs once in a blue moon, the manufacturer should pay on almost an "enterprise liability" basis. For me, the subtext was the court's willingness to suspend the normal rules to allow the one-family-in-a-million to receive no-fault insurance coverage, in effect, for their loss. It's an example of what Jim has called "echoes of enterprise liability," and he argues that these echoes are not so mischievous so long as they remain confined to their narrow spheres.

AARON: Jim, do you really approve of such lawlessness? You, of all people?

JIM: Let's just say I understand it. It doesn't upset me that much.

AARON: Well, I don't approve one bit. Even if *Ayers* is understandable, in most cases the heeding presumption works unfairly against the manufacturer. In any other area of the law it would be laughed out of court (just like that "subtext" jargon that Doug just threw at us).

JIM: My hunch is that when a products plaintiff tries to rely on the presumption in a case where common sense suggests that a warning wouldn't have made any difference, the court will take the case from the jury on causation grounds.

AARON: But in the "old days," that was easy because the court could say that the plaintiff had not carried the burden of production on but-for causation. But once the burden is on the defendant, via the heeding presumption, what's the court going to say?

DOUG: I guess that depends on whether you listen to the text or the subtext.

---

feet from where they had worked the previous evening, plaintiffs commenced pouring the Grow lacquer thinner on the tile floor and buffing the thinner with the electric buffer. During this operation, an explosion occurred, seriously injuring both plaintiffs and giving rise to the instant lawsuit.

Plaintiffs relied primarily on the declaration of plaintiff Powell. Powell declared that the lacquer thinner purchased from Standard Brands contained neither warnings nor safety instructions and that "Had anyone at Standard Brands advised us of the dangerous nature of lacquer thinner or of its highly flammable characteristics, I would not have used it on the job and would not have been using it at the time of my injury."

The trial court granted the motion and plaintiffs appeal from the summary judgment entered in favor of Standard Brands.

Discussion . . .

As best we understand it, plaintiffs assert on appeal that Standard Brands owed them a duty to warn them of the dangerous properties of its lacquer thinner, that it breached its duty to warn, and that its failure to warn was a legal proximate cause of the injuries suffered by plaintiffs. To our knowledge, no reported decision has held a manufacturer liable for its failure to warn of risks of using its product, where it is shown that the immediate efficient cause of injury is a product manufactured by someone else. Unfortunately, in addressing the merits of plaintiffs' important and novel contention, we find the meagre brief filed by plaintiffs' attorneys of little assistance. Needless to say, however, we believe our own research has produced a correct result. . . .

Standard Brands has not refuted plaintiffs' pleaded assertions that said defendant owed plaintiffs a duty to warn of risks of *its* product and that it breached its duty. However, the evidence is undisputed that the immediate efficient cause of plaintiffs' injuries was the explosion of a product manufactured not by Standard Brands but rather by Grow. The question posed is whether Standard Brands' failure to warn was a legal proximate cause of plaintiffs' injuries. We conclude, in the circumstances of this case, it was not. . . .

Where a defendant has committed a wrongful act, and where a third person also commits a later wrongful act, and both are alleged to have caused plaintiff's injuries, the courts have asked whether the subsequent act of the third party was a superseding cause that served to break the requisite chain of causation between defendant's wrongful act and the injury. Whether the act of the third person is a superseding cause depends in part on whether it (and plaintiff's injury) was reasonably foreseeable.

On the undisputed facts tendered in this case, we conclude the explosion of Grow's product, and plaintiffs' consequent injuries, were not reasonably foreseeable consequences of Standard Brands' failure to warn as a matter of law. We explain.

Although there appears to be some uncertainty about the knowledge required of a manufacturer to justify liability for failure to warn of *its* product it is clear the manufacturer's duty is restricted to warnings based on the characteristics of *the manufacturer's own product.* Understandably, the law does not require a manufacturer to study and analyze the products of others and to warn users of risks of those products. A manufacturer's decision to supply warnings, and the nature of any warnings, are therefore necessarily based upon and tailored to the risks of use of the manufacturer's own product. Thus, even where the manufacturer erroneously omits warnings, the most the manufacturer could reasonably foresee is that consumers might be subject to the risks of the manufacturer's own product, since those are the only risks he is required to know.

From the foregoing, it follows that if plaintiff's theory of liability (asserted on appeal) has any validity, it would be limited to situations where the risks of use of the product immediately causing injury are identical to the risks of use of the product previously used with inadequate warnings. No other risks are reasonably foreseeable. As a practical matter, a contrary conclusion would require each manufacturer to ascertain the risks of products manufactured by others within an industry and to warn of the highest risks a consumer might encounter. Such a requirement would place on each manufacturer an untoward duty and would penalize inventive manufacturers whose products are, in fact, of lower risk than other products in the industry.

We therefore believe the theory of liability now asserted by plaintiffs would require at a minimum that: (a) the product immediately causing injury (product B) was subject to the same generic description as the product previously used with inadequate warnings (product A), e.g., "lawnmower," "electric drill," "aspirin," etc.; (b) product B was generally used for the same purposes as product A by consumers; (c) product B's warnings were inadequate; and (d) *product B had risks of use identical to those of product A.* This theory of liability gains credence to the extent a generically identical product (with presumably identical risks of use) is made by a limited number of manufacturers in an industry, and there is an industry-wide practice of omitting warnings on the product. In such a situation, each manufacturer has reason to know that the risks of use associated with its product are the same as the risks of the other products and that a consumer will receive no adequate warnings from the other products.

In this case we need not decide whether a manufacturer who fails to warn of its product may be held liable for injuries immediately caused by the use of a product with the same generic description and identical risks of use, because it is clear plaintiffs' attorneys never pleaded facts necessary to support that legal theory, nor anything remotely resembling it, in the trial court. . . .

The complaint prepared by plaintiffs' attorneys did not plead that Standard Brands' absence of warnings caused plaintiffs to use a generically identical product, nor a product with the same risks of use, nor even a substantially similar product, without knowledge of its dangers. Indeed, the complaint pleads no relationship of similarity whatsoever between the Standard Brands and the Grow products. Rather, the complaint prepared by plaintiffs' attorneys states plaintiffs were using Standard Brands' product when an explosion occurred. The complaint tendered a theory that the Standard Brands product was the immediate efficient cause of injury, i.e., plaintiffs were using it when it exploded. That pleading was the one defendant had to encounter on its motion for summary judgment. Standard Brands showed, contrary to plaintiffs' pleading, plaintiffs were not using its product at the time of explosion. Standard Brands therefore refuted the only theory of causation pleaded by plaintiffs' attorneys. There was no other viable theory of causation pleaded, and the trial court had no duty to invent one. . . .

We conclude, on the facts pleaded and adjudicated on the motion for summary judgment, it was not reasonably foreseeable as a matter of law that Standard Brands' failure to warn of risks of its product would cause plaintiffs to suffer injuries while using the product of another. In the circumstances, the explosion of Grow's product was an intervening and superceding cause of injury to plaintiffs. Consequently, Standard Brands' failure to warn was not a proximate cause of plaintiffs' injuries as a matter of law. Standard Brands' motion for summary judgment was properly granted.

The judgment is affirmed.

Plaintiffs are obviously shooting for the moon when they attempt to hold one manufacturer liable for an injury caused by a *different* manufacturer's product. The argument has arisen frequently in the context of generic drugs, where federal regulations require generic drug manufacturers to issue warnings and instructions identical to their brand-name counterparts and where, as noted later in this chapter, federal preemption principles block plaintiffs from suing generic manufacturers. Faced with such constraints, plaintiffs have argued that brand-name manufacturers should bear liability even for harms caused to users of generic counterpart drugs. The overwhelming majority of courts reject this "innovator liability" theory. See, e.g., McNair v. Johnson & Johnson, 2015 WL 3935787 at *5 (S.D. Va. 2015) (gathering cases). But a handful of courts have flirted with it. See, e.g., Kellogg v. Wyeth, 762 F. Supp. 2d 694 (D. Vt. 2010) (brand name drug manufacturer owes a duty of care to adequately warn consumers of generic version of drug); Wyeth, Inc. v. Weeks, 150 So. 3d 649, 676 (Ala. 2014) (holding, in response to certified question, that "a brand-name-drug company may be held liable for fraud or misrepresentation (by misstatement or omission), based on statements it made in connection with the manufacture of a brand-name prescription drug, by a plaintiff claiming physical injury caused by a generic drug manufactured by a different company''); Conte v. Wyeth, Inc., 85 Cal. Rptr. 3d 299 (Cal. Ct. App. 2008) (holding that the name brand manufacturer's duty of care extends to patients whose doctors rely on its product information when prescribing the drug, whether or not the patient used the name brand or generic drug). Still, the *Wyeth* case was overturned by statute in Alabama in 2015 and the future of the "innovator liability" theory of recovery remains quite doubtful. See Brittany L. Raposa, Caveat Emptor: Protecting Inexpensive Generic Drugs at the Expense of Patient Safety, 27 No. 5 Health Law. 28, 31-32 (2015).

Earlier in this chapter, in connection with our discussion of Persons v. Salomon North America, Inc., we confronted a related but different issue: whether a seller or manufacturer has a duty to warn of dangers arising when its product is combined with another manufacturer's product, causing injury, and where neither product is, by itself, defective. A majority of jurisdictions have recognized such a duty. See, e.g., Bettencourt v. Hennessy Indus., Inc., 141 Cal. Rptr. 3d 167, 181 (Cal. Ct. App. 2012) ("[A] product manufacturer may be liable for harm caused by the product of another when the defendant's product contributes substantially to the harm. . . .") (citation omitted); Scheman-Gonzales v. Saber Mfg. Co., 816 So. 2d 1133 (Fla. App. Ct. 2002) (recognizing a duty to warn of the risk of explosion in loading a 16-inch tire onto the manufacturer's 16.5-inch rim); Rastelli v. Goodyear Tire & Rubber Co., 591 N.E.2d 222, 225-26 (N.Y. 1992) (acknowledging that where the combination of one sound product with another sound product creates a dangerous condition, the manufacturer of each product has a duty to warn). But see Firestone Steel Prods. Co. v. Barajas, 927 S.W.2d 608, 614 (Tex. 1996) (holding that a "manufacturer generally does not have a duty to warn or instruct about another manufacturer's products"); Schreiner v. Wieser Concrete Prods., Inc., 720 N.W.2d 525, 531 (Wis. Ct. App. 2006) ("Thus, other courts have [like this court] held a manufacturer only owes a duty to warn regarding its own products, not products it did not manufacture, sell or otherwise place in the stream of commerce.").

4.   Did the Plaintiff Suffer the Sort of Harm that an Adequate Warning Would Have Aimed at Preventing?

This is the failure-to-warn version of the "result within the risk" proximate cause issue presented in Section D of Chapter Two. In the authors' experience, it can be a "sleeper" issue, often obscured by the more vivid but-for issues of the sorts addressed in the preceding subsections. That is, the natural tendency is to focus on whether an adequate warning would have made any difference. This can be a difficult question to answer, as the heeding presumption cases bear witness. But when it is clear that a better warning would have prevented injury, it is tempting to conclude that the defendant's failure to warn has proximately caused the plaintiff's harm.

A Florida court may have resisted this impulse in Trek Bicycle Corp. v. Miguelez, ___ So. 3d ____, 2015 Fla. App. LEXIS 3833 (2015). The plaintiff was injured when his bike abruptly stopped due to road debris that hit the back sides of the carbon-fiber forks surrounding the bicycle's front wheel and became stuck in the front wheel's spokes.

The forks buckled, causing the bicycle to collapse. Plaintiff sued the bicycle manufacturer for failing to warn about the potential for the carbon fiber used in the bicycle's frame to crack and fail. The appellate court reversed the plaintiff's jury award, finding that the proximate cause of plaintiff's injury was not the defendant's failure to warn about the carbon fiber's weakness but the road debris that hit the plaintiff's bicycle. The court explained: "The possibility of encountering road debris in the manner that [the plaintiff] unfortunately experienced did not, however, have to do with the lack of warnings about carbon components, but had to do with the conditions of the road — conditions presented to all bicyclists regardless of the materials from which the bicycle is constructed, conditions certainly outside of the manufacturer's control." Id. at *2.

PROBLEM TWENTY-TWO

The facts in Problem Twenty-One supra, involving injury to Kathy Kritzik's eyes from wearing contact lenses for too long a period, are incorporated herein by reference.

The Kritziks have learned, since the episode with the contact lenses, that women who take birth control pills and women who go through pregnancy are subject to changes in the cornea. Continual daily use of contact lenses without correction for such changes may cause distortion of the cornea, a condition that corrects itself in several months when the lenses are no longer used. Women who take the pill should have their eyes checked more frequently than others to assure that such distortion does not take place. Unbeknownst to either Dr. Quell or Kathy's parents, Kathy had been taking birth control pills during the months preceding last Christmas. Neither Dr. Quell nor the Seenco booklet indicated to Kathy that contact lenses should be monitored more carefully for women who are taking birth control pills. Kathy insists that she would not have asked her parents for contact lenses had she been told of the possibility of corneal distortion connected with her taking birth control pills. "I didn't want my folks to know about my taking the pill," she explains.

The senior partner handling the case is concerned that the element of proximate cause may be too weak and that the case may be dismissed on a motion for summary judgment or a motion for directed verdict. She has asked you to assess the likelihood of getting to a jury. Indicate any further information that should be obtained. Assume that Ayers v. Johnson & Johnson, supra, is a decision of the high court in your jurisdiction.

E. FEDERAL PREEMPTION OF PRODUCT WARNING CLAIMS

As we have noted throughout this chapter, warning defect claims can be difficult to defend in light of doctrines such as the heeding presumption and the more general tendency to view warnings through the biased lens of hindsight. Perhaps for this reason the defense bar has sought refuge from warning claims through the constitutional doctrine of preemption, which works to entirely displace state common law liability when it applies. See Section I, Chapter Four, supra. The United States Supreme Court's involvement in preemption of state products liability claims began when plaintiffs brought suit against cigarette companies for failing to adequately warn

---

authors' dialogue 21

DOUG: The tobacco companies are finally getting their just due. After all the years of deception they are rightly being held accountable for fraud and misrepresentation.

AARON: I could not disagree with you more. Aspects of their conduct over the years have been reprehensible. But, in retrospect the tobacco litigation over the last decade has been a blot on American jurisprudence. After 1980 — almost four decades ago — one would have to have been brain dead not to know that cigarettes were deadly dangerous. Everyone but everyone knew about the dangers. There is just no causal relationship between any so-called misrepresentation and the injuries people suffered. If this were any product other than cigarettes the cases would have been laughed out of court.

DOUG: Are you telling me that cigarette companies who knew their product was as addictive as heroin yet suppressed that information for decades should walk free? Don't forget how far-reaching their campaign of manipulation was. They didn't just mislead the public. They lied to Congress. They bought and bullied scientists. They developed special advertisements to entice children, women, and minorities. I once had a former tobacco marketer tell my class that he researched ways to appeal to undereducated women with low self-esteem. His bosses told him that was a good demographic to target because the women wouldn't worry about health risks since they don't have hope for their future.

JIM: I'm not sure I would go as far as Aaron but I am troubled by the recent litigation. For those who began smoking in the 40's and 50's I can see valid suits. But we are now a half-century after the Surgeon General's Report. Everyone knew that it was hard to quit smoking. I cannot believe that an additional bit of information would have made a difference.

DOUG: Well, juries have found otherwise after listening to weeks of testimony and sifting through thousands of industry documents detailing their misdeeds. If you were on a jury and heard the evidence you might change your tune.

---

about the dangers associated with smoking. Since the passage of the Federal Cigarette Labeling and Advertising Act of 1965, 15 U.S.C. §§1331-1340 (hereinafter the Cigarette Act), which became effective January 1, 1966, most courts had ruled in favor of federal preemption — that is, they ruled against the recognition of a state-imposed common law duty to warn of the dangers of cigarettes in light of a perceived intent of Congress to preempt such claims. The relevant portion of the Cigarette Act, as amended in 1969, provides that "No requirement or prohibition based on smoking and health shall be imposed under state law with respect to the advertising or promotion of any cigarettes the packages of which are labeled in conformity with the provisions of this chapter." Id. §1334(b). In Cipollone v. Liggett Group, Inc., 893 F.2d 541 (3d Cir. 1990), *aff'd*, 505 U.S. 504 (1992), the Third Circuit upheld its earlier determination that the Cigarette Act impliedly preempts those state law damage claims that

AARON: Come on Doug. The tobacco companies have been painted as evil wrong-doers, murderers of millions of people. I don't disagree with that characterization. But being bad actors does not amount to causation. The job of the judiciary is to protect us from nonsensical conclusions based on prejudice. Even bad actors deserve a fair shake in court.

DOUG: What about the huckstering of cigarettes to young people and getting them hooked early on in life? They may have known but were not capable of fully understanding the risk.

AARON: These are the same young people who are old enough to vote and drive a car at the age of sixteen. Give me a break. For the last twenty-five years I have been confronting young men and women who stand outside the law school and smoke. When I ask them whether they fully under-stand the risks they say that they do but they enjoy smoking. Many people are willing to take risks that I would never do. I wouldn't ride a motorcycle or ski from the top of a mountain. But, more to the point, advertising is not illegal. Are you about to countenance suits against Coca-Cola for contributing to the obesity epidemic by failing to warn about the dangers of sugary drinks? Best estimates are that the medical costs of obesity run to the billions.

DOUG: Look, there are some industries — lead, asbestos, tobacco, and, yes, maybe even the high fructose corn syrup dealers — that create massive public health problems and then do everything they can to cover it up and continue pushing their deadly products. Why should those costs be dumped onto all of us through public and private insurance pools? If you really think that smokers and soda drinkers knowingly accept the risks of these products, why shouldn't they also have to pay for those risks through higher product prices?

AARON: You remember earlier I said Jim had a reputation for being "right of Attila the Hun"? Well you're starting to sound left of Ralph Nader.

"necessarily [depend] on the assertion that a party bear the duty to provide a warning to consumers in addition to the warning Congress has required on cigarette packages." Id. at 552.

Several federal courts of appeals followed *Cipollone*'s lead. See, e.g., Pennington v. Visitron Corp., 876 F.2d 414 (5th Cir. 1989); Palmer v. Liggett Group, 825 F.2d 620 (1st Cir. 1987); Roysdon v. R. J. Reynolds Tobacco Co., 849 F.2d 230 (6th Cir. 1987). However, some state courts disagreed with the decision. In Dewey v. R. J. Reynolds Tobacco Co., 577 A.2d 1239 (N.J. 1990), the Supreme Court of New Jersey held that, although plaintiff's decedent had not smoked defendant's cigarettes until 11 years after the passage of the Cigarette Act, the Act neither expressly nor impliedly preempted plaintiff's failure-to-warn claim.

The United States Supreme Court took up this thorny preemption problem in Cipollone v. Liggett Group, Inc., 505 U.S. 504 (1992). Justice Stevens, writing for a badly fractured court, held that the amended Cigarette Act preempts some but not all common law tort claims relating to tobacco products. Specifically, plaintiffs could not pursue liability for failure to warn insofar their claim alleged that defendant manufacturers' "advertising or promotions should have included additional, or more clearly stated, warnings." Id. at 524. Nor could plaintiffs pursue a claim for fraudulent misrepresentation insofar as the claim alleged that defendants "through their advertising, neutralized the effect of federally mandated warning labels." Id. at 527. On the other hand, the Court held that plaintiffs' claims were not preempted to the extent that they relied on defendants' "testing or research practices or other actions unrelated to advertising or promotion." Id. at 525. Likewise, plaintiffs' breach of express warranty claim was not preempted even though it relied heavily on statements made in defendants' advertisements. Such a claim, if successful, would not constitute an obligation "imposed under state law" within the meaning of the preemption provision, given that it would merely enforce promises voluntarily made by defendants. See id. at 526-27. Finally, plaintiffs also could pursue a theory of fraudulent misrepresentation to the extent it relied either "on a state-law duty to disclose [material] facts through channels of communication other than advertising or promotion," or on "state-law proscriptions on intentional fraud" whether or not contained within advertising or promotion. Id. at 528-29.

Taking their cue from the *Cipollone* decision, plaintiffs in cigarette litigation have based their post-1969 claims against tobacco companies not on failure to warn but on misrepresentation, express warranty, and violations of consumer protection statutes. See, e.g., Wright v. Brooke Group Ltd., 114 F. Supp. 2d 797, 824-825, 828 (N.D. Iowa 2000) (fraudulent concealment of the addictive nature of cigarettes in channels other than advertising and claims of fraudulent misrepresentation and express warranty are not preempted).

A more recent controversy over the reach of *Cipollone* concerns the litigation alleging that the cigarette companies fraudulently represented "lights" or "low tar" cigarettes as safer than regular cigarettes. The plaintiffs in these actions do not allege personal injury. Instead, they claim economic loss since they paid for cigarettes that were not, in fact, safer and were thus denied the benefit of the bargain. They claim that the tobacco companies knew that "light" cigarettes were not safer because smokers, by covering filter ventilation holes with their lips and fingers, taking larger or more frequent puffs, and holding the smoke in their lungs for longer periods of time, unknowingly ingest as much (or more) tar and nicotine as do smokers of regular cigarettes. In Brown v. Brown and Williamson Tobacco Corp., 479 F.3d 383 (5th Cir. 2007), the Court held that these claims were preempted by *Cipollone*. The opposite result was reached by Good v. Altria Group, Inc., 501 F.3d 29 (1st Cir. 2007). The United States granted certiorari to resolve the conflict between the circuits. In Altria Group, Inc. v. Good, 555 U.S. 70 (2008), the Court held that the plaintiff's claims that the tobacco companies misrepresented or fraudulently concealed critical information about "light" cigarettes were not preempted and that plaintiffs could pursue those claims under relevant state law. The Court rejected the argument of the tobacco companies that use of the descriptors "lights" and "low tar" was not inherently false and was more akin to the "warning neutralization" claims that *Cipollone* held to be preempted. The Supreme Court's holding in *Altria* has given life to the "lights" cases around the country that were on "hold" awaiting the preemption decision. See, e.g.,

Pearson v. Philip Morris Inc., 306 P.3d 665 (Or. Ct. App. 2014) (reversing, in light of *Altria*, district court holding that putative light cigarette class action was preempted and further reversing district court's denial of class certification).

NOTE: FDA-APPROVED WARNINGS

Wyeth v. Levine
555 U.S. 555 (2009)

Justice STEVENS delivered the opinion of the Court.

Directly injecting the drug Phenergan into a patient's vein creates a significant risk of catastrophic consequences. A Vermont jury found that petitioner Wyeth, the manufacturer of the drug, had failed to provide an adequate warning of that risk and awarded damages to respondent Diana Levine to compensate her for the amputation of her arm. The warnings on Phenergan's label had been deemed sufficient by the federal Food and Drug Administration (FDA) when it approved Wyeth's new drug application in 1955 and when it later approved changes in the drug's labeling. The question we must decide is whether the FDA's approvals provide Wyeth with a complete defense to Levine's tort claims. We conclude that they do not.

I

Phenergan is Wyeth's brand name for promethazine hydrochloride, an antihistamine used to treat nausea. The injectable form of Phenergan can be administered intramuscularly or intravenously, and it can be administered intravenously through either the "IV-push" method, whereby the drug is injected directly into a patient's vein, or the "IV-drip" method, whereby the drug is introduced into a saline solution in a hanging intravenous bag and slowly descends through a catheter inserted in a patient's vein. The drug is corrosive and causes irreversible gangrene if it enters a patient's artery.

Levine's injury resulted from an IV-push injection of Phenergan. On April 7, 2000, as on previous visits to her local clinic for treatment of a migraine headache, she received an intra-muscular injection of Demerol for her headache and Phenergan for her nausea. Because the combination did not provide relief, she returned later that day and received a second injection of both drugs. This time, the physician assistant administered the drugs by the IV-push method, and Phenergan entered Levine's artery, either because the needle penetrated an artery directly or because the drug escaped from the vein into surrounding tissue (a phenomenon called "perivascular extravasation") where it came in contact with arterial blood. As a result, Levine developed gangrene, and doctors amputated first her right hand and then her entire forearm. In addition to her pain and suffering, Levine incurred substantial medical expenses and the loss of her livelihood as a professional musician.

After settling claims against the health center and clinician, Levine brought an action for damages against Wyeth, relying on common-law negligence and strict-liability theories. Although Phenergan's labeling warned of the danger of gangrene and amputation following inadvertent intra-arterial injection, Levine alleged that the labeling was defective because it failed to instruct clinicians to use the IV-drip method of intravenous administration instead of the higher risk IV-push method. More broadly, she alleged that Phenergan is not reasonably safe for intravenous administration because the foreseeable risks of gangrene and loss of limb are great in relation to the drug's therapeutic benefits. . . .

Wyeth filed a motion for summary judgment, arguing that Levine's failure-to-warn claims were pre-empted by federal law. The court found no merit in either Wyeth's field pre-emption argument, which it has since abandoned, or its conflict pre-emption argument. With respect to the contention that there was an "actual conflict between a specific FDA order," . . . and Levine's failure-to-warn action, the court reviewed the sparse correspondence between Wyeth and the FDA about Phenergan's labeling and found no evidence that Wyeth had "earnestly attempted" to strengthen the intra-arterial injection warning or that the FDA had "specifically disallowed" stronger language. . . . The record, as then developed, "lack[ed] any evidence that the FDA set a ceiling on this matter." . . .

The evidence presented during the 5-day jury trial showed that the risk of intra-arterial injection or perivascular extravasation can be almost entirely eliminated through the use of IV-drip, rather than IV-push, administration. An IV drip is started with saline, which will not flow properly if the catheter is not in the vein and fluid is entering an artery or surrounding tissue. . . . By contrast, even a careful and experienced clinician using the IV-push method will occasionally expose an artery to Phenergan. . . . While Phenergan's labeling warned against intra-arterial injection and perivascular extravasation and advised that "[w]hen administering any irritant drug intravenously it is usually preferable to inject it through the tubing of an intravenous infusion set that is known to be functioning satisfactorily," . . . the labeling did not contain a specific warning about the risks of IV-push administration.

The trial record also contains correspondence between Wyeth and the FDA discussing Phenergan's label. The FDA first approved injectable Phenergan in 1955. In 1973 and 1976, Wyeth submitted supplemental new drug applications, which the agency approved after proposing labeling changes. Wyeth submitted a third supplemental application in 1981 in response to a new FDA rule governing drug labels. Over the next 17 years, Wyeth and the FDA intermittently corresponded about Phenergan's label. The most notable activity occurred in 1987, when the FDA suggested different warnings about the risk of arterial exposure, and in 1988, when Wyeth submitted revised labeling incorporating the proposed changes. The FDA did not respond. Instead, in 1996, it requested from Wyeth the labeling then in use and, without addressing Wyeth's 1988 submission, instructed it to "[r]etain verbiage in current label" regarding intra-arterial injection. . . . After a few further changes to the labeling not related to intra-arterial injection, the FDA approved Wyeth's 1981 application in 1998, instructing that Phenergan's final printed label "must be identical" to the approved package insert. . . .

Based on this regulatory history, the trial judge instructed the jury that it could consider evidence of Wyeth's compliance with FDA requirements but that such compliance did not establish that the warnings were adequate. He also instructed, without objection from Wyeth, that FDA regulations "permit a drug manufacturer to change a product label to add or strengthen a warning about its product without prior FDA approval so long as it later submits the revised warning for review and approval." . . .

Answering questions on a special verdict form, the jury found that Wyeth was negligent, that Phenergan was a defective product as a result of inadequate warnings and instructions, and that no intervening cause had broken the causal connection between the product defects and the plaintiff's injury. . . . It awarded total damages of $7,400,000, which the court reduced to account for Levine's earlier settlement with the health center and clinician. . . .

On August 3, 2004, the trial court filed a comprehensive opinion denying Wyeth's motion for judgment as a matter of law. After making findings of fact based on the trial record (supplemented by one letter that Wyeth found after the trial), the court rejected Wyeth's pre-emption arguments. . . .

The Vermont Supreme Court affirmed. . . .

II

The . . . question presented is whether federal law pre-empts Levine's claim that Phenergan's label did not contain an adequate warning about using the IV-push method of administration. . . .

III

Wyeth first argues that Levine's state-law claims are pre-empted because it is impossible for it to comply with both the state-law duties underlying those claims and its federal labeling duties. . . . The FDA's premarket approval of a new drug application includes the approval of the exact text in the proposed label. See 21 U.S.C. §355; 21 CFR §314.105(b) (2008). Generally speaking, a manufacturer may only change a drug label after the FDA approves a supplemental application. There is, however, an FDA regulation that permits a manufacturer to make certain changes to its label before receiving the agency's approval. Among other things, this "changes being effected" (CBE) regulation provides that if a manufacturer is changing a label to "add or strengthen a contraindication, warning, precaution, or adverse reaction" or to "add or strengthen an instruction about dosage and administration that is intended to increase the safe use of the drug product," it may make the labeling change upon filing its supplemental application with the FDA; it need not wait for FDA approval. §§314.70(c)(6)(iii)(A), (C).

Wyeth argues that the CBE regulation is not implicated in this case because a 2008 amendment provides that a manufacturer may only change its label "to reflect newly acquired information." 73 Fed. Reg. 49609. Resting on this language (which Wyeth argues simply reaffirmed the interpretation of the regulation in effect when this case was tried), Wyeth contends that it could have changed Phenergan's label only in response to new information that the FDA had not considered. And it maintains that Levine has not pointed to any such information concerning the risks of IV-push administration. Thus, Wyeth insists, it was impossible for it to discharge its state-law obligation to provide a stronger warning about IV-push administration without violating federal law. Wyeth's argument misapprehends both the federal drug regulatory scheme and its burden in establishing a pre-emption defense.

We need not decide whether the 2008 CBE regulation is consistent with the FDCA and the previous version of the regulation, as Wyeth and the United States urge, because Wyeth could have revised Phenergan's label even in accordance with the amended regulation. As the FDA explained in its notice of the final rule, " 'newly acquired information' " is not limited to new data, but also encompasses "new analyses of previously submitted data." . . . The rule accounts for the fact that risk information accumulates over time and that the same data may take on a different meaning in light of subsequent developments: "[I]f the sponsor submits adverse event information to FDA, and then later conducts a new analysis of data showing risks of a different type or of greater severity or frequency than did reports previously submitted to FDA, the sponsor meets the requirement for 'newly acquired information.'" . . .

The record is limited concerning what newly acquired information Wyeth had or should have had about the risks of IV-push administration of Phenergan because Wyeth did not argue before the trial court that such information was required for a CBE labeling change. Levine did, however, present evidence of at least 20 incidents prior to her injury in which a Phenergan injection resulted in gangrene and an amputation. . . . After the first such incident came to Wyeth's attention in 1967, it notified the FDA and worked with the agency to change Phenergan's label. In later years, as amputations continued to occur, Wyeth could have analyzed the accumulating data and added a stronger warning about IV-push administration of the drug.

Wyeth argues that if it had unilaterally added such a warning, it would have violated federal law governing unauthorized distribution and misbranding. Its argument that a change in Phenergan's labeling would have subjected it to liability for unauthorized distribution rests on the assumption that this labeling change would have rendered Phenergan a new drug lacking an effective application. But strengthening the warning about IV-push administration would not have made Phenergan a new drug. See 21 U.S.C. §321(p)(1) (defining "new drug"); 21 CFR §310.3(h). Nor would this warning have rendered Phenergan misbranded. The FDCA does not provide that a drug is misbranded simply because the manufacturer has altered an FDA-approved label; instead, the misbranding provision focuses on the substance of the label and, among other things, proscribes labels that fail to include "adequate warnings." 21 U.S.C. §352(f). Moreover, because the statute contemplates that federal juries will resolve most misbranding claims, the FDA's belief that a drug is misbranded is not conclusive. See §§331, 332, 334(a)-(b). And the very idea that the FDA would bring an enforcement action against a manufacturer for strengthening a warning pursuant to the CBE regulation is difficult to accept — neither Wyeth nor the United States has identified a case in which the FDA has done so. . . .

Of course, the FDA retains authority to reject labeling changes made pursuant to the CBE regulation in its review of the manufacturer's supplemental application, just as it retains such authority in reviewing all supplemental applications. But absent clear evidence that the FDA would not have approved a change to Phenergan's label, we will not conclude that it was impossible for Wyeth to comply with both federal and state requirements.

Wyeth has offered no such evidence. It does not argue that it attempted to give the kind of warning required by the Vermont jury but was prohibited from doing so by the FDA. And while it does suggest that the FDA intended to prohibit it from strengthening the warning about IV-push administration because the agency deemed such a warning inappropriate in reviewing Phenergan's drug applications, both the trial court and the Vermont Supreme Court rejected this account as a matter of fact. In its decision on Wyeth's motion for judgment as a matter of law, the trial court found "no evidence in this record that either the FDA or the manufacturer gave more than passing attention to the issue of" IV-push versus IV-drip administration. . . .

Impossibility pre-emption is a demanding defense. On the record before us, Wyeth has failed to demonstrate that it was impossible for it to comply with both federal and state requirements. The CBE regulation permitted Wyeth to unilaterally strengthen its warning, and the mere fact that the FDA approved Phenergan's label does not establish that it would have prohibited such a change.

IV

Wyeth also argues that requiring it to comply with a state-law duty to provide a stronger warning about IV-push administration would obstruct the purposes and objectives of federal drug labeling regulation. Levine's tort claims, it maintains, are preempted because they interfere with "Congress's purpose to entrust an expert agency to make drug labeling decisions that strike a balance between competing objectives." . . . We find no merit in this argument, which relies on an untenable interpretation of congressional intent and an overbroad view of an agency's power to pre-empt state law.

Wyeth contends that the FDCA establishes both a floor and a ceiling for drug regulation: Once the FDA has approved a drug's label, a state-law verdict may not deem the label inadequate, regardless of whether there is any evidence that the FDA has considered the stronger warning at issue. The most glaring problem with this argument is that all evidence of Congress' purposes is to the contrary. Building on its 1906 Act, Congress enacted the FDCA to bolster consumer protection against harmful products. . . . Congress did not provide a federal remedy for consumers harmed by unsafe or ineffective drugs in the 1938 statute or in any subsequent amendment. Evidently, it determined that widely available state rights of action provided appropriate relief for injured consumers. It may also have recognized that state-law remedies further consumer protection by motivating manufacturers to produce safe and effective drugs and to give adequate warnings.

Despite this evidence that Congress did not regard state tort litigation as an obstacle to achieving its purposes, Wyeth nonetheless maintains that, because the FDCA requires the FDA to determine that a drug is safe and effective under the conditions set forth in its labeling, the agency must be presumed to have performed a precise balancing of risks and benefits and to have established a specific labeling standard that leaves no room for different state-law judgments. In advancing this argument, Wyeth relies not on any statement by Congress, but instead on the preamble to a 2006 FDA regulation governing the content and format of prescription drug labels. In that preamble, the FDA declared that the FDCA establishes "both a 'floor' and a 'ceiling,'" so that "FDA approval of labeling . . . preempts conflicting or contrary State law." . . . It further stated that certain state-law actions, such as those involving failure-to-warn claims, "threaten FDA's statutorily prescribed role as the expert Federal agency responsible for evaluating and regulating drugs." . . .

This Court has recognized that an agency regulation with the force of law can pre-empt conflicting state requirements. See, e.g., Geier v. American Honda Motor Co., 120 S. Ct. 1913, (2000). In such cases, the Court has performed its own conflict determination, relying on the substance of state and federal law and not on agency proclamations of pre-emption. We are faced with no such regulation in this case, but rather with an agency's mere assertion that state law is an obstacle to achieving its statutory objectives. . . .

In prior cases, we have given "some weight" to an agency's views about the impact of tort law on federal objectives when "the subject matter is technica[l] and the relevant history and background are complex and extensive." Geier, 529 U.S., at 883, 120 S. Ct. 1913. Even in such cases, however, we have not deferred to an agency's conclusion that state law is pre-empted. Rather, we have attended to an agency's explanation of how state law affects the regulatory scheme. While agencies have no special authority to pronounce on pre-emption absent delegation by Congress, they do have a unique understanding of the statutes they administer and an attendant ability to make informed determinations about how state requirements may pose an "obstacle to the accomplishment and execution of the full purposes and objectives of Congress." . . .

Under this standard, the FDA's 2006 preamble does not merit deference. When the FDA issued its notice of proposed rulemaking in December 2000, it explained that the rule would "not contain policies that have federalism implications or that preempt State law." 65 Fed. Reg. 81103; see also 71 id., at 3969 (noting that the "proposed rule did not propose to preempt state law"). In 2006, the agency finalized the rule and, without offering States or other interested parties notice or opportunity for comment, articulated a sweeping position on the FDCA's pre-emptive effect in the regulatory preamble. The agency's views on state law are inherently suspect in light of this procedural failure.

Further, the preamble is at odds with what evidence we have of Congress' purposes, and it reverses the FDA's own longstanding position without providing a reasoned explanation, including any discussion of how state law has interfered with the FDA's regulation of drug labeling during decades of coexistence. The FDA's 2006 position plainly does not reflect the agency's own view at all times relevant to this litigation. Not once prior to Levine's injury did the FDA suggest that state tort law stood as an obstacle to its statutory mission. To the contrary, it cast federal labeling standards as a floor upon which States could build and repeatedly disclaimed any attempt to pre-empt failure-to-warn claims. For instance, in 1998, the FDA stated that it did "not believe that the evolution of state tort law [would] cause the development of standards that would be at odds with the agency's regulations." . . . It further noted that, in establishing "minimal standards" for drug labels, it did not intend "to preclude the states from imposing additional labeling requirements." . . .

In keeping with Congress' decision not to pre-empt common-law tort suits, it appears that the FDA traditionally regarded state law as a complementary form of drug regulation. The FDA has limited resources to monitor the 11,000 drugs on the market, and manufacturers have superior access to information about their drugs, especially in the postmarketing phase as new risks emerge. State tort suits uncover unknown drug hazards and provide incentives for drug manufacturers to disclose safety risks promptly. They also serve a distinct compensatory function that may motivate injured persons to come forward with information. Failure-to-warn actions, in particular, lend force to the FDCA's premise that manufacturers, not the FDA, bear primary responsibility for their drug labeling at all times. Thus, the FDA long maintained that state law offers an additional, and important, layer of consumer protection that complements FDA regulation. The agency's 2006 preamble represents a dramatic change in position. . . .

In short, Wyeth has not persuaded us that failure-to-warn claims like Levine's obstruct the federal regulation of drug labeling. Congress has repeatedly declined to pre-empt state law, and the FDA's recently adopted position that state tort suits interfere with its statutory mandate is entitled to no weight. Although we recognize that some state-law claims might well frustrate the achievement of congressional objectives, this is not such a case.

V

We conclude that it is not impossible for Wyeth to comply with its state and federal law obligations and that Levine's common-law claims do not stand as an obstacle to the accomplishment of Congress' purposes in the FDCA. Accordingly, the judgment of the Vermont Supreme Court is affirmed.

The concurring opinions of Justices Breyer and Thomas as well as the dissenting opinion of Justice Alito in which the Chief Justice and Justice Scalia joined are all omitted.

_____

The important question left open by *Wyeth* is what it will take to convince a court that a state failure-to-warn tort action is in conflict with FDA policy and deserves preemption. The crucial language in *Wyeth* is the Court's statement that "absent clear evidence that FDA would not have approved a change to [a] label we will not conclude that it was impossible for Wyeth to comply with both federal and state requirements." The Court said that the burden of establishing the "impossibility defense" is very demanding. The post-*Wyeth* case law does not portend well for the preemption defense, at least for brand name manufacturers. For instance, pharmaceutical manufacturers have raised the preemption defense in cases where adult plaintiffs committed suicide after taking anti-depressants such as Effexor and Paxil. The FDA extensively studied these widely used drugs and found that there was no evidence supporting the need for a warning of an increased risk of suicide for adults. In Mason v. Smithkline Beecham Corp., 596 F.3d 387 (7th Cir. 2010), the Court denied preemption in a case where a 23-year-old plaintiff committed suicide after taking Paxil, a commonly prescribed anti-depressant. The defendant presented substantial evidence that the FDA had refused citizens' petitions for suicide warnings for other than pediatric patients. Nonetheless, the Court held that the evidence fell short of the demanding "clear evidence" standard and allowed the case to go to trial on the issue of whether the drug manufacturer should have warned about the dangers of suicide. Accord Dorsett v. Sandoz, Inc., 2010 WL 1174204 (C.D. Cal. 2010). See also Reckis v. Johnson & Johnson, 28 N.E.3d 445 (Mass. 2015) (refusing to find that the FDA would have rejected a warning that over-the-counter children's Motrin could lead to life-threatening disease).

In a few cases district courts have decided pre-*Wyeth* that anti-depressant manufacturers presented sufficient evidence that the FDA would have rejected additional warnings of an increased risk of suicide to adults, thus preempting common law failure-to-warn claims; appellate courts reversed these decisions post-*Wyeth* to consider whether the evidence met the stringent standards set forth in *Wyeth*. See Dobbs v. Wyeth Pharmaceuticals, 530 F. Supp. 2d 1275 (W.D. Okla. 2008), *vacated* 606 F.3d 1269 (10th Cir. 2010) (Effexor); Miller v. Smithkline Beecham Corp., 2008 WL 510449 (N.D. Okla. 2008), *vacated* 381 F. App'x 776 (10th Cir. 2010); Colacicco v. Apotex, Inc., 521 F.3d 253 (3d Cir. 2008), *vacated* 556 U.S. 1101 (2009) (Paxil). The pharmaceutical manufacturers made very strong arguments that the FDA would have rejected warnings that these drugs presented an increased risk of suicide to adults and that, without preemption, drug manufacturers will be forced to submit warnings to the FDA that they know the FDA will reject and then ask the FDA to specifically reject them so they can support their claim of conflict preemption.

Another post-*Wyeth* issue concerns the question of whether the manufacturers of generic drugs have a common law obligation to warn if the warnings they provide are consistent with those approved for the brand-name drugs. The manufacturers of generic drugs contend that a provision of the Hatch-Waxman Amendment to the FDCA mandates that they conform to the warnings of the approved name-brand drug. They argue that they are not authorized to change warnings pursuant to the Change Being Effected (CBE) provisions that allow name-brand drug manufacturers to alter warnings. In Mensing v. Wyeth, Inc., 588 F.3d 603 (8th Cir. 2009), and Demahy v. Actavis, Inc., 593 F.3d 428 (5th Cir. 2010), the court found against preemption, concluding that generic manufacturers could take advantage of the CBE procedure and thus did not meet the standard for preemption set forth in *Wyeth*.

However, upon grant of certiorari in *Mensing*, the Supreme Court reversed and remanded the Eighth Circuit's decision. See PLIVA, Inc., v. Mensing, 131 S. Ct. 2567 (2011) (holding that federal law preempted state laws imposing upon generic drug manufacturers a duty to change a drug's label). On remand, the Eighth Circuit vacated Sections I, II, and IV (where it previously held that the FDCA did not preempt failure to warn claims) and reinstated Section III (where it held that holding name brand manufacturers liable for harm caused by generic manufactures stretches the concept of foreseeability too far). See Mensing v. Wyeth, Inc., 658 F.3d 867 (8th Cir. 2011). After *Mensing*, several courts have found preemption of failure-to-warn claims in cases against generic drug manufacturers. See Gaeta v. Perrigo Pharm. Co., 469 F. App'x 556 (9th Cir. 2012), *vacating* 630 F.3d 1225 (9th Cir. 2011) (concluding that the FDCA preempts failure-to-warn claims against generic manufacturers); Jacobsen v. Wyeth, LLC, No. CIV.A. 10-0823, 2012 WL 3575293 (E.D. La. Aug. 20, 2012) (dismissing plaintiff's failure-to-warn claims on preemption grounds in accordance with *Mensing*); Aucoin v. Amneal Pharm., LLC, No. CIV.A. 11-1275, 2012 WL 2990697 (E.D. La. July 20, 2012) (finding that the FDCA preempts design defect claims against generic manufacturers and rejecting similar arguments found in the *Mensing* dissent).

In Morris v. PLIVA, Inc.,713 F3d 774 (5th Cir. 2013), plaintiffs argued that defendant generic drug manufacturers should have more effectively communicated a warning against ingesting the drug metoclopramide for more than twelve weeks, a warning that was approved as a label change by the FDA in 2004 and as a "black box" warning in 2009. In plaintiffs' view, providing a special warning would not have violated the generic manufacturers' "duty of sameness" under federal law because the specific information sought to be included in the warning was approved by the FDA. However, because the brand-name manufacturers of metoclopramide themselves failed to issue any special warning based on the label change, the court held that plaintiffs' claims were preempted: "Under federal law, the inquiry is whether the brand-name manufacturer sent out a warning, not whether the proposed warning to be disseminated contains substantially similar information to the label." Id. at 777.

For academic writing on preemption see Catherine M. Sharkey, Tort-Agency Partnerships in an Age of Preemption, 15 Theoretical Inquiries L. 359 (2014) (discussing preemption analysis when state law claims seek to enforce standards parallel to, rather than different from or in addition to, federal agency standards); Daniel J. Meltzer, Preemption and Textualism, 112 Mich. L. Rev. 1 (2013) (discussing the surprising strength of purposivist, as opposed to textualist, statutory interpretation methods in the case of express preemption decisions); Erin O'Hara O'Connor & Larry E. Ribstein, Preemption and Choice-of-Law Coordination, 111 Mich. L. Rev. 647 (2013) (arguing that preemption analysis should consider whether states have evidenced tolerance of multiple or conflicting standards through their choice-of-law decisions); Catherine M. Sharkey, Inside Agency Preemption, 110 Mich. L. Rev. 521 (2012) (discussing growing importance of federal agency assessments of the scope of Congressional intent to preempt state tort law).

CHAPTER SIX

Express Warranty and Misrepresentation

This chapter introduces causes of action based on express warranty and misrepresentation. The first section focuses on the creation of express warranties and the requirements necessary to show breach. In reading the materials, readers should consider the thin line separating nonactionable statements about the performance and functions of a product from those that rise to the level of an express warranty or promise made about a product. Additionally, one should consider how an individual's reliance on certain statements factors into a court's decision about the nature of those statements. The second section of the chapter introduces misrepresentation, a tort close in spirit to the actions for breach of warranty and warning defect. All three actions can be seen as concerned with the quality of information that consumers hold when choosing to purchase and use a product. The concluding section considers more subtle ways in which manufacturer promotional efforts factor in tort litigation.

A. EXPRESS WARRANTY

Centuries ago, a body of law developed in England to regulate commercial dealings among merchants. The substance of this specialized "law merchant" drew heavily from the customs of the marketplace and reflected a shared desire to give effect to commercial agreements and to uphold the reasonable expectations of participants when deals broke down. Among the features of this complex body of law were "warranties"—obligations imposed by law on sellers of goods requiring them to stand behind the quality of their goods and to make buyers whole when the quality fell short of promised performance levels or reasonable expectations.

Given its practical significance, and the accompanying need for a uniform and predictable set of rules, the law merchant gradually came to be codified by statute. In the United States, the first great statute governing sales warranties was the Uniform Sales Act. Proposed in 1906, the Sales Act controlled commercial practices dealing with the sale of goods. Beginning in 1954, state legislatures replaced the Sales Act and other commercial law statutes with the Uniform Commercial Code (U.C.C., Code), Article 2 of which governs sale-of-goods transactions. Today, the law of commercial sales warranties is governed largely by the U.C.C. in the United States.

At about the same time that state legislatures began adopting the Code, state courts were engaged in developing the common law of products liability. Generally, under the Code's express warranty provision, a consumer may be able to recover for injuries suffered when a product fails to live up to a seller's *promises* regarding the quality, character, or performance of a good even if the buyer cannot prove that the *product* was defectively manufactured or designed, or marketed with insufficient warnings.

1.　What Is Warranted

Breach of an express warranty occurs when goods fail to conform to a promise made by the seller to the buyer regarding their character or their capacity to perform. Most express warranty claims arise from statements made in three contexts: (1) statements (written or oral) made by a seller to a buyer at or before the time of sale; (2) statements packaged with the goods at the time of sale; and (3) statements directed to the public at large, such as through advertising.

U.C.C. §2-313 sets forth the rules that determine how a warranty may be created.

Uniform Commercial Code

§2-313.　Express Warranties by Affirmation, Promise, Description, Sample

(1) Express warranties by the seller are created as follows:

(a) Any affirmation of fact or promise made by the seller to the buyer which relates to the goods and becomes part of the basis of the bargain creates an express warranty that the goods shall conform to the affirmation or promise.

(b) Any description of the goods which is made part of the basis of the bargain creates an express warranty that the goods shall conform to the description.

(c) Any sample or model which is made part of the basis of the bargain creates an express warranty that the whole of the goods shall conform to the sample or model.

(2) It is not necessary to the creation of an express warranty that the seller use formal words such as "warrant" or "guarantee" or that he have a specific intention to make a warranty, but an affirmation merely of the value of the goods or a statement purporting to be merely the seller's opinion or commendation of the goods does not create a warranty.

Baxter v. Ford Motor Co.
12 P.2d 409 (Wash. 1932)

HERMAN, J.

During the month of May, 1930, plaintiff purchased a model A Ford town sedan from defendant St. John Motors, a Ford dealer, who had acquired the automobile in question by purchase from defendant Ford Motor Company. Plaintiff claims that representations were made to him by both defendants that the windshield of the automobile was made of non-shatterable glass which would not break, fly, or shatter.

October 12, 1930, while plaintiff was driving the automobile through Snoqualmie Pass, a pebble from a passing car struck the windshield of the car in question, causing small pieces of glass to fly into plaintiff's left eye, resulting in the loss thereof. Plaintiff brought this action for damages for the loss of his left eye and for injuries to the sight of his right eye. The case came to trial, and, at the conclusion of plaintiff's testimony, the court took the case from the jury and entered judgment for both defendants. From that judgment, plaintiff appeals.

The principal question in this case is whether the trial court erred in refusing to admit in evidence, as against respondent Ford Motor Company, the catalogues and printed matter furnished by that respondent to respondent St. John Motors to be distributed for sales assistance. Contained in such printed matter were statements which appellant maintains constituted representations or warranties with reference to the nature of the glass used in the windshield of the car purchased by appellant. A typical statement, as it appears in appellant's exhibit for identification No. 1, is here set forth:

> Triplex Shatter-Proof Glass Windshield. All of the new Ford cars have a Triplex shatter-proof glass windshield — so made that it will not fly or shatter under the hardest impact. This is an important safety factor because it eliminates the dangers of flying glass — the cause of most of the injuries in automobile accidents. In these days of crowded, heavy traffic, the use of this Triplex glass is an absolute necessity. Its extra margin of safety is something that every motorist should look for in the purchase of a car — especially where there are women and children. . . .

Respondent Ford Motor Company contends that there can be no implied or express warranty without privity of contract, and warranties as to personal property do not attach themselves to, and run with, the article sold. . . .

In the case at bar, the automobile was represented by the manufacturer as having a windshield of non-shatterable glass "so made that it will not fly or shatter under the hardest impact." An ordinary person would be unable to discover by the usual and customary examination of the automobile whether glass which would not fly or shatter was used in the windshield. In that respect, the purchaser was in a position similar to that of the consumer of a wrongly labeled drug, who has bought the same from a retailer, and who has relied upon the manufacturer's representation that the label correctly set forth the contents of the container. For many years, it has been held that, under such circumstances, the manufacturer is liable to the consumer, even though the consumer purchased from a third person the commodity causing the damage. Thomas v. Winchester, 6 N.Y. 397, 57 Am. Dec. 455.

The rule in such cases does not rest upon contractual obligations, but rather on the principle that the original act of delivering an article is wrong, when, because of the lack of those qualities which the manufacturer represented it as having, the absence of which could not be readily detected by the consumer, the article is not safe for the purposes for which the consumer would ordinarily use it. . . .

Since the rule of caveat emptor was first formulated, vast changes have taken place in the economic structures of the English speaking peoples. Methods of doing business have undergone a great transition. Radio, bill boards and the products of the printing press have become the means of creating a large part of the demand that causes goods to depart from factories to the ultimate consumer. It would be unjust to recognize a rule that would permit manufacturers of goods to create a demand for their products by representing that they possess qualities which they, in fact, do not possess; and then, because there is no privity of contract existing between the consumer and the manufacturer, deny the consumer the right to recover if damages result from the absence of those qualities, when such absence is not readily noticeable. . . .

[Reversed and remanded.]

On retrial, Ford Motor Co. sought to introduce expert testimony that no auto manufacturer produced a better windshield at the time. The trial judge excluded the testimony and the appellate court affirmed. 35 P.2d 1090 (Wash. 1934). Why wasn't the expert testimony allowed in?

Courts have tried valiantly to distinguish between express warranties and mere sales puffery, though a consistent doctrine is hard to find. Scholar David Hoffman summarizes the prevailing opinion on puffery as "doctrinal chaos," arguing that courts have effectively created a "normative target that they are institutionally ill-suited to hit." David Hoffman, The Best Puffery Article Ever, 91 Iowa L. Rev. 1395, 1398 (2006). For example, consider In re FEMA Trailer Formaldehyde Product Liability Litigation, 2009 U.S. Dist. LEXIS 73368 (2009), in which plaintiff claimed injuries resulting from inhalation of formaldehyde vapors in emergency housing units provided by the Federal Emergency Management Agency in the wake of Hurricane Katrina. The basis of plaintiff's express warranty claim was that defendant's representative told her that a "chemical smell was nothing to worry about." The court held that the alleged statements were a "general opinion about or general praise of a product" and therefore did not constitute an express warranty. (Of note, the court also stated that because these representations were not mentioned in the original or amended complaint, the statements were given very little weight in finding for defendant.) Id. at *15. See also Mitchell v. GM LLC, 2014 U.S. Dist. LEXIS 43943 (W.D. Ky. 2014) (concluding that automaker's "general statements regarding [a] vehicle's quality, safety, and reliability are mere opinions, used to promote sales"); Wojcik v. Borough of Manville, 2010 WL 322893, at *3 (N.J. Super. A.D. 2010) (statements that helmet was "one of the best" and "top rated" is merely an opinion and not a warranty); Daugherty v. Sony Electronics, Inc., 2006 Tenn. App. LEXIS 53 (Tenn. Ct. App. 2006) (holding as a matter of law that defendant's statements that DVD players were "superior" and "set the standard" were puffery).

In determining whether statements constitute express warranties or puffery, should courts consider the degree of harm that could result if the statements are inaccurate? Cf. Pau v. Yosemite Park, 928 F.2d 880 (9th Cir. 1991) (bicycle leasing company's statement in an advertising brochure that a particular trail in Yosemite National Park offered "a safe and enjoyable cycling area" for use with the company's bikes could constitute an express warranty regarding the bikes with respect to a customer who died in an accident while riding on that trail); Drayton v. Jiffee Chemical Corp., 591 F.2d 352 (6th Cir. 1978) (advertising statement that household drain cleaning chemical was "safe" could constitute express warranty with respect to infant child disfigured after chemical was accidentally spilled on her).

PROBLEM TWENTY-THREE

Sarah Goldenberg, a bright and active six-year-old girl, suffered from a severe and relatively rare form of asthma. Any number of conditions, including shifts in temperament such as anger or excitement in anticipation of a coming event, could trigger an asthma attack. Many foods also posed a medical threat to Sarah. The foods to which Sarah was most allergic were milk and milk products. Although Sarah had a sweet tooth and loved chocolate, she knew that eating a chocolate bar was out of the question. Even the chocolate bars labeled "non-dairy" often contained slight traces of milk sufficient to trigger a severe allergic reaction, but in amounts so minute that they need not be reported on the label.

In light of Sarah's condition, the only chocolate bars that her parents would permit her to eat were kosher chocolate bars that were labeled "non-dairy." According to kosher dietary law, it is impermissible to eat dairy and meat derivative foods at the same time. Thus, kosher rabbinical supervision assures that even slight traces of dairy products are not present in chocolate that is labeled "kosher non-dairy." The Goldenbergs do not observe these dietary laws, but know that the strictness of the rabbinical supervision is the best assurance available to them that the candy Sarah eats contains no milk derivatives whatsoever.

Last fall, during a family get-together, Sarah's grandmother bought and gave to Sarah a kosher-certified non-dairy chocolate bar. The label of the bar read "kosher non-dairy." Apparently, the batch from which that bar came included a different emulsifier that was similar, but not precisely identical, to the emulsifier normally used. The rabbi performing the kosher supervision of ingredients did not pick up on the substitution, and thus was unaware that the particular batch contained a slight trace of milk powder. The problem was subsequently corrected, but not before the batch of chocolate bars containing the traces of milk powder reached the market and one bar was given to Sarah.

After consuming the chocolate bar, Sarah reacted violently to the trace of milk powder. Rushed to the emergency room of the nearest hospital, she died shortly after arrival. Sarah's parents consulted an attorney about bringing an action against Tasty Kosher Chocolates Inc., the manufacturer of the chocolate bar that triggered her fatal asthmatic attack. The Goldenbergs' attorney filed suit based on breach of express warranty.

You represent Tasty Kosher Chocolates Inc. In preparing your defense of this case, you consulted a rabbinic authority seeking to discover the religious ramifications that attend a consumer's innocent consumption of a non-kosher product. The rabbi tells you that if a purchaser relies on a competent rabbinic supervisor who certifies a product as kosher, then there is no moral culpability if the product turns out to be non-kosher. Nonetheless, the rabbi said, "It is unsettling to have eaten non-kosher food." You are about to file a motion for summary judgment. Making reasonable assumptions of fact where necessary, draft a memorandum in support of the motion.

2. Basis of the Bargain — The Reliance Controversy

Under the Uniform Sales Act, a plaintiff was required to prove her reliance on a seller's promise in order to state a claim for breach of an express warranty. The Act provided:

> Any affirmation of fact or any promise by the seller relating to the goods is an express warranty if the natural tendency of such affirmation or promise is to induce the buyer to purchase the goods, *and if the buyer purchases the goods relying thereon.* (emphasis added)

Under the Sales Act, regardless of how egregious a manufacturer's broken promise appeared, courts were unwilling to countenance a breach of express warranty claim absent a showing of reliance. For example, in McCully v. Fuller Brush Co., 415 P.2d 7 (Wash. 1966), plaintiff, while doing extensive cleaning, suffered permanent skin damage after immersing her bare hands in the defendant's household cleaning solution. Despite the undisputed evidence that several of the product's ingredients were well-known skin irritants, the product was labeled as being "Kind to Your Hands." The court held that plaintiff could not proceed under an express warranty theory where her evidence "f[ell] short of establishing the essential element of reliance." Id. at 11.

With the element of reliance drawing heavy fire from courts and academics, the U.C.C. did away with the term and replaced it instead with the nebulous "basis of the bargain" test. Whether this change was intended to preserve, modify, or displace altogether the element of reliance was unclear.

Cipollone v. Liggett Group, Inc.
893 F.2d 541 (3d Cir. 1990)

BECKER, Circuit Judge.

This appeal is from a final judgment in a protracted products liability case in which the plaintiff, Antonio Cipollone, seeks to hold Liggett Group, Inc., Lorillard, Inc., and Philip Morris, Inc., three of the leading firms in the tobacco industry, liable for the death from lung cancer of his wife, Rose Cipollone, who smoked cigarettes from 1942 until her death in 1984. . . .

Rose Cipollone was born in 1925 and began to smoke in 1942. She smoked Chesterfield brand cigarettes, manufactured by Liggett, until 1955. In her deposition, introduced into evidence at the trial, she stated that she smoked the Chesterfield brand to be "glamorous," to "imitate" the "pretty girls and movie stars" depicted in Chesterfield advertisements, and because the advertisements stated that Chesterfield cigarettes were "mild." Mrs. Cipollone stated that she understood the description of Chesterfield cigarettes as "mild" to mean that the cigarettes were safe.

Mrs. Cipollone also testified that she was an avid reader of a variety of magazines, frequently listened to the radio, and often watched television during the years that she smoked the Chesterfield brand. Although she could not specifically remember which Chesterfield advertisements she saw or heard during those years, Chesterfield advertisements appeared continuously in those media during that period. Several of these advertisements were introduced into evidence. The following copy appeared commonly in Chesterfield magazine advertisements during the year 1952:

PLAY SAFE Smoke Chesterfield.

NOSE, THROAT, and Accessory Organs not Adversely Affected by Smoking Chesterfields. First such report ever published about any cigarette. A responsible consulting organization has reported the results of a continuing study by a competent medical specialist and his staff on the effects of smoking Chesterfield cigarettes. A group of people from various walks of life was organized to smoke only Chesterfields. For six months this group of men and women smoked their normal amount of Chesterfields — 10 to 40 a day. 45% of the group have smoked Chesterfields continually from one to thirty years for an average of 10 years each. At the beginning and at the end of the six-months period each smoker was given a thorough examination, including X-ray pictures, by the medical specialist and his assistants. The examination covered the sinuses as well as the nose, ears and throat. The medical specialist, after a thorough examination of every member of the group, stated: "It is my opinion that the ears, nose, throat and accessory organs of all participating subjects examined by me were not adversely affected in the six-month period by smoking the cigarettes provided."

5 J.A. 21, 22 (c. 1952). The defendants stipulated that Mrs. Cipollone had seen many of these advertisements. . . .

In 1955, Mrs. Cipollone stopped smoking Chesterfield cigarettes and began to smoke L & M filter cigarettes, also made by Liggett. In response to a question as to why she switched to the L & M brand, Mrs. Cipollone stated that "[w]ell, they were talking about the filter tip, that it was milder and a miracle it would keep the stuff inside a trap, whatever." When asked why she desired the filter tip, she testified that "it was the new thing and I figured, well, go along [, and that] it was better [because t]he bad stuff would stay in the filter then." When asked whether concern about the "bad stuff" was due to a concern about her health, she stated "[n]ot really. . . . It was the trend. Everybody was smoking the filter cigarettes and I changed, too."

She also stated that although she could not remember any specific advertisements, she did "recall the ads and . . . remember the tips [and] the messages of a filter, a safer, something to that effect. . . . That it would filter the nicotine and the tar and the tobacco[, and t]hat it would be a cleaner and fresher smoke." Mrs. Cipollone also stated that she "recall[ed] seeing an ad that said doctors recommend you smoke . . . I think it was L & M's. . . . [T]hrough advertising, I was led to assume that they were safe and they wouldn't harm me. . . . There was lots of advertising. There was advertising everywhere. There was advertising in magazines, on billboards, in newspapers." . . .

With respect to [plaintiff's express warranty claim], the district court gave the following instructions to the jury:

> [P]laintiff must prove . . . that Liggett, prior to 1966, made one or more of the statements claimed by the plaintiff and that such statements were affirmations of fact or promises by Liggett . . . [and] that such statements were part of the basis of the bargain between Liggett and consumers like Rose Cipollone. . . .
>
> The law does not require plaintiff to show that Rose Cipollone specifically relied on Liggett's warranties.
>
> Ordinarily a guarantee or promise in an advertisement or other description of the goods becomes part of the basis of the bargain if it would naturally induce the purchase of the product and no particular reliance by the buyer on such statement needs to be shown. However, if the evidence establishes that the claimed statement cannot fairly be viewed as entering into the bargain, that is, that the statement would not naturally induce the purchase of a product, then no express warranty has been created.

4 J.A. at 232-34.

Liggett contends that this interpretation of "part of the basis of the bargain" is flawed because the jury should also have been instructed that Mrs. Cipollone's non-reliance on the advertisements would preclude those advertisements from becoming "part of the basis of the bargain." Liggett argues that the express warranty verdict must therefore be set aside. Although our interpretation of the precise meaning of "reliance" differs somewhat from Liggett's, we agree.

A

Authority on the question whether reliance is a necessary element of section 2-313 is divided. Although a few courts have held that reliance is not a necessary element of section 2-313, the more common view has been that it is, and that either a buyer must prove reliance in order to recover on an express warranty or the seller must be permitted to rebut a presumption of reliance in order to preclude recovery. Some treatise writers support this interpretation. No New Jersey court or panel of this court has squarely addressed the question.

The history of section 2-313(1)(a), although informative, fails to give a clear answer as to whether reliance is required. Section 2-313(1)(a) is an adaptation of section 12 of the Uniform Sales Act. A comparison of the two sections reveals that they are substantially the same except for the replacement of section 12's express reliance requirement with section 2-313(1)(a)'s basis of the bargain requirement. The district court reasoned that the omission of the word "reliance" from section 2-313(1)(a), in light of section 12's use of that word, implied that reliance was no longer an element of express warranties. See 693 F. Supp. at 213. Liggett contends that "if U.C.C. §2-313 wrought the radical change in New Jersey warranty law that the trial court has read into it," then "[o]ne would think that the New Jersey Study Comments would have at least made reference to it." Liggett Br. at 19. We note in this regard that the New Jersey Study Comment One to section 12A:2-313 states that "[t]his section of the Code is comparable to section 12 of the Sales Act (N.J.S.A. 46:30-18), except that it characterized the warranties of sample and description as express warranties." There is no reference to the reliance issue.

Liggett argues that reliance must have some place in the "basis of the bargain" determination. Thus, even if reliance should be assumed, based on what "would reasonably induce the purchase of a product," a defendant must have an opportunity to prove nonreliance. This position finds some support in the U.C.C. comments. U.C.C. Official Comment 3 states:

> In actual practice affirmations of fact made by the seller about the goods during a bargain are regarded as part of the description of those goods; hence no particular reliance on such statements need be shown in order to weave them into the fabric of the agreement. Rather, *any fact which is to take such affirmations, once made, out of the agreement requires clear affirmative proof.* The issue normally is one of fact. [Emphasis added.]

Moreover, comment 8 states that "all of the statements of the seller [become part of the basis of the bargain] *unless good reason is shown to the contrary.*" (Emphasis added.) The plain language of these comments supports Liggett's position, at least to the extent it indicates that a defendant must be given some opportunity to show that the seller's statements were not meant to be part of the basis of the bargain.

A final argument in support of a reliance requirement is found in the amicus brief. Without a reliance requirement, one runs the risk of draining the term "basis of the bargain" of all meaning, because the buyer's subjective state of mind becomes completely irrelevant. The district court instructed the jury that a statement could be considered part of the basis of the bargain if it "would naturally induce the purchase of the products." This instruction is completely objective and would permit a buyer to sue for breach of express warranty even if the seller's warranties were advertisements made in another state or country, and even if the buyer did not hear of the claims in these advertisements until the day that she walked into an attorney's office to bring suit for personal injury. It strains the language to say that a statement is part of the "basis" of the buyer's "bargain," when that buyer had no knowledge of the statement's existence.

The above arguments notwithstanding, it is possible to read the "basis of the bargain" requirement as requiring some subjective inducement of the buyer, without requiring a reliance finding. Requiring that the buyer *rely* on an advertisement, whether by imposing this burden initially on the buyer bringing suit, or by allowing the seller to rebut a presumption of reliance, puts a heavy burden on the buyer — a burden that is arguably inconsistent with the U.C.C. as a whole, with other comments to section 2-313 in particular, and with several commentators' suggestions in this area.

The reliance requirement does not comport well with U.C.C. Official Comment 7 to section 2-313. Comment 7 states that "[i]f language is used after the closing of the deal . . . the warranty becomes a modification, and need not be supported by consideration if it is otherwise reasonable and in order. . . ." N.J.S.A. §12A:2-313 U.C.C. Comment 7. If a post-closing promise — on which, by definition, a seller cannot rely in deciding to make a purchase — can create a warranty, then it is difficult to see why a pre-closing promise can create a warranty only if relied upon.

Additionally, a reliance requirement seems inconsistent with U.C.C. Official Comment 4 to section 2-313. Comment 4 states that "the whole purpose of the law of warranty is to determine what it is that the seller has in essence agreed to sell." N.J.S.A. §12A:2-313 U.C.C. Comment 4. Reliance is irrelevant to what a seller agrees to sell.

In light of these seemingly inconsistent mandates on the reliance question, some might argue that it is foolish to try to reconcile what is patently inconsistent. We reject this suggestion however, because we find it feasible to reconcile the competing arguments, and we believe that the New Jersey Supreme Court would want us to try. We believe that the most reasonable construction of section 2-313 is neither Liggett's reliance theory, which fails to explain how reliance can be relevant to "what a seller agreed to sell," or the district court's purely objective theory, which fails to explain how an advertisement that a buyer never even saw becomes part of the "basis of the bargain." Instead, we believe that the New Jersey Supreme Court would hold that a plaintiff effectuates the "basis of the bargain" requirement of section 2-313 by proving that she read, heard, saw or knew of the advertisement containing the affirmation of fact or promise. Such proof will suffice "to weave" the affirmation of fact or promise "into the fabric of the agreement," U.C.C. Comment 3, and thus make it part of the basis of the bargain. We hold that once the buyer has become aware of the affirmation of fact or promise, the statements are presumed to be part of the "basis of the bargain" unless the defendant, by "clear affirmative proof," shows that the buyer knew that the affirmation of fact or promise was untrue. We believe that by allowing a defendant to come forward with proof that the plaintiff did not believe in the warranty,[1] we are

---

1. If the defendant proves that the buyer did not believe in the warranty, the plaintiff should then be given the opportunity to show that the buyer nonetheless relied on the warranty. It is possible to disbelieve, but still rely on, the existence of a warranty. In this sense, the buyer can "buy" a lawsuit. Thus, if the buyer disbelieved the warranty, but could prove that she was relying on it when she bought the product, she could return the product for stipulated damages — for example, a refund — or economic damages — the difference between "the value of the goods accepted and the value the goods would have had if they had been warranted," U.C.C. §2-714. Such a buyer could not recover consequential damages, however. She would be barred by both U.C.C. §2-715 ("[I]f [the injured person] discover[s] the defect prior to his use, the injury would not proximately result from the breach of warranty."), and traditional contract principles, under which a buyer has a duty to mitigate damages and cannot recover for damages that she "could have avoided without undue risk, expense or humiliation," Restatement (Second) of Contracts §350(1) (1965). . . .

reconciling, as the New Jersey Supreme Court would want us to, the U.C.C. comments, the U.C.C. case law, and traditional contract principles, which serve as the background rules to the U.C.C. . . . . The relevant intent is that the statement be part of the basis of the bargain, and that, "as in the case of any contract term, is a question of the intent of the parties." Id. at 30.[2]

B

Applying our interpretation of section 2-313 to the case at bar, we conclude that the district court's jury instructions were erroneous for two reasons. First, they did not require the plaintiff to prove that Mrs. Cipollone had read, seen, or heard the advertisements at issue. Second, they did not permit the defendant to prove that although Mrs. Cipollone had read, seen, or heard the advertisements, she did not believe the safety assurances contained therein. We must therefore reverse and remand for a new trial on this issue. . . .

Do you understand footnote 34? Aren't the chances pretty good that any instruction a trial judge might give pursuant to this opinion will be found to be in error?

Cipollone is representative of the confusion engendered by the "basis of the bargain" terminology. See also Craig v. DaimlerChrysler Corp., 2008 WL 2816842, at *7-8 (S.D. Miss. 2008) (defendant not liable for breach of express warranty to repair any defect in the vehicle because there was no evidence that plaintiffs relied on the warranty when making purchase); Cole v. GMC, 484 F.3d 717, 726-727 (5th Cir. 2007) (reversing class certification because substantial split of authority on reliance requirement prevented the predominance of common issues necessary to allow class action). Some courts have interpreted the phrase synonymously with the old reliance requirement. See, e.g., American Tobacco Co. v. Grinnel, 951 S.W.2d 420, 436 (Tex. 1997) (" 'Basis of the bargain' loosely reflects the common-law express warranty requirement of reliance"); Phillips v. Ripley & Fletcher Co., 541 A.2d 946, 950 (Me. 1988) (holding that comments to Maine's version of U.C.C. §2-313 "meant to continue the uniform sales act requirement that the purchaser must show reliance on the affirmation in order to make out a cause of action for breach of a[n express] warranty"). Others hold that the enactment of U.C.C. §2-313 eliminated the need to prove reliance. See, e.g., Rosales v. FitFlop USA, LLC, 882 F. Supp. 2d 1168, 1178 (S.D. Cal. 2012) (noting that under California law when an advertisement is alleged to have created an express warranty, exposure to the advertisement but not actual reliance is required); Cavender v. American Home Prods. Corp., 2007 U.S. Dist.

---

2. Although we have emphasized the relevance of a buyer's *belief*, our construction of section 2-313 can be read as simply fleshing out the more commonly discussed *reliance* requirement with a framework of shifting presumptions and burdens of proof. Thus, in the context of advertisements claimed to be warranties, a plaintiff buyer must first prove that she saw the advertisements. This raises a (rebuttable) presumption of belief, which in turn raises an irrebuttable presumption of reliance. Next, a defendant seller may rebut the presumption of reliance, but only by proving that the plaintiff disbelieved the advertisement. Successfully proving disbelief creates a new rebuttable presumption of nonreliance. Finally, the plaintiff may rebut this presumption by proving reliance directly. Whether our holding is read as imposing a "belief" requirement or a "reliance" requirement thus is probably just a question of semantics, not substance.

LEXIS 33415 (E.D. Mo. 2007) (applying Kansas law) (no reliance is necessary to recover for breach of express warranty); Torres v. Northwest Eng'g Co., 949 P.2d 1004, 1014 (Haw. Ct. App. 1997) (finding it illogical for U.C.C. drafters to purposefully abandon Uniform Sales Act's reliance test and yet preserve reliance as required element in breach of express warranty claim).

For an exhaustive treatment of the issue, see James J. White & Robert S. Summers, Uniform Commercial Code, §§10-4 to 10-6 (6th ed. 2010); Steven Z. Hodaszy, Express Warranties Under the Uniform Commercial Code: Is There a Reliance Requirement?, 66 N.Y.U. L. Rev. 468 (1991). See also Katie McLaughlin, Another Argument "Pops Up" Against Reliance in Express Warranty Law, 28 J. L. & Com. 95 (2009); Kabir Masson, Paradox of Presumptions: Seller Warranties and Reliance Waivers in Commercial Contracts, 109 Colum. L. Rev. 503 (2009) (discussing recent trend that reliance waivers are unenforceable whereas seller waivers are presumptively enforceable); Donald J. Smythe, The Scope of a Bargain and the Value of a Promise, 60 S.C. L. Rev. 203 (2008) (arguing that reliance on express warranty should not be required).

Cipollone dealt with an express warranty allegedly created by a seller's statements made via advertising and the media. What if a manufacturer's promises or affirmations are not directed to the public at large, but are contained instead in documents accompanying the sale of a product? In Yarusso v. International Sport Marketing, Inc., 1999 WL 463531 (Del. Super. Ct. 1999), plaintiff sued the manufacturer of a protective helmet that he was wearing at the time of an off-road motorcycle accident, arguing that a defect in the helmet design enhanced injuries that he suffered. The jury found no negligence but did find that defendant-manufacturer breached an express warranty to plaintiff. In upholding the verdict, the appellate court noted:

> [I]n view of the evidence, in particular the testimony of Sundahl [a senior engineer at defendant], it is easy to see the basis for the jury's conclusion that a warranty was breached. Sundahl testified that the language in the owner's manual was "wrong." The owner's manual said that the "Moto-5 [helmet] is designed to absorb the force of a blow first by spreading it over as wide an area of the outer shell as possible, and by crushing the non-resilient inner liner." There was a factual issue as to whether the inner liner crushed. The jury apparently concluded that it did not. A breach of warranty was established. The next question was proximate cause. The plaintiff's expert, Stalnaker, testified that if there had been crush of the liner it would have absorbed a sufficient amount of the force of the fall to reduce it to a point where the plaintiff's anatomy could have tolerated it, without injury. The verdict was not against the weight of the evidence. [Id. at *4.]

In response to defendant's argument that the challenged statements could not have formed part of the basis of the bargain since they were read after purchase, the court stated:

> Express warranties arise by a seller's affirmation of fact or promise, description of the goods, or a sample or model. To create an express warranty, the representation must become a part of the "basis of the bargain." Proof of reliance is not necessary to create an express warranty. Any affirmation of fact or promise by the seller is presumed to be a part of the basis of the bargain, and the burden is on the manufacturer to show, by clear proof, that the parties did not intend their bargain to include these affirmations.

The affirmations and descriptions in the manual prepared by the manufacturer are part of what the seller has agreed to sell and became part of the basis of the bargain. In addition, the plaintiff testified that he had read the manual, was aware of the statements about the helmet and expected it to be true. Under these facts, the Court concludes that a jury could justifiably find that an express warranty had been made, that the express warranty was part of the basis for the bargain, and that the plaintiff relied on the warranty. . . . [Id. at *6.]

For supporting authority see Weinstat et al. v. Dentsply International, Inc. 103 Cal. Rptr. 3d 614, 629 (Cal. Ct. App. 2010) (holding that buyer need not read warranty before purchasing the product and that warranties delivered with the product form part of the basis of the bargain); Rite Aid Corp. v. Levy-Gray, 894 A.2d 563 (Md. 2006) (affirming a jury verdict against manufacturer on breach of express warranty claim, holding that instructional brochure given to patient in bag with medicine was part of basis of bargain and thus need not have been read by patient at time of sale). For contrary authority see Accurate Transmissions, Inc. v. Sonnax Indus., 2007 U.S. Dist. LEXIS 7956 (N.D. Ill. 2007) (denying motion for summary judgment because it was a question of fact whether catalogs containing disclaimers had been given to buyer at or before the time of sale and thus were part of the basis of the bargain).

Forbes v. General Motors Corp., 935 So. 2d 869 (Miss. 2006), finds some middle ground on this question. The court reversed summary judgment for defendant-manufacturer, holding that warranties in the owner's manual, although not read before purchase, could still be part of the basis of the bargain because the salesman had informed buyer of the warranties. The court stated, "It is . . . possible to rely on assertions [in the manual] without having actually read them. . . . Mr. Forbes did make his purchase conditional on one factor, the presence of a functional air bag. Forbes inquired about the presence of an air bag from the salesman . . . [and w]hile the salesman himself may not substantively assert facts making GM liable, here he was doing nothing more [than] conveying the express warranty to Forbes." Id. at 875. In weighing express warranty claims based on representations read or discovered after purchase, should courts consider whether a product was still within its valid return period at the time the consumer eventually receives a representation?

The conceptual problems raised by treating statements made in non-traditional bargaining settings under a one-size-fits-all express warranty provision are not lost on commentators. Professor James J. White, a preeminent commercial law scholar, argues in Freeing the Tortious Soul of Express Warranty Law, 72 Tul. L. Rev. 2089 (1998), that much of the analytical quagmire attending warranty claims results from the unhappy marriage of tort and contract principles. Observing that not all warranty claims are the same, Professor White calls for a revision to U.C.C. §2-313 that would "unbundle" the heretofore interwoven strands of express warranty liability depending on whether they are based on traditional contract notions, tort principles, or something different altogether. Under such a scheme, written or oral assurances made before or concurrently with a sales transaction would be governed by traditional contract principles. Post-sale statements accompanying the sale of goods, by virtue of being reduced to writing and anticipated by both the seller and buyer, would be enforceable by statute as though part of the contract for sale. Finally, liability for statements directed to the public at large, due to the "irrepressible minimum" of tort buried inside such claims, would require an unabashed showing of reliance as a prerequisite for recovery.

The National Conference of Commissioners on Uniform State Laws (NCCUSL) and the American Law Institute (ALI) — the two institutions responsible for preparing and approving the U.C.C. — drafted a revision of Article 2, including alterations to §2-313. Generally, they adopted Professor White's proposal for different standards, dependent on where the warranty appeared. The changes to §2-313 removed warranties contained in a good's packaging and warranties created by advertisements from the "basis of the bargain" test, which remained intact in §2-313. The reliance element was eliminated entirely with respect to "pass-through" statements included in the package, but reliance was retained regarding statements directed to the public at large. The proposed changes to Article 2 never received a warm welcome by state legislatures and in 2011 the American Law Institute, upon the recommendation of the Permanent Editorial Board for the U.C.C., withdrew the amendments.

NOTE: THE IMPLIED WARRANTY OF FITNESS FOR PARTICULAR PURPOSE

Another type of warranty that depends on firm expectations as to product quality is the implied warranty of fitness for particular purpose, U.C.C. §2-315. This warranty arises whenever the buyer relies on the seller's expertise in selecting a product to perform a particular purpose communicated by the buyer to the seller. Section 2-315 of the Uniform Commercial Code describes the warranty:

> Where the seller at the time of contracting has reason to know any particular purpose for which the goods are required and that the buyer is relying on the seller's skill or judgment to select or furnish suitable goods, there is . . . an implied warranty that the goods shall be fit for such purpose.

A significant difference between this type of implied warranty and an express warranty is that in connection with the latter, the seller does the talking, whereas in the former, the buyer does the talking. See, e.g., Moffitt v. Icynene, Inc., 407 F. Supp. 2d 591 (D. Vt. 2005) (plaintiff's failure to communicate special purpose to defendant precluded recovery for implied warranty of fitness of particular purpose). Thus, a warranty of fitness for particular purpose could be likened to an implied-in-fact promise by the seller that the goods will meet the buyer's unusual, but communicated, requirements. See, e.g., LePage v. E-One, Inc., 4 F. Supp. 3d 298 (D. Mass. 2014) (manufacturer of fire truck had no reason to know that attached aerial platform would be used by fireman inside station house causing him to strike the ceiling and suffer fatal injuries); Varner v. MHS, Ltd., 2 F. Supp. 3d 584 (M.D. Pa. 2014) (seller of nylon strap had no reason to know of workers' intent to use strap to move heavy equipment); Daniell v. Ford Motor Co., Inc., 581 F. Supp. 728 (D. N.M. 1984) (automobile manufacturer could not be held liable for psychological and physical injuries sustained when buyer crawled into trunk to commit suicide and remained in locked trunk for nine days as such use of trunk was highly extraordinary and not contemplated by buyer at the time of purchase). In most states, "[n]o warranty for a particular purpose is created if the intended use is no different from the ordinary use of the product." Rosenstern v. Allergan, Inc., 987 F. Supp. 2d 795, 804 (N.D. Ill. 2013) (implied warranty created when Botox manufacturer knew that some customers would use the product to treat temporomandibular joint syndrome). But see In re Atlas Roofing Corp. Chalet Shingle

Products Liability Litigation, 22 F. Supp. 3d 1322, 1329 (N.D. Ga. 2014) (noting that under South Carolina law plaintiffs could recover on an implied warranty of fitness for a particular purpose even if the purpose was identical to the product's ordinary usage).

B. MISREPRESENTATION

The tort of misrepresentation developed at common law in actions for fraud and deceit. To sustain a cause of action, the plaintiff had to establish that the defendant intended to mislead the plaintiff. See, e.g., Webster v. L. Romano Eng'g Corp., 34 P.2d 428, 430 (Wash. 1934). The Restatement (Second) of Torts recognized such intentional conduct as tortious but also laid out a lesser standard of negligent misrepresentation:

Restatement (Second) of Torts
(1965)

§310. CONSCIOUS MISREPRESENTATION INVOLVING RISK OF PHYSICAL HARM
An actor who makes a misrepresentation is subject to liability to another for physical harm which results from an act done by the other or a third person in reliance upon the truth of the representation, if the actor
(a) intends his statement to induce or should realize that it is likely to induce action by the other, or a third person, which involves an unreasonable risk of physical harm to the other, and
(b) knows
(i) that the statement is false, or
(ii) that he has not the knowledge which he professes.

§311. NEGLIGENT MISREPRESENTATION INVOLVING RISK OF PHYSICAL HARM
(1) One who negligently gives false information to another is subject to liability for physical harm caused by action taken by the other in reasonable reliance upon such information, where such harm results
(a) to the other, or
(b) to such third persons as the actor should expect to be put in peril by the action taken.
(2) Such negligence may consist of failure to exercise reasonable care
(a) in ascertaining the accuracy of the information, or
(b) in the manner in which it is communicated.

In products liability litigation, misrepresentation overlaps with express warranty and implied warranty of fitness for a particular purpose on the contract side, and with failure-to-warn on the tort side. Although for the most part these other doctrines cover the cases adequately, the tort of misrepresentation may be a useful weapon in a plaintiff's arsenal for several reasons. First, one need not be a party to a sales transaction to be held liable for misleading another into using a product in a way that causes injury or loss. It is more difficult to fit such product-related conduct by non-suppliers into the other contract or tort categories. Second, although tortious failure-to-warn doctrine may be adequate to cover personal injury or property losses, it may not be available to recover economic loss damages, and warranty actions may be difficult to establish since the seller may have cleverly worded his formal representations with regard to the performance capability of the product. The action for misrepresentation may fill the gap. Third, one must not forget that the contractual remedies may allow for more limited damages, be subject to more restrictive statutes of limitation, or be open to attack on such grounds as the parol evidence rule. And finally, the tort of misrepresentation may trigger remedies for malevolent conduct. It is, of course, possible to make the allegation of intentional or wanton misconduct in the context of a failure-to-warn case. Nonetheless, misrepresentation may more effectively characterize the true nature of the proceedings.

The Restatement sections set out above do not consider whether a faultless defendant should be strictly liable in tort for harm caused by false representations. Now that the privity requirement has been all but eliminated in express warranty cases involving personal injury or property damage, products liability plaintiffs have less occasion to make use of tort claims based on innocent misrepresentations. In any event, the Restatement (Second) of Torts includes a special rule imposing privity-free strict liability for innocent misrepresentations made by commercial product sellers:

§402B. Misrepresentation by Seller of Chattels to Consumer

One engaged in the business of selling chattels who, by advertising, labels, or otherwise, makes to the public a misrepresentation of a material fact concerning the character or quality of a chattel sold by him is subject to liability for physical harm to a consumer of the chattel caused by justifiable reliance upon the misrepresentation, even though

(a) it is not made fraudulently or negligently, and

(b) the consumer has not bought the chattel from or entered into any contractual relation with the seller.

Crocker v. Winthrop Laboratories
514 S.W.2d 429 (Tex. 1974)

REAVLEY, J.

Glenn E. Crocker became addicted to a new drug produced by Winthrop Laboratories and known as "talwin" which had been previously thought to be non-addictive. When he was in a weakened condition and his tolerance to drugs very low because of a period of detoxification, Crocker obtained an injection of a narcotic and died soon thereafter. His widow and representative, Clarissa Crocker, brought this action for damages due to his suffering while alive as well as for his wrongful death. She recovered judgment against Winthrop Laboratories in the trial court. The Court of Civil Appeals reversed and rendered judgment for the drug company, holding that while some of the facts found by the jury (including the positive misrepresentation by the drug company that talwin was non-addictive) would warrant the recovery, the additional finding that the drug company could not reasonably have foreseen Crocker's addiction (because of his unusual susceptibility and the state of medical knowledge when the drug was marketed), constituted a complete defense. We hold that the latter finding does not bar the recovery, and we affirm the judgment of the trial court.

In July of 1967 Glenn Crocker suffered a double hernia, as well as frostbite of two fingers, while working as a carpenter in a cold storage vault. He was then 49 years old and was not a user of drugs or alcohol. His hernia was successfully repaired. The circulation of blood in his fingers, however, was not restored. Skin grafts were done on the fingers in October, but it was necessary to amputate part of his thumb in November and part of his middle finger the following January (1968). Prior to November 23, 1967, when Dr. Mario Palafox amputated part of his thumb, the several doctors who had treated him had prescribed both demerol (a narcotic) and talwin for relief of pain without observing any cause to believe him to be then addicted to any drug. Crocker told Dr. Palafox that he liked the relief he received from talwin, and Dr. Palafox responded that this was fortunate because talwin had no addicting side effect.

Crocker did develop an addiction to talwin, however, and was able to obtain prescriptions from several doctors as well as to cross the Mexican border to Juarez and acquire the same drug without a prescription under the name of "sosigon." He was hospitalized on June 3, 1968 by a psychiatrist, Dr. J. Edward Stern, for a process of detoxification (to remove the toxic agents in his body) and treatment of his drug dependency. After six days in the hospital being withdrawn from talwin as well as all narcotics, and at a time when his tolerance for potent drugs was very low, Crocker walked out of the hospital and went to his home. Because of his agitated condition and the threats he made against his wife, he was finally successful in having her call Dr. Eugene Engel who, on June 10, 1968, came to the Crocker home and gave Mr. Crocker an injection of demerol. Crocker went to his bed for the last time.

Winthrop Laboratories first put talwin on the market in July of 1967 after extensive testing and approval by the Federal Drug Administration. The descriptive material on the new drug circulated by Winthrop Laboratories in 1967 gives no warning of the possibilities of addiction. There is a heading of a paragraph in the product information of the 1967 edition of Physicians' Desk Reference Book which reads: "Absence of addiction liability." This might be considered misleading, but in view of the evidence of verbal assurances as to the properties of talwin by the drug company's representative, there is no need to deal further with the printed materials. Dr. Palafox, a prominent orthopedic surgeon in El Paso, allowed Crocker to have liberal use of talwin and assured him that it was non-addictive because of the assurance by a representative of the drug company who had detailed the doctor on the nature of the drug. There had been an extended and specific conversation between the drug company representative and Dr. Palafox about talwin, and Dr. Palafox was told that talwin was as harmless as aspirin and could be given as long as desired. Dr. Palafox testified that the representative of the defendant insisted that talwin could have no addicting effect.

Subsequent experience has proved that talwin is an extremely useful drug for the relief of pain but that it cannot be regarded as non-addictive. Doctors Palafox and Stern had seen other patients dependent upon talwin. Dr. Arthur S. Keats, chairman of the Department of Anesthesiology at Baylor School of Medicine in Houston, who did original work on the drug and who testified during this trial on the call of the drug company, agreed with the attorney for Mrs. Crocker that "there are a tremendous number of people that do develop a talwin addiction."

Dr. Palafox was of the opinion that if he had not been assured of the non-addictive character of talwin, he could probably have avoided addiction or dependence by Crocker upon any drug.

Plaintiff's medical testimony depicted the addiction to talwin as a producing cause of the death of Crocker when taken together with the chain of events including the detoxification process and the injection of Demerol.

The findings of the jury included the following:

1. That the defendant failed to advise the public during the year 1967 that its drug talwin could cause physical dependence.
2. That the failure of the defendant to advise the public that the drug talwin could cause physical dependence made such drug unreasonably dangerous as marketed in 1967. The jury was instructed that a drug is unreasonably dangerous "if under all the circumstances under which it is marketed, it subjected the Plaintiff to an unreasonable risk of harm even though the manufacturer did not know and could not know of the risk involved."
3. That the defendant drug company represented to the medical profession during the year 1967 that its drug talwin would not cause physical dependence.
4. That such representation was relied upon by Dr. Mario Palafox in prescribing talwin for the deceased.
5. That the deceased became physically dependent upon the drug talwin.
6. That the physical dependence of Crocker on the drug talwin was a producing cause of his death. . . .

These findings, without more, would justify a recovery by the plaintiff under the rules of both sections 402A and 402B of the Restatement, Torts, Second. . . .

The carefully written opinion of the Court of Civil Appeals has correctly foreseen that we would apply Section 402B of the Restatement and that the judgment for plaintiff should be affirmed depending upon the effect to be given the findings of the jury in response to special issues 9 and 10. Those findings were as follows:

9. That Crocker's addiction or dependency upon talwin was an abreaction. Abreaction was defined as "an unusual reaction resulting from a person's unusual susceptibility to the product or intended effect of the product in question; that is, such person's reaction is different in the presence of the drug in question from that in the usual person. An abreaction is one in which an unusual result is produced by a known or theoretical mechanism of action. An abreaction is one which could not have been reasonably foreseen in an appreciable class or number of potential users prior to the time Glenn E. Crocker became addicted or dependent on talwin."
10. That at the time Crocker was taking talwin under doctors' prescriptions, the state of medical knowledge was such that Winthrop Laboratories could not have reasonably foreseen, in the exercise of ordinary care, that talwin would cause an addiction in an appreciable number of persons.

[The court concludes that the mere fact that the potentially endangered users were few in number should not preclude liability for failure to warn, but that the defendant cannot be held for failing to warn of risks not known or reasonably knowable at the time of sale.]

Liability of Winthrop Laboratories will be predicated upon the finding of misrepresentation that the drug would not cause physical dependence, a fact conceded by the attorney for the company in his jury argument, and upon the findings of reliance and causation. Whatever the danger and state of medical knowledge, and however rare the susceptibility of the user, when the drug company positively and specifically represents its product to be free and safe from all dangers of addiction, and when the treating physician relies upon that representation, the drug company is liable when the representation proves to be false and harm results. . . .

Judgment affirmed.

Not all jurisdictions accept the strict liability standard for misrepresentations as described in the Second Restatement §402B. See, e.g., DiBartolo v. Abbott Laboratories, 914 F. Supp. 2d 601, 623 (S.D.N.Y. 2012) (noting that New York specifically rejects the strict liability theory of §402B); Vitatoe v. Mylan Pharmaceuticals, Inc., 696 F. Supp. 2d 599, 606 (N.D. W. Va. 2010) (liability under §402B precluded by state tort reform statute). But some do. In Kirby v. B.I. Inc., 2003 U.S. Dist. LEXIS 16964 (N.D. Tex. Sept. 26, 2003), for instance, murder victim Karen Sawyer's estate sued the manufacturer of an ankle monitor after she was killed by her ex-boyfriend while he was out on bail for a less serious offense while wearing one of the company's monitors. The district court concluded that the company had made misrepresentations on their website about the capabilities of the ankle monitor which "gave [Sawyer] a false sense of security." Id at *23. In doing so, the misrepresentations were "a producing cause of Sawyer's death" and thus defendant-manufacturer could be found liable. Id. The court ultimately ascribed 20 percent of the fault in the victim's death to the defendant company for their misrepresentations, 70 percent to the murderer, and 10 percent to the victim. Id. at *46. Cf. discussion, supra Chapter Three, regarding fault allocation among intentional and nonintentional tortfeasors.

Most cases dealing with representations about product performance are covered under the express warranty provisions of U.C.C. §2-313. However, courts occasionally couch their decisions in both tortious misrepresentation as well as express warranty terminology. See, e.g., Hauter v. Zogarts, 534 P.2d 377 (Cal. 1975) (plaintiff entitled to recover under theory of misrepresentation or breach of express warranty for injury resulting from false assurances regarding safety of golf-ball training unit); Klages v. General Ordnance Equip. Corp., 367 A.2d 304, 306 (Pa. Super. Ct. 1976) (jury allowed to find defendant liable under either misrepresentation or breach of express warranty for false claims characterizing mace spray as having ability to "instantly stop and subdue entire groups"). In such cases, the semantic difference between the two theories may have an impact. "Misrepresentation" sounds more ominous and more tort-like than the bland terminology of "express warranty." Misrepresentation carries negative connotations to both judge and jury even when based in strict liability. For example, in the context of a misrepresentation claim, it is far easier to argue to a jury that the defendant's statements were "lies" (even if the defendant was not a liar). It is more difficult to attach such emotion-laden language to a breach of contract claim.

The American Law Institute attached the following caveat to §402B: "The Institute expresses no opinion as to whether the rule stated in this section may apply . . . where the representation is not made to the public, but to an individual. . . ." Clearly, §§310 and 311 of the Restatement (Second) set forth earlier, apply to representations made to individuals. (Indeed, those sections apply generally to representations made *by* individuals — even individuals not in the business of selling products.) Though the issue raised in the caveat to §402B is rarely addressed, there may be occasional indications that the section applies only to public misrepresentations. See, e.g., Lewis & Lambert Metal Contractors, Inc. v. Jackson, 914 S.W.2d 584, 590 (Tex. App. 1994) (holding that "Section 402B . . . does not apply to private misrepresentations").

According to its terms, §402B supports recovery only for "physical harm." Traditionally courts have refused to allow recovery for pure economic losses under tort claims of negligence or strict liability. Would a court today allow recovery under §402B (strict liability for innocent misrepresentation) for pure economic loss absent a showing of physical harm? In Ritter v. Custom Chemicides, Inc., 912 S.W.2d 128 (Tenn. 1995), the Supreme Court of Tennessee answered this question in the negative. See also Giddings & Lewis, Inc. v. Industrial Risk Insurers, 348 S.W.3d 729, 746 (Ky. 2011) (same under §9 of the Products Liability Restatement, reprinted below). Recovery for pure economic loss is allowed, however, when the plaintiff can prove either intentional or negligent misrepresentation. See, e.g., TGI Development, Inc. v. CV Reit, Inc., 665 So. 2d 366 (Fla. Dist. Ct. App. 1996).

Restatement (Third) of Torts: Products Liability
(1998)

§9. LIABILITY OF COMMERCIAL PRODUCT SELLER OR DISTRIBUTOR FOR HARM CAUSED BY MISREPRESENTATION

One engaged in the business of selling or otherwise distributing products who, in connection with the sale of a product, makes a fraudulent, negligent, or innocent misrepresentation of material fact concerning the product is subject to liability for harm to persons or property caused by the misrepresentation.

In Miller v. Pfizer Inc., 196 F. Supp. 2d 1095 (D. Kan. 2002), *aff'd*, 356 F.3d 1326 (10th Cir. 2004), plaintiff argued that §9 of the Products Liability Restatement disposes of the reliance requirement for claims for misrepresentation. In that case, parents of a child who committed suicide while being treated with Zoloft, a widely used antidepressant, argued that Pfizer was liable for misrepresentation because it had "gone to great lengths to reassure doctors that the violence and suicide problems they have heard about, mainly with its chief . . . competitor Prozac, would not occur with Zoloft." Id. at 1119. In response to defendant's claim that plaintiff could not prevail on a claim of misrepresentation absent evidence demonstrating that the prescribing physician had relied on the defendant's alleged misrepresentations, plaintiff contended that it was unnecessary under §9 to prove reliance on a product's misrepresentation. Rejecting plaintiff's argument, the court held that §9, in stating that the alleged harm must be "caused by the misrepresentation," does indeed require proof of a plaintiff's reliance on a product's misrepresentation. Id. at 1123. The district court cited to a prior decision by the Kansas Supreme Court that held that "[t]he reliance element of misrepresentation serves the function of causation in fact; that the misrepresentation causes someone to act or refrain from acting." Id. at 1120. Accord Wolfe v. McNeil-PPC, Inc., 773 F. Supp. 2d 561, 567, 573 (E.D. Pa. 2011) (holding that even if children's ibuprofen label instruction to "[s]ee box for complete information" amounted to a representation that the enclosed information was "complete," plaintiff had not demonstrated reliance on the representation); LaBelle v. Philip Morris, Inc., 243 F. Supp. 2d 508 (D. S.C. 2001) (applying Pennsylvania law) (summary judgment for defendant granted due to plaintiff's inability to show decedent's reliance on defendants' statements regarding the safety of smoking).

Courts appear to be split as to the kind of evidence necessary to establish the element of reliance on a claim of misrepresentation. In Williams v. Philip Morris, Inc., 48 P.3d 824 (Or. Ct. App.), *rev. denied*, 61 P.3d 938 (2002), plaintiff alleged that tobacco companies had engaged in decades-long conduct of deceptive advertising designed to lull consumers into the belief that cigarettes were not dangerous to one's health. Defendant claimed that there was insufficient evidence showing that plaintiff's decedent had relied on any misrepresentations it may have made. In upholding the jury's verdict in plaintiff's favor, the court said:

> There is evidence that Williams received the message that defendant intended to communicate and that the message affected his decision to continue smoking and not to make more serious efforts to overcome his addiction to cigarettes. Williams read the *Oregonian*, other newspapers and magazines, and watched television, all of which were media through which defendant conveyed its message. The evidence includes examples of newspaper stories describing the dangers of tobacco that also contain statements from industry spokespersons insisting that the dangers were not proved and at times attacking the validity of the research suggesting harmful effects. Industry newspaper advertisements conveyed the same message. For instance, in an article published in the *Oregonian* in 1991, an industry spokesman said that the dangers were not proven and argued that the money that the CTR spent on research showed how open-minded the industry was. [Id. at 834-835.]

The court pointed to specific evidence showing that Williams had, in fact, relied on the assurances of the tobacco companies that its cigarettes were safe. It is not clear from the opinion, however, whether the evidence regarding public statements conveyed through advertising and the media set forth in the language above would suffice to establish reliance on its own. See also Whitely v. Philip Morris, Inc., 117 Cal. App. 4th 635 (2004) (plaintiff did not have to prove that she heard or saw any specific misrepresentations to establish reliance; it is sufficient that the statements were issued to the public with the intent that those statements reach smokers or potential smokers and that the plaintiff was misled). However, in White v. R.J. Reynolds Tobacco Co., 109 F. Supp. 2d 424 (D. Md. 2000), the court made clear that a plaintiff could not establish reliance based on her exposure to alleged misrepresentations by the tobacco companies regarding the safety of smoking conveyed via publications and electronic media. The court said it would not presume reliance due merely to the fact that "[the plaintiff's decedent had] read the newspaper and magazines, watched television and listened to the radio where these misrepresentations were made. . . . The Court will not presume anything of the kind, because such a presumption would be nothing but speculation." Id. at 429. See also Commonwealth v. Ortho-McNeil-Janssen Pharmaceuticals, Inc., 52 A.3d 498, 502 (Pa. Commw. Ct. 2012) (although under Pennsylvania law reliance may be presumed where a misrepresentation is material, plaintiff still failed to demonstrate that it would have behaved differently with knowledge of the "true" facts surrounding a product); Wright v. Brooke Group Ltd., 114 F. Supp. 2d 797 (N.D. Iowa 2000) (plaintiff's fraudulent misrepresentation claim failed because he did not point to specific deceptive statements made at specific times upon which the plaintiff relied).

The *White* court also addressed the issue of whether representations made to and relied upon by third parties could support an action for misrepresentation when the plaintiff herself did not rely on such representations. The issue was left as a caveat to §402B and was not resolved in the Products Liability Restatement §9. The court in *White* had this to say in response to plaintiff's claim that the manufacturer should be liable for making allegedly false representations to government officials, physicians, and teachers who then passed on the misinformation to the plaintiff:

> Plaintiffs' argument fails because, under Maryland law, there is no fraudulent misrepresentation cause of action for statements made to third parties. . . . Even if there were such a cause of action, it would fail because plaintiffs do not have evidence (or even allegations) of reliance by those third persons allegedly deceived. Even in cases that have held that a defendant may be liable for an injury to a consumer for misrepresentations to someone else (*e.g.*, a person buys a product that is then used by her guest or child, who is injured by the product), the plaintiff must prove that the purchaser herself brought the product in reliance on the manufacturers' representations. *See* Restatement, Second, of Torts §402B cmt. *j*. [Id. at 430.]

Courts have also addressed the extent to which the "common knowledge doctrine" bars plaintiffs' misrepresentation claims when the risks of smoking are well known to the public. For example, in Wright v. Brooke Group Ltd., supra, the plaintiff brought an action against several cigarette manufacturers for misrepresenting the dangers of smoking. The defendants moved to dismiss, arguing that the risks associated with smoking are common knowledge and that, therefore, the plaintiff cannot show justifiable reliance as a matter of law. In denying the defendants' motion, the court noted that the plaintiff may have been defrauded by the defendants' attempts to refute the common knowledge of the harm and addictive nature of cigarettes. See also Whitely v. Philip Morris, Inc., supra, suggesting that the age and sophistication of a smoker may be relevant in determining whether the plaintiff's reliance was justifiable in light of the common knowledge doctrine.

For general discussions of the role of misrepresentation in products liability, see David G. Owen, Products Liability Law §3.2. (2d. ed. 2008); Jerry J. Phillips, Product Misrepresentation and the Doctrine of Causation, 2 Hofstra L. Rev. 561 (1974); Marshall S. Shapo, A Representational Theory of Consumer Protection: Doctrine, Function and Legal Liability for Product Disappointment, 60 Va. L. Rev. 1109 (1974).

C. OTHER MARKETING-BASED APPROACHES TO LIABILITY

The most significant source of product representations is Madison Avenue. Indeed, one of the authors has argued to his classes for years on end that much of products liability reflects the inability of American engineering to match the claims made for products by advertisers. However, it is no easy matter to establish that an advertising claim constitutes an express warranty. The question of which kinds of statements are puffing and constitute only "the seller's opinion or commendation of the goods," and which cross over the line and constitute a warranty has baffled the courts for decades. The legal staffs of the corporate giants take the trouble (in most instances) to see to it that advertisements remain on the right side of the line, if only by a hairsbreadth. See Jon D. Hanson & Douglas A. Kysar, Taking Behavioralism Seriously: Some Evidence of Market Manipulation, 112 Harv. L. Rev. 1420 (1999) (detailing arguably manipulative but difficult to police marketing practices by product manufacturers, including extensive case study of the tobacco industry).

Should the plaintiff include in a traditional products liability case based on defect, a plausible, although not likely winnable, express warranty or misrepresentation claim based on advertising? We think the answer is clearly "yes." The simple fact is that even if the express warranty claim cannot stand on its own, it is highly relevant to the overall issue of product safety. How a product is portrayed to the public is an important factor in determining how it will be used and what liberties consumers will take with it. Courts should be wary of allowing an inherently weak design case to be bolstered by an equally weak failure-to-warn claim. Here we ask whether it is right to bolster a weak design case with representational claims that may be unable to survive on their own. We think this raises a different question. Plaintiffs have every right and incentive to press the express warranty or misrepresentation claim as aggressively as possible. First, they may convince a court or a jury of its inherent merits. Second, in the event they do not, the issue of product portrayal is justifiably in the case on the overarching issue of product safety. See Products Liability Restatement §2, Comments *f* and *g*. In that sense, advertisements and promotional representations may be thought to serve as the "mood music" for determining product defect under traditional theories of liability.

It is difficult to support a thesis such as we have just set forth with case authority. But now and then a court comes up with language seemingly on point. In Hill v. Searle Laboratories, 884 F.2d 1064, 1070 (8th Cir. 1989), the plaintiff suffered injury when an IUD perforated her uterus and became partially embedded in her small bowel. A significant issue in the case was whether an IUD was an "unavoidably unsafe" drug in which case the seller would be exempt from strict liability. Id. at 1068. In a wonderfully confused opinion, the court denied the special drug exemption to IUDs for a host of reasons. One important factor was that "IUD manufacturers, through mass advertising and merchandising practices, generated a general sense of product quality, making it difficult for consumers to fully understand the risks involved with the use of an IUD." Id. at 1070. The court linked the representational background of the case to the underlying cause of action, suggesting that although neither might stand alone, both might stand together.

Two additional contexts in which product representations can give rise to liability deserve attention. First, a product whose risks are quite obvious and more than offset by corresponding benefits from normal use may occasionally find its way into the hands of a user who is predictably incapable of handling the product safely. (It might be said that such cases present a "mismatch" of product and user.) Sometimes the issue presented in such a case involves the design of the product itself. See Halliday v. Sturm, Ruger in Chapter Four, in which a young boy killed himself with his father's handgun. In other cases, the design of the packaging has been found defective because it did not adequately resist the efforts of a young child to open the package and consume its harmful contents.

The sorts of "mismatch" cases of interest here are those in which defendant's marketing techniques appear inadequate in trying to prevent the mismatch from occurring — where, for example, inherently and unavoidably dangerous products, designed for adult use, are marketed directly to children, or are marketed to adults without adequate reminders to keep the products out of the hands of children. The latter type of case, of course, may be subsumed under the "failure to instruct or warn" umbrella. But the former cannot so comfortably be characterized, and constitutes a separate category of defective marketing cases.

A case involving this sort of mismatch is Salvi v. Montgomery Ward & Co., 489 N.E.2d 394 (Ill. App. Ct. 1986), in which the plaintiff alleged that the defendant-manufacturer had defectively designed the safety on its BB gun and that the defendant-retailer had negligently sold the gun to the plaintiff's brother, then 14 years of age, whose carelessness eventually led to the plaintiff's being shot in the eye. The trial court sent both claims to the jury, which returned a verdict in favor of the manufacturer and against the retailer in the amount of $570,000. The container in which the BB gun was packaged warned that it should not be allowed in the possession of a child under the age of 16 without adult supervision. The accident occurred while the plaintiff's brother was cleaning the gun. Notwithstanding the fact that an Illinois statute set the age of 13 as the age below which it was criminal to sell an air gun to a minor, and the fact that the plaintiff's brother was over 15 years of age when the accident occurred, the court of appeals affirmed the verdict against the retailer. Referring to such cases as involving "negligent entrustment" of dangerous instrumentalities, other courts have reached the same result on similar facts. See, e.g., Moning v. Alfono, 254 N.W.2d 759 (Mich. 1977) (reserving as a jury question whether defendant's practice of marketing slingshots directly to children violated an obligation of due care to plaintiff injured by a missile fired by an 11-year-old using defendant's slingshot).

In some "mismatch" cases, plaintiffs claim that defendants not only negligently allowed the product mismatch to occur, but negligently *encouraged* it by targeting the mismatched group. Such claims were pressed in the weapons context prior to passage of lawsuit immunity legislation by the U.S. Congress in 2005. For instance, in Merrill v. Navegar, Inc., 89 Cal. Rptr. 2d 146 (Cal. Ct. App. 1999) *rev'd*, 28 P.3d 116 (Cal. 2001), plaintiffs claimed that defendant gun manufacturer negligently advertised its product in such a way as to increase their appeal to criminals by, for example, publicizing its product's nonglare finish, combat slash, threaded barrel suitable for silencers, flash muzzles and extension, and "excellent resistance to fingerprints." Plaintiffs argued that this marketing in turn caused a fatal shooting. The intermediate court found that defendant owed the public a duty not to create unreasonable risks by advertising firearms so as to appeal to persons with criminal purposes. On appeal, the Supreme Court of California reversed because plaintiffs had produced no evidence showing that the perpetrator of the fatal shooting had been influenced by defendant's advertisement, or that the perpetrator had even seen the advertisement. But see Ileto v. Glock, Inc., 349 F.3d 1191, 1200-01 (9th Cir. 2003) (allowing allegations that firearm manufacturer had specifically targeted illegal gun users to proceed under a nuisance or negligent distribution theory while recognizing that *Merrill* foreclosed a products liability claim).

A second category of defective marketing cases involves advertisements that encourage consumers to use a product in unsafe and gratuitously dangerous ways. One decision that comes very close to recognizing such a basis for liability is Leichtamer v. American Motors Corp., 424 N.E.2d 568 (Ohio 1981). The plaintiffs were injured when they drove a Jeep Model CJ-7 off the top of a ridge, flying almost 50 feet through the air and landing upside down near the bottom of the slope nearly 25 feet below. The plaintiffs argued that the defendant-manufacturer's advertising induced such user behavior, and that the roll bars should therefore have been able to withstand the great forces put upon them. Affirming judgment for plaintiffs, the court explained:

> Cited as exemplary of this "intentional incitement of unlawful conduct" was the sound track employed in the Jeep television commercials: "My Jeep CJ is the toughest rig around"; "That's Jeep guts — Guts to take you where only the toughest dares to go"; "Jeep guts — will take you places you have never been before"; "CJ-5 — will give the young couples the ride of their lives on the dunes and gutsy ground steering"; "All right, which one of you guys is going to climb that big old hill with me? I mean you guys aren't yellow, are you? Is it a steep hill? Yeah, little lady, you could say it's a steep hill. Let's try it. The King of the Hill, is about to discover the new Jeep CJ-7"; "That Jeep four-wheel drive is tough enough to go anywhere." . . . The television commercials relied upon by the Court of Appeals demonstrated an off-the-road use. The commercials are relevant to the foreseeable use of the vehicle and the unreasonable danger of the product when used as intended. [Id. at 579.]

In some negligent marketing cases, particularly in the area of prescription drugs, plaintiffs claim that their use of a product and resulting harm was caused by the distorting effects of defendant's "overpromotion" of its product. One of the clearest examples of a court grounding its decision on defendant's negligent "overpromotion" of a product is Stevens v. Parke, Davis & Co., 507 P.2d 653 (Cal. 1973), in which plaintiff recovered a substantial judgment based on the defendant's having induced her physician to negligently prescribe a dangerous drug that the physician knew full well was dangerous. The court concluded:

> We are satisfied from a review of the evidence . . . that the jury could reasonably find that [the doctor's] negligent prescription of Chloromycetin for Mrs. Stevens was a foreseeable consequence of the extensive advertising and promotional campaign planned and carried out by the manufacturer. The record reveals in abundant detail that Parke, Davis made every effort, employing both direct and subliminal advertising, to allay the fears of the medical profession which were raised by knowledge of the drug's dangers. It cannot be said, therefore, that [the doctor's] prescription of the drug despite his awareness of its dangers was anything other than the foreseeable consequence — indeed, the desired result — of Parke, Davis' over-promotion. [Id. at 664.]

Decades later, one court revisiting the issue of "overpromotion" in a prescription drug case cited *Stevens* for the proposition that "an adequate warning to the [medical] profession may be eroded or even nullified by overpromotion of the drug through a vigorous sales program which may have the effect of persuading the prescribing doctor to disregard the warnings given." Motus v. Pfizer, Inc., 196 F. Supp. 2d 984, 998 (C.D. Cal. 2001). However, as is often the case in negligent advertising cases (see also *Merrill*, supra), the *Motus* court granted defendant's motion for summary judgment because plaintiff had failed to produce evidence showing that defendant's marketing had persuaded, or even reached, the prescribing doctor. Despite this lack of recent success, plaintiffs continue to pursue "overpromotion" and negligent marketing theories in product liability cases involving pharmaceutical products. See, e.g., Lance v. Wyeth, 85 A.3d 434, 463 (Pa. 2014) (Eakin, J., dissenting).

Would any combination of the approaches explored in this section help plaintiff in the following scenario?

PROBLEM TWENTY-FOUR

John Lin is a thirteen-year-old skateboarding enthusiast. When he's not perfecting his 360 degree inward double heelflip at the local skate park, John is live-streaming professional skateboarding events to watch his favorite skaters shred rails and execute gravity-defying tricks on the half-pipe. When John is able to attend an event, he is sure to stop at the sponsor tents, including the Lightning Energy tent, where company representatives are always handing out free samples of Lightning's signature energy drink. In addition to sponsoring skateboarding events across the country, Lightning also sponsors many of John's favorite professional skateboarders, such as Shayna Taylor, whose skateboard deck and competition gear are emblazoned with the neon green Lightning Energy bolt logo. Lightning also runs a social networking website called Lightning Storm, where athletes between thirteen and twenty-one years old can submit videos and photos of themselves participating in extreme sports (such as skateboarding) for a chance to win free products and gear, or even to become a representative of the Lightning Energy brand. Lightning prominently features young Lightning Storm athletes in the ads John sees on other major social networking channels.

Because of Lightning's ubiquity in the skateboarding world, Lightning Energy is John's go-to beverage when he skates. He buys the drinks in bulk at the Lightning Energy website, where he learns from the product descriptions that Lightning Energy's beverages, with their proprietary Lightning Energy Blitz Boost, will quench his thirst, give him a bolt of energy to "power through" a strenuous workout, and even help him to restore and rehydrate after a "long, rough night." John particularly likes Greased Lightning, which the company describes as an energy booster just like a sports drink that relieves thirst particularly fast with its extra wide mouth and smooth flavor so "you can really swig it down."

The "boost" in Lightning Energy's beverages comes primarily from caffeine: each 24-ounce can contains about 240 milligrams of caffeine (comparable to the caffeine in nearly twelve regular cans of cola). The Lightning Energy Blitz Boost also contains other stimulants such as guarana, ginseng, and taurine, which can bolster the effects of caffeine. The American Academy of Pediatrics discourages the consumption of caffeine and other stimulants by children and adolescents, while the Food and Drug Administration (FDA) advises that healthy adults can safely consume up to 400 milligrams of caffeine per day.

Although studies are not conclusive on the safety of energy drinks and their high level of added caffeine, energy drinks are associated with a surge in emergency room visits. The U.S. Department of Health and Human Services' Drug Abuse Warning Network reported a nearly fourteen-fold increase in emergency visits related to energy drink consumption in the last six years. Furthermore, some experts have found that energy drinks have no "therapeutic benefit" and may expose children and youth to higher risk for adverse health consequences. Last year, the National Collegiate Athletic Association banned its member institutions from distributing caffeinated energy drinks like Lightning Energy to its student-athletes. Lightning Energy does print a small warning label on its can, advising "responsible" consumption, which Lightning suggests is two 24-ounce cans per day, and declaring that the drink is "not recommended for children, pregnant women, or people sensitive to caffeine."

Last week, after a particularly grueling skate session, John drank two 24-ounce cans of Greased Lightning. The two cans were the only energy drink or other caffeinated beverage John consumed that day. Shortly thereafter, John went into cardiac arrest and died. The autopsy report determined the cause of John's death as caffeine-induced cardiac arrhythmia.

John's tragic death is the most recent in a series of other reported deaths, illnesses, hospitalizations, and injuries involving Lightning Energy beverages. You are a Deputy City Attorney for the City of San Cristobal, where you head an affirmative litigation taskforce. Under state law, your office has the power to bring suits on behalf of residents, and your taskforce has decided to file a tort suit against Lightning Energy. You and your team brainstorm ideas: Is there a misrepresentation problem in the way Lightning suggested the health benefits of its products? Did Lightning's advertisements promote unsafe consumption of its beverages and inadequately convey the risks of consuming highly caffeinated energy drinks? How can you demonstrate that injured parties relied on Lightning's misrepresentations? Does the "common knowledge" or "open and obvious risk" doctrine come into play? What about Lightning's aggressive marketing toward adolescents like John? Draft a complaint articulating the theories under which your office might challenge Lightning Energy.

PART III
Special Problem Areas

Part III offers material concerning a variety of areas of special interest within products liability law. Chapter Seven examines rules applicable to distinctive subclasses of products, such as component parts, used products, or drugs and medical devices. Chapter Eight covers special elements of the plaintiff's recovery, such as claims for emotional distress or pure economic loss, as well as the U.S. Supreme Court's increasingly important constitutional jurisprudence on punitive damages recovery. Finally, Chapter Nine examines products liability in a global context, with attention to comparative products liability law as well as policy issues raised by the ever-escalating international movement of goods.

CHAPTER SEVEN

Special Products
and Product Markets

A. COMPONENT PARTS AND RAW MATERIALS

Comment *b* to §19 of the Products Liability Restatement, enlarging on the definition of "product," contains the general rule governing component parts: "Component parts are products, whether sold or distributed separately or assembled with other component parts. An assemblage of component parts is also, itself, a product. Raw materials are products, whether manufactured, such as sheet metal; processed, such as lumber; or gathered and sold or distributed in raw condition, such as unwashed gravel and farm produce." As sellers of products, sellers of component parts and raw materials are liable in tort for harm caused by product defects. If that were all there were to the story of component parts, it would hardly be deemed special enough to warrant separate treatment in a section of its own. Consider the following materials.

Zaza v. Marquess & Nell, Inc.
675 A.2d 620 (N.J. 1996)

This appeal presents the question of whether . . . a component part fabricator that builds a system component in accordance with the specifications of the owner, which component is not dangerous until it is integrated into the larger system, can be held strictly liable to an injured employee for the failure of the owner, installer-assembler, and training consultant to install safety devices and provide warnings. The Appellate Division[, reversing summary judgment for defendant,] found that such a fabricator could be held strictly liable. We now reverse.

I

On January 28, 1990, plaintiff Gerardo Zaza, an employee of Maxwell House Coffee (Maxwell House), a division of General Foods Manufacturing Corporation, discovered a clog in a quench tank located in the Hoboken plant. While working to repair the quench tank, hot molten water and carbon within the quench tank overflowed and landed on plaintiff's back, arms and upper extremities, causing second degree burns over twenty-one percent of plaintiff's body.

419

The quench tank is an integral part of a large, complex manufacturing process — the Maxwell House trecar-carbon regeneration system — which is used to produce decaffeinated coffee beans. The system contains a multiple hearth furnace, a quench tank, and numerous pipes, watering screws, scrubbers and fans. All of those parts must be fully integrated and assembled in order to create a properly working trecar-carbon regeneration system. It is a two-fold system. In the top portion of the system, the ultimate coffee product is made, and a byproduct (carbon) is reclaimed in the lower portion. The quench tank is located in the lower portion where the carbon regeneration process takes place. After the basic coffee product has been made in the top portion, the carbon, which has been heated in the multiple hearth furnace to 1700 degrees Fahrenheit, leaves the furnace through a large tube and enters the quench tank. At the same time the molten carbon enters the quench tank, cool water is pumped into the quench tank at the rate of twenty-two gallons per minute. The superheated carbon-water mixture moves through the quench tank for approximately thirty minutes, then exits the tank through two pipelines, and finally comes to rest in separate storage tanks where it is kept for future processing.

The initial designs for the quench tank were prepared by Maxwell House and were submitted to the engineering firm of Marquess and Nell, Inc., (Marquess) who prepared the final design plans. Marquess contracted with defendant International Sheet Metal & Plate Mfg., Inc. (International) for a fabricated quench-tank. Maxwell House hired Brennan Company, Inc. (Brennan) to assemble and integrate the trecar-carbon regeneration system. Calgon Carbon Company (Calgon) was hired to prepare training materials on how to operate the system and to educate Maxwell House employees in the use of the trecar-carbon regeneration system. William J. Merz, an engineer employed by Calgon, conducted a training session for Maxwell House employees on how to use the trecar-carbon regeneration system, including the quench tank. Plaintiff attended the training session.

The specifications on which defendant bid for the quench tank did not require that the fabricator prepare or install any safety devices. Rather, the specifications called for the fabricator to cut holes for the safety devices. The quench tank fabricated by defendant is best described as a stainless steel tank with holes in it. The tank also contains six flanges, which are devices used to hold pipes in place. The quench tank was sold to Maxwell for $7,400. When it was delivered to Maxwell House, professional installers had to connect water ingress piping, carbon extrusion piping and water discharge piping before it could be made operational.

The final plans and specifications for the trecar-carbon regeneration system incorporated three safety devices designed to avoid an overflow of the molten fluid out of the quench tank. These safety devices were to be installed by Maxwell House and Brennan. The devices included a spectacle shut-off valve, a high-level fluid sensor, and an overflow pipe. The spectacle shut-off valve was designed to stop the flow of the molten carbon from leaving the hearth furnace and entering the quench tank whenever personnel were working on the quench tank or associated piping. It was supposed to be located in the chute between the hearth furnace and the quench tank. The high-level fluid sensor was designed to trigger an alarm and light whenever the fluid level in the quench tank reached a dangerous level. The overflow pipe was to be located eight inches below the top of the quench tank and was designed to divert the fluids within the quench tank through a piping system to another location away from the user if the fluids reached a high level within the tank. It is uncontroverted that the installation of the overflow pipe would have prevented the quench tank from pouring out its molten contents on plaintiff.

Although all three safety devices were included in the design plans prepared by Marquess, none was actually in operation at the time plaintiff sustained his injuries. Brennan, the installer, claims that its function was to install and integrate the quench tank into the system based on the plans provided to it by Maxwell House, that Maxwell House decided to omit the safety devices recommended by Marquess, and that Maxwell House approved the installation. Maxwell House's decision to omit the safety devices appears to have been deliberate. Although the spectacle shut-off valve was on site and available when the tank was being installed, Maxwell House chose not to install it. When an engineer informed Maxwell House of the omission, the company chose to disregard the advice. . . .

II

We first focus on whether a fabricator, who produces a non-defective component part for an integrated manufacturing system in accordance with the designs and specifications of the owner, has a legal duty to ensure that the owner and installer-assembler properly integrate the component into the system. . . .

IV

Plaintiff contends that International had a non-delegable duty to see that Maxwell House and its team of hired professional assemblers properly integrated the quench tank into the trecar-carbon regeneration system. But the cases cited by plaintiff involved either suits against manufacturers of finished products or rebuilders of machinery. It was within the power of the defendants in those cases to install safety devices. In contrast, the fabricator of a component part that is not inherently dangerous has no control over whether the purchaser properly installs the component part into the final system.

Where a finished product is the result of work by more than one party, a court must examine at what stage installation of safety devices is feasible and practicable. In many jurisdictions, responsibility for installing a safety device is determined by reference to three criteria: (1) the trade custom indicating the party that normally would install the safety device; (2) the relative expertise of the parties, looking to which party is best acquainted with the design problems and safety techniques in question; and (3) practicality, focusing on the stage at which installation of the device is most feasible. See, e.g., Verge v. Ford Motor Co., 581 F.2d 384 (3d Cir. 1978) . . .

V

In its recent draft, the American Law Institute (A.L.I.) concluded that a component part manufacturer generally is not liable unless the component itself is defective or the component provider substantially participated in the design of the final product.

> [I]t would be unjust, impractical, and inefficient to impose liability solely on the ground that the manufacturer of the integrated product utilizes the component in a manner that renders the integrated product defective. To hold a component supplier to the same liability as the seller of the integrated product would require the component seller to

scrutinize another's product with respect to which the component seller has no role in developing. This would impose substantial costs on the component seller, who would have to develop sufficient sophistication to review the decisions of the business entity that already has assumed responsibility with regard to the integrated product.

[Restatement (Third) of Torts §10 cmt. *a* (Tentative Draft No. 3, 1996) (hereinafter Restatement, Tentative Draft).]

The majority of courts from other jurisdictions have held that a manufacturer of a component part, which is not dangerous until it is integrated by the owner into a larger system, cannot be held strictly liable to an injured employee for the failure of the owner and/or assembler to install safety devices, so long as the specifications provided are not so obviously dangerous that it would be unreasonable to follow them. For example, in Jordan v. Whiting Corp., 49 Mich. App. 481, 212 N.W.2d 324 (1973), *rev'd* in part on other grounds, 396 Mich. 145, 240 N.W.2d 468 (1976), a plaintiff brought suit against the manufacturer of component parts used in a crane. The plaintiff alleged that the assembled crane was defectively designed. However, the component parts were not in and of themselves defective. The trial court granted a directed verdict to the component part manufacturer and the verdict was affirmed on appeal. The appellate court stated:

> The obligation that generates the duty to avoid injury to another which is reasonably foreseeable does not — at least yet — extend to the anticipation of how manufactured components not in and of themselves dangerous or defective can become potentially dangerous dependent upon the nature of their integration into a unit designed, assembled, installed, and sold by another. [*Jordan,* supra, 212 N.W.2d at 328.] . . .

Plaintiff does not allege any manufacturing defect in the quench tank itself. The quench tank was not in and of itself dangerous or defective. It was a sheet metal tank with holes in it. Specifically, plaintiff's expert alleged that "the design of the Quench tank was improper in not including an overflow pipe and/or an automatic shutoff when the superheated carbon-water mixture reached a certain level in the Quench tank." . . .

[I]t was not feasible, practical, or reasonable for defendant, a sheet metal fabricator with no prior experience in the assembly and installation of trecar-carbon regeneration systems, to attach the safety devices to the quench tank. The safety devices could not have been incorporated into the quench tank at its factory. The shut-off valve was not located in or on the quench tank, but rather in the chute between the hearth furnace and the tank. Similarly, installation of the overflow line required that the tank be first installed in Maxwell House's plant. Further, defendant lacked the expertise required to attach the safety devices and to integrate the tank into the trecar-carbon regeneration system — a system that was actually composed of separate "systems" interfacing with one another. . . .

The design plans provided that the safety devices would be provided by others. International acted reasonably in relying on Maxwell House and its experienced assemblers, two entities with superior knowledge of the trecar-carbon regeneration system, to properly install the tank into the complicated system. Defendant had no control over the quench tank once it was sold and no control over the final assembly of the system. Maxwell House retained complete control over the design of the regeneration system and the quench tank's installation into the system.

It was not defendant's failure to attach the safety devices in the quench tank that caused plaintiff's injury. Defendant did exactly what it was paid $7,400 to do; its sole obligation was to produce a component part that was safe and satisfactory according to the specifications provided by Maxwell House. It did that. Under those circumstances, we find that International is not strictly liable for its failure to install the safety devices on the quench tank.

VII

Plaintiff also asserts that International had a duty to warn of the dangers of operating the quench tank without safety devices. . . .

The majority of jurisdictions also hold that a supplier of a component part that does not contain a latent defect has no duty to warn the subsequent assembler of any danger that may arise after the components are assembled. Mitchell v. Sky Climber Inc., 396 Mass. 629, 487 N.E.2d 1374, 1376 (1986); see Frazier v. Materials Transp. Co., 609 F. Supp. 933 (W.D. Pa. 1985); . . . For example, in . . . [Munger v. Herder Mfg. Corp., 456 N.Y.S.2d 271 (1982)], an employee of the Scott Paper Company was injured when the arm of a tension roll assembly in a paper machine fell upon him. The injured employee sued the four corporations that manufactured various components of the paper machine. The plaintiff argued that each of the component part manufacturers had a duty to foresee and warn employees that Scott might not post appropriate warnings. The court disagreed, holding that in the absence of any proof that the component designs were defective or that the parts were wrongfully manufactured, no public policy can be served by imposing liability on a manufacturer of specialized parts of a highly technical machine, particularly when, as here, the parts were created in accordance with the design, plans and specifications of the owner and assembler of the unit. Id. 456 N.Y.S.2d at 273. . . .

The prevailing view is that a manufacturer of a component part, not dangerous in and of itself, does not have a duty to warn an employee of the immediate purchaser of the component where the immediate purchaser is aware of the need to attach safety devices. Restatement, Tentative Draft §10 cmt. *b.* For example, in Crossfield v. Quality Control Equipment Co., 1 F.3d 701, 704 (8th Cir. 1993), the court held that, under Missouri law, the supplier of a non-defective chain for use in a machine that malfunctioned did not have a duty to warn. The court stated:

> To impose responsibility on the supplier of the chain in the context of the larger defectively designed machine system would simply extend liability too far. This would mean that suppliers would be required to hire machine design experts to scrutinize machine systems that the supplier had no role in developing. Suppliers would be forced to provide modifications and attach warnings on machines that they never designed nor manufactured. Mere suppliers cannot be expected to guarantee the safety of other manufacturers' machinery. [Ibid.] . . .

Holding defendant liable would impose on a component part fabricator, whose products were built in accordance with the designer's specifications and whose part when it left defendant's plant was not defective, the duty to investigate whether the use of its nondefective product would be made dangerous by the integration of that product into the complex system designed and installed by experts. Component fabricators would become insurers for the mistakes and failures of the owners and installers to follow their own plans. Defendant would have to retain an expert to determine whether each and every integrated manufacturing system that incorporates one of its sheet metal products is reasonably safe for its intended use. In Bond v. E.I. DuPont De Nemours & Co., 868 P.2d 1114, 1120 (Colo. App. 1993), the court in holding that a seller of Teflon integrated by the manufacturer in a prosthesis had no duty to warn observed: "there is little social utility in placing the burden on a manufacturer of component parts or supplier of raw materials against injuries caused by the final product when the component parts or raw materials themselves were not unreasonably dangerous." See also Kealoha v. E.I. DuPont de Nemours & Co., 844 F. Supp. 590, 594 (D. Hawaii 1994) ("Permitting plaintiffs to maintain a suit against the bulk suppier of inherently safe raw materials would lead to absurd consequences: there would be no end to potential liability if every manufacturer of nuts, bolts and screws could be held liable when this hardware was used in a defective product."). . . .

It would serve no useful purpose to hold defendant strictly liable to plaintiff for the failure of Maxwell House and its installer-assembler, Brennan, to install the safety devices or for its failure and the failure of its trainer, Calgon, to adequately warn plaintiff. Holding defendant liable would result in an unreasonable expansion of the products liability law. "In the developing steps towards higher consumer and user protection through higher trade morality and responsibility, the law should view trade relations realistically rather than mythically." Schipper v. Levitt and Sons, Inc., 44 N.J. 70, 99, 207 A.2d 314 (1965).

Accordingly, we reverse the judgment of the Appellate Division and grant summary judgment in favor of defendant International.

[Dissenting opinion omitted].

The court in *Zaza* refers to Restatement (Third) of Torts: Products Liability §10 (Tent. Draft No. 3, 1996). In the Restatement, finally approved and published in 1998, that section was slightly modified and renumbered.

Restatement (Third) of Torts: Products Liability
(1998)

---

§5. LIABILITY OF COMMERCIAL SELLER OR DISTRIBUTOR OF PRODUCT COMPONENTS FOR HARM CAUSED BY PRODUCTS INTO WHICH COMPONENTS ARE INTEGRATED

One engaged in the business of selling or otherwise distributing product components who sells or distributes a component is subject to liability for harm to persons or property caused by a product into which the component is integrated if:

(a) the component is defective in itself, as defined in this Chapter, and the defect causes the harm; or

(b)(1) the seller or distributor of the component substantially participates in the integration of the component into the design of the product; and

(2) the integration of the component causes the product to be defective, as defined in this Chapter, and

(3) the defect in the product causes the harm.

As *Zaza* points out §5 is firmly established in American law. See, e.g., In re Temporomandibular Joint (TMJ) Implants Products Liability Litigation, 97 F.3d 1050 (8th Cir. 1996), affirming summary judgment for a manufacturer of Teflon film incorporated into joint implants; the court reasoned that the failure of the Teflon product was not due to a flaw in the component part itself but because the implant manufacturer had made an erroneous decision to incorporate what turned out to be an unsuitable material into its implants. Thus, the film manufacturer could not be held strictly liable for implant failure. See also Artiglio v. General Electric Co., 71 Cal. Rptr. 2d 817 (Cal. Ct. App. 1998) (manufacturer of silicone used in breast implant has no duty to warn its customers as to danger of silicone in medical devices).

Component part manufacturers are, however, liable if the component is independently defective or if the component manufacturer becomes sufficiently involved in the integration of the component part and that integration causes the final product to be defective. What constitutes substantial integration sufficient to impose liability has been the subject of litigation. See, e.g., Roberts v. Performance Site Mgmt., Inc., 2004 WL 1196140 (Ohio Ct. App. 2004) (court affirmed grant of summary judgment for defendant by deciding that merely advertising did not constitute sufficient involvement to acquire a duty to warn). See also Smith v. Robin America, Inc., 484 Fed. App'x 908 (5th Cir. 2012) (applying Texas law) (granting component part manufacturer summary judgment because minimal technical advice to product manufacturer did not constitute substantial participation in the integration of the component in the design of the product); Brookshire Bros. Holdings, Inc. v. Total Containment Inc., 2006 U.S. Dist. LEXIS 62576, *20 (W.D. La. 2006) (case sent to jury to decide if ''[the defendant's] representatives work[ing] extensively with Dayco and Cleveland Tubing . . . educating both companies about handling and processing engineering thermoplastics like [defendant's component material]'' was sufficient involvement to attach strict liability when underground flexpipes began to leak causing loss of property).

When a component part is alleged to be defective because of inadequate warnings, the question of whether the manufacturer owes a duty to warn is especially interesting because the immediate purchaser—the manufacturer of the final assembled product—is typically a sophisticated purchaser who knows as much as, or more than, the component seller about the relevant risks. Does the component manufacturer owe a duty to warn the purchaser? What about end users of the final product?

Comment *b* to §5 assesses the component seller's duty to warn:

[W]hen a sophisticated buyer integrates a component into another product, the component seller owes no duty to warn either the immediate buyer or ultimate consumers of dangers arising because the component is unsuited for the special purpose to which the buyer puts it. To impose a duty to warn in such a circumstance would require that component sellers monitor the development of products and systems into which their components are to be integrated. . . . Courts have not yet confronted the question of whether, in combination, factors such as the component purchaser's lack of expertise and ignorance of the risks of integrating the component into the purchaser's product, and the component supplier's knowledge of both the relevant risks and the purchaser's ignorance thereof, give rise to a duty on the part of the component supplier to warn of risks attending integration of the component into the purchaser's product. Whether the seller of a component should be subject to liability for selling its product to one who is likely to utilize it dangerously is governed by principles of negligent entrustment.

Regarding warnings to end users, the Texas Supreme Court in Humble Sand & Gravel, Inc. v. Gomez, 146 S.W.3d 170, 190 (Tex. 2004), recites six factors for a court to weigh to determine if a warning is necessary: "(1) the dangerous condition of the product; (2) the purpose for which the product is used; (3) the form of any warnings given; (4) the reliability of the third party as a conduit of necessary information about the product; (5) the magnitude of the risk involved; and (6) the burdens imposed on the supplier by requiring that he directly warn all users." The court remanded the case for a new trial so that the parties could more explicitly address these factors to determine if a silica supplier is required to warn end users of the dangers of silicosis. See also Union Carbide Corp. v. Aubin, 97 So. 3d 886 (Fla. Dist. Ct. App. 2012) (whether manufacturer of component has a duty to warn users of dangers posed by integrated product is a question governed by Products Liability Restatement §2, Comment i); Satterfield v. Morris, 2014 WL 2744687 (D.S.C. 2014) (no liability for failure to warn by manufacturer of denatured alcohol which was later integrated into eco-gel fuel because component manufacturer did not know the formula of end product).

Courts have differed sharply as to whether a manufacturer whose original product (such as a pump, valve, or engine) was used with asbestos-containing component parts (such as gaskets, packing material, or external insulation), should be liable when the product was repaired using asbestos from another manufacturer. In these cases, plaintiffs allege injury from exposure to the replacement asbestos but sue the manufacturer of the original product (e.g., pump, valve, engine) for failing to warn about asbestos in the original product. They contend that defendant knew the original product would be repaired using asbestos and that defendant's failure to warn was the proximate cause of the injury. Two recent opinions take polar opposite views. Compare O'Neil v. Crane Co., 266 P.3d 982 (Cal. 2012) (defendant not liable for failing to warn when injuries caused by component it did not manufacture), with Schwartz v. Abex Corp., 2015 WL 3387824 (E.D. Pa. 2015) (holding that Pennsylvania law would impose liability on the manufacturer of a product containing asbestos who negligently failed to warn of asbestos dangers for injuries caused when the original asbestos was replaced with material from another manufacturer and the injury to plaintiff arose from the replacement asbestos). Both opinions contain exhaustive treatment of prior authority.

A third opinion, Quirin v. Lorillard Tobacco Co., 17 F. Supp. 3d 760 (N.D. Ill. 2014), takes a middle ground. It would impose a duty on a valve manufacture where it manufactured a product that "by necessity contained asbestos components and where the asbestos-containing material would necessarily be replaced." Id. at 769-70. Where the original product was not defective, the mere fact that it was foreseeable that at some later time asbestos might be used to repair the product should not impose liability on seller of the original product. Simonetta v. Viad Corp., 195 P.3d 127 (Wash. 2008) (en banc) (manufacturer of an evaporator machine had no duty to warn users of risks associated with asbestos insulation that manufacturer knew would be used to encapsulate a machine upon installation in ship). For scholarly commentary, see James A. Henderson, Jr., Seller of Safe Products Should Not Be Required to Rescue Users From Risks Presented by Other, More Dangerous Products, 37 SW. U. L. Rev. 595 (2008).

authors' dialogue 22

AARON: Remember how we were going to handle component parts in the Restatement when we started?

JIM: I sure do. We were simply going to state the obvious — that component parts are products, in their own right. And we followed through on our plan. The third sentence in Comment *b* to §19 says that "Component parts are products, whether sold or distributed separately or assembled with other component parts." And Comment *b* also says that raw materials are products, whether manufactured, processed, or simply gathered and sold in their natural state. But we didn't see any need for a separate section on the subject of component parts.

DOUG: So how did the subject get onto your radar screen to wind up in §5?

AARON: I seem to recall that one of our advisers urged us to look into it. John Frank, a lawyer from Phoenix, I think.

JIM: You're right, Aaron, except John wasn't an adviser. He's a member of the ALI Council, the governing body that screens and supervises all the Restatement work of the Institute.

AARON: Whatever. I just remember that he was the one who told us it was a "hot" topic and we ought to look into it. At first, I don't think we understood what he was talking about. Of course if a defective component gets incorporated into a product, it makes the product defective, also. Who needs a special section to make that clear? But we went ahead and read some cases and realized that it was at least arguable that the manufacturer of a nondefective component should be liable when the component's inclusion in an integrated product makes the integrated product defective. That was the aspect that we hadn't understood earlier.

DOUG: Does the focus on the component manufacturer's "substantial participation" in the integration of the ultimate product seem at odds with the general maxim in products liability law that we focus on the product rather than the manufacturer's conduct?

JIM: Maybe Doug, but how else would you have it? Remember the *Cronin* decision in California, in Chapter One? (See p. 22, supra.) Defective bread racks in a bakery truck collapsed and harmed the plaintiff in a minor fender bender. Remember how the plaintiff joined General Motors, the manufacturer of the truck chassis, along with Olson, the company who assembled the bread truck? When we discussed *Cronin* in class, we couldn't figure any way, except searching for deep pockets, that GM could be liable for the failure of the bread racks. Maybe there was evidence that GM was actively involved in the truck assembly.

AARON: But that wouldn't be enough under §5 unless GM's chassis somehow contributed to making the bread racks weaker.

JIM: You're right. No wonder the plaintiff agreed to dismiss GM from the *Cronin* case prior to trial.

For an article employing a "cheapest cost avoider" approach in determining the liability of component manufacturers, see David A. Fischer, Product Liability: A Commentary on the Liability of Suppliers of Component Parts and Raw Materials, 53 S.C. L. Rev. 1137 (2002). An exploration of the duties of component part suppliers (especially in Texas) can be found in Victor E. Schwartz, et al., Getting the Sand Out of the Eyes of the Law: The Need for a Clear Rule for Sand Suppliers in Texas After Humble Sand & Gravel, Inc. v. Gomez, 37 St. Mary's L.J. 283 (2006).

B. PRESCRIPTION DRUGS AND MEDICAL DEVICES

Liability for harm caused by prescription drugs and medical devices is generally predicated on the failure of the manufacturer to adequately warn the prescribing physician of risks associated with the use of the product. Manufacturers and other distributors are liable for manufacturing defects, but most cases involve failure to warn. Less often, though with increasing frequency, plaintiffs claim that the manufacturer should have warned them directly. Even less often, plaintiffs claim that a prescription drug was defectively designed.

1. Liability Based on Failure to Warn

a. Warning the Health Care Provider

Any analysis of liability for prescription drugs must begin with the following comment to §402A of the Restatement of Torts (Second).

Restatement (Second) of Torts
(1965)

---

§402A. SPECIAL LIABILITY OF SELLER OF PRODUCT FOR PHYSICAL HARM TO USER OR CONSUMER

COMMENT:

k. Unavoidably unsafe products. There are some products which, in the present state of human knowledge, are quite incapable of being made safe for their intended and ordinary use. These are especially common in the field of drugs. An outstanding example is the vaccine for the Pasteur treatment of rabies, which not uncommonly leads to very serious and damaging consequences when it is injected. Since the disease itself invariably leads to a dreadful death, both the marketing and the use of the vaccine are fully justified, notwithstanding the unavoidable high degree of risk which they involve. Such a product, properly prepared, and accompanied by proper directions and warning, is not defective, nor is it *unreasonably* dangerous. The same is true of many other drugs, vaccines, and the like, many of which for this very reason cannot legally be sold except to physicians, or under the prescription of a physician. It is also true in particular of many new or experimental drugs as to which, because of lack of time and opportunity for sufficient medical experience, there can be no assurance of safety, or perhaps even of purity of ingredients, but such experience as there is justifies the marketing and use of the drug notwithstanding a medically recognizable risk. The seller of such products, again with the qualification that they are properly prepared and marketed, and proper warning is given, where the situation calls for it, is not to be held to strict liability for unfortunate consequences attending their use, merely because he has undertaken to supply the public with an apparently useful and desirable product, attended with a known but apparently reasonable risk.

In the several decades following promulgation of §402A by the American Law Institute, Comment *k* was interpreted by courts to limit the duty of drug manufacturers to providing adequate warnings to the physicians who prescribe drugs and who make sure that the right drugs reach the right patients. Under the so-called "learned intermediary rule," manufacturers need not warn patients directly. The learned intermediary rule retains its vitality in the vast majority of courts. See Tyree v. Boston Scientific Corp., 56 F. Supp. 3d 826 (S.D. W. Va. 2014) n.3 (48 states adhere to learned intermediary rule). Several courts have applied the doctrine to cases involving prescription medical devices. See, e.g., Ellis v. C.R. Bard, Inc., 311 F.3d 1272 (11th Cir. 2002) (morphine-drip pump); Hurley v. Heart Physicians, 898 A.2d 777, 784 (Conn. 2006) (pacemaker). When the drug manufacturer advertises directly to consumers, a few states recognize a duty to warn consumers in addition to doctors. See discussion infra, this chapter. The Products Liability Restatement sets out the traditional learned intermediary rule in this way:

Restatement (Third) of Torts: Products Liability
(1998)

---

§6. LIABILITY OF COMMERCIAL SELLER OR DISTRIBUTOR FOR HARM CAUSED BY DEFECTIVE PRESCRIPTION DRUGS AND MEDICAL DEVICES

(a) A manufacturer of a prescription drug or medical device who sells or otherwise distributes a defective drug or medical device is subject to liability for harm to persons caused by the defect. A prescription drug or medical device is one that may be legally sold or otherwise distributed only pursuant to a health-care provider's prescription.

(b) For purposes of liability under Subsection (a), a prescription drug or medical device is defective if at the time of sale or other distribution the drug or medical device:

. . .

(3) is not reasonably safe due to inadequate instructions or warnings as defined in Subsection (d).

. . .

(d) A prescription drug or medical device is not reasonably safe due to inadequate instructions or warnings if reasonable instructions or warnings regarding foreseeable risks of harm are not provided to:

(1) prescribing and other health-care providers who are in a position to reduce the risks of harm in accordance with the instructions or warnings. . . .

COMMENT:

. . .

b. Rationale. The obligation of a manufacturer to warn about risks attendant to the use of drugs and medical devices that may be sold only pursuant to a health-care provider's prescription traditionally has required warnings directed to health-care providers and not to patients. The rationale supporting this "learned intermediary" rule is that only health-care professionals are in a position to understand the significance of the risks involved and to assess the relative advantages and disadvantages of a given form of prescription-based therapy. The duty then devolves on the health-care provider to supply to the patient such information as is deemed appropriate under the circumstances so that the patient can make an informed choice as to therapy. Subsection (d)(1) retains the "learned intermediary" rule. . . .

d. Manufacturers' liability for failure adequately to instruct or warn prescribing and other health-care providers. Failure to instruct or warn is a major basis of liability for manufacturers of prescription drugs and medical devices. When prescribing health-care providers are adequately informed of the relevant benefits and risks associated with various prescription drugs and medical devices, they can reach appropriate decisions regarding which drug or device is best for specific patients. Sometimes a warning serves to inform health-care providers of unavoidable risks that inhere in the drug and medical device. By definition, such a warning would not aid the health-care provider in reducing the risk of injury to the patient by taking precautions in how the drug is administered or the medical device is used. However, warnings of unavoidable risks allow the health-care provider, and thereby the patient, to make an informed choice whether to utilize the drug or medical device. Beyond informing prescribing health-care providers, a drug or device manufacturer may have a duty under the law of negligence to use reasonable measures to supply instructions or warnings to nonprescribing health-care providers who are in positions to act on such information so as to reduce or prevent injury to patients.

Sterling Drug, Inc. v. Yarrow
408 F.2d 978 (8th Cir. 1969)

BECKER, C.D.J.

[The plaintiff, a South Dakota housewife, brought an action against Sterling Drug, Inc., claiming that her vision had been permanently damaged by the use of "Aralen," a prescription drug manufactured and sold by the defendant for use in the treatment of rheumatoid arthritis and other diseases. The plaintiff claimed that Sterling had been negligent in testing, manufacturing, and marketing the drug, and in failing to warn the public, the plaintiff, her physician, and retail druggists of the potential dangers from use of the drug. Sitting without a jury, the trial judge found that the defendant had negligently failed to warn the plaintiff's prescribing physician, and entered judgment for $180,000. The plaintiff had begun using Aralen in 1958, when her physician, Dr. Olson, had been introduced to Aralen by one of Sterling's traveling salesmen or "detail men." The plaintiff used the drug on a daily basis until October 19, 1964, when it was discontinued on the advice of Dr. Olson at the time of a complete physical examination. The physical examination was made at the suggestion of the plaintiff's ophthalmologist, who had observed a deterioration of the plaintiff's vision and suspected that it might be caused by the medications she was taking. At no time up to and including October 19, 1964, had Dr. Olson read or heard of any warnings concerning irreversible vision loss (chloroquine retinopathy) caused by taking Aralen, except from the plaintiff's ophthalmologist. Nevertheless, he discontinued the plaintiff's medication on October 19, 1964. A follow-up examination in January, 1965, revealed a marked deterioration in the plaintiff's condition.

The opinion outlines the advancements in knowledge of the side effects of chloroquine phosphate (marketed by the appellant under the registered trademark name "Aralen") prior to October 19, 1964. Beginning in 1957, reports in various medical journals indicated that the drug was causing, or might be causing, side effects of the sort suffered by the plaintiff. The opinion continues:]

The evidence strongly supports the findings of the trial court that appellant usually communicates its product information to physicians prescribing its products:

(1) by "detail men," who are specially trained field representatives engaged in selling and promoting the use of its products by personal calls in which oral presentations are made and literature and samples delivered,

(2) by listings of drugs in an annually published advertising medium known as Physicians' Desk Reference,

(3) by "product cards" which are mailed and distributed by detail men to physicians and are available at medical conventions and hospital exhibits, and

(4) by special letters mailed to physicians.

The evidence summarized in part hereinabove also strongly supports the finding of the trial court that, beginning in 1957, medical publications suggested some connection between retinal eye changes and chloroquine; that from the medical publications this connection became increasingly evident by the year 1959 and reasonably apparent in the year 1962; that in 1961 reports that the retinal changes associated with the drug were irreversible began to appear. . . .

The record shows that appellant was contemporaneously aware of the reports, summarized above, that chloroquine phosphate caused irreversible retinal damage in a substantial percentage of those using the recommended dosage for rheumatoid arthritis for extended periods of time. The evidence supports the findings of fact of the trial court concerning the limited nature of warnings given by appellant to those prescribing the drug. These findings of fact are not clearly erroneous within the meaning of Rule 52(a) F.R. Civ. P.

On this record of the medical reports summarized above, the trial court would have been warranted in holding that the warnings on the product cards and in the Physicians' Desk Reference concerning irreversible retinal damage did not always, in the relevant period, represent the full state of the reported medical knowledge in respect to the percentage of patients affected, the irreversibility of the retinal damage and the toxicity of the recommended drug in affected cases. (This is mentioned because appellant contends that the judgment below should be reversed outright on the ground that a submissible case of failure to warn was not made on any theory.)

Dr. Foley, appellant's Medical Director and Vice-President, testified that in August 1962, because of appearance of additional reports of side effects of chloroquine, that he, and other members of appellant's staff, felt that appellant should add additional information in the literature on the drug. To do so (he testified) appellant's staff consulted with the Food and Drug Administration until January 1963, finally developing the letter, the "Dear Doctor" letter. In the meantime, no special warning was given physicians. During this period appellant's staff was unwilling to accept the accuracy of the percentages of affected patients reported in the medical literature, and questioned the figures. Finally in January 1963, through its advertising department, appellant contracted with a mailing service, specializing in mailings to the medical profession, for the mailing of the "Dear Doctor" letter to all physicians and hospital personnel in the United States. Some 248,000 copies of the letter were reproduced, were mailed in envelopes addressed by addressograph plates and sent by first class mail. The letter read as follows:

IMPORTANT DRUG PRECAUTIONS
Dear Doctor:
The recent experience of various investigators has shown that Aralen® (brand of chloroquine), used alone or as an adjunct to other drugs and therapeutic measures, may be very helpful in the management of patients with lupus erythematosus or rheumatoid arthritis. Although many physicians have found that the incidence of serious side effects is lower than that encountered with other potent agents that are often employed in such patients, certain ocular complications have sometimes been reported during prolonged daily administration of chloroquine. Therefore, when chloroquine or any other antimalarial compound is to be given for long periods, it is essential that measures be taken to avoid or minimize these complications.
Thus initial and periodic (trimonthly) ophthalmologic examinations (including expert slit-lamp, fundus and visual field studies) should be performed. The initial examination will reveal if any visual abnormalities, either coincidental or due to the disease, are present and will establish a base line for further assessment of the patient's vision. Should corneal changes occur (which are thought to be reversible and which sometimes even fade on continuance of treatment), the advantages of withdrawing the drug must be weighed in each case against the therapeutic benefits that may accrue from continuation of treatment (sometimes a severe relapse follows withdrawal). If visual disturbances occur — which are not fully explainable by difficulties of accommodation or corneal opacities — and particularly if there is any suggestion of visual field restriction or retinal change, administration of the drug should be stopped immediately and the patient closely observed for possible progression.
We should like to request your cooperation in reporting to Winthrop Laboratories or to the Food and Drug Administration any patients in your own practice who have developed impairment of vision or retinal change during or subsequent to the administration of chloroquine.
A reference card of a convenient size for filing is enclosed. It contains information on the various indications for Aralen (including lupus erythematosus, rheumatoid arthritis, malaria and amebiasis), dosage, side effects and precautions.

Very truly yours,
WINTHROP LABORATORIES
/s/ E.J. Foley
E. J. Foley, M.D.
Vice President
Medical Director . . .

The direct and circumstantial evidence amply supports a finding that, prior to October 19, 1964, Dr. Olson was not aware of the dangers of irreversible retinal damage from prolonged use of the drug. There was ample direct evidence from Dr. Olson, and opinion evidence from qualified professional witnesses, to support the findings that Dr. Olson (and other general practitioners) receive so much literature on drugs that it is impossible to read all of it; that Dr. Olson relied on detail men, medical conventions, medical journals and conversations with other doctors for information on drugs he was prescribing; that Dr. Olson was inundated with literature and product cards of various manufacturers; that a change in literature and an additional letter were insufficient to present new information to Dr. Olson; that detail men visit physicians at frequent intervals and could give an effective warning which would affirmatively notify the doctor of the dangerous side effects of chloroquine phosphate on the retina. These findings of fact were not clearly erroneous. . . .

Appellant contends that in this case the trial court adopted an erroneous view that the law required appellant to warn of dangers of the use of Aralen by the most effective method; that, therefore, the ultimate determination of the fact that appellant breached a duty to warn by the most effective method (by detail men) was induced by application of an erroneous legal standard, a standard higher than the admitted duty to make reasonable efforts to warn. Amicus curiae [Pharmaceutical Manufacturers Association] supports appellant by a post-trial extra-record affidavit on the number of detail men on the detail force of 136 companies producing 90 percent of the output of prescription drugs in the United States. Amicus curiae argues that "the trial court has, in effect, asserted that a drug manufacturer should personally notify, by use of detail men, each of the nation's 248,000 physicians of new warning information on a prescription drug"; that this is an unreasonable duty.

This extra-record information is not all judicially noticeable, but will be assumed to be true for the purposes of this appeal, since it does not require reversal of the trial court.

We hold that appellant and amicus curiae have misconstrued the memorandum opinion of the trial court, and have taken out of context a portion of the memorandum dealing with the trial court's reasoning in the fact finding process of applying the standard of reasonableness. The trial court clearly applied, recognized and expressly enunciated the undisputed standard of a duty to make reasonable efforts to warn the medical profession of the side effects of the drug. . . .

This does not mean that every physician in the United States must have been given an immediate warning by a personal messenger. But it does mean that the trial court was justified in finding that it was unreasonable to fail to instruct the detail men, at least, to warn the physicians on whom they regularly called of the dangers of which appellant had learned, or in the exercise of reasonable care should have known. In none of the arguments of appellant, and of amicus curiae, and in none of the expert testimony offered by appellant is there an explanation of the reason the available detail men were not instructed to give such warnings in the course of their regular calls. . . .

The "Dear Doctor" letter could have been reasonably found to be lacking in emphasis, timeliness and attention inviting qualities. A reasoning mind could find that appellant's warning actions were unduly delayed, reluctant and lacking in a sense of urgency, and therefore unreasonable under the circumstances. While a warning in February 1963 in an attention inviting letter would probably have been timely in this case if promptly received and heeded by appellee's physician, it could be inferred that a reasonably earlier warning, with greater intensity could well have reached appellee's physician directly, or indirectly through other professional channels such as conversations with other doctors and discussions at conventions. The delay in issuance of the "Dear Doctor" letter from August 1962 to February 1963, its wording, and the manner of its circulation could be found unreasonable considering the magnitude of the risk involved. The trier of the fact could reasonably conclude that the urgency of the circumstances reasonably required more than the relatively slow action and relative lack of emphasis employed in composing and circulating the "Dear Doctor" letter. The longer the warning was delayed the greater the risk became. Further Dr. Rice, former Director of Medical Research of appellant, offered as an expert witness, could give no explanation of the failure to send the letter by registered or certified mail. . . .

None of the assignments of error are supported by the record in this case. . . .

The judgment of the trial court is affirmed.

The court in *Yarrow* applied a negligence test in determining the defendant's legal responsibility for failing to warn. Would the same test be applied today, in this era of "strict liability?" We address this question of the doctrinal basis of failure-to-warn liability in Chapter Five, in the broader context of nonprescription products. The overwhelming majority of courts apply negligence as the doctrine-of-choice in failure-to-warn cases involving prescription drugs. See, e.g., Martin v. Hacker, 628 N.E.2d 1308 (N.Y. 1993). The Supreme Court of California applied strict liability in Carlin v. Superior Court, 920 P.2d 1347 (Cal. 1996).

As with all failure-to-warn claims, prescription drug cases require the plaintiff to show but-for proximate causation. In Weilbrenner v. Teva Pharmaceuticals USA, Inc., 2010 U.S. Dist. LEXIS 22161 (M.D. Ga. 2010), the plaintiff took the defendant's antibiotic as a treatment for acne, which caused her to develop a disorder that led to partial vision loss. She alleged that the defendant did not adequately warn doctors of the potential dangers of the drugs or provide adequate instructions for its use. The defendant moved for summary judgment, arguing that the warnings were adequate and that any inadequacy did not proximately cause the plaintiff's injuries because her doctor admitted in his testimony that he had not read the label or other prescribing information immediately before prescribing her the drug. In denying summary judgment, the court concluded that because the doctor's testimony did not rule out the possibility that he had read the prescribing information at some previous point in his career — even though he had no specific recollection of reviewing such material — the issue of whether or not he had read the label was for the jury.

In Dietz v. Smithkline Beecham Corp., 598 F.3d 812 (11th Cir. 2010), the trial court granted summary judgment for the defendant on the issue of proximate causation. The plaintiff's husband, Dietz, committed suicide shortly after he began taking the defendant's anti-depressant, Paxil. Plaintiff argued that the defendant did not adequately address the risk of suicide in its warnings. The court of appeals upheld the district court's granting of summary judgment, stating:

> Appellant cannot demonstrate that [the defendant's] alleged failure to warn [Dietz's doctor] about increased suicide risks associated with Paxil proximately caused Dietz to commit suicide. The doctor provided explicit, uncontroverted testimony that, even [if] provided with [more specific] warnings, he still would have prescribed Paxil for Dietz's depression. Pursuant to Georgia's learned intermediary doctrine, this assertion severs any potential chain of causation through which Appellant could seek relief, and Appellant's claims thus fail. [Id. at 815.]

Accord Miller v. Alza Corp., 759 F. Supp. 2d 929, 936 (S.D. Ohio 2010); Rimbert v. Eli Lilly & Co., 577 F. Supp. 2d 1174, 1196 (D. N.M. 2008).

Did the court in *Dietz* affirm because the doctor's testimony was uncontroverted? Might not a reasonable jury have disbelieved his self-serving testimony and come to a different result regarding what he would have done if given more explicit warnings? What is going on here?

b. Warning the Patient Directly

An intriguing question is whether drug manufacturers must warn patients directly. An early leading case is Reyes v. Wyeth Laboratories, Inc., 498 F.2d 1264 (5th Cir.), *cert. denied,* 419 U.S. 1096 (1974), in which the manufacturer of an oral polio vaccine was held liable for having failed directly to warn the plaintiff, who contracted polio from vaccine taken at a free public health clinic. See also Cunningham v. Charles Pfizer & Co., Inc., 532 P.2d 1377 (Okla. 1974), in which the Supreme Court of Oklahoma held that a drug manufacturer could be held strictly liable under §402A for having failed to warn a child's parents of the risks of contracting polio from the defendant's polio vaccine. The vaccine was administered in a mass immunization program, and the defendant had warned the medical society sponsoring the program. See generally Marc A. Franklin & Joseph E. Mais, Jr., Tort Law and Mass Immunization, 65 Cal. L. Rev. 754 (1977).

In light of the fact that federal law mandates that manufacturers warn patients about the risks associated with taking birth control pills, plaintiffs have sought to abrogate the traditional rule that warnings to the doctor are sufficient. They have been largely unsuccessful. Where the warnings to the physician were more elaborate than those given directly to the patient and the patient suffered a side effect from the birth control pills not listed in the direct warning to the patient, courts have still relied on the learned intermediary rule to deny recovery on the grounds that notwithstanding the federal mandate to warn patients, a drug manufacturer has no common law duty to warn the patient directly. See Skill v. Martinez, 91 F.R.D. 498 (D.N.J. 1981), *aff'd,* 677 F.2d 368 (3d Cir. 1982) (oral contraceptives); West v. Searle & Co., 806 S.W.2d 608 (Ark. 1991) (oral contraceptives); Martin v. Ortho Pharm. Corp., 661 N.E.2d 352 (Ill. 1996). See also Odom v. G.D. Searle & Co., 979 F.2d 1001 (4th Cir. 1992) (intrauterine devices); Terhune v. A.H. Robins Co., 577 P.2d 975 (Wash. 1978) (intrauterine device). But see Lukaszewicz v. Ortho Pharm. Corp., 510 F. Supp. 961 (D. Wis. 1981) (denying an oral contraceptive manufacturer's motion to dismiss because federal regulations require manufacturers to warn the patient as well as the physician).

In cases in which courts require drug companies to warn consumers directly, the question of the adequacy of warnings presents problems usually not encountered when warnings are directed only at learned intermediaries. Thus, in MacDonald v. Ortho Pharm. Corp., 475 N.E.2d 65 (Mass.), *cert. denied,* 474 U.S. 920 (1985), the plaintiffs claimed that the warnings contained on the pill dispenser label and in a booklet that a young mother received along with defendant's oral contraceptive pills were inadequate, resulting in massive injuries to her from a pill-induced stroke. As required by the then-effective regulations promulgated by the United States Food and Drug Administration (FDA), the pill dispenser she received was labeled with a warning that "oral contraceptives are powerful and effective drugs which can cause side effects in some users and should not be used at all by some women," and that "[t]he most serious known side effect is abnormal blood clotting which can be fatal.'' Id. at 66. The warning also referred MacDonald to a booklet which she obtained from her gynecologist, and which was distributed by Ortho pursuant to FDA requirements.

The defendant's booklet contained the following information:

> Blood clots occasionally form in the blood vessels of the legs and the pelvis of apparently healthy people and may threaten life if the clots break loose and then lodge in the lung or if they form in other vital organs, such as the brain. It has been estimated that about one woman in 2,000 on the pill each year suffers a blood clotting disorder severe enough to require hospitalization. The estimated death rate from abnormal blood clotting in healthy women under 35 not taking the pill is 1 in 500,000, whereas for the same group taking the pill it is 1 in 66,000. For healthy women over 35 not taking the pill, the rate is 1 in 200,000 compared to 1 in 25,000 for pill users. Blood clots are about three times more likely to develop in women over the age of 34. For these reasons it is important that women who have had blood clots in the legs, lungs or brain not use oral contraceptives. Anyone using the pill who has severe leg or chest pains, coughs up blood, has difficulty breathing, sudden severe headache or vomiting, dizziness or fainting, disturbances of vision or speech, weakness or numbness of an arm or leg, should call her doctor immediately and stop taking the pill. [Id. at 66-67, n.4.]

The jury returned a verdict for plaintiffs, and the trial court entered j.n.o.v. for defendant on the ground that the defendant owed no duty to warn the patient directly.

On appeal, the Supreme Judicial Court held that the defendant owed the patient a duty to warn her of the dangers inherent in using the pill. The court then turned to an issue not reached below — the adequacy of the defendant's warnings:

> Ortho argues that reasonable minds could not differ as to whether MacDonald was adequately informed of the risk of the injury she sustained by Ortho's warning that the oral contraceptives could cause "abnormal blood clotting which can be fatal" and further warning of the incremental likelihood of hospitalization or death due to blood clotting in "vital organs, such as the brain." We disagree. . . . We cannot say that this jury's decision that the warning was inadequate is so unreasonable as to require the opposite conclusion as a matter of law. The jury may well have concluded, in light of their common experience and MacDonald's testimony, that the absence of a reference to "stroke" in the warning unduly minimized the warning's impact or failed to make the nature of the risk reasonably comprehensible to the average consumer. Similarly, the jury may have concluded that there are fates worse than death, such as the permanent disablement suffered by MacDonald, and that the mention of the risk of death did not, therefore, suffice to apprise an average consumer of the material risks of oral contraceptive use. [Id. at 71.]

A vigorous dissent argued against recognizing a duty on the part of prescription drug manufacturers to warn patients directly. Following *MacDonald,* Massachusetts courts have limited the manufacturers' duty to warn patients directly to oral contraceptives. For example, in Linnen v. A.H. Robins Co., 2000 WL 89379 (Mass. Super. Ct. 1999), the court held that the drug manufacturer had no duty to warn the patient directly about the risks associated with diet pills. The court disagreed with the plaintiff's argument that the peculiar characteristics of oral contraceptives also applied to diet drugs, finding that the prescription of fen-phen constituted an "ordinary interaction between a doctor and patient." Id. at 3.

With the advent of commercial advertising of prescription drugs in newspapers, magazines, and television, it was only a matter of time before a plaintiff would argue that for drugs marketed directly to patients that adequate warnings of risks associated with the use of such drugs be communicated directly to them.

Perez v. Wyeth Laboratories Inc.
734 A.2d 1245 (N.J. 1999)

O'Hern, J.

Our medical-legal jurisprudence is based on images of health care that no longer exist. At an earlier time, medical advice was received in the doctor's office from a physician who most likely made house calls if needed. The patient usually paid a small sum of money to the doctor. Neighborhood pharmacists compounded prescribed medicines. Without being pejorative, it is safe to say that the prevailing attitude of law and medicine was that the "doctor knows best."

Pharmaceutical manufacturers never advertised their products to patients, but rather directed all sales efforts at physicians. In this comforting setting, the law created an exception to the traditional duty of manufacturers to warn consumers directly of risks associated with the product as long as they warned health-care providers of those risks.

For good or ill, that has all changed. Medical services are in large measure provided by managed care organizations. Medicines are purchased in the pharmacy department of supermarkets and often paid for by third-party providers. Drug manufacturers now directly advertise products to consumers on the radio, television, the Internet, billboards on public transportation, and in magazines. For example, a recent magazine advertisement for a seasonal allergy medicine in which a person is standing in a pastoral field filled with grass and goldenrod, attests that to "TAKE [THE PRODUCT]" is to "TAKE CLEAR CONTROL." Another recent ad features a former presidential candidate, encouraging the consumer to "take a little courage" to speak with "your physician." The first ad features major side effects, encourages the reader to "talk to your doctor," and lists a brief summary of risks and contraindications on the opposite page. The second ad provides a phone number and the name of the pharmaceutical company, but does not provide the name of the drug.

The question in this case, broadly stated, is whether our law should follow these changes in the marketplace or reflect the images of the past. We believe that when mass marketing of prescription drugs seeks to influence a patient's choice of a drug, a pharmaceutical manufacturer that makes direct claims to consumers for the efficacy of its product should not be unqualifiedly relieved of a duty to provide proper warnings of the dangers or side effects of the product.

I

The Norplant System (Norplant)

This appeal concerns Norplant, a Food and Drug Administration (FDA)-approved, reversible contraceptive that prevents pregnancy for up to five years. The Norplant contraceptive employs six thin, flexible, closed capsules that contain a synthetic hormone, levonorgestrel. The capsules are implanted under the skin of a woman's upper arm during an in-office surgical procedure characterized by the manufacturer as minor. A low, continuous dosage of the hormone diffuses through the capsule walls and into the bloodstream. Although the capsules are not usually visible under the skin, the outline of the fan-like pattern can be felt under the skin. Removal occurs during an in-office procedure, similar to the insertion process. . . .

According to plaintiffs, Wyeth began a massive advertising campaign for Norplant in 1991, which it directed at women rather than at their doctors. Wyeth advertised on television and in women's magazines such as Glamour, Mademoiselle and Cosmopolitan. According to plaintiffs, none of the advertisements warned of any inherent danger posed by Norplant; rather, all praised its simplicity and convenience. None warned of side effects including pain and permanent scarring attendant to removal of the implants. Wyeth also sent a letter to physicians advising them that it was about to launch a national advertising program in magazines that the physicians' patients may read.

Plaintiffs cite several studies published in medical journals that have found Norplant removal to be difficult and painful. One study found that thirty-three percent of women had removal difficulty and forty percent experienced pain. Another study found that fifty-two percent of physicians reported complications during removal. Medical journals have catalogued the need for advanced medical technicians in addition to general surgeons for Norplant removal. Plaintiffs assert that none of this information was provided to consumers.

In 1995, plaintiffs began to file lawsuits in several New Jersey counties claiming injuries that resulted from their use of Norplant. Plaintiffs' principal claim alleged that Wyeth, distributors of Norplant in the United States, failed to warn adequately about side effects associated with the contraceptive. Side effects complained of by plaintiffs included weight gain, headaches, dizziness, nausea, diarrhea, acne, vomiting, fatigue, facial hair growth, numbness in the arms and legs, irregular menstruation, hair loss, leg cramps, anxiety and nervousness, vision problems, anemia, mood swings and depression, high blood pressure, and removal complications that resulted in scarring.

Class action certification was denied. All New Jersey Norplant cases were consolidated in Middlesex County. Eventually, twenty-five New Jersey Norplant cases involving approximately fifty Norplant users were pending in the Superior Court in Middlesex County.

After a case management conference, plaintiffs' counsel sought a determination of whether the learned intermediary doctrine applied. Pursuant to that conference, five bellwether plaintiffs were selected to challenge defendant's motion for summary judgment concerning the learned intermediary doctrine. The trial court dismissed plaintiffs' complaints, concluding that even when a manufacturer advertises directly to the public, and a woman is influenced by the advertising campaign, "a physician is not simply relegated to the role of prescribing the drug according to the woman's wishes." Consequently, the court held that the learned intermediary doctrine applied. Ibid. According to the court, the physician retains the duty to weigh the benefits and risks associated with a drug before deciding whether the drug is appropriate for the patient. . . .

Plaintiffs appealed. . . . The Appellate Division affirmed the trial court's grant of summary judgment in favor of defendants and its determination that the learned intermediary doctrine applied. . . .

We granted plaintiffs' petition for certification. 156 N.J. 410 (1998). . . .

II

Direct-to-Consumer Advertising

It is paradoxical that so pedestrian a concern as male-pattern baldness should have signaled the beginning of direct-to-consumer marketing of prescription drugs. Upjohn Company became the first drug manufacturer to advertise directly to consumers when it advertised for Rogaine, a hair-loss treatment. Jon D. Hanson & Douglas A. Kysar, Taking Behavioralism Seriously: Some Evidence of Market Manipulation, 112 Harv. L. Rev. 1420, 1456 (1999). The ad targeted male consumers by posing the question, "Can an emerging bald spot . . . damage your ability to get along with others, influence your chance of obtaining a job or date or even interfere with your job performance?" Ibid. (footnotes omitted). A related ad featured an attractive woman asserting suggestively, "I know that a man who can afford Rogaine is a man who can afford me." Ibid. (footnote omitted).

Advertising for Rogaine was the tip of the iceberg. Since drug manufacturers began marketing directly to consumers for products such as prescription drugs in the 1980s, "almost all pharmaceutical companies have engaged in this direct marketing practice." . . .

Pressure on consumers is an integral part of drug manufacturers' marketing strategy. From 1995 to 1996, drug companies increased advertising directed to consumers by ninety percent. . . ." John F. Kamp, senior vice president of the American Association of Advertising Agencies, said that prescription drug companies spent $1.3 billion on print and broadcast advertising aimed at consumers last year, up from $843 million in 1997. . . .

IV

How Has the Law Responded to These Changes?

A. The New Restatement (Third) of Torts Has Left the Issue to "Developing Case Law."

Parallel to the developments in drug marketing, the American Law Institute was in the process of adopting the Restatement (Third) of Torts: Products Liability (1997). The comment to Section 6 explains that subsection (d)(1) sets forth the traditional rule of the learned intermediary that drug and medical device manufacturers are liable for failing to warn of a drug's risks only when the manufacturer fails to warn the health-care provider of risks attendant to a specific drug. Restatement, supra, §6(d) comment *a.* That same comment also notes that subsection (d)(2) reflects decisional law and provides limited exceptions to the traditional rule by requiring manufacturers to warn patients in certain circumstances. Ibid. Because situations may exist when the health-care provider assumes a "much-diminished role as an evaluator or decisionmaker," it is appropriate to impose a duty on the manufacturer to warn the patient directly. Id. at §6d comment *b.* Despite the early effort to provide an exception to the doctrine in the case of direct marketing of pharmaceuticals to consumers, the drafters left the resolution of that issue to "developing case law." Id. at §6d comment *e.* One commentator described the Restatement's approach as a "tepid endorsement" of the learned intermediary doctrine. Charles J. Walsh et al., The Learned Intermediary Doctrine: The Correct Prescription for Drug Labeling, 48 Rutgers L. Rev. 821, 869 (1994). Thus, under the new Restatement, "warnings may have to be provided to a health-care provider or even to the patient," depending on the circumstances. William A. Dreier, The Restatement (Third) of Torts: Products Liability and the New Jersey Law — Not Quite Perfect Together, 50 Rutgers L.J. 2059, 2097 (1998). . . .

C. Direct Advertising of Drugs to Consumers Alters the Calculus
of the Learned Intermediary Doctrine. . . .

A . . . recent review summarized the theoretical bases for the [learned intermediary] doctrine as based on four considerations.

First, courts do not wish to intrude upon the doctor-patient relationship. From this perspective, warnings that contradict information supplied by the physician will undermine the patient's trust in the physician's judgment. Second, physicians may be in a superior position to convey meaningful information to their patients, as they must do to satisfy their duty to secure informed consent. Third, drug manufacturers lack effective means to communicate directly with patients, making it necessary to rely on physicians to convey the relevant information. Unlike [over the counter products], pharmacists usually dispense prescription drugs from bulk containers rather than as unit-of-use packages in which the manufacturer may have enclosed labeling. Finally, because of the complexity of risk information about prescription drugs, comprehension problems would complicate any effort by manufacturers to translate physician labeling for lay patients. For this reason, even critics of the rule do not suggest that pharmaceutical companies should provide warnings only to patients and have no tort duty to warn physicians. [Lars Noah, Advertising Prescription Drugs to Consumers: Assessing the Regulatory and Liability Issues, 32 Ga. L. Rev. 141, 157-159 (1992).]

Consumer-directed advertising of pharmaceuticals . . . belies each of the premises on which the learned intermediary doctrine rests.

First, the fact that manufacturers are advertising their drugs and devices to consumers suggests that consumers are active participants in their health care decisions, invalidating the concept that it is the doctor, not the patient, who decides whether a drug or device should be used. Second, it is illogical that requiring manufacturers to provide direct warnings to a consumer will undermine the patient-physician relationship, when, by its very nature, consumer-directed advertising encroaches on that relationship by encouraging consumers to ask for advertised products by name. Finally, consumer-directed advertising rebuts the notion that prescription drugs and devices and their potential adverse effects are too complex to be effectively communicated to lay consumers. Because the FDA requires that prescription drug and device advertising carry warnings, the consumer may reasonably presume that the advertiser guarantees the adequacy of its warnings. Thus, the common law duty to warn the ultimate consumer should apply. [Susan A. Casey, Comment, Laying an Old Doctrine to Rest: Challenging the Wisdom of the Learned Intermediary Doctrine, 19 Wm. Mitchell L. Rev. 931, 956 (1993) (footnotes omitted).] . . .

Obviously, the learned intermediary doctrine applies when its predicates are present. "In New Jersey, as elsewhere, we accept the proposition that a pharmaceutical manufacturer generally discharges its duty to warn the ultimate users of prescription drugs by supplying physicians with information about the drug's dangerous propensities." Had Wyeth done just that, simply supplied the physician with information about the product, and not advertised directly to the patients, plaintiffs would have no claim against Wyeth based on an independent duty to warn patients. The question is whether the absence of an independent duty to warn patients gives the manufacturer the right to misrepresent to the public the product's safety.

D. Prescription Drug Manufacturers that Market their Products Directly to Consumers Should Be Subject to Claims by Consumers if their Advertising Fails to Provide an Adequate Warning of the Product's Dangerous Propensities.

In reaching the conclusion that the learned intermediary doctrine does not apply to the direct marketing of drugs to consumers, we must necessarily consider that when prescription drugs are marketed and labeled in accordance with FDA specifications, the pharmaceutical manufacturers should not have to confront "state tort liability premised on theories of design defect or warning inadequacy." Note, A Question of Competence: The Judicial Role in the Regulation of Pharmaceuticals, 103 Harv. L. Rev. 773, 773 (1990). We draw much of this summary concerning the specifics of FDA pharmaceutical regulation from the brief of amicus curiae, the Pharmaceutical Research and Manufacturers of America. Because such regulations may change from day-to-day, our commentary concerning the current regulations may soon become moot. . . .

FDA regulations are pertinent in determining the nature and extent of any duty of care that should be imposed on pharmaceutical manufacturers with respect to direct-to-consumer advertising. Presently, any duty to warn physicians about prescription drug dangers is presumptively met by compliance with federal labeling. See N.J.S.A. 2A:58C-4. That presumption is not absolute. Nevertheless, FDA regulations serve as compelling evidence that a manufacturer satisfied its duty to warn the physician about potentially harmful side effects of its product.

We believe that in the area of direct-to-consumer advertising of pharmaceuticals, the same rebuttable presumption should apply when a manufacturer complies with FDA advertising, labeling and warning requirements. That approach harmonizes the manufacturer's duty to doctors and to the public when it chooses to directly advertise its products, and simultaneously recognizes the public interest in informing patients about new pharmaceutical developments. Moreover, a rebuttable presumption that the duty to consumers is met by compliance with FDA regulations helps to ensure that manufacturers are not made guarantors against remotely possible, but not scientifically-verifiable, side-effects of prescription drugs, a result that could have a "significant anti-utilitarian effect." Michael D. Green, Statutory Compliance and Tort Liability: Examining the Strongest Case, 30 U. Mich. J.L. Ref. 461, 466-67 (1997) (noting that over deterrence in drug advertising context could impede and delay manufacturers from research and development of new and effective drugs, force beneficial drugs from market, lead to shortages in supplies and suppliers of pharmaceuticals, and create unnecessary administrative costs).

We believe that this standard is fair and balanced. For all practical purposes, absent deliberate concealment or nondisclosure of after-acquired knowledge of harmful effects, compliance with FDA standards should be virtually dispositive of such claims. By definition, the advertising will have been "fairly balanced." This presumptive effect is in accordance with legislative intent that we discern from the punitive damages provision of the Products Liability Act. See L. 1987, c. 142, §5(c). That provision prohibits, in the case of the sale of pharmaceutical products, an award of punitive damages if there has been compliance with FDA labeling and pre-marketing requirements, impliedly reserving compensatory damages for those rare cases when the presumption is overcome. N.J.S.A. 2A:58C-5(c).

V

The final issues in this case concern proximate cause, that is, whether misinformation actually affected these patients and, if so, whether the intervention of the physician (without whom the product may not reach the patient) breaks the chain of causation. . . .

Although the physician writes the prescription, the physician's role in deciding which prescription drug is selected has been altered. With the arrival of direct-to-consumer advertising, patients now enter physician's offices with "preconceived expectations about treatment because of information obtained from DTC [direct-to-consumer] advertisements." Tamar V. Terzian, Direct-to-Consumer Prescription Drug Advertising, 25 Am. J.L. & Med. 149, 157 (1999). Consequently,

> [p]hysicians may relent to patient pressure, even if it is not in the best interest of the patient. In fact, physicians state that they are increasingly asked and pressured by their patients to prescribe drugs that the patient has seen advertised. For example, the diet drug combinations known as fen-phen was prescribed despite little hard scientific evidence of its potential side-effects. Physicians are under attack for prescribing the pills too often and too readily to inappropriate patients. Physicians argue that it is not their fault; rather, they claim pushy patients, prodded by DTC advertisements, pressed, wheedled, begged and berated them for quick treatments. This scenario comes at a time when physicians cannot afford to lose patients, because their income is already strained by managed care cost cutting. Physicians complain that it is impossible to compete with pharmaceutical companies' massive advertising budgets, and resign themselves to the fact that if consumers make enough noise, they will eventually relent to patient pressure. [Id. at 157-58 (footnotes omitted).]

We disagree that these "ads change the physician into 'simply a functionary, filling out prescriptions[,]' " but we must examine whether the changed relationship affects the finding of proximate cause. . . .

Courts have differed in their application of the learned intermediary doctrine in cases in which the defendant claimed that the prescribing physician knew of the risk that the manufacturer did not warn about. Some courts have applied a presumption that the physician would not have prescribed the product if an adequate warning had been given. The defendant may then rebut the presumption with evidence that the physician's decision would not have been affected by such a warning. Other courts have refused to create such a presumption, and have required the plaintiff to prove that an adequate warning would actually have changed the physician's decision. The courts have also differed in the quantum of proof a defendant must establish to show that the physician would have prescribed the drug even if the manufacturer had warned of the risk. . . . [Richard J. Heafey & Don M. Kennedy, Products Liability: Winning Strategies and the User, §10.03 (1999).]

However, we must consider as well a case in which a diabetic patient might have been influenced by advertising to request a drug from a physician without being warned by the manufacturer or the physician of the special dangers posed to a diabetic taking the drug. If an overburdened physician does not inquire whether the patient is a diabetic, the question remains whether the manufacturer should be relieved entirely of responsibility. In the case of direct marketing of drugs, we believe that neither the physician nor the manufacturer should be entirely relieved of their respective duties to warn. Pharmaceutical manufacturers may seek contribution, indemnity or exoneration because of the physician's deficient role in prescribing that drug. In each case, a jury must resolve the close questions of whether a breach of duty has been a proximate cause of harm, and how that causative harm, if found, may be apportioned among culpable defendants. In our experience, jurors are extremely skilled at sorting out the justly and legally responsible parties. . . .

The judgment of the Appellate Division is reversed and the matter is remanded to the Law Division for further proceedings.

[Dissenting opinion of Pollack, J. is omitted.]

Is *Perez* well reasoned? Even if it is, it has not been influential. Only one state court has followed it. See State ex. rel. Johnson v. Johnson Corp. v. Karl, 647 S.E.2d 899 (W. Va. 2007). In Rimbert v. Eli Lilly & Co., 577 F. Supp. 2d 1174, 1214-1224 (D.N.M. 2008), the federal district court predicted that New Mexico would reject the learned intermediary doctrine in large part because of the rise of direct-to-consumer advertising and other changes in the market for health care services. But these cases remain the exception: In the absence of direct-to-consumer advertising the almost unanimous rule is that there is no duty to warn consumers directly of risks associated with a drug, see Tyree, *supra* at n.3 (counting 48 jurisdictions adopting the learned intermediary rule), and even with direct advertising only two states have imposed a duty to warn consumers directly.

The possibility of a direct-to-consumer advertising exception to the learned intermediary doctrine has generated a great deal of discussion among scholars and commentators. For arguments against such an exception, see Lars Noah, Advertising Prescription Drugs to Consumers: Assessing the Regulatory and Liability Issues, 32 Ga. L. Rev. 141 (1997). For arguments in favor of an exception, see Ashley Porter, Old Habits Die Hard, Reforming the Learned Intermediary Doctrine in the Era of Direct to Consumer Advertising, 43 McGeorge L. Rev. 433 (2012). Even in New Jersey, where *Perez* recognizes a duty to warn patients directly, one commentator argues that "despite the apparently pro-plaintiff language of the Perez opinion, the New Jersey Supreme Court has announced a rather conservative rule." William A. Drier, Direct-To-Consumer Advertising Liability: An Empty Gift to Plaintiffs, 30 Seton Hall L. Rev. 806, 808 (2000).

Subsection (d)(2) of §6 of the Products Liability Restatement recognizes a duty to warn patients directly "when the manufacturer knows or has reason to know that health-care providers will not be in a position to reduce the risks of harm in accordance with the instructions or warnings [given to them.]" Comment *e* to §6 addresses the issue:

> *e. Direct warnings to patients.* Warnings and instructions with regard to drugs or medical devices that can be sold legally only pursuant to a prescription are, under the "learned intermediary" rule, directed to health-care providers. Subsection (d)(2) recognizes that direct warnings and instructions to patients are warranted for drugs that are dispensed or administered to patients without the personal intervention or evaluation of a health-care provider. An example is the administration of a vaccine in clinics where mass inoculations are performed. In many such programs, health-care providers are not in a position to

evaluate the risks attendant upon use of the drug or device or to relate them to patients. When a manufacturer supplies prescription drugs for distribution to patients in this type of unsupervised environment, if a direct warning to patients is feasible and can be effective, the law requires measures to that effect.

Although the learned intermediary rule is generally accepted and a drug manufacturer fulfills its legal obligation to warn by providing adequate warnings to the health-care provider, arguments have been advanced that in two other areas courts should consider imposing tort liability on drug manufacturers that fail to provide direct warnings to consumers. In the first, governmental regulatory agencies have mandated that patients be informed of risks attendant to the use of a drug. A noted example is the FDA requirement that birth control pills be sold to patients accompanied by a patient package insert. In the second, manufacturers have advertised a prescription drug and its indicated use in the mass media. Governmental regulations require that, when drugs are so advertised, they must be accompanied by appropriate information concerning risk so as to provide balanced advertising. The question in both instances is whether adequate warnings to the appropriate health-care provider should insulate the manufacturer from tort liability.

Those who assert the need for adequate warnings directly to consumers contend that manufacturers that communicate directly with consumers should not escape liability simply because the decision to prescribe the drug was made by the health-care provider. Proponents of the learned intermediary rule argue that, notwithstanding direct communications to the consumer, drugs cannot be dispensed unless a health-care provider makes an individualized decision that a drug is appropriate for a particular patient, and that it is for the health-care provider to decide which risks are relevant to the particular patient. The Institute leaves to developing case law whether exceptions to the learned intermediary rule in these or other situations should be recognized. . . .

Does a physician cooperating with a pharmaceutical manufacturer in clinical drug trials function as a traditional learned intermediary on behalf of participating patients or as more of a marketing agent with conflicting interests, such that the manufacturer should have a duty to warn patients directly? See Rodriguez v. Gilead Sciences, Inc., 2015 WL 236621 (S.D. Tex. 2015) (reviewing case law and denying defendant manufacturer's motion for summary judgment).

2. Liability for Defective Drug Designs

Brown v. Superior Court (Abbott Laboratories)
751 P.2d 470 (Cal. 1988)

Mosk, J.

In current litigation several significant issues have arisen relating to the liability of manufacturers of prescription drugs for injuries caused by their products. Our first and broadest inquiry is whether such a manufacturer may be held strictly liable for a product that is defective in design. . . .

authors' dialogue 23

JIM: I'm not sure the Products Restatement does enough with the subject of drug companies warning patients directly. I recall that our early drafts included a provision recognizing such a duty when drug manufacturers advised directly to consumers. We had a few cases and thought that that was the direction the law would take.

AARON: Yeah. But a majority of our advisers urged us not to push things. Especially the members who were judges, who argued that we should leave it to the courts to work out sensible solutions. "Handle it in a comment," they advised. "Leave the black letter flexible on the issue."

JIM: You know better than I that we didn't put issues to a formal vote with the advisers. But I remember the discussions you're talking about. The judges made a persuasive case for going easy in the black letter. Especially coming from the judges, the argument carried weight. They had no substantive stake — simply an institutional commitment to reaching the right position. Given what has transpired since the Products Liability Restatement was drafted, it appears that the judges were correct in advising us not to adopt a direct duty to warn consumers in the black letter.

AARON: That touches on the question of the proper role of the Reporters and the Institute regarding developing areas of the law. We felt an obligation to reflect not only existing case law, but also the Institute's sense of what rules were reasonable and where the law was headed.

DOUG: Of course, when William Prosser introduced §402A into the Second Restatement he could only point to a couple cases supporting strict products liability. He sensed a trend sweeping the nation and, sure enough, §402A became the most cited section of any ALI Restatement project in any field of law. Whether that outcome would have happened without Prosser's intervention is hard to say. The Restatements are part of the very process of legal development that they try to merely "restate." So, who knows? Maybe if §6 of the Products Liability Restatement came down strongly in support of a duty to warn consumers for directly advertised drugs, the rule in *Perez* might have taken off.

JIM: That sounds like *your* wishful thinking Doug. At any rate, the hardest aspect of §6 in this regard was §6(c), dealing with prescription drug design liability. We saw a trend in favor of exposure to liability but had to pull a coherent rule together from what was available. It certainly has been a controversial topic among scholars.

AARON: When we get to the drug design materials in the book, the students can judge for themselves if what we did makes sense. Time will tell.

---

authors' dialogue 24

DOUG: Jim and Aaron, can you figure out why it is that the *Perez* case has not caught on? If drug companies advertise their pills as if they were M&M chocolates, why should they not be held liable for failing to warn directly to consumers?

AARON: I remember doing an interview for a TV news show after *Perez* was decided and I predicted that it would sweep the country. Boy, was I wrong.

JIM: Even more mystifying: You hardly even see cases raising the issue. Strange.

AARON: I once wrote a short article saying that if we were to view drug advertising as a public good since it informs consumers about the availability of drugs to cure ailments and gets them to see their doctors then a direct duty to warn would put a burden on drug manufacturers that they could not meet. It is easy to communicate to consumers the benefits of a drug. But there are so many potential side effects that every case would raise a jury question as to the adequacy of the warning. Courts did not want to get into that mess.

JIM: That's an interesting argument but it's too cute. I doubt that explains why *Perez* has had such a poor run. I see nothing in the cases that even hints that you are right.

DOUG: I want to pick up on what Jim said. The absence of cases raising the issue is telling. Perhaps, the drug manufacturers sensing the possible liability for failing to warn consumers directly have done the intelligent thing. They have strengthened the warnings to consumers both in print and in TV advertising. There is a marked difference in the quality of warnings about side effects over what was the case ten to fifteen years ago. I can't document it but I know from watching a lot of golf tournaments that it feels right.

JIM: You mean that the threat of tort liability actually had some effect? That should make some folks feel good. Tort law deters bad conduct.

DOUG: Whether tort law deters individuals is questionable. But institutions can and do react to the threat of massive liability. It's the magic of market incentives, properly disciplined.

A.   Strict Liability in General

The doctrine of strict liability had its genesis in a concurring opinion by Justice Roger Traynor in Escola v. Coca-Cola Bottling Co. (1944) 24 Cal. 2d 453, 461, 150 P.2d 436. He suggested that a manufacturer should be absolutely liable if, in placing a product on the market, it knew the product was to be used without inspection, and it proved to have a defect that caused injury. The policy considerations underlying this suggestion were that the manufacturer, unlike the public, can anticipate or guard against the recurrence of hazards, that the cost of injury may be an overwhelming misfortune to the person injured whereas the manufacturer can insure against the risk and distribute the cost among the consuming public, and that it is in the public interest to discourage the marketing of defective products. This court unanimously adopted

Justice Traynor's concept in Greenman v. Yuba Power Products, Inc. (1963) 59 Cal. 2d 57, 62, holding a manufacturer strictly liable in tort and using the formulation of the doctrine set forth in *Escola.*

Strict liability differs from negligence in that it eliminates the necessity for the injured party to prove that the manufacturer of the product which caused injury was negligent. It focuses not on the conduct of the manufacturer but on the product itself, and holds the manufacturer liable if the product was defective. . . .

This court refined and explained application of the principle in Cronin v. J.B.E. Olson Corp. (1972) 8 Cal. 3d 121, and Barker v. Lull Engineering Co. (1978), 20 Cal. 3d 413 (hereafter *Barker*). In *Cronin,* we rejected the requirement of section 402A that the defect in a product must be "unreasonably dangerous" to the consumer in order to invoke strict liability, holding that the requirement "rings of negligence" (8 Cal. 3d at p.132) and that the showing of a defect which proximately caused injury is sufficient to justify application of the doctrine.

Barker defined the term "design defect" in the context of strict liability. In that case the plaintiff was injured while operating a piece of heavy construction equipment, and claimed that a safety device called an "outrigger" would have prevented the accident. We held that the defendant could be held liable for a defect in design.

Barker identified three types of product defects. (20 Cal. 3d at p.428.) First, there may be a flaw in the manufacturing process, resulting in a product that differs from the manufacturer's intended result. The archetypal example of such a defect was involved in *Escola,* supra, 24 Cal. 2d 453, where a Coca-Cola bottle exploded. Such a manufacturing defect did not exist in the heavy equipment that caused the injury in *Barker,* and is not alleged in the present case.

Second, there are products which are "perfectly" manufactured but are unsafe because of the absence of a safety device, i.e., a defect in design. This was the defect alleged in *Barker.* It held that a product is defectively designed if it failed to perform as safely as an ordinary consumer would expect when used as intended or in a manner reasonably foreseeable, or if, on balance, the risk of danger inherent in the challenged design outweighs the benefits of the design. (20 Cal. 3d at p.430) Plaintiff asserts this test should be applied in the present case because DES contained a design defect.

The third type of defect identified in *Barker* is a product that is dangerous because it lacks adequate warnings or instructions. According to plaintiff, defendants here failed to warn of the dangers inherent in the use of DES. We are concerned, therefore, with the second and third types of defects described in *Barker.*

B.   Strict Liability and Prescription Drugs

Even before *Greenman* was decided, the members of the American Law Institute, in considering whether to adopt a rule of strict liability, pondered whether the manufacturer of a prescription drug should be subject to the doctrine. (38 ALI Proc. 19, 90-92, 98 (1961).) During a rather confusing discussion of a draft of what was to become section 402A, a member of the institute proposed that drugs should be exempted from strict liability on the ground that it would be "against the public interest" to apply the doctrine to such products because of "the very serious tendency to stifle medical research and testing." Dean Prosser, who was the reporter for the Restatement Second of Torts, responded that the problem was a real one, and that he had it in mind in drafting section 402A. A motion to exempt prescription drugs from the section was defeated on the suggestion of Dean Prosser that the problem could be dealt with in the comments to the section. However, a motion to state the exemption in a comment was also defeated. (38 ALI Proc. 19, 90-98, supra.) At the next meeting of the institute in 1962, section 402A was approved together with comment *k* thereto. (41 ALI Proc. 227, 244 (1962).)

The comment provides that the producer of a properly manufactured prescription drug may be held liable for injuries caused by the product only if it was not accompanied by a warning of dangers that the manufacturer knew or should have known about. . . .

Comment *k* has been analyzed and criticized by numerous commentators. While there is some disagreement as to its scope and meaning, there is a general consensus that, although it purports to explain the strict liability doctrine, in fact the principle it states is based on negligence. (E.g., Schwartz, Unavoidably Unsafe Products (1985) 42 Wash. & Lee L. Rev. 1139, 1141; McClellan, Drug Induced Injury (1978) 25 Wayne L. Rev. 1, 2.) That is, comment *k* would impose liability on a drug manufacturer only if it failed to warn of a defect of which it either knew or should have known. This concept focuses not on a deficiency in the product — the hallmark of strict liability — but on the fault of the producer in failing to warn of the dangers inherent in the use of its product that were either known or knowable — an idea which "rings of negligence," in the words of *Cronin,* supra, 8 Cal. 3d 121, 132.

Comment *k* has been adopted in the overwhelming majority of jurisdictions that have considered the matter.

We are aware of only one decision that has applied the doctrine of strict liability to prescription drugs. (Brochu v. Ortho Pharmaceutical Corp. (1st Cir. 1981) 642 F.2d 652, 654-657.) Most cases have embraced the rule of comment *k* without detailed analysis of its language. A few, notably Kearl v. Lederle Laboratories, 172 Cal. App. 3d 812 [,218 Cal. Rptr. 453 (1985)] (hereafter *Kearl*), have conditioned application of the exemption stated therein on a finding that the drug involved is in fact "unavoidably dangerous," reasoning that the comment was intended to exempt only such drugs from strict liability. . . .

We appear, then, to have three distinct choices:

(1)   to hold that the manufacturer of a prescription drug is strictly liable for a defect in its product because it was defectively designed, as that term is defined in *Barker,* or because of a failure to warn of its dangerous propensities even though such dangers were neither known nor scientifically knowable at the time of distribution;

(2)   to determine that liability attaches only if a manufacturer fails to warn of dangerous propensities of which it was or should have been aware, in conformity with comment *k;* or

(3)   to decide, like *Kearl* and Toner v. Lederle Laboratories, supra, 732 P.2d 297, 303-309, that strict liability for design defects should apply to prescription drugs unless the particular drug which caused injury is found to be "unavoidably dangerous."

We shall conclude that:

(1)   a drug manufacturer's liability for a defectively designed drug should not be measured by the standards of strict liability;

(2) because of the public interest in the development, availability, and reasonable price of drugs, the appropriate test for determining responsibility is the test stated in comment *k;* and

(3) for these same reasons of policy, we disapprove of the holding of *Kearl* that only those prescription drugs found to be "unavoidably dangerous" should be measured by the comment *k* standard and that strict liability should apply to drugs that do not meet the description.

1. Design Defect

Barker, as we have seen, set forth two alternative tests to measure a design defect: first, whether the product performed as safely as the ordinary consumer would expect when used in an intended and reasonably foreseeable manner, and second, whether, on balance, the benefits of the challenged design outweighed the risk of danger inherent in the design. In making the latter determination, the jury may consider these factors: "the gravity of the danger posed by the challenged design, the likelihood that such danger would occur, the mechanical feasibility of a safer alternative design, the financial cost of an improved design, and the adverse consequences to the product and to the consumer that would result from an alternative design." (20 Cal. 3d at p.431.)

Defendants assert that neither of these tests is applicable to a prescription drug like DES. As to the "consumer expectation" standard, they claim, the "consumer" is not the plaintiff but the physician who prescribes the drug, and it is to him that the manufacturer's warnings are directed. A physician appreciates the fact that all prescription drugs involve inherent risks, known and unknown, and he does not expect that the drug is without such risks. We agree that the "consumer expectation" aspect of the *Barker* test is inappropriate to prescription drugs. While the "ordinary consumer" may have a reasonable expectation that a product such as a machine he purchases will operate safely when used as intended, a patient's expectations regarding the effects of such a drug are those related to him by his physician, to whom the manufacturer directs the warnings regarding the drug's properties. The manufacturer cannot be held liable if it has provided appropriate warnings and the doctor fails in his duty to transmit these warnings to the patient or if the patient relies on inaccurate information from others regarding side effects of the drug.

The second test, which calls for the balancing of risks and benefits, is inapposite to prescription drugs, according to defendants, because it contemplates that a safer alternative design is feasible. While the defective equipment in *Barker* and other cases involving mechanical devices might be "redesigned" by the addition of safety devices, there is no possibility for an alternative design of a drug like DES, which is a scientific constant compounded in accordance with a required formula. (See *Sindell,* 26 Cal. 3d at p.605.)

We agree with defendants that *Barker* contemplates a safer alternative design if possible, but we seriously doubt their claim that a drug like DES cannot be "redesigned" to make it safer. For example, plaintiff might be able to demonstrate at trial that a particular component of DES rendered it unsafe as a miscarriage preventative and that removal of that component would not have affected the efficacy of the drug. Even if the resulting product, without the damaging component, would bear a name other than DES, it would do no violence to semantics to view it as a "redesign" of DES.

Or plaintiff might be able to prove that other, less harmful drugs were available to prevent miscarriage; the benefit of such alternate drugs could be weighed against the advantages of DES in making the risk/benefit analysis of *Barker*. As the Court of Appeal observed, defendants' attempt to confine the issue to whether there is an "alternative design" for DES poses the problem in an "unreasonably narrow" fashion. (See Comment, The Failure to Warn Defect (1983), 17 U.S.F. L. Rev. 743, 755-762.). . . .

It is indisputable, as plaintiff contends, that the risk of injury from such drugs is unavoidable, that a consumer may be helpless to protect himself from serious harm caused by them, and that, like other products, the cost of insuring against strict liability can be passed on by the producer to the consumer who buys the item. Moreover, as we observe below, in some cases additional testing of drugs before they are marketed might reveal dangerous side effects, resulting in a safer product.

But there is an important distinction between prescription drugs and other products such as construction machinery . . . the producers of which were held strictly liable. In the latter cases, the product is used to make work easier or to provide pleasure, while in the former it may be necessary to alleviate pain and suffering or to sustain life. Moreover, unlike other important medical products (wheelchairs, for example), harm to some users from prescription drugs is unavoidable. Because of these distinctions, the broader public interest in the availability of drugs at an affordable price must be considered in deciding the appropriate standard of liability for injuries resulting from their use.

Perhaps a drug might be made safer if it was withheld from the market until scientific skill and knowledge advanced to the point at which additional dangerous side effects would be revealed. But in most cases such a delay in marketing new drugs — added to the delay required to obtain approval for release of the product from the Food and Drug Administration — would not serve the public welfare. Public policy favors the development and marketing of beneficial new drugs, even though some risks, perhaps serious ones, might accompany their introduction, because drugs can save lives and reduce pain and suffering.

If drug manufacturers were subject to strict liability, they might be reluctant to undertake research programs to develop some pharmaceuticals that would prove beneficial or to distribute others that are available to be marketed, because of the fear of large adverse monetary judgments. Further, the additional expense of insuring against such liability — assuming insurance would be available — and of research programs to reveal possible dangers not detectable by available scientific methods could place the cost of medication beyond the reach of those who need it most. . . .

The possibility that the cost of insurance and of defending against lawsuits will diminish the availability and increase the price of pharmaceuticals is far from theoretical. Defendants cite a host of examples of products which have greatly increased in price or have been withdrawn or withheld from the market because of the fear that their products would be held liable for large judgments.

For example, according to defendant E.R. Squibb & Sons, Inc., Bendectin, the only antinauseant drug available for pregnant women, was withdrawn from sale in 1983 because the cost of insurance almost equalled the entire income from sale of the drug. Before it was withdrawn, the price of Bendectin increased by over 300 percent. (132 Chemical Week (June 12, 1983) p.14.)

Drug manufacturers refused to supply a newly discovered vaccine for influenza on the ground that mass inoculation would subject them to enormous liability. The government therefore assumed the risk of lawsuits resulting from injuries caused by the vaccine. (Franklin & Mais, Mass Immunization Programs (1977) 65 Cal. L. Rev. 754, 769 et seq.; Feldman v. Lederle Laboratories (1983) 460 A.2d 203, 209.) One producer of diphtheria-tetanus-pertussis vaccine withdrew from the market, giving as its reason "extreme liability exposure, cost of litigation and difficulty of continuing to obtain adequate insurance." (Hearing Before Subcom. on Health and the Environment of House Com. on Energy and Commerce on Vaccine Injury Compensation, 98th Cong., 2nd Sess. (Sept. 10, 1984) p.295.) There are only two manufacturers of the vaccine remaining in the market, and the cost of each dose rose a hundredfold from 11 cents in 1982 to $11.40 in 1986, $8 of which was for an insurance reserve. The price increase roughly paralleled an increase in the number of lawsuits from one in 1978 to 219 in 1985. (232 Science (June 13, 1986) p.1,339.) Finally, a manufacturer was unable to market a new drug for the treatment of vision problems because it could not obtain adequate liability insurance at a reasonable cost. (N.Y. Times (Oct. 14, 1986) p.10.)

There is no doubt that, from the public's standpoint, these are unfortunate consequences. And they occurred even though almost all jurisdictions follow the negligence standard of comment k. It is not unreasonable to conclude in these circumstances that the imposition of a harsher test for liability would not further the public interest in the development and availability of these important products.

We decline to hold, therefore, that a drug manufacturer's liability for injuries caused by the defective design of a prescription drug should be measured by the standard set forth in *Barker*.

2. Failure to Warn

For these same reasons of policy, we reject plaintiff's assertion that a drug manufacturer should be held strictly liable for failure to warn of risks inherent in a drug even though it neither knew nor could have known by the application of scientific knowledge available at the time of distribution that the drug could produce the undesirable side effects suffered by the plaintiff. . . .

3. The Kearl Test

One further question remains in this aspect of the case. Comment k, as we have seen, provides that the maker of an "unavoidably unsafe" product is not liable for injuries resulting from its use if the product is "properly prepared, and accompanied by proper directions and warning." With the few exceptions noted above, the courts which have adopted comment k have viewed all prescription drugs as coming within its scope.

Kearl suggested that not all drugs are "unavoidably dangerous" so as to merit the protection of the negligence standard of comment k, and it devised a test to separate those which meet that description from those which do not. It held that the question whether a drug should be exempt from strict liability as "unavoidably dangerous" presents a mixed question of law and fact which should be decided on the basis of evidence to be taken by the trial judge out of the presence of the jury. The judge should determine, after hearing the evidence,

(1) whether, when distributed, the product was intended to confer an exceptionally important benefit that made its availability highly desirable;

(2)   whether the then-existing risk posed by the product was both "substantial" and "unavoidable"; and

(3)   whether the interest in availability (again measured as of the time of distribution) outweighs the interest in promoting enhanced accountability through strict liability design defect review.

If these questions are answered in the affirmative the liability of the manufacturer is tested by the standard of comment *k;* otherwise, strict liability is the applicable test.

The Court of Appeal in the present case refused to adopt this approach on the ground that it required the trial judge to decide questions of fact which were ordinarily left to the jury, and that it presented the specter of inconsistent verdicts in various trial courts: in one case the question of liability for injuries caused by a specific drug would be tested by a negligence standard, while in another, involving the same drug, the judge might conclude that strict liability was the appropriate test.

We acknowledge that there is some appeal in the basic premise of *Kearl.* It seems unjust to grant the same protection from liability to those who gave us thalidomide as to the producers of penicillin. If some method could be devised to confine the benefit of the comment *k* negligence standard to those drugs that have proved useful to mankind while denying the privilege to those that are clearly harmful, it would deserve serious consideration. But we know of no means by which this can be accomplished without substantially impairing the public interest in the development and marketing of new drugs, because the harm to this interest arises in the very process of attempting to make the distinction. . . .

Kearl gives the manufacturer a chance to avoid strict liability. But the eligibility of each drug for favorable treatment must be tested at a trial, with its attendant litigation costs, and the drug must survive two risk/benefit challenges, first by the judge and then by the jury. In order to vindicate the public's interest in the availability and affordability of prescription drugs, a manufacturer must have a greater assurance that his products will not be measured by a strict liability standard than is provided by the test stated in *Kearl.* Therefore, we disapprove the portion of *Kearl* which holds that comment *k* should not be applied to a prescription drug unless the trial court first determines that the drug is "unavoidably dangerous."

In conclusion, and in accord with almost all our sister states that have considered the issue, we hold that a manufacturer is not strictly liable for injuries caused by a prescription drug so long as the drug was properly prepared and accompanied by warnings of its dangerous propensities that were either known or reasonably scientifically knowable at the time of distribution. . . .

The judgment of the Court of Appeal is affirmed.

In the jurisdictions that have adopted comment *k,* most apply it on a case-by-case basis as an affirmative defense. In Ortho Pharmaceutical Corp. v. Heath, 722 P.2d 410 (Colo. 1986), *overruled on other grounds,* Armentrout v. FMC Corp., 842 P.2d 175 (Colo. 1992), the court found that it was possible to make out a design defect case against a drug manufacturer based on risk-utility balancing "without regard to the availability of warnings." It did, however, allow the jury to hear evidence as to whether the drug in question was an "unavoidably unsafe product" within the meaning of Restatement of Torts (Second) §402A, comment *k.*

Some courts adopt a straightforward risk-utility test in determining the prima facie element of design defect. In Mack v. Amerisource Drug Corp., 2009 U.S. Dist. LEXIS 109705 (D. Md. 2009), the plaintiffs alleged that their daughter died of cardiac arrhythmia caused by taking the defendant's drug for autoimmune diseases. They did not assert a claim for failure-to-warn. Instead, they made a claim for defective design, asserting that the drug's side effects were great enough to render it unreasonably dangerous. The trial court, granting summary judgment for the defendant, concluded:

> At the hearing on summary judgment . . . , Plaintiffs' counsel proffered several miscellaneous documents, including internal corporate memoranda and correspondence from [the defendant] that referred to the exhibited side effects of [the drug]. However, such documents do not militate for the submission of the defect issue to a jury. The fact that a drug may exhibit certain adverse side effects does not, by itself, create an issue of material fact on whether the drug is unreasonably dangerous. . . . In the face of the drug's apparent advantages, Plaintiffs would need to provide a much greater evidentiary showing to establish that the medication's attendant risks outweigh its benefits — a necessary showing under the "risk/utility" test. [Id. at 15-16.]

Restatement (Third) of Torts: Products Liability
(1998)

§6. LIABILITY OF COMMERCIAL SELLER OR DISTRIBUTOR FOR HARM CAUSED BY DEFECTIVE PRESCRIPTION DRUGS AND MEDICAL DEVICES

(a) A manufacturer of a prescription drug or medical device who sells or otherwise distributes a defective drug or medical device is subject to liability for harm to persons caused by the defect. . . .

(b) For purposes of liability under Subsection (a), a prescription drug or medical device is defective if at the time of sale or other distribution the drug or medical device:

. . .

(2) is not reasonably safe due to defective design as defined in Subsection (c) . . .

(c) A prescription drug or medical device is not reasonably safe due to defective design if the foreseeable risks of harm posed by the drug or medical device are sufficiently great in relation to its foreseeable therapeutic benefits that reasonable health-care providers, knowing of such foreseeable risks and therapeutic benefits, would not prescribe the drug or medical device for any class of patients. . . .

COMMENT:

b. Rationale. . . . The traditional refusal by courts to impose tort liability for defective designs of prescription drugs and medical devices is based on the fact that a prescription drug or medical device entails a unique set of risks and benefits. What may be harmful to one patient may be beneficial to another. Under Subsection (c) a drug is defectively designed only when it provides no net benefit to any class of patients. Courts have concluded that as long as a drug or medical device provides net benefits to some persons under some circumstances, the drug or device manufacturer should be required to instruct and warn health-care providers of the foreseeable risks and benefits. Courts have also recognized that the regulatory system governing prescription drugs is a legitimate mechanism for setting the standards for drug design. In part, this deference reflects concerns over the possible negative effects of judicially imposed liability on the cost and availability of valuable medical technology. This deference also rests on two further assumptions: first, that prescribing health-care providers, when adequately informed by drug manufacturers, are able to assure that the right drugs and medical devices reach the right patients; and second, that governmental regulatory agencies adequately review new prescription drugs and devices, keeping unreasonably dangerous designs off the market.

Nevertheless, unqualified deference to these regulatory mechanisms is considered by a growing number of courts to be unjustified. An approved prescription drug or medical device can present significant risks without corresponding advantages. At the same time, manufacturers must have ample discretion to develop useful drugs and devices without subjecting their design decisions to the ordinary test applicable to products generally under §2(b). Accordingly, Subsection (c) imposes a more rigorous test for defect than does §2(b), which does not apply to prescription drugs and medical devices. The requirement for establishing defective design of a prescription drug or medical device under Subsection (c) is that the drug or device have so little merit compared with its risks that reasonable health-care providers, possessing knowledge of risks that were known or reasonably should have been known, would not have prescribed the drug or device for any class of patients. Thus, a prescription drug or medical device that has usefulness to any class of patients is not defective in design even if it is harmful to other patients. Because of the special nature of prescription drugs and medical devices, the determination of whether such products are not reasonably safe is to be made under Subsections (c) and (d) rather than under §§2(b) and 2(c). . . .

f. Manufacturers' liability for defectively designed prescription drugs and medical devices. Subsection (c) reflects the judgment that, as long as a given drug or device provides net benefits for a class of patients, it should be available to them, accompanied by appropriate warnings and instructions. Learned intermediaries must generally be relied upon to see that the right drugs and devices reach the right patients. However, when a drug or device provides net benefits to no class of patients — when reasonable, informed health-care providers would not prescribe it to any class of patients — then the design of the product is defective and the manufacturer should be subject to liability for harm caused.

A prescription drug or device manufacturer defeats a plaintiff's design claim by establishing one or more contexts in which its product would be prescribed by reasonable, informed health-care providers. That some individual providers do, in fact, prescribe defendant's product does not in itself suffice to defeat the plaintiff's claim. Evidence regarding the actual conduct of health-care providers, while relevant and admissible, is not necessarily controlling. The issue is whether, objectively viewed, reasonable providers, knowing of the foreseeable risks and benefits of the drug or medical device, would prescribe it for any class of patients. Given this very demanding objective standard, liability is likely to be imposed only under unusual circumstances. The court has the responsibility to determine when the plaintiff has introduced sufficient evidence so that reasonable persons could conclude that plaintiff has met this demanding standard.

In James A. Henderson, Jr. & Aaron D. Twerski, Drug Designs Are Different, 111 Yale L.J. 151 (2001), two of the authors of this casebook wrote a spirited defense of the

Restatement position on drug design.[1] Recently, the authors revisited the issue in an article entitled Drug Design Liability, Farewell to Comment k, 67 Baylor L. Rev. ___ (2015). They had this to say:

> There can be no doubt that the confused language of Comment k has spawned chaos in the decisional law of drug design liability. Courts have embraced at least eight different standards for drug design liability. Relying on Comment k, they have variously held that manufacturers of prescription drugs are entitled to escape liability for drug designs completely; that they are entitled to escape from strict liability claims but not from claims of negligence; that before a court allows a manufacturer to escape liability for an unavoidably unsafe drug it must make a threshold decision as to whether the drug in question confers an exceptionally important benefit that makes its availability highly desirable; that it is the plaintiff's burden to prove that the risks of a particular drug outweigh its benefits; that it is a defendant's burden to prove that a drug's benefits outweigh its risks; that a drug may deemed defectively designed if its risks outweigh its benefits with regard only to a particular plaintiff or class of patients; that plaintiff may establish a drug design defect by introducing a reasonable alternative design that has not yet been approved by the Food and Drug Administration and that plaintiffs can establish liability if an alternative FDA-approved drug is as effective as, and safer than, the drug in question.

The authors then examine what could be the basis of a drug design claim:

> Several cases [here] suggested that drug manufacturers, like other product manufacturers, could be held liable for failing to adopt a reasonable alternative design that would have avoided harm to the patient. For good reason the overwhelming majority of scholars agree that courts are incapable of administering such a test, dependent as the test is on a judicial determination that the FDA would have approved the proposed alternative drug. Anyone proposing a change in the molecular structure of an already-approved drug must present the proposed altered molecule to the FDA for approval, thus initiating the selfsame review that is required for a new drug. The new-drug approval process generally takes ten to fifteen years, during which time the FDA reviews countless tests that check the drug for safety and efficacy, utilizing thousands of patients. The current cost of bringing a new drug to market runs between 1.2–1.8 billion dollars. Because of the rigor of the process, only a small percentage of drugs initially proposed to the FDA eventually receive final approval. No court could, even in a trial of much greater duration than normal, determine that a supposedly safer alternative drug would have been approved by the FDA. Of course, if another drug company has already marketed an FDA-approved drug that has greater benefits and fewer risks than the drug in question, liability may be imposed on the seller of the drug that harmed the plaintiff. In that instance, a court would be comparing two FDA-approved drugs rather than seeking to establish that a drug that has not undergone the FDA-approval process should be considered as an alternative. In that circumstance, the court would not be required to replicate the administrative approval process and the case would presumably be adjudicable. . . .
>
> A significant number of courts take the position that a drug can be declared to be defectively designed if, from an overall perspective, its risks outweigh its benefits. Several considerations reveal why this sort of macro risk-utility balancing is inadvisable. First, to undertake an analysis of the overall social value of a drug for all uses would require highly complex evidentiary inquiry. A court would have to look at all potential uses of the drug for ailments that bear no relation to the case at bar. Potentially, many

---

1. In main the article responds to a critique by George Conk, Is There a Design Defect in the Restatement (Third) of Torts Products Liability, 109 Yale L.J. 151 (2001).

illnesses would have to be considered, together with all the possible benefits and detriments of the drug for each such illness. The trial would closely resemble a roving inquiry into all the issues that a regulator might have considered in deciding whether to allow the drug on the market. Second, and perhaps more important, for a court to decide that a particular drug's overall risks outweigh its overall benefits would mean that even if the drug was highly valuable for one or more distinct classes of users, the court might strike down the design as defective and thus by implication not worthy of being prescribed even for those who would benefit from its consumption.

One might respond to the just-described difficulties by sheltering drug manufacturers from macro risk-utility liability if the drug is found to provide exceptional benefits. But such a threshold requirement would deny the benefits of lifestyle drugs to those who value them. To impose design liability on such drugs because they can cause serious side-effects would effectively bar them from the market. Thus a young man in his early twenties who finds himself balding; or an eighteen year-old who is unable to date because his or her face is pockmarked with acne; would be denied a drug essential to their well-being as they define it because a court decides that the drug does not present exceptional, life-or-death medical benefits. Such denials strike the authors as overly paternalistic. Drugs rarely have third-party effects, so the choice should be the patient's to make. If the drug manufacturer adequately warns physicians about the risks associated with lifestyle drugs then the risk created by misprescription of such drugs or devices should be dealt with by a malpractice action against the physician who ignores those warnings rather than by a design case against the manufacturer.

For these reasons, the authors reaffirm their belief that the only plausible design defect claim is the one articulated in §6(c): If the foreseeable risks of harm are sufficiently great that reasonable health-care provides would not prescribe the drug for any class of patients then it can be considered to be defectively designed. Federal courts sitting in diversity have predicted that their respective state high courts would adopt §6(c). See Mills v. Bristol-Myers, 2011 WL 4708850, *2 (D. Ariz. 2011) ("Courts in this District apply the Restatement (Third) of Torts' definition of an unreasonably safe prescription drug or medical device to Arizona design defect claims."); Madsen v. American Home Products Corp., 477 F. Supp. 2d 1025, 1037 (E.D. Mo. 2007) (predicting that Iowa would adopt §6(c)). Some courts have rejected §6(c). See, e.g., Bryant v. Hoffmann La Roche Inc., 585 S.E.2d 723, 727 (Ga. Ct. App. 2003); In Re Fosomax Products Liability Litigation, 742 F. Supp. 2d 460, 471-72 (S.D.N.Y. 2010) (refusing to adopt §6(c) without an affirmative indication that Supreme Court of Florida would do so).

In Lance v. Wyeth, 85 A.3d 434 (Pa. 2014), the Pennsylvania Supreme Court explicitly adopted §6(c) as the governing rule of the case. Plaintiff's decedent, a 35-year-old woman, had taken Redux, a weight-reducing pill, from January through April of 1997. The plaintiff alleged that Wyeth knew or should have known that Redux caused pulmonary hypertension (PPH). Plaintiff did not predicate her claim on failure to warn; rather her claim was that, notwithstanding the warning, Redux was so dangerous that no physician "knowing the risk and benefits of the drug would have prescribed the drug for any class of patients." Id. at 447. The court acknowledged that drug design liability cannot be based on a claim that a pharmaceutical manufacturer should have developed a reasonable alternative design, noting that it is beyond judicial competence to replicate the FDA process for approval of new drugs. However, the court saw no reason to shield drug manufacturers from design liability when a pharmaceutical manufacturer was negligent in marketing a drug that did not benefit any class of patients.

3. Pharmacists' Liability for Prescription Products

Pharmacists have frequently been afforded special protection by courts in products liability actions. Consider the limited circumstances under which the Products Liability Restatement imposes liability on retail sellers of prescription drugs:

Restatement (Third) of Torts: Products Liability
(1998)

§6. LIABILITY OF COMMERCIAL SELLER OR DISTRIBUTOR FOR HARM CAUSED BY DEFECTIVE PRESCRIPTION DRUGS AND MEDICAL DEVICES

. . .

(e) A retail seller or other distributor of a prescription drug or medical device is subject to liability for harm caused by the drug or device if:

(1) at the time of sale or other distribution the drug or medical device contains a manufacturing defect as defined in §2(a); or

(2) at or before the time of sale or other distribution of the drug or medical device the retail seller or other distributor fails to exercise reasonable care and such failure causes harm to persons.

COMMENT:

h. Liability of retail seller of prescription drugs and medical devices for defective designs and defects due to inadequate instructions or warnings. The rule governing most products imposes liability on wholesalers and retailers for selling a defectively designed product, or one without adequate instructions or warnings, even though they have exercised reasonable care in marketing the product. See §1, Comment *e,* and §2, Comment *o.* Courts have refused to apply this general rule to nonmanufacturing retail sellers of prescription drugs and medical devices and, instead, have adopted the rule state in Subsection (e). That rule subjects retailers to liability only if the product contains a manufacturing defect or if the retailer fails to exercise reasonable care in connection with distribution of the drug or medical device. In so limiting the liability of intermediary parties, courts have held that they should be permitted to rely on the special expertise of manufacturers, prescribing and treating health-care providers, and governmental regulatory agencies. They have also emphasized the needs of medical patients to have ready access to prescription drugs at reasonable prices.

Traditionally, pharmacists are not held liable for injuries as long as a prescription is accurately filled. See, e.g., Johnson v. Walgreen, Co., 675 So. 2d 1036 (Fla. Dist. Ct. App. 1996); Morgan v. Wal-Mart Stores, Inc., 30 S.W.3d 455 (Tex. App. 2000). Pharmacists may also have a duty to be alert for obvious errors on the face of the prescription. See, e.g., Powers v. Thobani, 903 So. 2d 275 (Fla. Dist. Ct. App. 2005) (reversing dismissal of claim that pharmacist was negligent for refilling prescriptions that were written too frequently). Horner v. Spalitto, 1 S.W.3d 519 (Mo. Ct. App. 1999) (holding that pharmacist owed a higher standard of care than accurately filling a prescription when prescription called for three times the normal dosage); McKee v. American Home Prods. Corp., 782 P.2d 1045 (Wash. 1989). Courts often rely on the learned intermediary doctrine in finding that patients are expected to rely upon their physicians, not their pharmacists, for warnings. As the *McKee* court reasoned, "[r]equiring the pharmacist to warn of potential risks associated with a drug would interject the pharmacist into the physician-patient relationship and interfere with ongoing treatment." Id. at 712.

However, courts are finding the learned intermediary doctrine less persuasive as pharmacists take on greater responsibilities than merely measuring and dispensing prescriptions, and pharmacists have been found liable for failure to warn drug users under special circumstances. For example, courts may find that pharmacies willfully undertake a duty to warn customers of the dangers associated with the drugs they sell. In Cottam v. CVS Pharmacy, 764 N.E.2d 814 (Mass. Sup. Ct. 2002), the defendant pharmacy had voluntarily distributed a list of potential side effects associated with a certain prescription drug. The pharmacy did not represent that the list was exhaustive. Nonetheless, in affirming judgment on a verdict finding the defendant to have been negligent, the appellate court found that when a pharmacy undertakes to warn customers of some potential side effects of a drug, it undertakes to warn of all known side effects. See also Baker v. Arbor Drug, 544 N.W.2d 727 (Mich. Ct. App. 1996) (finding that a pharmacy undertakes a duty to warn where it advertises the efficacy of its drug interaction computer database in protecting consumers). But see Kasin v. Osco Drug, Inc., 728 N.E.2d 77 (Ill. App. Ct. 2000).

On the more general subject of the liability of manufacturers of prescription drugs, see generally Michael D. Green, Safety as an Element of Pharmaceutical Quality: The Respective Roles of Regulation and Tort Law, 42 St. Louis U. L.J. 163 (1998); James A. Henderson, Jr., Prescription Drug Design Liability Under the Proposed Restatement (Third) of Torts: A Reporter's Perspective, 48 Rutgers L. Rev. 471 (1996); Aaron D. Twerski, Liability for Direct Advertising of Drugs to Consumers: An Idea Whose Time Has Not Come, 33 Hofstra L. Rev. 1149 (2005); Lars Noah, This is Your Products Liability Restatement on Drugs, 74 Brook. L. Rev. 839 (2009).

C. USED PRODUCTS

1. *The Tort Rules Governing Liability*

Crandell v. Larkin and Jones Appliance Co.
334 N.W.2d 31 (S.D. 1983)

DUNN, J.

This is an appeal from a judgment entered by the trial court granting a motion to dismiss a products liability action against a commercial seller of used products. We reverse and remand.

On February 4, 1978, Gloria (Mrs. A. L.) Crandell (appellant) purchased a used Coronado clothes dryer from Larkin and Jones Appliance Company, Inc. (appellee). The dryer, which was displayed on appellee's sales floor, had a tag affixed to it which described the machine as "Larkin and Jones Quality Reconditioned Unit" which was

"Tag-Tested" and "Guaranteed." In addition to these written representations, the salesman assured appellant that the dryer carried a ninety-day guarantee for "workmanship, parts and labor." Appellant purchased the dryer because of the guarantee and the $100 price tag. Appellee apparently delivered and installed the dryer that same day.

Late in the afternoon of February 18, 1978, appellant asked her son to put a blanket in the dryer to dry. Fifteen to twenty minutes later appellant noticed smoke coming through the furnace vents in her bedroom. Appellant ran to the utility room in the basement and saw the room was full of smoke, apparently coming from the dryer. Appellant opened the dryer door with wet towels because flames were coming out the front. Appellant's attempts to smother the flames in the drum with the wet towels was unsuccessful. Appellant then called the fire department. By the time of their arrival, the fire had spread to other areas of the utility room and had also caused significant smoke damage throughout appellant's home. Total damages to appellant's property as a result of the fire were in excess of $25,000.

Several days prior to the fire, appellant noticed the dryer had apparently overheated a load of clothing. To compensate for this, appellant put the heat selector dial on a lower setting and continued to use the dryer. According to appellant, the thought of a fire did not even occur to her.

Fire department personnel testified the sole ignition source of the fire was inside the dryer. Other expert testimony established that the fire originated in the dryer when the blanket being dried became so hot that it ignited.

None of the theories for recovery which were presented to the trial court were accepted. Appellant now appeals, contending the trial court erred in not finding appellee strictly liable and in not finding that appellee breached express and implied warranties. We address each contention in turn.

We adopted the strict liability theory, as set forth in Restatement (Second) of Torts: §402A, in Engberg v. Ford Motor Company, 87 S.D. 196, 205 N.W.2d 104 (1973), and thereby created a new cause of action in tort. Restatement (Second) of Torts §402A neither expressly includes nor excludes commercial sellers of used products from its coverage. Rather, its coverage applies to "one who sells any product." We have not determined whether the strict liability doctrine should be broadened to cover the commercial sale of used products. We now undertake that inquiry.

Courts and commentators disagree as to whether strict liability should apply to a commercial seller of used products. Courts rejecting strict liability for used products have primarily dealt with fact patterns which did not involve guarantees or reconditioned, rebuilt, or recapped products. In Rix v. Reeves, 23 Ariz. App. 243, 245, 532 P.2d 185, 187 (1975), a case involving the sale of a used wheel, the court specifically limited its holding when it stated: "By used products we do not refer to products rebuilt by a manufacturer, nor do we mean to imply that there is never any liability when used products are sold."

More recently the Oregon Supreme Court in Tillman v. Vance Equipment Co., 286 Or. 747, 596 P.2d 1299 (1979), came to the same conclusion in a case involving the sale of a used crane "as is" which was inspected and approved by the purchaser. There, the court was reluctant to hold every commercial used-goods dealer responsible for injuries caused by defects in its goods. The court stated:

> We conclude that holding every dealer in used goods responsible regardless of fault for injuries caused by defects in his goods would not only affect the prices of used goods; it would work a significant change in the very nature of used goods markets. Those markets,

generally speaking, operate on the apparent understanding that the seller, even though he is in the business of selling such goods, makes no particular representation about their quality simply by offering them for sale. *If a* buyer *wants some assurance of quality, he typically either bargains for it in the specific transaction or seeks out a dealer who routinely offers it* (by, for example, providing a guarantee, limiting his stock of goods to those of a particular quality, advertising that his used goods are specially selected, or in some other fashion). The flexibility of this kind of market appears to serve legitimate interests of buyers as well as sellers.

We are of the opinion that the sale of a used product, without more, may not be found to generate the kind of expectations of safety that the courts have held are justifiably created by the introduction of a new product into the stream of commerce. 286 Or. at 755-56, 596 P.2d at 1303-04 (emphasis added, footnote omitted).

We agree with the rationale provided by these courts to the extent it applies to the broad commercial used-product market. We believe, however, that those used-product merchants who rebuild or recondition goods are subject to the strict liability doctrine. The application of strict liability to sellers of used products, who rebuild or recondition those products, helps to protect the reasonable expectations of consumers.

Appellant alleges the trial court erred in finding that recovery was precluded under strict liability because it was not established that the defect caused the accident. . . .

At trial, appellant presented two expert witnesses to testify as to the existence of a defect and the cause of the fire. Both witnesses were professors of electrical engineering at the South Dakota School of Mines and Technology in Rapid City, South Dakota. The witnesses examined the dryer after the fire and prepared a report documenting their findings. That report and their testimony concluded that the clothes dryer was defective. They found that contact points on the thermostats were pitted and in a very deteriorated condition. The witnesses believed that the two thermostats malfunctioned, thereby allowing the heat element to rise to temperatures high enough to cause the blanket to ignite. This evidence, coupled with the knowledge that a properly functioning dryer would not start a blanket on fire, leads us to conclude the dryer was defective. As one of the experts noted: "I don't know how I could reach a conclusion other than the dryer is defective if the thing (blanket) you put in it catches fire."

As to causation, we can find no credible evidence to support the trial court's position that causation was not established. Here, it is undisputed that appellant did not tamper with or misuse the dryer prior to the fire. Expert testimony established that the dryer was defective and identified the exact components, the thermostats, that failed to function properly allowing the temperature inside the drum to reach temperatures high enough to cause a fire. In our view, this evidence goes well beyond the preponderance requirement in establishing causation.

Finally, we look to the requirement that the defect existed when the product was in appellee's hands. Contrary to appellee's assertion, it was not necessary to show appellee created the defect, but only that the defect existed when the product was distributed by and under appellee's control. Evidence produced at trial provides sufficient circumstantial evidence to meet this requirement. First, and most obvious, the fire occurred within two weeks of leaving appellee's hands. Second, one of the experts testified that in his opinion one of the thermostats became inoperative quite some time prior to the fire. In his opinion, the back-up thermostat eventually became so worn that it too failed to function properly. Finally, it was established at trial that the wrong type of thermostats were in the dryer at the time of sale. According to the expert testimony, this improper equipment also contributed to the fire's inception. We believe this evidence establishes the existence of a defect while the product was in the hands of appellee.

All this aside, however, appellee would have us believe that strict liability is negated in this case because appellant assumed the risk by continuing to use the machine after it overheated on one occasion. At the close of trial, appellee moved to amend its pleadings to allege the defense of assumption of the risk. The trial court in its memorandum opinion and findings of fact and conclusions of law specifically excluded the use of this defense theory. Lacking a notice of review, we must conclude this issue is not preserved for appeal. Even if the trial court had approved the use of the assumption of the risk defense, however, there was no credible evidence to support such a defense theory. While appellant acknowledged the dryer on one occasion dried her clothing so that they were "abnormally hot," she simply turned the heat selector to a lower setting. We do not find this an abnormal reaction and cannot imagine that a reasonable person, by so reacting, would thereby assume the risk of a fire starting in the dryer. . . .

For all the reasons set forth above, we reverse the judgment of the trial court and remand this case for entry of a judgment awarding damages in accordance with the stipulation agreed to by the parties.

All the Justices concur.

Restatement (Third) of Torts: Products Liability
(1998)

---

§8. LIABILITY OF COMMERCIAL SELLER OR DISTRIBUTOR OF DEFECTIVE USED PRODUCTS

One engaged in the business of selling or otherwise distributing used products who sells or distributes a defective used product is subject to liability for harm to persons or property caused by the defect if the defect:

> (a) arises from the seller's failure to exercise reasonable care; or
> (b) is a manufacturing defect under §2(a) or a defect that may be inferred under §3 and the seller's marketing of the product would cause a reasonable person in the position of the buyer to expect the used product to present no greater risk of defect than if the product were new; or
> (c) is a defect under §2 or §3 in a used product remanufactured by the seller or a predecessor in the commercial chain of distribution of the used product; or
> (d) arises from a used product's noncompliance under §4 with a product safety statute or regulation applicable to the used product.

A used product is a product that, prior to the time of sale or other distribution referred to in this Section, is commercially sold or otherwise distributed to a buyer not in the commercial chain of distribution and used for some period of time.

NOTE: TORT AND CONTRACT—SOMETHING OLD, SOMETHING NEW

The controversy that swirls around the issue of whether strict liability ought to apply to used products reveals a strange ambivalence that pervades the entire field of products liability. We have already seen that the vast majority of courts have placed products liability firmly within the scope of tort law. Only a small minority draw the doctrinal basis for strict liability from the Uniform Commercial Code. Try as we may, however, it is impossible to totally divorce products liability law from contract law. The fact remains that the buyer of a product is not a stranger to the transaction. The buyer purchases the product for value. Expectations with regard to quality and performance of a product are at least partially, and often significantly, a function of price and other terms. Putting aside express warranties, one has different expectations when purchasing a Rolls Royce than when purchasing a Yugo. To be sure, tort law has triumphed on one important issue: When a new product fails to meet a manufacturer's own standard for product quality it is considered defective. Both the Rolls Royce and the Yugo must be free of manufacturing defects.

When we turn to used products, it is much more difficult to disregard contract norms. First, used products markets tend to be almost perfect. One can, for example, purchase a used car for $100 to $30,000. It is clear that expectations change along the price spectrum. But pinpointing what consumer expectations are at any given price is no easy task. Second, it is far from certain that a commercial seller of used products is in a better position than the buyer to discover latent manufacturing defects or weaknesses that arise from extended product use. Third, there is a real possibility that the imposition of strict liability on commercial sellers of used goods will drive the prices of such products so high that consumers will prefer to buy used products on a private and individual basis from classified advertisements in local newspapers. Since strict liability does not apply to private noncommercial sales, such private sales would not reflect a strict liability price hike. On the other hand, private sellers also lack the resources to make any kind of sophisticated inspection of the products they sell. It would be difficult to make out a case of negligence against a noncommercial seller. The net effect of imposing strict liability on commercial sellers might be to drive purchasers of used goods to buy from less responsible, noncommercial sellers who do not have the expertise to undertake "reasonable inspection." More rather than fewer dangerous used products will reenter the stream of commerce.[2]

Notwithstanding the foregoing arguments, a substantial number of courts do impose strict liability for the sale of used products. See, e.g., Gaumer v. Rossville Truck And Tractor Co., 257 P.3d 292 (Kan. 2011) (after comprehensive survey of authority pro and con, court concludes that Kansas Product Liability Act imposes strict liability on used product sellers). See also Gonzalez v. Rutherford Corp., 881 F. Supp. 829 (E.D.N.Y. 1995); Jordan v. Sunnyslope Appliance Propane & Plumbing Supplies Co., 660 P.2d 1236 (Ariz. Ct. App. 1983); Ferragamo v. Massachusetts Bay Transp. Auth., 481 N.E.2d 477 (Mass. 1985); Turner v. International Harvester Co., 336 A.2d 62 (N.J. Super. Ct. App. Div. 1975); Hovenden v. Tenbush, 529 S.W.2d 302 (Tex. Ct. Civ. App. 1975); Thompson v. Rockford Machine Tool Co., 744 P.2d 357 (Wash. Ct. App. 1987); Nelson by Hibbard v. Nelson Hardware, Inc., 467 N.W.2d 518 (Wis. 1991). Not surprisingly, these cases place heavy emphasis on the ability of the commercial used product seller to spread the risk.

The opposing view denying strict liability is well set forth in Peterson v. Idaho First Nat'l Bank, 791 P.2d 1303, 1306 (Idaho 1990). See also Peterson v. Superior Court,

---

2. For a full exposition of this thesis, see James A. Henderson, Jr., Extending the Boundaries of Strict Products Liability: Implications of the Theory of the Second Best, 128 Pa. L. Rev. 1036 (1980). See also Nelson by Hibbard v. Nelson Hardware, Inc., 467 N.W.2d 518, 529-530 (Wis. 1991).

899 P.2d 905, 914-916 (Cal. 1995); Tillman v. Vance Equip. Co., 596 P.2d 1299 (Or. 1979). The Supreme Court of Oklahoma followed *Tillman* in refusing to apply strict liability doctrine to the seller of a used shuttle bus. Allenberg v. Bentley Hedges Travel Serv., Inc., 22 P.3d 223 (Okla. 2001). In so doing, the court noted that the policy considerations supporting strict liability for manufacturers and distributors of new products did not support liability for sellers of used products. Id. at 230.

A few courts, like *Crandell,* attempt to straddle the line. In a somewhat narrower opinion than *Crandell,* the New Jersey Supreme Court held that strict liability applies to defective repairs or replacement of parts performed by a dealer who sells used products. Realmuto v. Straub Motors, 322 A.2d 440 (N.J. 1974). See also Wynia v. Richard-Ewing Equip. Co., 17 F.3d 1084 (8th Cir. 1994) (applying South Dakota law and finding that *Crandell* is still the governing rule in South Dakota); Peterson v. Lou Bachrodt Chevrolet Co., 329 N.E.2d 785 (Ill. 1975). See generally William L. Humes, Note, Application of Strict Liability in Tort to the Retailers of Used Products: A Proposal, 16 Okla. City U. L. Rev. 373 (1991) (discussing policy considerations of imposing strict liability on used product sellers); Antonio J. Senagore, The Benefits of Limiting Strict Liability for Used-Product Sellers, 30 N. Ill. U. L. Rev. 349 (2010).

2. The Role of Disclaimers in Determining Liability for Used Products

We have set forth the controversy concerning the imposition of strict liability against used product sellers. We have yet to focus on a very practical question. Many, if not most, used product sales are accompanied by disclaimers. The sellers usually sell the products "as is." Should disclaimers between the seller and buyer be honored to negate liability to the buyer or third parties injured by the used product? Your first reaction might well be — have you lost your marbles? The subject under discussion is liability for harm caused by defective products. And everyone knows that disclaimers are not worth the paper they are written on. Well, not so fast. There is a story to be told. At the end of the story you will have to decide whether disclaimers should be given some effect with regard to the sale of used products. But, for starters, why are disclaimers not effective to protect a seller from liability arising from the sale of a new product?

To understand the ins and outs of disclaimers we have no alternative but to set forth several sections of the U.C.C. and the comments thereto.

UNIFORM COMMERCIAL CODE

§2-316. EXCLUSION OR MODIFICATION OF WARRANTIES

(1) Words or conduct relevant to the creation of an express warranty and words or conduct tending to negate or limit warranty shall be construed wherever reasonable as consistent with each other; but subject to the provisions of this Article on parol or extrinsic evidence (Section 2-202) negation or limitation is inoperative to the extent that such construction is unreasonable.

(2) Subject to subsection (3), to exclude or modify the implied warranty of merchantability or any part of it the language must mention merchantability and in case of a writing must be conspicuous, and to exclude or modify any implied warranty of fitness the exclusion must be by a writing and conspicuous. Language to

exclude all implied warranties of fitness is sufficient if it states, for example, that "There are no warranties which extend beyond the description on the face hereof."

(3) Notwithstanding subsection (2)

(a) unless the circumstances indicate otherwise, all implied warranties are excluded by expressions like "as is," "with all faults" or other language which in common understanding calls the buyer's attention to the exclusion of warranties and makes plain that there is no implied warranty; and

(b) when the buyer before entering into the contract has examined the goods or the sample or model as fully as he desired or has refused to examine the goods there is no implied warranty with regard to defects which an examination ought in the circumstances to have revealed to him; and

(c) an implied warranty can also be excluded or modified by course of dealing or course of performance or usage of trade.

(4) Remedies for breach of warranty can be limited in accordance with the provisions of this Article on liquidation or limitation of damages and on contractual modification of remedy (Sections 2-718 and 2-719).

OFFICIAL COMMENT

1. This section is designed principally to deal with those frequent clauses in sales contracts which seek to exclude "all warranties, express or implied." It seeks to protect a buyer from unexpected and unbargained language of disclaimer by denying effect to such language when inconsistent with language of express warranty and permitting the exclusion of implied warranties only by conspicuous language or other circumstances which protect the buyer from surprise. . . . This Article treats the limitation or avoidance of consequential damages as a matter of limiting remedies for breach, separate from the matter of creation of liability under a warranty. If no warranty exists, there is of course no problem of limiting remedies for breach of warranty. Under subsection (4) the question of limitation of remedy is governed by the sections referred to rather than by this section. . . .

§2-302. UNCONSCIONABLE CONTRACT OR CLAUSE

(1) If the court as a matter of law finds the contract or any clause of the contract to have been unconscionable at the time it was made the court may refuse to enforce the contract, or it may enforce the remainder of the contract without the unconscionable clause, or it may so limit the application of any unconscionable clause as to avoid any unconscionable result.

(2) When it is claimed or appears to the court that the contract or any clause thereof may be unconscionable the parties shall be afforded a reasonable opportunity to present evidence as to its commercial setting, purpose and effect to aid the court in making the determination.

OFFICIAL COMMENT

1. This section is intended to make it possible for the courts to police explicitly against the contracts or clauses which they find to be unconscionable. In the past such policing has been accomplished by adverse construction of language, by manipulation of the rules of offer and acceptance or by determinations that the clause is contrary to public policy or to the dominant purpose of the contract. . . . The principle is one of the

prevention of oppression and unfair surprise (Cf. Campbell Soup Co. v. Wentz, 172 F.2d 80 (3d Cir. 1948)) and not of disturbance of allocation of risks because of superior bargaining power. . . .

§2-719. Contractual Modification or Limitation of Remedy

(1) Subject to the provisions of subsections (2) and (3) of this section and of the preceding section on liquidation and limitation of damages,

(a) the agreement may provide for remedies in addition to or in substitution for those provided in this Article and may limit or alter the measure of damages recoverable under this Article, as by limiting the buyer's remedies to return of the goods and repayment of the price or to repair and replacement of non-conforming goods or parts; and

(b) resort to a remedy as provided is optional unless the remedy is expressly agreed to be exclusive, in which case it is the sole remedy.

(2) Where circumstances cause an exclusive or limited remedy to fail of its essential purpose, remedy may be had as provided in this Act.

(3) Consequential damages may be limited or excluded unless the limitation or exclusion is unconscionable. Limitation of consequential damages for injury to the person in the case of consumer goods is prima facie unconscionable but limitation of damages where the loss is commercial is not.

OFFICIAL COMMENT

3. Subsection (3) recognizes the validity of clauses limiting or excluding consequential damages but makes it clear that they may not operate in an unconscionable manner. Actually such terms are merely an allocation of unknown or undeterminable risks. The seller in all cases is free to disclaim warranties in the manner provided in Section 2-316.

What gives? Are disclaimers unconscionable or not? Read carefully §2-316, comment 1 and §2-719, comment 3. Got it? How does U.C.C. §2-302 fit into this picture? If after chewing these sections over you believe that disclaimers of strict liability are OK under the Code, you have some allies. In Ford Motor Co. v. Moulton, 511 S.W.2d 690, 693 (Tenn.), *cert. denied,* 419 U.S. 870 (1974), the Tennessee Supreme Court upheld the validity of a disclaimer even though the claim was for personal injuries arising from a defective steering column. *Moulton is* apparently still in force in Tennessee. See McCullough v. General Motors Corp., 577 F. Supp. 41 (W.D. Tenn. 1982).

But most courts disagree. Starting with Henningsen v. Bloomfield Motors Co., 161 A.2d 69 (N.J. 1960), discussed in Chapter One, supra, tort courts have been decidedly hostile toward disclaimers. In striking down a disclaimer of the implied warranty of merchantability that was part of the standard automobile sale agreement, the *Henningsen* court waxed eloquent:

The gross inequality of bargaining position occupied by the consumer in the automobile industry is thus apparent. There is no competition among the car makers in the area of the express warranty. Where can the buyer go to negotiate for better protection? Such control and limitation of his remedies are inimical to the public welfare and, at the very least, call for great care by the courts to avoid injustice through application of strict common-law principles of freedom of contract. Because there is no competition among the motor vehicle manufacturers with respect to the scope of protection guaranteed to the buyer, there is no incentive on their part to stimulate good will in that field of public relations. Thus, there is lacking a factor existing in more competitive fields, one which tends to guarantee the safe construction of the article sold. Since all competitors operate in the same way, the urge to be careful is not so pressing. . . . 161 A.2d at 87-95.

Strong stuff. Would you feel any different if auto companies or other competitors engaged in a warranty war? Shouldn't you be given the option of purchasing a car with or without a disclaimer, thus enjoying the benefit of a discounted price if you seek to buy the product sans the warranty? Is the *Henningsen* reasoning consistent with §2-302?

In any event, the law is quite clear. Professors White and Summers have it right when they conclude ''that whenever a consumer's blood is spilled, even wild horses could not stop a sympathetic court from plowing through the most artfully drafted and conspicuously printed disclaimer clause in order to grant relief.'' Handbook on the Law of the Uniform Commercial Code 485 (4th ed. 1994). See also Ford Motor Co. v. Tritt, 430 S.W.2d 778 (Ark. 1968); Walsh v. Ford Motor Co., 298 N.Y.S.2d 538 (N.Y. Sup. Ct. 1969); Tuttle v. Kelley-Springfield Tire Co., 585 P.2d 1116 (Okla. 1978).

Restatement (Third) of Torts: Products Liability
(1998)

---

§18. DISCLAIMERS, LIMITATIONS, WAIVERS, AND OTHER CONTRACTUAL EXCULPATIONS AS DEFENSES TO PRODUCTS LIABILITY CLAIMS FOR HARM TO PERSONS

Disclaimers and limitations of remedies by product sellers or other distributors, waivers by product purchasers, and other similar contractual exculpations, oral or written, do not bar or reduce otherwise valid products liability claims against sellers or other distributors of new products for harm to persons.

If you are quite ready to bury disclaimers in personal injury products liability cases altogether, consider the role of disclaimers in used products cases. Assume that a court decides to apply strict liability to used products. Now further assume that the seller has clearly disclaimed liability by selling the product ''as is.'' Should persons injured by the used product have a cause of action against the commercial used product seller? Cf. §8 of the Products Liability Restatement, supra.

Before jumping to conclusions, it is worth taking a moment to consider how courts treat warnings in products liability cases. Both disclaimers and warnings are communications from the seller to the buyer about the product. Warnings have a rather good reputation in products liability law. Manufacturers who are honest and straightforward about a product's performance capabilities are, in general, treated with considerable solicitude. Disclaimers for new products, as noted earlier, have gotten a very bad rap. Why is that?

Warnings convey specific information to a buyer about avoiding risk in using the product. In some cases warnings inform the consumer that there is a basic nonreducible risk that cannot be avoided. In either event, with an eye to a specific set of harms, the consumer is told the limitations of the product. It is a real-world communication, the kind of information that would be conveyed by a good friend or a neighbor. Disclaimers are made of different stuff. They might be taken as a communication by the seller to the buyer that the seller has little confidence in his wares and that the buyer should lower his expectations for product performance. But with new products that just isn't the case. The disclaimer is a legal artifice created by the law of contracts for the seller to walk away from any problems that may arise with regard to the product. Where consumer expectations remain high, notwithstanding the disclaimer, courts are not willing to let lawyer's talk deprive consumers of their legitimate expectations.

But aren't used-product disclaimers somewhat different? When a commercial used-product seller markets a three-year-old product "as is," the seller may be telling the buyer that the product has been subject to significant wear and tear and the buyer ought to have drastically reduced expectations for it. The analogy to a pure no-duty argument in tort is compelling. The disclaimer in this context may be more than a legal artifice. Admittedly, the seller is not in a position to specifically warn about the problems that may arise. The seller does not, in fact, know when and how they may surface. But the communication is not merely lawyer's talk. The seller is, so to speak, rubbing the buyer's nose into the realities of the sale, telling the buyer that he must be on full alert. "It's your baby, not mine."

Having made the distinction, we note its shortcomings. Some used products bear hefty price tags. A two-year-old, low-mileage Cadillac or Lexus may sell for more than many other new cars do. Doesn't price reflect expectations? On the other hand, once the expectations are something less than perfect, should we not allow contract a fairly free hand in working out the equities between the buyer and seller?

This story has a satisfactory ending. Many courts recognize disclaimers for used-product sales. See, e.g., Harber v. Altec Industries Inc. 812 F. Supp. 954 (W.D. Mo.), *aff'd,* 5 F.3d 339 (8th Cir. 1993); LaRosa v. Superior Court, 176 Cal. Rptr. 224 (Cal. Ct. App. 1981) (strict liability inapplicable against seller of used punch press sold "as is" when press malfunctioned and caused personal injuries to plaintiff); Tillman v. Vance Equipment Company, 596 P.2d 1299 (Or. 1979) (strict liability inapplicable in personal injury action against seller of used crane sold "as is" where defect existed at time of manufacture). But some disagree. See, e.g., Gonzalez v. Rutherford Corp., 881 F. Supp. 829 (E.D. N.Y. 1995).

The authors struggled with the issue in drafting §8 of the Products Liability Restatement. Liability for manufacturing defects in used products depends on whether a reasonable person would "expect the used product to present no greater risk of defect than if the product were new." However, rather than giving a disclaimer conclusive effect and thus barring claims for personal injury, comment *k* to §8 takes the position that a disclaimer is a factor which may bear on the reasonable buyer's expectations as to whether the product presents no greater risk of defect than if it were new. An earlier draft had given conclusive effect to disclaimers for used products, but that position was rejected by the ALI membership.

PROBLEM TWENTY-FIVE

Your client, American Alarm Systems Inc. (AAS), manufactures and markets smoke alarms nationally. It advertises its products in trade journals as well as in popular magazines. Recently, AAS sold 1,000 of its Jiffy Smoke Alarm units to General Merchandise, Inc. In the contract of sale, AAS specifically disclaimed all express warranties and the implied warranty of merchantability. In a separate clause AAS agreed to replace any defective smoke alarm and specifically disclaimed any liability for personal injury or other consequential damages. General Merchandise sold 200 of the Jiffy Smoke Alarms to Home Safe, Inc., a large retailer of home safety systems (locks, burglar alarms, smoke alarms, etc.) in Los Alamos, New California. General Merchandise's sale contract with Home Safe was identical to that which AAS had made with General Merchandise.

When the units arrived at Home Safe, they were offered for sale for $35 each. Two units were removed from the boxes and placed on a display shelf. Two months later, after most of the units had been sold, Home Safe put the two display units on special sale for $15. The sign next to the units read "Display Models $35." The $35 was crossed out and $15 was written under it. The sign also said "Before You Take the Unit Home, Test It on Our Smoke Alarm Tester."

Jack Resnick had just moved into a new office and warehouse complex out of which he ran a computer sales and service business. Over the years, Resnick had cultivated several lucrative accounts for which he did data processing. He sold both hardware and software in addition to servicing these data processing accounts. Resnick was always in the market for a bargain. When he saw the two Jiffy Smoke Alarms on sale for $15 at the Home Safe store, he took them off the shelf and tested them on the testing machine. They seemed to be operating properly. He purchased both units and took them to his new place of business, where he installed one in the warehouse and one in the storeroom where he kept the computer discs for the data processing accounts.

On December 4, Resnick was working late in the outer office adjacent to the disc storeroom and a short walk from the warehouse. Around 8:30 P.M. he smelled smoke. He dashed into the warehouse and found it filled with smoke. The alarm was ringing. He ran back into the office to call the fire department, and then ran into the storeroom in which the computer discs were stored, seeking to save as many as he could. The alarm in the storeroom was not ringing, although the storeroom was filled with smoke. He pulled as many of the discs as possible from the storeroom, but finally was forced by the heat and smoke to leave the building. When the fire department came they found him standing across the street, complaining of sharp pains in his chest. He was taken to the hospital, where doctors found serious lung damage from the smoke inhalation.

Resnick's ill-fated attempt to save the computer discs proved to be useless. Most of the discs were destroyed by the heat and smoke. The cost of reproducing the data stored on the destroyed discs will be well over $250,000. In addition, the computer hardware losses exceed $550,000. Some, but not all, of the hardware losses are covered by fire insurance.

Resnick's major factual premise — that the smoke alarm in the storeroom did not sound — will be difficult to refute. It should have sounded well before Resnick smelled smoke. Had it sounded, the noise given off would have been loud enough that Resnick would have certainly heard it, even if he had been sleeping at the time. The alarm in the warehouse appears to have been too far away for Resnick to hear until he entered the warehouse building. The Jiffy Smoke Alarm in the storeroom was substantially destroyed in the fire; it reveals nothing about why it failed to work. AAS is concerned about its potential liability in this case. It is also interested in your opinion as to whether it can recoup potential losses from others in the distributive chain.

authors' dialogue 25

DOUG: Aaron and Jim, how did the used products section in the Products Liability Restatement come about? It's a fairly intricate set of provisions which tells
me there might be a story behind it.

JIM: Ah yes, that one was a challenge. I remember that we alternated responsibility for drafting the used products section. Aaron came up with the first
draft, which applied Sections 1 and 2 to used products, judging them as
though they were new at the time of sale by the commercial used product
seller. At the same time, the seller could disclaim liability in whole or part
even for personal injuries. Our idea was that the standard for judging the
defectiveness of a used product was so fact sensitive — how old was the
product, what condition was it in, and the like — that it was best to let the
parties work it out via contract. We had caselaw that seemed to back us up,
although it was admittedly ambiguous. We had a neat, clean draft that we
thought got the job done by deferring the important decisions to the used
product market.

AARON: And then the advisers came down on us like a ton of bricks. They just
would not accept the idea that disclaimers should be given dispositive
effect. They agreed that the cases showed that the terms of the sales contract, including disclaimer language, should affect the seller's liability, pro
and con. But they insisted that courts should determine defectiveness, not
the parties. I got so upset with their dismissive attitude, I asked Jim to take
over the next draft.

JIM: And I didn't do much better. I got us all bogged down in trying to occupy the
middle ground with a complicated structure that even I had a hard time
understanding. The advisers didn't like that much better than our first draft.
So we took various drafts to the next three Annual Meetings and had lengthy
debates that led to redrafts on top of redrafts.

AARON: I remember at the last Annual Meeting of the Institute at which our
project was scheduled to be considered, when we were looking to get
final approval, we asked the President, Charlie Wright,[3] to announce on
our behalf that the membership could approve §8 or reject it, but that we
had been through 14 or 15 drafts over a three-year period and we were
not going to try our hand again. We thought §8 was a good proposal and
faithful to the cases. But we were burned out on the subject of used
products liability.

JIM: And then the membership approved §8 without further discussion. Go
figure.

---

3. Charles Alan Wright, a world-renowned legal academic at the University of Texas for more than
45 years, was President of the American Law Institute during the Products Liability Restatement
project. He died in 2000, after the Products Restatement had been published.

Based upon the Code sections and comments reproduced supra, prepare a memorandum outlining the legal position of AAS.

D. FOOD, NONPRESCRIPTION DRUGS, AND COSMETICS

1. Food Products

It may seem obvious that one engaged in the business of selling or otherwise distributing food products accompanied by manufacturing, design, or instructional defects can be found strictly liable for resulting harm. Yet, in food cases, it is often unclear whether a harm-causing ingredient constitutes a product defect or not. Consider the California Supreme Court's decision in Mix v. Ingersoll Candy Co., 59 P.2d 144 (Cal. 1936), in which the court directed a verdict for a restauranteur for injuries sustained by a customer who had swallowed a fragment of a chicken bone contained in a chicken pie. Did the presence of the bone in the chicken pie constitute a defect? The court explained, "Bones which are natural to the type of meat served cannot legitimately be called a foreign substance and a consumer who eats meat dishes ought to anticipate and be on his guard against the presence of such bones." Id. The court in *Mix* adopted what came to be known as the "foreign-natural" test for determining whether a harm-causing ingredient contained in food constitutes a defect. A strong majority of courts today, however, rely on the concept of "consumer expectations" instead of the "foreign-natural" test to decide such manufacturing defect cases. See, e.g., Kolarik v. Cory Int'l Corp., 721 N.W.2d 159, 165 (Iowa 2006) (rejecting foreign-natural test for olive pit in stuffed olive). While the naturalness or foreignness of a harmful object will be a relevant consideration in determining reasonable expectations, it will not be controlling. See, e.g., Jackson v. Nestle-Beich, Inc., 589 N.E.2d 547 (Ill. 1992). In that case a plaintiff broke his tooth on a pecan shell imbedded in a chocolate covered pecan candy; the Supreme Court affirmed the reversal of summary judgment for the defendant, holding that the foreign-natural test, which would operate as a complete bar on these facts, should not be applied. See also Rudloff v. Wendy's Rest. of Rochester, Inc., 821 N.Y.S.2d 358, 367 (Buffalo City Ct. 2006) (applying reasonable expectations test, indicating that whether object is foreign to food pertains to "whether the plaintiff should have expected to find it in his or her food").

California, the originator of the foreign-natural test in Mix v. Ingersoll Candy Co., supra, has revisited the issue in a lengthy and prolix opinion. In Mexicali Rose v. Superior Court, 822 P.2d 1292 (Cal. 1992), the court held that:

> The strict foreign-natural test . . . should be rejected as the exclusive test for determining liability when a substance natural to food injures a restaurant patron. We conclude instead that in deciding the liability of a restauranteur for injuries caused by harmful substances in food, the proper tests to be used by the trier of facts are as follows:
>
> If the injury-producing substance is natural to the preparation of the food served, it can be said that it was reasonably expected by its very nature and the food cannot be determined unfit or defective. A plaintiff in such a case has no cause of action in strict liability or implied warranty. If however, the presence of the natural substance is due to a restauranteur's failure to exercise due care in food preparation, the injured patron may sue under a negligence theory.
>
> If the injury-causing substance is foreign to the food served then the injured patron may also state a cause of action in implied warranty and strict liability, and the trier of fact will determine whether the substance (i) could be reasonably expected by the average consumer and (ii) rendered the food unfit or defective. [Id. at 1303.]

Dissenting opinions asserted that the court's decision was badly out of harmony with the vast majority of authority throughout the country, and argued that there was no good reason for not simply applying a consumer expectation test to both foreign and natural substances. See id. at 1304-1316.

Restatement (Third) of Torts: Products Liability
(1998)

§7. Liability of Commercial Seller or Distributor for Harm Caused by Defective Food Products

One engaged in the business of selling or otherwise distributing food products who sells or distributes a food product that is defective under §2, §3, or §4 is subject to liability for harm to persons or property caused by the defect. Under §2(a), a harm-causing ingredient of the food product constitutes a defect if a reasonable consumer would not expect the food product to contain that ingredient.

COMMENT:

a. General applicability of §§2, 3, and 4 to food products. Except for the special problems identified in Comment *b,* liability for harm caused by defects in commercially distributed food products are determined under the same rules generally applicable to non-food products. A food product may contain a manufacturing defect under §2(a), as when a can of peas contains a pebble; may be defectively designed under §2(b), as when the recipe for potato chips contains a dangerous chemical preservative; or may be sold without adequate warnings under §2(c), as when the seller fails to inform consumers that the dye applied to the skins of oranges contains a well-known allergen. Section 3 may allow a plaintiff to reach the trier of fact when, unable to identify the specific defect, the plaintiff becomes violently ill immediately after consuming the defendant's food product and other causes are sufficiently eliminated. And §4 may apply when a commercially distributed food product fails to conform to applicable safety statutes or administrative regulations.

b. The special problem under §2(a). When a plaintiff suffers harm due to the presence in food of foreign matter clearly not intended by the product seller, such as a pebble in a can of peas or the pre-sale spoilage of a jar of mayonnaise, the claim is readily treated under §2(a), which deals with harm caused by manufacturing defects. Food product cases, however, sometimes present unique difficulties when it is unclear whether the ingredient that caused the plaintiff's harm is an unanticipated adulteration or is an inherent aspect of the product. For example, is a one-inch chicken bone in a chicken enchilada, or a fish bone in fish chowder, a manufacturing defect or, instead, an inherent aspect of the product? The analytical problem stems from the circumstance that food products in many instances do not have specific product designs that may be used as a basis for determining whether the offending product ingredient constitutes a departure from design, and is thus a manufacturing defect. Food recipes vary over time, within the same restaurant or other commercial food-preparation facility, from facility to facility, and from locale to locale.

Faced with this indeterminacy, some courts have attempted to rely on a distinction between "foreign" and "natural" characteristics of food products to determine liability. Under that distinction, liability attaches only if the alleged adulteration is foreign rather than natural to the product. Most courts have found this approach inadequate, however. Although a one-inch chicken bone may in some sense be "natural" to a chicken enchilada, depending on the context in which consumption takes place, the bone may still be unexpected by the reasonable consumer, who will not be able to avoid injury, thus rendering the product not reasonably safe. The majority view is that, in this circumstance of uncertainty, the issue of whether a food product containing a dangerous but arguably natural component is defective under §2(a) is to be determined by reference to reasonable consumer expectations within the relevant context of consumption. A consumer expectations test in this context relies upon culturally defined, widely shared standards that food products ought to meet. Although consumer expectations are not adequate to supply a standard for defect in other contexts, assessments of what consumers have a right to expect in various commercial food preparations are sufficiently well-formed that judges and triers of fact can sensibly resolve whether liability should be imposed using this standard.

Restatement §7 has received much support because of its majority stance. See Schafer v. JLC Food Sys., Inc., 695 N.W.2d 570, 575 (Minn. 2005) (following reasonable expectations test in §7). Does the Restatement contradict itself by relying on consumer expectations in §7 but rejecting them as the standard for defective designs generally in §2(b)?

Finally, one interesting area of food-related products liability that is still developing deals with the purveyors of fast food. A few self-described "victims" have brought actions against fast food providers seeking to recover for their fast-food-related ill health under such theories as failure to warn, breach of implied warranty, and misrepresentation. Thus far, however, these lawsuits have had limited success. See Pelman v. McDonald's Corp., 396 F.3d 508 (2d Cir. 2005) (plaintiff alleged sufficient facts to survive 12(b)(6) motion on complaint seeking to recover from McDonald's for deceptive advertisements of its food products). See also Jada J. Fehn, The Assault on Bad Food: Tobacco-Style Litigation As an Element of the Comprehensive Scheme to Fight Obesity, 67 Food & Drug L.J. 65 (2012).

2. Nonprescription Drugs and Cosmetics

Because nonprescription drugs and cosmetics do not fall within the complex scheme of FDA regulation applied to prescription drugs and medical devices, one might expect them to be subject to a products liability regime similar to the system applicable to nonprescription products generally. The surprise comes when one discovers that nonprescription drugs and cosmetics are subjected to a specific set of liability rules all their own. For example, in Kaempfe v. Lehn & Fink Products, 249 N.Y.S.2d 840 (N.Y. App. Div. 1964), aff'd, 231 N.E.2d 294 (N.Y. 1967), the plaintiff sought to recover for injuries suffered from the application of a spray-on deodorant. The product contained aluminum sulfate, which caused the plaintiff to suffer a fairly severe allergic reaction. The deodorant contained no manufacturing defect, and the label on the can stated that the deodorant contained aluminum sulfate. The label also stated that the deodorant was "safe for normal skin." No warning was given that the deodorant might cause allergic reactions in sensitive users. The trial court submitted plaintiff's failure-to-warn claim to the jury, which returned its verdict for the plaintiff. On appeal, the court reversed and ordered judgment for the defendant. Stressing that only one in 150,000 users of the product would suffer such a reaction, the appellate court concluded (249 N.Y.S.2d at 846-847):

> In light of the foregoing, the plaintiff, as the basis for imposing upon defendant a special duty of warning, was bound at the very least to show (1) that she was one of a substantial number or of an identifiable class of persons who were allergic to the defendant's product, and (2) that defendant knew, or with reasonable diligence should have known of the existence of such number or class of persons. There was, however, a failure of proof as to both of these requirements. Furthermore, it does not appear that a special warning here would have been effective for any purpose. . . .
>
> The statement that the product contained a particular sulphate was adequate to warn any and all persons who knew that they had an allergy with respect to the same. As to those persons, an additional express warning not to use the product would serve no purpose. Specific words of caution would be meaningless as to those, such as the plaintiff, who did not know of their allergy to the particular sulphate. The plaintiff's prior use of deodorants containing the particular ingredient did not yield any manifestations of sensitivity and she expected none when she applied the defendant's product. So, it is difficult to see that a special warning in general terms of danger to the infinitesimal few with an allergy would be of any help or have persuaded plaintiff here from the purchase and use of defendant's merchandise. Under the circumstances, the special warning would have been wholly ineffective. And the defendant should not be held negligent in failing to give a warning which would have served no purpose.

In *Daley v. McNeil Consumer Prods. Co.*, 164 F. Supp. 2d 367 (S.D.N.Y. 2001), the plaintiff sued the manufacturer of Lactaid for failure to warn after the plaintiff allegedly suffered an allergic reaction from consuming the product to aid in her digestion of milk. In granting the defendant's motion for summary judgment with respect to the plaintiff's failure-to-warn claim, the court cited *Kaempfe,* supra, noting that there is no duty to warn of potential reactions unless a product contains an ingredient "to which a substantial number of the population are allergic." 164 F. Supp. 2d at 374. See also *Smallwood v. Clairol, Inc.*, 2005 U.S. Dist. LEXIS 2726 (S.D.N.Y. 2005) (summary judgment for defendant because plaintiff produced no evidence of similar reactions in other consumers from hair-coloring product).

For a critique of the "appreciable number" limitation, see David A. Fischer, Products Liability—The Meaning of Defect, 39 Mo. L. Rev. 339, 354-355 (1974). For treatments of the broader issues raised in this section, see generally Page Keeton, Products Liability—Drugs and Cosmetics, 25 Vand. L. Rev. 131 (1972); see also James A. Henderson, Jr., Process Norms in Products Litigation: Liability for Allergic Reactions, 51 U. Pitt. L. Rev. 761 (1990), in which the author concludes that although sudden, unexpected allergic reactions affect victims in much the same ways as do manufacturing defects, the traditional approach of limited liability is appropriate because courts could not cope institutionally with a more robust liability system for allergic reaction injuries.

The Products Liability Restatement addresses these issues in a Comment to §2(c), the basic failure-to-warn provision:

> *k. Warnings: adverse allergic or idiosyncratic reactions.* Cases of adverse allergic or idiosyncratic reactions involve a special subset of products that may be defective because of inadequate warnings. Many of these cases involve nonprescription drugs and cosmetics. However, virtually any tangible product can contain an ingredient to which

some persons may be allergic. Thus, food, nonprescription drugs, toiletries, paint, solvents, building materials, clothing, and furniture have all been involved in litigation to which this Comment is relevant. . . .

The general rule in cases involving allergic reactions is that a warning is required when the harm-causing ingredient is one to which a substantial number of persons are allergic. The degree of substantiality is not precisely quantifiable. Clearly the plaintiff in most cases must show that the allergic predisposition is not unique to the plaintiff. In determining whether the plaintiff has carried the burden in this regard, however, the court may properly consider the severity of the plaintiff's harm. The more severe the harm, the more justified is a conclusion that the number of persons at risk need not be large to be considered "substantial" so as to require a warning. Essentially, this reflects the same risk-utility balancing undertaken in warnings cases generally. But courts explicitly impose the requirement of substantiality in cases involving adverse allergic reactions.

The ingredient that causes the allergic reaction must be one whose danger or whose presence in the product is not generally known to consumers. When both the presence of an allergenic ingredient in the product and the risks presented by such ingredient are widely known, instructions and warnings about that danger are unnecessary. When the presence of the allergenic ingredient would not be anticipated by a reasonable user or consumer, warnings concerning its presence are required. Similarly, when the presence of the ingredient is generally known to consumers, but its dangers are not, a warning must be given.

Finally, as required in Subsection (c), warnings concerning risks of allergic reactions that are not reasonably foreseeable at the time of sale need not be provided. . . .

ILLUSTRATION:

13. XYZ produces an over-the-counter nonprescription medicine containing aspirin, a well-known allergen to which a substantial minority of persons are sensitive. XYZ may reasonably assume that those who are allergic to aspirin are aware of their allergy or that, if they are not aware, warnings of possible allergic reactions would not be heeded. Thus, it is necessary to warn only of the fact that the medicine contains aspirin.

Congress has enacted the Food and Drug Administration Modernization Act, 111 Stat. 2296 (1997), which contains a provision preempting state regulation of nonprescription drug warnings. 21 U.S.C.S. §379s. Under this statute, state and local governments are precluded from creating warning requirements for nonprescription drugs different that those mandated by federal regulation. Although §379s(d) states that "[nothing] in this section shall be construed to modify or otherwise affect any action or the liability of any person under the product liability law of any state," at least one court has interpreted the Act to preempt failure to warn claims. See Green v. BDI Pharmaceuticals, 803 So. 2d 68 (La. Ct. App. 2001). In *Green*, the plaintiffs brought action against the manufacturer of an over-the-counter stimulant alleging that the manufacturer failed to warn of the addictive propensities of its product, which contained epinephrine. The trial court granted the manufacturer's motion for summary judgment, and the appellate court affirmed. The court found that the manufacturer had included all federally required warnings on its label for products containing epinephrine and that the manufacturer should prevail as a matter of law because §379s was intended to preempt state law. The court neglected to discuss §379s(d), which appears to insulate products liability actions from the effects of the statute. It is unclear whether other courts will also find that federal law has preempted failure-to-warn claims regarding nonprescription drugs and cosmetics. See, e.g., Astiana v. Hain Celestial Group, Inc., 783 F.3d 753, 759 (9th Cir. 2015) (holding, in the context of claim that defendant's use of the term "natural" for cosmetics was false and misleading, that the FDCA does not preempt state laws designed to prevent deceptive advertising).

CHAPTER EIGHT

Special Elements of the Products Liability Plaintiff's Recovery

A. RECOVERY FOR PURE EMOTIONAL UPSET

Tort law generally has had more than its share of difficulties in deciding whether to permit recovery for pure emotional upset not caused by physical harm to the victim. Products liability cases have increased the problem exponentially. Unlike garden-variety mental distress cases that involve a small number of victims and injury-triggering events within a limited period of time, generic product defects can affect untold numbers of victims whose injuries may play out over decades.

Before tackling the problems arising from products cases, it is necessary briefly to review the state of the law generally with regard to recovery in tort for emotional upset. Beginning with State Rubbish Collectors Ass'n v. Siliznoff, 240 P.2d 282 (Cal. 1952), most U.S. jurisdictions have recognized a cause of action for the intentional infliction of severe emotional distress not caused by physical harm to the victim. See, e.g., Eckenrode v. Life of Am. Ins. Co., 470 F.2d 1 (7th Cir. 1972).

The cause of action for negligent infliction of emotional distress has had a more checkered history. Several jurisdictions simply refuse to recognize a duty to avoid negligently inflicted emotional distress. See, e.g., Dowty v. Riggs, 385 S.W.3d 117 (Ark. 2010); Boyles v. Kerr, 855 S.W.2d 593 (Tex. 1993). Even courts that recognize a duty have attached some kind of objective filter to limit liability for negligent distress claims. One such approach is to require that plaintiffs demonstrate physical harm resulting from their mental distress in order to bring suit. See, e.g., Sullivan v. Boston Gas Co., 605 N.E.2d 805 (Mass. 1993). In terms of mental distress claims by bystanders who witness a relative being injured by a tortious act, many courts have required that plaintiff's witnessing of the traumatic event be in the so-called "zone of danger." See, e.g., Asaro v. Cardinal Glennon Memorial Hosp., 799 S.W.2d 595 (Mo. 1995); Bovsun v. Sanperi, 461 N.E.2d 843 (N.Y. 1984); Boryszewski v. Burke, 882 A.2d 410 (N.J. App. Div. 2005). Other courts have been more lenient in accommodating plaintiffs' emotional distress claims. See, e.g., Dillon v. Legg, 441 P.2d 912 (Cal. 1968) (rejecting "zone of danger" test and allowing recovery by closely related, eyewitness bystanders); Corgan v. Muehling, 574 N.E.2d 602 (Ill. 1991) (allowing recovery for mental distress to bystander not in zone of danger). In Thing v. La Chusa, 771 P.2d 814 (Cal. 1989), though, the Supreme Court of California held that contemporary viewing of the accident was an absolute prerequisite for bystander recovery. For the most part, these restrictions are well entrenched in most jurisdictions and there does not appear to be a groundswell to adopt more liberal approaches.

The rise of products liability litigation has not significantly disturbed the judiciary's traditional approach to mental distress claims. In fact, the standard product-related mental distress cases often did not differ analytically from the one-on-one negligent mental distress cases. For instance, in Walker v. Clark Equip. Co., 320 N.W.2d 561 (Iowa 1982), the Supreme Court of Iowa recognized plaintiff's right to recover for her distress over watching an allegedly defective forklift crush her brother. In that case, there was little reason to distinguish the role of the manufacturer of the defective product from that of the negligent automobile driver responsible for inflicting mental distress on a sibling-bystander. So long as the plaintiff was entitled to recover for the mental anguish caused by a defendant's negligence, it mattered little whether the horrific sight resulted from products or non-product-related misconduct. See also Wallace v. Parks Corp., 629 N.Y.S.2d 570 (1995) (distinguishing between compensable and non-compensable products liability mental distress claims based on traditional zone-of-danger-test). Some courts, however, are not as quick to engraft traditional mental distress analyses onto products liability claims. See, e.g., Pasquale v. Speed Products Eng'g, 654 N.E.2d 1365 (Ill. 1995) (holding that bystander/witness to his wife's gory death could not recover for his own emotional distress in a strict products liability action, notwithstanding Illinois precedent allowing such recovery in claims based on negligence).

Some products liability cases involve plaintiffs who were more than mere bystanders. The following New York decision presents a particularly vivid example.

Kennedy v. McKesson Co.
448 N.E.2d 1332 (N.Y. 1983)

MEYER, J.

A complaint which alleges that plaintiff, a dentist, delivered to defendants for repair an anesthetic machine he had purchased from them, that defendants were negligent in replacing the color-coded decals on the machine with the result that, intending to administer oxygen to a patient, plaintiff in fact administered nitrous oxide, causing the death of the patient, that as a result plaintiff's mental condition was such that he was unable to carry on his professional work and because of the damage to his reputation was obliged to withdraw from practice states a valid cause of action permitting recovery by plaintiff for such pecuniary loss as may be proved but not permitting recovery for the emotional injury claimed to have resulted. The order of the Appellate Division (88 A.D.2d 785, 451 N.Y.S.2d 530) should, therefore, be modified, with costs to the appellant, to reinstate so much of the complaint as seeks to recover damages for other than emotional injuries and, as so modified, affirmed.

I

The complaint, the sufficiency of which is the subject of this appeal, alleges the following facts: Plaintiff is a dental surgeon. Defendant Hradil is an employee of defendant Norton-Starr, Inc. Norton is a distributor of products of defendant McKesson Company. Plaintiff bought through Hradil a McKesson anesthetic machine. In

September, 1976, he arranged through Hradil and Norton for the overhaul and adjustment of the machine. When the machine was returned the color-coded identification decals for the oxygen and nitrous oxide connections had been reversed and defendants had failed to install, or inform plaintiff that they could install, connectors of different sizes for the oxygen and nitrous oxide which would have prevented improper connection of the machine. On December 10, 1976, plaintiff removed four wisdom teeth from the mouth of a patient and upon completion of the extraction adjusted the machine to administer 100 percent oxygen to the patient. In fact the patient received 100 percent nitrous oxide as a result of which she died. A civil action against plaintiff for damages for wrongful death of the patient resulted, and there was a criminal investigation all of which resulted in plaintiff's mental ill health, damaged his reputation, and caused him permanently to withdraw from practice.

Defendants moved to dismiss the complaint for failure to state a cause of action. Supreme Court held that defendants having breached a duty owed to plaintiff, he was entitled to recover for emotional harm as well as for any pecuniary loss sustained. The Appellate Division reversed and dismissed the complaint holding that no cause of action was stated when emotional harm results indirectly through the reaction of the plaintiff to injury negligently caused to another.

II

Dismissal of the complaint was clearly erroneous, for Becker v. Schwartz, 46 N.Y.2d 401, 413, 413 N.Y.S.2d 895, 386 N.E.2d 807 and Johnson v. State of New York, 37 N.Y.2d 378, 383, 372 N.Y.S.2d 638, 334 N.E.2d 590 both recognized that a plaintiff who states a cause of action in his own right predicated upon a breach of duty flowing from defendant to plaintiff may recover the pecuniary expenses he has borne as a result of that breach.

The more difficult question is whether damages for emotional injury are recoverable. Examination of our decisions involving recovery for emotional harm reveals three distinct lines of cases. The first recognizes that when there is a duty owed by defendant to plaintiff, breach of that duty resulting directly in emotional harm is compensable even though no physical injury occurred. That principle had its beginning in Ferrara v. Galluchio, 5 N.Y.2d 16, 176 N.Y.S.2d 996, 152 N.E.2d 249. That was a malpractice action in which plaintiff recovered from defendant, a specialist in X-ray therapy, for radiodermatitis caused by excessive radiation, the sum of $25,000, which included $15,000 for mental anguish arising from cancerphobia induced by a dermatologist's advice to plaintiff that she should be checked every six months because of the possibility that cancer might develop. We held (at p.21, 176 N.Y.S.2d 996, 152 N.E.2d 249) that "[f]reedom from mental disturbance is now a protected interest in this State" and that the evidence presented a sufficient guarantee of germaneness to permit the jury to pass upon the claim. It was extended in Battalla v. State of New York, 10 N.Y.2d 237, 219 N.Y.S.2d 34, 176 N.E.2d 729 [failure properly to lock ski-lift belt], Johnson v. State of New York, 37 N.Y.2d 378, 372 N.Y.S.2d 638, 334 N.E.2d 590, supra [false information that plaintiff's mother had died] and Lando v. State of New York, 39 N.Y.2d 803, 385 N.Y.S.2d 759, 351 N.E.2d 426 [failure for 11 days to recover plaintiff's daughter's body] to allow recovery for emotional injury by a plaintiff to whom a direct duty was owed, even though unlike plaintiff Ferrara, plaintiffs Battalla, Johnson and Lando incurred no physical injury. At least under the circumstances of those cases, we held, the sophistication of the medical profession and the likelihood of genuine and serious mental distress arising from the circumstances of the case warranted allowing the jury to weed out spurious claims, though there was no contemporaneous physical harm to provide an index of reliability.

The second group of cases has its genesis in Tobin v. Grossman, 24 N.Y.2d 609, 301 N.Y.S.2d 554, 249 N.E.2d 419. The issue there was whether the operator of a motor vehicle who caused injury to plaintiff's two-year-old son owed a duty also to plaintiff on the basis of which she could recover for her injuries due to shock and fear for her child even though she did not view the accident. After extended discussion of foreseeability of the injury, proliferation of claims, fraudulent claims, inconsistency of the zone of danger rule, unlimited liability, unduly burdensome liability, and the difficulty of circumscribing the area of liability, we declined to recognize the claimed duty because "there appears to be no rational way to limit the scope of liability" other than drawing arbitrary distinctions (24 N.Y.2d, at p.618, 301 N.Y.S.2d 554, 249 N.E.2d 419), and "[t]here are too many factors and each too relative to permit creation of only a limited scope of liability or duty" (supra, at p.619, 301 N.Y.S.2d 554, 249 N.E.2d 419). Similar cases are Lafferty v. Manhasset Med. Center Hosp., 54 N.Y.2d 277, 445 N.Y.S.2d 111, 429 N.E.2d 789 dismissing an action by a daughter-in-law who witnessed a negligent blood transfusion of her mother-in-law and participated in the ensuing efforts to save the mother-in-law, and Vaccaro v. Squibb Corp., 52 N.Y.2d 809, 436 N.Y.S.2d 871, 418 N.E.2d 386 dismissing a complaint by the mother of a child born with severe birth defects as the claimed result of the mother's ingestion of a drug, which alleged no physical injury to the mother.

The third branch of the emotional injury decisions involves the violation of a duty to plaintiff which results in physical injury to a third person but only financial or emotional harm or both to the plaintiff. Progenitor in that line is Howard v. Lecher, 42 N.Y.2d 109, 397 N.Y.S.2d 363, 366 N.E.2d 64, in which recovery was sought for the emotional (but not financial, see, supra, 397 N.Y.S.2d 363, 366 N.E.2d 64) injury to the parents of a two-year-old child afflicted with Tay-Sachs disease whom they had had to watch degenerate and die. We held that a complaint which alleged defendant obstetrician's awareness of plaintiffs' eastern European lineage and consequent susceptibility of their offspring to the disease and his failure to take or evaluate a history or to cause proper tests to be made, failed to state a cause of action. Notwithstanding the presence in *Howard* of a duty of the doctor to the parents absent in *Tobin* (supra), we denied recovery on the policy reasoning of *Tobin*. Becker v. Schwartz and Park v. Chessin, 46 N.Y.2d 401, 413 N.Y.S.2d 895, 386 N.E.2d 807, involved claims on behalf of the parents of children born with Down's Syndrome and polycystic kidney disease resulting from claimed similar malpractice of the obstetrician involved. Though we upheld the parents' claim for pecuniary damages resulting from the duty flowing from defendants to them, we refused to permit recovery for psychic or emotional harm because, as in *Howard*, to do so would have "inevitably led to the drawing of artificial and arbitrary boundaries" (46 N.Y.2d, at pp.413-414, 413 N.Y.S.2d 895, 386 N.E.2d 807, quoting from Howard v. Lecher, 42 N.Y.2d, at p.113, 397 N.Y.S.2d 363, 366 N.E.2d 64).

The rule to be distilled from those cases is that there is no duty to protect from emotional injury a bystander to whom there is otherwise owed no duty, and, even as to a participant to whom a duty is owed, such injury is compensable only when a direct, rather than a consequential, result of the breach. The fear and upset induced by being left suspended high above the ground on an insecure ski lift is compensable, but that which results from the death of a patient under the circumstances described in the instant complaint is not. It will not do to argue as did the dissenters below that the injury here was inflicted directly upon plaintiff and the death of the patient was only an unintended result of defendant's breach of duty. The duty in *Howard* and in *Becker* (supra) was as direct and the resulting deaths as unintended as in the present case.

Nor is it an answer to suggest as do the dissenters here that plaintiff seeks recovery not because he observed the patient die but because he was, as a result of defendant's negligence, the very instrument of her death, and that *Becker* can be distinguished by reason of its reference to the mitigating joy of parenting a child "that even an abnormality cannot fully dampen" (46 N.Y.2d, at pp.414-415, 413 N.Y.S.2d 895, 386 N.E.2d 807). The mothers, if not the fathers, involved in *Howard* (supra) and *Becker* were equally, though more painfully because over a much longer period, the cause of death of their infants, and the speculativeness of damage was only one among many of the policy factors considered in *Tobin* in the search for a "rational practical boundary for liability" (24 N.Y.2d, at p.618, 301 N.Y.S.2d 554, 249 N.E.2d 419). Moreover, the dissent's repeated reference to liability to more than one person (at pp.508, 509, 462 N.Y.S.2d 425, 426, 448 N.E.2d 1336, 1337) misconceives the court's holding in this case, which is simply that recovery for breach of duty includes damages for emotional injury only to the extent that that injury results directly rather than consequentially. Thus, had defendant's breach resulted in gases escaping from the machine and ruining a family manuscript or portrait, plaintiff's recovery would be limited to the value of the physical item; recovery of the sentimental or emotional loss consequent upon its destruction would not be permitted (Lake v. Dye, 232 N.Y. 209, 214, 133 N.E. 448; Furlan v. Rayan Photo Works, 171 Misc. 839, 12 N.Y.S.2d 921; Twersky v. Pennsylvania R.R. Co., 152 Misc. 300, 273 N.Y.S. 328; Valentino v. Nasio Studio, 136 Misc. 826).

If the distinction thus drawn appears overfine that is the inevitable result of the fact that the drawing of any line necessarily differentiates between close cases. But to extend the rule as plaintiff argues and as would the dissenters here and below would be not only to ignore stare decisis but also to face Trial Judges and juries with a distinction extremely difficult, if not impossible, to articulate or conceptualize. It would, moreover, be anomalous, allowing recovery for emotional injury by the dentist but denying such recovery to members of the patient's family.

For the foregoing reasons, the order of the Appellate Division should be modified, with costs to appellant, to reinstate so much of the complaint as seeks to recover damages for other than emotional injuries and, as so modified, affirmed.

JASEN, J. (dissenting in part).

I am compelled to dissent because I believe the complaint in this action alleges a valid cause of action not only for pecuniary loss resulting from loss of professional reputation, but also alleges a valid cause of action for emotional injury suffered by a person to whom the defendants owed a duty which lies despite any separate liability that defendants would have to another person also injured by their negligence.

This case is before us on the basis of the defendants' motions to dismiss for failure to state a cause of action. We are thus obligated to give the complaint a liberal construction, assuming the allegations to be true. (Underpinning & Foundation Constructors v. Chase Manhattan Bank, N.A., 46 N.Y.2d 459, 386 N.Y.S.2d 1319, 414 N.E.2d 298; Cohn v. Lionel Corp., 21 N.Y.2d 559, 289 N.Y.S.2d 404, 236 N.E.2d 634.) The threshold question before this court, I believe, is whether or not the necessary elements of a tort have been pleaded — that is, whether facts sufficient to conclude that the defendants owed the plaintiff a duty and they breached that duty, resulting in a foreseeable injury to the plaintiff — are alleged. Assuming that all the necessary elements of a cause of action sounding in tort have been alleged in the complaint, the motion to dismiss must be denied unless the injury plaintiff seeks to recover for is not recognized in this State.

The majority, by allowing the plaintiff to pursue his cause of action for injury to his reputation and the resultant pecuniary loss apparently agrees that the defendants owed the plaintiff a duty which according to the allegations in the complaint was breached. Since the same factual allegations support the cause of action for emotional distress, the plaintiff should also be allowed to continue to pursue that cause of action unless recovery for nonphysical injury is barred by public policy. I can only conclude that the implication of the majority's holding is that a cause of action alleging an injury of emotional distress is no longer cognizable under New York law, at least in those cases where the defendant is also liable to another person for physical injury caused by the same negligent acts.

My disagreement with the majority's conclusion is twofold. In the first instance, I find it logically inconsistent to say that the plaintiff can recover for one type of injury flowing from the breach of a duty owed him, but that he cannot recover for a different type of injury flowing from that same breach. The majority, despite this logical inconsistency, concludes that this result is mandated by this State's policy, as expressed in previous opinions of this court, which limits the scope of duty when three people are involved in a situation causing injury. I do not agree that the precedent of this court or the policy embodied in those decisions does mandate such a result. Indeed, a deference to both policy and stare decisis requires that plaintiff's cause of action for emotional injury not be dismissed.

To my mind, this case is more properly aligned with Battalla v. State of New York, 10 N.Y.2d 237, 219 N.Y.S.2d 34, 176 N.E.2d 729 and its progeny than the line of cases coming under the rationale and policy of Tobin v. Grossman, 24 N.Y.2d 609, 301 N.Y.S.2d 554, 249 N.E.2d 419. The first line of cases recognized liability for emotional injury as a result of the defendant's breach of its duty to the plaintiff. The second line of cases limits liability so that third parties cannot recover for emotional injuries resulting from observing the physical injury sustained by another person as a result of the defendant's breach of the duty owed that other person. This case, I believe, is readily distinguishable from the second line of cases so that this plaintiff should be allowed to pursue his remedy under Battalla v. State of New York (supra). Furthermore, I see no basis for concluding that a third line of cases has developed which arguably bars one plaintiff from recovering for his emotional injuries merely because the tort-feasor is also liable for physical injuries sustained by a third person even when the defendant has breached its duty to both persons.

In Vitolo v. Dow Corning Corp., 634 N.Y.S.2d 362 (N.Y. 1995), a New York trial court considered motions to dismiss the complaint in a case brought by a surgeon who had implanted silicone breast prostheses, manufactured by the defendant, in over 1,800 women between 1978 and 1991. In January 1992, the FDA banned further such use of the silicone implants. Plaintiff alleged that use of the defective implants had adversely affected his business by subjecting him to numerous lawsuits, damaging his professional reputation and significantly distracting him from his occupation by requiring him to testify in pending litigation. Plaintiff additionally sought recovery for the accompanying emotional strain he was forced to bear. The defendant relied on Kennedy v. McKesson Co., supra, in moving to dismiss the plaintiff's claims against the breast implant manufacturer. The plaintiff sought to distinguish *Kennedy* on the ground that the defendant in that case provided a service, whereas here the defendant in this case was a product manufacturer. The trial court, citing *Kennedy*, granted defendant's motion to dismiss in connection with all claims except those based on alleged damage to plaintiff's professional practice and reputation.

B. RECOVERY FOR PURE ECONOMIC LOSS

It is axiomatic that a defendant is liable for all harms to persons or property proximately caused by a product defect. Economic losses flowing from harm to persons or property, such as lost earning capacity or lost rental values, are typically recoverable in tort. "Pure economic loss," on the other hand, is a court's shorthand reference to the situation in which the plaintiff suffers economic loss that does not flow from physical harm to the plaintiff's person or property, such as economic loss caused by a product failing to operate properly (e.g., a faulty fuse causing an assembly line to halt production for several hours). The question here is whether the rules determining recovery for this type of pure economic loss should be governed by contract rather than tort principles.

Pure economic loss has traditionally been recoverable in contract actions, including products actions based on breach of warranty. These are "true" warranty claims under the U.C.C., subject to privity requirements and disclaimers. Almost from the outset of judicial recognition of strict tort liability, courts have been besieged by plaintiffs seeking to recover pure economic loss on the basis of tort rather than only on the basis of breach of warranty. (Newsworthy recent examples have included Toyota's recall troubles and BP's massive Gulf oil spill.) Bearing in mind that the Uniform Commercial Code permits the recovery of consequential economic losses when a warranty has been breached, why have plaintiffs who suffer pure economic loss pressed tort actions? In most cases, plaintiffs are seeking to escape from the negative effects of three code provisions that govern contract actions: (1) the Code statute of limitations that runs in contract actions from the time of delivery of the product, (2) the Code provisions that permit disclaimer of contract warranties or limitation of remedies, or (3) the privity of contract requirement that immunizes nonprivity defendants from liability. These impediments can be avoided if the case sounds in tort; they will remain as good defenses if the case sounds in contract warranty.

Tort statutes of limitations typically begin to run from the time of injury or from the time that a reasonable person should have discovered such injury; contract statutes of limitations run from time of sale. Thus, if the plaintiff can convince a court to "tortify" the claim, an action that would otherwise be time-barred under U.C.C. §2-725(1) (four years from tender of delivery) may still be very much alive. Similarly, "tortification" may aid a plaintiff in escaping contractual disclaimers and limitations on liability. Courts have generally been hostile to disclaimers and limitation of remedies in cases that sound in tort. Finally, privity of contract remains an obstacle in many states for cases that do not have a personal injury component.

The case law and much of the literature on pure economic loss are often difficult to follow. Rather than focusing on the appropriateness of applying the Code rule or the tort rule to a given fact pattern and articulating the policy grounds for so doing, the discussion seems to concern itself with the typology of the injury and/or the injury-producing event. Is the loss more tort-like or contract-like in nature? It often seems that courts are seeking to determine whether, in the world of Platonic forms, the case will be relegated to the room that houses tort cases or the one that houses contract claims.

East River Steamship Corp. v. Transamerica Delaval, Inc.
476 U.S. 858 (1986)

BLACKMUN, J., delivered the opinion of the Court.

In this admiralty case, we must decide whether a cause of action in tort is stated when a defective product purchased in a commercial transaction malfunctions, injuring only the product itself and causing purely economic loss. The case requires us to consider preliminarily whether admiralty law, which already recognizes a general theory of liability for negligence, also incorporates principles of products liability, including strict liability. Then, charting a course between products liability and contract law, we must determine whether injury to a product itself is the kind of harm that should be protected by products liability or left entirely to the law of contracts.

I

In 1969, Seatrain Shipbuilding Corp. (Shipbuilding), a wholly owned subsidiary of Seatrain Lines, Inc. (Seatrain), announced it would build the four oil-transporting supertankers in issue — the T.T. Stuyvesant, T.T. Williamsburgh, T.T. Brooklyn, and T.T. Bay Ridge. Each tanker was constructed pursuant to a contract in which a separate wholly owned subsidiary of Seatrain engaged Shipbuilding. Shipbuilding in turn contracted with respondent, now known as Transamerica Delaval, Inc. (Delaval), to design, manufacture, and supervise the installation of turbines (costing $1.4 million each, see App. 163) that would be the main propulsion units for the 225,000-ton, $125 million, ibid., supertankers. When each ship was completed, its title was transferred from the contracting subsidiary to a trust company (as trustee for an owner), which in turn chartered the ship to one of the petitioners, also subsidiaries of Seatrain. Queensway Tankers, Inc., chartered the Stuyvesant; Kingsway Tankers, Inc., chartered the Williamsburgh; East River Steamship Corp. chartered the Brooklyn; and Richmond Tankers, Inc., chartered the Bay Ridge. Each petitioner operated under a bareboat charter, by which it took full control of the ship for 20 or 22 years as though it owned it, with the obligation afterwards to return the ship to the real owner. Each charterer assumed responsibility for the cost of any repairs to the ships.

The Stuyvesant sailed on its maiden voyage in late July 1977. On December 11 of that year, as the ship was about to enter the Port of Valdez, Alaska, steam began to escape from the casing of the high-pressure turbine. That problem was temporarily resolved by repairs, but before long, while the ship was encountering a severe storm in the Gulf of Alaska, the high-pressure turbine malfunctioned. The ship, though lacking its normal power, was able to continue on its journey to Panama and then

San Francisco. In January 1978, an examination of the high-pressure turbine revealed that the first-stage steam-reversing ring virtually had disintegrated and had caused additional damage to other parts of the turbine. The damaged part was replaced with a part from the Bay Ridge, which was then under construction. In April 1978, the ship again was repaired, this time with a part from the Brooklyn. Finally, in August, the ship was permanently and satisfactorily repaired with a ring newly designed and manufactured by Delaval.

The Brooklyn and the Williamsburgh were put into service in late 1973 and late 1974, respectively. In 1978, as a result of the Stuyvesant's problems, they were inspected while in port. Those inspections revealed similar turbine damage. Temporary repairs were made, and newly designed parts were installed as permanent repairs that summer. . . .

II

The charterers' second amended complaint, filed in the United States District Court for the District of New Jersey, invokes admiralty jurisdiction. It contains five counts alleging tortious conduct on the part of respondent Delaval and seeks $3.03 million in damages, App. 73, for the cost of repairing the ships and for income lost while the ships were out of service. The first four counts, read liberally, allege that Delaval is strictly liable for the design defects in the high-pressure turbines of the Stuyvesant, the Williamsburgh, the Brooklyn, and the Bay Ridge, respectively. The fifth count alleges that Delaval, as part of the manufacturing process, negligently supervised the installation of the astern guardian valve on the Bay Ridge. The initial complaint also had listed Seatrain and Shipbuilding as plaintiffs and had alleged breach of contract and warranty as well as tort claims. But after Delaval interposed a statute of limitations defense, the complaint was amended and the charterers alone brought the suit in tort. The non-renewed claims were dismissed with prejudice by the District Court. Delaval then moved for summary judgment, contending that the charterers' actions were not cognizable in tort.

The District Court granted summary judgment for Delaval, and the Court of Appeals for the Third Circuit, sitting en banc, affirmed. East River S.S. Corp. v. Delaval Turbine, Inc., 752 F.2d 903 (1985). The Court of Appeals held that damage solely to a defective product is actionable in tort if the defect creates an unreasonable risk of harm to persons or property other than the product itself, and harm materializes. Disappointments over the product's quality, on the other hand, are protected by warranty law. Id., at 908, 909-910. The charterers were dissatisfied with product quality: the defects involved gradual and unnoticed deterioration of the turbines' component parts, and the only risk created was that the turbines would operate at a lower capacity. Id., at 909. See Pennsylvania Glass Sand Corp. v. Caterpillar Tractor Co., 652 F.2d 1165, 1169-1170 (CA3 1981). Therefore, neither the negligence nor the strict liability claims were cognizable.

Judge Garth concurred on "grounds somewhat different," 752 F.2d, at 910, and Judge Becker, joined by Judge Higginbotham, concurred in part and dissented in part. Id., at 913. Although Judge Garth agreed with the majority's analysis on the merits, he found no strict liability claim presented because the charterers had failed to allege unreasonable danger or demonstrable injury.

Judge Becker largely agreed with the majority's approach, but would permit recovery for a "near miss," where the risk existed but no calamity occurred. He felt that the first count, concerning the Stuyvesant, stated a cause of action in tort. The exposure of the ship to a severe storm when the ship was unable to operate at full power due to the defective part created an unreasonable risk of harm.

We granted certiorari to resolve a conflict among the Courts of Appeals sitting in admiralty. . . .

III . . .

B . . .

When torts have occurred on navigable waters within the United States, the Court has imposed an additional requirement of a "maritime nexus" — that the wrong must bear "a significant relationship to traditional maritime activity." See Executive Jet Aviation, Inc. v. City of Cleveland, 409 U.S. 249, 268, 93 S. Ct. 493, 504, 34 L. Ed. 2d 454 (1972); Foremost Ins. Co. v. Richardson, 457 U.S. 668, 102 S. Ct. 2654, 73 L. Ed. 2d 300 (1982). We need not reach the question whether a maritime nexus also must be established when a tort occurs on the high seas. Were there such a requirement, it clearly was met here, for these ships were engaged in maritime commerce, a primary concern of admiralty law. . . .

C . . .

The Courts of Appeals sitting in admiralty overwhelmingly have adopted concepts of products liability, based both on negligence, Sieracki v. Seas Shipping Co., 149 F.2d 98, 99-100 (CA3 1945), *aff'd* on other grounds, 328 U.S. 85, 66 S. Ct. 872, 90 L. Ed. 1099 (1946), and on strict liability, Pan-Alaska Fisheries, Inc. v. Marine Constr. & Design Co., 565 F.2d 1129, 1135 (CA9 1977) (adopting Restatement (Second) of Torts §402A (1965)). Indeed, the Court of Appeals for the Third Circuit previously had stated that the question whether principles of strict products liability are part of maritime law "is no longer seriously contested." Ocean Barge Transport Co. v. Hess Oil Virgin Islands Corp., 726 F.2d 121, 123 (CA3 1984) (citing cases).

We join the Courts of Appeals in recognizing products liability, including strict liability, as part of the general maritime law. This Court's precedents relating to injuries of maritime workers long have pointed in that direction. . . . Our incorporation of products liability into maritime law, however, is only the threshold determination to the main issue in this case.

IV

Products liability grew out of a public policy judgment that people need more protection from dangerous products than is afforded by the law of warranty. See Seely v. White Motor Co., 63 Cal. 2d 9, 15, 45 Cal. Rptr. 17, 21, 403 P.2d 145, 149 (1965). It is clear, however, that if this development were allowed to progress too far, contract law would drown in a sea of tort. See G. Gilmore, The Death of Contract 87-94 (1974). We must determine whether a commercial product injuring itself is the kind of harm against which public policy requires manufacturers to protect, independent of any contractual obligation.

A

The paradigmatic products-liability action is one where a product "reasonably certain to place life and limb in peril," distributed without reinspection, causes bodily injury. See, e.g., MacPherson v. Buick Motor Co., 217 N.Y. 382, 389, 111 N.E. 1050, 1051, 1053 (1916). The manufacturer is liable whether or not it is negligent because "public policy demands that responsibility be fixed wherever it will most effectively reduce the hazards to life and health inherent in defective products that reach the market." Escola v. Coca Cola Bottling Co., 24 Cal. 2d, at 462, 150 P.2d, at 441 (concurring opinion).

For similar reasons of safety, the manufacturer's duty of care was broadened to include protection against property damage. See Marsh Wood Products Co. v. Babcock & Wilcox Co., 207 Wis. 209, 226, 240 N.W. 392, 399 (1932); Genesee County Patrons Fire Relief Assn. v. L. Sonneborn Sons, Inc., 263 N.Y. 463, 469-473, 189 N.E. 551, 553-555 (1934). Such damage is considered so akin to personal injury that the two are treated alike. See Seely v. White Motor Co., 63 Cal. 2d, at 19, 45 Cal. Rptr., at 24, 403 P.2d, at 152.

In the traditional "property damage" cases, the defective product damages other property. In this case, there was no damage to "other" property. Rather, the first, second, and third counts allege that each supertanker's defectively designed turbine components damaged only the turbine itself. Since each turbine was supplied by Delaval as an integrated package, see App. 162-163, each is properly regarded as a single unit. "Since all but the very simplest of machines have component parts, [a contrary] holding would require a finding of 'property damage' in virtually every case where a product damages itself. Such a holding would eliminate the distinction between warranty and strict products liability." Northern Power & Engineering Corp. v. Caterpillar Tractor Co., 623 P.2d 324, 330 (Alaska 1981). The fifth count also alleges injury to the product itself. Before the high-pressure and low-pressure turbines could become an operational propulsion system, they were connected to piping and valves under the supervision of Delaval personnel. See App. 78, 162-163, 181. Delaval's supervisory obligations were part of its manufacturing agreement. The fifth count thus can best be read to allege that Delaval's negligent manufacture of the propulsion system — by allowing the installation in reverse of the astern guardian valve — damaged the propulsion system. Cf. Lewis v. Timco, Inc., 736 F.2d 163, 165-166 (CA5 1984). Obviously, damage to a product itself has certain attributes of a products-liability claim. But the injury suffered — the failure of the product to function properly — is the essence of a warranty action, through which a contracting party can seek to recoup the benefit of its bargain.

B

The intriguing question whether injury to a product itself may be brought in tort has spawned a variety of answers. At one end of the spectrum, the case that created the majority land-based approach, Seely v. White Motor Co., 63 Cal. 2d 9, 45 Cal. Rptr. 17, 403 P.2d 145 (1965) (defective truck), held that preserving a proper role for the law of warranty precludes imposing tort liability if a defective product causes purely monetary harm. See also Jones & Laughlin Steel Corp. v. Johns-Manville Sales Corp., 626 F.2d 280, 287 and n.13 (CA3 1980) (citing cases).

At the other end of the spectrum is the minority land-based approach, whose progenitor, Santor v. A and M Karagheusian, Inc., 44 N.J. 52, 66-67, 207 A.2d 305, 312-313 (1965) (marred carpeting), held that a manufacturer's duty to make nondefective products encompassed injury to the product itself, whether or not the defect created an unreasonable risk of harm. See also LaCrosse v. Schubert, 72 Wis. 2d 38, 44-45, 240 N.W.2d 124, 127-128 (1976). The courts adopting this approach, including the majority of the Courts of Appeals sitting in admiralty that have considered the issue, e.g., Emerson G.M. Diesel, Inc. v. Alaskan Enterprise, 732 F.2d 1468 (CA9 1984), find that the safety and insurance rationales behind strict liability apply equally where the losses are purely economic. These courts reject the Seely approach because they find it arbitrary that economic losses are recoverable if a plaintiff suffers bodily injury or property damage, but not if a product injures itself. They also find no inherent difference between economic loss and personal injury or property damage, because all are proximately caused by the defendant's conduct. Further, they believe recovery for economic loss would not lead to unlimited liability because they think a manufacturer can predict and insure against product failure. See Emerson G.M. Diesel, Inc. v. Alaskan Enterprise, 732 F.2d, at 1474.

Between the two poles fall a number of cases that would permit a products-liability action under certain circumstances when a product injures only itself. These cases attempt to differentiate between "the disappointed users . . . and the endangered ones," Russell v. Ford Motor Co., 281 Or. 587, 595, 575 P.2d 1383, 1387 (1978), and permit only the latter to sue in tort. The determination has been said to turn on the nature of the defect, the type of risk, and the manner in which the injury arose. See Pennsylvania Glass Sand Corp. v. Caterpillar Tractor Co., 652 F.2d 1165, 1173 (CA3 1981) (relied on by the Court of Appeals in this case). The Alaska Supreme Court allows a tort action if the defective product creates a situation potentially dangerous to persons or other property, and loss occurs as a proximate result of that danger and under dangerous circumstances. Northern Power & Engineering Corp. v. Caterpillar Tractor Co., 623 P.2d 324, 329 (1981).

We find the intermediate and minority land-based positions unsatisfactory. The intermediate positions, which essentially turn on the degree of risk, are too indeterminate to enable manufacturers easily to structure their business behavior. Nor do we find persuasive a distinction that rests on the manner in which the product is injured. We realize that the damage may be qualitative, occurring through gradual deterioration or internal breakage. Or it may be calamitous. Compare Morrow v. New Moon Homes, Inc., 548 P.2d 279 (Alaska 1976), with Cloud v. Kit Mfg. Co., 563 P.2d 248, 251 (Alaska 1977). But either way, since by definition no person or other property is damaged, the resulting loss is purely economic. Even when the harm to the product itself occurs through an abrupt, accident-like event, the resulting loss due to repair costs, decreased value, and lost profits is essentially the failure of the purchaser to receive the benefit of its bargain — traditionally the core concern of contract law. See E. Farnsworth, Contracts §12.8, pp. 839-840 (1982).

We also decline to adopt the minority land-based view espoused by Santor and Emerson. Such cases raise legitimate questions about the theories behind restricting products liability, but we believe that the countervailing arguments are more powerful. The minority view fails to account for the need to keep products liability and contract law in separate spheres and to maintain a realistic limitation on damages.

C

Exercising traditional discretion in admiralty, see Pope & Talbot, Inc. v. Hawn, 346 U.S. 406, 409, 74 S. Ct. 202, 204, 98 L. Ed. 143 (1953), we adopt an approach similar to Seely and hold that a manufacturer in a commercial relationship has no duty under either a negligence or strict products-liability theory to prevent a product from injuring itself.

> The distinction that the law has drawn between tort recovery for physical injuries and warranty recovery for economic loss is not arbitrary and does not rest on the 'luck' of one plaintiff in having an accident causing physical injury. The distinction rests, rather, on an understanding of the nature of the responsibility a manufacturer must undertake in distributing his products. [Seely v. White Motor Co., 63 Cal. 2d, at 18, 45 Cal. Rptr., at 23, 403 P.2d, at 151.]

When a product injures only itself the reasons for imposing a tort duty are weak and those for leaving the party to its contractual remedies are strong.

The tort concern with safety is reduced when an injury is only to the product itself. When a person is injured, the "cost of an injury and the loss of time or health may be an overwhelming misfortune," and one the person is not prepared to meet. Escola v. Coca-Cola Bottling Co., 24 Cal. 2d, at 462, 150 P.2d, at 441 (concurring opinion). In contrast, when a product injures itself, the commercial user stands to lose the value of the product, risks the displeasure of its customers who find that the product does not meet their needs, or, as in this case, experiences increased costs in performing a service. Losses like these can be insured. Society need not presume that a customer needs special protection. The increased cost to the public that would result from holding a manufacturer liable in tort for injury to the product itself is not justified. Cf. United States v. Carroll Towing Co., 159 F.2d 169, 173 (CA2 1947).

Damage to a product itself is most naturally understood as a warranty claim. Such damage means simply that the product has not met the customer's expectations, or, in other words, that the customer has received "insufficient product value." See J. White and R. Summers, Uniform Commercial Code 406 (2d ed. 1980). The maintenance of product value and quality is precisely the purpose of express and implied warranties. See U.C.C. §2-313 (express warranty), §2-314 (implied warranty of merchantability), and §2-315 (warranty of fitness for a particular purpose). Therefore, a claim of a nonworking product can be brought as a breach-of-warranty action. Or, if the customer prefers, it can reject the product or revoke its acceptance and sue for breach of contract. See U.C.C. §§2-601, 2-608, 2-612.

Contract law, and the law of warranty in particular, is well suited to commercial controversies of the sort involved in this case because the parties may set the terms of their own agreements. The manufacturer can restrict its liability, within limits, by disclaiming warranties or limiting remedies. See U.C.C. §§2-316, 2-719. In exchange, the purchaser pays less for the product. Since a commercial situation generally does not involve large disparities in bargaining power, cf. Henningsen v. Bloomfield Motors, Inc., 32 N.J. 358, 161 A.2d 69 (1960), we see no reason to intrude into the parties' allocation of the risk.

While giving recognition to the manufacturer's bargain, warranty law sufficiently protects the purchaser by allowing it to obtain the benefit of its bargain. See J. White and R. Summers, supra, ch. 10. The expectation damages available in warranty for purely economic loss give a plaintiff the full benefit of its bargain by compensating for forgone business opportunities. See Fuller and Perdue, The Reliance Interest in Contract Damages: 1, 46 Yale L.J. 52, 60-63 (1936); R. Posner, Economic Analysis of Law §4.8 (3d ed. 1986). Recovery on a warranty theory would give the charterers their repair costs and lost profits, and would place them in the position they would have been in had the turbines functioned properly. See Hawkins v. McGee, 84 N.H. 114, 146 A. 641 (1929). Thus, both the nature of the injury and the resulting damages indicate it is more natural to think of injury to a product itself in terms of warranty.

A warranty action also has a built-in limitation on liability, whereas a tort action could subject the manufacturer to damages of an indefinite amount. The limitation in a contract action comes from the agreement of the parties and the requirement that consequential damages, such as lost profits, be a foreseeable result of the breach. See Hadley v. Baxendale, 9 Ex. 341, 156 Eng. Rep. 145 (1854). In a warranty action where the loss is purely economic, the limitation derives from the requirements of foreseeability and of privity, which is still generally enforced for such claims in a commercial setting. See U.C.C. §2-715; J. White and R. Summers, Uniform Commercial Code 389, 396, 406-410 (2d ed. 1980).

In products-liability law, where there is a duty to the public generally, foreseeability is an inadequate brake. Cf. Petitions of Kinsman Transit Co., 388 F.2d 821 (CA2 1968). See also Perlman, Interference with Contract and Other Economic Expectancies: A Clash of Tort and Contract Doctrine, 49 U. Chi. L. Rev. 61, 71-72 (1982). Permitting recovery for all foreseeable claims for purely economic loss could make a manufacturer liable for vast sums. It would be difficult for a manufacturer to take into account the expectations of persons downstream who may encounter its product. In this case, for example, if the charterers — already one step removed from the transaction — were permitted to recover their economic losses, then the companies that subchartered the ships might claim their economic losses from the delays, and the charterers' customers also might claim their economic losses, and so on. "The law does not spread its protection so far." Robins Dry Dock & Repair Co. v. Flint, 275 U.S. 303, 309, 48 S. Ct. 134, 135, 72 L. Ed. 290 (1927). And to the extent that courts try to limit purely economic damages in tort, they do so by relying on a far murkier line, one that negates the charterers' contention that permitting such recovery under a products-liability theory enables admiralty courts to avoid difficult linedrawing. Cf. Ultramares Corp. v. Touche, 255 N.Y. 170, 174 N.E. 441 (1931); State ex rel. Guste v. M/V Testbank, 752 F.2d 1019, 1046-1052 (CA5 1985) (en banc) (dissenting opinion), *cert. pending*, No. 84-1808. . . .

D . . .

Thus, whether stated in negligence or strict liability, no products-liability claim lies in admiralty when the only injury claimed is economic loss. [Affirmed.]

In Saratoga Fishing Co. v. J.M. Martinac & Co., 520 U.S. 875 (1997), the Supreme Court clarified what constitutes injury to the "product itself" under *East River*, as well as how recovery would be affected if the party seeking damages is not the initial purchaser of the product. In that case, an individual purchased a boat from the defendant-manufacturer and subsequently added certain equipment to the boat. The individual then sold the boat to the plaintiff. Sometime thereafter the boat sank due to an engine-room fire that resulted from a defectively designed hydraulic system supplied to the defendant-manufacturer by a component supplier. Characterizing the additional equipment as "other property" rather than the "product itself," the Supreme Court held that the plaintiff could recover for the physical damage to the equipment added by the initial purchaser explaining that:

> When a Manufacturer places an item in the stream of commerce by selling it to an Initial User, that item is the "product itself" under East River. Items added to the product by the Initial User are therefore "other property," and the Initial User's sale of the product to a Subsequent User does not change these characterizations. [Id. at 1786.]

The Court justified its holding on several grounds. For one, the Court reasoned that to hold the manufacturer liable for damage to the equipment added by the initial purchaser only when the initial purchaser still possessed the product "makes the scope of a manufacturer's liability turn on what seems . . . a fortuity." Id. at 1787. Moreover, the Court noted that subsequent purchasers are not as able as initial purchasers to adjust the risks of harm by contractual agreement, and it is likely more difficult for initial purchasers (consumers) to offer a warranty to subsequent purchasers on used products. Id. Finally, the Court did not agree with the respondents' contention that its holding would expose manufacturers to too great a potential of tort liability. The Court explained that "a host of other tort principles, such as foreseeability, proximate cause, and the 'economic loss' doctrine already do . . . limit liability in important ways." Id. In fact, earlier in the opinion the Court stated that preventing subsequent purchasers from recovering for damage to equipment added by initial purchasers would create a "tort damage immunity beyond that set by any relevant precedent." Id. at 1787.

The Products Liability Restatement adopts the economic loss rule set forth in *East River* and *Saratoga Fishing*.

Restatement (Third) of Torts: Products Liability
(1998)

---

§21. DEFINITION OF HARM TO PERSONS OR PROPERTY: RECOVERY FOR ECONOMIC LOSS

For purposes of the Restatement, harm to persons or property includes economic loss if caused by harm to:

    (a) the plaintiff's person; or

    (b) the person of another when harm to the other interferes with an interest of the plaintiff protected by tort law; or

    (c) the plaintiff's property other than the defective product itself.

COMMENT:

e. Harm to the plaintiff's property other than the defective product itself. A defective product that causes harm to property other than the defective product itself is governed by the rules of this Restatement. What constitutes harm to other property rather than harm to the product itself may be difficult to determine. A product that nondangerously fails to function due to a product defect has clearly caused harm only to itself. A product that fails to function and causes harm to surrounding property has clearly caused harm to other property. However, when a component part of a machine or a system destroys the rest of the machine or system, the characterization process becomes more difficult. When the product or system is deemed to be an integrated whole, courts treat such damage as harm to the product itself. When so characterized, the damage is excluded from the coverage of this Restatement. A contrary holding would require a finding of property damage in virtually every case in which a product harms itself and would prevent contractual rules from serving their legitimate function in governing commercial transactions.

Most courts have adopted the view expressed in *East River* and the Products Liability Restatement and deny recovery when the defective component causes damage to the product into which it is integrated. One court, however, has held that the economic loss rule applies even when there is damage to adjoining property when such damage was foreseeable to the contracting parties at the time they entered into their contractual relationship. Arena Holdings Charitable LLC v. Harman Professional, Inc., 785 F.3d 292 (8th Civ. 2015) (applying North Dakota law).

Some courts reject *East River* and allow recovery for damage to the product itself when such damage is brought about by a sudden and highly dangerous occurrence that endangers the consumer. See, e.g., American Fire & Casualty Co. v. Ford Motor Co., 588 N.W.2d 437 (Iowa 1999) (truck caught fire causing damage to the truck and its contents; court held that economic loss rule applies only to a product that disappoints consumer expectations and does not apply to a defective product that endangers others); Lloyd v. General Motors Corp., 916 A.2d 257 (Md. 2007) (exception to general no-recovery rule where defective product creates a substantial and unreasonable risk of death or personal injury; plaintiff may recover monetary costs of repairing collapse-prone, dangerous seat backs in defendant's vehicles).

Plaintiffs may recover under contract even where they might not in tort. For example, in In re Bisphenol-A Polycarbonate Plastic Prods. Liab. Litig., 2010 U.S. Dist. LEXIS 3904 (W.D. Mo. 2010), the plaintiffs in a class action brought claims for breach of implied warranty of merchantability against manufacturers of baby bottles that contained bisphenol-A, a substance found to pose a risk of adverse health effects, especially to developing infants and children. They did not assert a products liability claim for personal injuries; instead they sought to recover costs for having bought bottles they could no longer use after learning that the bottles contained a harmful chemical. The defendants argued in a motion to dismiss that the plaintiffs' claims for breach of warranty should fail because the plaintiffs did not allege that they were physically injured by the bottles. The court denied the motion, holding that the plaintiffs' claims were sufficient because they asserted both that they paid for the products without knowing they contained a harmful substance and that they would not have bought the products if they had known of the relevant risks.

Plaintiffs have argued that the economic loss rule should be limited to commercial transactions between sophisticated business entities, but consumers who have suffered economic loss should be allowed to bring products liability actions to recover pure economic loss. Courts have not been hospitable to these entreaties. See, e.g., Alejandre v. Bull, 153 P.3d 864 (Wash. 2007).

One class of economic loss cases remains a puzzlement. Owners of buildings that have incurred significant costs when required by law to undertake asbestos abatement have been successful in getting courts to allow them to bring actions in tort for their economic loss. Had the plaintiffs been limited to their U.C.C. warranty actions, they would have been time-barred. Typically, asbestos was installed several decades before a suit was brought, well beyond the four years from tender of delivery provided by U.C.C. §2-725(1). Under tort law the statute of limitations does not generally begin to run until discovery of the injury. Courts have held that asbestos insulation integrated into the building is damage to other property; see, e.g., City of Greenville v. W.R. Grace & Co., 827 F.2d 975 (4th Cir. 1987); Board of Educ. of City of Chicago v. A. C. & S., Inc., 546 N.E.2d 580 (Ill. 1989); see also Richard G. Ausness, Tort Liability for Asbestos Removal Costs, 73 Or. L. Rev. 505 (1994). It is almost impossible to reconcile the finding that damage caused by asbestos fully integrated into a building constitutes damage to "other property" with *East River* and its progeny.

Furthermore, the asbestos cases remain problematic in that they allow recovery for damages before any injury has become manifest. Asbestos causes harm to human lungs and related tissue when tiny fibrous particles circulate in the ambient air. Abatement anticipates that at some time in the future asbestos may crumble and the fibers then released will cause lung cancer. In non-asbestos cases courts have refused to allow recovery in tort even if a product may become dangerous in the future. See, e.g., In re Bridgestone/Firestone, Inc., 288 F.3d 1012, 1016-1017 (7th Cir. 2002) (no tort action for tires that are more prone to blowout in the future); In re General Motors Type III Door Latch Litig. v. General Motors Corp., 2001 WL 103434 (N.D. Ill. 2002) (no recovery in tort for dangerously defective door latches that have yet to cause injury). Accord Ziegelmann v. DaimlerChrysler Corp., 649 N.W.2d 556 (N.D. 2002).

Burglar alarm and fire alarm cases have caused courts to confront the economic loss question in nontraditional settings. In Lobianco v. Property Protection, Inc., 437 A.2d 417 (Pa. 1981), plaintiff sued for the value of jewelry stolen from her home when a burglar alarm system installed by the defendant failed to work. Although the alarm system malfunctioned within the 90-day warranty period, the court refused recovery under the contract because it specifically limited damages to repairs and excluded recovery for loss or damages to possessions, persons, or property. Plaintiff then sought to avoid the contract by couching her cause of action in strict tort liability. The trial court dismissed this claim as well on the ground that the alarm system was "not dangerous and did not cause any physical harm to [plaintiff] or her property." The appellate court spurned the trial court's rationale:

> Suppose that the burglar, or burglars, who took appellant's jewelry had broken the mirror on her dressing table. If we were to accept the lower court's reasoning, and construe "physical harm" as requiring appellant to prove damage to her property, we should conclude that the mirror had suffered physical harm but the jewelry had not. This conclusion would be artificial; it would make the outcome of the case depend on happenstance, with no reference to the reason Section 402A was adopted. [Id. at 422.]

Nonetheless, the court dismissed the strict tort liability claim, finding that the purposes supporting strict liability would not be served by applying §402A to this case:

> . . . Homeowners are not "otherwise defenseless victims" of burglar alarm manufacturers in the same sense that a buyer of an automobile, for example, may be the victim

of the automobile manufacturer. If the property is valuable, the homeowner may insure it. To apply Section 402A to the present case would in practical effect excuse the homeowner from having to insure the property and would shift the risk of its loss to the burglar alarm manufacturer. This would represent a less, not more, equitable allocation of the risk. The homeowner, not the manufacturer, knows what property is in the home, and its value; the manufacturer does not. Even if the manufacturer were to find out what property was in the home before installing the burglar alarm system, the homeowner could, and probably would, add other property, without notice to the manufacturer. As between the homeowner and the manufacturer, the manufacturer is more "defenseless" than the homeowner.

Courts treat smoke alarm failures differently. Thus, in Butler v. Pittway Corp., 770 F.2d 7 (2d Cir. 1985), a homeowner sought to recover when two smoke alarms failed to go off in time to warn the owner of a fire. Plaintiff sued for the damage that would have been avoided had the alarms sounded. The district court held that the damage was economic loss that could not be recovered under strict tort liability. The Second Circuit reversed. The court of appeals found that a smoke alarm that did not go off at the proper time was an unreasonably dangerous product and that the damage suffered constituted "property damage" within the meaning of §402A. Similarly, in Laaperi v. Sears, Roebuck & Co., Inc., 787 F.2d 726 (1st Cir. 1986), the First Circuit affirmed a judgment in excess of $1 million against the seller of a smoke detector for failing to warn the buyer that in the event that a fire resulted from a short circuit, the alarm, which was powered by electrical current, might not function. Three youngsters were killed and one was injured when the alarm failed to sound. It was plaintiff's contention that, had he been warned about this danger, he would have purchased a battery-powered smoke detector as a back-up or taken some other precaution, such as wiring the detector to a circuit of its own, in order to better protect his family in the event of an electrical fire.

PROBLEM TWENTY-SIX

The owners of The King's Table, a popular restaurant maintaining a thriving business in Ithaca, New California, suddenly discovered the presence of polychlorinated biphenyl, or PCB (a toxic chemical which is a known carcinogen), in the basement of their building. The PCB originated in lubricating oil that had clogged gas meters. In order to alleviate the problem, the Consolidated Electric Company (ConEl), who had sold the gas to the restaurant and was responsible for maintaining the gas meters, sent an environmental clean-up team to The King's Table. The members of the clean-up team were dressed in protective clothing and gas masks, and looked like spacemen from Mars. The local newspapers photographed the scene and local television stations covered the event. Marie Witkins, a longtime tenant who lived on the second floor above the restaurant, had contracted cancer shortly before the time of the incident. After learning of the PCB in the basement, Witkins sued ConEl for causing her disease. Apparently as a result of the adverse publicity surrounding the entire episode, business at The King's Table has fallen off sharply. Customers have been scared away from the premises by the PCB risk and the attendant fear of cancer. Although the restaurant will survive the episode, the losses in revenues and goodwill are substantial.

The standard contract between ConEl and its customers, in effect in this case, limits liability to direct losses and disclaims liability for consequential losses. King's Table, Inc., which owns and operates the restaurant, is a closely held family corporation.

Lloyd Rangsten, president and majority stockholder, has contacted a senior partner of the law firm in which you are an associate about bringing an action against ConEl. The partner called you in this morning and told you that she has strong reservations about whether the complaint can withstand attack. But she is desirous of bringing an action if there is even a respectable chance that the case can go forward. Lloyd Rangsten is a long-time friend whom the partner wants to help. She says "Look, even if there is only a 5 percent chance of success I want to pursue it. ConEl may be afraid of another tort action and may be willing to settle to avoid the negative publicity. Lloyd is in bad financial shape and even a $20,000-$30,000 settlement would be meaningful. Find me a hook."

Considering the preceding materials, determine whether there is a plausible cause of action on behalf of Lloyd Rangsten and the other King's Table stockholders against ConEl, and what course of action you would recommend.

Charles W. Wolfram, Modern Legal Ethics*
594-596 (1986)

The "warm zeal" with which a lawyer is to urge a client's interests is part of the very model of an advocate. But professional rules and substantive law impress limits on a lawyer's zeal. To what extent must a lawyer decline to take steps in litigation for a client that are not warranted by the facts or existing law? May a lawyer, for example, file an action against a defendant solely to gain the advantage of the nuisance value of a settlement for some portion of the defendant's anticipated defense costs? Reciprocally, may a lawyer assert a defense if it is legally insupportable but when the plaintiff's travels on the road to ultimate success will require an extended period of time during which the defendant will have the interest-free use of the money sought? Those and similar questions ask whether, and to what extent, a lawyer should serve as a filter of clients' desires to take aggressive moves in litigation.

The lawyer codes have consistently reflected the position that not every client wish to litigate should be furthered by a lawyer. Following 1908 Canon 30, the 1969 code, in DR 7-102(A)(1), provides that a lawyer shall not take action in behalf of a client "when he knows or it is obvious that such action would serve merely to harass or maliciously injure another." Further, under DR 7-102(A)(1) a lawyer is not to assert a claim or defense "unwarranted under existing law" unless it is supported by a good-faith argument for the alternation of existing law. In 1983 Model Rule 3.1 these separate statements are collapsed into a single standard that limits a lawyer to actions or other steps in litigation that are "not frivolous," a standard that explicitly includes actions based on a good-faith argument to alter existing law. Probably in recognition of the attention currently being given to limiting discovery abuses, a separate provision, MR 3.4(d), specifically provides that a lawyer should not make "frivolous" discovery requests or fail to make "reasonably diligent" efforts to comply with proper discovery requests by another party.

Those professional standards can very likely do little to restrain advocates from taking steps that, based on other calculations, seem in the best interests of clients.

*Reprinted from Charles W. Wolfram, Modern Legal Ethics (1986) with permission of the West Publishing Company.

Judicial statements can be found requiring lawyers to question clients closely about doubtful claims, to refuse to assist clients in groundless litigation, and to withdraw if not satisfied that a client's position has merit. But discipline is rarely imposed for violations of the anti-harassment rules and then mainly for moves in litigation that sometimes seem more psychopathic than nasty, that involve patently fraudulent schemes, or that arise in limited areas in which courts express a special concern for lawyer forthrightness.

The approach of the common law, essentially, was to leave a party oppressed by bad-faith litigation to the costly solace of victory and, possibly, to limited tort remedies such as that for malicious abuse of civil process. Asserted fears of chilling litigant access to the courts have thus far prevented much effective relief from such tort-based concepts. Courts also possess a traditional power to enjoin litigation but only in the rare case of extremely vexing and repeated frivolous suits.

The professional standards and the common-law reticence about harassment in litigation have been largely overtaken by recent developments in other arenas, particularly involving fee-shifting for bad-faith litigation. It has become apparent, as complaints about abusive litigation have been heard recently on all sides, that the state of affairs permitted by existing professional and tort regulation is not tolerable. One response has been the judicial development and extension of the doctrine empowering courts to require a party, or the party's lawyer, to pay the legal fees of an adversary oppressed by bad-faith litigation. Another has been the assertion by courts of the power to screen papers and positions of litigants and, on the motion of an aggrieved party or at the court's own behest, to impose sanctions, including fee awards, against a party who engages in harassing or otherwise inappropriate litigation. The sanctions available in those and similar contexts include, in addition, damages, cost sanctions, dismissal or default, and similar preclusion orders against the client.

Note that, as Professor Wolfram observes, not only plaintiffs' lawyers but also defendants' lawyers can be liable for overzealous litigation. A lawyer can also act unreasonably in refusing to pursue a case. Professor Underwood reviews cases in which attorneys were found liable for malpractice for failing to do adequate research before advising that a claim was not likely to be successful and for failing to advise potential clients of an approaching expiration of the statute of limitations. See generally Richard H. Underwood, Taking and Pursuing a Case: Some Observations Regarding "Legal Ethics" and Attorney Accountability, 74 Ky. L.J. 173 (1985-1986).

C. RECOVERY IN TOXIC TORTS LITIGATION: SPECIAL PROBLEMS

1. Increased Risk of Future Injury

The advent of toxic torts litigation presented significant complications for plaintiffs in seeking adequate redress for their injuries. Unlike the standard tort case in which a plaintiff suffers an immediately cognizable injury, exposure to toxic substances often introduces latent risks that may or may not manifest themselves later into potentially fatal or debilitating diseases. The litigation against the manufacturers of asbestos is paradigmatic. Though exposure to asbestos fibers unquestionably enhances a plaintiff's chance of contracting cancer or mesothelioma, the overall possibility of contracting such diseases is remote. Even where a plaintiff suffers from asbestosis, a condition that impairs respiratory functions, the possibility of developing cancer or mesothelioma is relatively small.

In the past, plaintiffs seeking recovery for asbestos-related injuries were placed in a pincers. On the one hand, plaintiffs were pressed by the firmly embedded "single action rule" of torts. This rule, in order to reduce repetitive litigation, requires plaintiffs to consolidate all of their claims for damages against a certain defendant in a single action. Claims for injuries that are not addressed in the litigation are subsequently barred. Plaintiffs who came down with pleural thickening or asbestosis were therefore required to seek recovery for all future harms that might arise. But when they attempted to do so they were faced with the argument that they could not establish that such future harms were probable to eventuate. On the other hand, if they waited until they developed cancer or mesothelioma, they were told that the statute of limitations had begun to run at the onset of pleural thickening or asbestosis. Plaintiffs were thus caught between the Scylla of bringing a timely, yet not fully ripe claim for damages and the Charybdis of bringing a fully matured, yet possibly time-barred action.

Not surprisingly, plaintiffs sought some creative avenues to seek adequate compensation. One such approach was to seek redress for the increased risk of harm a plaintiff faced as a result of exposure to a defendant's toxic substances even though the plaintiff did not currently suffer from a disease or illness. Though courts struggled for a way to allow plaintiffs to recover in full, they were unnerved by the prospect of chipping away at the core principle of tort law that a plaintiff suffer a cognizable injury as a precondition to bringing suit.

Mauro v. Raymark Industries, Inc.
561 A.2d 257 (N.J. 1989)

STEIN, J.

I

Plaintiffs, Roger Mauro (hereinafter plaintiff) and Lois Mauro, his wife, instituted this action against several manufacturers of asbestos products based on injuries allegedly sustained as a result of inhalation of asbestos fibers in the course of Mauro's employment at Ancora State Psychiatric Hospital. Mauro testified that he was employed as a repairman and later as a plumber-steam fitter. From 1964 until the mid-to-late 1970s he used or was exposed to materials containing asbestos manufactured by defendants, including pipe covering and asbestos cement. The exposure occurred when he was ripping out old insulation material and installing new insulation. He testified that defendants' products contained no warnings.

In 1981 plaintiff and his co-workers participated in tests conducted by the New Jersey Department of Health to determine the prevalence of asbestos-related disease among plumbers and steam fitters in state institutions. Plaintiff was informed by Dr.

Peter Gann, the department's Chief of Occupational Medicine, that although the results of his physical examination and lung function test were "normal," he had bilateral thickening of both chest walls and calcification of the diaphragm. Dr. Gann's letter informing plaintiff of his condition stated: "[Y]our exposure to asbestos has been significant and there is some evidence that this exposure may increase the risk of development of lung cancer." . . .

In its charge to the jury at the conclusion of the trial, the trial court rejected Mauro's claim for enhanced risk of developing cancer. . . .

However, the court permitted the jury to consider Mauro's claim for damages caused by emotional distress relating to his fear of developing cancer, provided the jury found that Mauro sustained an asbestos-related injury. The court also permitted the jury to consider Mauro's claim for damages caused by his present medical condition, as well as the cost of future medical surveillance. . . .

The Appellate Division affirmed. . . .

II

It is important to recognize at the outset that the rule of law advocated by plaintiffs, i.e., that tort victims should have a present cause of action for a significant but unquantified enhanced risk of future injury, represents a significant departure from traditional, prevailing legal principles. . . .

The long-standing rule in New Jersey is that prospective damages are not recoverable unless they are reasonably probable to occur. The rationale for adopting this standard was explained by Justice Francis, then sitting in the Appellate Division, in Budden v. Goldstein, 43 N.J. Super. 340, 346-47, 128 A.2d 730 (1957):

> In the admeasurement of damages, it is well known that no recovery can be allowed for possible future consequences of an injury inflicted by a wrongdoer. In order for suggested future results to be includible as an element of damage, it must appear that they are reasonably certain or reasonably probable to follow. . . . [M]any of the authorities throughout the country use the expression "reasonably certain" or "reasonable certainty" as the test and consider "reasonably probable" or "reasonable probability" inadequate and erroneous; others accept the latter statement. Our cases do not seem to have dealt specifically with the question of whether the two have the same significance in relation to quantum of proof, and so may be used interchangeably. It seems to us that in a resolution of the conflicting interests involved, reasonable probability is the just yardstick to be applied. Basically, our view comes down to this: a consequence of an injury which is possible, which may possibly ensue, is a risk which the injured person must bear because the law cannot be administered so as to do reasonably efficient justice if conjecture and speculation are to be used as a measure of damages. On the other hand, a consequence which stands on the plane of reasonable probability, although it is not certain to occur, may be considered in the evaluation of the damage claim against the defendant. In this way, to the extent that men can achieve justice through general rules, a just balance of the warring interests is accomplished.

Although most of the courts that have addressed claims for enhanced-risk damages in toxic-tort cases have applied the general rule requiring proof that the threatened injury be probable, commentators on the subject have generally encouraged recognition of an enhanced-risk cause of action in such cases even if the threat of contingent harm is less than probable, or is unquantified.

[D]efendants asserted at oral argument that plaintiff's claim premised on enhanced risk of disease had been fully adjudicated by submission to the jury of the claims for medical surveillance and emotional distress, contending that there were no other components of the enhanced-risk cause of action. Defendants' argument misconceives the essential nature of a claim predicated on enhanced risk of disease. Simply stated, it is a claim for damages based on a prospective injury, conceptually analogous to the claim of a personal-injury plaintiff with a damaged knee to recover damages for the prospective onset of an arthritic condition that may result from the knee injury. Under our case law, the personal-injury plaintiff conceivably could claim medical-surveillance damages and emotional-distress damages on the basis that the knee injury might cause arthritis, but could not recover damages for the prospective arthritic condition—the "enhanced risk" of arthritis—unless its occurrence was established as a matter of reasonable medical probability. Thus, the fact that Mauro's claims for medical surveillance and emotional distress, attributable to his enhanced risk of cancer, were submitted to the jury does not exhaust his claim for damages based on the prospective occurrence of cancer—the "enhanced risk" of cancer. The question before us is whether that component of the claim should have been submitted to the jury in the absence of evidence establishing the future occurrence of cancer as a reasonable medical probability. We hold that the prospective-cancer component of plaintiff's enhanced-risk claim was properly withheld from the jury.

Although the weight of authority compellingly argues against recognition of an enhanced-risk-of-cancer claim by a plaintiff with an asbestos-related injury absent proof that satisfies the standard of reasonable medical probability, our analysis would be incomplete without consideration of policy arguments that oppose the general rule. Foremost among these is the concern that deferral of the prospective-injury claim may preclude any recovery when the disease eventually occurs because of the substantial difficulties inherent in attempting to prove causation in toxic-tort cases. If the enhanced-risk claim is [invariably] deferred, a plaintiff asserting the claim when the second injury occurs will inevitably confront the defense that the injury did not result from exposure to toxic chemicals but was "the product of intervening events or causes."

Recognition of a claim for significantly enhanced risk of disease would also enhance the tort-law's capacity to deter the improper use of toxic chemicals and substances, thereby addressing the contention that tort law cannot deter polluters who view the cost of proper use or disposal as exceeding the risk of tort liability. . . .

Other considerations weigh in favor of limiting recognition of enhanced-risk claims to those that prove to a reasonable medical probability the likelihood of future injury. Those claims that fail to meet this standard, if presented to juries, would require damage awards for diseases that are prospective, speculative, and less than likely to occur. The more speculative the proof of future disease, the more difficult would be the juries' burden of calculating fair compensation. Inevitably, damage awards would be rendered for diseases that will never occur, exacting a societal cost in the form of higher insurance premiums and higher product costs. . . .

In our view, removal of the statute-of-limitations and single-controversy doctrines as a bar to the institution of suit when the disease for which plaintiff is at risk ultimately occurs enhances the quality of the remedy that tort law can provide in such cases. If the disease never occurs, presumably there will be no claim and no recovery. If it does occur, the resultant litigation will involve a tangible claim for present injury, rather than a speculative claim for future injury. Hence, juries will be better able to award damages in an amount that fairly reflects the nature and severity of the plaintiff's injury. . . .

By adapting the statute-of-limitations and the single-controversy doctrines to the realities of toxic-tort cases, we have ameliorated the potential unfairness of applying the reasonable-probability standard to this type of litigation. Moreover, our case law affords toxic-tort plaintiffs the right to receive full compensation for any provable diminution of bodily health, accommodating all damage claims attributable to present injury and deferring compensation only for disease not yet incurred and not reasonably probable to occur. Recognition of present claims for medical surveillance and emotional distress realistically addresses significant aspects of the present injuries sustained by toxic-tort plaintiffs, and serves as an added deterrent to polluters and others responsible for the wrongful use of toxic chemicals. . . .

Judgment affirmed.

Traditionally, courts have tended to agree with the majority in *Mauro* and have refused recovery for future harm unless the plaintiff has produced evidence for the jury to find that such harm is more probable than not to occur. See, e.g., Pollock v. Johns-Manville Sales Corp., 686 F. Supp. 489 (D.N.J. 1988). While Judge Handler would have permitted the plaintiff in *Mauro* to reach the jury although the chance of future harm was less than 51 percent, he did not state whether the plaintiff should recover 100 percent of the future harm or only a percentage equivalent to the probability that the harm will occur. Perhaps implicit in his opinion is the thought that the rule in *Mauro* would reduce, but not eliminate, the plaintiff's recovery based on the evidence relating to the chance of future harm.

In Patriello v. Kalman, 576 A.2d 474 (Conn. 1990), the Supreme Court of Connecticut overruled an earlier decision that, like *Mauro*, had held that the plaintiff could recover for future harm only if the probability of the harm exceeded 50 percent. The plaintiff's evidence in *Patriello* was that there was an 8 to 16 percent chance of future injury. The court ruled that the plaintiff who suffers a "present injury which has resulted in an increased risk of future harm is entitled to compensation to the extent that the future harm is likely to occur." 576 A.2d at 484. The court made it clear that the plaintiff could recover, not the full amount of the harm should it occur, but a reduced amount based on the probability of future harm. The court did not specifically address the issue of what the plaintiff's recovery should be if the chance of future harm exceeds 50 percent, but dictum indicates that the plaintiff in such a case might recover in full. Can you think of any arguments for reducing recovery in all cases in which the chance of future harm is less than 100 percent?

Because allowing claims for future harm carries the risk of imposing liability on defendants for an injury that never materializes, an increasing number of courts are basing those damages on the percentage probability that the harm will occur. See, e.g., Dillon v. Evanston Hosp., 771 N.E.2d 357(Ill. 2002); Alexander v. Scheid, 726 N.E.2d 272 (Ind. 2000). Arguments for allocating damages between the plaintiff and defendant based on the chances of future injury are made in Joseph H. King, Causation, Valuation and Chance in Personal Injury Torts Involving Preexisting Conditions and Future Consequences, 90 Yale L.J. 1353 (1981); Andrew R. Klein, A Model for Enhanced Risk Recovery in Tort, 56 Wash. & Lee L. Rev. 1173 (1999).

Mauro is representative of a long line of cases that have accommodated toxic tort plaintiffs by eliminating the single-controversy doctrine. In the overwhelming majority of jurisdictions, plaintiffs need no longer fear that a subsequent action for the development of a more serious disease will be barred by a previous suit. So long as they are distinct injuries, a plaintiff will be allowed to seek recovery as illnesses manifest themselves. See, e.g., Carroll v. Owens-Corning Fiberglass Corp., 37 S.W.3d 699 (Ky. 2000) (holding that cancer and asbestosis are separate diseases that independently trigger the running of statutes of limitations relative to their discoveries); Sopha v. Owens-Corning Fiberglas Corp., 601 N.W.2d 627, 642 (Wis. 1999) ("The diagnosis of a malignant asbestos-related condition creates a new cause of action" distinct from the initial development of a nonmalignant asbestos-related condition). But see Troum v. Newark Beth Israel Med. Center, 768 A.2d 177 (N.J. Super Ct. App. Div. 2001) (holding that HIV and AIDS are different stages of "a single pathology"; the statute of limitations begins to run once the plaintiff becomes aware of his or her HIV-positive status). See generally James A. Henderson, Jr. & Aaron D. Twerski, Asbestos Litigation Gone Mad: Exposure-Based Recovery for Increased Risk, Mental Distress, and Medical Monitoring, 53 S.C. L. Rev. 815, 821 n.22 (2002) (listing authority); Andrew R. Klein, Fear of Disease and the Puzzle of Futures Cases in Tort, 35 U.C. Davis L. Rev. 965 (2002).

2. Recovery for Emotional Upset

A revitalized strain of emotional distress claims has arisen from the flood of toxic torts cases that have swamped judicial dockets. Plaintiffs, unable to demonstrate any physical injury arising from their exposure to hazardous substances and barred from recovering for increased risks, have sought to develop a cause of action that would allow them to recover without having to wait until they developed cancer or mesothelioma.

Metro-North Commuter R.R. Co. v. Buckley
521 U.S. 424 (1997)

Justice BREYER, delivered the opinion of the Court.

The basic question in this case is whether a railroad worker negligently exposed to a carcinogen (here, asbestos) but without symptoms of any disease can recover under the Federal Employers' Liability Act (FELA or Act), . . . for negligently inflicted emotional distress. We conclude that the worker before us here cannot recover unless, and until, he manifests symptoms of a disease. . . .

I

Respondent, Michael Buckley, works as a pipefitter for Metro-North, a railroad. For three years (1985-1988) his job exposed him to asbestos for about one hour per working day. During that time Buckley would remove insulation from pipes, often covering himself with insulation dust that contained asbestos. Since 1987, when he attended an "asbestos awareness" class, Buckley has feared that he would develop cancer — and with some cause, for his two expert witnesses testified that, even after taking account of his now-discarded 15-year habit of smoking up to a pack of cigarettes per day, the exposure created an *added* risk of death due to cancer, or to other asbestos-related diseases of either 1 percent to 5 percent (in the view of one of plaintiff's experts), or 1 percent to 3 percent (in the view of another). Since 1989, Buckley has received periodic medical check-ups for cancer and asbestosis. So far, those check-ups have not revealed any evidence of cancer or any other asbestos-related disease.

Buckley sued Metro-North under the FELA, a statute that permits a railroad worker to recover for an "injury . . . resulting . . . from" his employer's "negligence." 45 U.S.C. §51. He sought damages for his emotional distress and to cover the cost of future medical check-ups. His employer conceded negligence, but it did not concede that Buckley had actually suffered emotional distress, and it argued that the FELA did not permit a worker like Buckley, who had suffered no physical harm, to recover for injuries of either sort. After hearing Buckley's case, the District Court dismissed the action. The court found that Buckley did not "offer sufficient evidence to allow a jury to find that he suffered a real emotional injury." . . . And, in any event, Buckley suffered no "physical impact;" hence any emotional injury fell outside the limited set of circumstances in which, according to this Court, the FELA permits recovery. Id., at 620; see Consolidated Rail Corporation v. Gottshall, 512 U.S. 532. . . .

Buckley appealed, and the Second Circuit reversed. 79 F.3d 1337 (1996). Buckley's evidence, it said, showed that his contact with the insulation dust (containing asbestos) was "massive, lengthy, and tangible," id., at 1345, and that the contact "would cause fear in a reasonable person," id., at 1344. Under these circumstances, the court held, the contact was what this Court in *Gottshall* had called a "physical impact" — a "physical impact" that, when present, permits a FELA plaintiff to recover for accompanying emotional distress. The Second Circuit also found in certain of Buckley's workplace statements sufficient expression of worry to permit sending his emotional distress claim to a jury. . . .

II

The critical question before us in respect to Buckley's "emotional distress" claim is whether the physical contact with insulation dust that accompanied his emotional distress amounts to a "physical impact" as this Court used that term in *Gottshall*. In *Gottshall*, an emotional distress case, the Court interpreted the word "injury" in FELA §1, a provision that makes "[e]very common carrier by railroad . . . liable in damages to any person suffering injury while . . . employed" by the carrier if the "injury" results from carrier "negligence." . . .

The Court stated that "common-law principles," where not rejected in the text of the statute, "are entitled to great weight" in interpreting the Act, and that those principles "play a significant role" in determining whether, or when, an employee can recover damages for "negligent infliction of emotional distress." . . .

[I]t recognized that the common law of torts does not permit recovery for negligently inflicted emotional distress *unless* the distress falls within certain specific categories that amount to recovery-permitting exceptions. The law, for example, does permit recovery for emotional distress where that distress accompanies a physical injury. . . . The Court then held that FELA §1, mirroring the law of many States, sometimes permitted recovery "for damages for negligent infliction of emotional distress," . . . and, in particular, it does so where a plaintiff seeking such damages satisfies the common law's "zone of danger" test. It defined that test by stating that the law permits "recovery for emotional injury" by

> "those plaintiffs who sustain a physical impact as a result of a defendant's negligent conduct, or who are placed in immediate risk of physical harm by that conduct." Id., at 547-548 . . . (emphasis added).

The case before us, as we have said, focuses on the italicized words "physical impact." The Second Circuit interpreted those words as including a simple physical contact with a substance that might cause a disease at a future time, so long as the contact was of a kind that would "cause fear in a reasonable person." . . . In our view, however, the "physical impact" to which *Gottshall* referred does not include a simple physical contact with a substance that might cause a disease at a substantially later time — where that substance, or related circumstance, threatens no harm other than that disease-related risk.

First, *Gottshall* cited many state cases in support of its adoption of the "zone of danger" test quoted above. And in each case where recovery for emotional distress was permitted, the case involved a threatened physical contact that caused, or might have caused, immediate traumatic harm. [Citing authority.]

Second, *Gottshall's* language, read in light of this precedent, seems similarly limited. 512 U.S. at 555 . . . ("zone of danger test . . . is consistent with FELA's central focus on physical perils"). . . .

Taken together, language and cited precedent indicate that the words "physical impact" do not encompass every form of "physical contact." And, in particular, they do not include a contact that amounts to no more than an exposure — an exposure, such as that before us, to a substance that poses some future risk of disease and which contact causes emotional distress only because the worker learns that he may become ill after a substantial period of time.

Third, common-law precedent does not favor the plaintiff. Common law courts do permit a plaintiff who suffers from a disease to recover for related negligently caused emotional distress, . . . and some courts permit a plaintiff who exhibits a physical symptom of exposure to recover. . . . But with only a few exceptions, common law courts have denied recovery to those who, like Buckley, are disease and symptom free. [Citing authority.]

Fourth, the general policy reasons to which *Gottshall* referred — in its explanation of why common law courts have restricted recovery for emotional harm to cases falling within rather narrowly defined categories — militate against an expansive definition of "physical impact" here. Those reasons include: (a) special "difficulty for judges and juries" in separating valid, important claims from those that are invalid or "trivial," *Gottshall*, 512 U.S. at 557 . . . (b) a threat of "unlimited and unpredictable liability," ibid.; and (c) the "potential for a flood" of comparatively unimportant, or "trivial," claims, ibid.

To separate meritorious and important claims from invalid or trivial claims does not seem easier here than in other cases in which a plaintiff might seek recovery for typical negligently caused emotional distress. The facts before us illustrate the problem. The District Court, when concluding that Buckley had failed to present "sufficient evidence to allow a jury to find . . . a real emotional injury," pointed out that, apart from Buckley's own testimony, there was virtually no evidence of distress. . . . Indeed, Buckley continued to work with insulating material "even though . . . he could have transferred" elsewhere, he "continued to smoke cigarettes" despite doctors' warnings, and his doctor did not refer him "either to a psychologist or to a social worker." . . . The Court of Appeals reversed because it found certain objective corroborating evidence, namely "workers' complaints to supervisors and investigative bodies." 79 F.3d at 1346. Both kinds of "objective" evidence — the confirming and disconfirming evidence — seem only indirectly related to the question at issue, the existence and seriousness of Buckley's claimed emotional distress. Yet, given the difficulty of separating valid from invalid emotional injury claims, the evidence before us may typify the kind of evidence to which parties and the courts would have to look.

The Court in *Gottshall* made a similar point:

"Testing for the 'genuineness' of an injury alone . . . would be bound to lead to haphazard results. Judges would be forced to make highly subjective determinations concerning the authenticity of claims for emotional injury, which are far less susceptible to objective medical proof than are their physical counterparts. To the extent the genuineness test could limit potential liability, it could do so only inconsistently." 512 U.S. at 552. . . .

More important, the physical contact at issue here — a simple (though extensive) contact with a carcinogenic substance — does not seem to offer much help in separating valid from invalid emotional distress claims. That is because contacts, even extensive contacts, with serious carcinogens are common. See e.g., Nicholson, Perkel & Selikoff, Occupational Exposure to Asbestos: Population at Risk and Projected Mortality — 1980-2030, 3 Am. J. Indust. Med. 259 (1982) (estimating that 21 million Americans have been exposed to work-related asbestos); U.S. Dept. of Health and Human Services, 1 Seventh Annual Report on Carcinogens 71 (1994) (3 million workers exposed to benzene, a majority of Americans exposed outside the workplace); Pirkle, et al., Exposure of the U.S. Population to Environmental Tobacco Smoke, 275 JAMA 1233, 1237 (1996) (reporting that 43% of American children lived in a home with at least one smoker, and 37% of adult nonsmokers lived in a home with at least one smoker or reported environmental tobacco smoke at work). They may occur without causing serious emotional distress, but sometimes they do cause distress, and reasonably so, for cancer is both an unusually threatening and unusually frightening disease. See Statistical Abstract of United States 94 (1996) (23.5 percent of Americans who died in 1994 died of cancer); American Cancer Society, Cancer Facts & Figures — 1997, p.1 (half of all men and one third of all women will develop cancer). The relevant problem, however, remains one of evaluating a claimed emotional reaction to an *increased* risk of dying. An external circumstance — exposure — makes some emotional distress more likely. But how can one determine from the external circumstance of exposure whether, or when, a claimed strong emotional reaction to an *increased* mortality risk (say from 23% to 28%) is reasonable and genuine, rather than overstated — particularly when the relevant statistics themselves are controversial and uncertain (as is usually the case), and particularly since neither those exposed nor judges or juries are experts in statistics? The evaluation problem seems a serious one.

The large number of those exposed and the uncertainties that may surround recovery also suggest what *Gottshall* called the problem of "unlimited and unpredictable liability." Does such liability mean, for example, that the costs associated with a rule of liability would become so great that, given the nature of the harm, it would seem unreasonable to require the public to pay the higher prices that may result? Cf. Priest,

The Current Insurance Crisis and Modern Tort Law, 96 Yale L.J. 1521, 1585-1587 (1987). The same characteristics further suggest what *Gottshall* called the problem of a "flood" of cases that, if not "trivial," are comparatively less important. In a world of limited resources, would a rule permitting immediate large-scale recoveries for widespread emotional distress caused by fear of future disease diminish the likelihood of recovery by those who later suffer from the disease? Cf. J. Weinstein, Individual Justice in Mass Tort Litigation 10-11, 141 (1995); Schuck, The Worst Should Go First: Deferral Registries in Asbestos Litigation, 15 Harv. J. L. & Pub. Pol'y 541 (1992).

We do not raise these questions to answer them (for we do not have the answers), but rather to show that general policy concerns of a kind that have led common law courts to deny recovery for certain classes of negligently caused harms are present in this case as well. That being so, we cannot find in *Gottshall's* underlying rationale any basis for departing from *Gottshall's* language and precedent or from the current common-law consensus. That is to say, we cannot find in *Gottshall's* language, cited precedent, other common law-precedent, or related concerns of policy, a legal basis for adopting the emotional-distress recovery rule adopted by the Court of Appeals.

Buckley raises several important arguments in reply. He points out, for example, that common law courts do permit recovery for emotional distress where a plaintiff has physical symptoms; and he argues that his evidence of exposure and enhanced mortality risk is as strong a proof as an accompanying physical symptom that his emotional distress is genuine.

This argument, however, while important, overlooks the fact that the common law in this area does not examine the genuineness of emotional harm case by case. Rather, it has developed recovery-permitting categories the contours of which more distantly reflect this, and other, abstract general policy concerns. The point of such categorization is to deny courts the authority to undertake a case by case examination. The common law permits emotional-distress recovery for that category of plaintiffs who suffer from a disease (or exhibit a physical symptom), for example, thereby finding a special effort to evaluate emotional symptoms warranted in that category of cases — perhaps from a desire to make a physically injured victim whole or because the parties are likely to be in court in any event. In other cases, however, falling outside the special recovery-permitting categories, it has reached a different conclusion. The relevant question here concerns the validity of a rule that seeks to redefine such a category. It would not be easy to redefine "physical impact" in terms of a rule that turned on, say, the "massive, lengthy, [or] tangible" nature of a contact that amounted to an exposure, whether to contaminated water, or to germ-laden air, or to carcinogen-containing substances, such as insulation dust containing asbestos. But, in any event, for the reasons we have stated . . . we cannot find that the common law has done so. . . .

Finally, Buckley argues that the "humanitarian" nature of the FELA warrants a holding in his favor. We do not doubt that, the FELA's purpose militates in favor of recovery for a serious and negligently caused emotional harm. Cf. *Gottshall*, 512 U.S. at 550, 114 S. Ct., at 2407-2408. But just as courts must interpret that law to take proper account of the harms suffered by a sympathetic individual plaintiff, so they must consider the general impact, on workers as well as employers, of the general liability rules they would thereby create. Here the relevant question concerns not simply recovery in an individual case, but the consequences and effects of *a rule of law that would permit that recovery*. And if the common law concludes that a legal rule permitting recovery here, from a tort law perspective, and despite benefits in *some* individual cases, would on balance cause more harm than good, and if we find that judgment reasonable, we cannot find that conclusion inconsistent with the FELA's humanitarian purpose.

[The Court went on in Part III to consider and ultimately reject Buckley's contention that a lump sum recovery for medical monitoring costs was sustainable even absent exhibitions of symptoms or disease.]

IV

For the reasons stated, we reverse the determination of the Second Circuit, and we remand the case for further proceedings consistent with this opinion.

It is so ordered.

[Justice GINSBURG's concurrence in the judgment in part and dissent in part is omitted.]

Though *Metro-North* held that mere exposure to asbestos was not an "injury" within the meaning of the FELA, the Court did not address what type of physical impact *could* substantiate an award for emotional upset. At least a partial answer to the question was provided by the Court in Norfolk & Western Railway Co. v. Ayers, 538 U.S. 135 (2003). The action was nearly identical to the one brought in *Metro-North*. Plaintiffs, exposed to asbestos fibers, brought an action under the FELA seeking compensation for their fear of developing cancer. However, unlike the plaintiff in *Metro-North* who had merely been exposed to asbestos, the plaintiffs in *Ayers* had actually contracted asbestosis. The majority relied heavily on this difference in sustaining plaintiffs' recovery for emotional upset, recalling that *Metro-North* "sharply distinguished exposure-only plaintiffs from 'plaintiffs who suffer from a disease,' and stated, unambiguously, that '[t]he common law permits emotional distress for [the latter] category.'"

The dissent, authored by Justice Kennedy, criticized the majority opinion for ignoring the realities of the asbestos litigation. Taking note of the FELA's purpose to provide adequate compensation for injured federal employees, the dissent argued that it would be inequitable to provide the plaintiffs substantial monetary relief from a finite and dwindling pool of assets required to satisfy the claims of all potential claimants. Moreover, to allow recovery for the fear of contracting cancer based on the development of asbestosis would be to sanction damages based on little more than speculation:

> The majority . . . would permit recovery because "[t]here is an undisputed relationship between exposure to asbestos sufficient to cause asbestosis, and asbestos-related cancer." . . . To state that some relationship exists without examining whether the relationship is enough to support recovery, however, ignores the central issue in this case. There is a fundamental premise in this case — conceded, as I understand it, by all parties — and it is this: There is no demonstrated causal link between asbestosis and cancer. . . . The incidence of asbestosis correlates with the less-frequent incidence of cancer among exposed workers, . . . but this does not suffice. Correlation is not causation. Absent causation, it is difficult to conceive why asbestosis is any more than marginally more suitable a predicate for recovering for fear of cancer than the fact of mere exposure. This correlation the Court relies upon does not establish a direct link between asbestosis and asbestosis-related cancer, and it does not suffice under common-law precedents as a predicate condition for recovery of damages based upon fear. [Ayers, 538 U.S. at. at 1232.]

As *Ayers* demonstrates, courts are often called upon to perform some rather difficult line-drawing in determining what constitutes the principle "injury" to which parasitic mental distress claims may attach. In cases involving asbestos, some courts have extended the boundary beyond asbestosis to include other asbestos-induced physiological changes in the lungs. See, e.g., McCleary v. Armstrong World Indus., Inc., 913 F.2d 257 (5th Cir. 1990) (applying Texas law) (pleural fibrosis); Herber v. Johns-Manville Corp., 785 F.2d 79 (3d Cir. 1986) (applying New Jersey law) (pleural thickening constitutes sufficient impact to warrant recovery for emotional distress damages). A majority of courts maintain more stringent standards and will not allow recovery for asymptomatic pleural thickening. See, e.g., Simmons v. Pacor, 674 A.2d 232, 237 (Pa. 1996) ("asymptomatic pleural thickening is not a compensable injury which gives rise to cause of action"). For an example of a court employing a similar analysis in relation to a mental distress claim for the fear of contracting AIDS, see Johnson v. Am. Nat'l Red Cross, 578 S.E.2d 106 (Ga. 2003) (holding that plaintiff must establish actual exposure to an infectious agent in order to recover damages for emotional upset).

A line of cases has emerged in which plaintiffs have brought products liability actions seeking recovery for the mental distress associated with exposure to HIV. For example, in Coca-Cola v. Hagan, 813 So. 2d 167 (Fla. Dist. App. Ct. 2002), the plaintiff sued the defendant manufacturer because a bottle of Coca-Cola that the plaintiff consumed appeared to have a used condom inside. Later tests indicated that the substance inside the bottle was, in fact, mold, and the plaintiffs tested negative for HIV six months after the incident. Nevertheless, the plaintiff sought to recover for the emotional strain of fearing for six months that he had contracted HIV. In barring the plaintiff's recovery, the court summarized the majority and minority positions in fear-of-AIDS cases. Under the majority view, the plaintiff must show that the virus was present and that the contact between the material containing the virus and the plaintiff was a medically accepted channel for the transmission of the disease. Under the minority view, the plaintiff is required to show only that it was likely that the virus was present. The *Hagan* court concluded that the plaintiff satisfied neither of these tests. Similarly, in Johnson v. American Nat'l Red Cross, 578 S.E.2d 106 (Ga. 2003), the plaintiff sued the Red Cross for emotional distress damages after it supplied blood for a transfusion that did not meet Red Cross guidelines because the donor had spent an extended period of time in Africa. The court denied recovery because the plaintiff failed to prove "actual exposure" to HIV. See also Parker v. Wellman, 230 Fed. App'x 878 (11th Cir. 2007) (applying Georgia law) (denying recovery for exposure to toxic substance because such exposure, although it increased the risk of future disease, is not an injury in itself).

For a general treatment of damages for emotional distress, see Robert L. Rabin, Pain and Suffering and Beyond: Some Thoughts on Recovery for Intangible Loss, 55 DePaul L. Rev. 359 (2006).

3. *Medical Monitoring*

We have seen that courts have generally been reluctant to grant plaintiffs recovery for latent harms that have not matured into cognizable physical injuries. A strong majority have thus rejected claims for increased risk of harm or for mental distress arising from fear of developing cancer when the plaintiff is asymptomatic. Plaintiffs have, however, succeeded in many jurisdictions in pressing their claim for the costs of medically monitoring their conditions after exposure to highly toxic substances. One of the first cases to recognize a cause of action for medical monitoring was In re Paoli R.R. Yard PCB Litig., 916 F.2d 829 (3d Cir. 1990) (applying Pennsylvania law) (*Paoli I*). In that case, plaintiff railroad workers who were exposed to polychlorinated biphenyls (PCBs) brought an action against a litany of defendants involved either in the manufacture of PCBs or the operation of the railroad yard. Framing the issue as "not whether it is reasonably probable that plaintiffs will suffer harm in the future, but rather whether medical monitoring is, to a reasonable degree of medical certainty, necessary in order to diagnose properly the warning signs of disease," id. at 851, the court articulated several policy reasons for allowing plaintiffs to recover the costs of medical monitoring. Many courts have followed in *Paoli I*'s footsteps since then. The following case from the New York Court of Appeals reflects the conflicting views on this controversial issue.

Caronia v. Philip Morris USA, Inc.
5 N.E.3d 11 (N.Y. 2013)

PIGOTT, J.

The United States Court of Appeals for the Second Circuit has asked us to determine whether this State recognizes an independent equitable cause of action for medical monitoring and, if so, what the elements, appropriate statute of limitations and accrual date are for that particular cause of action.

I

Plaintiffs, who are all over the age of 50, are current and/or former smokers of Marlboro cigarettes with histories of 20 pack-years or more. None of the plaintiffs has been diagnosed with lung cancer, nor are they currently "under investigation by a physician for suspected lung cancer." Plaintiffs commenced this putative class action against Philip Morris USA, Inc. in federal court asserting claims sounding in negligence, strict liability and breach of the implied warranty of merchantability. Plaintiffs requested equitable relief, namely, the creation of a court-supervised program, at Philip Morris's expense, that would provide them with Low Dose CT Scanning of the chest (LDCT), which plaintiffs claim is a type of medical monitoring that assists in the early detection of lung cancer. [The Second Circuit asked the New York Court of Appeals to decide whether an independent cause of action for medical monitoring exists in New York]. The Second Circuit certified the following questions of law:

"(1) Under New York Law, may a current or former longtime heavy smoker who has not been diagnosed with a smoking-related disease, and who is not under investigation by a physician for such a suspected disease, pursue an independent equitable cause of action for medical monitoring for such a disease?

"(2) If New York recognizes such an independent cause of action for medical monitoring,

"(A) What are the elements of that cause of action?

"(B) What is the applicable statute of limitations, and when does that cause of action accrue?" (715 F3d 417, 450 [2013]).

We answer the first certified question in the negative, and decline to answer the second certified question as academic.

II

Plaintiffs do not claim to have suffered physical injury or damage to property. They assert, rather, that they are at an "increased risk" for developing lung cancer and would benefit from LDCT monitoring, which they claim would allow them to discover the existence of cancers at an earlier stage, leading to earlier treatment.

A threat of future harm is insufficient to impose liability against a defendant in a tort context (*see* Prosser & Keeton, Torts §30 at 165 [5th ed 1984]). The requirement that a plaintiff sustain physical harm before being able to recover in tort is a fundamental principle of our state's tort system (*see Kimbar v. Estis*, 1 NY2d 399, 403 [1956] [no action will lie in negligence absent a "resultant injury to plaintiff"]; *see also Voss v. Black & Decker Mfg. Co.*, 59 NY2d 102, 106-107 [1983] [plaintiff must sustain injury or damage before being able to recover under a strict products liability theory]). The physical harm requirement serves a number of important purposes: it defines the class of persons who actually possess a cause of action, provides a basis for the factfinder to determine whether a litigant actually possesses a claim, and protects court dockets from being clogged with frivolous and unfounded claims. . . .

The Appellate Divisions have consistently found that medical monitoring is an element of damages that may be recovered only after a physical injury has been proven, i.e., that it is a form of remedy for an *existing* tort. For instance, in *Abusio v Consolidated Edison Co. of N.Y.*, 656 N.Y.S.2d 371 (2d Dept. 1997), (1997) . . . where the plaintiffs brought a negligence cause of action arising out of exposure to toxins, the Court concluded that the trial court properly set aside the damage awards for emotional distress and medical monitoring, holding that although plaintiffs established that they were exposed to toxins, they failed to establish that they had a "rational basis" for their fear of contracting the disease, i.e., they failed to establish a "clinically demonstrable presence of [toxins] in the plaintiff's body, or some indication of [toxin]-induced disease, i.e., some physical manifestation of [toxin] contamination" 656 N.Y.S.2d 371. . . .

The highest courts in our sister states are divided on whether an independent cause of action for medical monitoring should lie absent any allegation of present physical injury or damage to property. Some have refused to recognize such equitable claims for the imposition of a court-supervised medical monitoring program absent such injury or harm (*see Henry v. Dow Chem. Co.*, 76, 701 NW2d 684, 690 [Mich. 2005] [reaffirming "the principle that a plaintiff must demonstrate a present physical injury to person or property in addition to economic losses that result from that injury in order to recover under a negligence theory" (emphasis omitted)]; *see also Lowe v. Philip Morris USA, Inc.*, 183 P3d 181, 187 [Ore. 2008] ["negligent conduct that results only in a significantly increased risk of future injury that requires medical monitoring does not give rise to a claim for negligence"]). Others, however, have dispensed with the physical injury requirement and have recognized an independent medical monitoring cause of action (*see Donovan v. Philip Morris USA, Inc.*, . . . 914 NE2d 891, 901-903 [2009] [concluding that the cause of action is in tort, not equity]; *Bower v Westinghouse Elec. Corp.*, . . . 522 SE2d 424, 431-433 [1999] [holding that a plaintiff who does not allege a present physical injury may recover future medical monitoring costs]; *Redland Soccer Club, Inc. v. Department of the Army & Dept. of Defense of the U.S.*,

696 A2d 137, 145-146 [1997] [stating that the injury in a medical monitoring claim is an economic one]; *Burns v. Jaquays Min. Corp.*, . . . 752 P2d 28, 33 [Ct App 1988]).

Plaintiffs ask us to follow the second line of cases — *Donovan* in particular — and recognize a cause of action for medical monitoring because Philip Morris's "wrong," i.e., its alleged failure to design a safer cigarette that delivers lower amounts of tar, should not be without a remedy. Although "the desire to provide an avenue to redress wrongs is . . . an important consideration underlying our tort jurisprudence, the recognition that there has been an interference with an interest worthy of protection has been the beginning, not the end, of our analysis" (*Ortega v. City of New York*, 9 NY3d 69, 78 [2007]). This Court undoubtedly has the authority to recognize a new tort cause of action, but that authority must be exercised responsibly, keeping in mind that a new cause of action will have both "foreseeable and unforeseeable consequences, most especially the potential for vast, uncircumscribed liability" (*Madden v. Creative Servs.*, 84 NY2d 738, 746 [1995] [citations omitted]).

> "Tort liability . . . depends on balancing competing interests: the question remains who is legally bound to protect plaintiffs' right at the risk of liability. . . . To identify an interest deserving protection does not suffice to collect damages from anyone who causes injury to that interest . . . Not every deplorable act . . . is redressable in damages" (*id.* at 746 [citation, internal quotation marks and brackets omitted]).

We do not deny that there are significant policy reasons that favor recognizing an independent medical monitoring cause of action. There is certainly "an important public health interest in fostering access to medical testing" for those whose exposure has resulted in an increased risk of disease, and such testing could lead to early detection and treatment, not only mitigating future illness but also reducing the cost to the tortfeasor (*Bower*, . . . 140, 522 S.E.2d at 431, quoting *Potter v. Firestone Tire & Rubber Co.*, . . . 1008, 863 P2d 795, 824 [1993]). However, "the potential systemic effects of creating a new, full-blown, tort law cause of action" cannot be ignored (*Metro-North Commuter R. Co. v. Buckley*, 521 US 424, 443-444 [1997] [refusing to recognize a tort claim for medical monitoring costs where the plaintiff was exposed to asbestos but had not manifested symptoms of a disease]). For instance, dispensing with the physical injury requirement could permit "tens of millions" of potential plaintiffs to recover monitoring costs, effectively flooding the courts while concomitantly depleting the purported tortfeasor's resources for those who have actually sustained damage (*id.* at 442-444). Moreover, it is speculative, at best, whether asymptomatic plaintiffs will ever contract a disease; allowing them to recover medical monitoring costs without first establishing physical injury would lead to the inequitable diversion of money away from those who have actually sustained an injury as a result of the exposure.

From a practical standpoint, it cannot be overlooked that there is no framework concerning how such a medical monitoring program would be implemented and administered. Courts generally lack "the technical expertise necessary to effectively administer a program heavily dependent on scientific disciplines such as medicine, chemistry, and environmental science" (*Henry*, . . . 701 NW2d at 698-699). The legislature is plainly in the better position to study the impact and consequences of creating such a cause of action, including the costs of implementation and the burden on the courts in adjudicating such claims (*see* Schwartz, *Medical Monitoring: The Right Way and the Wrong Way*, 70 Mo. L. Rev. at 382-385).

III

We conclude that the policy reasons set forth above militate against a judicially-created independent cause of action for medical monitoring. Allowance of such a claim, absent any evidence of present physical injury or damage to property, would constitute a significant deviation from our tort jurisprudence. That does not prevent plaintiffs who have in fact sustained physical injury from obtaining the remedy of medical monitoring. Such a remedy has been permitted in this State's courts as consequential damages, so long as the remedy is premised on the plaintiff establishing entitlement to damages on an already existing tort cause of action. Accordingly, we answer the first certified question in the negative, and we decline to answer the second certified question as academic.

Chief Judge LIPPMAN (dissenting).

Rarely are we presented with a case more worthy of the age-old maxim that equity will not suffer a wrong without a remedy. Where, as here, it is within the Court's power to provide a vehicle for plaintiffs to seek equitable relief capable of forestalling profound suffering and death, judicial hesitance and legislative deference only serve to thwart the ends of justice. Because I believe that overall fairness demands that New York recognize an independent equitable medical monitoring cause of action for smokers who can prove that their enhanced risk of cancer was caused by the wrongful conduct of tobacco companies, I dissent and would answer the first certified question in the affirmative.

Relief in the form of medical monitoring has developed in response to "a world in which people regularly encounter environmental toxins, the effects of which are largely unknown" (*Recent Cases, Supreme Judicial Court of Massachusetts Recognizes Cause of Action for Medical Monitoring of Tobacco Users*, 123 Harv. L Rev 1771, 1771 [2010]), and the "growing recognition that exposure to toxic substances . . . may cause substantial injury which should be compensable even if the full effects are not immediately apparent" (*Donovan v. Philip Morris USA, Inc.*, . . . 914 NE2d 891, 901 [2009], citing *Hansen v. Mountain Fuel Supply Co.*, 858 P2d 970, 977 [Utah 1993]). It is undisputed in the scientific community and conceded by defendant Philip Morris — albeit only since 1999 — that cigarettes are a lethal and addictive product which contain cancer-causing carcinogens. Lung cancer is the leading cause of cancer death in the United States, and smoking is responsible for between 80 and 90 percent of lung cancer deaths. Moreover, the high mortality rate in lung cancer patients is largely due to the latent nature of the disease, whose symptoms typically manifest only after the cancer has metastasized, at which point survival rates are in the single digits. However, advances in imaging technology have resulted in the development of Low-Dose Computerized Tomography scanning of the chest (LDCT), a monitoring method widely acknowledged in the medical community as allowing for the detection of lung cancer tumors at a much earlier stage than previously possible. LDCT can detect cancer when it is still localized, at a point when surgery and/or chemotherapy have vastly higher success rates. The significance of this technological advancement cannot be overstated. It is a critical development in our society's medical knowledge that has the potential of transforming lung cancer into a survivable disease.

Furthermore, plaintiffs have submitted expert evidence attesting that Marlboro cigarettes expose smokers to excessive and unreasonably dangerous levels of carcinogens. These experts also contend that, since the time Marlboro cigarettes were first sold, it was technologically feasible for Philip Morris to design a cigarette which delivered a dramatically lower amount of tar but were equally "pleasurable," reducing exposure to carcinogenic agents by 100 fold without reducing the product's "utility."

We are thus presented with a defendant who has allegedly engaged in long-term and continuing misconduct and plaintiffs who, as a proximate result of that wrongdoing, have allegedly reached a risk level threshold for lung cancer at which medical experts believe LDCT screening is "reasonable and necessary" to facilitate early detection so as to avert terrible suffering and near-certain death. Legal recovery eludes these plaintiffs, however, because they do not manifest the kind of physical, symptomatic injury traditionally required for a valid tort claim. Furthermore, plaintiffs are unlikely to manifest symptoms of lung cancer unless and until the disease is at an advanced stage, at which point mortality rates are high and the only treatments available would be aimed at extending their lives, not saving them. . . .

In sum, where a defendant's alleged misconduct causes severe harm, and the opportunity exists to save lives and alleviate suffering, countervailing public policy considerations must be extraordinarily compelling to justify such an "absolute failure of justice" (*Strusburgh v. Mayor of City of N.Y.*, 87 NY 452, 456 [1882]). The majority's justifications fall short of the mark.

In refusing to recognize an independent equitable action for medical monitoring, the majority raises the specter of a flood of frivolous claims brought by asymptomatic plaintiffs, leading to the "inequitable diversion of money away from those who have actually sustained an injury as a result of the exposure" (majority op at 451). This fear is unfounded. As an initial matter, the surest way to safeguard against frivolous claims and limitless liability is to carefully tailor the elements of a cause of action, which is by no means an insurmountable challenge here. The first step is to prescribe an alternatively defined injury requiring definite and identifiable proof. Plaintiffs urge us to define the injury as the enhanced risk of cancer recognized by medical experts according to specifically defined thresholds of age (at least 50 years old) and exposure to carcinogens (at least 20 pack-years). Such an approach neither opens the litigation floodgates nor unduly burdens the courts. Indeed, linking the injury element to standards recognized in the scientific community is a familiar judicial exercise in the context of claims related to latent injury due to exposure to toxic substances. . . .

Beyond circumscribing the alternative injury requirement, the claim's scope would be further curtailed by the other enumerated elements. For instance, plaintiffs would still have the burden of proving defendant's tortious conduct, however defined. . . . Furthermore, despite the uncontroverted medical evidence that nicotine's addictive qualities, combined with the additives in cigarettes which enhance those propensities, put the addictive nature of cigarettes on par with cocaine and heroin (*see e.g. Evans v. Lorillard Tobacco Co.*, 465 Mass 411, 420, 990 NE2d 997, 1009 [2013]), smoking cigarettes undeniably involves a conscious (not to mention legal) act of exposure to carcinogens. Heavy smokers are thus different from individuals whose exposure to toxic substances is wholly inadvertent. In this sense, smokers' claims for medical monitoring could be further restricted by the availability of tort defenses such as contributory negligence.

The majority's position that the proposed cause of action threatens a deluge of frivolous claims is also undermined by the fact that plaintiffs would need to prove: (1) the existence of an efficacious method of screening for early detection which not only (2) conforms with the medical standard of care but (3) is also reasonably necessary given the enhanced risk of cancer (*see e.g. Hansen*, 858 P2d at 979-980).

In this case, these requirements would, among other things, necessitate proof that, had Philip Morris marketed and sold "safer" cigarettes, plaintiffs would have smoked them. A recent case of this Court evidences the difficulty of supplying such proof (*Adamo v Brown & Williamson Tobacco Corp.*, 11 NY3d 545 [2008] [plaintiffs failed to establish tobacco manufacturer's liability in a product liability action where there was no proof that the proposed alternative design (a "safer" cigarette) was equivalent in "function" or "utility" in terms of providing smokers with equivalent satisfaction]). When properly tailored, the cause of action would set a high bar for plaintiffs to meet, dispelling concerns of any onslaught of meritless litigation. . . .

Finally, establishing a court-administered fund to finance a medical surveillance program is a "highly appropriate exercise of the Court's equitable powers" (*Ayers*, 106 NJ at 608, 525 A2d at 608). In reaching a contrary conclusion, the majority claims that courts lack the requisite expertise to administer a program "dependent on scientific disciplines" and that "there is no framework concerning how such a medical monitoring program would be implemented and administered" (majority op at 452). In fact, valuable guidance on the administration of medical monitoring programs has been provided by the courts that have granted such relief. For example, almost 15 years ago a Florida appellate court outlined specific guidelines to follow in running a medical monitoring fund (*see Petito v A.H. Robins Co., Inc.*, 750 So 2d 103, 107 [Fla. Dist. Ct. App. 1999]). In adopting the *Petito* framework, the Court of Appeals of Maryland recently summarized the following steps that may be appropriate for courts to follow if plaintiffs can demonstrate an entitlement to medical monitoring relief:

"(1) appoint a plan administrator; (2) with the administrator's advice, approve an advisory panel of persons qualified and knowledgeable in the relevant medical field or fields to supervise, among other things, the persons who consume or undergo medication and treatment, and select a list of skilled and neutral examining physicians to perform the medical tests; (3) establish a time frame for those eligible to obtain the monitoring; and (4) authorize the plan administrator to pay the reasonable amounts of claims based on submitted reports and findings by the monitoring physicians" (*Exxon Mobil Corp. v Albright*, . . . 71 A3d 30, 81 [2013], citing *Petito*, 750 So 2d at 106).

These and similar guidelines provide useful roadmaps for administering a medical monitoring program.

As the majority opinion in *Caronia* notes courts, disagree as to the wisdom of mandating medical monitoring absent physical manifestation of injury. Thus, in Lewis v. Lead Indus. Ass'n, 793 N.E.2d 869 (Ill. Ct. App. 2003), the court held that an award for medical monitoring was appropriate where plaintiffs alleged that they currently suffered an injury that could not be detected except by future monitoring, but was not appropriate for the purpose of detecting an injury that might develop in the future. But, in Sinclair v. Merck & Co., Inc., 948 A.2d 587 (N.J. 2008), the New Jersey Supreme Court rejected a claim for medical monitoring by patients who took VIOXX, a drug that had been withdrawn from the market because it allegedly caused cardiovascular problems. The Court held that the New Jersey Product Liability Act required proof of physical injury and that the claimants could not meet that criteria.

In Donovan v. Philip Morris USA, Inc., 914 N.E.2d 891 (Mass. 2009), the plaintiffs brought a class action in federal court alleging that they suffered from a substantially increased risk of developing lung cancer as a result of smoking cigarettes negligently manufactured, designed, and marketed by the defendant. They sought a court-supervised program, paid for by the defendant, to provide them with newly developed diagnostic medical technology that would detect lung cancer at an early stage. The defendant argued that Massachusetts law requires a plaintiff to plead and prove a present physical injury to recover in tort. The federal district court certified the question to the Massachusetts high court of "[whether] the plaintiffs' suit for medical monitoring, based on subclinical effects of exposure to cigarette smoke and increased risk of lung cancer, state[s] a cognizable claim and/or permit[s] a remedy under Massachusetts state law." Id. at 894-95. The Massachusetts high court held that a plaintiff may recover with proof that:

> (1) The defendant's negligence (2) caused (3) the plaintiff to become exposed to a hazardous substance that produced, at least, subcellular changes that substantially increased the risk of serious disease, illness, or injury (4) for which an effective medical test for reliable early detection exists, (5) and early detection, combined with prompt and effective treatment, will significantly decrease the risk of death or the severity of the disease, illness or injury, and (6) such diagnostic medical examinations are reasonably (and periodically) necessary, conformably with the standard of care, and (7) the present value of the reasonable cost of such tests and care, as of the date of the filing of the complaint. Id. at 902 (citation omitted).

A significant rearguard movement questions the wisdom of awarding medical monitoring costs where plaintiffs have not suffered a cognizable physical injury. Some of the more powerful arguments against recognizing an action for medical monitoring costs were laid out in the Supreme Court's decision in *Metro-North*, supra. Specifically, the Court had reservations that:

> [T]ens of millions of individuals may have suffered exposure to substances that might justify some form of substance-exposure-related medical monitoring . . . And that fact, along with uncertainty as to the amount of liability, could threaten both a 'flood' of less important cases (potentially absorbing resources better left available to those more seriously harmed . . .) and the systemic harms that can accompany "unlimited and unpredictable liability."[Id. at 442.]

The Kentucky Supreme Court rejected an action for medical monitoring in Wood v. Wyeth-Ayerst Laboratories, 82 S.W.3d 849 (Ky. 2002). Plaintiff, a "Fen-Phen" diet drug consumer, sought recovery for the costs of monitoring against the highly publicized and acknowledged risks of heart valve abnormalities linked to the use of the drug. After weighing the arguments on both sides, the court found the analysis in *Metro-North* persuasive and was unwilling to depart from a long line of precedent holding that a plaintiff suffer physical injury as a prerequisite to the accrual of an action. Id. at 853. Accord Lowe v. Philip Morris USA, Inc., 183 P.3d 181 (Ore. 2008); Hinton v. Monsanto Co., 813 So. 2d 827 (Ala. 2001); Henry v. Dow Chem. Co., 701 N.W.2d 684 (Mich. 2005); Badillo v. Am. Brands, Inc., 16 P.3d 435 (Nev. 2001). See also In re Berg Litig., 293 F.3d 1127 (9th Cir. 2002) (finding that plaintiffs not entitled to recover under Price-Anderson Act for medical monitoring costs associated with the risk of contracting cancer as a result of exposure to nuclear radiation absent plaintiffs' showing of present physical injury).

authors' dialogue 26

JIM: Is there any way to fix the asbestos mess short of intervention by Congress?

AARON: I doubt it. As long as state courts are willing to award mental distress damages and medical monitoring for anyone ever exposed to asbestos, we will continue throwing company after company into bankruptcy. Asbestos plaintiffs have begun targeting anyone and everyone that had any connection with asbestos as potential defendants. Almost all of the asbestos manufacturers are already in bankruptcy. Now automobile manufacturers and other users of asbestos are being sued on the grounds that they should have known about the dangers of asbestos and should not have used them in their products. For example, brake linings in trucks and cars contained small amounts of asbestos. Employees of garages and auto repair shops now claim that they were exposed to asbestos and are entitled to either mental distress damages or medical monitoring. It's just never-ending.

DOUG: Hold it, Aaron. You are overstating the problem. Very few courts allow mental distress damages for exposure to asbestos. There must be some physical manifestation of asbestos-related injury in the body of the plaintiff. *Metro-North* is really the law in most all states on this issue.

AARON: OK. But what about asymptomatic pleural thickening? Some states allow recovery for mental distress even though the likelihood of anyone contracting asbestosis or mesothelioma is very remote. And what about asbestosis? *Ayers* allowed recovery for mental distress because the plaintiff feared that he would contract cancer or mesothelioma. There are enough asbestosis cases to break the bank.

JIM: I agree with Aaron that asymptomatic pleural thickening should not support an action for mental distress, but why wasn't the court right in *Ayers*? Asbestosis is a serious disease and fear of developing cancer or mesothelioma is not stretched.

AARON: The problem is that asbestosis is a label that doctors can easily place on even the most minor of changes in lung pathology. If it becomes the key to recovery, doctors can easily conform the facts to the pleadings without violating their Hippocratic oath. It is all in the eyes of the beholder.

JIM: I give up. The only way to clean up the asbestos mess is through congressional action. Asbestos is unique. We can't and shouldn't mess up traditional tort law principles to deal with a once-in-a-century problem.

DOUG: I'm not sure I agree that asbestos is unique, Jim. Asbestos caused a massive public health problem, yes, but so do lead paint, cigarettes, and handguns. And each of those industries has also had substantial influence in Congress over the years, part of the reason victims and public advocates end up turning to the courts for recourse. Maybe an effort to "mess up traditional tort law" is just what we need?

Professors Henderson and Twerski, in their article Asbestos Litigation Gone Mad: Exposure-Based Recovery for Increased Risk, Mental Distress, and Medical Monitoring, 53 S.C. L. Rev. 815 (2002), offer a rejoinder to the oft-repeated policy arguments supporting medical monitoring:

> But if the social benefits derived from court-sanctioned medical monitoring are questionable to the point of being dubious, the serious negative impacts of such liability on the business firms involved cannot be doubted. Given that negligently distributed or discharged toxins can be perceived to lie around every corner in the modern industrialized world, and their effects on risk levels are at best speculative, the potential tort claims involved are inherently limitless and endless. When courts require plaintiffs to prove that they have been, or are likely to become, physically injured as a result of exposures to asbestos or other toxic substances, defendants' potential liabilities are contained within natural boundaries. In contrast, in the medical monitoring context, there are no such natural boundaries. . . .
>
> Another inescapable implication of the inherent vagueness and open-endedness of medical monitoring litigation is that the courts will face, in the long run, an overwhelming flood of litigation in this area. . . . The West Virginia Supreme Court may believe that it "did justice" in Bower by adopting an ostensibly sensible rule of liability with which lower courts will be able to render medical monitoring decisions that are fair, rational, and manageable. But surely Bower has unwittingly brought upon the West Virginia judiciary the potential for a plague of future litigation of questionable substantive benefit with which it is institutionally incapable of dealing. . . . [Id at 844-846.]

The authors return (more briefly) to the subject in their article Reaching Equilibrium in Tobacco Litigation, 62 S.C. L. Rev. 67 (2010).

Putting to one side the wisdom of allowing recovery for medical monitoring, the West Virginia court in *Bower* left open the question of whether medical monitoring costs should be paid to plaintiffs who actually avail themselves of the services or whether the cost of medical monitoring should be paid to plaintiffs in a lump sum. When courts award lump-sum payments they may be utilized for vacations to Florida rather than for the purposes for which they were awarded. A fair number of courts demand that courts monitor the payment for services actually rendered. See, e.g., Potter v. Firestone Fire & Rubber Co., 863 P.2d 795, 824 n.23 (Cal. 1993); Redland Soccer Club, Inc. v. Department of the Army, 696 A.2d 137, 196 n.9 (Pa. 1997); Hansen v. Mountain Fuel Supply Co., 858 P.2d 970, 981 (Utah 1993).

For further scholarship on the issue, see Mark Geistfeld, The Analytics of Duty: Medical Monitoring and Related Forms of Economic Loss, 88 Va. L. Rev. 1921 (2002); John C. P. Goldberg & Benjamin C. Zipursky, Unrealized Torts, 88 Va. L. Rev. 1625 (2002); Andrew R. Klein, Rethinking Medical Monitoring; 64 Brook. L. Rev. 1 (1998); Victor E. Schwartz et al., Medical Monitoring — Should Tort Law Say Yes?, 34 Wake Forest L. Rev. 1057 (1999). An extensive survey of medical monitoring appears in 17 A.L.R.5th 327 (2015).

D.   RECOVERY OF PUNITIVE DAMAGES

1.   Legal Standards and Limits Under State Law

Courts award punitive damages to punish defendants for egregious wrongdoing. Punitive damages are not aimed at compensating the injured plaintiff; they are given in addition to compensatory damages, and courts will not award them in the absence of compensatories. See, e.g., Green v. Schutt Sports Mfg. Co., 2010 U.S. App. LEXIS 5482 (5th Cir. 2010) (holding that, because the jury found against plaintiff on his only claim for which compensatory damages could be awarded, the trial court's failure to submit to the jury plaintiff's claim for punitive damages based on gross negligence was harmless error). Punitive damages have been the subject of heated debate among products liability lawyers, judges, and scholars, and in recent years punitive awards have drawn the attention of the Supreme Court. The place to begin is with the factual predicates on which punitive damages are most often based.

The standard for punitive damages varies from jurisdiction to jurisdiction. In Owen-Illinois, Inc. v. Zenobia, 601 A.2d 633 (Md. 1992), the Maryland high court rejected "gross negligence" as the standard for awarding punitive damages, deeming it too broad and likely to produce excessively high awards. The court concluded that "[i]n a non-intentional tort action [such as a products liability claim for failing to warn of the dangers of asbestos products], the trier of facts may not award punitive damages unless the plaintiff has established that the defendant's conduct was characterized by evil motive, intent to injure, ill will, or fraud, i.e., 'actual malice. . . .'" Id. at 652. The court also imposed a heightened, "clear and convincing" standard of proof. One judge dissented. While he agreed with the new evidentiary standard, he felt that the new substantive standard goes too far and will deny punitive awards to deserving plaintiffs. Other tests for awarding punitive damages include "conscious disregard for the consequences" (Ford Motor Co. v. Stubblefeld, 319 S.E.2d 470 (Ga. Ct. App. 1984)); "evil mind" (including evil acts, spiteful motive, or outrageous, oppressive, or intolerant conduct creating a substantial risk of tremendous harm) (Volz v. Coleman Co., Inc., 748 P.2d 1191 (Ariz. 1987)); and "wanton disregard for safety" (Axen v. American Home Prods. Corp., 974 P.2d 224 (Or. Ct. App. 1999)). All of these tests require something more than mere negligence on the part of the defendant. Either the conduct must be intentional, or it must exhibit awareness of, and indifference toward, significant attendant risks, often termed "recklessness."

In Jablonski v. Ford Motor Co., 923 N.E.2d 347 (Ill. Ct. App. 2010), the plaintiff and her husband were severely injured when they were rear-ended and their car's gas tank caught fire. The husband died of his injuries. During trial, the plaintiff brought claims for defective design and failure-to-warn, presenting evidence that the defendant knew their cars' gas tanks were especially susceptible to post-crash fires after high-speed rear-end collisions. In fact, some of the defendant's own researchers and engineers had, with the risk for gas tank fires in mind, recommended a safer design. The defendant also knew of other similar gas tank fires but did not warn consumers or change the design. The jury returned a general verdict for the plaintiff and awarded both compensatory and punitive damages. The defendant argued on appeal that the plaintiff's evidence was insufficient to meet the Illinois standard of "willful and wanton conduct" to grant punitive damages. The Appellate Court of Illinois upheld the jury's award, ruling that the plaintiff presented a prima facie case for punitive damages by showing that the defendant, with knowledge of the defect and that it was likely to cause injury, failed to warn consumers or to remedy the defective design.

Many courts are quite insistent that the behavior of the defendant be truly egregious before imposing punitive damages. Thus in Ford v. GACS Inc., 265 F.3d 670 (8th Cir. 2001), GACS, the manufacturer of a ratchet system for securing cars to automobile transporters was held not to have acted with "wantonness or bad motive" by continuing to manufacture a product despite knowledge of some injuries. The court found that: (1) "the fact that [GACS] worked to design a safer system belies the level of reckless indifference or conscious disregard for the safety of others necessary to support an award of punitive damages" even though GACS chose not to market the safer design; (2) a ten percent chance that an individual driver would be injured by the system in a single year did not establish that the manufacturer was aware that the system was "unreasonably dangerous;" (3) GACS's decision to continue marketing the device because its major customer had approved only that type of device was motivated by considerations of utility and not by bad faith.

Similarly, in Bonnette v. Conoco Inc., 837 So. 2d 1219 (La. 2003), a refinery that knowingly sold asbestos-contaminated dirt to contractors for use in a residential development, was not "wanton and reckless" in failing to inform anyone that the dirt was contaminated because the refinery did not violate any state environmental regulations. Since the particular type of construction was not regulated by the state environmental protection agency (the "DEQ"), the refinery had not violated any environmental regulations by failing to warn that the dirt was contaminated. Furthermore, the refinery's actions after plaintiffs discovered the contamination were "in excess" of what the DEQ "would have required of them." The court held that the refinery's conduct did not satisfy the statutory "wanton and reckless conduct" standard necessary to impose punitive damages stemming from the handling of toxic substances:

> Although the actions of [the defendant,] including his failure to take any steps to inform anyone of the presence of asbestos on the site, leave much to be desired, it is clear that [defendant's] actions were not in violation of any DEQ regulation. Because [defendant] acted in compliance with DEQ regulations in effect during the events at issue, we cannot say that defendant's conduct was highly unreasonable or that it involved an extreme departure from ordinary care.

States have utilized a wide range of other techniques to rein in what are believed to be excessive punitive damages. A strong majority have legislation regulating punitive damages. Many of these states require plaintiffs to meet a heightened burden of proof to be entitled to punitive damages. Most require "clear and convincing evidence" of wrongdoing. Colorado requires proof equivalent to the criminal standard: "beyond a reasonable doubt." See Colo. Rev. Stat. §13-25-127(2). In addition, at least eight states and the District of Columbia have imposed the "clear and convincing" evidence standard by judicial decision.

A strong minority of states have statutes that limit the dollar amount of punitive damage awards, either by imposing an absolute cap on punitive damages or by limiting punitive damages to some multiple of compensatory damages. Massachusetts, Nebraska, New Hampshire, and Washington do not recognize punitive damages as a common law remedy. Louisiana awards punitive damages by statute only and in limited circumstances. In at least one state, Georgia, punitive damages arising out of a products liability suit are exempt from the statutory cap. Ga. Code Ann. §51-12-5.1(e)(1). See also Lewellen v. Franklin, 441 S.W.3d 136 (Mo. 2014) (holding that state statute that imposed a cap on punitive damages of $500,000 or five times net amount of judgment awarded to plaintiff violates state constitutional right to a trial by jury).

At least five states have enacted statutes that exempt drug manufacturers or sellers from liability for punitive damages if the drug that caused injury was labeled, manufactured, marketed, and distributed in compliance with FDA regulations.

Three states, Connecticut, Kansas, and Ohio, require the court to determine the amount of punitive damages after a jury's finding that punitive damages are appropriate. A number of states have provisions for a separate proceeding to determine the amount of punitive damages to be awarded.

The subject of punitive damages has attracted considerable scholarly commentary. See generally Dan Markel, Retributive Damages: A Theory of Punitive Damages as Intermediate Sanction, 94 Cornell L. Rev. 239 (2009); Dan Markel, How Should Punitive Damages Work?, 157 U. Pa. L. Rev. 1383 (2009); Anthony J. Sebok, Punitive Damages: From Myth to Theory, 92 Iowa L. Rev. 957 (2007); Theodore Eisenberg et al., Juries, Judges, and Punitive Damages: Empirical Analysis Using the Civil Justice Survey of State Courts 1992, 1996, and 2001 Data, 3 J. Empirical Legal Stud. 263 (2006); Benjamin C. Zipursky, A Theory of Punitive Damages, 84 Tex. L. Rev. 105 (2005) (attributing controversial nature and tentative constitutional status of punitive damages to ambivalence regarding nongovernmental plaintiffs' rights to inflict quasi-criminal punishment on civil defendants); Michael L. Rustad & Thomas H. Koenig, Taming the Tort Monster: The American Civil Justice System as a Battleground of Social Theory, 68 Brook. L. Rev. 1 (2002) (contending that the need for tort reform is overblown; reviewing the history of punitive damages and concluding that "[t]ort retrenchment is jeopardizing the social role of tort law in protecting the public from corporate and individual misbehavior").

2. *Federal Constitutional Control of Punitive Damages*

State Farm Mutual Automobile Insurance Co. v. Campbell
538 U.S. 408 (2003)

Justice KENNEDY delivered the opinion of the Court.

We address once again the measure of punishment, by means of punitive damages, a State may impose upon a defendant in a civil case. The question is whether, in the circumstances we shall recount, an award of $145 million in punitive damages, where full compensatory damages are $1 million, is excessive and in violation of the Due Process Clause of the Fourteenth Amendment to the Constitution of the United States.

I

In 1981, Curtis Campbell (Campbell) was driving with his wife, Inez Preece Campbell, in Cache County, Utah. He decided to pass six vans traveling ahead of them on a two-lane highway. Todd Ospital was driving a small car approaching from the opposite direction. To avoid a head-on collision with Campbell, who by then was driving on the wrong side of the highway and toward oncoming traffic, Ospital swerved onto the shoulder, lost control of his automobile, and collided with a vehicle driven by Robert G. Slusher. Ospital was killed, and Slusher was rendered permanently disabled. The Campbells escaped unscathed. . . .

In the ensuing wrongful death and tort action, Campbell insisted he was not at fault. Early investigations did support differing conclusions as to who caused the accident, but "consensus was reached early on by the investigators and witnesses that Mr. Campbell's unsafe pass had indeed caused the crash." . . . Campbell's insurance company, petitioner State Farm Mutual Automobile Insurance Company (State Farm), nonetheless decided to contest liability and declined offers by Slusher and Ospital's estate (Ospital) to settle the claims for the policy limit of $50,000 ($25,000 per claimant). State Farm also ignored the advice of one of its own investigators and took the case to trial, assuring the Campbells that "their assets were safe, that they had no liability for the accident, that [State Farm] would represent their interests, and that they did not need to procure separate counsel." . . . To the contrary, a jury determined that Campbell was 100 percent at fault, and a judgment was returned for $185,849, far more than the amount offered in settlement.

At first State Farm refused to cover the $135,849 in excess liability. Its counsel made this clear to the Campbells: "'You may want to put for sale signs on your property to get things moving.'" . . . Nor was State Farm willing to post a supersedeas bond to allow Campbell to appeal the judgment against him. Campbell obtained his own counsel to appeal the verdict. During the pendency of the appeal, in late 1984, Slusher, Ospital, and the Campbells reached an agreement whereby Slusher and Ospital agreed not to seek satisfaction of their claims against the Campbells. In exchange the Campbells agreed to pursue a bad faith action against State Farm and to be represented by Slusher's and Ospital's attorneys. The Campbells also agreed that Slusher and Ospital would have a right to play a part in all major decisions concerning the bad faith action. No settlement could be concluded without Slusher's and Ospital's approval, and Slusher and Ospital would receive 90 percent of any verdict against State Farm.

In 1989, the Utah Supreme Court denied Campbell's appeal in the wrongful death and tort actions. . . . State Farm then paid the entire judgment, including the amounts in excess of the policy limits. The Campbells nonetheless filed a complaint against State Farm alleging bad faith, fraud, and intentional infliction of emotional distress. The trial court initially granted State Farm's motion for summary judgment because State Farm had paid the excess verdict, but that ruling was reversed on appeal. . . . On remand State Farm moved *in limine* to exclude evidence of alleged conduct that occurred in unrelated cases outside of Utah, but the trial court denied the motion. At State Farm's request the trial court bifurcated the trial into two phases conducted before different juries. In the first phase the jury determined that State Farm's decision not to settle was unreasonable because there was a substantial likelihood of an excess verdict.

Before the second phase of the action against State Farm we decided BMW of North America, Inc. v. Gore, 517 U.S. 559, L. Ed. 2d 809 (1996), and refused to sustain a $2 million punitive damages award which accompanied a verdict of only $4,000 in compensatory damages. Based on that decision, State Farm again moved for the exclusion of evidence of dissimilar out-of-state conduct. . . . The trial court denied State Farm's motion. . . .

The second phase addressed State Farm's liability for fraud and intentional infliction of emotional distress, as well as compensatory and punitive damages. The Utah Supreme Court aptly characterized this phase of the trial:

"State Farm argued during phase II that its decision to take the case to trial was an 'honest mistake' that did not warrant punitive damages. In contrast, the Campbells introduced evidence that State Farm's decision to take the case to trial was a result of a national scheme to meet corporate fiscal goals by capping payouts on claims company wide. This scheme was referred to as State Farm's 'Performance, Planning and Review,' or PP & R, policy. To prove the existence of this scheme, the trial court allowed the Campbells to introduce extensive expert testimony regarding fraudulent practices by State Farm in its nation-wide operations. Although State Farm moved prior to phase II of the trial for the exclusion of such evidence and continued to object to it at trial, the trial court ruled that such evidence was admissible to determine whether State Farm's conduct in the Campbell case was indeed intentional and sufficiently egregious to warrant punitive damages." . . .

Evidence pertaining to the PP&R policy concerned State Farm's business practices for over 20 years in numerous States. Most of these practices bore no relation to third-party automobile insurance claims, the type of claim underlying the Campbells' complaint against the company. The jury awarded the Campbells $2.6 million in compensatory damages and $145 million in punitive damages, which the trial court reduced to $1 million and $25 million respectively. Both parties appealed.

The Utah Supreme Court sought to apply the three guideposts we identified in *Gore*, supra, . . . and it reinstated the $145 million punitive damages award. Relying in large part on the extensive evidence concerning the PP&R policy, the court concluded State Farm's conduct was reprehensible. The court also relied upon State Farm's "massive wealth" and on testimony indicating that "State Farm's actions, because of their clandestine nature, will be punished at most in one out of every 50,000 cases as a matter of statistical probability," . . . and concluded that the ratio between punitive and compensatory damages was not unwarranted. Finally, the court noted that the punitive damages award was not excessive when compared to various civil and criminal penalties State Farm could have faced, including $10,000 for each act of fraud, the suspension of its license to conduct business in Utah, the disgorgement of profits, and imprisonment. . . . We granted certiorari. . . .

II

We recognized in Cooper Industries, Inc. v. Leatherman Tool Group, Inc., 532 U.S. 424, . . . that in our judicial system compensatory and punitive damages, although usually awarded at the same time by the same decisionmaker, serve different purposes. . . . Compensatory damages "are intended to redress the concrete loss that the plaintiff has suffered by reason of the defendant's wrongful conduct." . . . (citing Restatement (Second) of Torts §903, pp.453-454 (1979)). By contrast, punitive damages serve a broader function; they are aimed at deterrence and retribution. *Cooper Industries*, supra. . . .

While States possess discretion over the imposition of punitive damages, it is well established that there are procedural and substantive constitutional limitations on these awards. . . . The reason is that "elementary notions of fairness enshrined in our constitutional jurisprudence dictate that a person receive fair notice not only of the conduct that will subject him to punishment, but also of the severity of the penalty that a State may impose." . . . To the extent an award is grossly excessive, it furthers no legitimate purpose and constitutes an arbitrary deprivation of property. . . .

Although these awards serve the same purposes as criminal penalties, defendants subjected to punitive damages in civil cases have not been accorded the protections applicable in a criminal proceeding. This increases our concerns over the imprecise manner in which punitive damages systems are administered. We have admonished that "punitive damages pose an acute danger of arbitrary deprivation of property. Jury instructions typically leave the jury with wide discretion in choosing amounts, and the presentation of evidence of a defendant's net worth creates the potential that juries will use their verdicts to express biases against big businesses, particularly those without strong local presences." ...

In light of these concerns, in *Gore* supra, ... we instructed courts reviewing punitive damages to consider three guideposts: (1) the degree of reprehensibility of the defendant's misconduct; (2) the disparity between the actual or potential harm suffered by the plaintiff and the punitive damages award; and (3) the difference between the punitive damages awarded by the jury and the civil penalties authorized or imposed in comparable cases. ... We reiterated the importance of these three guideposts in *Cooper Industries* and mandated appellate courts to conduct *de novo* review of a trial court's application of them to the jury's award. ... Exacting appellate review ensures that an award of punitive damages is based upon an "'application of law, rather than a decisionmaker's caprice.'" ...

III

Under the principles outlined in BMW of North America, Inc. v. Gore, this case is neither close nor difficult. It was error to reinstate the jury's $145 million punitive damages award. We address each guidepost of *Gore* in some detail.

A

"The most important indicium of the reasonableness of a punitive damages award is the degree of reprehensibility of the defendant's conduct." ... We have instructed courts to determine the reprehensibility of a defendant by considering whether: the harm caused was physical as opposed to economic; the tortious conduct evinced an indifference to or a reckless disregard of the health or safety of others; the target of the conduct had financial vulnerability; the conduct involved repeated actions or was an isolated incident; and the harm was the result of intentional malice, trickery, or deceit, or mere accident. ... The existence of any one of these factors weighing in favor of a plaintiff may not be sufficient to sustain a punitive damages award; and the absence of all of them renders any award suspect. It should be presumed a plaintiff has been made whole for his injuries by compensatory damages, so punitive damages should only be awarded if the defendant's culpability, after having paid compensatory damages, is so reprehensible as to warrant the imposition of further sanctions to achieve punishment or deterrence. ...

Applying these factors in the instant case, we must acknowledge that State Farm's handling of the claims against the Campbells merits no praise. The trial court found that State Farm's employees altered the company's records to make Campbell appear less culpable. State Farm disregarded the overwhelming likelihood of liability and the near-certain probability that, by taking the case to trial, a judgment in excess of the policy limits would be awarded. State Farm amplified the harm by at first assuring the Campbells their assets would be safe from any verdict and by later telling them, postjudgment, to put a for-sale sign on their house. While we do not suggest there was error in awarding punitive damages based upon State Farm's conduct toward the Campbells, a more modest punishment for this reprehensible conduct could have satisfied the State's legitimate objectives, and the Utah courts should have gone no further.

This case, instead, was used as a platform to expose, and punish, the perceived deficiencies of State Farm's operations throughout the country. The Utah Supreme Court's opinion makes explicit that State Farm was being condemned for its nationwide policies rather than for the conduct directed toward the Campbells. 65 P.3d at 1143 ("The Campbells introduced evidence that State Farm's decision to take the case to trial was a result of a national scheme to meet corporate fiscal goals by capping payouts on claims company wide"). This was, as well, an explicit rationale of the trial court's decision in approving the award, though reduced from $145 million to $25 million. . . . ("[T]he Campbells demonstrated, through the testimony of State Farm employees who had worked outside of Utah, and through expert testimony, that this pattern of claims adjustment under the PP&R program was not a local anomaly, but was a consistent, nationwide feature of State Farm's business operations, orchestrated from the highest levels of corporate management").

The Campbells contend that State Farm has only itself to blame for the reliance upon dissimilar and out-of-state conduct evidence. The record does not support this contention. From their opening statements onward the Campbells framed this case as a chance to rebuke State Farm for its nationwide activities. . . . ("You're going to hear evidence that even the insurance commission in Utah and around the country are unwilling or inept at protecting people against abuses"); . . . ("[T]his is a very important case. . . . It transcends the Campbell file. It involves a nationwide practice. And you, here, are going to be evaluating and assessing, and hopefully requiring State Farm to stand accountable for what it's doing across the country, which is the purpose of punitive damages"). This was a position maintained throughout the litigation. In opposing State Farm's motion to exclude such evidence under *Gore*, the Campbells' counsel convinced the trial court that there was no limitation on the scope of evidence that could be considered under our precedents. . . .

A State cannot punish a defendant for conduct that may have been lawful where it occurred. . . . Nor, as a general rule, does a State have a legitimate concern in imposing punitive damages to punish a defendant for unlawful acts committed outside of the State's jurisdiction. Any proper adjudication of conduct that occurred outside Utah to other persons would require their inclusion, and, to those parties, the Utah courts, in the usual case, would need to apply the laws of their relevant jurisdiction. Phillips Petroleum Co. v. Shutts, 472 U.S. 797. . . .

Here, the Campbells do not dispute that much of the out-of-state conduct was lawful where it occurred. They argue, however, that such evidence was not the primary basis for the punitive damages award and was relevant to the extent it demonstrated, in a general sense, State Farm's motive against its insured. Brief for Respondents 46-47 ("Even if the practices described by State Farm were not malum in se or malum prohibitum, they became relevant to punitive damages to the extent they were used as tools to implement State Farm's wrongful PP&R policy"). This argument misses the mark. Lawful out-of-state conduct may be probative when it demonstrates the deliberateness and culpability of the defendant's action in the State where it is tortious, but that conduct must have a nexus to the specific harm suffered by the plaintiff. A jury must be instructed, furthermore, that it may not use evidence of out-of-state conduct to punish a defendant for action that was lawful in the jurisdiction where it occurred. . . .

For a more fundamental reason, however, the Utah courts erred in relying upon this and other evidence: The courts awarded punitive damages to punish and deter conduct that bore no relation to the Campbells' harm. A defendant's dissimilar acts, independent from the acts upon which liability was premised, may not serve as the basis for punitive damages. A defendant should be punished for the conduct that harmed the plaintiff, not for being an unsavory individual or business. Due process does not permit courts, in the calculation of punitive damages, to adjudicate the merits of other parties' hypothetical claims against a defendant under the guise of the reprehensibility analysis, but we have no doubt the Utah Supreme Court did that here. . . . Punishment on these bases creates the possibility of multiple punitive damages awards for the same conduct; for in the usual case nonparties are not bound by the judgment some other plaintiff obtains. . . .

The Campbells have identified scant evidence of repeated misconduct of the sort that injured them. Nor does our review of the Utah courts' decisions convince us that State Farm was only punished for its actions toward the Campbells. Although evidence of other acts need not be identical to have relevance in the calculation of punitive damages, the Utah court erred here because evidence pertaining to claims that had nothing to do with a third-party lawsuit was introduced at length. Other evidence concerning reprehensibility was even more tangential. For example, the Utah Supreme Court criticized State Farm's investigation into the personal life of one of its employees and, in a broader approach, the manner in which State Farm's policies corrupted its employees. . . . The Campbells attempt to justify the courts' reliance upon this unrelated testimony on the theory that each dollar of profit made by underpaying a third-party claimant is the same as a dollar made by underpaying a first-party one. . . . For the reasons already stated, this argument is unconvincing. The reprehensibility guidepost does not permit courts to expand the scope of the case so that a defendant may be punished for any malfeasance, which in this case extended for a 20-year period. In this case, because the Campbells have shown no conduct by State Farm similar to that which harmed them, the conduct that harmed them is the only conduct relevant to the reprehensibility analysis.

B

Turning to the second *Gore* guidepost, we have been reluctant to identify concrete constitutional limits on the ratio between harm, or potential harm, to the plaintiff and the punitive damages award. *Gore*, supra, at 582, 116 S. Ct. 1589 ("[W]e have consistently rejected the notion that the constitutional line is marked by a simple mathematical formula, even one that compares actual *and potential* damages to the punitive award");. . . . We decline again to impose a bright-line ratio which a punitive damages award cannot exceed. Our jurisprudence and the principles it has now established demonstrate, however, that, in practice, few awards exceeding a single-digit ratio between punitive and compensatory damages, to a significant degree, will satisfy due process. In *Haslip*, in upholding a punitive damages award, we concluded that an award of more than four times the amount of compensatory damages might be close to the line of constitutional impropriety. 499 U.S., at 23-24. . . . We cited that 4-to-1 ratio again in *Gore*. 517 U.S., at 581. . . . The Court further referenced a long legislative history, dating back over 700 years and going forward to today, providing for sanctions of double, treble, or quadruple damages to deter and punish. . . . While these ratios are not binding, they are instructive. They demonstrate what should be obvious: Single-digit multipliers are more likely to comport with due process, while still achieving the State's goals of deterrence and retribution, than awards with ratios in range of 500 to 1, . . . or, in this case, of 145 to 1.

Nonetheless, because there are no rigid benchmarks that a punitive damages award may not surpass, ratios greater than those we have previously upheld may comport with due process where "a particularly egregious act has resulted in only a small amount of economic damages." . . . The converse is also true, however. When compensatory damages are substantial, then a lesser ratio, perhaps only equal to compensatory damages, can reach the outermost limit of the due process guarantee. The precise award in any case, of course, must be based upon the facts and circumstances of the defendant's conduct and the harm to the plaintiff.

In sum, courts must ensure that the measure of punishment is both reasonable and proportionate to the amount of harm to the plaintiff and to the general damages recovered. In the context of this case, we have no doubt that there is a presumption against an award that has a 145-to-1 ratio. The compensatory award in this case was substantial; the Campbells were awarded $1 million for a year and a half of emotional distress. This was complete compensation. The harm arose from a transaction in the economic realm, not from some physical assault or trauma; there were no physical injuries; and State Farm paid the excess verdict before the complaint was filed, so the Campbells suffered only minor economic injuries for the 18-month period in which State Farm refused to resolve the claim against them. The compensatory damages for the injury suffered here, moreover, likely were based on a component which was duplicated in the punitive award. Much of the distress was caused by the outrage and humiliation the Campbells suffered at the actions of their insurer; and it is a major role of punitive damages to condemn such conduct. Compensatory damages, however, already contain this punitive element. . . .

The Utah Supreme Court sought to justify the massive award by pointing to State Farm's purported failure to report a prior $100 million punitive damages award in Texas to its corporate headquarters; the fact that State Farm's policies have affected numerous Utah consumers; the fact that State Farm will only be punished in one out of every 50,000 cases as a matter of statistical probability; and State Farm's enormous wealth. . . . Since the Supreme Court of Utah discussed the Texas award when applying the ratio guidepost, we discuss it here. The Texas award, however, should have been analyzed in the context of the reprehensibility guidepost only. The failure of the company to report the Texas award is out-of-state conduct that, if the conduct were similar, might have had some bearing on the degree of reprehensibility, subject to the limitations we have described. Here, it was dissimilar, and of such marginal relevance that it should have been accorded little or no weight. The award was rendered in a first-party lawsuit; no judgment was entered in the case; and it was later settled for a fraction of the verdict. With respect to the Utah Supreme Court's second justification, the Campbells' inability to direct us to testimony demonstrating harm to the people of Utah (other than those directly involved in this case) indicates that the adverse effect on the State's general population was in fact minor.

The remaining premises for the Utah Supreme Court's decision bear no relation to the award's reasonableness or proportionality to the harm. They are, rather, arguments that seek to defend a departure from well-established constraints on punitive damages. While States enjoy considerable discretion in deducing when punitive damages are warranted, each award must comport with the principles set forth in *Gore*. Here the argument that State Farm will be punished in only the rare case, coupled with reference to its assets (which, of course, are what other insured parties in Utah and other States must rely upon for payment of claims) had little to do with the actual harm sustained by the Campbells. The wealth of a defendant cannot justify an otherwise unconstitutional punitive damages award. . . . ("[Wealth] provides an open-ended basis for inflating awards when the defendant is wealthy. . . . That does not make its use unlawful or inappropriate; it simply means that this factor cannot make up for the failure of other factors, such as 'reprehensibility,' to constrain significantly an award that purports to punish a defendant's conduct''). The principles set forth in *Gore* must be implemented with care, to ensure both reasonableness and proportionality.

C

The third guidepost in *Gore* is the disparity between the punitive damages award and the "civil penalties authorized or imposed in comparable cases." . . . We note that, in the past, we have also looked to criminal penalties that could be imposed. . . . The existence of a criminal penalty does have bearing on the seriousness with which a State views the wrongful action. When used to determine the dollar amount of the award, however, the criminal penalty has less utility. Great care must be taken to avoid use of the civil process to assess criminal penalties that can be imposed only after the heightened protections of a criminal trial have been observed, including, of course, its higher standards of proof. Punitive damages are not a substitute for the criminal process, and the remote possibility of a criminal sanction does not automatically sustain a punitive damages award.

Here, we need not dwell long on this guidepost. The most relevant civil sanction under Utah state law for the wrong done to the Campbells appears to be a $10,000 fine for an act of fraud. . . . an amount dwarfed by the $145 million punitive damages award. The Supreme Court of Utah speculated about the loss of State Farm's business license, the disgorgement of profits, and possible imprisonment, but here again its references were to the broad fraudulent scheme drawn from evidence of out-of-state and dissimilar conduct. This analysis was insufficient to justify the award.

IV

An application of the *Gore* guideposts to the facts of this case, especially in light of the substantial compensatory damages awarded (a portion of which contained a punitive element), likely would justify a punitive damages award at or near the amount of compensatory damages. The punitive award of $145 million, therefore, was neither reasonable nor proportionate to the wrong committed, and it was an irrational and arbitrary deprivation of the property of the defendant. The proper calculation of punitive damages under the principles we have discussed should be resolved, in the first instance, by the Utah courts.

The judgment of the Utah Supreme Court is reversed, and the case is remanded for proceedings not inconsistent with this opinion.

It is so ordered.

[The dissenting opinions by Justices SCALIA and THOMAS are omitted.]

[Justice GINSBURG (dissenting) reviews the evidence of State Farm's conduct and finds it to be outrageous.]

The Court dismisses the evidence describing and documenting State Farm's PP&R policy and practices as essentially irrelevant, bearing "no relation to the Campbells' harm." . . . It is hardly apparent why that should be so. What is infirm about the Campbells' theory that their experience with State Farm exemplifies and reflects an overarching underpayment scheme, one that caused "repeated misconduct of the sort that injured them," . . . ? The Court's silence on that score is revealing: Once one

authors' dialogue 27

DOUG: This whole line of Supreme Court cases on punitive damages feels like a radical intrusion into the traditional right of state courts to decide tort-related issues. Am I the only one who is troubled by that?

JIM: You know, Doug, punitives aren't the only area where the Court has been acting in something of a tort reform capacity. After all, some of the federal preemption decisions wipe out state common-law causes of action entirely. But, I won't quibble with you that the Court's constitutionalization of punitive damages review is a major development. My take is that the court saw punitive awards playing an unacceptably large role in tort litigation. Whether they were right or not is debatable. My colleague, the late Ted Eisenberg, did a study on actual punitive damage awards and found that punitives rarely exceeded the amount awarded in compensatories.

AARON: I actually heard Ted present the work you're describing Jim. It was impressive. But, my recollection is that Ted did not take into account the influence of potential punitive damages on settlements. Punitives have an *in terrorem* effect on defendants. Nobody is willing to bet the house as long as there is a real possibility that punitive damages will be huge and unrestricted. Even after cases like *State Farm* and *Philip Morris*, I still read about jury awards of punitive damages running into the hundreds of millions of dollars that have been upheld by the trial judge. And in one recent cigarette case a jury in Florida awarded the widow of a chain smoker $23 billion in punitive damages. Admittedly these awards will almost certainly be drastically cut back after appellate review. But the noise gets to be awfully loud.

DOUG: Back in 1994 a jury in Anchorage, Alaska issued one of the first of these modern "blockbuster" punitive damages judgments – a $5 billion award against Exxon for the Valdez oil spill. When the award was announced one the plaintiffs' lawyers turned around and hugged his three-year-old son. At that point, a lawyer for Exxon whispered to him, "He'll be in college before you get any of that money." Guess what? After two more decades of courtroom battles, the Supreme Court eventually reduced the award to $500 million, one tenth of one percent of the initial amount. My point is, I think defendants are sophisticated enough to know that a jury's initial award bears only a slight relationship to what they will eventually have to pay.

AARON: You may be right that many tort defendants are sophisticated actors who won't panic just because a blockbuster award is announced. But there are still costs to the judicial system itself when juries appear to be ordering massive shifts of money in unpredictable ways. It's partly for that reason that the Supreme Court has stepped in, telling the world that it will no longer countenance business as usual with regard to punitives. Lower courts have begun responding by cutting back sharply on punitive damage awards, or at least by giving them much greater scrutiny and oversight. When it is all said and done, punitive damages will continue to play a role in our tort system but the appearance of a free-for-all will be gone.

recognizes that the Campbells did show "conduct by State Farm similar to that which harmed them," . . . it becomes impossible to shrink the reprehensibility analysis to this sole case, or to maintain, at odds with the determination of the trial court, . . . that "the adverse effect on the State's general population was in fact minor," ante, at 1525.

Evidence of out-of-state conduct, the Court acknowledges, may be "probative [even if the conduct is lawful in the state where it occurred] when it demonstrates the deliberateness and culpability of the defendant's action in the State where it is tortious. . . ." Other acts" evidence concerning practices both in and out of State was introduced in this case to show just such "deliberateness" and "culpability." The evidence was admissible, the trial court ruled: (1) to document State Farm's "reprehensible" PP&R program; and (2) to "rebut [State Farm's] assertion that [its] actions toward the Campbells were inadvertent errors or mistakes in judgment." . . . Viewed in this light, there surely was "a nexus" . . . between much of the "other acts" evidence and "the specific harm suffered by [the Campbells]." . . .

When the Court first ventured to override state-court punitive damages awards, it did so moderately. The Court recalled that "in our federal system, States necessarily have considerable flexibility in determining the level of punitive damages that they will allow in different classes of cases and in any particular case." *Gore*, 517 U.S., at 568 . . . Today's decision exhibits no such respect and restraint. No longer content to accord state-court judgments "a strong presumption of validity." . . . the Court announces that "few awards exceeding a single-digit ratio between punitive and compensatory damages, to a significant degree, will satisfy due process." . . . Moreover, the Court adds, when compensatory damages are substantial, doubling those damages "can reach the outermost limit of the due process guarantee." . . . In a legislative scheme or a state high court's design to cap punitive damages, the handiwork in setting single-digit and 1-to-1 benchmarks could hardly be questioned; in a judicial decree imposed on the States by this Court under the banner of substantive due process, the numerical controls today's decision installs seem to me boldly out of order.

. . .

I remain of the view that this Court has no warrant to reform state law governing awards of punitive damages. . . . Even if I were prepared to accept the flexible guides prescribed in *Gore*, I would not join the Court's swift conversion of those guides into instructions that begin to resemble marching orders. For the reasons stated, I would leave the judgment of the Utah Supreme Court undisturbed. . . .

Will punitive awards exceeding single-digit ratios pass constitutional scrutiny? The majority in *State Farm* imply that a few double-digit (or higher) awards, presumably involving reprehensible defendant conduct, might do so. Although the intermediate appellate courts in California continue to recognize the possibility that an award might exceed a single-digit ratio, in fact they have reduced punitive awards to single digit ratios with regularity since *State Farm*. See, e.g., Gober v. Ralph, 40 Cal. Rptr. 3d 92 (Cal. Ct. App. 2006) (reducing punitive damages to six times compensatory damages); Grassilli v. Barr, 48 Cal. Rptr. 3d 715 (Cal. Ct. App. 2006) (reducing punitives from an eight-to-one ratio to a four-to-one ratio); Henley v. Philip Morris, Inc., 9 Cal. Rptr. 3d 29 (Cal. Ct. App. 2004) (reducing punitive damages to six to one); Bardis v. Oates, 14 Cal. Rptr. 3d 89 (Cal. Ct. App. 2004) (reducing punitive damages to a nine-to-one ratio); Textron Fin. Corp. v. National Union Ins. Co. of Pittsburgh, Pa., 13 Cal. Rptr. 3d 586 (Cal. Ct. App. 2004) (reducing punitive damages to a four-to-one ratio); Romo v. Ford Motor Co., 6 Cal. Rptr. 3d 793 (Cal. Ct. App. 2003) (reducing punitive damages to a five-to-one ratio). But see Bullock v. Philip Morris USA, Inc., 42 Cal. Rptr. 3d 140 (Cal. Ct. App. 2006) (holding that ratio of 33 to 1 was not excessive because the defendant's conduct was extremely reprehensible in light of the "scale and profitability of the course of misconduct").

Philip Morris USA v. Williams
127 S. Ct. 1057, 549 U.S. 346 (2007)

Justice BREYER delivered the opinion of the Court.

The question we address today concerns a large state-court punitive damages award. We are asked whether the Constitution's Due Process Clause permits a jury to base that award in part upon its desire to *punish* the defendant for harming persons who are not before the court (e.g., victims whom the parties do not represent). We hold that such an award would amount to a taking of "property" from the defendant without due process.

I

This lawsuit arises out of the death of Jesse Williams, a heavy cigarette smoker. Respondent, Williams' widow, represents his estate in this state lawsuit for negligence and deceit against Philip Morris, the manufacturer of Marlboro, the brand that Williams favored. A jury found that Williams' death was caused by smoking; that Williams smoked in significant part because he thought it was safe to do so; and that Philip Morris knowingly and falsely led him to believe that this was so. The jury ultimately found that Philip Morris was negligent (as was Williams) and that Philip Morris had engaged in deceit. In respect to deceit, the claim at issue here, it awarded compensatory damages of about $821,000 (about $21,000 economic and $800,000 noneconomic) along with $79.5 million in punitive damages.

The trial judge subsequently found the $79.5 million punitive damages award "excessive," and reduced it to $32 million. Both sides appealed. The Oregon Court of Appeals rejected Philip Morris' arguments and restored the $79.5 million jury award. Subsequently, Philip Morris sought review in the Oregon Supreme Court (which denied review) and then here. We remanded the case in light of State Farm Mut. Automobile Ins. Co. v. Campbell, 123 S. Ct. 1513 (2003). The Oregon Court of Appeals adhered to its original views. And Philip Morris sought, and this time obtained, review in the Oregon Supreme Court.

Philip Morris then made two arguments relevant here. First, it said that the trial court should have accepted, but did not accept, a proposed "punitive damages" instruction that specified the jury could not seek to punish Philip Morris for injury to other persons not before the court. In particular, Philip Morris pointed out that the plaintiff's attorney had told the jury to "think about how many other Jesse Williams in the last 40 years in the State of Oregon there have been. . . . In Oregon, how many people do we see outside, driving home . . . smoking cigarettes? . . . [C]igarettes . . . are going to kill ten [of every hundred]. [And] the market share of Marlboros [i.e., Philip Morris] is one-third [i.e., one of every three killed]." In light of this argument, Philip Morris asked the trial court to tell the jury that "you may consider the extent of harm suffered by others in determining what [the] reasonable relationship is" between any punitive award and "the harm caused to Jesse Williams" by Philip Morris' misconduct, "[but] you are not to punish the defendant for the impact of its alleged misconduct on other persons, who may bring lawsuits of their own in which other juries can resolve their claims. . . ." The judge rejected this proposal and instead told the jury that "[p]unitive damages are awarded against a defendant to punish misconduct and to deter misconduct," and "are not intended to compensate the plaintiff or anyone else for damages caused by the defendant's conduct." In Philip Morris' view, the result was a significant likelihood that a portion of the $79.5 million award represented punishment for its having harmed others, a punishment that the Due Process Clause would here forbid.

Second, Philip Morris pointed to the roughly 100-to-1 ratio the $79.5 million punitive damages award bears to $821,000 in compensatory damages. Philip Morris noted that this Court in *BMW* emphasized the constitutional need for punitive damages awards to reflect (1) the "reprehensibility" of the defendant's conduct, (2) a "reasonable relationship" to the harm the plaintiff (or related victim) suffered, and (3) the presence (or absence) of "sanctions," e.g., criminal penalties, that state law provided for comparable conduct. And in *State Farm*, this Court said that the longstanding historical practice of setting punitive damages at two, three, or four times the size of compensatory damages, while "not binding," is "instructive," and that "[s]ingle-digit multipliers are more likely to comport with due process." 123 S. Ct. 1513. Philip Morris claimed that, in light of this case law, the punitive award was "grossly excessive."

The Oregon Supreme Court rejected these and other Philip Morris arguments. In particular, it rejected Philip Morris' claim that the Constitution prohibits a state jury "from using punitive damages to punish a defendant for harm to nonparties." 127 P.3d 1165, 1175 (2006). And in light of Philip Morris' reprehensible conduct, it found that the $79.5 million award was not "grossly excessive."

Philip Morris then sought certiorari. It asked us to consider, among other things, (1) its claim that Oregon had unconstitutionally permitted it to be punished for harming nonparty victims; and (2) whether Oregon had in effect disregarded "the constitutional requirement that punitive damages be reasonably related to the plaintiff's harm." We granted certiorari limited to these two questions.

For reasons we shall set forth, we consider only the first of these questions. We vacate the Oregon Supreme Court's judgment, and we remand the case for further proceedings.

II

This Court has long made clear that "[p]unitive damages may properly be imposed to further a State's legitimate interests in punishing unlawful conduct and deterring its repetition." *BMW*, 116 S. Ct. 1589. At the same time, we have emphasized the need to avoid an arbitrary determination of an award's amount. Unless a State insists upon proper standards that will cabin the jury's discretionary authority, its punitive damages system may deprive a defendant of "fair notice . . . of the severity of the penalty that a State may impose," *BMW*, supra; it may threaten "arbitrary punishments," i.e., punishments that reflect not an "application of law" but "a decisionmaker's caprice," *State Farm*, supra; and, where the amounts are sufficiently large, it may impose one State's (or one jury's) "policy choice," say as to the conditions under which (or even whether) certain products can be sold, upon "neighboring States" with different public policies, *BMW*, supra.

For these and similar reasons, this Court has found that the Constitution imposes certain limits, in respect both to procedures for awarding punitive damages and to amounts forbidden as "grossly excessive." See Honda Motor Co. v. Oberg, 114 S. Ct. 2331 (1994) (requiring judicial review of the size of punitive awards); Cooper Industries, Inc. v. Leatherman Tool Group, Inc., 121 S. Ct. 1678 (2001) (review must be de novo); *BMW*, supra (excessiveness decision depends upon the reprehensibility of the defendant's conduct, whether the award bears a reasonable relationship to the actual and potential harm caused by the defendant to the plaintiff, and the difference between the award and sanctions "authorized or imposed in comparable cases"); *State Farm*, supra (excessiveness more likely where ratio exceeds single digits). Because we shall not decide whether the award here at issue is "grossly excessive," we need now only consider the Constitution's procedural limitations.

III

In our view, the Constitution's Due Process Clause forbids a State to use a punitive damages award to punish a defendant for injury that it inflicts upon nonparties or those whom they directly represent, i.e., injury that it inflicts upon those who are, essentially, strangers to the litigation. For one thing, the Due Process Clause prohibits a State from punishing an individual without first providing that individual with "an opportunity to present every available defense." Lindsey v. Normet, 92 S. Ct. 862 (1972). Yet a defendant threatened with punishment for injuring a nonparty victim has no opportunity to defend against the charge, by showing, for example in a case such as this, that the other victim was not entitled to damages because he or she knew that smoking was dangerous or did not rely upon the defendant's statements to the contrary.

For another, to permit punishment for injuring a nonparty victim would add a near standardless dimension to the punitive damages equation. How many such victims are there? How seriously were they injured? Under what circumstances did injury occur? The trial will not likely answer such questions as to nonparty victims. The jury will be left to speculate. And the fundamental due process concerns to which our punitive damages cases refer — risks of arbitrariness, uncertainty and lack of notice — will be magnified.

Finally, we can find no authority supporting the use of punitive damages awards for the purpose of punishing a defendant for harming others. We have said that it may be appropriate to consider the reasonableness of a punitive damages award in light of the *potential* harm the defendant's conduct could have caused. But we have made clear that the potential harm at issue was harm potentially caused *the plaintiff.* . . .

Respondent argues that she is free to show harm to other victims because it is relevant to a different part of the punitive damages constitutional equation, namely, reprehensibility. That is to say, harm to others shows more reprehensible conduct. Philip Morris, in turn, does not deny that a plaintiff may show harm to others in order to demonstrate reprehensibility. Nor do we. Evidence of actual harm to nonparties can help to show that the conduct that harmed the plaintiff also posed a substantial risk of harm to the general public, and so was particularly reprehensible — although counsel may argue in a particular case that conduct resulting in no harm to others nonetheless posed a grave risk to the public, or the converse. Yet for the reasons given above, a jury may not go further than this and use a punitive damages verdict to punish a defendant directly on account of harms it is alleged to have visited on nonparties.

Given the risks of unfairness that we have mentioned, it is constitutionally important for a court to provide assurance that the jury will ask the right question, not the wrong one. And given the risks of arbitrariness, the concern for adequate notice, and the risk that punitive damages awards can, in practice, impose one State's (or one jury's) policies (e.g., banning cigarettes) upon other States — all of which accompany awards that, today, may be many times the size of such awards in the 18th and 19th centuries — it is particularly important that States avoid procedure that unnecessarily deprives juries of proper legal guidance. We therefore conclude that the Due Process Clause requires States to provide assurance that juries are not asking the wrong question, i.e., seeking, not simply to determine reprehensibility, but also to punish for harm caused strangers.

IV

Respondent suggests as well that the Oregon Supreme Court, in essence, agreed with us, that it did not authorize punitive damages awards based upon punishment for harm caused to nonparties. We concede that one might read some portions of the Oregon Supreme Court's opinion as focusing only upon reprehensibility. But the Oregon court's opinion elsewhere makes clear that that court held more than these few phrases might suggest.

The instruction that Philip Morris said the trial court should have given distinguishes between using harm to others as part of the "reasonable relationship" equation (which it would allow) and using it directly as a basis for punishment. The instruction asked the trial court to tell the jury that "you *may* consider the extent of harm suffered by others *in determining what [the] reasonable relationship is*" between Philip Morris' punishable misconduct and harm caused to Jesse Williams, "*[but] you are not to punish the defendant for the impact of its alleged misconduct on other persons, who may bring lawsuits of their own* in which other juries can resolve their claims. . . ." And as the Oregon Supreme Court explicitly recognized, Philip Morris argued that the Constitution "prohibits the state, acting through a civil jury, from using punitive damages to punish a defendant for harm to nonparties." 127 P.3d, at 1175.

The court rejected that claim. In doing so, it pointed out (1) that this Court in *State Farm* had held only that a jury could not base its award upon "dissimilar" acts of a defendant. 127 P.3d, at 1175-1176. It added (2) that "[i]f a jury cannot punish for the conduct, then it is difficult to see why it may consider it at all." 127 P.3d, at 1175, n. 3. And it stated (3) that "[i]t is unclear to us how a jury could 'consider' harm to others, yet withhold that consideration from the punishment calculus." Ibid.

The Oregon court's first statement is correct. We did not previously hold explicitly that a jury may not punish for the harm caused others. But we do so hold now. We do not agree with the Oregon court's second statement. We have explained why we believe the Due Process Clause prohibits a State's inflicting punishment for harm caused strangers to the litigation. At the same time we recognize that conduct that risks harm to many is likely more reprehensible than conduct that risks harm to only a few. And a jury consequently may take this fact into account in determining reprehensibility.

The Oregon court's third statement raises a practical problem. How can we know whether a jury, in taking account of harm caused others under the rubric of reprehensibility, also seeks to *punish* the defendant for having caused injury to others? Our answer is that state courts cannot authorize procedures that create an unreasonable and unnecessary risk of any such confusion occurring. In particular, we believe that where the risk of that misunderstanding is a significant one — because, for instance, of the sort of evidence that was introduced at trial or the kinds of argument the plaintiff made to the jury — a court, upon request, must protect against that risk. Although the States have some flexibility to determine what *kind* of procedures they will implement, federal constitutional law obligates them to provide *some* form of protection in appropriate cases.

V

As the preceding discussion makes clear, we believe that the Oregon Supreme Court applied the wrong constitutional standard when considering Philip Morris' appeal. We remand this case so that the Oregon Supreme Court can apply the standard we have set forth. Because the application of this standard may lead to the need for a new trial, or a change in the level of the punitive damages award, we shall not consider whether the award is constitutionally "grossly excessive." We vacate the Oregon Supreme Court's judgment and remand the case for further proceedings not inconsistent with this opinion.

It is so ordered.

Justice STEVENS, dissenting.

The Due Process Clause of the Fourteenth Amendment imposes both substantive and procedural constraints on the power of the States to impose punitive damages on tortfeasors. I remain firmly convinced that the cases announcing those constraints were correctly decided. In my view the Oregon Supreme Court faithfully applied the reasoning in those opinions to the egregious facts disclosed by this record. . . .

Whereas compensatory damages are measured by the harm the defendant has caused the plaintiff, punitive damages are a sanction for the public harm the defendant's conduct has caused or threatened. There is little difference between the justification for a criminal sanction, such as a fine or a term of imprisonment, and an award of punitive damages. . . . And while in neither context would the sanction typically include a pecuniary award measured by the harm that the conduct had caused to any third parties, in both contexts the harm to third parties would surely be a relevant factor to consider in evaluating the reprehensibility of the defendant's wrongdoing. We have never held otherwise.

In the case before us, evidence attesting to the possible harm the defendant's extensive deceitful conduct caused other Oregonians was properly presented to the jury. No evidence was offered to establish an appropriate measure of damages to compensate such third parties for their injuries, and no one argued that the punitive damages award would serve any such purpose. To award compensatory damages to remedy such third-party harm might well constitute a taking of property from the defendant without due process. But a punitive damages award, instead of serving a compensatory purpose, serves the entirely different purposes of retribution and deterrence that underlie every criminal sanction. . . .

While apparently recognizing the novelty of its holding, the majority relies on a distinction between taking third-party harm into account in order to assess the reprehensibility of the defendant's conduct — which is permitted — from doing so in order to punish the defendant "directly" — which is forbidden. This nuance eludes me. When a jury increases a punitive damages award because injuries to third parties enhanced the reprehensibility of the defendant's conduct, the jury is by definition punishing the defendant-directly-for third-party harm. A murderer who kills his victim by throwing a bomb that injures dozens of bystanders should be punished more severely than one who harms no one other than his intended victim. Similarly, there is no reason why the measure of the appropriate punishment for engaging in a campaign of deceit in distributing a poisonous and addictive substance to thousands of cigarette smokers statewide should not include consideration of the harm to those "bystanders" as well as the harm to the individual plaintiff. The Court endorses a contrary conclusion without providing us with any reasoned justification.

I would affirm [the Supreme Court of Oregon's] judgment.

Justice THOMAS, dissenting.

I join Justice GINSBURG's dissent in full. I write separately to reiterate my view that "'the Constitution does not constrain the size of punitive damages awards.'" State Farm Mut. Automobile Ins. Co. v. Campbell, (THOMAS, J., dissenting). It matters not that the Court styles today's holding as "procedural" because the "procedural" rule is simply a confusing implementation of the substantive due process regime this Court has created for punitive damages. . . . Today's opinion proves once again that this Court's punitive damages jurisprudence is "insusceptible of principled application." BMW of North America, Inc. v. Gore, (SCALIA, J., joined by THOMAS, J., dissenting).

Justice GINSBURG, with whom Justice SCALIA and Justice THOMAS join, dissenting. The purpose of punitive damages, it can hardly be denied, is not to compensate, but to punish. Punish for what? Not for harm actually caused "strangers to the litigation," the Court states, but for the *reprehensibility* of defendant's conduct, *ante*, at 1063-1064. "[C]onduct that risks harm to many," the Court observes, "is likely more reprehensible than conduct that risks harm to only a few." The Court thus conveys that, when punitive damages are at issue, a jury is properly instructed to consider the extent of harm suffered by others as a measure of reprehensibility, but not to mete out punishment for injuries in fact sustained by nonparties. The Oregon courts did not rule otherwise. They have endeavored to follow our decisions, . . . and have "depri-ve[d][no jury] of proper legal guidance." Vacation of the Oregon Supreme Court's judgment, I am convinced, is unwarranted. . . .

For the reasons stated, and in light of the abundant evidence of "the potential harm [Philip Morris'] conduct could have caused," I would affirm the decision of the Oregon Supreme Court.

The Supreme Court never reached the issue of excessiveness-based-on-ratio in Philip Morris USA v. Williams. On remand, the Oregon Supreme Court affirmed the $79.5 million punitive damage award. Surprisingly, the Oregon Court found that the plaintiff's request for instructions in the original trial was inadequate on state grounds and thus the constitutional issue dealing with the problem of punitive damages based on injury to non-party victims was moot. See Williams v. Philip Morris Inc., 176 P.3d 1255 (Or. 2008). After originally granting certiorari to review the Oregon Supreme Court decision on remand, 128 S. Ct. 2904 (2008), the U.S. Supreme Court subsequently dismissed certiorari as improvidently granted (2009). In Schwarz

v. Philip Morris Inc., 2015 WL 4275360 (Or. Ct. App. 2015), an intermediate court in Oregon upheld against constitutional challenges a punitive damages award of $25 million for a suit that had garnered less than $180,000 of compensatory damages.

Whether the Supreme Court will allow trial courts to impose substantial, high-ratio punitive awards in favor of products liability plaintiffs suffering personal injury is not clear. On the one hand, the four dissenting Justices in *Williams* voted to uphold a punitive award based on nearly a 100-to-1 ratio. It would take only one more vote to establish the principle that, at least in personal injury cases involving allegedly egregious conduct, the ratio-based approach considered in *State Farm* does not apply. On the other hand, the *Williams* restrictions on the conduct for which plaintiffs may ask juries to punish defendants may dampen somewhat attempts by plaintiffs hereafter to inflame the passions of juries by arguing that defendant companies deserve to pay hugely for all the harm they have done to so many other victims. Moreover, the Supreme Court has yet to address an issue that has for decades been recognized as troublesome: the unfairness of punishing a defendant multiple times, in a succession of tort actions by different plaintiffs, for the same egregious conduct. Assuming that, when the Court finally addresses the issue of successive, arguably redundant punishment, it will attempt to place due-process-based restrictions on multiple punishments, and such restrictions will further limit the power of state courts to allow huge punitive damages awards.

For more recent scholarship on the constitutional control of punitive damages, see Benjamin Michael, Constitutional Limitations on Punitive Damages: Ambiguous Effects and Inconsistent Justifications, 66 Vand. L. Rev. 961 (2014); N. William Hines, Marching To A Different Drummer: Are Lower Courts Faithfully Implementing The Evolving Due Process Guideposts To Catch And Correct Excessive Punitive Damages Awards?, 62 Cath. U. L. Rev. 371 (2013).

CHAPTER NINE

Products Liability in a Global Context

Although the developments in products liability law that most directly affect American consumers and firms involve claims brought in American courts based on events that have occurred within this country, students of products liability law cannot afford to ignore the international dimensions of the field. Transportation and communications technologies, not to mention the role of international trade agreements, have intensified the interdependence of national economies and created a truly global marketplace. According to the U.S. Census Bureau, between the United States and China alone, the value of annual bilateral trade has risen from $7.7 billion in 1985 to $590.6 billion in 2014. The increasing movement of goods across borders raises questions for injured consumers regarding whom they can sue, in which forum, and under what system of products liability law. The lack of harmony among trading partners with respect to product safety regulations and liability laws also gives rise to challenging policy questions regarding the impact on national economic competitiveness and the appropriateness of protective trade measures.

The first part of this chapter offers comparative perspective on products liability systems, with particular attention to the rules and practices that have emerged in Europe and Japan; the second part examines some policy implications of these diverging rules and practices, including the question of whether the U.S. liability system unduly burdens its domestic business firms and whether imported products should be subjected to special scrutiny or compensatory measures on account of perceived differences in national product safety systems.

A. PRODUCTS LIABILITY LAW BEYOND THE UNITED STATES

Mathias Reimann, Liability for Defective Products at the Beginning of the Twenty-First Century: Emergence of a Worldwide Standard?*
51 Am. J. Comp. L. 751 (Fall 2003)

A Search for Global Developments

In the last few decades, the compensation for harm inflicted by defective products has been an important political and legal agenda in the majority of the economically

---

* This article is a revised and abbreviated version of the General Report presented at the XVIth Congress of the International Academy of Comparative Law in Brisbane, Australia, on July 19, 2002. The

developed nations. Following the American example set in the 1960s and 1970s, many countries have reformed their laws and moved towards stricter standards of liability. While we have countless studies of the respective national laws and even quite a few collections on regional developments, we lack comparative overview of the worldwide situation. The main purpose of this Report is to provide a picture of the status quo on a global basis. In particular, its goal is to compare the various national laws in theory and practice in order to assess how much uniformity there is among them, how much diversity remains, and whether there are any global developments. . . .

Countries Considered

In its survey of the status quo and its search for global developments, this Report draws on the laws of over forty countries. It relies primarily on the twenty-two national reports received. Consulting various additional sources, the Report also considers the law of about two dozen other jurisdictions although the available information about them is often not as comprehensive as in the national reports. These additional sources also supplemented the information provided in the various national reports themselves. . . .

Conditions of Liability

Under which conditions can the victim hold a defendant liable? As a rule, the plaintiff has a cause of action only if the item in question was a "product" (a), had a "defect" (b), was put on the market by the defendant in an already defective condition (c), and caused the plaintiff's harm (d). Regarding several of these conditions, victims may benefit from a shifted burden of proof (e). As a rule, the special product liability regimes do not expressly require a showing of fault but that does not mean that liability under them is always truly strict.

a. Product

What counts as a "product" is by and large a fairly simple question — not because there is universal agreement (there is not) but because the answer follows from statutory or other definitions. The prototypical concept at the heart of modern product liability law is that of a moveable and tangible good resulting from industrialized mass-production. Most regimes limit the definition of a product to moveables. For the European Union, the EC-Directive dictates this result; in the United States it is generally accepted; and many other countries follow suit; jurisdictions which include buildings, like Cyprus, Israel and Taiwan, are the exception. Component parts generally count, even if built into other objects (moveables or buildings). But systems differ on whether unprocessed agricultural products are included because they often do not result from "industrialized mass-production."

---

authors believe that the Report from which this text is excerpted is the best short summary of foreign products liability law available. The heavily footnoted, longer version, and the book in which it appears, are recommended reading for products liability mavens.

Whatever the specific definition of "product," if the item in question in a particular case is covered, the respective special (strict) liability regime will apply; otherwise, a plaintiff must look to the general tort or contract remedies.

b. Defect

If the definition of a "product" is perhaps the easiest problem among the conditions of liability, the determination of what constitutes a "defect" is probably the most difficult. Three factors complicate the matter: the panoply of formulated definitions, the competition between two basic tests, and the existence of three defect types suggesting different treatment.

First, there is a considerable diversity of definitions in the various product liability regimes. Some of these definitions are not very helpful to begin with because they are terribly imprecise or outright tautological. In addition, several systems eschew the notion of a "defect" altogether but rather ask whether the product was "dangerous," had a "safety deficiency" or created an (undue) "risk." The variety of approaches is also illustrated by the fact that different regimes weigh even the non-compliance with mandatory safety regulations differently: some consider such a violation conclusive while others regard it as a rebuttable presumption or simply as mere evidence of defectiveness.

Second, most systems ultimately tend to rely on one of two tests. The first of these tests looks to justified consumer expectations: roughly speaking, a product is defective if it is more dangerous than the average consumer has reason to anticipate. This test prevails in the majority of jurisdictions. It rules supreme in Europe where it is codified in art. 6(2) of the EC Directive and consequently applies in all EU member states as well as in most other European countries; it was also adopted in jurisdictions around the world, including Australia, Brazil, China, Japan, Korea, Malaysia, Peru, the Philippines, Quebec, and Taiwan. The other major approach is the risk-utility analysis. It renders a product defective if its risks outweigh its utility. To put it more colloquially: there is a defect if the product is more dangerous than absolutely necessary in light of its purpose. This test tends to dominate in the United States. There, it lies at the heart of the Third Restatement and looks like the trend of the future. Yet, it would be wrong neatly to divide the world into separate geographic spheres governed by different tests. The consumer expectation paradigm is also used in the United States, often in combination with the risk-utility analysis, and the risk-utility analysis is occasionally used in other countries as well, albeit mostly to define negligence in general tort law. Thus the difference is really one of emphasis: on the risk-utility approach in the United States, on the consumer expectation test in the rest of the world. Both tests have been praised and criticized for their advantages and disadvantages but a substantive evaluation is beyond the purpose of this Report.

Third, there are three basic types of defects which may call for different treatment: manufacturing defects, design defects, and insufficient warnings (sometimes called instruction defects). While these categories are almost generally recognized in theory by scholars and often even by courts, legal systems differ as to their recognition on the level of blackletter law. The majority of specialized product liability regimes do not distinguish between them. Thus the EC-Directive applies the same rules to all defect types, as do the many statutes modeled after it in jurisdictions inside and outside of Europe. In most of the respective countries, it also seems that courts actually do approach all defects under the same rules. A minority of countries apply different approaches to the various categories. Such differentiation is pervasive in the United States where liability for manufacturing defects tends to be considerably stricter than in design and warning cases, but the distinction is apparently also persistent (in spite of the EC Directive) in Italian law and built into the Russian Consumer Protection Act. In short, with regard to different defect categories, there is considerable uniformity on the level of product liability theory but persistent difference on the level of positive rules. . . .

Burden of Proof

According to almost universally accepted principles of civil procedure, the plaintiff must plead, and in case of doubt prove, the elements of his or her cause of action. This would normally require the plaintiff to establish that the defendant put a defective product into circulation which then caused the plaintiff's harm. Yet, matters are not so simple because most regimes shift some of the burden of proof to the defendant, albeit in different ways. There is, once more, essentially an American and a European approach with the rest of the world following one or the other or falling in between.

The American approach is that the plaintiff bears the burden of proof regarding all these conditions in principle but that courts can also ease that burden concerning all the requirements in an individual case. The main device used for that purpose is the venerable doctrine of res ipsa loquitur which is widely shared among common law jurisdictions. This doctrine exists in various versions but essentially boils down to one basic idea: if, under the circumstances of the case, common sense strongly suggests that things were as the plaintiff says, the court may presume that they were so even if the plaintiff cannot really prove it. The strength of this presumption varies. It may amount to a fairly weak inference which the defendant can destroy by presenting no more than a plausible alternative explanation, or it can lead to a fully reversed burden of proof which the defendant can overcome only by substantial evidence. Originally developed for issues of negligence, American courts also have employed this doctrine to establish the existence of a defect (at the time the product was put on the market) and concerning cause. The Third Restatement openly endorses this approach.

The European model, as codified in the EC Directive, is more categorical. It divides the conditions of liability into two groups and assigns burdens of proof according to unambiguous rules. Art. 4 states that the plaintiff has to establish defect, harm, and the causal connection between them. Art. 7 then provides a list of items which the defendant may prove in order to exonerate himself, among them "that he did not put the product into circulation" and "that, having regard to the circumstances, it is probable that the defect which caused the damage did not exist at the time when the product was put into circulation by him or that this defect came into being afterwards." Such are the ground rules throughout Western Europe and, often with modifications, in many jurisdictions elsewhere.

Which approach is more helpful to a plaintiff in distress? At first glance, the American model may look friendlier to victims: it allows easing the burden of proof not only concerning a few more or less marginal issues but also where it really counts in most cases: regarding defectiveness and causation. In comparison, the European Directive seems tough on plaintiffs when it comes to these core issues and tinkers with burdens of proof only in questions that will rarely arise to begin with, such as whether the defendant really put the product on the market. Yet, how plaintiffs will actually fare under these two approaches cannot be answered in any general fashion because it all depends on how the respective models work out in practice. Under the American model, the plaintiff's situation turns on the particular version of res ipsa loquitur employed, the facts of the individual case, the inclination of the judge, and, frequently, the mood of the jury. Under the European approach, it is contingent on what is really required "to prove" defectiveness and causation. The Directive leaves that for the adopting countries to decide under their general rules and many courts in these countries actually ease the burden of proof quite considerably, sometimes in ways that closely resemble the res ipsa loquitur doctrine. . . .

Negligence? (Or: How Strict Is Products Liability?)

Among the conditions of liability, we have not mentioned negligence. The clear majority of special product liability regimes today do not require the plaintiff to show that the defendant was at fault. This is particularly true where these regimes are statutory. Thus the EC Directive seeks to impose liability without fault as do the numerous statutes that adopt its basic design as well as many others that were drafted more or less independently. In the United States, where the area is essentially governed by caselaw, this used to be the ground rule as well. Section 402A of the Second Restatement, which most courts accepted and many continue to follow, was adamant that liability was independent from fault. To be sure, the strict liability paradigm does not entirely sweep the field: Canadian and Indian law is clearly predicated on negligence; the Third Restatement in the United States sometimes speaks in terms of reasonableness and foreseeability; and in some Latin American countries, the question whether product liability rests on fault is disputed. Still, the majority rule is otherwise: at least if taken at face value, most special product liability regimes today are in principle based on strict liability.

Yet, this does not mean that liability is always truly strict in the sense of "completely independent of negligence." Instead, how strict it really is depends on the type of defendant, the kind of defect, as well as on the jurisdiction involved.

Liability is usually truly strict regarding certain defendants: some actors may be liable even though they had nothing to do with the design, manufacture, or labeling of the product. Under the European approach, this is true for distributors who put their trademark on products made by others, importers, and sometimes even sellers if no other defendant is available in the European Union. In the United States, they include all post-manufacturing links in the chain of distribution, even a small-time retailer. All such defendants have usually done is distribute the product in one way or another, and that, in and of itself, violates no duty of care.

Furthermore, liability is normally truly strict for certain defects: in the vast majority of regimes, manufacturing defects trigger liability regardless of due care. Where an individual specimen of a mass-produced item deviates from the series in a negative (and possibly dangerous) way, the defectiveness is established and no other standard is necessary to ascertain it. A manufacturer bears the risk of such a defect. Of course, one could say that he has a duty of care not to let defective products slip through. But this is just another way of restating the same rule: since this duty is absolute, liability for its violation is strict.

Beyond these two areas, however, doubts begin to arise. When it comes to the liability of manufacturers for design defects and insufficient warnings, strict liability is often tempered with elements normally associated with negligence. Jurisdictions vary as to how openly they acknowledge these elements.

The European approach is more clandestine: it proclaims strict liability but nonetheless implicitly relies on notions of due care in at least two ways. First, it considers a product defective if it is "not as safe as a person is entitled to expect, taking all circumstances into account." But making (and releasing) such a product smacks of negligence. This is not to say that it makes no difference whether one looks to the defendant's conduct or to the product's defect but in design and instruction cases, both are flipsides of the same coin: the manufacturer's conduct results in the product's substandard nature. Second, the crucial moment to judge the product's defectiveness is "the time when it was put into circulation"; in particular, as we shall see, the defendant can escape liability by showing that the defect was unavoidable given the technical or scientific knowledge at the time. In other words, if the defendant did everything possible back then, he will not be liable today, even if the product has since turned out to be unreasonably dangerous. Again, liability really turns on blameworthiness. A truly strict regime would judge purely the product, and it would do so purely at the time of the judgment (or, at most, at the time of the accident). This Report is not the place to enter into the discussion whether these fault-related considerations turn the EC Directive's approach (and others modeled after it) partially into a camouflaged negligence regime or whether liability is still strict in principle. Be that as it may, there is no denying that under it, courts cannot decide design and warning cases without applying some kind of reasonableness standard. At the minimum, strict liability is somewhat ameliorated. . . .

Defenses

Even if the plaintiff establishes that the defendant distributed a product in an already defective condition which caused the plaintiff's harm, the manufacturer or seller can raise various affirmative defenses. Most special product liability regimes allow at least four defenses while excluding several others.

Plaintiff's Conduct

To begin with, the defendant can always claim that the harm was really the result of the plaintiff's own doing. This defense comes in many forms, shapes, and sizes. Most often it is simply a form of the general doctrines of assumption of risk or contributory/comparative negligence. Doubts about the compatibility of the defendant's strict liability with the defendant's contributory fault have been laid to rest.

The plaintiff's conduct often consists of misusing or altering the product, of a failure to heed instructions or warnings, etc. Depending on the jurisdiction and the circumstances, such conduct will normally lead to a reduction of compensation but can sometimes also wipe out the plaintiff's claim altogether. At least in some countries, however, this defense is not as easily allowed as under general tort rules because the defendant has to reckon with a certain degree of carelessness or ignorance by consumers. . . .

Development Risks

In most jurisdictions a manufacturer or seller can also avail himself of the so-called development risk defense: he will not be liable if he proves that the defect was not avoidable given the scientific and technical knowledge at the time the product was put into circulation (but only later as such knowledge developed further). The EC Directive allows this defense. While it also permits the member states to exclude it, all but two have chosen to keep it, sometimes in questionable versions. Most other countries which have followed the European model provide for the defense as well. . . . In practice, however, the development risk defense seems to be of very limited relevance. At least in Europe, litigation involving it is rare. Problems are by and large limited to drug cases in which side effects become knowable only after a product has already caused the harm. And if the defense is construed as narrowly as the EC Directive suggests, escaping liability will be very difficult anyway. . . .

The Reality of Litigation and Compensation: The United States v. the Rest of the World

[T]he United States is no longer the only country with tough product liability rules. Almost all industrialized nations have them today. Yet, when we turn from the law on the books to the law in action, we see a very different picture. As far as the reality of litigation and compensation is concerned, it is still the United States versus the Rest of the World. Whether one looks at the number of suits filed or the amount of compensation awarded, the United States is a world apart. No other country comes even close. . . .

The Volume of Litigation

Victims in the United States bring product liability suits in numbers unheard of anywhere else. As a result, product liability litigation in the United States is big business while it is of marginal importance in the Rest of the World. This is true both in absolute and relative terms.

Product Liability Actions in United States Courts

Between 1975 and 1997, product liability litigation in the United States exploded. In less than a quarter century, the annual number of cases filed in the federal courts alone rose from 2,393 to 32,856. For reasons that are not quite clear, it has since dropped to about 15,000 per year. In addition, there are the cases filed in the state courts. While there are no directly corresponding data for the state judiciary, studies suggest that they carry about half the burden of product liability litigation. This means that ca. 30,000 actions based on product defects are currently filed in American courts per year— about one for 9,000 inhabitants. . . .

The Rest of the World

Nothing like this exists anywhere else in the world. [D]ata are scarce and may be unreliable but it is clear that no other country has a comparable number of product liability suits, not even in relative terms. To be sure, "the Rest of the World" is a big and diverse place. But whatever the differences among the various countries, they are dwarfed by the differences between them as a group and the United States.

Where the respective national reports submitted speak to this point, their message is imprecise but unequivocal. The number of product liability suits ranges from "modest" and "quite low" to "very rare" and "almost no officially reported cases." It may not mean much that there are "very few cases" in developing countries like Peru or

India but even in rich nations like Belgium, Canada, Korea and Switzerland, product liability litigation simply does not play a significant role. This is confirmed by the one jurisdiction outside of the United States for which we have more specific data, i.e., Japan. Between 1945 and 1994, a total of about 200 product liability judgments were reported in Japan, and that included appeals; fifty or so additional cases were filed in the mid- and late 1990s. This means that there are at the very most a dozen reported product liability decisions per year for a country with about half the population and half the economic output of the United States. In Japan as elsewhere, the subject as a whole simply "does not occupy the prominent place that one would expect it to play in a dense technological society with a highly developed system of judicial redress." As one of the leading experts in comparative product liability law put it, even in Europe, "few lawyers can make a living out of product liability and only a few more will ever come across a product liability case." . . .

The Size of Awards

Recovery in the United States

American tort judgments, especially for personal injury, have a well-deserved reputation for being high. This is particularly true in product liability cases. In fact, compensation for injury caused by products on average significantly exceeds awards in other personal injury cases, such as medical malpractice.

In 1999, the mean (average) award in product liability actions was $3,045,908, the highest judgment came to $285,000,000. These numbers include compensation for pain and suffering but not punitive damages. They show that American product liability victories can easily, and often do, result in judgments well in excess of a million dollars. This does not necessarily mean that plaintiffs are being overcompensated. Long-term medical care costs are high, lost income alone can quickly exceed a million dollars over a lifetime, not to mention great pain and suffering in catastrophic injury cases; and one must not forget that a substantial portion of the overall award goes to the plaintiff's lawyer as a contingency fee. But it does mean that the American product liability system transfers enormous amounts of money from defendants to plaintiffs. Of course, most cases are settled but settlements are based on predicted outcomes in court because parties bargain "in the shadow of the law." . . .

Compensation Elsewhere

Like litigation rates, damage awards in the rest of the world are significantly lower. The range is broad, however, because some systems award fairly substantial damages while others are incredibly cheap.

National Reports and other statements in the literature are unanimous that damage awards in the respective jurisdictions are modest. This holds true for rich, industrial countries like Belgium, France, Italy, Japan, Korea, and Spain as well as for developing ones like India, Indonesia, or Peru. Concrete numbers are, once again, hard to come by. But even though they allow only occasional glimpses, these glimpses show that the size of judgments remains well below what is common in the United States. Take, again, Japan, a country with at least comparable costs of living. The highest product liability judgment entered in the 1990s amounted to 45 million yen (ca. $364,000) under the Civil Code and 44 million yen (ca. $356,000) under the Product Liability Act. Belgian courts allowed the victim of an exploding soda bottle BEF 500,000 (ca. $11,000) for pecuniary loss, BEF 3,000 (ca. $70) for pain and suffering, and a further BEF 15,000 (ca. $370) for "aesthetic impairment." In Brazil, judgments sometimes amounted to $25,000 in the 1990s but courts have become less generous since. In Spain, average claims are under $5000 although the highest judgment did come to $1 million. The only country where personal injury awards can also amount to millions of dollars seems to be Canada. There, judgments have exceeded Can. $5 mill. (ca. US $3.3 mill.) in catastrophic cases. Still, on average, even Canadian judgments are "usually significantly below recovery levels in the US." . . .

A major reason why judgments in the rest of the world are so much lower than in the United States is that most non-American courts will award only the pecuniary damages clearly documented and add comparatively low sums for pain and suffering. There is, as far as the national reports indicate, no jurisdiction outside of the United States where a plaintiff can currently recover more than about $300,000 for non-pecuniary damages, even in the most catastrophic cases. Courts in many countries also set awards for pain and suffering according to unofficial schedules and thus stay within generally accepted, and usually fairly low, limits. . . .

The Institutional, Procedural, and Social Environment: A Search for Explanations

What explains the dramatically different practical impact of (strict) product liability rules, especially the higher litigation volume, in the United States versus the Rest of the World? There is no simple answer. Trying to resolve the question involves a good deal of speculation; moreover, there are many factors at work, often in changing combinations, and depending on the jurisdiction involved. . . .

The practical impact of product liability (and other) law depends primarily on the broader legal and social context. It is one thing to bring an action in a system where courts are socially activist, procedures allow vigorous prosecution of claims, the bar is specialized, victims rely primarily on civil damages for their recovery, and product liability cases make headlines. It is quite another to file a suit in a country where courts emphasize restraint, procedural rules disfavor aggressive litigation, attorneys do not specialize, first party insurance covers most losses, and the public does not care. In short, an understanding of product liability law in action requires that we consider it in its institutional (I.), procedural (II.), professional (III.), insurance (IV.) and broader social environment (V.).

I. Institutions

. . . As far as institutions are concerned, the great dividing line is between the jurisdictions that use a civil jury in product liability claims and those that do not.

The former group is exceedingly small because the United States is its only full-fledged member. Almost all product liability cases that go to trial in an American court are decided by a lay jury. Plaintiffs have the right to ask for one and routinely do so. Juries can also sit in Australia and Canada but they do not play nearly as important a role as in the United States. In Australian or Canadian product liability cases, jury trials are not the rule but the exception. They exist only in some provinces or territories, and juries are more tightly controlled by judges than is common in the United States.

The membership in the non-jury group is much more numerous: it contains all of the remaining countries considered in this Report (as well as many more). In other words, jury trials in product liability cases are allowed only in a tiny minority of countries and regularly held only in one. Still, since this one country is the jurisdiction with by far the largest litigation volume, juries decide a huge portion, and perhaps even the majority, of product liability cases on a worldwide level.

The fact that most product liability actions are filed where juries decide them is no coincidence. Juries are a great attraction for plaintiffs. To be sure, jurors are not nearly as biased in the victims' favor as is commonly perceived: even in American jury trials, plaintiffs lose more often than they win. In fact, some studies suggest that juries may be more favorably inclined towards defendants than judges, at least on the issue of liability, although there is reason to believe that juries may be more generous in assessing damages, especially if the defendant is a deep pocket. In the end, the most important concern about juries is not what they do but what they might do. Their unpredictability threatens a losing defendant with a potentially catastrophic verdict. Rather than gamble, most manufacturers or sellers prefer to avoid the risk and settle, even at high cost. . . .

II. Procedures

What are the most influential procedural features in products liability cases? As with jury trials on the institutional level, we can see that for plaintiffs, the United States offers several advantages over most other legal systems. In particular, filing a complaint is cheap (1.), discovery rights are powerful (2.), and collective actions allow the pooling of resources (3.).

1. The Costs of Filing

In the United States, it is cheap to file a lawsuit. Court fees are very low, service of process can be achieved by mail, and attorneys typically take personal injury cases on a contingency fee basis, i.e., usually without an up-front retainer. As a result, the start-up cost for plaintiffs is minimal and easily within reach of most victims. To be sure, many product liability suits become phenomenally expensive — but only if they proceed further.

In most other countries, beginning a lawsuit is much more costly. Filing a $1,000,000 action in Japan requires not only a court fee of about $5,000 but also an up-front retainer of about $35,000 payable to the plaintiff's lawyer. Even in Germany, the court fee for a DM 1,000,000 (ca. $500,000) suit in 1999, was DM 5,905 (almost $3,000) and the lawyer's fee (just for filing the case) came to another DM 6,225 (ca. $3,100). In countries like Japan or Germany, it is less likely that expenses will spin out of control later on but the financial entry-barrier is significant. . . .

2. Discovery Rights

American law provides the most extensive discovery rights in the world. For better or worse, American rules "enable plaintiffs to press claims that are initially supported by little or no evidence, and that would not give rise to litigation in systems with more restrictive evidence-taking procedures." Way before trial, a party can orally question witnesses under oath (depositions), request written responses to a list of questions (interrogatories), and demand the delivery of files (document production). Under the Federal Rules of Civil Procedure, the opponent must even identify and hand over proof on his own motion.

No other legal system provides the parties with such powerful discovery instruments. In civil law countries, there is simply nothing at all like a pre-trial discovery process. A party must essentially put the initial case together without any cooperation from the other side. Once in court, he or she can ask the judge to request certain documents from the opponent, to subpoena witnesses, or to allow examinations, but without an explicit order by the court, neither the opponent nor third parties are normally under an obligation to assist the plaintiff. Under this approach, it is obviously very difficult, if not impossible, for a victim or her lawyer to investigate a product liability case. To be sure, in some jurisdictions with a civilian procedural system, recent reforms have somewhat strengthened the parties' rights to obtain evidence from the other side, as in Japan, Germany, and Spain. But these measures do not even approach an American-style discovery regime, and it remains to be seen whether they will have much of an impact in practice.

More substantial pre-trial discovery rights typically exist in common law systems. Opponents are normally obligated to produce specified documents, to answer interrogatories, and sometimes even to submit to depositions. In some countries, these rights can be quite extensive. In Canada, for example, they resemble the American approach and are considered "generally effective."

Still, as all national reporters agree, none of these systems go as far as discovery rules in the United States. Most importantly, it is only in the United States that a party can search broadly for evidence yet unknown: "The information sought need not be admissible at the trial," instead it is enough that it "appears reasonably calculated to lead to the discovery of admissible evidence." This allows a product liability plaintiff to go on a "fishing-expedition" in the defendant's records in the mere hope of finding a "smoking gun," i.e., a crucial piece of incriminating evidence. American product liability law is full of examples where such a find was indeed made and where the defendant paid a tremendous price.

3. Collective Procedures

. . . To what extent do legal systems allow representatives to bring a product liability claim for others?

The answer to this question varies greatly among the jurisdictions considered in this Report. The range of models and the resultant procedural diversity is quite bewildering. Greatly simplifying, one can put the various approaches into three major categories.

The first category consists of regimes which allow a representative plaintiff to sue for the damages suffered by all similarly situated victims, and which give the judgment res judicata effect for all of them, whether named as parties or not. Such actions are often allowed in the common law world. The prototype is the American class action, especially in the federal courts. In the United States, it has been employed in product liability litigation with some regularity, although obtaining class certification is not easy in light of the courts' frequent reluctance to entertain mass tort suits. Since 1992, class actions have also been allowed in the federal courts of Australia. In Canada, three provinces permit such actions while several others allow representative suits of a somewhat similar nature. A roughly comparable, albeit somewhat different, approach is the group litigation procedure in England, Wales, and Ireland. Finally, the so-called representative suits in India are by and large the functional equivalents of class actions since their outcomes are also "binding on all persons on whose behalf, or for whose benefit, the suit is instituted." Interestingly, today these types of collective proceedings are spreading beyond the common law orbit albeit in modified forms and limited to consumer claims. In Spain, designated consumer organizations can now sue on behalf of consumer victims and obtain a judgment for damages with binding effect on all those similarly situated; this allows essentially a class action led by a public interest organization. A similar class action regime exists in Brazil. A partial representative action is allowed in the Netherlands: qualified associations can sue a defendant to establish the wrongfulness of certain conduct. Actions for damages still have to be brought by the respective victims but they can build on the previous declaratory judgment and only need to prove individual causation and damages.

The second category comprises regimes under which representatives pursue claims for damages suffered by themselves and others but where the judgment binds only the named parties. In principle, this approach is based on the joinder of plaintiffs (which is allowed in most countries under varying conditions) and just adds the feature that these plaintiffs delegate the prosecution of their case to a representative. In most legal systems, the representative is one of the plaintiffs themselves. This is true in several Asian countries, such as China, Korea, Malaysia, and Taiwan. In some other jurisdictions, injured persons may also assign their claims to a consumer protection group which can then represent them in court (pro bono) and, in case of victory, will distribute the proceeds to the assignors. This option exists in Taiwan and Austria.

The last type of collective proceedings comprises a large and highly diverse variety of actions brought by representatives of common interests who sue for collective relief. They may seek compensation for the group itself, an injunction against a manufacturer or seller to withdraw a product, or simply the vindication of the public interest at large. Proceedings of this nature differ as to their prerequisites and precise effect but are now permitted in several countries. In Europe, for example, Denmark, France, Greece, Italy, Poland, Portugal, and Spain allow them in various forms; they are also possible in Brazil, India, and Peru. They express broader consumer protection policies but do not generate damage judgments for individuals. . . .

III. Legal Representation and Its Cost

Product liability plaintiffs need lawyers. If victims can cheaply find a lawyer, more of them will hire one. If they owe nothing in case of defeat, more of them will sue. And if their lawyer is determined and specialized, more of them will win. In short, how product liability law functions in practice depends in no small part on the rules and realities of legal representation.

1. Contingency and Success Fees

. . . The United States is not the only country to allow [lawyer fee arrangements contingent on client's recovery]. But nowhere else, it seems, are they as broadly permitted and as commonly used. Where they are allowed at all, they are often more restricted by law or at least not as common in practice. In many jurisdictions, they do not exist at all.

Contingency fee arrangements are possible in some Canadian provinces but their use is not as common as south of the border. They are also allowed, at least to some extent, in Israel, Korea, South Africa, and, surprisingly, in a few European countries like Greece and Finland; even England has lately introduced them. In addition, a variation of the contingency fee, the no-win-no-fee approach, is becoming increasingly common in some jurisdictions, including Australia, England, and Spain. While the lawyer does not receive a share of the award but a scheduled or hourly fee if the case is won, he or she receives nothing if the case is lost. As under a contingency fee arrangement, the lawyer bears the risk so that potential clients are more likely to hire him or her.

Several other countries, including Belgium, France, and Japan, outlaw contingency agreements but permit a success fee. The lawyer receives his regular remuneration regardless of the outcome but can charge an additional percentage if the client wins. Such an arrangement lowers the client's cost risk only slightly and is unlikely to have a great impact on the willingness to hire counsel.

Finally, many countries, especially in the civil law orbit, strictly prohibit any kind of contingency agreements. They consider it unethical and dangerous for a lawyer to have any financial stake in the outcome of a case. This does not necessarily mean that clients have to pay their lawyers whether they win or not (that depends on the rules about cost allocation between winners and losers — infra 2.). But it does mean that the client bears the risk of having to pay at least his own lawyer in full even if the litigation avails him nothing.

2. The Basic Cost Allocation Rules

A victim's willingness to sue also depends more generally on who has to pay whose lawyer under which circumstances. . . . In terms of basic cost allocation, the United States rule is straightforward: each side pays its own lawyer, regardless of outcome. This is, again, highly favorable to plaintiffs. Not only do they owe their own lawyer nothing if they lose, they are not liable for the other side's fee either. As far as litigation expenses are concerned, losing costs plaintiffs nothing. As a result, suing is (financially) virtually risk free. Consequently, victims are quite willing to take their case to court.

Most other countries surveyed for this Report take a very different approach: the loser pays both his and the winner's attorney fees. To be sure, there are several jurisdictions which follow the American rule and, even under some loser-pays-all systems, liability for the opponent's costs may be limited in one way or another. But in the clear majority of nations, a plaintiff must reckon with having to pay for several items if he loses: court costs, his own lawyer's fees, and (at least to some extent) those of his opponent's counsel as well. Facing this risk, victims will think twice before they sue.

3. The Specialization of the Bar

. . . The American bar is not only huge, it is also highly specialized. Even in the absence of formal categories or official qualification requirements, there is, in the personal injury field, a rather sharp division into plaintiffs' lawyers and defense attorneys, and the line is rarely crossed. Moreover, there is a high degree of specialization even within these groups, especially within the plaintiffs' bar. Not only do many of its members focus exclusively on products liability cases, some even specialize more narrowly on particular products, such as pharmaceuticals, asbestos or, more recently, tobacco. This degree of specialization engenders high expertise concerning the respective industry, its production processes, testing procedures, licensing standards, and safety record. In addition, specialists in certain areas often share information through formal or informal nationwide networks. If there is something wrong with a product, it doesn't escape these expert attorneys for long. Furthermore, they often command enormous financial resources, either as members of large firms with multimillion dollar budgets, or through combining forces with other law offices. As a result, the plaintiffs' bar in the United States has both the expertise and the financial resources to take on billion dollar corporations — and to defeat them.

There is no comparable bar in other jurisdictions. In most countries, there is very little specialization to begin with, and certainly none on product liability. As we have seen, litigation of that type is usually too scarce to concentrate on. In some nations, some lawyers specialize on personal injury claims or consumer issues but that still covers a very broad range of cases. . . .

4. Expert Witnesses

. . . In the United States, expert testimony is virtually indispensable in most cases and constitutes a major element in a product liability suit. Experts are hired and paid by the parties. Courts can also appoint them but normally do not exercise that power. Accordingly, experts are partisan. The advantage of this approach is that they are normally highly specialized, often extremely knowledgeable, and thus potentially very helpful in finding the factual truth. The downside is that they are expensive, often biased, and that both sides routinely appoint their own, resulting in the proverbial battle of experts in the courtroom.

There are partisan experts outside of the United States as well. They are widely used in common law systems but also quite frequent in Japan and Quebec. But even there, one does not find such a culture of expert testimony nor such an outright industry of expert witnesses as in the United States.

In other, especially civil law, countries, experts have a very different status and function. They are selected and appointed by the court. The parties can, and sometimes do, present their own experts but that makes them suspect of bias so that courts are reluctant to trust them; a tribunal will rather rely its own candidate. His or her job is to assist the judge in understanding and evaluating the evidence. Consequently, an expert is expected to be neutral, objective, and reliable. Whether judges often accept the experts' views too uncritically, is a different question.

The regular use, great specialization, and vigorous efforts of expert witnesses in the United States often enable American victims and their lawyers to identify product defects that litigants in other countries would overlook or at least could not prove. This, again, favors more product liability actions, at least in cases involving claims large enough to make the employment of experts worthwhile. Where the defect is real and the claim is meritorious, experts have a salutary effect. But they can also help lawyers to occupy the courts, and even to blackmail defendants, with far-fetched allegations based on junk science or mere speculation.

IV. The Role of Insurance

Much, if not most, of the personal injury or property damage resulting from defective products is ultimately covered by insurance. . . .

1. First-Party Insurance

While some plaintiffs sue to vindicate their rights and have their day in court, most people bring damage claims to recoup their loss. But if the victims' loss is already covered by first-party insurance, a suit against the tortfeasor is unlikely. In some systems such a suit is simply foreclosed by statute (insurance takes precedence over tort law) although this is the exception. Most jurisdictions leave it to the injured person where to look for compensation. This choice, however, is rather obvious because it is usually much easier, cheaper, and faster to pursue a claim against one's own insurance than to win a lawsuit (and then to execute a judgment) against a tortfeasor.

When it comes to the extent of first-party insurance coverage, there is a significant difference between the United States on the one hand and the majority of countries surveyed for this Report on the other: on the whole, Americans enjoy less coverage not only than Western Europeans but also than citizens in many other parts of the world. This is particularly true regarding the consequences of personal injury, i.e., medical expenses, loss of income, and long-term disability.

In the United States, accident victims are not nearly protected comprehensively. In 1997, 16 percent of all Americans and 37 percent of the low-income population had no health coverage at all, and the number kept rising. Only 66 percent of the adult workforce have disability benefits, and these benefits are usually less than ample. All States have enacted workers compensation schemes but the compensation they pay is fairly low and often insufficient to make ends meet. Overall, social and workers insurance cover only about three-fifths of the economic consequences of accidents, forcing victims to bear the remaining 40 percent themselves. To be sure, in comparison with many other, especially poorer, countries, these numbers are quite respectable. But they seem low from a Western European, Australian, Canadian, or Japanese perspective.

Virtually throughout Western Europe, the bulk of the financial consequences of personal injuries (whether caused by defective products or something else) are covered under a large variety of public, semi-public or work-related insurance schemes, ranging from tax-funded national health insurance to fairly generous unemployment benefits and long-term disability pensions. Of course there are still variations among the countries: for example, social insurance rights are probably most comprehensive in Scandinavia but seem to be less so in Spain. Still, the "level and scope of social security provisions in Europe is generally high." In addition, several European countries have created publicly or privately funded no-fault compensation systems for injuries related to specific types of products: the Scandinavian countries for drugs, France for asbestos and HIV infected blood, and more than half a dozen nations for vaccines. Finally, many individuals have supplemental coverage through their employer or under privately bought policies.

In many non-European countries, there is also broad first-party coverage. In Australia, "universal health insurance plus significant workers' compensation coverage" absorb most of the financial consequences of accidents. In Canada there is not only "universal access to high quality health care" most of which is funded by the government but also "coverage for loss of income from the federally regulated employment insurance plan." And in Japan, "national and private health insurance is widespread and comprehensive." The situation in Israel is similar. On the whole, accident victims are fairly well protected.

As a result of these variations in the level of social insurance, many victims of product related accidents find themselves in rather different economic positions depending on where they live. In the United States, a significant portion of their basic needs will often be left uncovered, and a tort suit against the manufacturer or seller may be their only (and often vain) hope to recoup the loss. In countries with stronger welfare systems, as in Western Europe, Canada, or Japan, the victim's basic needs are likely to be taken care of. . . .

2. Liability Insurance

If manufacturers or sellers have third party insurance, they are more likely to face product liability claims for three reasons. First, victims will see them as more willing to pay since the money comes from someone else. Second, they are deeper pockets because they are worth the value of their own assets plus the policy limit. Third, chances to win in court may be higher because the court, and especially a jury, will be more inclined to hold someone liable if it knows or assumes that he does not really have to foot the bill. In some jurisdictions, the victim can also sue the insurer directly although this is rather the exception. Still, an insured defendant is a more attractive target.

Comparing how many manufacturers or other potential product liability defendants are insured in different countries is difficult because information is scarce and often based on estimates. The data available for this Report, however, do not suggest that there is a significant and pervasive difference between the United States and the Rest of the World in this regard. Thus, from what we know, there is no reason to assume that Americans sue more frequently because most of their defendants are insured while victims elsewhere tend to refrain from suing because manufacturers have no coverage.

Liability insurance could still have a major impact on litigation rates for an entirely different reason: perhaps American insurers are less willing to pay, forcing victims to sue their clients, while European and other carriers pay more easily, saving their clients the trouble of litigation. The reason may be that American insurers usually face much larger claims that are worth fighting about while European and other carriers look at more modest demands which may be less costly to pay than to dispute. If this is true, liability insurance compounds the impact of claim size on litigation rates: American plaintiffs are more likely to sue not only because they have more to win but also because insurers are less willing to satisfy their claims without going to court. . . .

The following article examines Professor Reimann's hypotheses about comparative products liability law in the context of Japan. The selection is heavily edited and readers are again advised to consult the full published article for additional depth and detail.

J. Mark, Ramseyer, Liability for Defective Products: Comparative Hypotheses and Evidence from Japan
61 Am. J. Comp. L. 617 (2013)

In North American legal circles, products liability law generates enormous tension. Americans file many claims and litigate many products liability suits. To the law's critics, their claiming and litigating has turned the field into a Miltonian bog where industries whole have sunk — and occasionally vanished outright.

Products liability does not have this effect in other rich democracies. Europe and Japan have products liability law, too. They maintain rules much like those in the United States. Yet few Europeans or Japanese litigate products liability suits. Few file claims. No industries disappear. And no critics bewail any 'crisis' in products liability.

Why the contrast? Why do Americans file so many suits while people in other wealthy democracies file so few? In an intriguing comparative meditation on cross-national patterns of law and litigation, Mathias Reimann advances a number of promising explanations. Through his forty-five-country comparison, Reimann nicely weighs likely reasons for the cross-national contrasts. I apply Reimann's hypotheses to evidence from Japan, and explore what they might tell us about the micro-level divergence between Japan and the United States.

As Reimann notes, the reason for the Japanese-American contrast does not lie in legal doctrine: on the substantive law of products liability, the United States and Japan do not significantly diverge. Instead, the reasons for the contrast apparently turn on aspects of American procedure (nicely identified by Reimann) that encourage merit-less demands. Litigation rates are not lower in Japan because of a Japanese pathology: Japanese law does not block valid claims. Instead, rates are higher in the United States because of a distinctly American dysfunction: American law facilitates efforts by claimants to collect amounts to which they are not legally entitled. They are higher in the United States, in short, because plaintiffs (often not victims) can manipulate the courts to extort payoffs from defendants (who may have done little, if anything, wrong).

I. The Product Liability 'Problem'

Critics argue that products liability litigation in the United States has left several industries devastated. It has raised costs, hiked prices, and slashed revenues. It has caused firms to cut research. It has chased some enterprises from the field. If the court judgments had simply ordered compensation for the losses the firms had imposed on others, perhaps they had it coming. The law just forced them to internalize costs they had tried to externalize on the public. According to the critics, however, the law did nothing of the sort. Instead, plaintiffs mostly used the threat of massive court verdicts to extort settlements from firms that had done little if anything wrong. At the least, this drove up the prices of products; at its worst, it actually lowered their overall safety.

II. The Reimann Inquiry

A. Introduction

The reasons for the contrast, writes Reimann, do not lie in legal doctrine. The rich democracies do not maintain products liability law that differs at any substantial level. Instead, the reasons lie in the claiming behavior ostensibly based on that law. The puzzle is why that claiming behavior could diverge so widely when the underlying law converges so closely. With a focus on Japan, consider first the convergence in doctrine (and the effect on product safety; see Section B), and then the divergence in practice (both in — and outside of court; see Section C).

B. Convergence in Doctrine

2. Legal Doctrine in Japan

The points Reimann makes about legal doctrine through his forty-five country survey nicely capture the gist of products liability law in Japan as well. Since 1995,

Japanese courts have held product liability claims to a strict liability standard. The legislature modeled the law on the European Community directive of 1985, and at its heart lies Section 3: "A manufacturer must pay compensation for any damages to the life, health, or property of another person, if those damages were caused by a defect in a product that it manufactured, processed, or imported. . . ." The rule governs disputes over products sold after July 1, 1995. As with its European antecedent, it does not apply to services.

Even without the 1995 statute, Japanese injured by defective products could sue. Prior to the statute, they could bring products liability claims under the standard rules of tort or contract. Since 1995 they can still sue under tort or contract, but they can add claims under the new products liability statute to boot.

Basic Japanese tort law dates to the 1896 Civil Code. Modeled after the German equivalent, the Code mandates a negligence regime for torts (Sec. 709): "He who infringes a right of another, either intentionally or negligently, must compensate that person for any damages he causes."

To determine whether a defendant has acted negligently, the courts often (not always) adopt a test close to Learned Hand's formula in Carroll Towing. Due care is the care that 'a person of ordinary care would show under the circumstances,' explained the Japanese Supreme Court, and those circumstances typically require people to weigh risks, costs, and benefits.

In fact, negligence under the Civil Code can sometimes approach strict liability in practice. Take a 1994 dispute over a Panasonic television set that caught fire. The Osaka District Court went out of its way to insist that it did not hold Panasonic to strict liability. All the same, it declared that the firm had a duty to sell television sets that were safe for normal use; that a television which catches fire is not safe; and that—given the fire—it would 'presume' that Panasonic had produced the set negligently. Panasonic could avoid liability only if it proved that it had not been negligent. Unable to rebut the presumption, Panasonic lost.

Conversely, strict liability under the new statute can sometimes resemble negligence. The point has been particularly true for the design defects, as Reimann explained. Whether a design is 'defective' under Section 3 of the Japanese products liability statute turns on its reasonably intended use. 'Reasonableness,' in turn, introduces a cost-benefit analysis close to the negligence rule itself.

Prior to the 1995 statute, plaintiffs could often also sue in contract. They still can. Japanese courts sometimes declare safety an 'implied' contract term. Lack of safety then constitutes a 'hidden defect.' The analysis turns on Sections 570 and 566 of the Civil Code:

Sec. 570: If the object of a sales contract contains a hidden defect, the provisions of Sec. 566 shall apply [by analogy]. . . .

Sec. 566: If the object of a sales contract is encumbered [by a competing legal claim], if the buyer does not know [of that competing claim], and if [that claim] prevents him from fulfilling the purpose of the contract, he may void the purchase. [If the buyer cannot void the purchase,] he may demand compensation for his damages.

Take a family that bought a toy archery set. When the suction cup at the end of one of the arrows came off, a daughter blinded her brother. The family collected from the retailer, the retailer collected from distributor, the distributor collected from the wholesaler, and the wholesaler sued the manufacturer for indemnity. The manufacturer had an obligation to sell a safe archery set, the court reasoned. Because the set—in retrospect—had not been safe, the manufacturer was liable.

Sometimes courts just duck fine distinctions entirely. The strict liability rule in the new statute may require a quasi-negligence analysis. The negligence rule in the Civil Code may approach strict liability. And as scholars in law and economics have noted for decades, the two regimes have similar efficiency characteristics anyway. Given the interpretive overlap and the crude similarity between the two, modern courts in Japan sometimes just ignore the new statute and stay with what they know.

Rather than learn the new rules, in other words, modern courts may just apply the law they know well. When a plaintiff sued a cosmetics firm under both general tort rules and products liability, the district court held the firm liable in negligence without worrying about the products liability statute. When a defendant sold a plaintiff contaminated dumplings, the plaintiff sued in contract and products liability. The district court held the defendant liable in contract without bothering to apply the products liability statute. And when a plaintiff sued Fuji Heavy Industries (Subaru) over an engine-compartment fire, the district court held the firm liable without even distinguishing the different legal regimes.

4. Whether Doctrine Affects Safety

Scholars have claimed that the 1995 strict products liability statute increased product safety. They argue that manufacturers responded to the law by making products safer.

Yet if manufacturers improved safety, no evidence of it appears in accident reports. Consider the data collected by the national network of Consumer Centers. According to Consumer Center data, the 1995 statute did nothing of that sort. The statute did not cover all purchases; it covered products but excluded services. If it promoted safety, then the number of product-related accidents should have fallen relative to the number of service-related accidents. It did not.

That the law would not have raised product safety is exactly what theory (and common sense) would have suggested. Both the United States and Japan have mostly competitive markets, and both have mostly rich consumers. Product safety is a normal good, the demand for which rises with income. In both countries, consumers will mostly want safe products. Even without strict products liability, the manufacturers that survive in these markets will tend to be the firms that offer that safety (and given that the courts had already interpreted the Civil Code to impose rules close to strict liability, the 1995 statute did not radically change the law anyway).

C. Divergence in Practice

2. Litigating in Japan

Exactly as Reimann notes, the contrast in litigating practice between the United States and Japan is massive. In the United States, Mitchell Polinsky and Steven Shavell estimate that plaintiffs file about 80,000 suits per year. In Japan, hardly anyone sues for defective products.

Consider then the contrast: Polinsky and Shavell place the annual number of American product liability suits at 80,000; extrapolations from the annual number of published product liability opinions in Japan range from under 100 to a little over 300. The United States has a population of 304 million; Japan has 128 million. Apparently, the United States has over 100 times as many product liability suits per capita as Japan.

3. Claiming in Japan

If Japanese litigate much less frequently than Americans, they also seem to claim less frequently. Out-of-court claims are obviously hard to track on any systematic basis. As a crude proxy, however, consider evidence from the insurance industry.

Insurance premiums will reflect the amounts firms pay on products liability claims. After all, if a firm wants to insure against products liability, it will buy its coverage on a private market. Insurers will quote the firm rates that depend on industry, coverage, annual sales — and expected liability.

Japanese firms pay more claims than appear in court statistics, but still not many. Our discussion above suggested that Japanese consumers file at most 100-300 products liability suits a year. Insurers actually pay 500 to 1,100 claims a year. Yet the effect on total liability remains trivial. A plastic-goods manufacturer can buy insurance on the private market at about 400 yen per million yen in sales. If it sells a gadget for 1000 yen, the price will include products liability coverage costing 0.4 yen. In U.S. dollars, if it sells a gadget for $12, the price will include insurance costs of 0.5¢.

4. The Significance of the Japanese-American Contrast

Ask then the obvious normative question: do Japanese claim too seldom? Are victims of defective products systematically failing to recover their damages in Japan? The data suggest not. Instead, they suggest that they file claims about as often as one would expect, given the number of serious accidents.

Relatively few people suffer serious injuries from defective products. Every year, 6,600 non-elderly Japanese die in non-traffic-related accidents, and another several thousand suffer serious injuries but do not die. Only some of these victims are killed or injured by defective products. If Japanese file 2,000 product-defect claims a year, the number suggests that most people with substantial product liability claims probably assert them.

III. The Reimann Hypotheses

To explain the contrast in 'law in action,' Reimann offers several factors that might account for the cross-national divergence.

IV. Exploring the Hypotheses with Japanese Data

A. Introduction

Reimann's hypotheses roughly group themselves into three sets. The first set explain why plaintiffs elsewhere might file fewer lawsuits, but do not explain why they might assert fewer claims (sec. B). The second set are ambiguous: under some conditions they could reflect an American court system that works better than courts elsewhere, but they could also reflect a legal system that works worse (sec. C). The third set implies that the high litigation rates in the United States result from the way the legal system rewards fraud and abuse (sec. D).

Let us consider what the data from Japan suggest about each of these hypotheses.

B. Suing Compared To Claiming

Reimann's first three hypotheses plausibly suggest that litigation rates are high in the United States because Americans negotiate through the courts, while victims elsewhere negotiate outside the courts. These hypotheses explain why plaintiffs elsewhere might file fewer suits than Americans, in other words, but not why they might assert fewer claims. They go to the fraction of claims that people pursue in court, but not to the total number of claims they pursue. Recall the three:

(1) Americans sue first, talk later.
(2) American courts charge lower filing fees.
(3) American claimants have fewer alternative fora.

If it accurately captured the United States-Japan contrast, hypothesis (1) would explain lower litigating rates in Japan, but not lower claiming rates. The hypothesis asserts that Americans who intend to pursue a loss first file suit. Then, but only then, do they approach the manufacturer to begin serious negotiations. They use the suit to signal their earnestness, but intend actually to collect their damages out of court. Elsewhere, claimants approach the manufacturer first, and sue only if the manufacturer seems unresponsive.

Hypotheses (2) and (3) help explain why Americans may actually file first. Because fees are low, filing a complaint costs very little. Americans file the suit, Reimann implies, on the 'why not' principle. By contrast, where filing fees are high, claimants might wait to file to see whether the defendant will pay voluntarily.

As the discussion above suggests, however, Japanese seem not just to file fewer suits than Americans. They also (though the evidence from insurance data is obviously only suggestive) seem to indicate that that Japanese file fewer claims. They file about as many claims as one might expect, given accident rates. Yet they apparently file many fewer claims than their American peers. Reimann may be right about hypotheses (1) through (3), but they do not explain the Japanese-American contrast.

C. The Legal System Works

2. Damages

Turn first to the level of damages. According to hypothesis (4), victims in the United States sue more often than victims elsewhere because American courts more often award full damages. In other words, in the United States, those who suffer massive injuries can sue to recover a correspondingly large amount; they are thus more likely [to] pursue their claims than victims in jurisdictions that grant less than full recovery.

The hypothesis does not explain the Japanese-American contrast. Although American courts do award generous compensatory damages, in routine cases they do not award more than Japanese courts. Reimann reports that the mean products liability award in U.S. courts in 1999 was $3,045,908. Unfortunately, this misleads. Reimann takes his numbers from his American country report, which relies on 1993-99 trial verdicts.

Alexander Tabarrok and Eric Helland more plausibly report 1993 median product liability awards of $260,000. To hold the claim-mix constant, however, focus on wrongful death claims. Frank Cross and Charles Silver find that tort claims in Texas (1988-2003; 'mono-line general liability, commercial auto liability, Texas commercial, medical professional liability, and other professional liability') pay a median $199,586 for wrongful death. Payouts begin at $172,445 for children, rise to $263,864 for victims in their 30s, and fall to $139,693 for those over age 80.

By any of these measures American courts do not award higher product liability damages in routine cases than Japanese courts. They do grant a few stratospherically high awards—no tort claimant in Japan has ever collected the $285 million that skewed the mean in Reimann's account. But Japanese courts do award generous amounts on a regular basis, amounts that would compare favorably to the more quotidian American cases. In wrongful death claims, for example, successful Japanese product liability plaintiffs in reported cases collect a mean 61 million yen per case. At the late 2012 exchange rate of 81.3 yen/$, this comes to $750,000.

3. Lawyer Costs

Hypothesis (5) suggests that victims sue in the United States because American lawyers are cheap. In truth, they are no cheaper than Japanese lawyers.

As evidence for the accessibility of American attorneys, scholars regularly cite the use of contingency fees. Attorneys may offer to represent their clients on a contingency fee basis—but they do not promise to represent all victims. They agree to represent a victim only if the probability of success is high enough to enable them to recover both the market value of their legal services, and the market interest on the risky advance of those services.

Japanese law does not ban contingency fees, and the bar does not set prices. By custom, litigators tend to couple a fixed retainer upfront with a contingent percentage of the eventual outcome. The practice is not mandatory, though, and (as the survey results below show) most lawyers charge only a modest initial retainer anyway. Instead, they collect the bulk of their fee through the contingent component.

Japanese attorneys do not earn extraordinarily high incomes. According to an anonymous 2010 bar association survey, Japanese attorneys reported a mean income of about 14.7 million yen ($181,000, at the then-current exchange rate of 81 yen/$), and a median income of 9.6 million yen ($118,000). Adjusted for age, they just barely earn more than white-collar business executives, and substantially less than physicians. In the United States, salaried lawyers (obviously excluding the AmLaw 500 partners) earned a median salary of $112,760 in 2010. Of all 21,000 Japanese attorneys (salaried and partners) in 2004, only 404 paid taxes of over 10 million yen—implying a taxable income of about $390,000. Only one lawyer made at least $6 million.

4. Discovery

The theory behind the expansive discovery regime in the United States (hypothesis (6)) is simple: sometimes defendants control evidence that plaintiffs need (or vice versa) to prove their case. The notion that without discovery wronged victims could not effectively recover misses the way judges conduct trials outside the Anglo-American world. In a jurisdiction like Japan, a judge controls the trial. He structures it through discontinuous sessions held about once a month. At each session, he hears evidence, discusses the case, and then tells the parties what evidence to bring to the next session. If a plaintiff can convince him that the defendant controls access to evidence the plaintiff needs to prove his case, the judge can simply tell the defendant to bring it to the next meeting. Plaintiffs cannot conduct 'fishing expeditions,' to be sure, but if they need information the judge can simply tell the defendant to bring it.

To induce defendants to comply with these orders, judges in jurisdictions like Japan use burdens of proof and presumptions. If a judge thinks that the defendant holds crucial evidence, he can switch the burden of proof. The judge can 'presume' a fact against the defendant unless he introduces evidence sufficient to rebut the presumption.

In medical malpractice, for example, physicians often control the information patients will need to prove negligence. Japanese judges do not order discovery, but they do sometimes presume that the doctor was negligent. They let him avoid liability only if he can show that he exercised appropriate care. In malpractice cases, as Takashi Uchida put it, the courts sometimes 'lighten the burden of proof through a method known as the presumption of negligence.'

Through strategic shifts in burdens of proof and presumptions, Japanese judges can accomplish most of what discovery gives plaintiffs in the United States. When they do, they accomplish it at far lower cost to the parties, and with far lower risk that the plaintiff might harass the defendant into settlement.

5. Class Actions

Japan does not have class actions. As Reimann notes, neither do most countries. Instead, Japanese judgments bind victims only if they appear as named plaintiffs. By contrast, anyone falling within the ambit of an American class may collect on a judgment, even if the person did nothing in the case at all.

Unfortunately, this logic misleads as well. American lawyers simply bring too few class actions to explain the cross-national difference in litigation rates. Remember that there are 80,000 products liability suits in the United States, but only 100-300 in Japan. Of the 80,000 suits, only a trivial number are class actions. With 40 federal consumer class actions, even if plaintiffs filed 10 times more class actions in state court the number would not begin to explain the difference between 'the U.S. and the Rest.'

6. Health Insurance

Hypothesis (8) implies that American claimants will more likely sue because they will less likely have health insurance. Uninsured victims have higher out-of-pocket expenses, higher compensable damages, and thus more reason to sue. If a smaller fraction of Americans have health insurance, then a higher fraction has these higher levels of out-of-pocket losses. By contrast, covered by national health insurance, European and Japanese victims have less reason to sue.

Logical as this hypothesis may seem, it again misleads. First, about 80 to 85 percent of Americans do have health insurance. The 15-20 percent uninsured are disproportionately poor and uneducated — exactly the portion of the population least likely to pursue a claim in court. Second, even insured Americans sometimes file claims for medical expenses anyway. When they do, they may file them because their insurer holds the right to pursue the claim under subrogation. Americans are more likely to sue because their insurers pursue their subrogated claims.

D. The Legal System Rewards Extortion

1. Introduction

More plausibly, Reimann's factors suggest a darker, more abusive logic to American litigation patterns. Litigation rates are not higher in the United States because American courts more effectively help victims recover their losses. They are higher because the courts facilitate extortion by the plaintiffs' bar. Consider the abusive potential: although median American judgments are not higher than in Japan, a small number of spectacularly high judgments badly skew the mean. Punitive damages can raise the idiosyncratic awards even higher. Class actions let strategic attorneys turn trivial injuries into massive claims. And discovery lets the plaintiff's attorney relentlessly distract the defendant through grinding demands.

Together, these factors let abusive attorneys file claims so large that risk-averse managers may decide to settle even meritless claims rather than bet the firm. Perhaps the defendant did no wrong; perhaps the victim suffered no harm; or perhaps the defendant simply caused far less harm than the plaintiff claimed.

2. Damages, Discovery, Class Actions, Again

Remember the following hypotheses:

(4) American courts award high damages.
(6) American courts allow generous discovery.
(7) American courts permit class actions.

Consider the abusive potential: each of these factors has the potential to help plaintiffs extort a settlement from not-at-fault manufacturers. The key lies in the effect that the risk of a brutally large award can have on settlement incentives. First, although American judges do not usually grant high compensatory damages, they do occasionally award spectacular amounts. By contrast, Japanese judges rely on a standard formula to keep tort awards uniform. Second, American courts occasionally (but perhaps more rarely today than before) award punitive damages. Courts elsewhere do not.

Third, American courts sometimes also let the plaintiffs' bar inflate demands by filing claims as class actions. Even if any one plaintiff could claim only a trivial injury, an attorney who files on behalf of a class can demand massive amounts. If a plaintiff class successfully files and certifies a suit big enough to bankrupt the firm if it wins, many managers will try to settle — even if the class has only miniscule odds of winning.

And throughout the process, American judges let plaintiffs erode a defendant's resistance through a steady and grinding stream of costly discovery demands. In part, discovery is expensive because it is run by attorneys whose time costs a lot of money. In part, however, it is also expensive because of how badly it can distract a firm from delivering the products and services at the heart of its business. Rather than risk a judgment that could bankrupt the firm, rather than endure the long, grinding discovery, and rather than take a chance on either, many firms settle to make a plaintiff go away. That, in turn, encourages product liability suits in the first place.

3. Juries and Judges

The ability of attorneys and claimants to extort unwarranted settlements in U.S. courts does not just reflect the high idiosyncratic award, caustic discovery demands, or the occasional class action. It also turns on two distinctively American aspects of the civil trial: juries and elected judges.

First, whereas American courts try product liability (and other tort) cases before juries, Japanese courts try civil cases before professional judges. In this, Japan is no outlier. Civil law countries have long avoided civil juries, and today even most common-law countries do.

The civil jury is central to the problems that plague American products liability. Aggressive attorneys do not file products liability cases randomly. Instead, they pick the courts where they know juries award the most inflated recoveries. Prominent plaintiffs' lawyer (and now convicted felon) Richard (Dickie) Scruggs called them 'magic' jurisdictions:

> The trial lawyers have established relationships with the judges that are elected; they're State Court judges; they're populists. They've got large populations of voters [who serve on the juries] who are in on the deal, they're getting their piece in many cases. And so, it's a political force in their jurisdiction, and it's almost impossible to get a fair trial if you're a defendant in some of these places.

Second, where Japanese courts use only judges appointed by the national government, American plaintiffs try many products liability cases before popularly elected state judges. Who decides whether a judge keeps his job matters. Successful legislators answer to their local constituencies — and so do elected judges. Out-of-state corporations do not vote. Local juries do. The electoral mechanism affects outcomes.

The American civil procedural system sometimes lets attorneys use civil juries to extract large payments from out-of-state defendants; elected judges sometimes acquiesce to the scheme; and the idiosyncratic spectacular verdict and class action magnify the combined effect of those two factors.

V. Conclusions

Americans sue much more readily than Japanese. And as Mathias Reimann notes, Americans sue much more readily than people in most other wealthy democracies. Americans file some 80,000 products liability suits per year. Japanese file 100-300. The reason for the contrast does not lie in the substantive law. As Reimann rightly explains, on the law of products liability, the United States, Japan, and most wealthy democracies maintain very similar rules.

Instead, the reason for the cross-national divergence lies in other aspects of the legal system. Together, these aspects suggest that the American litigation rate in products liability is not high because American victims can readily collect compensation. It is high because American claimants can use the courts to extort funds, even when they lack a meritorious claim. Although median American verdicts are not high, courts sometimes award spectacularly high compensatory awards. Courts sometimes award high punitive awards. Attorneys can sometimes inflate trivial claims to extortionate levels through the class action. They can sometimes harass defendants through constant, grinding discovery.

Given all this, rather than bet the firm against a low-probability, but high-magnitude, disaster, managers often settle a case to make a claimant go away. In part, they settle out of simple risk-aversion. But they also settle because they know that juries and elected judges can — and sometimes do — award plaintiffs large amounts simply to redistribute wealth from out-of-town corporations to local friends, neighbors, and voters.

This section has focused on Europe and Japan because those jurisdictions' products liability systems have been the most studied and discussed within the U.S. legal academic literature. For a useful collection of articles on foreign products liability more generally, see Symposium on Products Liability: Comparative Approaches & Transnational Litigation, 34 Tex. Int'l L.J. 1 (1999). For additional contributions, see Marta Infanito, Making European Tort Law: The Game and Its Players, 18 Cardozo J. Int'l & Comp. L. 45 (2010); Joel Slawotsky, Liability For Defective Chinese Products Under the Alien Tort Claims Act, 7 Wash. U. Global Stud. L. Rev. 519 (2008); Thomas Rouhette, The Availability of Punitive Damages in Europe: Growing Trend or Non-Existing Concept, 74 Def. Couns. J. 320 (2007); Jane Stapleton, Bugs in Anglo-American Products Liability, 53 S.C. L. Rev. 1225 (2002); Simon Taylor, The Harmonisation of European Product Liability Rules: French and English Law, 48 Int'l & Comp. L.Q. 419 (1999).

B. POLICY CHALLENGES POSED BY A GLOBALLY INTEGRATED PRODUCT MARKETPLACE

Professor Ramseyer's article is just one of a litany of studies that have criticized the products liability law of the United States. As critiques of the U.S. products liability system have grown, Congress and state legislatures have responded with a series of reforms. At the federal level, Congress has passed a number of laws aimed at relieving specific industries from the burden of products liability litigation, such as the General Aviation Revitalization Act of 1994, the Biomaterials Access Assurance Act of 1998, the Homeland Security Act of 2002, and the Protection of Lawful Commerce in Arms Act of 2005. States, too, have enacted a variety of reforms to products liability law aimed at making their jurisdiction more competitive for business activity. These reforms are motivated in part by concern that the comparative generosity of products liability law to plaintiffs in the United States leaves domestic business firms at a disadvantage to foreign competitors. Sections 1 and 2 of this Part analyze the sparse evidence and inconclusive analysis in the literature on products liability law's impact on the competitiveness and innovative capacity of firms.

At the same time that concerns have been raised that U.S. products liability law is too harsh on product manufacturers, many commentators also worry that foreign product safety systems may be too lax. Spurred by sometimes sensationalist media coverage of hazards posed by imported products, consumers and politicians argue that greater regulatory oversight abroad or scrutiny at the border during importation is necessary to avoid serious harm. Section 3 treats these and related issues concerning the safety of globally traded goods.

1. *The Impact of Products Liability Law on the Competiveness of Firms*

There can be no doubt that the American products liability system imposes uniquely high costs on firms distributing products in this country. Earlier in this Chapter, we sketched some of the reasons in our discussion of the substantive and procedural differences between the products liability laws of the United States and other jurisdictions. In sum, the scope of liability faced by firms operating within the United States is significantly greater than that burdening firms in Europe and Japan. American manufacturers are also more likely to be held liable for injuries arising from older products already on the market not equipped with modern safety devices. International competitors will be less concerned with such liability since very few older products of foreign origin exist in the United States. See Randolph J. Stayin, The U.S. Product Liability System: A Competitive Advantage to Foreign Manufacturers, 14 Can.-U.S. L.J. 193, 199 (1988). In addition, suits can be instituted in the United States much more readily than in other nations. Stayin argues that the procedural ease with which lawsuits may be brought against domestic manufacturers

> confers an advantage upon foreign manufacturers which makes them less accountable than U.S. manufacturers to persons injured by their products, which results in unprotected American users of foreign products, lower insurance costs to be included in the prices of foreign products and loss of market share for U.S. manufacturers. [Id. at 204.]

As Stayin suggests, American firms must insure against liability to a greater extent than their foreign counterparts. Indeed, a 1984 International Trade Administration study found that domestic machine manufacturers had products liability insurance costs 20 to 100 times greater in their respective home markets than did similar foreign firms in their respective home markets. Even when competing in international markets, many American companies, by failing to purchase separate insurance for foreign coverage, do not reap the benefits of lower premium payments associated with foreign markets.

In addition to paying higher tort claims and insurance premiums, American firms are inundated by less obvious costs, such as deductible sums and awards above insurance policy limits. Other significant costs include legal expenses, settlement payments, and product safety testing expenditures. Firms may also engage in socially wasteful behavior designed to evade liability, the costs of which are difficult to estimate.

Obviously American firms must be more attentive than foreign manufacturers to their potential liability. But what does this mean in terms of product costs and prices? Selected industries and municipalities are certainly hit hard because of the perceived risk associated with their goods and services. Indeed, even marginal increases in costs and prices can be very damaging to firms participating in highly competitive markets with relatively undifferentiated products. Furthermore, smaller businesses may suffer more than larger, diversified firms that are better able to absorb the costs of liability insurance. Peter Huber believes that the impact of products liability law on costs and prices is significant:

> [The $80 billion annual "liability tax"] is one of the most ubiquitous taxes we pay, now levied on virtually everything we buy, sell, and use. The tax accounts for 30 percent of the price of a stepladder and over 95 percent of the price of childhood vaccines. It is responsible for one-quarter of the price of a ride on a Long Island tour bus and one-third of the price of a small airplane. It will soon cost large municipalities as much as they spend on fire and sanitation services. . . .
>
>   Because of the tax, you cannot use a sled in Denver city parks or a diving board in New York City schools. You cannot buy an American Motors "CJ" Jeep or a set of

construction plans for novel airplanes from Burt Rutan, the pioneering designer of the Voyager. . . . [From Huber, Liability: The Legal Revolution and Its Consequences 1-2 (1988).]

But the aggregate effects of the liability system on product costs and prices may not be as significant as Huber suggests, despite the severe impact of liability on certain individual products and industries. As Robert E. Litan notes, the "liability tax" on average comprises only two percent of the cost of all products and services sold within the United States. See Litan, The Liability Explosion and American Trade Performance: Myths and Realities, in Tort Law and the Public Interest: Competition, Innovation, and Consumer Welfare (Peter H. Schuck, ed. 1991). Moreover, Huber's $80 billion liability figure, which he seems to pull out of thin air, is only half the story. That estimate does not represent the net impact on U.S. living standards, which Litan contends is the appropriate measure of the competitive effect of the current products liability system. Benefits of the liability system include improved standards of quality control, safer products for consumers, healthier workplace environments, and an arguably more "just" distribution of wealth. Thus, the infrequency with which products cases are litigated in other jurisdictions such as Japan is not necessarily desirable, given the fairness and efficiency goals served by the consistent imposition of strict liability. When considered in their entirety, Litan argues, these benefits could potentially outweigh the negative impact of increased liability costs.

Admittedly, little empirical evidence exists regarding the safety benefits accruing from the U.S. products liability scheme. Defenders of the system can point to the withdrawal of the Ford Pinto and the Dalkon Shield from the market as instances where the system presumably worked; but few conclusions can be drawn from such isolated occurrences. In an attempt to analyze these benefits empirically, George Priest found little evidence that increased liability promotes safety. See George Priest, Products Liability Law and the Accident Rate, in Liability: Perspectives and Policy, at 184-222 (Robert E. Litan & Clifford Winston, eds. 1988). To be sure, daunting methodological challenges face any such survey. But even if Priest is mistaken and significant safety benefits do exist, their value is certainly diminished by the high administrative costs of the tort liability system.

Surveying studies quantifying the legal costs related to product liability litigation, Professors Polinsky and Shavell conclude that "for each dollar that an accident victim receives in a settlement or judgment, it is reasonable to assume that a dollar of legal and administrative expenses is incurred." A. Mitchell Polinsky & Steven Shavell, The Uneasy Case for Product Liability, 123 Harv. L. Rev. 1437, 1470 (2010). Polinsky and Shavell argue that market forces and government regulation sufficiently protect consumers from dangerous products and that first-party insurance sufficiently compensates victims for harm. Responding to Polinsky and Shavell's "striking conclusion" that products liability law may be unnecessary, Professors Goldberg and Zipursky argue that the evidence is still inconclusive regarding the deterrent effect of products liability, and that many products liability plaintiffs lack sufficient insurance and require litigation to receive compensation. Importantly, though, Goldberg and Zipursky criticize Polinsky and Shavell for evaluating the tort system in isolation from market forces and government regulation:

There is plenty of reason to believe that these three modes of 'regulation' influence one another. The filing of litigation is presumably sometimes necessary for the discovery of the newsworthy story behind a product's dangers, and litigation can itself be news that focuses consumer attention on alleged product dangers and attracts regulatory attention. News of alleged product-related injuries can foment litigation and regulation. The enactment of regulation can generate news coverage and litigation. Given these probable synergies, it is almost certainly a mistake to posit that, once tort law is removed from the bundle of regulatory sticks, market and regulatory forces will have the same deterrent effect that they now have. [John C.P. Goldberg & Benjamin C. Zipursky, The Easy Case for Products Liability: A Response to Professors Polinsky and Shavell, 123 Harv. L. Rev. 1919 (2010).]

Rather than draw "common sense" conclusions from examining the increasing trade deficit and the differences between the American, European Community, and Japanese products liability systems, Litan attempts to determine exactly what affects a country's "competitiveness." In order to assess the impact of the products liability system on a nation's competitiveness, he says, one must

> determine how its citizens' living standards are affected when its trade is balanced. Bangladesh may import no more than it exports, but it is hardly "competitive" with industrialized nations whose living standards are far higher. Conversely, nations such as the United States may enjoy rising living standards largely by running trade deficits and borrowing from abroad to do so. Only by measuring our rate of improvement in living standards relative to other countries *when our trade is balanced* can we know how competitive we truly are.
>
> The analytical distinction between competitiveness and trade performance has important implications for how one thinks about the international impact of the U.S. tort system. Perhaps most significant, it demonstrates that however adverse an impact liability trends may have on U.S. firms, *the tort system will not permanently affect the nation's overall trade deficit unless it also somehow affects domestic saving and investment.* [Litan at 130.]

Noting that any effects of liability trends on savings and investment are minimal, Litan concludes that using the trade balance to assess the impact of liability trends is nonsensical. As was mentioned earlier, some firms and industries will bear a greater burden of the liability explosion:

> [T]he liability tax should encourage certain types of imports and discourage certain exports. But . . . this does *not* mean that the overall trade balance will be affected. Any initial negative effects on the trade balance will increase the supply of dollars on the world market, thereby reducing the value of the dollar. After some period of adjustment, other exports will rise and other imports will fall. The aggregate trade balance will remain unchanged. [Litan at 140.]

To assume, by examining international trade statistics, that products liability contributes significantly to the plight of American manufacturers competing abroad thus ignores other relevant factors and cause-and-effect relationships. American firms certainly bear higher liability costs than their foreign counterparts. But the magnitude of this burden is difficult to assess in light of the dearth of statistical evidence on the subject. According to Litan, many factors, in addition to liability influencing firms' costs and pricing decisions, render inadequate any attempt to conclusively establish the tort system's effects.

Some scholars have relied on variation among jurisdictions *within* the United States in an effort to tease out the economic impact of products liability law. Joanna Shepherd observes that state-level reforms may provide enough empirical data to measure the competitive impact of product liability schema. See Joanna Shepherd, Products Liability and Economic Activity: An Empirical Analysis of Tort Reform's Impact on Businesses, Employment, and Production, 66 Vand. L. Rev. 257 (2013). Employing a sophisticated regression methodology, she finds that certain state-level reforms were strongly associated with increases in economic activity in the states that enacted them:

> Several reforms that restrict the scope of products liability have a significant impact on economic activity. Statutes of repose that limit the period for which manufacturers and product sellers are liable for product defects are associated with statistically significant increases in both the number of small businesses and the amount of employment in manufacturing industries. . . . Similarly, comparative negligence reforms that reduce damage awards when plaintiffs engage in negligent activity affect economic activity. These reforms are associated with statistically significant increases in the number of small manufacturing businesses and manufacturing production. [Id. at 313.]

Shepherd finds, however, that not all reforms to products liability law have had a significant positive effect on economic activity; in fact, Shepherd finds that some reforms had a negative impact:

> Other reforms have a weaker and less consistent relationship with economic activity. . . . [R]eforms to joint and several liability are associated with decreases in the number of businesses and level of production in both manufacturing industries and the larger category of high-risk industries that includes the retail, distribution, wholesale, and insurance industries. Similarly, punitive damage caps are associated with decreases in the amount of employment in both definitions of high-risk industries. However, the results are not statistically significant across all specifications, casting doubt on the reliability of the findings. [Id. at 313-314.]

Frank Cross, using state rankings of the tort system published by two pro-defendant organizations — the Chamber of Commerce and the Pacific Research Institute — in a regression analysis, finds that tort law is "at least not harming" the economies of states with low rankings. Frank B. Cross, Tort Law and the American Economy 96 Minn. L. Rev. 28, 89 (2011).

2.   *Effects of Products Liability Law on Product Innovation*

Even if the direct costs of liability are relatively insignificant, products liability law may reduce America's competitiveness by discouraging product innovation. Many observers believe that the threat of liability has a stifling effect on the research and development of new products because of the unforeseen risks these products might pose. Rather than venture into untested waters, it is argued, manufacturers opt to continue producing older designs whose risks are typically knowable. As Stayin summarizes,

> [T]hrough the suspicious-looking glass of our product liability law, attorneys too often see the risks rather than the benefits. They advise their clients that the new development

may be too risky, too new, with no precedent to follow in a broad area of technology. . . . This thinking leads to a status quoism that prefers staying with a proven product rather than taking a chance with something new, more advanced and more competitive. Adoption of a new, safer technology implicitly involves acknowledgement that the previous technology was not as safe as possible. There is a perception that it is safer to stay with an established product than risk lawsuits with an unknown product which may also stimulate lawsuits with respect to established product lines. [Stayin at 206.]

Peter W. Huber echoes a similar sentiment, but focuses more on the capabilities and tendencies of jurors rather than the risk-averseness of corporate managers and the attorneys advising them:

Jurors can make reasonably sensitive judgments about people — even about professionals — because we are all in the people-judging business every day of our lives. But jurors are not experts about technology itself, and intuition here is a terrible guide. When a juror is asked to categorize technologies — as distinct from their inventors and managers — as good, bad, or ugly, the answers follow a quite predictable pattern. Age, familiarity, and ubiquity are the most powerful legitimizing forces known to the layperson. The inexpert juror is predisposed at every turn to identify technologies that are novel, exotic, unfamiliar, or adventuresome as unwelcome and fraught with danger — in short, defective. [Huber at 157.]

Evidence regarding the influence of liability on innovation is even more speculative and anecdotal than that concerning economic competiveness. Canvassing the history of litigation related to planes and automobiles, Kyle Graham contends that ''Huber's argument applies to some innovations far better than it does to others,'' and that many innovations ''have benefited, early on in their diffusion, from the perception that they were less risky than they ultimately proved to be.'' Kyle Graham, Of Frightened Horses and Autonomous Vehicles: Tort Law and its Assimilation of Innovations 52 Santa Clara L. Rev. 1241, 1268 (2012).

The presence of many complex factors that affect the decision of whether or not to market a new product makes analyzing such developments particularly difficult. Moreover, assessing the consequences of the absence of action — that is, the failure to develop new products — is not currently feasible. Thus, much of the literature in the field is brimming with case studies of firms and trades, such as the pharmaceutical and textile industries, that have absorbed a disproportionate impact of the products liability revolution. Alfred W. Cortese and Kathleen L. Blaner, for example, list 30 instances of ''anti-competitive effects'' of American products liability law, including plant closings, discontinued product lines, decisions not to market new products, and discontinued research. Cortese & Blaner, The Anti-Competitive Impact of U.S. Product Liability Laws: Are Foreign Businesses Beating Us at Our Own Game?, 9 J.L. & Com. 167, 198-202 (1989). Their evidence seems to bear out Litan's previously mentioned observation that products liability law may affect the composition of trade. Most of Cortese and Blaner's examples involve either sporting goods, pharmaceuticals, or component parts in motor vehicles and aircraft.

Nonetheless, some empirical evidence on the link between products liability and innovation is available. A popular approach is to sample corporate managers to assess the effect of products liability on their decisions to introduce new goods. In one such survey, 19 percent of the respondents reported that they dropped a product line because of the high risks associated with it, while 16 percent said they decided against developing a new product because of liability fears. Another survey revealed that 57 percent of the managers polled agreed that all-important innovative technology is not being produced for fear of crippling lawsuits. See Stayin at pp. 204-205. Top-level corporate complaints, however, should be received with a certain skepticism, as the respondents may have self-interested reasons for blaming external forces for problems.

Fortunately, more extensive statistical research exists. In Rationalizing the Relationship between Product Liability and Innovation, in Tort Law and the Public Interest (Peter Schuck, ed. 1991), W. Kip Viscusi and Michael J. Moore compare products liability costs (the ratio of premiums per policy to industry sales) with various measures of innovation and new product introductions. Though they determine that increasing liability costs do dampen innovative strategies, the effect is not so devastating as the criticisms of corporate executives would lead one to believe. With guarded optimism, they conclude:

> The statistical evidence indicates that the relationships are much more complex than is generally believed. By most measures we have examined, innovators bear a larger share of the product liability burden. On the other hand, there is no evidence that their share is escalating dramatically. Moreover, product liability has increased incentives for introducing product design changes that outweigh liability's depressing effect on the introduction of products with new attributes other than those relating to safety. [Id. at 123.]

Another comprehensive project, edited by Huber and Litan, examines the link between liability law and safety and innovation in five selected contexts: motor vehicles, medical malpractice, prescription drugs, chemical development, and general aviation. See The Liability Maze (Peter W. Huber & Robert E. Litan, eds. 1991). Regarding safety, most of the authors in the study conclude that factors outside the tort system — such as regulation, industry-imposed standards, and bad publicity — are primarily responsible for influencing product safety. With respect to innovation, however, most of the authors find a positive correlation between sharply rising liability costs and diminished innovation. For example, general aviation manufacturers, long burdened by skyrocketing liability, have ceased new developments and, in some cases, production altogether. Though Huber and Litan make clear that tort law may reduce innovation in those particular industries hardest hit by liability, their study does not address products liability law's effect on American manufacturing in general.

The effects of products liability law on innovation may be potentially more damaging to America's long-run competitive well-being than are marginal cost and price increases induced by exposure to tort liability. Once again, however, an absence of empirical research makes such conclusions difficult, if not impossible, to assess. Quantifying the countless other variables that affect product innovation — trade barriers, government involvement in and regulation of industry, consumer demand, unstable world financial markets, and so on — would be next to impossible. In a RAND study conducted for the Institute for Civil Justice, Peter Reuter found "surprisingly little evidence suggesting that liability currently hinders international competitiveness." See Peter Reuter, The Economic Consequences of Expanded Corporate Liability: An Exploratory Study (1988). In accordance with Huber and Litan's findings, however, Reuter's research suggests that certain industries (like sporting goods) do constitute exceptions.

For recent law review commentary on the product innovation question, see James A. Henderson, Jr., Tort vs. Technology: Accommodating Disruptive Innovation, 47 Ariz.

St. L.J. __ (2015); Gideon Parchomovsky and Alex Stein, Torts and Innovation, 107 Mich. L. Rev. 285 (2008) (claim that tort law has an adverse effect on innovation); Benjamin H. Barton, Tort Reform, Innovation, and Playground Design, 58 Fla. L. Rev. 265 (2006) (products liability has not retarded innovation but in some markets has led to a rise in innovation); Deborah J. LaFetra, Freedom, Responsibility and Risk: Fundamental Principles Supporting Tort Reform, 36 Ind. L. Rev. 645 (2003) (arguing that products liability litigation has stifled innovation).

3. Does the Global Marketplace Need a Global Regulator?

Of growing concern in recent years has been the safety and quality of goods that move through global trading channels. Much of the concern has focused on products emanating from China, which has suffered from a perception that the country's regulatory standards and government enforcement mechanisms are comparatively weak. See Huanan Liu, William A. Kerr & Jill E. Hobbs, Product Safety, Collateral Damage and Trade Policy Responses: Restoring Confidence in China's Exports, 43 J. World Trade 97 (2009). Isolated but widely-reported product safety episodes have fostered this perception at the same time that China's role in international goods manufacturing has vastly expanded. For instance, in August 2007, the world's largest toy company Mattel recalled 19 million toys because they contained such dangerous features as lead paint and small, powerful magnets that could harm children if swallowed. Infant formula, candy, and food products from China have been found on multiple occasions to contain the harmful chemical melamine, with an alleged six infants deaths resulting from such tainted products in 2008. Since 2009, thousands of U.S. residents have claimed health and economic damage due to defective Chinese-made drywall, which emits harmful sulfurous gases. See In re Chinese-Manufactured Drywall Products Liability Litigation, 2014 WL 4809520 (E.D. La. 2014). More recently, a major U.S. home improvement retailer stopped all sales of Chinese-manufactured flooring products and issued thousands of indoor air quality test kits to its customers after reports that the products were leaking unsafe levels of formaldehyde.

A consumer injured by an imported product may face numerous hurdles before holding the foreign manufacturer accountable. For instance, the consumer must locate a defendant that is both solvent and amenable to jurisdiction. See, e.g., Book v. Doublestar Dongfeng Tyre Co., Ltd., 860 N.W.2d 576 (Iowa 2015) (court could constitutionally exercise jurisdiction over Chinese firms that allegedly sold defective tires). In many cases, the ultimate manufacturer of the product will be difficult, if not impossible, to identify. Even if the identity of the manufacturer is known, the firm may have no assets in the United States, may not be amenable to service of process, or may simply boycott the proceedings and refuse to pay any judgments against it. See, e.g., Taiwanese Candy Firm Held Liable in Child's Death, L.A. Times, July 12, 2003, available at http://articles.latimes.com/2003/jul/12/local/me-candy12 (noting that plaintiffs were unlikely to collect on judgments arising out of toddlers' choking deaths from a candy manufactured in Taiwan). Consumer plaintiffs naturally target U.S.-based distributors and retailers to avoid these challenges. See, e.g., Vita v. Rooms to Go Louisiana Corp., 2014 WL 6835913 (E.D. La. 2014) (applying "apparent manufacturer" doctrine under Louisiana Product Liability Act to seller of glass table that had been manufactured in China). However, the concentration of attention on these domestic defendants can quickly exhaust their available resources. For instance, in the

Chinese drywall case, many of the U.S. importers, distributors, and sellers of the defective drywall are "out of business, bankrupt, or possess insufficient assets to satisfy a judgment." Stephanie Glynn, Toxic Toys and Dangerous Drywall: Holding Foreign Manufacturers Liable for Defective Products–the Fund Concept, 26 Emory Int'l L. Rev. 317, 318 (2012).

Even if plaintiff does successfully identify and obtain jurisdiction over a solvent foreign manufacturer, the possibility still exists that a U.S. court will decline to hear the case due to the doctrine of *forum non conveniens*. Sometimes applied in the products liability context, this doctrine is a discretionary device that enables courts to decline to exercise jurisdiction in cases where, through an equitable balancing of multiple factors, the dispute seems more appropriately adjudicated in a foreign jurisdiction. See Piper Aircraft Co. v. Reyno, 454 U.S. 235 (1981). Finally, even if plaintiffs do secure a favorable verdict in the foreign jurisdiction after their initial suit is dismissed on forum non conveniens grounds, they may be unable to enforce the verdict domestically if U.S. courts do not view the foreign forum as adequately protective of a defendant's due process rights. See Osorio v. Dole Food Co., 665 F. Supp. 2d 1307 (S.D. Fla. 2009), *aff'd*, 635 F.3d 1277 (11th Cir. 2011) (detailing fatal shortcomings in Nicaraguan liability law and court proceedings against the defendant, which had years earlier successfully argued that toxic exposure suits filed in the United States should be dismissed in favor of litigation in Nicaragua).

Perhaps in part because of these barriers to effective litigation against foreign product manufacturers, commentators and policymakers rarely promote products liability law as the sole or primary means of ensuring the safety and quality of imported products. Instead, attention tends to focus on improving regulatory oversight, both by stepping up inspection at the border by U.S. regulators and by helping to build regulatory capacity in foreign jurisdictions. According to one report, U.S. Food and Drug Administration officials examine less than two percent of imported food products and rarely visit food manufacturers in China. See Jason J. Czarnezki, Global Environmental Law: Food Safety & China, 25 Geo. Int'l Envtl. L. Rev. 261, 267 (2013). On the other hand, some observers worry that such increased scrutiny might operate as a barrier to trade with adverse consequences to both domestic consumers and foreign workers. From this perspective, public desire for increased safety standards gets hijacked by domestic industry and their representatives who implement laws and policies in ways that act as hidden restraints on trade. Such opportunities to exploit public outcry are seen as all too easily generated, given various cognitive biases that afflict the public's perceptions of risk and a zealous media that readily feeds the hysteria. See Cass R. Sunstein & Timur Kuran, Availability Cascades and Risk Regulation, 51 Stan. L. Rev. 683 (1999).

This "Baptists and Bootleggers" story[1] is overdone. Legitimate safety concerns do exist with imported products, just as they do with domestic products. For instance, children in the United States have been harmed by high exposure to lead from spices imported from India. See Cristiane Gurgel Lin et al., Pediatric Lead Exposure From Imported Indian Spices and Cultural Powders, 125 Pediatrics e828, e829 (2010). The

---

1. This term, popular in economics and public choice literatures, captures the notion that temperance in America resulted from an unlikely political coalition that included Baptists who supported banning the legal sale of alcohol for moral reasons and Bootleggers who supported it in order to increase their profits. See Bruce Yandle, Bootleggers and Baptists: The Education of a Regulatory Economist, 7 Reg. no. 3 (1983).

harder question is not whether such safety issues sometimes exist, but rather how to address them in a way that ensures appropriate levels of safety without unduly burdening increased trade and economic growth. Many argue that the only logical and globally equitable solution is the creation of internationally harmonized product safety standards. Indeed, the World Trade Organization actively encourages the development of such standards by generally insulating domestic regulations from trade scrutiny if the regulations comport with a standard developed by an appropriate international body. One prominent such body is the Codex Alimentarius, a United Nations-sponsored organization of member nations and observer entities that develops internationally recognized standards, codes of practice, guidelines, and other recommendations relating to food products, food production, and food safety. Naturally, such a bold vision of global regulatory harmonization attracts objections from all quarters, ranging from those who believe the Codex is too weak without international enforcement powers as well as standard-setting authority to those who see in the Codex nothing less than a powerful global conspiracy to undermine local and traditional food practices.

For more background on food products liability and import regulation, especially regarding the United States and China, see Alexia Brunet Marks, Check Please: How Legal Liability Informs Food Safety Regulation, 50 Houston L. Rev. 3 (2013); Chenglin Liu, The Obstacles of Outsourcing Imported Food Safety to China, 43 Cornell Int'l L.J. 249 (2010).

PROBLEM TWENTY-SEVEN

In 2013, investigators discovered mislabeled horsemeat in packages of frozen beef burgers sold in various Irish and British supermarkets. While horsemeat has not been found to be unsafe for human consumption, its consumption violates cultural taboos and norms in many European countries. Moreover, twenty-three out of twenty-seven samples of beef burgers in these supermarkets also contained pig DNA. Since pork is considered a taboo food product in the Jewish and Muslim religions, the scandal caused uproar, leading certain segments of the population to decry the corrosion of food safety measures. Indeed, public confidence in commercial food safety declined sharply, wreaking havoc on European markets.

That same year, over sixteen thousand deceased pigs were found floating in the Huangpu River in China not far from Shanghai. The pigs were traced back to a factory farm that was dumping the carcasses into the river illicitly, and some of the pigs tested positive for porcine cirovirus, a disease that has not yet been shown to have effects on humans. Many in the global community viewed this event as an indicator of much larger problems concerning the enforcement of food health and safety regulations in China.

These food safety issues abroad have started to worry U.S. consumers, including many from the district in which you serve as a United States Representative. Your constituents have reached out to you, wondering whether lax food safety measures around the world, combined with expanding free trade practices, are putting them and their families at risk.

Your legislative aides have proposed two pieces of legislation in response to the food safety issue:

(1)   For any food product offered for sale in the United States, the exporter of the good must present a certificate of product safety law equivalency. The certificate must verify the product's origins and the system of national products liability and safety regulation to which the manufacturer is subject abroad. The U.S. Food and Drug Administration, in cooperation with the U.S. Department of State, will maintain a table rating the robustness of each nation's products liability and safety regulation scheme on a scale of 1-5. If the exporting company has a lower score than the national average of the United States, then the exporting company must pay an import tax equal to an estimate by U.S. regulators of the amount of the product's expected accident costs over and above comparable U.S. products. Proceeds from the tax will be directed to the State Department's "rule of law" program which attempts to enhance legal accountability, regulatory capacity, and government transparency in other nations.

(2)   For any food product offered for sale within the United States, the exporting company must agree to be bound by the products liability law of the state within which the company's product is sold or consumed, submit to jurisdiction for civil claims that arise out of harms caused by the product in any jurisdiction where it is sold or consumed, and post an "import quality assurance bond" that will serve to guarantee payment of all products liability awards against the exporting company.

Decide whether you would like to sponsor one of the proposed approaches, modify it, or offer your own.

We close on a speculative note. If products liability law in the United States was motivated — as is often proclaimed — by a desire to shift focus away from the conduct of the manufacturer and toward the defective nature of the product itself, how far might the idea of a *product's* liability extend?

Consider the growing problem of electronic waste, often known as e-waste. See Hannah G. Elisha, Addressing the E-Waste Problem: The Need for Comprehensive Federal E-Waste Regulation Within the United States, 14 Chap. L. Rev. 145 (2010). Driven by rapid growth in the production, purchase, and disposal of goods such as flat screen televisions, laptop computers, and cell phones, the world generates tens of millions of tons of e-waste per year. Currently, the largest receiving sites for e-waste are located in Africa and Asia, where thousands of individuals sift through the electronic debris in search of scrap metal that can be sold for profit.

Despite creating economic opportunities for people living on the margin, e-waste is notorious for containing toxins, including lead, mercury, and other known carcinogens. When electronics are burned, ground into dust, or handled without appropriate safety equipment — as they frequently are at dumping sites in lesser developed nations — they release these toxins into the air and water, causing damage to the environment, as well as severe health effects for the individuals who work and live there. See Jennifer Chen, The Efficiency and Management of the International Trade in Electronic Waste: Is There a Better Plan than a Ban?, 21 N.Y.U. Envtl. L.J. 142 (2014). Despite these known adverse effects, the e-waste trade is a lucrative one, and many industrialized countries, including the United States, have not developed comprehensive regulatory mechanisms to reduce or even track e-waste trade. See Jeffrey M. Gaba, Exporting Waste: Regulation of the Export of Hazardous Wastes from the United States, 36 Wm. & Mary Envtl. L. & Pol'y Rev. 405 (2012).

To what extent should e-waste harms be considered product-caused harms? On the one hand, a manufacturer could be said to satisfy all appropriate duties under products liability law if the manufacturer's product is safely handled to the point of disposal. See, e.g., Thompson v TCI Products Co., 2015 WL 321400 (N.D. Okla. 2015) (no duty as matter of law to plaintiff's decedent who died after cutting with a torch into an unmarked secondhand barrel of defendant's paint solvent and the barrel exploded); Monsanto v. Reed, 950 S.W.2d 811 (Ky. 1997) (dismissing products liability claims against battery transformer manufacturers for harms to salvage workers caused by PCBs in the batteries). On the other hand, one might argue that certain kinds of post-disposal harms remain quite foreseeable to the manufacturer, including those associated with e-waste which have been widely reported in the media and by government agencies. Perhaps for this reason many countries in Europe and some U.S. states have devised "extended producer responsibility" laws under which manufacturers of products are required to retake possession of and safely handle products at the end of their useful lives. See Noah Sachs, Planning the Funeral at the Birth: Extended Producer Responsibility in the European Union and the United States, 30 Harv. Envtl. L. Rev. 51 (2006).

Still — foreseeable or not — does the failure of the global economic trading system to protect e-waste dumping site workers reflect a failure by the electronics industry or a more widespread failure by *all* those who participate in the life cycle of electronics products?

PROBLEM TWENTY-EIGHT

Some time in the near future, following rapid technological breakthroughs in the industry, two American cellphone companies announce a new promotion: For a low monthly fee, customers can sign up to trade in their cellphones for new, updated models as often as they choose at deeply discounted rates. The promotion is a huge success, and millions of American consumers sign up for it.

With their brief usable life and planned obsolescence, cellphones manufactured by these two brands rapidly become the most common product in the e-waste market. However, the phones contain high amounts of chromium deep inside their cases, and while the chromium has no contact with phone users, it leaks out of the phones when they are disposed of at e-waste dumping sites abroad. The chromium seeps into the air and water supplies of nearby villages, and causes health issues, including organ failure and even death.

As exports of these temporary phones grows to several million tons of weight annually, legal scholars and activists begin to question whether the companies manufacturing the phones should be subject to liability for the harms caused by toxic chemicals in their products after disposal. Courts, however, refuse to apply liability in such cases, reasoning that the degradation of these phones in landfills is not a foreseeable use of the product, that injuries are resulting not from the product but from a substantial alteration of the product, and that manufacturers owe no duty to "downstream" victims exposed to products after their useful lives.

You work as an executive in the corporate social responsibility department of one of the two cellphone companies behind the temporary phone promotion. Although you doubt that courts will shift from their current stance of hesitance to impose liability on manufacturers for "downstream" product-caused harms, you are concerned that Congress and state legislatures will act in response to mounting public concern and international outrage.

The chief executive officer of your company has asked you to brainstorm possible responses to the situation. She has asked you to think specifically of proposals that would enable the temporary phone promotion to continue while both minimizing the risk of overseas chromium exposure and maintaining the low overall production cost that is essential to the success of the promotion. She has also stressed that your company's long-term vision is to make the temporary phone promotion available to consumers throughout the world, not only those who live in relatively affluent countries. "Think creatively," she tells you, "The world is counting on us."

Table of Cases

Principal cases are in italics.

Table of Statutes and Other Authorities

Index

Indemnity
  rights up the distribution chain, 62-64
Independent contractor
  indemnity rights, 62-63
Information sales
  strict liability, 36
Informed choice
  case, 335
  warnings, 331
    meat grinder, 335-339
Injury
  enhanced, 113
Innovation
  U.S. liability system effects on, 564-567
Inspection failure
  retailer liability, 56
Instructions. *See also* Defective marketing; Duty to
    warn
  failure, prescription drugs and medical devices,
    manufacturer liability, 430
  warnings vs., 309
Insurance
  costs for American firms vs. foreign counterparts,
    561-562
  health, 557
  insurance company practices, punitive damages,
    517-526
  international product liability claims, 548-550,
    557
  strict liability, 20
Intentional tort
  occupational disease, 73
  workers' compensation bar, 69
International perspectives. *See* Foreign products
    liability law; Global context
IUD
  causing harm, 103-104
  express warranty based on advertising, 412

Japan, 550-560
  burdens of proof, 557
  claiming, 554, 555
  class actions and, 557
  damages, 555-556
  discovery, 556-557
  health insurance, 557
  implied contract term, 552
  juries and judges, 558-559
  lawyer costs, 556
  legal doctrine, 551-553
  litigating practice, 553
  medical malpractice, 557
  negligence, 552, 557
  number of suits filed, 553
  presumptions, 557
  significance of Japanese-American contrast, 554

strict liability, 552, 553
  suing vs. claiming, 555
  tort law, 442
Joint and several liability
  allocating responsibility, 52-56
  market-share theory, 107
  noneconomic damages, 54
  percentage threshold, 54
  tort exceptions, 53-54
Judicial review
  defective design, 158
Juries and judges, 558-559

Kill switch
  state of the art design, 189
Knowledge
  defective design, 165
  risk-utility balance, 165
  time-based defenses, 150-154
Korean Air Lines disaster
  navigation system defect, 287-288
Kosher chocolate
  warranty, 395

Ladder defect
  design defect, 166
  duty to warn, 353
Language problem
  duty to warn, 357
Lacquer thinner
  duty to warn case, 371-375
Latex gloves
  design defect, 186
Lawnmower
  defective design, 165-166
Lawyer. *See* Attorney
Lead paint
  market share liability, 108
Learned intermediary rule, 429-430, 434, 435, 437-
    444, 454, 458
Legal standard
  defective design, 157
Liability. *See also* Manufacturing defects; Strict
    liability
  failure to warn, 357-358
  generic product risks, 155-307
  joint and several, 52-56
  limitations on, 120
Limited liability rule. *See* Shareholder liability
Litigation
  Japan vs. United States, 553
  United States vs. rest of world, 541-542, 553, 554,
    557-559
  volume, 541-542, 553, 554, 557-559
Loss of a chance, 113